T0301337

Advanced
Bond Portfolio
Management

THE FRANK J. FABOZZI SERIES

Advanced
Bond Portfolio
Management

Best Practices in Modeling and Strategies

FRANK J. FABOZZI

LIONEL MARTELLINI

PHILIPPE PRIAULET

EDITORS

WILEY
John Wiley & Sons, Inc.

ISBN-13 978-0-471-67890-8
ISBN-10 0-471-67890-2

10 9 8 7 6 5 4 3 2 1

Contents

Preface

Bonds, also referred to as fixed income instruments or debt instruments, have always been and will likely remain particularly predominant in institutional investors' allocation because they are typically the asset class most correlated with liability structures. However, they have evolved from straight bonds characterized by simple cash flow structures to securities with increasingly complex cash flow structures that attract a wider range of investors. In order to effectively employ portfolio strategies that can control interest rate risk and enhance returns, investors and their managers must understand the forces that drive bond markets, and the valuation and risk management practices of these complex securities.

In the face of a rapidly increasing complexity of instruments and strategies, this book aims at presenting state-of-the-art of techniques related to portfolio strategies and risk management in bond markets. (Note that throughout the book, we use the terms "fixed income securities" and "bonds" somewhat interchangeably.) Over the past several years, based on the collective work of numerous experts involved in both practitioner and academic research, dramatic changes have occurred in investment best practices and much progress has been made in our understanding of the key ingredients of a modern, structured, portfolio management process. In this book, these ingredients that continue to shape the future of the bond portfolio management industry will be reviewed, with a detailed account of new techniques involved in all phases of the bond portfolio management process. This includes coverage of the design of a benchmark, the portfolio construction process, and the analysis of portfolio risk and performance.

The book is composed of six parts.

Part One provides general background information on fixed income markets and bond portfolios strategies. Chapter 1 by Frank Jones provides a general classification of bond portfolio strategies, emphasizing the fact that bond portfolio strategies, just like equity portfolio strategies, can be cast within a simple asset management setup, or alternatively and arguably more fittingly, cast within a more general asset-liability management context. The chapter not only covers standard active and passive bond portfolio strategies; it also provides the reader with an introduction to some of the new frontiers in institutional portfolio management, including an overview of the core-satellite approach as well as an introduction to portable alpha strategies.

In Chapter 2, Leland Crabbe and Frank Fabozzi offer a thorough and detailed analysis of liquidity and trading costs in bond markets. While active trading is meant to generate outperformance, it can also result in efficiency loss in the presence of market frictions. Because it is quite often that the presence of such frictions may transform a theoretically sound active bond portfolio decision into a costly and inefficient dynamic trading strategy, one may actually argue that the question of *implementation* of bond portfolio management decisions is of an importance equal to that of the *derivation* of such optimal decisions. The elements they present in Chapter 2 are useful ingredients in a bond portfolio optimization process that accounts for the presence of trading costs.

A first view on the fundamental question of the design of fixed income benchmarks in the context of active bond portfolio strategies is provided by Bülent Baygün and Robert Tzucker in Chapter 3. They begin by explaining how different methods can be used in the process of benchmark construction, with a key distinction between rule-based methods meant to ensure that the benchmark truthfully represents a given sector of the market, and optimization methods to ensure that the benchmark is an efficient portfolio. They then explore various aspects of the active portfolio management process, which allows managers to transform their view on various factors affecting bond returns into meaningful and coherent portfolio decisions.

Part Two is entirely devoted to the first, and perhaps most important, phase in the bond portfolio management process: the design of a strategy benchmark. In Chapter 4 Chris Dialynas and Alfred Murata presents a useful reminder of the fact that existing commercial indices contain implicit allocation biases; they then explore the market conditions and factors that result in outperformance of one versus another bond index. Overall, the chapter conveys the useful message that selecting a benchmark accounts for most of the eventual portfolio performance.

Lev Dynkin, Jay Herman, and Bruce Phelps revisit the question of bond benchmarks from a liability-based standpoint in Chapter 5. Existing commercial indices are not originally designed to serve as proper benchmarks for institutional investors; instead they are meant to represent specific given sectors of the bond markets. Because commercial indices are inadequate benchmarks for institutional investors, the question of the design of customized benchmarks that would properly represent the risks faced by an institution in the presence of liability constraints is a key challenge. Dynkin, Herman, and Phelps introduce the modern techniques involved in the design of such customized bench-marks with an emphasis on liability-matching though the presentation of conceptual underpinnings as well as practical illustrations.

Risk budgeting in a fixed income environment process is explained in Chapter 6 by Frederick Dopfel; he carefully explains how investors may usefully implement an optimal allocation of resources across managers based on efficient spending of an active risk budget perceived as the maximum amount of deviation between the manager's benchmark and the actual portfolio. A key distinction is made between style risk on the one hand and active risk/residual risk on the other hand. *Style risk* (also called *misfit risk*) is the deviation between a manager's portfolio and the benchmark return that is caused by different strategic factor exposures in the manager's portfolio with respect to the benchmark. *Active risks* involve the budgeting of abnormal returns with respect to residual risk (also known as *alpha risk*) which is the deviation between a manager's portfolio and the benchmark return that is due to security selection and/or factor timing skills exercised by the manager.

The presentation of the toolbox of the modern bond portfolio manager is the subject of Part Three. In particular, this part of the book covers various aspects of fixed income modeling that will provide key ingredients in the implementation of an efficient portfolio and risk management process. In this respect, the chapters in this part of the book set forth critical analytical concepts and risk concepts that will be used in the last three parts of the book. Chapters in those parts provide a more detailed focus on some of the risk factors introduced in there. In the first chapter in Part Three, Chapter 7, Philip Obazee presents a detailed introduction to option-adjusted spread (OAS) analysis, a useful analytical relative value concept employed in the context of security selection strategies, particularly in analysis of securities backed by a pool of residential mortgage loans (i.e., residential mortgage-backed securities).

Chapter 8 offers a thorough account of the design of factor models used for risk analysis of bond portfolios, with an emphasis not only on individual risk components but also on how they relate to each other. The authors, Ludovic Breger and Oren Cheyette, provide as an illustration an application in the context of risk analysis of several well-known bond indices.

In Chapter 9, Lev Dynkin and Jay Hyman follow up on this question by exploring how such factor models can be used in the context of bond portfolio strategies. In particular, they demonstrate how active bond portfolio managers can optimize in a relative risk-return space the allocated active risk budget through the use of a factor analysis of deviations between a portfolio and a benchmark portfolio.

Part Four focuses on interest rate risk management, arguably the dominant risk factor in any bond portfolio. The main object of attention for all bond portfolio managers is the time-varying shape of the term structure of interest rates. In Chapter 10, Bennett Golub and Leo Tilman provide an insightful discussion of how to measure the plausibility, in terms of comparison with historical data, of various scenarios about the future evolution of the term structure. They use principal component analysis of past changes in the term structure's shape (level, slope, and curvature) as a key ingredient for the modeling of future changes.

In Chapter 11, the coeditors along with Michael Luo build on such a factor analysis of the time-varying shape of the term structure to explain how bond portfolio managers can improve upon duration-based hedging techniques by taking into account scenarios that are not limited to changes in interest rate level, but instead account for general changes in the whole shape of the term structure of interest rates. Farshid Jamshidian and Yu Zhu in Chapter 12 take the reader beyond an *ex post* analysis of interest rate risk and present an introduction to modeling techniques used in the context of stochastic simulation for bond portfolios, with an application to Value-at-Risk and stress-testing analysis.

The focus in Part Five is on the question of credit risk management, another dominant risk factor for the typical bond portfolio managers who invests in spread products. In Chapter 13, Sivan Mahadevan, Young-Sup Lee, Viktor Hjort, David Schwartz, and Stephen Dulake provide a first look at the question of credit risk management emphasizing the similarities and differences between quantitative approaches to credit risk analysis and more traditional fundamental analysis. By comparing and contrasting fundamental credit analysis with various quantitative approaches, they usefully prepare the ground for subsequent chapters dedicated to a detailed analysis of various credit risk models.

In Chapter 14, Donald van Deventer begins with a thorough discussion of both structural models and reduced form models, emphasizing the benefits of the latter, more recent, approach over Merton-based credit risk models. In Chapter 15, he explains how these models can be used for the pricing and hedging of credit derivatives that have become a key component of the fixed income market.

Wesley Phoa revisits structural models in Chapter 16. These models are the most adapted tools for an analysis of the relationship between prices of stock and bonds issued by the same company. In Chapter 17, David Soronow concludes this analysis of credit risk with a focus on the use of credit risk models in the context of bond selection strategies. He provides convincing evidence of the ability for a portfolio manager to add value in a risk-adjusted sense on the basis of equity-implied risk measures, such as those derived from structural models.

After these analyses of interest rate and credit risk analysis in the context of bond portfolio management, the last part of this book, Part Six, focuses on additional risk factors involved in the management of an international bond portfolio. Lee Thomas in Chapter 18 makes a strong case for global bond portfolio management, with a detailed analysis of various bond markets worldwide, and a discussion of the benefits that can be gained from strategic as well as tactical allocation decisions to these markets.

The specific challenges involved in the management of a multicurrency portfolio and the related impacts in terms of benchmark design and portfolio construction are covered in Chapter 19. The chapter, coauthored by Srichander Ramaswamy and Robert Scott, also provides detailed discussion of the generation of active bets based on fundamental macro and technical analysis, as well as a careful presentation of the associated portfolio construction and risk analysis process. In Chapter 20, Maria Mednikov Loucks, John A. Penicook, and Uwe Schillhorn conclude the book with a specific focus on emerging market debt. Once again, the reader is provided with a detailed analysis of the various elements of a modern bond portfolio process applied to emerging market debt investing, including all aspects related to the design of a benchmark, the portfolio construction process, as well as the analysis of risk and performance.

Overall, this book represents a collection of the combined expertise of more than 30 experienced participants in the bond market, guiding the reader through the state-of-the-art techniques used in the analysis of bonds and bond portfolio management. It is our hope, and indeed our belief, that this book will prove to be a useful resource tool for anyone with an interest in the bond portfolio management industry.

The views, thoughts and opinions expressed in this book should not in any way be attributed to Philippe Priaulet as a representative, officer, or employee of Natexis Banques Populaires.

Frank Fabozzi
Lionel Martellini
Philippe Priaulet

About the Editors

Frank J. Fabozzi is the Frederick Frank Adjunct Professor of Finance in the School of Management at Yale University. Prior to joining the Yale faculty, he was a Visiting Professor of Finance in the Sloan School at MIT. Professor Fabozzi is a Fellow of the International Center for Finance at Yale University and the editor of the *Journal of Portfolio Management*. He earned a doctorate in economics from the City University of New York in 1972. In 1994 he received an honorary doctorate of Humane Letters from Nova Southeastern University and in 2002 was inducted into the Fixed Income Analysts Society's Hall of Fame. He earned the designation of Chartered Financial Analyst and Certified Public Accountant.

Lionel Martellini is a Professor of Finance at EDHEC Graduate School of Business and the Scientific Director of Edhec Risk and Asset Management Research Center. A former member of the faculty at the Marshall School of Business, University of Southern California, Dr. Martellini is a member of the editorial board of the *Journal of Portfolio Management* and the *Journal of Alternative Investments*. He conducts active research in quantitative asset management and derivatives valuation which has been published in leading academic and practitioner journals and has coauthored books on topics related to alternative investment strategies and fixed income securities. He holds master's degrees in Business Administration, Economics, Statistics and Mathematics, as well as a Ph.D. in Finance from the Haas School of Business, University of California at Berkeley.

Philippe Priaulet is the head of global strategy at Natexis Banques Populaires. Related to fixed-income asset management and derivatives pricing and hedging, his research has been published in leading academic and practitioner journals. He is the coauthor of books on fixed-income securities and both an associate professor in the Department of Mathematics of the University of Evry Val d'Essonne and a lecturer at ENSAE. Formerly, he was a derivatives strategist at HSBC, and the head of fixed-income research in the Research and Innovation Department of HSBC-CCF. He holds a master's degrees in business administration and mathematics as well as a Ph.D. in financial economics from the University Paris IX Dauphine.

Contributing Authors

Bülent Baygün	Barclays Capital
Ludovic Breger	MSCI Barra
Oren Cheyette	MSCI Barra
Leland E. Crabbe	Consultant
Chris P. Dialynas	Pacific Investment Management Company
Frederick E. Dopfel	Barclays Global Investors
Stephen Dulake	
Lev Dynkin	Lehman Brothers
Frank J. Fabozzi	Yale University
Bennett W. Golub	BlackRock Financial Management, Inc.
Viktor Hjort	Morgan Stanley
Jay Hyman	Lehman Brothers
Farshid Jamshidian	NIB Capital Bank and FELAB, University of Twente
Frank J. Jones	San Jose State University and International Securities Exchange
Young-Sup Lee	Morgan Stanley
Michael Luo	Morgan Stanley
Sivan Mahadevan	Morgan Stanley
Lionel Martellini	EDHEC Graduate School of Business
Maria Mednikov Loucks	Black River Asset Management
Alfred Murata	Pacific Investment Management Company
Philip O. Obazee	Delaware Investments
John A. Penicook, Jr.,	UBS Global Asset Management
Bruce D. Phelps	Lehman Brothers
Wesley Phoa	The Capital Group Companies
Philippe Priaulet	HSBC and University of Evry Val d'Essonne
Srichander Ramaswamy	Bank for International Settlements
Robert Scott	Bank for International Settlements
Uwe Schillhorn	UBS Global Asset Management
David Schwartz	
David Soronow	MSCI Barra

Lee R. Thomas	Allianz Global Investors
Leo M. Tilman	Bear Stearns
Robert Tzucker	Barclays Capital
Donald R. van Deventer	Kamakura Corporation
Yu Zhu	China Europe International Business School and Fore Research & Management, LP

PART

One

Background

Overview of Fixed Income Portfolio Management

Frank J. Jones, Ph.D.
Professor of Finance
Department of Accounting & Finance
San Jose State University
and
Vice Chairman, Board of Directors
International Securities Exchange

This chapter provides a general overview of fixed income portfolio management. More specifically, investment strategies and portfolio performance analysis are described. A broad framework is provided rather than a deep or exhaustive treatment of these two aspects of fixed income portfolio management.

A discussion of the risks associated with investing in fixed income securities is not provided in this discussion. They are, however, provided in other chapters of this book. Exhibit 1.1, nonetheless, provides a summary of the risk factors that affect portfolio performance.

FIXED INCOME INVESTMENT STRATEGIES

Fixed income investment strategies can be divided into three approaches. The first considers fixed income investment strategies that are basically the same as stock investment strategies. This is a pure asset management approach and is called the *total return approach*. The second approach

3

EXHIBIT 1.1   Summary of Risk Factors

Risk Factors	Risk Factor Measurement	Market Changes that Affect Risk Factors
Market Risk	Duration	Change in Yield Levels—Parallel Change in Yield Curve
Yield Curve Risk	Convexity/Distribution of Key Rate Durations (Bullet, Barbell, Ladder, et al.)	Change in Slope and Shape of Yield Curve
Exposure to Market Volatility	Convexity • Negatively convex assets (e.g., callables)/portfolios are adversely affected by volatility • Positively convex assets (e.g., putables)/portfolios are benefited by volatility	Market Volatility • Historical, based on past actual prices or yields • Expected, as indicated by implied volatility of options
Sector Allocation	Percent allocation to each macrosector, microsector, and security and the option-adjust spread (OAS) of each	Change in option-adjusted spreads (OAS) of macrosectors, microsectors, and individual securities
Credit Risk	Average credit rating of portfolio and its sectors	Changes in credit spreads (e.g., spread between Treasuries versus AAA corporates; or spread between AAA corporates versus BBB corporates); also specific company rating changes
Liquidity Risk	Typically measured by the bid/ask price spread—that is, the difference between the price at which a security can be bought and sold at a point in time The liquidity of a security refers to both it marketability (the time it takes to sell a security at its market price, e.g., a registered corporate bond takes less time to sell than a private placement) and the stability of the market price	Different securities have inherently different liquidity (e.g., Treasuries are more liquid than corporates). The liquidity of all securities, particularly riskier securities, decreases during periods of market turmoil.
Exchange Rate Risk	Changes in the exchange rate between the U.S. dollar and the currency in which the security is denominated (e.g., yen or euro)	Volatility in the exchange rate increases the risk of the security. For a U.S. investor, a strengthening of the other currency (weakening of the U.S. dollar) will be beneficial to a U.S. investor (negative to a U.S. investor) who holds a security denominated in the other currency

considers features unique to bonds—that is, fixed coupons and a defined time to maturity and maturity value, which relates these cash flows to many of the liabilities or products of an institution. We refer to this approach as the *liability funding strategy*.[1] This is an *asset liability management* (ALM) approach. This third approach unifies and specifies the first two types. It represents a surplus optimization strategy that, as discussed, includes both beta and alpha management. We refer to this as the *unified approach*.

Total Return Approach

The total return approach (TRA), the most common approach to asset management, is an investment strategy that seeks to maximize the *total rate of return* (TRR) of the portfolio. The two component returns of the TRR are the income component and the capital gains component. Despite the different risks associated with these two components of the TRR, they are treated fungibly in TRA.

TRR strategies for bonds, as well as stocks, are based on their own risk factors. In the TRR approach, the TRR for the fixed income portfolio is compared with the TRR of a benchmark selected as the basis for evaluating the portfolio (discussed in more detail below). The risk factors of the benchmark should be similar to those of the bond portfolio.

Overall, however, two different portfolios, or a portfolio and a benchmark that have different risk factors, will experience different TRRs due to identical market changes. A portfolio manager should calculate or measure the risk factor *ex ante* and either be aware of the differential response to the relevant market change or, if this response is unacceptable to the portfolio manager, to alter the exposure to the risk factor by portfolio actions.

Thus, changes in market behavior may affect the performance of the portfolio and the benchmark differently due to their differences in risk factors. The specification measurement of a portfolio's risk factors and the benchmark's risk factors are critical in being able to compare the performance of the portfolio and benchmark due to market changes. This is the reason the risk factors of a bond portfolio and its benchmark should be very similar. A methodology for doing so is described in Chapter 9.

Having selected a benchmark, being aware of the risk factors of the portfolio, and having calculated the risk factors for the benchmark, a portfolio manager must decide whether he or she wants the portfolio to

---

[1] This strategy is also referred to as the *interest rate risk portfolio strategy* by Robert Litterman of Goldman Sachs Asset Management.

replicate the risk factors of the benchmarks or to deviate from them. Replicating all the risk factors is called a *passive strategy*; deviating from one or more of the risk factors is called an *active strategy*.

That is, a portfolio manager could be passive with respect to some risk factors and active with respect to others—there is a large number of combinations given the various risk factors. Passive strategies require no forecast of future market changes—both the portfolio and benchmark respond identically to market changes. Active strategies are based on a forecast, because the portfolio and benchmark will respond differently to market changes. In an active strategy, the portfolio manager must decide in which direction and by how much the risk factor value of the portfolio will deviate from the risk factor value of the benchmark on the basis of expected market changes.

Consequently, given multiple risk factors, there is a pure passive strategy, and there are several hybrid strategies that are passive on some risk factors and active on others.

Exhibit 1.2 summarizes the passive strategy and some of the common active strategies. The active strategies relate to various fixed income risk factors. An active fixed income manager could be active relative to any set of these risk factors, or all of them. This chapter does not provide a thorough discussion of any one of these strategies. However, some stylized comments on some of the common strategies are provided.

EXHIBIT 1.2   Passive and Active Strategies

Strategy	Description	Comment
PASSIVE		
Indexation (pure passivity)	Replicate all risk factors in the "index" or benchmark	The only certain way to accomplish this is to buy all the securities in the index in amounts equal to their weight in the index. While this can easily be done in the stock market, say for the S&P 500 Index by buying all 500 stocks in the appropriate amounts, it is difficult to do so in the fixed income market. For example, the Lehman Aggregate Bond Index is based on approximately 6,000 bonds, many of them quite illiquid.

EXHIBIT 1.2 (Continued)

Strategy	Description	Comment
ACTIVE		
Market Timing	Deviate from duration of the benchmark	If the portfolios have a greater duration than the benchmark: • It outperforms the benchmark during market rallies • It underperforms during market contractions • Vice versa
Yield Curve Trades	Replicate duration of the benchmark, but vary the convexity and yield curve exposure by varying the composition of key rate durations	Bullets outperform during yield curve steepenings; barbells outperform during yield curve flattenings
Volatility Trades	Deviates from optionality of benchmarks: • Callables are more negatively convex than bullets. • Putables are more positively convex than bullets.	Volatility increases benefit putables (which are long an option) and negatively affect callables (which are short an option)
Asset Allocation/Sector Trades	Deviate from macrosector, microsector or security weightings of benchmark: • Macro—overall sectors (Treasuries; agencies; corporates; MBS; ABS; Municipals) • Microcomponents of a macrosector (e.g., utilities versus industrials in corporate sector) • Securities—overweight/underweight individual securities in a microsector (e.g., Florida Power and Light versus Niagara Mohawk in corporate utility sector)	Deviations based on option-adjusted spread (OAS) of sectors, subsectors and securities relative to historical averages and fundamental projection; can use breakeven spreads (based on OAS) as a basis for deviations On overweights, spread tightening produces gain; spread widening produces losses; and vice versa
Credit Risk Allocations	Deviate from average credit rating of macrosector or microsectors and composites thereof	Credit spreads typically widen when economic growth is slow or negative Credit spread widening benefits higher credit rating, and vice versa Can use spread duration as basis for deviations
Trading	Short-term changes in specific securities on the basis of short-term price discrepancies	Often short-term technicals, including short-term supply/demand factors, cause temporary price discrepancies

Market Timing

Few institutions practice market timing by altering the duration of their portfolio based on their view of yield changes. Few feel confident that they can reliably forecast interest rates. A common view is that market timing adds much more to portfolio risk than to portfolio return, and that often the incremental portfolio return is negative. The duration of their portfolio may, however, inadvertently change due to yield changes through the effect of yield changes on the duration of callable or pre-payable fixed income security, although continual monitoring and adjustments can mitigate this effect.

Credit Risk Allocations

Institutions commonly alter the average credit risk of their corporate bond portfolio based on their view of the credit yield curve (i.e., high quality/low quality yield spreads widening or narrowing). For example, if they believe the economy will weaken, they will upgrade the quality of their portfolio.

Sector Rotation

Institutions may rotate sectors, for example, from financials to industrials, on the basis of their view of the current valuation of these sectors and their views of the prospective economic strength of these sectors.

Security/Bond Selection

Most active institutional investors maintain internal credit or fundamental bond research staffs that do credit analysis on individual bonds to assess their overevaluation or underevaluation. A portfolio manager would have benefited greatly if they had avoided Worldcom before the bankruptcy during June 2002 (at the time Worldcom had the largest weight in the Lehman Aggregate) or General Motors or Ford before downgraded to junk bond status in June 2005. Security/bond selection can also be based on rich/cheap strategies (including long-short strategies) in Treasury bonds, mortgage-backed securities or other fixed income sectors.

Core Satellite Approach

As indicated above, the active/passive decision is not binary. A passive approach means that all risk factors are replicated. However, an active approach has several subsets by being active in any combination of risk factors. There is another way in which the active/passive approach is not binary.

An overall fixed income portfolio may be composed of several specific fixed income asset classes. The overall portfolio manager may choose to be passive in some asset classes, which are deemed to be very efficient and have little potential for generating alpha. Other asset classes, perhaps because they are more specialized, may be deemed to be less efficient and have more potential for generating alpha. For example, the manager may choose to use a "core" of U.S. investment-grade bonds passively managed via a Lehman Aggregate Index and "satellites" of actively managed bonds such as U.S. high-yield bonds and emerging market debt. Such core satellite approaches have become common with institutional investors.

These and other fixed income investment strategies are commonly used by institutional investors. Note, however, that the TRR approach relates to an external benchmark, not to the institution's internal liabilities or products. That is why the TRR approach is very similar for bonds and stocks.

Now consider evaluating an institution's investment portfolio relative to its own liabilities or products. Because the cash flows of these liabilities or products are more bond-like than stock-like, bond investment strategies assume a different role in this context.

Liability Funding Approach

The benchmark for the TRR approach is an external fixed income return average. Now consider a benchmark based on an institution's internal liabilities or products. Examples of this would be a defined benefit plan's retirement benefit payments; a life insurance company's actuarially determined death benefits; or a commercial bank's payments on a book of fixed-rate certificate of deposits (CDs). In each case, the payments of the liability could be modeled as a stream of cash outflows. Such a stream of fixed outflows could be funded by bonds which provide known streams of cash outflows, not stocks that have unknown streams of cash flows. Consider the investment strategies for bonds for funding such liabilities.

The first such strategy would be to develop a fixed income portfolio whose duration is the same as that of the liability's cash flows. This is called an *immunization strategy*. An immunized portfolio, in effect, matches of the liability due to market risks only for parallel shifts in the yield curve. If the yield curve steepens (flattens), however, the immunized portfolio underperforms (outperforms) the liability's cash flows.

A more precise method of matching these liability cash flows is to develop an asset portfolio which has the same cash flows as the liability. This is called a *dedicated portfolio strategy*. A dedicated portfolio has more constraints than an immunized portfolio and, as a result, has a lower return. Its effectiveness, however, is not affected by changes in the slope of the yield curve. But if non-Treasury securities are included in the portfolio, this strategy as well as the immunization strategy, are exposed to credit risk.

A somewhat simplified version of a dedicated portfolio is called a *laddered portfolio*. It is used frequently by individual investors for retirement planning. Assume an investor with $900,000 available for retirement is 60 years old, plans to retire at age 65, and wants to have funds for 10 years. The investor could buy $100,000 (face or maturity value) each of zero-coupon bonds maturing in 5, 6, 7..., and 14 years. Thus, independent of changes in yields and the yield curve during the next 10 years, the investor will have $100,000 of funds each year. To continue this approach for after age 75, the investor could buy a new 10-year bond after each bond matures. These subsequent investments would, of course, depend on the yields at that time. This sequence of bonds of different maturities, which mature serially over time, is a laddered portfolio. (Some analysts liken a laddered portfolio to a stock strategy called dollar-cost averaging.) The 10-year cash flow receipt is a "home-made" version of a *deferred fixed annuity* (DFA). If the cash flows began immediately, it would be a version of an *immediate fixed annuity* (IFA).

An even simpler strategy of this type is called *yield spread management*, or simply *spread management*. Suppose a commercial bank issued a 6-month CD or an insurance company wrote a 6-month *guaranteed investment contract* (GIC). The profitability of these instruments (ignoring the optionality of the GIC) would depend on the difference between the yield on the asset invested against these products (such as 6-month commercial paper or 6-month fixed-rate notes) and the yield paid on the products by the institution. Spread management is managing the profitability of a book of such products based on the assets invested in to fund these products. In the short term, profitability will be higher if low quality assets are used; but over the longer run, there may be defaults which reduce the profitability.

Overall, while both bonds and stocks can be used for the TRR strategy, only bonds are appropriate for many liability funding strategies because of their fixed cash flows, both coupon and maturity value.

Unified Approach[2]

A recent way of considering risk and corresponding return is by disaggregating risk and the corresponding return into three components. Litterman calls this approach "active alpha investing."

---

[2] This section draws from Robert Litterman, "Actual Alpha Investing," open letter to investors, Goldman Sachs Asset Management (three-part series).

The first type is the risk and desired return due to the institution's or individual's liabilities. A portfolio is designed to match the liabilities of the institution whose return matches or exceeds the cost of the liabilities. Typically, liabilities are bond-like and so the matching portfolio is typically a fixed income portfolio. Examples of this are portfolios matching defined benefit pensions, whole life insurance policies, and commercial bank floating-rate loans.

The second risk/return type is a portfolio that provides market risk: either stock market risk (measured by beta) or bond market risk (measured by duration). The return to this portfolio is the stock market return (corresponding to the beta achieved) or the bond market return (corresponding to the duration achieved). The *market risk portfolio* could also be, rather than a pure beta or duration portfolio, a combination of a beta portfolio for stocks and a duration portfolio for bonds; that is, an asset allocation of market risk. In practice, the beta portfolio is typically achieved by an S&P 500 product (futures, swaps, etc.) for a beta of one, and the duration portfolio by a Lehman Aggregate product (futures, swaps, etc.) for a duration equal to the duration of the Lehman Aggregate. These betas or duration could also be altered from these base levels by additional (long or short) derivatives.

The third risk/return type is the *alpha portfolio* (or *active risk portfolio*). Alpha is the return on a portfolio after adjusting for its market risk, that is, the risk-adjusted return or the excess return.[3] Increasingly more sophisticated risk-factor models have been used to adjust for other types of risk beyond market risk in determining alpha (e.g., two-, three-, and four-factor alphas). For now, we will assume that the beta or duration return on the one hand and alpha return on the other hand go together in either a stock portfolio or a bond portfolio singularly. That is, by selecting a passive (or indexed) stock where the market return for stocks is the S&P 500 return and for bonds is the Lehman Aggregate return, one obtains either the stock market beta return or bond return duration and no alpha. Selecting an active stock portfolio, one has both the stock market beta and the prospects for an alpha, either positive or negative. Similarly for active fixed income funds and bond market duration and alpha returns.

So far, we have considered the market return (associated with beta or duration) as being part of the same strategy as the alpha return. There are two exceptions to this assumption. The first is market neutral funds. Market neutral funds are usually hedge funds which achieve market neutrality by taking short positions in the stock and/or bond mar-

---

[3] For a stock portfolio: Alpha = Portfolio return − Beta (Market return − Risk-free return). For a bond portfolio: Alpha = Portfolio return − Duration (Market return − Risk-free return).

kets. Thus, they have no market return and their entire return is an alpha return. By being market neutral, they have separated market return (beta or duration) from alpha return.

The second exception is an extension of market-neutral hedge funds and is discussed in the next section.

Portable Alpha

We have assumed that for stock and bond portfolios, the market return (due to beta or duration) is part of the same strategy as the alpha return. But market neutral hedge funds separate the market return from the alpha return by taking short and long positions in the markets via derivatives. However, portfolio managers could also separate the market return from the alpha return by taking short positions in the market via derivatives.

To understand how, consider the following example. Assume that the *chief investment officer* (CIO) of a firm faces liabilities that require a bond portfolio to fund liabilities. Further assume that the CIO considers the firm's bond portfolio managers to be not very talented. In contrast, the firm has stock managers who the CIO considers to be very talented. What should the CIO do? The CIO should index the firm's bond portfolio, thereby assuring that the untalented bond managers do not generate negative alpha, while providing the desired overall bond market returns. By using long positions in bond derivatives (e.g., via futures, swaps, or exchange-traded funds), the untalented bond managers could be eliminated. The CIO could then permit the firm's talented stock managers to run an active stock portfolio, ideally generating a positive alpha. In addition, at the CIO level, the CIO could eliminate the undesired stock market risk by shorting the stock market (e.g., via S&P 500 futures, swaps, or exchange-traded funds). The CIO could then "port" the stock portfolio alpha to the passive bond portfolio and achieve excess returns on the firm's passive bond portfolio. The final overall portfolio would consist of a long bond position using bond derivatives, an active stock portfolio, and a short S&P 500 position using derivatives. This is the *portable alpha* concept. This concept has recently become popular in the "search for alpha."

The opposite could also be the case for the CIO with an equity mandate (for example, the manager of a P&C insurance company portfolio or an equity indexed annuity portfolio): an untalented stock managers and a talented bond managers. In this case, the CIO could index the firm's stock portfolio, let the bond managers run an active portfolio, eliminate the stock managers, hedge the market risk of the bond portfolio at the CIO level with short bond derivatives and "port" the bond portfolio alpha to an indexed stock portfolio.

The portable alpha concept is a natural extension of advances in disaggregating overall returns into liability matching returns, market returns, and alpha returns and has provided considerable additional flexibility to asset managers. Specifically, a CIO can search for alpha in places that are not associated with beta. The beta portfolio is typically determined by the type of institution (e.g., pension fund, insurance company or endowment). However, alpha—in a market-neutral portfolio—can be obtained anywhere such as in stocks, bonds, hedge funds, real estate, and the like.

The total return approach is typical for portfolios with no clear liability such as mutual funds. Bonds are often used in the total return approach for a pure active portfolios, a pure passive portfolio or a combination as in the core satellite approach. The liability funding approach is typical for portfolios which have specific liabilities such as pension funds or, to a lesser extent, insurance companies. Bonds are typically used in the liability funding approach because some institutions have liabilities which are similar to bonds. These approaches are the two traditional portfolio investment approaches.

The recent unified approach (called *active alpha investing* by Litterman) begins with, in effect, the liability funding approach, using this approach to fund an institution's liabilities. Having funded the liabilities, the unified approach disaggregates the market (or beta) risk and the alpha risk using derivatives (long and short) to achieve an excess return over the liability funding return. The beta and alpha returns are essentially surplus optimization strategies. The unified approach, as with the liability funding approach, applies to institutions whose liabilities are known. In addition to pension funds and insurance companies, it could apply to foundations and endowments.

The role of bonds in the unified approach is varied. Certainly, bonds are used to fund liabilities. In addition, passive bond portfolios could be used in the market portfolio, for example through a *Lehman aggregate exchange-traded fund* (ETF). Finally, bonds could be a portion of the alpha portfolio, for example fixed income market-neutral hedge funds, high-yield bonds, or emerging market bonds.

Overall the total return approach and the liability funding approach are the traditional approaches. The unified approach (or active alpha approach) is more recent, more flexible, and requires liquid derivatives instruments. It may also provide more latitude and more responsibility to the CIO and portfolio mangers. Managing market risk should be easy and cheap. Managing alpha risk may be difficult and more expensive.

EX POST PORTFOLIO EVALUATION ANALYSIS

Assume that a portfolio has been developed corresponding to a specified investment strategy. Time has passed and the portfolio has performed. The portfolio and its performance must now be evaluated. The analysis of the portfolio's performance is referred to as an *ex post analysis*. There are three parts of the portfolio evaluation: selection of a benchmark, evaluation of returns, and evaluation of risks as measured in terms of tracking error.

Selection of a Benchmark

Before one can evaluate how a portfolio did, one has to know what it was supposed to do. Suppose a portfolio manager says, "My portfolio returned 6.5% in 2004. Wasn't that good?" In 2004 a 6.5% return was excellent for a short-term bond fund but terrible for a high-yield bond fund. To answer the question posed by the portfolio manager, one needs a benchmark for comparison. That is, one needs to know "what" the portfolio manager was trying to do.

Answering the "what" question involves selecting a benchmark, that is a portfolio—actual or conceptual—whose return can be used as a basis of comparison. In the above example, it could be a short-term, investment-grade bond portfolio, a high-yield bond portfolio, or a broad taxable, investment-grade bond portfolio.

There are three fundamentally different kinds of benchmarks. The first kind is a market index or market portfolio. In this case a sponsor of an index—such as Standard and Poor's, Lehman Brothers, or Dow Jones—specifies an initial portfolio and revises it according to some rules or practices and periodically or continually calculates the market capitalization-weighted (usually) prices and returns on the portfolio. This is a simulated portfolio, not an actual portfolio and, thus, has no expenses or transaction costs associated with it. The Lehman Brothers Aggregate Index, High Yield Index, Municipal Index, and Intermediate Term Index are examples of bond market indexes.

The second kind of benchmark is managed portfolios that are actual portfolios whose actual returns—usually after expenses and transaction costs—are collected and averaged for similar types of actual portfolios. For example, Morningstar and Lipper categorize fixed income mutual funds into cells, collect return data on these funds, and average the returns for funds in a cell on a market capitalization-weighted basis and then report these averages. Examples of such managed portfolio indexes are Morningstar's short-term, high-quality bond index; intermediate-term, low-quality bond index; and intermediate-term, intermediate-quality bond index—all averages of mutual funds with these characteristics. Instead of using asset portfolios as a benchmark, the liabilities or products of an institution may be used as the basis of the benchmark. This is the third kind of benchmark. The liabilities are specified, the returns on the liabilities are determined, and the marked capitalization-weighted return on the liabilities is used as a benchmark. With the poor performance of defined benefit pension plan since 2000, plan sponsors are beginning to use the calculated return on their pension liabilities as a benchmark or basis of comparison for their investment portfolios used to fund these pension benefits.

Finally, consider a fairly recent type of investment strategy that has no stock- or bond-related benchmarks. It is called an *absolute return portfolio*. In the limit such portfolios have a duration of zero and/or a beta of zero. That is, it responds to neither the overall bond market nor stock market. It achieves these characteristics, typically by taking short positions. As a frame of reference, a short-term interest rate—such as the *London interbank offered rate* (LIBOR)—is typically used as a benchmark for absolute return strategies.

Evaluation of Return: Attribution Analysis

Consider now *relative return portfolios*—that is, portfolios for which a benchmark has been specified, one of the three types of benchmarks specified in the previous section—and consider the portfolio's return relative to its benchmark. The return on the portfolio minus the return on the benchmark—typically called the *excess return*—is the return on the portfolio *relative to* the return on the benchmark. Implicitly, the relative portfolio return has been adjusted for risk because the benchmark should have approximately the same risk as the portfolio if the benchmark has been selected correctly.

If the excess return on the portfolio is positive, the portfolio has *outperformed* the benchmark (again, approximately on a risk adjusted basis); if negative, the portfolio has *underperformed*. Such outperformance and underperformance is used, not only to evaluate the portfolio, in general, but to compensate portfolio managers in particular.

The next question is how the outperformance or underperformance occurred. Was it due to market timing, that is taking a market bet, either bull or bear? Was it due to sector selection? Was it due to security selection?

Does it make any difference what the reason for outperformance or underperformance was? Yes it does. If the outperformance was due to market timing, the positive performance may not continue. Many—

including this author—believe that returns due to market timing are less persistent (that is, more of a gamble) than other types of returns. Outperformance due to individual bond selection may be preferable since such positive returns may be more persistent. In this case, with respect to compensation, the CIO may want to give the firm's fundamental bond analysts responsible for the outperformance an additional bonus.

Another reason that the source of the return makes a difference is that many portfolio managers have limitations on different sources of return (e.g., credit risk, duration mismatches, etc.) that are specified in their investment guidelines or prospectuses.

If knowledge of the causes of the outperformance or underperformance of a portfolio is important, how are these causes determined? To be specific, one tries to "attribute" the excess return (positive or negative) to specific risk factors, or deviations from the benchmark. This is conducted by a statistical exercise called *attribution analysis*. Exhibit 1.3 depicts a very simple type of attribution analysis. For example, if the excess return of a portfolio was 1.5%, the attribution analysis might conclude that 0.6% was due to market timing, 0.2% to sector selection, and 0.7% to security selection. In practice, one might also be interested in which particular sector and security overweights and underweights were responsible for these returns. A more detailed attribution analysis could answer these questions as well.

Risk: Tracking Error

In the previous section, in calculating excess return relative to a benchmark, we implicitly assumed that the managed portfolio and the benchmark had the same total risk. That is, it is assumed that the outperformance or underperformance was due to manager skill in deviating from various risk factors, not to differences in overall risk. But this is not usually the case. The total risk of the portfolio is typically dif-

EXHIBIT 1.3 Attribution Analysis

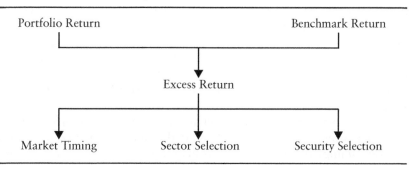

ferent from that of the benchmark. How different are the risks? What is the metric for measuring this difference?

To answer these questions, consider a simple example. While there have been various measures of risk proposed in the literature, risk is typically measured by the standard deviation of returns (SD). Suppose that the benchmark for a portfolio is the S&P 500 Index and that its SD is approximately 18%. Assume that the SD of the managed portfolio is 20%. Is the incremental risk of the managed portfolio the excess of the risk of the managed portfolio (P) over the risk of the benchmarks (B); that is, $SD(P) - SD(B) = 20\% - 18\% = 2\%$? Of course not. This calculation ignores the fundamental result of Markowitz diversification—it ignores the effect of diversification. In this case, taking the differences of the risk ignores the relationship of the return pattern of the portfolio and the return pattern of the benchmark. Are these return patterns perfectly correlated, in which case the benchmark is a good one? Or are the return patterns very imperfectly correlated, in which case the benchmark is not a good one?

So what is the best way to determine the risk of a portfolio's return relative to a benchmark's return. We will denote $R(P)$ as the portfolio's return and $R(B)$ the benchmark's return. The most obvious way is to calculate the difference in these returns, $R(P) - R(B)$, and determine the standard deviation—the risk—of this difference, that is $SD[R(P) - R(B)]$. This construct, that is, the standard deviation of the difference in the portfolio return and the benchmark return, is called *tracking error* (*TE*) of the portfolio's return relative to the benchmark's return.

A second way to determine the tracking error is to use the statistical equation for the risk a portfolio of two or more securities that requires the correlation coefficient of the returns on these securities. In this context, the portfolio would consist of a 100% long position (+100%) in the managed portfolio and a 100% short position (-100%) in the benchmark. Examples of this method are considered in the appendix to this chapter. These two approaches are perfectly statistically equivalent. Both start with the returns of the portfolio and benchmark over time. The first approach—the approach usually used in practice—calculates the differences in return over time and then calculates the mean and SD of these differences. The second approach calculates the mean of each return, the correlation between these returns, and then the standard deviation of the difference from the standard statistical equation used in the appendix at the end of this chapter.

Overall, the standard deviation of the difference in returns is called the tracking error of the return of a managed portfolio *relative to* its benchmark. Thus, the *standard deviation of the difference in the returns* of the managed portfolio and the benchmark, *not the difference in the standard deviations* of the returns on the managed portfolio and the benchmarks is a metric for the relative risk of a managed portfolio relative to its benchmark.

Exhibit 1.4 provides general guidelines for the magnitude of the tracking error and the degree of active risk of a portfolio relative to its benchmarks. Thus, a tracking error (standard deviation) of 0% indicates an indexed portfolio; a tracking error of 2% indicates a portfolio, which has little tracking risk relative to its benchmark; and a tracking error of 6% indicates a significant amount of tracking risk. Returning to a previous concept, the greater the tracking error, the greater the potential for alpha (either positive or negative). Thus, a portfolio with a tracking error of 0% has no potential for alpha generation.

CONCLUSION

The fundamentals of fixed income investment strategies include many of the same elements of stock investment strategies, but also some unique features. These unique features are due to the different cash flows for bonds, specifically their defined coupons and maturity values. There have been advances in the concepts and practices for both fixed income and stock investment strategies, and these advances have tended to unify the treatment of fixed income and stock investment strategies. Nevertheless, there are unique aspects of fixed income investment strategies due to their exact coupon and maturity cash flows. Fixed income investment strategies are myriad and have many applications.

EXHIBIT 1.4 Magnitudes of Tracking Error
Tracking Error (TE) for Degree of Activity of an Active Portfolio

TE	Strategy
0%	Passive Portfolio (Indexed)
1%–2%	"Index plus" strategy
2%–4%	Moderate risk strategy
4%–7%	Fairly active strategy
Over 8%	Very aggressive strategy

Note: TE measured in terms of the number of standard deviations.

APPENDIX

Equation for Alternative Method for Computing Tracking Error

The tracking error of a portfolio (P) relative to a benchmark (B) can be calculated from the standard equation for the risk of a combination of variables. This equation for two asset types, P and B, is

$$SD(P, B) = W(P)^2 SD(P)^2 + W(B)^2 SD(B)^2 + 2 \times CORR \times W(P) \times W(B) \times SD(P) \times SD(B)$$

where $W(.)$ is the weight of the asset type in the portfolio, $SD(.)$ is the standard deviation of the asset type, and $CORR$ is the correlation coefficient between the two asset types.

In this application of a managed portfolio, P, and a benchmark, B, $W(P) = +1$ and $W(B) = -1$. Also, $SD(P, B)$ is the tracking error (TE) of P relative to B.

The following table shows the tracking error of P relative to B for two different combinations of risks of P and B (20%/18% and 18%/18%) and three different correlation coefficients $(CORRs)$ between P and B:

A. $SD(P) = SD(B) = 18\%$	$W_P = 1; W_B = -1$
$CORR\ (P, B)$	$SD(P, B)$ (TE)
+1	0%
0.9	8.1%
0	25%

B. $SD(P) = 20\%$ $SD(B) = 18\%$	
$CORR\ (P, B)$	$W_P = 1; W_B = -1$ $SD(P, B)$ (TE)
+1	2%
0.9	8.7%
0	26.9%

Note that for a perfect benchmark $(CORR = +1)$, the tracking error is equal to the difference between $SD(P)$ and $SD(B)$ (0% in A and 2% in B). But for $CORR(P, B)$ less than +1, the tracking error becomes greater than this difference as $CORR\ (P, B)$ decreases.

CHAPTER 2

Liquidity, Trading, and Trading Costs

Leland E. Crabbe, Ph.D.
Consultant

Frank J. Fabozzi, Ph.D., CFA
Frederick Frank Adjunct Professor of Finance
School of Management
Yale University

A goal of active portfolio management is to achieve a better performance than a portfolio that is simply diversified broadly. To this end, portfolio managers make informed judgments about bond market risks and expected returns, and align their portfolios accordingly by trading bonds in the secondary market. By definition, portfolios that are actively managed are portfolios that are actively traded.

While trading can improve performance, any active portfolio strategy must account for the cost of trading and for the vagaries of liquidity. In this chapter, we show that trading costs and liquidity are inextricably linked though the bid-ask spread. The cost of trading depends on that bid-ask spread, as well as duration and the frequency of turnover. While trading costs can be measured, they cannot be known with certainty because the bid-ask spread could be wide or narrow

The authors benefited from helpful comments by William Berliner, Anand Bhattacharya, Ludovic Breger, Howard Chin, Joseph DeMichele, Sri Ramaswamy, and Yu Zhu.

when trades are executed. In fact, the bid-ask spread changes over time, it varies across issuers, and it depends on the size of the transaction. That uncertainty about the cost of trading creates risk—liquidity risk— and that liquidity risk, in turn, gives rise to a risk premium. Consequently, illiquid bonds have higher yields than liquid bonds, not only because their wider bid-ask spreads imply a higher cost of trading but also because investors require compensation for the uncertainty about trading costs. The importance of this relation between the degree of liquidity risk and the level of yield spreads cannot be understated.

Bond liquidity has a pervasive influence on portfolio management. Liquidity affects not only the cost of trading, but it also gives rise to creative trading strategies. Liquidity not only plays a role in determining the level of spreads, but also in establishing relative value between different sectors of the fixed income market. Indeed, because liquidity contributes to portfolio risks and because trading costs subtract from portfolio returns, portfolios that optimize across the spectrum of known risks and returns will have an optimal amount of liquid bonds and an optimal turnover ratio. Decisions about trading and portfolio liquidity are part of the asset allocation decision.

In this chapter, we analyze liquidity and trading costs from several perspectives. We begin with a description of the secondary market, focusing on the role of dealers in determining the bid-ask spread. We also review the spread arithmetic used to measure the excess return on a bond swap, and we build on this arithmetic to incorporate the cost of trading. The concepts and methodology we provide in this chapter can also be applied to bond portfolio optimization by maximizing portfolio expected returns taking into account trading costs.

LIQUIDITY AND TRADING COSTS

Among portfolio managers, liquidity is an incessant topic of discussion. Sometimes, fluctuations in liquidity occur as a rational response to observable changes in macroeconomic trends or corporate sector risks. But more often than not, liquidity evaporates for reasons that seem hidden, trivial, or inexplicable. History teaches that liquid markets can quickly become illiquid. Corporate bond markets, in particular, have a history of alternating from periods of confidence and transparency—with multiple dealer quotes, heavy secondary market volume, and tight bid-ask spreads—to periods of gloom and uncertainty characterized by low trading volumes and wide bid-ask spreads, or worse "offer without." At times of extreme illiquidity, corporate bond salespeople are slow to return phone calls, corporate bond traders seem to spend an inordinate amount of time in the bathroom, and corporate bond portfolio managers mutter the mantra "the Street is not my friend." Portfolio managers, most of whom are educated to believe that financial markets are efficient, learn through experience that bond market liquidity is capricious, illusive, and maddening.

Conceptual Framework

Although liquidity is difficult to understand, it does not defy analysis. Our analysis begins with a list of observations about liquidity. First and most obvious, investors need to be paid for liquidity risk. Liquidity or, to be more precise, illiquidity can be viewed as a risk that reduces the flexibility of a portfolio. Liquidity risk should be reflected in the yield spread on a bond relative to its benchmark: the greater the illiquidity, the wider the spread. In this respect, liquidity risk is no different than other bond risks such as credit risk or the market risk of embedded options. Greater risks require wider spreads.

Second and equally obvious, bonds that are difficult to analyze are less liquid than standard bonds. For example, corporate bonds are less liquid than Treasuries, and bonds with unusual redemption features are less liquid than bullet bonds. Similarly, complex collateralized mortgage obligation bond classes are less liquid than planned amortization class bonds. In general, bonds that are difficult to analyze trade less frequently, have wider bid-ask spreads, and have a narrower base of potential buyers. Investors need to be paid for the effort it takes to analyze a complex bond.

Third, market liquidity depends on the size of the transaction. An investor may find it easy to sell $2 million of bonds at the bid side of the market, but a sale of $10 million might come at a concession to the bid side, and a sale of $50 million would typically require a large concession and a good deal of patience.

Fourth, liquidity varies over time. Stable markets are usually liquid markets. In stable markets, bid-ask spreads are relatively narrow, and size does not generally imply a large concession in price. By contrast, volatile markets, especially bear markets, are notoriously illiquid. During bear markets, bid-ask spreads widen, and it often becomes all but impossible to trade in large size.

Fifth, bid-side liquidity causes more angst and sleepless nights than offered-side liquidity.

The Institutional Market Structure: Bond Dealers and the Bid-Ask Spread

Trading is costly. To understand why trading generates costs, it helps to explore the mechanics and structure of the secondary market. In the bond market, most trades are directed through bond dealers, mainly investment banks, rather than through exchanges or on electronic platforms. Bond dealers serve as intermediaries between investors, standing ready to buy and sell securities in the secondary market.

The cost of trading is measured by the bid-ask spread. Most major bond dealers are willing to provide *indicative* "two-sided" (bid-ask) quotes for all but the most obscure bonds. For example, a dealer might quote a Ford 5-year bond as "80–78, 5-by-10," indicating that the dealer would be willing to buy $5 million of the Ford bond at a spread of 80 basis points above the 5-year Treasury, and sell $10 million of the same bond at a 78-basis-point spread. Clearly, bonds that have narrow bid-ask spreads have good liquidity. Liquidity depends not only on the magnitude of the bid-ask spread, but also on the depth of the market, as measured by the number of dealers that are willing to make markets, and also by the size that can be transacted near the quoted market. For example, an "80–78, 5-by-5" market quoted by three dealers is more liquid than an "80–78, 1-by-2" market quoted by only one dealer.

An indicative bid-ask quote is not the same as a firm market. In practice, an investor and a dealer usually haggle back and forth several times before agreeing to the terms of trade. The haggling process may take several minutes, several hours, or even several days; in many cases, the haggling concludes without an agreement to trade.

On any given day, a dealer may provide dozens of indicative quotes, but the number of actual trades may be quite small. In fact, most corporate bonds and mortgaged-backed securities do not trade every day, or even once a month. Moreover, trading tends to be concentrated in a limited number of bonds.

For example, in the corporate bond market trading tends to be concentrated in:

- Bonds that have recently been placed in the new issue market
- Bonds that are close substitutes for recent new issues (e.g., swapping an old GM 5-year for a new Ford 5-year)
- Bonds of large and frequent corporate borrowers such as the major banking, telecommunications, auto, and financial companies
- Bonds of companies that are involved in important events such as a merger, a rating change, an earnings surprise, or an industry shock

For these types of bonds, dealers generally provide liquid markets with tight bid-ask spreads (e.g., XYZ Corporation 10-year 97–95, $10 million-by-$10 million). Moreover, dealers prefer to hold inventories in bonds that have high turnover, deep demand, transparent pricing, and close substitutes. Dealers' preference for liquid bonds in itself acts to narrow the bid-ask spread. Liquidity begets liquidity.

For less liquid bonds, indicative quotes are not firm markets, bid-ask spreads are wide, and transaction amounts tend to be small. The vast majority of corporate bonds trade only infrequently. For most individual corporate bonds, the market is neither smooth nor continuous.

In the securitized product markets—agency and nonagency residential *mortgage-backed securities* (MBS), commercial MBS, *asset-backed securities* (ABS), and *collateralized debt obligations* (CDO)—there are varying degrees of liquidity. In these markets, there is a lower spread to a benchmark for issuers where there is greater transparency of deal information, particularly credit and severity loss information.

In the agency mortgage market, trading tends to be concentrated in agency pass-throughs because this sector has a TBA market. In the nonagency mortgage market, liquidity is better for:

- Bonds from newer deals issued by large originators with well-established shelves and servicing (i.e., "known entities")
- Tranches that are fairly generic in terms of both their structures and loan attributes (e.g., 3-year sequential off jumbo loan collateral)
- Bonds with coupons and note rates (i.e., weighted average coupons) close to prevailing market levels
- Bonds from structures with very broad and deep investor bases (e.g., LIBOR-based floaters with minimal cap exposure)

In the ABS sector, there are differences in liquidity by sector. There is excellent liquidity for credit cards and auto loan/lease backed securities. There is medium liquidity for home equity loan backed securities because of increasing concerns over loose underwriting standards and the bursting of a potential housing bubble leading to spread widening. There is low/poor liquidity for sectors that have experienced credit events (e.g., manufactured housing loans, aircraft leases, and franchise loans). There are also differences between issuers within the ABS sector. For instance, for credit cards, Citigroup will trade tighter to some small bank securitizing its credit card receivables. Liquidity is higher for well-rated servicers, well-capitalized issuers, more-frequent issuers, and those issuers that provide detailed information on their deals.

Relative to other ABS, the CMBS sector (the fastest-growing sector of the Lehman Aggregate Index) has a few larger benchmark issues that trade with a very high degree of liquidity. There is less variability in structure in today's CMBS market between different deals. As a result, to some extent all 9- to 10-year average life triple-A-rated tranches are somewhat fungible. This allows for these deals to also trade very liquidly. More recent issues tend to exhibit a higher degree of liquidity than previous issues as they are fresher in investor's minds. More-seasoned deals, lower-credit tranches, single-property type, or deals with property type concentration trade less liquidly.

For credit products there seems to be far more bid in competition activity in the secondary markets of both ABS and CMBS than in the corporate market. The ABS and CMBS sectors are largely insulated from corporate credit event risk. Historically, there has been only modest spread widening during credit crises at the parent level (e.g., Ford/GMAC ABS versus Ford/GMAC debentures) and there is greater exposure to risk of regulatory changes (e.g., interest rate limits on consumer debt).

For mezzanine and subordinated tranches in CDO deals, the tranches are typically acquired by investors that seek to buy and hold, thereby limiting liquidity. This has led this sector to be very much a new issue market, with much less secondary trading than the other securitized sectors.

Coordination and Information Problems: Understanding Trading Costs

Trading costs exist because of market imperfections. Two of the most important market imperfections are coordination problems and information problems. Coordination problems arise because buy and sell orders do not arrive simultaneously; rather, dealers must hold securities in inventory until they can arrange placements with investors. Holding bond inventories is costly because inventories must be financed. In addition to the cost of carrying inventories, dealers face uncertainty about the time required to place their holdings with new investors. When a dealer buys a bond in the secondary market, he or she faces the risk that the bond may remain in inventory for a day, a week, a month, or even longer. At most investment banks, the cost of carrying inventories rises over time because risk managers penalize stale inventories with higher capital charges. The bid-ask spread serves to compensate dealers for the cost of holding inventory and for the uncertainty about the holding period.

Information problems are another underlying source of trading costs. The more difficult it is for dealers and investors to analyze a bond, the longer will a dealer expect to hold the bond in inventory, and the greater will be the cost of trading. In the case of corporate bonds, the information that investors analyze can be divided into two categories: (1) information that is specific to the corporate borrower and (2) information that is specific to the bond issue. Investors analyze a variety of types of information about a borrower, such as its leverage ratios, cash flow, management expertise, litigation risk, credit ratings, cyclical risk, and industry risk. Holding other factors constant, bid-ask spreads are wider for companies that are difficult to analyze.

Along with analyzing information that is specific to the borrower, investors also evaluate information that is specific to the bond issue, such as its face value, maturity, covenants, seniority, and option and redemption features. Other factors held constant, bonds with standard features have low information costs because they are relatively easy to evaluate. Conversely, a complicated security will have lower liquidity and higher information costs, even if other securities issued by the same borrower are very liquid. In the case of securitized products, the dealer must have the transaction modeled and must be able to analyze the collateral's prepayment behavior and default/recovery rates.

As a consequence of these information and coordination problems, the magnitude of the bid-ask spread varies over time and across issuers due to a number of factors such as those described as follows.

Slope of the Yield Curve   As noted, bond inventories must be financed. Inventories become more expensive to finance when the yield curve flattens, because the money market serves as dealers' main source of funding. As a result, to compensate for the higher cost of carry, dealers widen bid-ask spreads when the curve flattens. A flat yield curve may also affect liquidity and the bid-ask spread indirectly through other channels. First, a flattening of the curve often spurs investors to reallocate funds to the money markets and away from bond markets. When funds flow out of the bond market, spreads must widen to equate supply and demand. Second, the yield curve generally flattens during the late stage of the business cycle, when the Fed raises short rates to quell inflationary pressures. In the case of corporate bonds, credit ratings, corporate earnings, and corporate spreads display strong cyclical patterns, and those patterns are highly correlated with the slope of the yield curve.[1] Greater uncertainty about the economy gives rise to higher information costs and wider bid-ask spreads.

Market Volatility   Orderly markets are liquid markets. When the market is calm, yield spreads exhibit low volatility and bid-ask spreads are relatively narrow. At those times, dealers often carry large inventories, but inventories tend to turn over quickly. In orderly markets, dealers earn steady profits from a high volume of turnover, rather than from a wide bid-ask margin. By contrast, in times of market turmoil, such as the 1998 hedge fund crisis, dealers face greater uncertainty about the depth of investor demand for spread products and about credit risk in the cor-

---

[1] See Chapter 10 in Leland Crabbe and Frank J. Fabozzi, *Managing a Corporate Bond Portfolio* (New York: John Wiley & Sons, 2002).

porate sector. The same was observed in Spring 2004 in the mortgage market with the collapse of one hedge fund, Granite Capital, that invested in complex mortgage products. At times when markets are risky, dealers and investors become more risk averse. Consequently, in volatile markets, as dealers become reluctant to hold large inventories, bid-ask spreads widen.

Ratings   During most of the 1990s, Disney's bonds were quoted with a tighter bid-ask spread than Time Warner's bonds. Both were large, well-known companies, and both were in the same industry, but Time Warner carried a lower credit rating. The risk of credit deterioration exists for all companies, but the risk becomes more crucial for lower-rated companies. For a high-rated company, a small mistake in a cash flow projection may have no discernible effect on credit risk, but for lower-rated companies the margin for error is slim. In general, low-rated bonds have wider bid-ask spreads than high-rated bonds.

Industry and Sector   In some industries, each company may have unique business risks that are difficult to analyze. For example, each company in the Real Estate Investment Trust sector requires intensive credit research. In that industry, credit quality can vary markedly across companies due to differences in management, regional exposure, and tenant diversification. When the company-specific risk dominates the industry risk, information costs are high and bid-ask spreads wide. In other industries, such as oil production, the industry risk generally dominates the company-specific risks.

Name Recognition   Information about large companies, such as Ford and Citigroup, is broadly disseminated in the media and financial markets. Consequently, well-known companies face lower information problems, and, other factors held equal, their bonds trade with tighter bid-ask spreads.

Structure   In the secondary market, simpler is better. The bullet bond, the simplest bond, trades with a tighter bid-ask spread than a bond with a complex structure. For example, noncallable bonds typically trade with tighter bid-ask spreads than callable bonds of the same issuer. Callable bonds are less liquid because their duration can change significantly when interest rates change. Investors often disagree about which models are appropriate to analyze bonds with complex structures. In the corporate bond market, investors would prefer to focus solely on analyzing credit risk, rather than bond structures. As a result of these information problems, the market for complex bonds is not as deep as it is for bullet bonds, which gives rise to wider bid-ask spreads.

An Analytical Framework

The analytical tools to measure trading costs are the same tools that are used for all fixed income investments. As usual, duration is the most important tool. Long-duration bonds usually have higher trading costs than bonds with short durations.

Probability theory is the other key tool for measuring trading costs. In fixed income strategy, investors frequently use probability distributions to characterize uncertain events (e.g., a 70% probability that the Fed cuts the funds rate by 25 basis points at the next FOMC meeting). Those same probability tools can be applied to characterize the uncertainty about trading costs. Specifically, the timing of a trade, the size of the bid-ask spread, and the depth of the market are not known with certainty, but the uncertainty can be described by probability distributions. For example, when a portfolio manager buys a bond, he or she knows that the bond may be sold before maturity. The bond may have a 1% probability of being sold on the next day, a 10% probability of being sold over the next month, and a 50% probability over the next year. The portfolio manager likewise knows that the bond's bid-ask spread may be wide or narrow at the time he or she wants to sell. Furthermore, the amount of bonds that can be sold at the bid side of the market also can be described by a probability distribution. There may be, for example, an 80% probability of selling $1 million at the bid-side spread, but only a 30% chance of selling $10 million at that spread. These probability distributions cannot be observed directly, but they can be inferred from historical data or subjectively estimated using scenario analysis. Portfolio managers can use these probability distributions to estimate the cost of trading.

CORPORATE BOND SWAPS

Trading has measurable costs and potential benefits. In this section, we quantify the potential benefits, with a review of the spread arithmetic of a bond swap. Specifically, we derive the basic formulas for excess returns and breakeven spreads. In subsequent sections, we use this framework to quantify the costs of a bond swap—specifically, the trading costs—and later we expand the cost/benefit framework to a broader portfolio context.

A Review of Spread Duration Math

Investors decide to trade when they conclude that doing so will enhance portfolio returns or reduce risk. Many investors are "yield hogs." They love to swap from low-yielding to high-yielding bonds. Although yield is a key element of the decision to trade, it is not the only element, and it is often not the most important element. Indeed, one of the first lessons of fixed income investing is the distinction between a bond's yield and its return: because markets fluctuate, yields can differ substantially from subsequent returns.

Similarly, a key lesson in bond portfolio management is that a bond's yield spread can differ substantially from its subsequent *excess return*. Frequently, corporate bonds and other spread products look "cheap" when they have a large yield spread above U.S. Treasuries or other high-quality bonds, but the realized excess return depends on a number of factors, not just the spread.

To identify the factors that contribute to excess returns, we begin with a simple example of a bond swap. In our example, the investor is buying Bond A and selling Bond B. Initially, we will analyze the general case where the bonds do not necessarily have equal durations, and we will not address the cost of trading. Later in this chapter, we analyze duration-neutral swaps and trading costs, as well as the role of uncertainty.

Over a 1-year horizon, the total return on Bond A (TR_A) is approximately equal to its coupon (C_A) plus the percentage change in price $(\Delta P_A/P_A)$:[2]

$$TR_A \approx C_A + \Delta P_A/P_A \qquad (2.1)$$

Since the percentage change in price is approximately equal to the change in yield (ΔY_A) times the *end-of-period* duration $D_{A,t+1}$, or, suppressing the time subscript for now, D_A, the total return on Bond A can be rewritten as:[3]

$$TR_A \approx C_A - D_A \, \Delta Y_A \qquad (2.2)$$

When Bond A is a par bond, its coupon equals the yield on its Treasury benchmark $(Y_{A,\text{Treas}})$ plus a spread (S_A):

$$C_A = Y_{A,\text{Treas}} + S_A \qquad (2.3)$$

---

[2] In this chapter, the formulas for total returns, excess returns, and breakevens are not exact, but only approximations, in part because the returns depend on the reinvestment rate assumption. For short investment horizons, the reinvestment rate usually has only a small effect on returns. More importantly, the return calculations do not account for convexity.

[3] Of course, the end-of-period duration cannot be known at the beginning of the investment horizon because the horizon duration depends on the horizon Treasury yield and the horizon spread. Those horizon yields and spreads can be estimated from forward rates.

By definition, the change in the yield on Bond A (ΔY_A) is equal to the change in the Treasury yield plus the change in spread:

$$\Delta Y_A = \Delta Y_{A,\text{Treas}} + \Delta S_A \qquad (2.4)$$

Substituting equations (2.3) and (2.4) into equation (2.2) results in a formula for the total return on Bond A in terms of its spread, horizon duration, and Treasury benchmark yield:

$$TR_A \approx (Y_{A,\text{Treas}} + S_A) - D_A (\Delta Y_{A,\text{Treas}} + \Delta S_A) \qquad (2.5)$$

Similarly, the total return on Bond B can be approximated in terms of its spread, horizon duration, and Treasury benchmark yield:

$$TR_B \approx (Y_{B,\text{Treas}} + S_B) - D_B (\Delta Y_{B,\text{Treas}} + \Delta S_B) \qquad (2.6)$$

When an investor buys Bond A and sells Bond B, the Excess Return (ER) on the swap is equal to the difference in the total returns. Subtracting equation (2.6) from equation (2.5) results in:

$$\begin{aligned} ER &= TR_A - TR_B \\ &= (Y_{A,\text{Treas}} + S_A) - D_A(\Delta Y_{A,\text{Treas}} + \Delta S_A) \\ &\quad - (Y_{B,\text{Treas}} + S_B) - D_B(\Delta Y_{B,\text{Treas}} + \Delta S_B) \end{aligned} \qquad (2.7)$$

Rearranging terms gives:

$$\begin{aligned} ER &\approx (Y_{A,\text{Treas}} - Y_{B,\text{Treas}}) + (S_A - S_B) - D_A(\Delta Y_{A,\text{Treas}} - \Delta Y_{B,\text{Treas}}) \\ &\quad + (D_B - D_A)\Delta Y_{B,\text{Treas}} - D_A(\Delta S_A - \Delta S_B) + (D_B - D_A)\Delta S_B \end{aligned} \qquad (2.8)$$

Equation (2.8) shows that the excess return on the bond swap depends on six factors:

1. Slope of the Treasury curve $= Y_{A,\text{Treas}} - Y_{B,\text{Treas}}$
2. Slope of the spread curve $= S_A - S_B$
3. Change in the Treasury curve $= D_A (\Delta Y_{A,\text{Treas}} - \Delta Y_{B,\text{Treas}})$
4. Change in the spread curve $= D_A (\Delta S_A - \Delta S_B)$
5. Direction of Treasury rates $= (D_B - D_A)\Delta Y_{B,\text{Treas}}$
6. Direction of spreads $= (D_B - D_A)\Delta S_B$

Four of these factors can move over the investment horizon: the change in the Treasury curve; the change in the spread curve; the direction of Treasuries; and the direction of spreads. The change in the spread curve is only one of the moving parts that determines the return on a bond swap![4] Therefore, a bond swap can be an imprecise and risky strategy to capture a wide yield spread when the swapped bonds have different durations.

Duration-Neutral Swaps

Fortunately, the arithmetic of a bond swap becomes simplified when both bonds have roughly the same duration. In that case, we can make use of the following relations:

$$D_B = D_A = D \tag{2.9}$$

and

$$Y_{A,\text{Treas}} = Y_{B,\text{Treas}} \tag{2.10}$$

In words equation (2.9) says that we have selected two bonds, A and B, that have the same duration and, therefore, as indicated by equation (2.10) both bonds are spread over the same benchmark Treasury yield. After substituting these relations into equation (2.8), we arrive at a simplified expression for the return pickup on a bond swap over the 1-year horizon. The excess return is equal to the spread between Bond A and Bond B minus the duration times the change in the spread:

$$ER \approx (S_A - S_B) - D(\Delta S_A - \Delta S_B) \tag{2.11}$$

Equation (2.11) shows that the excess return can be attributed to two factors: the spread and the market move. The first term, $(S_A - S_B)$, is the spread, and the second term, $D\,(\Delta S_A - \Delta S_B)$, is the market move, which captures the change in the spread curve, scaled by duration. As a result of constructing a duration-neutral swap, the excess return has only one moving part, the market move. In descriptive terms:

$$\text{Excess return} = \text{Spread} + \text{Market move} \tag{2.12}$$

For example, consider a swap in which the investor sells Bond B at 50 basis points and swaps into Bond A at 80 basis points. Therefore, the Spread is 30 basis points. The bonds are estimated to have a duration of about five after a 1-year holding period. If the spread between Bond A and Bond B tightens by 20 basis points, then the Market Move will con-

---

[4] For a discussion of a change in the spread curve, see Chapter 8 in Crabbe and Fabozzi, *Managing a Corporate Bond Portfolio*.

tribute 100 basis points to the excess return. The excess return would sum to 130 basis points:

$$ER = (80 - 50) - 5(-20) = 130 \text{ bps} \qquad (2.13)$$

Of course, the realized excess return may differ from the excess return that the investor expected. In our example, the investor expects to earn 130 basis points by swapping from Bond B to Bond A, but that expectation is premised on the forecast of a 20 basis point spread narrowing. The realized return could be greater or less than 130 basis points, depending on whether the spread between Bond A and Bond B tightens by more or less than the 20 basis point forecast.

Rather than focusing on a single forecast for the excess return, some investors prefer to examine a variety of scenarios and to assign probabilities to those scenarios. For example, the horizon spread can be characterized by a probability distribution, with M different possible outcomes, each with a probability of m_i. Under this method, the excess return given by equation (2.11) can be rewritten as:

$$\text{Excess return} = (S_A - S_B) - D \sum_{i=1}^{M} m_i (\Delta S_{A,i} - \Delta S_{B,i}) \qquad (2.14)$$

Exhibit 2.1 shows several scenarios for the excess return derived from alternative views about the horizon spread between Bonds A and B. In this analysis, the investor believes a 20 basis point spread tightening has the highest probability, 40%, and under that scenario the excess return is 130 basis points. However, if the spread between Bond A and Bond B were to *widen* by 20 basis points, rather than tighten by 20

EXHIBIT 2.1 Excess Return on a Bond Swap under Alternative Spread Scenarios
Spread – Duration × (Change in spread) = Excess return

Spread (bps)	Duration (end of period)	Change in Spread (bps)	Excess Return (bps)	Probability
		−40	230	0.10
		−20	130	0.40
30	5	0	30	0.25
		20	−70	0.15
		40	−170	0.10
		Expected Excess Return	55 bps	

basis points, the excess return would be –70 basis points. The expected excess return, weighted by the probabilities across all scenarios, is 55 basis points. To develop a more rigorous approach to forecasting excess returns, some portfolio managers model historical data on yield spreads to estimate probability distributions.

Breakeven Analysis

In many cases, investors measure the risk of a bond swap in terms of the breakeven. The breakeven indicates how much spreads have to change in order for a bond swap to have an excess return equal to zero. Thus, by setting equation (2.11) equal to zero and solving for the spread change, we see that the breakeven is equal to the initial spread between Bonds A and B divided by the end-of-period duration:

$$\text{Breakeven spread change} \approx (S_A - S_B)/D \qquad (2.15)$$

To calculate a breakeven, let us continue with the example in which the investor sells Bond B at 50 basis points and swaps into Bond A at 80 basis points. That bond swap will break even if the spread between Bond A and Bond B widens from its current level of 30 basis points to 36 basis points over the 1-year horizon:

$$\text{Breakeven spread change} \approx (80 - 50)/5 = 6 \text{ bps} \qquad (2.16)$$

In this example, the initial spread of 30 basis points is exactly offset by a market move of –30 basis points.

The breakeven spread is an important concept, but it is an incomplete measure of risk. The breakeven measures how much spreads could widen before a bond swap loses money, but it does not measure the likelihood of losing money. The breakeven tells us nothing about probabilities or volatility. If spreads are very volatile, a bond swap may have a high probability of busting through the breakeven. Conversely, if volatility is low, the breakeven may have little relevance. The breakeven represents only one point on the probability distribution of possible outcomes for excess returns. The probability distribution of spreads, and the implied distribution of excess returns, provides a much more comprehensive measure of risk.[5]

Swaps between Corporates and Treasuries

Spread arithmetic becomes even more simplified when an investor swaps from a Treasury to a corporate bond with a similar duration. For exam-

---

[5] Spread volatility is discussed in Chapter 7 of Crabbe and Fabozzi, *Managing a Corporate Bond Portfolio*.

ple, if Bond B is the benchmark Treasury bond, it will have a spread of zero ($S_B = 0$), and the excess return on the bond swap simplifies to:

$$ER \approx S_A - D\Delta S_A \qquad (2.17)$$

Likewise, the equation for the breakeven spread to Treasuries becomes, simply, Spread divided by duration:

$$\text{Breakeven spread to Treasury} \approx S_A/D \qquad (2.18)$$

For example, if Bond A has a spread of 80 basis points and an end-of-period duration of 5, its spread could widen by 16 basis points over a 1-year horizon (from 80 basis points to 96 basis points), and the bond's return would just break even with the return on a comparable Treasury. Again, the breakeven spread to Treasuries is a limited measure of risk because it represents only one point on the distribution of possible returns versus Treasuries.

Shorter Investment Horizons

In the previous analysis, we calculated the excess return under the assumption of a 1-year investment horizon. That calculation can be modified easily to accommodate shorter investment horizons, such as one quarter or one month. Shorter investment horizons affect the calculated excess return in two ways. First, the return attributed to the spread will be reduced because the spread will be earned over a shorter time period. Second, the return attributed to the market move will be larger because the end-of-period duration will be slightly greater.

In general, to accommodate a shorter investment horizon, the excess return given by equation (2.11) can be reexpressed as:

$$ER \approx (S_A - S_B)(H/12) - D(\Delta S_A - \Delta S_B) \qquad (2.19)$$

where H is the investment horizon measured in months.

To illustrate the importance of the investment horizon, let us continue with the example where an investor sells Bond B at 50 basis points and swaps into Bond A at 80 basis points. Now, instead of using a 1-year holding period, let us assume a 3-month horizon. In this case, the expected duration at the horizon would be 5.5, larger than the duration of 5 under the 1-year investment horizon. If the spread between Bond A and Bond B tightens by 20 basis points, then the bond swap will result in a return pickup of 117.5 basis points:

$$ER \approx (80 - 50)(3/12) - 5.5 (-20) = 117.5 \text{ bps} \qquad (2.20)$$

In this example, it is interesting to note that the 117.5 basis point return pickup over this 3-month horizon is less than the 130 basis point excess return under the previous example of the 1-year horizon, even though spreads tightened by 20 basis points in both examples. In terms of attribution, the spread contributed 7.5 basis points over the 3-month horizon, compared with 30 basis points over the 1-year horizon, while the market move contributed 110 basis points, compared with 100 basis points over the longer horizon. Thus, the impact of earning 30 basis points of spread for a shorter period of time more than offset the benefit of a larger end-of-period duration. Of course, the 12.5 basis point difference in excess returns is specific to this example. By changing the assumptions about the duration, the initial spread, or the spread change, it is easy to construct alternative scenarios in which the excess return is larger over a shorter time horizon.

The formula for the breakeven spread, likewise, needs to be modified when the investment horizon is less than one year. Specifically, a more general expression for the breakeven spread is:

$$\text{Breakeven} \approx (S_A - S_B)(H/12)(1/D) \tag{2.21}$$

Likewise, a general approximation for the breakeven spread to Treasuries is:

$$\text{Breakeven spread to Treasury} \approx S_A \, (H/12)(1/D) \tag{2.22}$$

For example, under a 3-month horizon, a bond with an 80 basis point spread to Treasuries and a 5.5 end-of-period duration could widen by 3.6 basis points (from 80 to 83.6) and just break even with Treasuries. By contrast, over a 1-year horizon, the breakeven was 16 basis points. Short investment horizons imply thin breakevens. In turn, thin breakevens barely cover the cost of trading.

Updating Spread Duration Math to Account for Trading Costs and Liquidity

Up to this point, we have calculated the excess return without accounting for liquidity risk. In effect, we have assumed that (1) trading has no cost; (2) the bid-ask spread is zero; and (3) the only factors influencing the excess return on a bond swap are the spread and the market move. To account for trading costs, we can include them explicitly as a component of the excess return:

$$\text{Excess return} \approx \text{Spread} + \text{Market move} - \text{Trading cost} \tag{2.23}$$

Trading cost is equal to the *beginning-of-period* duration (D_t) times the bid-ask spread (BA):

$$\text{Trading cost} = D_t \times BA \qquad (2.24)$$

Similarly, the formula for the excess return, equation (2.11), can be re-expressed as:

$$ER \approx (S_A - S_B) - D_{t+1}(\Delta S_A - \Delta S_B) - D_t \times BA \qquad (2.25)$$

Note that while both the market move and the trading cost depend on duration, these durations are not equivalent. In the analysis, Bonds A and B are traded at the beginning of the period, at time t, when their durations are D_t, but the market move is measured at the end of the investment horizon, at time $t+1$, when their durations are D_{t+1}. In general, D_t is greater than D_{t+1}.

To illustrate the importance of trading costs, let us continue with our example of the swap from Bond B to Bond A. Assume that the bid-ask for Bond A is 80–76, and that the bid-ask for Bond B is 50–47. The investor believes the bid-side spread between Bond A and Bond B will tighten by 20 basis points. Both bonds have a duration of 5.5 today, at the time they are traded, but at the end of one year their durations fall to 5. The investor currently owns Bond B, which can be sold at the 50 basis point bid-side spread. The investor is evaluating the expected return of swapping to Bond A, which can be purchased at the offered side spread of 76 basis points. After Bond A is purchased, it will be marked in the investor's portfolio at the bid-side spread of 80 basis points. Thus, the act of trading created an immediate, negative return of 22 basis points: the 4 basis point bid-ask spread times the 5.5 duration. Therefore, over a 1-year investment horizon, the expected excess return, inclusive of the 22 basis points in trading cost, is 108 basis points:

$$\begin{aligned} ER &\approx (80 - 50) - 5(-20) - 5.5(4) \\ &= 108 \text{ bps} \end{aligned} \qquad (2.26)$$

Accounting for Uncertainty

The previous example assumes that the bid-ask spread is known with certainty, but for reasons outlined earlier in the chapter, bid-ask spreads change over time. A thorough analysis of trading costs must account for the uncertainty about the bid-ask. In our example, the investor believes that Bond B, quoted at 50–47, has a 3 basis point bid-ask spread, but the exact bid-ask cannot be known for certain until a dealer makes a market. In some cases, the investor might be able to tighten the bid-ask by haggling with a dealer or by shopping around to multiple dealers. The haggling might reduce the bid-ask spread to 2 basis points or 1 basis point. However, it is also possible that the 50–47 quoted market might evaporate when it comes time for a dealer to commit capital. The real market might be 51–46, or if the size of the trade is large, 53–45. Similarly, although a dealer may quote an 80–76 market for Bond A, the true bid-ask can only be discovered by testing a dealer for a bid or offer.

One way to analyze the problem of uncertainty about the bid-ask spread is to frame the problem in terms of probabilities. Specifically, rather than assigning a single value to the bid-ask spread, we can describe it by a probability distribution in which there are N different bid-ask spreads, each with a probability of p_i. This framework allows us to rewrite equation (2.24) as:

$$\text{Trading cost} = D \sum_{i=1}^{N} p_i BA_i \qquad (2.27)$$

In our example of the swap from Bond B to Bond A, the investor may believe the probability of executing a trade with a 4-basis-point bid-ask is 60%. However, there may be a 30% probability that the tradable bid-ask spread is 5 basis points, and a 10% probability that the bid-ask is 3 basis points. Substituting these values into (27) gives an expected trading cost of about 23 basis points.

$$\begin{aligned}\text{Trading cost} &= 5.5 \times (0.6 \times 4 \text{ bps} + 0.3 \times 5 \text{ bps} + 0.1 \times 3 \text{ bps}) \\ &= 23.1 \text{ bps}\end{aligned} \qquad (2.28)$$

Portfolio Trading Cost

In a portfolio context, trading costs depend not only on the duration and the bid-ask spread, but also on the portfolio turnover. Specifically, the equation for trading cost (2.24) can be modified for the portfolio context in the following manner:

$$\begin{aligned}&\text{Portfolio trading cost} \\ &= \text{Portfolio duration} \times \text{Bid ask} \times \text{Portfolio turnover}\end{aligned} \qquad (2.29)$$

where portfolio turnover is measured by:

$$\begin{aligned}\text{Portfolio turnover} = (&\text{Market value of buys} + \text{Market value of sells})/ \\ &(2 \times \text{Market value of portfolio})\end{aligned} \qquad (2.30)$$

For example, suppose an investor manages a $500 million corporate bond portfolio with a weighted average duration of 5. Over the course of a year, our investor turns the portfolio over 80% (roughly $400 million buys and $400 million sales) and pays an average bid-ask spread of 3 basis points. In this example, the cost of trading would amount to 12 basis points:

$$\text{Portfolio trading cost} = 5 \times 3 \text{ bps} \times 0.8 = 12 \text{ bps} \qquad (2.31)$$

For this $500 million portfolio, the 12-basis-point cost of trading translates into $600,000 per year (which, by coincidence, just happens to equal the annual bonus of an average bond salesperson). A portfolio manager spends 12 basis points trading hopes that that cost will be recouped through prescient investment decisions. For the market as a whole, however, trading is a zero-sum game, in which the gains to portfolio managers and traders with good skills are balanced by losses to players with bad luck.[6]

Exhibit 2.2 shows the portfolio cost of trading for a variety of alternative assumptions about portfolio duration, turnover, and the bid-ask spread. The results are intuitive. Trading costs are high for portfolios with long durations, high turnover ratios, and wide bid-ask spreads. For example, a portfolio with an 8-year duration and a 200% turnover ratio will incur 48 basis points in trading costs per year if the average trade is executed with a 3 basis point bid-ask spread. Only skilled portfolio managers have the ability to recoup sizable trading costs.

Liquidity Risk in a Portfolio Context

Uncertainty pervades portfolio management. Just as investors can never be absolutely certain about the direction of the interest rates or the size of the bid-ask spread, they also face uncertainty about their portfolio turnover. An investor may plan to turn his portfolio over 80% per year, but he or she knows that the actual turnover ratio could be higher or lower, depending on a number of factors, such as the vagaries of monetary policy, the liquidity of bond dealers, and the incidence of negative credit events. To account for uncertainty about turnover, we can modify the previous analysis by assuming T different turnover ratios, each with a probability of q_j. This framework allows us to express the portfolio trading cost as a function of an uncertain bid-ask spread and an uncertain turnover ratio:

---

[6] Actually, trading is a slightly negative-sum game due to dead-weight costs such as transfer fees and back-office expenses.

EXHIBIT 2.2 The Portfolio Cost of Trading (basis points)
Portfolio Duration = 3

Bid-Ask Spread (bps)	Annual Portfolio Turnover				
	25%	50%	100%	200%	400%
1	0.8	1.5	3.0	6.0	12.0
3	2.3	4.5	9.0	18.0	36.0
5	3.8	7.5	15.0	30.0	60.0

Portfolio Duration = 5

Bid-Ask Spread (bps)	Annual Portfolio Turnover				
	25%	50%	100%	200%	400%
1	1.3	2.5	5.0	10.0	20.0
3	3.8	7.5	15.0	30.0	60.0
5	6.3	12.5	25.0	50.0	100.0

Portfolio Duration = 8

Bid-Ask Spread (bps)	Annual Portfolio Turnover				
	25%	50%	100%	200%	400%
1	2.0	4.0	8.0	16.0	32.0
3	6.0	12.0	24.0	48.0	96.0
5	10.0	20.0	40.0	80.0	160.0

$$\text{Portfolio trading cost} = D \sum_{i=1}^{N} p_i BA_i \sum_{j=1}^{T} q_j \text{Turnover}_j \quad (2.32)$$

At first glance, the introduction of probabilities into the calculation of trading costs seems silly. After all, a portfolio with a 100% turnover ratio has the same expected trading cost as another portfolio with a 50% probability of 75% turnover and a 50% probability of 125% turnover. Likewise, a 4 basis point bid-ask spread with 100% certainty has the same expected cost as a 1 basis point bid-ask spread with a 25% probability and a 5 basis point spread with a 75% probability. Rather than introducing probabilities, why not just keep the analysis simple and express the bid-ask and the turnover as a weighted average?

Although it is true that the average bid-ask spread and the average turnover ratio measure the cost of trading, the averages hide the inherent uncertainty in the trading process. The most basic concept in finance is that investors do not like uncertainty. For example, corporate bond investors do not like the uncertainty that some of their bonds may be downgraded or default. To compensate for the uncertainty about credit risk, investors demand a yield premium in excess of the default and downgrade probabilities. Likewise, investors do not like uncertainty about trading in the secondary market. Investors would prefer to pay a 4-basis-point bid-ask with certainty, rather than take the risk that the bid-ask could be higher or lower than 4 basis points, and only equal 4 basis points on average. To some degree, the yield spread on a corporate bond is payment to investors for the risk that the bid-ask may differ significantly from the average, or expected value.

The fact that liquidity risk, itself, commands a risk premium is of crucial importance. Yield spreads on corporate bonds compensate investors not only for the measurable costs of trading, which can be calculated with risk-neutral pricing by equation (2.32), but also for the uncertainty about liquidity and trading costs. Part of the spread on a corporate bond represents an uncertainty risk premium. Sometimes, the uncertainty risk premium is called a liquidity risk premium, or premium to risk-neutral pricing. Two bonds may have the same fundamental risks (e.g., they may both have BBB ratings), but if one bond is less liquid it will have a wider yield spread. This is the key reason why liquidity is important to monitor. Liquidity affects not only the size of the bid-ask spread, but also the level of the yield spread.

CONCLUSION

When investing in a spread product, we need to be paid for what we know. We know that yields on corporate bonds and other spread products must be high enough to compensate for the cost of trading. We know that trading costs depend on duration, turnover, and the bid-ask spread. We also demand to be paid for what we do not know. We do not know the frequency of turnover or the magnitude of the bid-ask spread. And we face the risk that the bid-ask will gap wider at the moment we want to trade in size. We need to be paid for uncertainty.

Rational portfolio managers understand that trading is costly. Trading, in effect, transfers performance from investors' portfolios to the bonus pools of bond dealers. Trading eats into the yield spread on a non-Treasury or some other high-quality benchmark security: It drives a wedge between a bond's spread and its expected excess return. This is not to say that portfolio managers should abandon active portfolio strategies to avoid trading costs. Rather, portfolio managers should merely recognize that the benefits of active strategies must be weighed against the costs of trading.

CHAPTER 3

Portfolio Strategies for Outperforming a Benchmark

Bülent Baygün, Ph.D.
Head of U.S. Fixed Income Strategy
Barclays Capital

Robert Tzucker
U.S. Portfolio and Inflation Strategist
Barclays Capital

Increasingly, fund managers and more importantly chief investment officers are looking to measure the performance of portfolios and portfolio managers in an objective fashion. We believe that the best way to approach the problem is to adopt a "beat the benchmark" approach. The first question that this approach raises is: "What is an appropriate benchmark?" We address this in this chapter where we discuss six widely recognized academic principles of a good index and also look at a quantitative technique to achieve this goal. A good index should be:

- Relevant to the investor
- Representative of the market
- Transparent in rules with consistent constituents
- Investible and replicable
- Based on high data quality
- Independent

The second question that we address in this chapter follows naturally from the first, which is: "How does one beat a benchmark?" There are countless strategies that can be employed to outperform a benchmark. In this chapter we focus on balancing the risk versus return in a portfolio by employing a constrained optimization decision framework. This strategy involves taking views on:

- Forward interest rates
- Economic scenarios
- Yield curve
- Asset allocation
- Duration
- Risk tolerance
- Issue selection
- Spread relationships

SELECTING THE BENCHMARK INDEX

Selecting a benchmark by which to measure performance can be as important as the individual investment decisions themselves. The benchmark index is the basis against which all allocation decisions are made, including duration and curve positioning among others. Not only is the index used as a way to evaluate the relative performance of the manager, but it should be considered the best "passive" way to achieve the goals of the fund. If an inappropriate benchmark is selected relative to the goals of the fund, the manager may perform well against the index but fall short of the desired level of return of the fund. We discuss examples of this later in the chapter.

In the current environment there are myriad index providers, each with a different set of qualifying criteria defining the market. Selecting the appropriate index depends upon the needs of the fund. There are some widely recognized academic principles of what constitutes a good index. The major ones are discussed in the following sections. Later in the chapter, we discuss the pros and cons of defining a custom index and methods to accomplish that task while applying the principles given below.

Principle 1: Relevance to the Investor

Any index chosen as a benchmark must be a relevant investment for the investor. One of the most common examples of relevance is the quest to avoid a "natural concentration" between the business risk of the sponsoring entity and the invested portfolio. For example, a defense contractor would seek to benchmark its pension fund to an index with a low concentration of defence-related businesses. For this purpose many investors use custom indices, excluding specific industries that cause natural concentration, while creating a benchmark. Another example that continues to gain traction is the choosing of an appropriate benchmark for a pension fund. In order to reduce volatility in its funding gap (or limit the possibility of creating a large funding gap), a pension fund manager may wish to use a portfolio of liabilities as a benchmark. The characteristics of the portfolio should closely resemble those of the actual pension fund liabilities. If, for example, the pension fund benchmarks to an index with too short of a duration (pension liabilities typically have very long durations), a move lower in rates could adversely affect its funding gap, even if the fund happens to outperform the index.

Principle 2: Representative of the Market

A good benchmark should provide an accurate picture of the market it claims to represent. For example, if in a market most of the issues of a particular rating or industry sector are below the index size threshold, the performance of the index will be very different from the performance of the market. Hence two indices, with different minimum thresholds, could exhibit vastly different industry and/or ratings distribution and consequently a vastly different risk/return profile.

Principle 3: Transparent Rules and Consistent Constituents

One of the definitions of a bond index is that it is a rules-based collection of bonds. It is, therefore, imperative that the rules defining the index are transparent and are applied objectively and in a consistent fashion. It is often tempting to bend the rules to accommodate particular market situations such as avoiding undue concentrations of a particular issuer or industry. For example, the downgrade of KPN in September 2001 left it teetering on the edge of the investment grade threshold. This raised concerns among some high-yield fund managers that KPN would account for over a quarter of the euro high-yield universe were it to make the transition into high yield. These investors sought changes in the index in the form of sector and issuer caps to address this particular situation. If such caps are implemented, they violate the principles that define a good index.

The treatment of unrated paper for investment grade indices falls under this category. Many index providers include unrated paper in investment grade indices on the premise that if these instruments were to be rated they would end up in the investment grade. The other area where many index providers often vary from each other is the treatment of split-rated bonds, both for the rating tier they represent, as well as to determine whether they form part of the investment grade universe or not.

Principle 4: Investible and Replicable

An investor should be able to replicate the index and its performance with a small number of instruments as well as with relatively low transaction costs and without moving the market too much. For this reason the index constituents should be a set of bonds that have standard features, are liquid and trade actively in the secondary market. The ability to invest in the index through derivative instruments such as futures and total return swaps is an added attraction of an index.

Indices with higher threshold levels typically contain fewer illiquid instruments and are thus easy to replicate for obvious reasons, and very often easy to beat as well. The reason for the latter is explained by the presence of a liquidity premium. Everything else being the same, bonds which are more liquid tend to trade at tighter levels than bonds which are less liquid, and the difference is known as the "liquidity premium." Indices that have more liquid bonds have lower yields than those with less liquid bonds, and consequently generate lower returns, which in turn implies that they are easier to outperform.

Principle 5: High Quality Data

It goes without saying that an index is only as good as the data—both prices and static information—that is used to calculate it. Even a well-constituted and well-calculated index is unlikely to represent the moves of the market if it uses distorted prices. Unlike the equity market, where price transparency is high, there have historically been major impediments for getting true market prices for bonds and other *over-the-counter* (OTC) instruments. Most bond indices are proprietary indices that use in-house pricing, and are hence highly susceptible to be distorted by the presence/absence of long/short positions on the trading book. Often, bonds where the trader has no position are not marked actively and reflect an indicative price and, for that reason, produce erroneous results for return and other calculations. To avoid these pitfalls it is therefore important to ensure that index pricing is from an accurate and reliable source.

Principle 6: Independence

One of the reasons equity indices are so popular is that the prices used to calculate them are from an independent and a quasi-regulatory source. Independent indices also make index and bond-level data available from multiple sources. This encourages the development of after-index products including derivatives, as there are multiple dealers active in the market and the resulting competition is good for all participants.

As many market participants observe, the above-mentioned principles are not entirely compatible, and thus create the need to strike the right balance. For example, in the quest to be representative of the market one could sacrifice liquidity of the instruments constituting the index. However, when striking the balance, one has to consider that for an index to be used as a benchmark, the ability to buy the constituent instruments is paramount. Therefore, we argue that principle 4 is more important than principle 2.

CREATING A CUSTOM INDEX

It may be that there are no indices currently constructed that meet the exact needs of the investor. In this case, constructing an index from scratch, or combining multiple indices may very well be worth the time and effort in order to determine the appropriate benchmark. There are several methods that can be employed to create the benchmark index. We will discuss creating a rules-based index as well as using mean/variance frontier analysis to create the appropriate asset class mix within the index.

Rules-Based Indices

For this exercise we take a look at an actual index, the rules used to create the index, and how the index can be customized to better suit individual managers. We start by examining the Barclays Capital Global Inflation-Linked Bond Index. This index is a market value weighted index that tracks the performance of inflation-linked bonds meeting specific credit and issue specific criteria. In the next sections, we look at some of the individual rules governing this index and describe the relevance of each to the above mentioned principles. These rules are reasonably common in creating indices and can be applied in many situations.

Market Type

In this index, the debt must be domestic government only, meaning that it must be issued by a government in the currency of that country. This rule pertains to principles 2, 3, and 4 above in that it is a clear description of the type of debt allowed (principle 3), representative of the market of inflation-linked debt (principle 2), and can be invested in easily through cash or total return swaps (principle 4).

Inflation Index

The inflation index of each issue must be a commonly used domestic inflation measure. For example, in the United States, not-seasonally adjusted CPI would be an acceptable index. This rule eliminates the risk of having a bond that uses a suspect means of indexing, following principle 3, increasing transparency.

Rating

The rule for this index requires the foreign currency debt rating of the country to be AA–/Aa3 or better to be included in the index (S&P or Moody's, whichever is lower). This would exclude certain sovereign debt such as Greece, which meets the first two index rules, but has only a single-A rating. The Barclays Global Inflation-Linked Index is designed to have only high-grade sovereign issuance and, therefore, excludes higher-risk sovereigns.

Aggregate Face Value

The aggregate face value of any particular debt issue meeting the other rules must be at least worth $1 billion. In order to create stability and keep bonds from entering and leaving the index frequently, a rule can be imposed that if the bond falls below 90% of that lower limit it will be removed. This prevents bonds from arbitrarily dropping out due to routine currency fluctuations. Rules of this nature are typically devised under principle 4 to reduce transaction costs and increase the replicability of the index.

Percentage of Index

Issues meeting all the previous criteria will be included in the index based upon their market value weight in U.S. dollars at the rebalancing date (typically the last day of the month). This market value weighting scheme is very popular among indexers for various reasons. First, it is easy to replicate. Second, typically relative market size will also determine relative liquidity. As a result, a smaller market has smaller weights; so, to replicate the index, a manager does not have as much problem sourcing the issues, which keeps costs lower. Although it is a useful rule, it may be problematic with principle 1, as the construction using market weights may not be an optimal benchmark for an active manager. We explore this issue further in the next section.

Perhaps a manager has a global inflation-linked mandate but is not permitted to invest in issues that have longer than 10 years to maturity. Using the Global Inflation-Linked Index as a benchmark would violate principle 1 discussed previously due to the irrelevance of the index. It would be unfair to evaluate a manager's performance relative to this benchmark because in the case of a rally, the longer bonds would likely outperform and the portfolio would unfairly be penalized. Likewise, a sell-off would favor the portfolio as longer duration assets underperformed. Instead, a rule can be created to bucket the index into maturities of less than 10-years and maturities of greater than 10-years. Now, the manager can be benchmarked more appropriately and performance more accurately measured. This is a relatively simple example of how rules-based index creation can be used to customize an index, so we will move on to more complicated problems next.

Using Mean/Variance Analysis to Customize an Index

Portfolio theory can play an important role in setting a benchmark for measuring performance. Traditionally, managers use efficient frontiers as a way of determining the most appropriate allocation of assets given either certain return targets or risk limits. Because historical data can only yield one efficient frontier with multiple efficient portfolios, by defining risk limits or targeted returns, the efficient portfolio can be used as a passive benchmark against which to perform tactical asset allocation. Rather than benchmarking against an index that uses arbitrary weighting based on the market value of the constituents, this method allows a manager to make decisions versus a historically efficient allocation, perhaps improving the decision making process. A custom index can also be useful when trying to optimize allocation in concert with the core operations of a business. For example, a bank with a core loan portfolio that would like to use its excess capital to generate returns to supplement their income may need to include that loan portfolio as an asset in the mean/variance analysis construct the most appropriate benchmark.

Setting up the Problem

In order to create a custom index using mean/variance analysis, certain restrictions will have to be placed on the amount of the index that can consist of a given asset. This prevents, for example, U.S. Agency bonds from becoming such a big part of the index that it is impossible to replicate in any size. If so desired, constraints on the size of the assets can also keep at least a nominal allocation to assets that may disappear from the solution if not otherwise constrained. Using minimum inclusion constraints makes sense to a manager that has a mandate to diversify into a certain asset or number of assets to some degree. Once the constraints have been determined, the efficient frontier can be solved using iterative solving software.

Several decisions have to be made before performing the mean variance analysis. First, and arguably most important, the asset classes need to be chosen. In this example, we take the view of a fixed income portfolio manager that is mandated to invest in a combination of non-callable U.S. Agency bonds (Fannie Mae, Freddie Mac, Federal Home Loan Bank, etc.), TIPS (Treasury Inflation-Indexed Securities), and U.S. Treasuries. Because there are few indices that describe this universe, creating a custom index may provide the best alternative in this case.

The next step is to determine the constraints that should be imposed on the asset classes to make certain that the index meets the investable and replicable criteria from the previously described rules. The most straightforward way to determine appropriate maximum weights for each asset class is to look at the securities' weight as a proportion of the total weight of all of the asset classes and make a judgement as to a realistic percentage that could be invested based on the size of assets under management. For this exercise, we assume we have $5 billion under management. Comparing this number to the size of each of the classes of assets we are using looks very small. Exhibit 3.1 shows the relative sizes of our investable asset classes. It is immediately clear that our $5 billion under management is dwarfed by the size of securities outstanding, so we are not necessarily constrained by size. However, for the sake of prudence, our index should not consist entirely of one asset, so we will limit the analysis to use no more than 80% of any asset.

Finally, we set up the problem statement so that we can solve for the most efficient index allocation. To accomplish our goal, we perform a constrained optimization by minimizing the variance (risk) of the portfolio for different levels of returns (Markowitz model). The problem we are trying to solve is:

EXHIBIT 3.1 Gauging the Size of the Market

Asset Class	Market Value Outstanding ($ billion)	Percentage of Total
U.S. Treasuries (> 1yr to maturity)	2,000	66%
TIPS	320	11%
U.S. Agency non-callable	690	23%

Source: Barclays Capital, *The Yieldbook.*

Minimize:

$$w^T C w$$

Subject to:

$w^T \mu = \mu_P$
$w_i \leq 0.8$
$\Sigma w_i = 1$ for all i
$w_i > 0$

where:

w = asset weight vector
C = covariance matrix
μ = expected return vector
μ_P = targeted expected return

The next step is to solve the problem. If a desired return target or a desired risk level is known, the problem can be solved for just one desired return level. If the desired level of return or risk is unknown, the frontier can be created and an efficient mix chosen after evaluating the different portfolio constructions. One thing to remember is that the portfolio return cannot be higher than the highest returning asset as long as no short positions are allowed, which is an assumption we are making, nor can it be lower than the lowest returning asset. To keep things simple and illustrate the point, we have decided to use the minimum risk portfolio as the benchmark. Exhibit 3.2 shows the efficient frontier as well as the market value weighted index on a historical risk/return basis. It is obvious that the market-value-weighted index is less than efficient, falling far below the frontier. The minimum risk portfolio gives us an advantage on expected return and expected risk.

The minimum risk portfolio consists of 26% Treasuries, 54% Agencies, and 20% TIPS. This contrasts starkly from the market-value-weighted index which consisted mostly of Treasury debt. One clear advantage of using this new benchmark is that if we choose to have no tactical views and purely match the benchmark, the expected performance of our portfolio is much better than with a market value weighted index. Another advantage is that the additive value of tactical asset allocation choice can clearly be measured in terms of additional return or reduced risk versus the frontier, which takes into account much more information than a market value weighted index when constructed. An investor using this technique can develop a custom bench-

EXHIBIT 3.2 Efficient Frontier and the Minimum Risk Portfolio

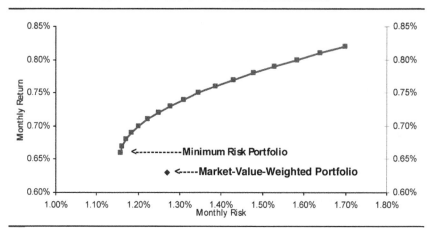

Source: Barclays Capital, *The Yieldbook.*

mark for almost any purpose—whether it is to balance risk with the core business or to assist in asset liability management—and generate a meaningful investment hurdle with which to measure performance.

BEATING THE BENCHMARK INDEX

Once the index is selected, the next step is to manage the portfolio around that index while trying to outperform it—or generate "alpha." The starting point in a typical investment strategy is a core view on the economy (GDP growth, inflation expectations, consumer behavior, employment picture, etc.), which forms the basis of calls on asset prices going forward. For instance, in an environment where employment is rising, inflationary pressures are building, and there is a general surge in asset valuations, the Fed is likely to react by hiking rates, which in turn should give rise to higher rates and a flattening along the entire yield curve. Under these assumptions one could surmise, based on historical relationships, that high-quality asset spreads to Treasuries should widen. Therefore, a portfolio that is structured for this scenario (our "base case") likely would have a short duration bias relative to the index, have curve flattening exposure and be underweight spread products.

So far the above approach has taken into account only one dimension of investment decisions, namely return. Before executing the strategy, we would want to assess the risks to the portfolio should the markets behave differently than what is depicted in the base case scenario. Typically, that involves stress-testing the portfolio under alternative (risk) scenarios. In other words, one would shock the curve and spreads in different ways and monitor the performance of the portfolio. If performance fell short of the risk guidelines, then one would go back and fix the portfolio in such a way to mitigate the problem—more often than not using ad-hoc techniques—and then run the stress test on the revised portfolio. This process would be repeated until desirable risk characteristics are obtained. As an alternative to this iterative process, one could adopt a more formal quantitative framework that aims to optimize some performance criterion, incorporating the base case as well as the risk scenarios at the same time. That is the approach we will describe below, as we have found it to be a very effective way to make informed investment decisions.

Choosing Scenarios for the Optimization

The forwards should play a central role in the selection of the scenarios. This is a very subtle but important point that may be easily overlooked. Let us explain with some examples: If all the scenarios considered had rates higher than the forwards, the resulting optimal portfolio would undoubtedly have a short duration bias. Similarly, if all the scenarios gave rise to, say, flatter curves than the forwards, then one would end up with flattener positions in the portfolio. That is because in this framework risk assessment is limited to the scenarios under consideration. When all the scenarios are stacked on one side of the forwards it is tantamount to saying "there is no risk of rates being lower (or the curve being steeper) than the forwards." As a result, it would appear as if a portfolio that is short duration (or is fully loaded in flatteners) does not have any potential downside risk—the very characteristic of being optimal. However, it is clear that the portfolios constructed using these lopsided scenarios do not capture the risks in a realistic manner. The same is true when selecting the spread and breakeven scenarios for a portfolio that involves Agencies and TIPS.

　　With this in mind, we consider four scenarios that bracket the current forwards.[1] We will not provide a description of the economic backdrop for each one of the scenarios, but suffice it to say that each one depicts significantly different economic conditions giving rise to a broad range of rate and spread changes for the third quarter of 2005 (see Exhibits 3.3 through 3.6). In particular, there are two bearish and two bullish scenarios. In terms of curve movements, two of the scenarios depict a flattening of the curve across all maturities (vis à vis the forwards), while one sub-

---

[1] All pricing is as of June 21, 2005.

sumes a steepening, and another one has steepeners in the front-end and flatteners from the 5-year on out. Similarly, swap spreads to Treasuries and Agency/Libor spreads, as well as TIPS breakevens encompass enough variety across the breadth of the scenarios.

EXHIBIT 3.3 Three-Month Treasury Forecasts for Different Scenarios

	Yield Levels (%)	Yield Changes (bps)				
	Current on 6/21	Base Case	Stable Inflation	High Inflation	Growth Slowdown	Forwards
2 yr	3.70	35	10	55	−10	10
5 yr	3.84	36	1	71	−19	7
10 yr	4.06	29	−16	74	−31	4
30 yr	4.34	21	−24	76	−34	2

Source: Barclays Capital.

EXHIBIT 3.4 Three-Month Swap Spread Forecasts (bps) for Different Scenarios

	Current	Base Case	Stable Inflation	High Inflation	Growth Slowdown
2 yr	35	34	32	42	30
5 yr	40	42	37	47	34
10 yr	40	42	37	48	34
30 yr	42	43	38	50	34

Source: Barclays Capital.

EXHIBIT 3.5 Three-Month Agency-Libor Spread Forecasts (bps) for Different Scenarios

	Current	Base Case	Stable Inflation	High Inflation	Growth Slowdown
2 yr	−18	−20	−18	−22	−16
5 yr	−19	−20	−19	−23	−17
10 yr	−7	−9	−4	−12	−3
30 yr	−4	−6	−2	−9	0

Source: Barclays Capital.

EXHIBIT 3.6   Three-Month TIPS Breakeven (%) and Inflation Forecasts for Different Scenarios

	Current	Base Case	Stable Inflation	High Inflation	Slow Growth
Jan 07	2.49	2.53	2.35	2.63	2.82
Jan 10	2.43	2.50	2.30	2.61	2.61
Jan 15	2.34	2.43	2.27	2.60	2.42
Jan 25	2.52	2.58	2.43	2.79	2.52
NSA CPI					
June		194.8	194.7	195.0	194.9
July		195.1	194.8	195.4	195.7

Choosing the Optimization Criterion

Now that the scenarios are defined, the next step is to define the criterion for optimization. The parameters to optimize over are the market value weights of the issues in the universe of eligible securities. Popular choices for the optimization criterion include the following:

- *Maximize expected return.* This approach requires assigning (subjective) probabilities to the various scenarios. This approach has the advantage of being intuitive: most people already have some sense of what scenarios are more likely than others, and like to be able to impose those biases in the way they run their portfolio. Furthermore, it is easy to see the connection between the structure of the portfolio and the probabilities. The disadvantage is that because the criterion is based on average performance across the scenarios, one could not be assured of risks staying below allowable limits in specific scenarios unless there are additional explicit constraints. Another potential downside is that guessing some sensible probabilities adds another layer of subjectivity to what is already a rather subjective process—that is, the choice of a set of scenarios.
- *Maximize return under a specific scenario.* This is a very effective criterion when one has a strong conviction about a certain scenario. The remaining scenarios are treated as risk scenarios, for which underperformance constraints are imposed. The existence of those constraints allows one to balance risks versus return.
- *Maximize the worst case return (maxmin).* This is the most conservative approach that one would employ when (1) the objective is primarily to replicate the benchmark as closely as possible, say for liability matching; or (2) one does not proclaim to have a strong view about

the market. Instead of investing based on a specific view, the investor aims for gains across all the scenarios, however modest they may be. This is not the approach that will generate home runs. As long as the scenarios are representative of a broad range of outcomes, the investor should be able to generate modest but consistent returns versus the benchmark.

In our experience, we have found that the maxmin criterion, by its conservative nature, helps limit the volatility of the returns over time. However, the margin of outperformance may be less than desirable for some investors, despite the attractive risk characteristics. Therefore, we leave that criterion aside for now, though we note that it may be an invaluable approach for liability management applications in particular.

There is an interesting relationship between the other two criteria. More specifically, in the absence of any risk constraints under the other scenarios, maximizing return under a specific scenario (e.g., the base case) would be equivalent to assigning a 100% probability to that one scenario and maximizing expected return. Surely, performance could well be dismal under some of the risk scenarios, in particular those that are the "opposite" of the favored scenario. Think of what maximizing return for a bearish scenario would do to performance if a bullish scenario were to materialize. On the other hand, if one were to impose some loss constraints in the risk scenarios, and make those constraints ever more stringent, there would come a point where the optimal portfolio begins to change character and look more like a portfolio driven by the risk scenarios rather than the base-case scenario. At the extreme, where one constrains the portfolio to have a high positive return in the risk scenario, while still maximizing the base case, the result would be the same as if one were maximizing expected return while assigning 100% probability to the risk scenario! In other words, there is a correspondence between the probabilities assigned to various scenarios in the expected return maximization case and the risk constraints in the single-scenario maximization case. As a side note, the two approaches are classified as linear optimization problems, in that both the objective functions and the constraints are linear functions of the optimization parameters (i.e., the market value weights).

We prefer the criterion of maximizing return under a specific scenario subject to loss constraints under the risk scenarios. The reason is twofold: we like to be able to impose the loss constraints explicitly (as we want a clear handle on the risks we are taking) and we do not want to create another layer of subjectivity by having to guess probabilities. Yet, we emphasize that what we are doing would be equivalent to maximizing expected return *under a specific choice of probabilities.*

Defining the Constraints

There are several dimensions in which one could impose constraints on the portfolio. These include duration bands, partial duration bounds, sector allocation constraints, issue weights (both in terms of the percentage of the portfolio, and relative to the float available in the market) and loss constraints as we discussed above.

Duration Bands

Most real-money portfolios cannot deviate significantly from the benchmark duration. The typical band would be 0.25 to 0.5 on either side of the benchmark duration.[2] The duration decision is facilitated by gauging how much the base case performance improves for an incremental change in duration; that is, if the improvement is marginal beyond a certain duration deviation, then taking additional duration risk is not warranted.

Partial Duration

Typically, unless one imposes some explicit constraints, the optimal portfolio has allocations in all but a few maturity buckets. As a result, the portfolio has an implicit underweight (relative to the benchmark) in those buckets where there is no allocation. If that is not desirable, for fear that relative valuation changes not accounted for in the scenarios may cause tracking error, then one might choose to constrain the partial durations to remain close to those of the benchmark. Of course, curbing potential mismatch comes at a cost: the more constraints one imposes, the less the portfolio can deviate from the benchmark, limiting its upside potential.

Asset Allocation Weights

In a multi-asset portfolio, such as one comprised of Treasuries, agencies, and TIPS, the portfolio manager typically overweights or underweights a specific asset relative to the benchmark to generate alpha. The deviation from the benchmark, especially in spread products, typically has some bounds on it, such as between 90% and 110% of the benchmark allocation, and so on. For example, if agencies were 54% of the benchmark, then the allocation into agencies would have to stay between 48.6% and 59.4% of the portfolio.

Loss Constraints

As we discussed above, the objective is to maximize performance under a base-case scenario, subject to loss constraints under the risk scenarios. The more stringent the constraints, the more the portfolio has to honor

---

[2] Sometimes the band is expressed as a percentage of the benchmark duration.

them and move away from a structure geared for optimal performance under the base case alone. The choice of the loss constraint depends on how it affects performance under the base case. For instance, if by allowing an incremental loss of 10 bps in the risk scenarios, performance in the base case improves by more than 10 bps, then one should relax the loss constraint. However, if the performance improvement is significantly less than the potential incremental risk one takes on, then it is better to use the more restrictive loss constraint.

Issue Weights

In general, one would be better served diversifying the holdings in a portfolio across a large enough set of issues, rather than having concentrated allocations into just a handful of them. Furthermore, when defining the issue size limits in the portfolio, one may need to take into account the total float available in each issue and ensure that no more than a certain percentage of the float is owned by the portfolio. This makes intuitive sense as it will help prevent the portfolio from being subject to technical anomalies in one or two issues. In short, we believe it is advisable to impose a constraint such as "no issue should be more than 10% of the portfolio or 20% of the float."

Putting It All Together: The Optimal Portfolio

We demonstrate the process we have outlined so far with a couple of specific examples. To illustrate the duration decision, separately from the sector allocation decision, we use the Citigroup Treasury Index as the benchmark. As a second example, we turn to sector allocation and choose the minimum risk portfolio defined earlier as the benchmark. To recap, the benchmark consists of 26% Treasuries, 54% Agencies and 20% TIPS in market value terms. In both optimization problems, our objective is to construct a portfolio that is projected to outperform the benchmark in the base case, subject to the following constraints:

- Duration: within −0.5 to 0.5 years around the benchmark
- Asset allocation weights: within ±20% around the benchmark allocation
- Allowable losses: up to −30 bps versus the benchmark
- Issue weights: no one issue to be more than 10% of the portfolio size in market value terms

The Duration Decision

There is interplay between the duration decision and the maximum losses allowed. The final decision depends on the improvement in performance in the base case. Exhibit 3.7 illustrates the point. Each one of the

EXHIBIT 3.7   Excess Return as a Function of Duration and Loss Tolerance

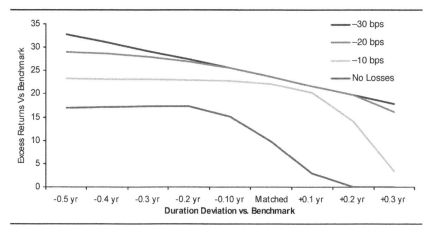

profiles corresponds to a different level of losses allowed (the loss constraint) and shows the excess return versus the benchmark as a function of the duration deviation. Clearly, when no losses are allowed (the bottom profile), base-case performance improves as duration is shortened—after all, the base case is a bearish move in rates—but up to a certain point. For instance, when duration is matched to the benchmark, the projected excess return is 10 bps, while with a –0.1-year duration deviation the excess return reaches 15 bps. However, in going from –0.1 to –0.2-year, the improvement is a mere 2 bps. Furthermore, there is no incremental improvement for shortening duration past –0.2-year. Therefore, if one favored a very conservative strategy and allowed no losses, shortening duration by 0.1yr would be the way to go.

If the loss constraint is relaxed, there is a marked improvement in performance. For instance in the case where a 10 bp loss is allowed and portfolio duration is matched to the benchmark, excess return is 22 bps. In other words, the return pickup relative to the "no loss" case is 12 bps (22 – 10 bps), 2 bps higher than the concession given in terms of loss tolerance. It does not seem to make sense to shorten duration in this case, as performance is topped out at 23 bps with any kind of duration mismatch.

Now comes the judgement call. Using the no-loss, matched-duration case as the baseline, we can either (1) boost performance by 12 bps, by taking on the risk of a 10 bps loss but no duration, or (2) add 5 bps of return, by taking on a 0.1-year duration short but no projected losses. We would contend that the latter is a better choice in this case as it does not require making a compromise in terms of loss tolerance (at least within the confines of the scenarios used). However, one could easily argue that targeting a bigger upside potential while relaxing the risk constraints by a small margin is preferable, especially considering that the gains could be attained with no duration mismatch. Having stated our preference, we leave the decision to our readers.

The Optimal Portfolio in a Multi-Asset Setting

When constructing the portfolio that comprises Treasuries, agencies and TIPS, we arrive at a clear conclusion following a similar reasoning as in the Treasury-only case: there is no need for duration mismatch, or for allowing losses. The reason is that there are more degrees of freedom in this optimization, as one can enhance performance by choosing to overweight/underweight assets versus one another in addition to, or in lieu of, taking on duration and curve positions.

Because of the asset allocation weight constraints, no one asset can be fully excluded from the portfolio, which makes for good diversification characteristics. Exhibit 3.8 shows the allocation into each one of the assets in the optimization universe. In this case, the portfolio maintains an overweight in TIPS, and an underweight in Treasuries and agencies versus the benchmark, and also has an allocation into cash (10%). The reason for the inclusion of cash is that the portfolio benefits from having a barbelled curve position (i.e., overweight in short and long maturity buckets, underweight in intermediate maturities) since the base case involves curve flattening.[3] By taking a position in cash, and coupling that with a bigger position (further out) in the back end of the curve, one can improve exposure to flattening, which is what is happening here. Exhibit 3.9 shows the allocation into different maturity buckets along the curve in each one of the assets, relative to the benchmark composition. It is interesting to note that in the 2022–2028 maturity bucket, the optimal portfolio consists of overweights in TIPS versus Treasuries—roughly, a long TIPS breakeven position. In the longest maturity bucket, there is a preference for agencies versus Treasuries and TIPS, which is essentially a long spread position.

EXHIBIT 3.8 Percentage of the Market Value Allotted into Each Asset

	Portfolio	Benchmark	Overweight (Underweight)
Treasury	11%	26%	–15%
Agency	40%	54%	–14%
TIPS	39%	20%	19%
Cash	10%	0%	10%

---

[3] Barbelled positions tend to outperform bullets in a curve flattening environment.

EXHIBIT 3.9   Optimal Portfolio Market Value Over/Underweights Along the Yield Curve

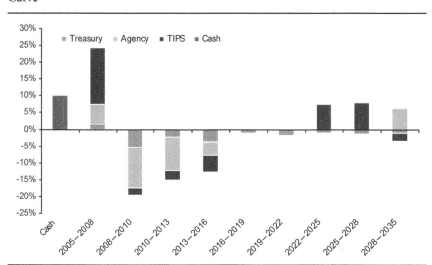

CONCLUSION

The selection of a benchmark index is a process that can carry as much importance as the optimization of the portfolio itself. Above all else, the index should be relevant to the investor. The goals of the fund should be considered and, if necessary, a customized index should be created to meet the specific needs of the manager. When constructing an index using a rules-based method, it is always important to take into account the replicability of the index, the transparency of the rules created and it should be representative of the market. Construction of a custom index can be achieved through mean/variance analysis to meet the needs of almost any investor. Using this method allows the manager to measure performance against the most efficient "passive" allocation of assets, which should eventually lead to better, more informed investment decisions.

Once the benchmark is selected, using optimization techniques is a very potent approach to balance risk versus return in a portfolio versus the benchmark. It allows one to change risk parameters, monitor the associated change in excess returns, gauge the interplay between duration, curve positioning and asset allocation, all in a well-defined and consistent framework. Notwithstanding the fact that the framework is highly quantitative, there are certainly some steps in the analysis that require a judgement call, such as the choice of certain constraints, the decision about what duration/risk tolerance combination to use, etc. The choice of the scenarios to be used in the optimization is also critical, in that one should ensure that they cover a wide range of possibilities, bracketing the forwards. The projected performance numbers, and more to the point, the risk assessment, is only as good as the quality of the set of scenarios selected. Once intuition is gained about how to generate realistic scenarios, and what kind of risk constraints to employ, the discipline of analyzing risks and returns in a unified framework proves invaluable.

Two

Benchmark Selection and Risk Budgeting

The Active Decisions in the Selection of Passive Management and Performance Bogeys

Chris P. Dialynas
Managing Director
Pacific Investment Management Company

Alfred Murata
Vice President
Pacific Investment Management Company

The asset allocation decision is perhaps a plan sponsor's most important decision. Within the scope of that decision, the selection of investment managers and performance bogeys are critical. Traditional asset allocation methods are based on studies of relative returns and risk over long periods of time. Performance periods, however, both for the plan itself and the investment manager entrusted with the funds, are based upon relatively short time spans. As such, there is an inherent inconsistency in the investment process.

In this chapter, the active bond management process is explored and contrasted with the "passive management" option. We also examine the differences in index composition. We will see that successful bond management, whether active or passive, depends on good long-term economic

The authors express their gratitude to the research department at Lehman Brothers for their effort in providing data.

forecasting and a thorough understanding of the mathematical dynamics of fixed income obligations. Likewise, selection of a performance bogey depends on similar considerations as well as the liability structure of the plan itself.

ACTIVE BOND MANAGEMENT

Active management of bond portfolios capitalizes on changing relationships between bonds to enhance performance. Realized interest rate volatility and changes in implied volatility induce divergences in relative bond prices. Because volatility, by definition, allows for opportunity, the fact that active bond managers as a class underperformed passive indices during the first half of 1986, the second half of 1998, and the calendar year 2002 (three of the most volatile periods in the bond market in the past 50 years) seems counterintuitive. What went wrong then? What should we expect in the future?

Active bond managers employ their own methods for relative value analysis. Common elements among most managers' analyses are historical relationships, liquidity considerations, and market segmentation. Market segmentation allegedly creates opportunities, and historical analysis provides the timing cue. The timing of strategic moves is important because there is generally an opportunity cost associated with every strategy. Unfortunately, because the world is in perpetual motion and constant evolution, neither market segmentation nor historical analysis is able to withstand the greater forces of change. Both methods, either separately or jointly, are impotent.

The dramatic fluctuations in realized and implied interest rate volatility show that the world is changing and evolving more quickly. Paradoxically, many active managers are using methods voided by volatility to try to capitalize on volatility.

The mistakes of active bond managers and the asset allocation decisions of many plan sponsors have been costly. As a result, a significant move from active to passive (or indexed) management has occurred and an initiative to better asset-liability duration management is underway. Does this move make sense? To understand relative performance differentials between passive and active managers, we need to dissect the active and passive portfolios and reconstruct the macroeconomic circumstances. The issue of macro-asset-allocation of defined benefit pension plans is beyond this chapter's scope. First, we review the characteristics of callable and noncallable bonds and their expected price performance in various interest rate environments. Next, we examine the composition of popular bond market indices and their expected performance in various interest rate environments. Third, we discuss historical interest rate movements, and the resulting impact on the performance of several bond market indices. We conclude by analyzing the impact that historical interest rate movements have had on bond market index selection.

PERFORMANCE CHARACTERISTICS OF CALLABLE AND NONCALLABLE BONDS

An issuer of a callable bond retains the right to call the bond—consequently the holder of the callable bond is short a call option. To compensate the holder of the callable bond for being short the call option, the callable bond will have an income advantage versus a noncallable bond of the same duration, which essentially is the option premium.

We recall that convexity is a measure of a bond's expected outperformance or underperformace, relative to its duration, given an instantaneous change in rates. Given an instantaneous change in interest rates, a bond with zero convexity is expected to perform in line with its duration, while a bond with positive convexity is expected to outperform its duration, and a bond with negative convexity is expected to underperform its duration. Noncallable bonds have higher convexity than callable bonds. Consequently, given an instantaneous change in rates, noncallable bonds should outperform comparable duration callable bonds, due to the convexity advantage. On the other hand, to compensate for the poorer convexity, callable bonds have a yield advantage versus noncallable bonds. Consequently, callable bonds should outperform comparable duration noncallable bonds in infinitesimally short periods in which rates are unchanged. Exhibit 4.1 characterizes the expected relative performance of callable and noncallable bonds in an infinitesimally short time horizon, as a function of changes in interest rates.

EXHIBIT 4.1 Expected Relative Performance of Callable and Noncallable Bonds in an Infinitesimally Short Period as a Function of Changes in Interest Rates

Change in Interest Rates		
Decrease	No Change	Increase
Noncallable	Callable	Noncallable

Expected relative performance over an infinitesimally short time horizon
Legend:

Callable   Callable bond outperforms.
Noncallable   Noncallable bond outperforms.

An extended period of time can be divided into infinitesimally short periods, whereby interest rates change in some periods (during which noncallable bonds outperform, due to the convexity advantage), and rates are unchanged in other periods (during which callable bonds outperform, due to the yield advantage). Consequently, callable bonds should outperform noncallable bonds over an extended period of time if the yield advantage outweighs the convexity disadvantage. This will be the case in the event that interest rates are less volatile than expected (i.e., realized volatility is below expectations). In the event that realized interest rate volatility is in line with expectations, callable bonds should perform in line with noncallable bonds, while noncallable bonds should outperform callable bonds in the event that realized interest rate volatility exceeds expectations. Exhibit 4.2 summarizes the expected relative performance of callable and noncallable bonds over an extended time horizon, as a function of realized interest rate volatility.

The poorer convexity of a callable bond relative to a noncallable bond is due to the call option embedded within the callable bond. The value of the embedded option increases as implied volatility increases, and decreases as implied volatility decreases. Consequently, callable bonds should outperform noncallable bonds when implied volatility decreases, and callable bonds should underperform noncallable bonds when implied volatility increases. Exhibit 4.3 summarizes the expected relative performance of callable and noncallable bonds, as a function of changes in implied volatility.

The call features of the bond universe are summarized in Exhibit 4.4.

EXHIBIT 4.2 Expected Relative Performance of Callable and Noncallable Bonds as a Function of Realized Volatility

Realized Volatility of Interest Rates		
Less than Expected	Inline with Expectations	More than Expected
Callable	Tie	Noncallable

Expected relative performance over an extended time horizon
Legend:

Tie	Callable bond performs inline with noncallable bond.
Callable	Callable bond outperforms.
Noncallable	Noncallable bond outperforms.

EXHIBIT 4.3   Expected Relative Performance of Callable and Noncallable Bonds as a Function of Changes in Implied Volatility

Change in Implied Interest Rate Volatility		
Decrease	Unchanged	Increase
Callable	Tie	Noncallable

Expected relative performance
Legend:

Tie	Callable bond performs inline with noncallable bond.
Callable	Callable bond outperforms.
Noncallable	Noncallable bond outperforms.

EXHIBIT 4.4   Call Features of the Bond Universe

Issue Type	Refunding Protection	Call Protection	Refunding Price	Current Call Price
Treasury	Maturity[a]	Maturity	NA	NA
Traditional Agency	Maturity	Maturity	NA	NA
Traditional Industrial	10 Years	None	Premium	Premium
Traditional Utility	5 Years	None	Premium	Premium
Traditional Finance	10 Years[b]	None	Premium	Premium
GNMA Pass-Through	None	None	100	100
FNMA Pass-Through	None	None	100	100
FHLMC PC	None	None	100	100
CMO	None	None	100	100
Title XI	None[c]	None[c]	100[c]	100[c]
PAC CMO	Within Prepayment Range[d]	None Outside Range	100	100
TAC CMO	Within Prepayment Range[d]	None Outside Range	100	100

[a] Some 30-year government bonds were issued with 25 years of call protection.
[b] A decline in receivables may permit an immediate par call.
[c] Default negates any refunding or call protection.
[d] Call protected within a prespecified range of prepayment rates on the collateral.

Mortgages are callable bonds, where the call option is imperfectly exercised. While mortgagors have the opportunity to call (prepay) their mortgage at any time, this option is imperfectly exercised as a result of numerous factors such as the fixed costs of refinancing a mortgage, mortgagors' costs of monitoring current mortgage rates, and the requirement that a mortgagor call (prepay) one's mortgage when moving. Despite the fact that the call option is imperfectly exercised, in general, mortgages are less convex than noncallable bonds of similar duration. The poorer convexity is due to the negative correlation of prepayment speeds with changes in interest rates. As interest rates decline, borrowers have an increased incentive to refinance their mortgages (and consequently prepayment rates increase); in contrast, if interest rates rise, borrowers have a reduced incentive to refinance their mortgages (and consequently prepayment rates decline). From the bondholder's perspective, the negative correlation of prepayment speeds to changes in interest rates is exactly the opposite of what would be desirable. To compensate bondholders for the poorer convexity, mortgages generally have a significant income advantage versus noncallable bonds of similar duration, where the income advantage is directly related to the expected volatility of interest rates.

The convexity of a mortgage is principally dependent upon the interest rate on the underlying mortgage relative to current mortgage rates. If the interest rate on a mortgage is significantly above current mortgage rates, the mortgagor will have an incentive to call (prepay) their existing mortgage and refinance at the lower, current mortgage rate—because the mortgagor can save money by refinancing. Mortgages with significantly above-market interest rates that trade well above par are called *premium* mortgages and are likely to have fast prepayment rates. On the other hand, if the interest rate on a mortgage is significantly below current mortgage rates, the mortgagor will not have an incentive to call (prepay) their existing mortgage and refinance at the higher, current mortgage rate. Mortgages with significantly below-market interest rates that will trade well below par are called "discount" mortgages and are likely to have slow prepayment rates. The future prepayment behavior of mortgages with interest rates close to current mortgage rates are the most difficult to predict. While there is little current incentive to refinance a mortgage that has an interest rate that is close to current mortgage rates, the incentive to refinance increases substantially if mortgage rates decline. Mortgages with interest rates that are close to current mortgage rates trade close to par and are called "cusp coupon" mortgages. Given the sensitivity of cusp coupon mortgage prepayments to changes in mortgage rates, cusp coupon mortgages have poorer convexity than both premium and discount mortgages—which is demonstrated by the fact that their durations are most sensitive to changes in both mortgage rates and prepayment assumptions. Exhibit 4.5 summarizes the characteristics of premium, cusp and discount mortgages.

Exhibit 4.6 plots the historical monthly total return of the Lehman Mortgage Index as a function of changes in the 5-year constant maturity treasury rate. This graph only includes data where the Lehman Mortgage Index ended the previous month in the $101 to $104 range (in this price range, we view the index as a whole as a cusp coupon mortgage). We note that the index has exhibited positive duration (returns increased as the 5-year constant maturity treasury rate decreased) and has exhibited negative convexity (an increase in interest rates more negatively impacted performance than a decrease in interest rates positively impacted performance).

Exhibit 4.7 plots the historical monthly total return of the Lehman Mortgage Index as a function of changes in the 5-year constant maturity treasury rate. This graph only includes data where the Lehman Mortgage Index ended the previous month below $90 (mortgages trading below $90 are well within the threshold of being considered discount mortgages). We note that the index has exhibited positive duration (returns increased as the 5-year constant maturity treasury rate decreased) and has exhibited positive convexity (an increase in interest rates less negatively impacted performance than a decrease in interest rates positively impacted performance).

Exhibits 4.6 and 4.7 show the historical performance of cusp coupon and discount mortgages as function of changes in interest rates. Given the negative convexity of cusp coupon mortgages and the positive convexity of discount mortgages, we see that cusp coupon mortgages behave more like callable bonds than do discount mortgages. We now discuss fixed income indices.

FIXED INCOME INDICES

While numerous fixed income indices are currently popular, three indices have attracted significant sponsorship over time. The Salomon Brothers Long Corporate Index was a popular bond market bogey during the early 1980s. The index is comprised primarily of high-quality, long-term (10+ year maturity) corporate bonds. Due to its long duration (approximately 7.5 years in the early 1980s), index returns were very poor as interest rates rose. Following the poor returns of the index in the early 1980s, the Salomon Brothers Long Corporate Index became perceived as being too risky and not representative of the market's distribution of

EXHIBIT 4.5 Characteristics of Premium, Cusp Coupon and Discount Mortgages

Type of Mortgage	Mortgage Rate	Dollar Price	Expected Prepayment Rates Under Various Changes in Market Mortgage Rates			Convexity
			Market Mortgage Rates Decline	Market Mortgage Rates Unchanged	Market Mortgage Rates Increase	
Premium	Well above market	Well above par	Fast	Fast	Fast	Fair
Cusp	Close to market	Close to par	Fast	Medium	Slow	Poor
Discount	Well below market	Well below par	Slow	Slow	Slow	Fair

EXHIBIT 4.6   Historical Performance of Cusp Coupon Mortgages as a Function of Interest Rate Changes

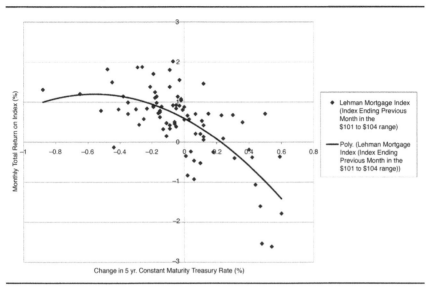

EXHIBIT 4.7   Historical Performance of Discount Mortgages as a Function of Interest Rate Changes

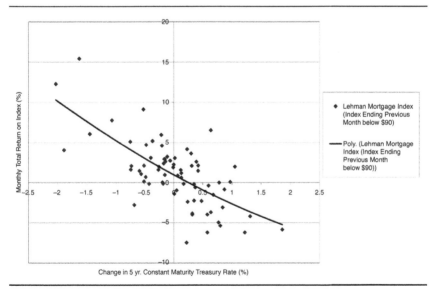

bonds. Consequently, many market participants switched to the lower duration (approximately 5.0 years) Lehman Brothers Government Corporate (LBGC) (now Lehman Brothers Government Credit) Index. The LBGC is primarily composed of government and agency securities. It also includes investment grade corporate bonds, and SEC-registered, U.S. dollar denominated, sovereign, supranational, foreign agency, and foreign local government bonds. As the mortgage backed securities market expanded in the late 1980s, the Lehman Brothers Aggregate (LBAG) Index became the most widely used index. The primary difference between the LBAG and the LBGC is inclusion of fixed-rate, agency-guaranteed, mortgage-backed securities in the LBAG, in addition to all of the securities included within the LBGC, with index weights determined in accordance with the proportion of outstanding bonds.

Exhibit 4.8 shows the historical composition of the LBAG and LBGC since inception.

EXHIBIT 4.8   Historical Composition of LBAG and LBGC

Semi-annual Period Ending	LBAG Duration (yrs)	LBGC Duration (yrs)	LBAG Yield (%)	LBGC Yield (%)	LBAG Corporate Concentration (%)	LBGC Corporate Concentration (%)	LBAG MBS Concentration (%)	LBAG MBS Index Price ($)	LBAG 10+ yrs. Maturity Concentration (%)	LBGC 10+ yrs. Maturity Concentration (%)
Jun-76	N/A	N/A	8.10	8.03	42.7	46.8	4.7	94.59	N/A	N/A
Dec-76	N/A	N/A	6.99	6.90	41.8	46.2	5.2	101.52	N/A	N/A
Jun-77	N/A	N/A	7.37	7.27	40.9	46.1	6.7	98.65	N/A	N/A
Dec-77	N/A	N/A	8.04	7.95	38.8	44.6	8.3	95.34	N/A	N/A
Jun-78	N/A	N/A	8.89	8.81	36.6	42.6	9.1	90.62	N/A	N/A
Dec-78	N/A	N/A	9.80	9.78	35.5	41.9	10.1	89.83	N/A	N/A
Jun-79	N/A	N/A	9.24	9.18	35.3	41.6	10.3	91.82	N/A	N/A
Dec-79	N/A	N/A	11.19	11.08	32.5	38.7	11.3	82.72	N/A	N/A
Jun-80	N/A	N/A	10.18	10.09	31.4	37.7	12.1	86.80	N/A	N/A
Dec-80	N/A	N/A	13.03	12.95	30.0	35.7	11.8	75.77	N/A	N/A
Jun-81	N/A	N/A	14.53	14.48	28.2	33.6	12.0	69.38	N/A	N/A
Dec-81	N/A	N/A	14.64	14.53	26.0	30.8	11.4	68.25	N/A	N/A
Jun-82	N/A	N/A	14.94	14.92	25.1	29.8	12.0	70.70	N/A	N/A
Dec-82	N/A	N/A	10.95	10.75	24.8	29.9	13.0	87.28	N/A	N/A
Jun-83	N/A	N/A	11.22	11.03	24.0	29.6	14.9	87.26	N/A	N/A
Dec-83	N/A	N/A	11.79	11.61	21.3	26.6	16.5	86.68	N/A	N/A
Jun-84	N/A	N/A	13.77	13.64	19.6	24.3	16.4	78.69	N/A	N/A
Dec-84	N/A	N/A	11.37	11.16	19.7	24.6	16.7	89.32	N/A	N/A
Jun-85	N/A	N/A	10.19	9.95	19.3	24.3	17.8	95.58	N/A	N/A
Dec-85	N/A	N/A	9.31	9.11	19.1	24.2	18.5	101.08	N/A	N/A
Jun-86	N/A	N/A	8.31	8.02	19.9	25.4	18.8	100.99	N/A	N/A
Dec-86	N/A	N/A	7.75	7.60	18.9	25.1	22.5	103.43	N/A	N/A

EXHIBIT 4.8   (Continued)

Semi-annual Period Ending	LBAG Duration (yrs)	LBGC Duration (yrs)	LBAG Yield (%)	LBGC Yield (%)	LBAG Corp-orate Concen-tration (%)	LBGC Corp-orate Concen-tration (%)	LBAG MBS Concen-tration (%)	LBAG MBS Index Price ($)	LBAG 10+ yrs. Maturity Concen-tration (%)	LBGC 10+ yrs. Maturity Concen-tration (%)
Jun-87	N/A	N/A	8.64	8.47	17.9	24.7	25.5	97.04	N/A	N/A
Dec-87	N/A	N/A	9.08	8.80	17.6	24.6	26.1	96.21	N/A	N/A
Jun-88	N/A	N/A	9.01	8.80	17.8	25.0	26.4	96.91	N/A	N/A
Dec-88	N/A	N/A	9.68	9.47	17.5	23.9	26.5	95.06	N/A	N/A
Jun-89	4.52	4.55	8.77	8.47	17.0	23.2	26.4	98.80	N/A	N/A
Dec-89	4.56	4.71	8.62	8.33	19.1	26.3	27.3	99.78	N/A	N/A
Jun-90	4.62	4.72	8.96	8.72	19.0	26.5	28.5	98.80	N/A	N/A
Dec-90	4.55	4.76	8.52	8.24	18.0	25.3	28.7	100.52	N/A	N/A
Jun-91	4.63	4.78	8.40	8.11	18.4	26.0	29.1	100.88	N/A	N/A
Dec-91	4.15	4.93	6.70	6.38	16.6	24.2	29.1	106.50	N/A	N/A
Jun-92	4.42	4.91	6.87	6.54	16.9	24.5	29.3	105.26	N/A	N/A
Dec-92	4.50	5.01	6.64	6.27	16.9	24.5	29.3	104.84	N/A	N/A
Jun-93	4.38	5.27	5.78	5.46	17.4	25.0	28.6	106.01	22.9	32.8
Dec-93	4.77	5.34	5.82	5.49	16.8	23.9	28.1	104.43	24.3	34.5
Jun-94	4.87	4.98	7.41	7.12	16.2	23.2	28.7	96.95	29.6	42.4
Dec-94	4.67	4.83	8.21	8.03	16.0	22.9	28.9	94.37	26.7	38.3
Jun-95	4.58	5.04	6.61	6.35	16.7	23.6	28.0	100.74	22.6	31.8
Dec-95	4.47	5.28	6.01	5.74	17.5	24.9	28.5	102.49	21.0	29.9
Jun-96	4.76	5.04	6.95	6.71	17.5	25.2	29.6	99.10	23.6	34.1
Dec-96	4.65	5.10	6.69	6.44	17.8	25.7	29.6	100.34	19.7	28.4
Jun-97	4.62	5.08	6.79	6.60	18.6	26.8	29.9	100.48	19.4	28.0
Dec-97	4.42	5.33	6.24	6.03	19.3	28.1	30.2	102.24	20.8	30.2
Jun-98	4.47	5.46	6.08	5.88	20.7	30.0	30.2	101.99	21.5	31.3
Dec-98	4.44	5.58	5.65	5.35	21.8	32.0	30.7	101.98	21.6	31.7
Jun-99	4.88	5.47	6.55	6.29	20.7	32.3	33.4	98.68	20.9	32.7
Dec-99	4.92	5.30	7.16	6.96	21.5	34.0	34.2	96.45	20.4	32.3
Jun-00	4.91	5.38	7.24	7.03	19.9	31.8	34.4	96.49	18.4	29.4
Dec-00	4.58	5.51	6.43	6.19	20.6	33.5	35.1	100.10	18.1	29.5
Jun-01	4.75	5.47	6.15	5.84	22.8	37.3	35.1	100.41	17.2	28.2
Dec-01	4.54	5.40	5.60	5.19	23.1	38.0	35.4	101.53	16.5	27.1
Jun-02	4.29	5.34	5.27	4.96	22.5	37.7	36.5	102.79	15.0	25.1
Dec-02	3.79	5.41	4.06	3.76	22.3	36.5	35.0	104.46	14.9	24.5
Jun-03	3.95	5.58	3.56	3.23	23.2	37.8	34.2	104.10	15.1	24.6
Dec-03	4.50	5.45	4.15	3.73	22.2	36.9	35.6	102.35	19.1	31.8
Jun-04	4.77	5.21	4.64	4.27	20.5	34.3	35.8	100.39	14.4	24.1
Dec-04	4.34	5.22	4.38	4.09	20.6	34.1	35.1	101.80	12.8	21.2
Jun-05	4.16	5.26	4.48	4.24	20.1	33.0	34.4	101.37	13.0	21.3

Exhibit 4.9 plots the historical yield of the LBAG and LBGC. We note that LBAG has historically been the higher yielding index, where the yield differential has increased over time, and has averaged 31.2 bps from December 1999 until June 2005.

Exhibit 4.10 plots the historical durations of the LBAG and LBGC. We note that LBGC has historically been the higher duration index (with the LBGC averaging a duration 0.97 years longer than the LBAG from December 1999 until June 2005). The duration of the LBAG over time has been much more volatile than the duration of the LBGC due to the inclusion of negatively convex MBS in the LBAG. The volatility of LBAG duration has increased over time as the MBS concentration of the LBAG has increased.

The inclusion of mortgage-backed securities in the LBAG has two effects: First, it causes the LBAG to seek yield in place of convexity (as mortgages are short the prepayment option); and second it causes the LBAG to have less credit risk (given the smaller percentage of lower-rated corporate bonds in the LBAG due to the inclusion of agency-guaranteed, mortgage-backed securities). As the concentration of MBS in the LBAG has increased over time, the LBAG's yield advantage relative to the LBGC has increased, while its convexity has deteriorated. Exhibit 4.11 plots the LBAG's yield advantage relative to LBGC versus the MBS concentration of the LBAG.

EXHIBIT 4.9   Historical Yield of LBAG and LBGC

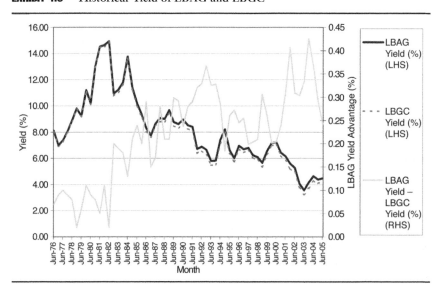

EXHIBIT 4.10   Historical Duration of LBAG and LBGC

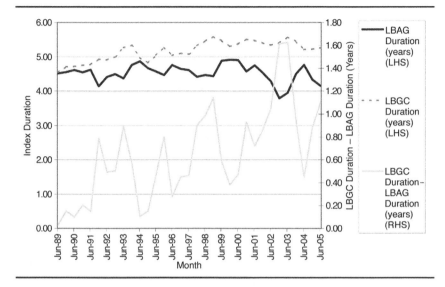

EXHIBIT 4.11   LBAG Yield Advantage Relative to LBGC versus LBAG MBS Concentration

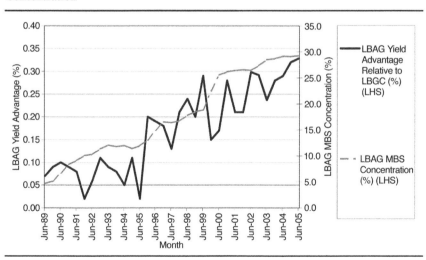

We would expect the LBAG to outperform the LBGC when interest rates are stable (because the extra yield should more than compensate for the poorer convexity), or when credit spreads are widening (because the LBAG should suffer less from the widening in credit spreads than the LBGC given the smaller proportion of lower-rated corporate bonds). Conversely, we would expect the LBGC to outperform the LBAG when interest rate volatility is high, or when credit spreads are tightening. Note that changes in credit spreads and changes in interest rate volatility are positively correlated, which should cause the performance of the LBAG and LBGC to be closer aligned than would be implied by changes in interest rate volatility and credit spreads alone. This relationship can be observed in Exhibit 4.12, which plots the Lehman Credit Index Treasury OAS versus treasury implied volatility. The graph shows that every 1 basis point increase in Treasury implied volatility coincided with a 1.9 basis point widening of the Lehman Credit Index Treasury OAS during the period of February 1995 to June 2005.

Exhibit 4.13 compares the expected relative performance of the LBAG and LBGC under various interest rate environments when credit spreads are unchanged. Note the similarities to Exhibits 4.2 and 4.3, where the LBGC can be viewed as a noncallable bond, and the LBAG can be viewed as a callable bond.

Exhibit 4.14 compares the expected relative performance of the LBGC and LBAG as a function of changes in implied volatility and credit spreads.

EXHIBIT 4.12 Lehman Credit Index Treasury OAS versus Treasury Implied Volatility, February 1995 to June 2005

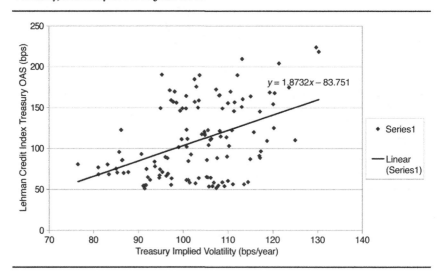

EXHIBIT 4.13   Expected Relative Performance of LBAG and LBGC as a Function of Changes in Implied Volatility and Level of Realized Volatility

		Realized Volatility		
		Less than Expected	Inline with Expectations	More than Expected
Change in Implied Volatility	Decrease	LBAG	LBAG	NA
	No Change	LBAG	TIE	LBGC
	Increase	NA	LBGC	LBGC

Expected relative performance
Legend:

LBAG   LBAG outperforms LBGC.
LBGC   LBGC outperforms LBAG.
TIE   LBAG and LBGC perform inline with one another.
NA   Ambiguous.

EXHIBIT 4.14   Expected Relative Performance of LBAG and LBGC as a Function of Changes in Implied Volatility and Credit Spreads

		Change in Credit Spreads		
		Spreads Widen	Spreads Unchanged	Spreads Tighten
Change in Implied Volatility	Decrease	LBAG	LBAG	NA
	No Change	LBAG	TIE	LBGC
	Increase	NA	LBGC	LBGC

Expected relative performance over an infinitesimally short time horizon
Legend:

LBAG   LBAG outperforms LBGC.
LBGC   LBGC outperforms LBAG.
TIE   LBAG and LBGC perform inline with one another.
NA   Ambiguous.

As previously discussed, mortgages are callable bonds, where the call option is imperfectly exercised. Despite the fact that the call option is imperfectly exercised, mortgages in general have poorer convexity than noncallable bonds of similar duration. The mortgage universe can be divided into three types of mortgages: (1) those with mortgage rates significantly above current market mortgage rates (premium mortgages); (2) those with mortgage rates significantly below current market mortgage rates (discount mortgages); and (3) those with mortgage rates close to current market mortgage rates (cusp coupon mortgages). Given the sensitivity of cusp coupon mortgage prepayments to changes in mortgage rates, cusp coupon mortgages have poorer convexity than both premium and discount mortgages. Consequently, the convexity of the LBAG will be closest to that of the LBGC when the mortgages in the LBAG are either discount or premium mortgages, and the convexity of the LBAG will be farthest from that of the LBGC when the mortgages in the LBAG are cusp coupon mortgages. We now compare the composition and performance of the LBGC and the LBAG over time in Exhibit 4.15.

EXHIBIT 4.15   Historical Review: LBAG versus LBGC

1976–1982
Interest-rate change from 8% to 14.5% moved the call features out of the money. However, the change in interest rates is so large that the duration of callable bonds increased substantially. This, combined with a substantial increase in volatility, led to the outperformance of noncallable portfolios.

1982–1986
The steep decline in interest rates and the virtually unchanged level of high volatility favored noncallable over callable portfolios by a wide margin. The options became in-the-money and shortened the duration of the callable portfolio, revealing the dramatic effects of negative convexity.

1976–1986
While interest rates declined only modestly, the tremendous increase in volatility served to make the option more valuable. A countervailing effect of callable issues' income advantage did not offset their decrease in principal value created by the option over short investment horizons.

1986–1989
During the first half of this period, the increase in interest rates swamped the increase in volatility. Callable bonds outperformed noncallables during this subperiod. During the second half of the period rates declined and volatility declined. The drop in rates dominated and callables performed best. There were ambiguous results for the full period. Rates increased modestly and volatility was largely unchanged.

EXHIBIT 4.15   (Continued)

1990–1992
Intermediate interest rates declined gradually throughout the period. Despite the Gulf War and a U.S. recession in 1991, volatility declined causing callable bonds to outperform non-callable bonds. The relatively range-bound path of interest rates helped the LBAG outperform the LBGC during the period. While the Fed Funds rate was lowered 525 bps from 8.25% in June of 1990 to 3.00% in September of 1992, 10-year Treasury rates remained primarily in a 6¾% to 8¼% range. As a result, mortgage repayments remained benign. Fortunately, the LBAG started the decade with solid convexity due to a mortgage pool that was the least negatively convex in June of 1990 than at any point in the 1990s (65% of the GNMA mortgage universe traded at or below par).

1992–1995
Interest rates moved down and then up and then down again in this highly volatile period, which was marked by a U.S. recovery and the Fed's aggressive monetary stance against inflation. By June of 1992, only 3.5% of the GNMA mortgage universe was priced at or below par. The negative convexity of the mortgage universe during this timeframe caused the LBGC to sharply outperform the LBAG as interest rates fell and volatility increased from 1992 to 1993. Throughout 1994, the Fed was vigilant in its fight against inflation causing volatility to remain high. Long-term interest rates moved up in 1994, but then fell in 1995 once inflation was no longer a threat to the U.S. economy. The LBGC continued to lead the LBAG near the end of this period due to its longer duration.

1995–1997
Ten-year interest rates remained range-bound between 5½% and 6½%. Volatility remained calm. The LBAG outperformed the LBGC due to the range-bound nature of interest rates during the period and a more positively convex mortgage universe (by June 1996, 52% of the GNMA mortgage universe was priced at or below par).

1997–1999
This period was marked by the Asian Contagion, the IMF's bailout of Russia, the LTCM crisis and a liquidity scare which lead to the decade's low in interest rates, rising risk premiums, soaring volatility, and widening credit spreads. Mortgage prepayments surged and the mortgage universe became its most negatively convex ever in the decade with only 3% of the GNMA mortgage universe trading at or below par by December of 1998. The Fed lowered by Fed Funds rate to 4.75% and 10-year Treasury rates approached 4½% by the end of 1998. The LBGC outperformed the LBAG throughout this period due to a sharp rise in volatility.

1999
Interest rates moved up sharply throughout 1999 as the Fed took away its 75 bps of easing in 1998 by tightening 75 bps in 1999, taking the Fed Funds rate back up to 5.50%. Ten-year Treasury rates soared almost 2% to end the decade at 6.44%. While interest rates rose, volatility came down. Fears of a Y2K induces liquidity crush were contained by the Fed's aggressive actions. The LBAG outperformed the LBGC due to a shorter duration and callable bonds outperformed noncallable bonds as volatility declined.

EXHIBIT 4.15   (Continued)

2000–2002
The Federal Reserve Bank provided an abundant amount of liquidity in late 1999 as a precaution toward possible problems in the financial markets because of potential "Y2K" related events. The monetary base and M1 growth peaked at a 20% annual rate. The Y2K transition was ultimately a nonevent. As the Fed withdrew the liquidity, the markets became more volatile, spreads widened and the stock markets declined abruptly. The NASDAQ declined from its early 2000 peak by 70% in 2001. The S&P Index declined by 36%. Bond defaults rate doubled by November 2002. VIX volatility increased from 20% in January 2000, to 45% in November 2002. Spreads on BBB bonds widened from 1.50% to 3.50%. Ten-year interest rates started at 6.25% and ended at 4.00%. The LBAG outperformed the LBGC on a duration-adjusted basis as the volatility associated with credit risk dominated the effect on mortgages in the LBAG of increased interest rate volatility.

The September 2001 terrorist attack on the United States further exacerbated the contractionary bias. Globally, central banks responded by expanding liquidity and, in the United States, the fiscal deficit expanded considerably as a result of increased defense spending and counter-cyclical tax cuts.

2002–2004 (November 2002 to June 2003 and July 2003 to December 2004 subperiods)
In November 2002, the Fed once again came to the rescue reducing interest rates and aggressively expanding the money supply in an attempt to save the credit markets. The episode was a replay of the Fed's response function to the LTCM crisis, the Y2K fears and the September 2001 attacks. This time, however, the participation of foreign investors in the U.S. markets was much greater than it had been in the past and is even greater today. The Fed's pseudo guarantee of corporate credit resulted in an immediate, large contraction in credit spreads, a reduction in interest rates and then a return to the 4.0% level on the 10-year Treasury note. The yield curve steepened and then flattened when the Fed began to raise rates. Real interest rates declined across the yield curve as a result of the deflationary fears.

Ten-year nominal yields fell from 4.00% to 3.10% from November 2002 to June 2003, and rose to 4.10% at yearend 2004. BBB spreads fell from 3.50% in November 2002 to 1.6% in June 2003, and to 1% in December 2004. Real rates on 10-year TIPS bonds fell from 4.125% to 1.7% in June 2003 and remained near that rate, and VIX volatility fell from 45% in November 2002 to 18% in June 2003, and to 12% by December 2004. Volatility of 10-year Treasuries fell from 37% in 2002 to 32% in June 2003, and to 20% in December 2004. Prepayment rates on premium mortgages surged, and 100% of the mortgage market traded at a premium by October 2002—reducing the effective duration of the LBAG by 23% from the June 2000 level. By December 2004, the duration of the LBAG had increased by 15% from the October 2002 level, as prepayment rates declined and new current coupon mortgages were added to the index.

The dramatic improvement in the credit market as delineated by the compression in BBB credit spreads swamped the improvement in mortgage valuation resulting from a decline in interest rate volatility and the LBGC performance exceeded that of the LBAG by 0.41% on a duration-adjusted basis from November 2002 to June 30, 2003. However, from July 1, 2003, to December 2004, the LBAG performed inline with the LBGC as both mortgage spreads and credit spreads compressed.

COMPARISON OF COMPOSITION AND PERFORMANCE OF THE LBGC AND LBAG OVER TIME

We observe relative bogey performance in Exhibit 4.16. The LBAG index is the higher yielding, less convex, and less credit-sensitive index. Consequently, as previously discussed, we would expect the LBAG to outperform the LBGC (on a duration-adjusted basis) when interest rates are stable (because the extra yield should more than compensate for the poorer convexity), or when credit spreads are widening (because the LBAG should suffer less from the widening in credit spreads than the LBGC, given the smaller proportion of credit-sensitive corporate bonds).

Exhibit 4.17 plots the historical duration-adjusted performance of the LBAG relative to the LBGC versus changes in treasury implied volatility. The graph shows that every 1-basis-point increase in treasury implied volatility coincided with 0.32 basis points of underperformance of the LBAG relative to the LBGC—the negative correlation was to be expected, given that the LBAG is less convex than the LBGC.

Exhibit 4.18 plots the historical duration-adjusted performance of the LBAG relative to the LBGC versus changes in Lehman Credit Index OAS. The graph shows that every 1 basis point of widening in the Lehman Credit Index OAS coincided with 0.40 basis points of outperformance of the LBAG relative to the LBGC—the positive correlation was is to be expected, given that the LBAG is less credit-sensitive than the LBGC.

FIXED INCOME INDEX SELECTION

Bogey selection may be a plan sponsor's most important decision, as the choice of an index as a bogey is an implicit forecast of both interest rates and volatility. The selection of the bogey incorporates decisions regarding the duration, convexity, and composition of the portfolio. Similarly, fixed income portfolio management necessarily requires an interest-rate forecast, a volatility forecast, and a set of analytical models that calculate the future value of individual securities and portfolios of securities based upon those forecasts, as it is the confluence of volatility changes and interest rate movements that is predominate driver of bond values.[1]

Those who are required to select a performance bogey for their fund have a difficult choice. The bogey performs the role of directing the risk of the assets. The choice involves a trade-off between a bogey that (1) replicates the proportional distribution of bonds in the market; (2) has

---

[1] For a rigorous discussion, see Chris P. Dialynas and D. Edington, "Bond Yield Spreads Revisited," *Journal of Portfolio Management* (Fall 1992), pp. 68–75.

EXHIBIT 4.16 Historical Review: LBAG versus LBGC

Semi-annual Period Ending	Lehman Credit Index Treasury OAS (bps)	Change in Lehman Credit Index Treasury OAS (bps)	Treasury Implied Volatility (bps/year)	Change in Treasury Implied Volatility (bps/year)	10 Yr. Constant Maturity Treasury Rate (%)	Change in Constant Maturity Treasury Rate (%)	LBAG Total Return (%)	LBGC Total Return (%)	LBAG Excess Return vs. Treasuries (%)	LBGC Excess Return vs. Treasuries (%)	LBAG Outperformance vs. LBGC (%)
Jun-76	N/A	N/A	N/A	N/A	7.86	(0.15)	5.04	5.06	N/A	N/A	N/A
Dec-76	N/A	N/A	N/A	N/A	6.87	(0.99)	10.05	10.02	N/A	N/A	N/A
Jun-77	N/A	N/A	N/A	N/A	7.28	0.41	2.21	2.21	N/A	N/A	N/A
Dec-77	N/A	N/A	N/A	N/A	7.69	0.41	0.80	0.77	N/A	N/A	N/A
Jun-78	N/A	N/A	N/A	N/A	8.46	0.77	0.14	0.18	N/A	N/A	N/A
Dec-78	N/A	N/A	N/A	N/A	9.01	0.55	1.26	0.99	N/A	N/A	N/A
Jun-79	N/A	N/A	N/A	N/A	8.91	(0.10)	6.50	6.60	N/A	N/A	N/A
Dec-79	N/A	N/A	N/A	N/A	10.39	1.48	(4.29)	(4.06)	N/A	N/A	N/A
Jun-80	N/A	N/A	N/A	N/A	9.78	(0.61)	8.45	8.21	N/A	N/A	N/A
Dec-80	N/A	N/A	N/A	N/A	12.84	3.06	(5.29)	(4.77)	N/A	N/A	N/A
Jun-81	N/A	N/A	N/A	N/A	13.47	0.63	0.17	0.71	N/A	N/A	N/A
Dec-81	N/A	N/A	N/A	N/A	13.72	0.25	6.09	6.53	N/A	N/A	N/A
Jun-82	N/A	N/A	N/A	N/A	14.30	0.58	6.84	6.42	N/A	N/A	N/A
Dec-82	N/A	N/A	N/A	N/A	10.54	(3.76)	24.14	23.19	N/A	N/A	N/A
Jun-83	N/A	N/A	N/A	N/A	10.85	0.31	4.92	4.82	N/A	N/A	N/A
Dec-83	N/A	N/A	N/A	N/A	11.83	0.98	3.29	3.02	N/A	N/A	N/A
Jun-84	N/A	N/A	N/A	N/A	13.56	1.73	(1.67)	(1.21)	N/A	N/A	N/A
Dec-84	N/A	N/A	N/A	N/A	11.50	(2.06)	17.11	16.41	N/A	N/A	N/A
Jun-85	N/A	N/A	N/A	N/A	10.16	(1.34)	10.98	10.56	N/A	N/A	N/A
Dec-85	N/A	N/A	N/A	N/A	9.26	(0.90)	10.05	9.73	N/A	N/A	N/A
Jun-86	N/A	N/A	N/A	N/A	7.80	(1.46)	9.05	9.95	N/A	N/A	N/A
Dec-86	N/A	N/A	N/A	N/A	7.11	(0.69)	5.69	5.13	N/A	N/A	N/A

EXHIBIT 4.16 (Continued)

Semiannual Period Ending	Lehman Credit Index Treasury OAS (bps)	Change in Lehman Credit Index Treasury OAS (bps)	Treasury Implied Volatility (bps/year)	Change in Treasury Implied Volatility (bps/year)	10 Yr. Constant Maturity Treasury Rate (%)	Change in Constant Maturity Treasury Rate (%)	LBAG Total Return (%)	LBGC Total Return (%)	LBAG Excess Return vs. Treasuries (%)	LBGC Excess Return vs. Treasuries (%)	LBAG Outperformance vs. LBGC (%)
Jun-87	N/A	N/A	N/A	N/A	8.40	1.29	(0.16)	(0.44)	N/A	N/A	N/A
Dec-87	N/A	N/A	N/A	N/A	8.99	0.59	2.92	2.75	N/A	N/A	N/A
Jun-88	N/A	N/A	N/A	N/A	8.92	(0.07)	4.99	4.60	N/A	N/A	N/A
Dec-88	N/A	N/A	N/A	N/A	9.11	0.19	2.76	2.85	N/A	N/A	N/A
Jun-89	74.4	N/A	N/A	N/A	8.28	(0.83)	9.19	9.22	(0.01)	(0.01)	0.00
Dec-89	97.2	22.8	N/A	N/A	7.84	(0.44)	4.89	4.58	0.24	(0.07)	0.31
Jun-90	87.7	(9.5)	N/A	N/A	8.48	0.64	2.82	2.42	0.65	0.24	0.40
Dec-90	151.1	63.4	N/A	N/A	8.08	(0.40)	5.96	5.73	(0.65)	(0.69)	0.04
Jun-91	101.7	(49.4)	N/A	N/A	8.28	0.20	4.47	4.25	0.97	0.77	0.20
Dec-91	107.2	5.5	N/A	N/A	7.09	(1.19)	11.04	11.39	(0.50)	(0.11)	(0.39)
Jun-92	86.7	(20.5)	N/A	N/A	7.26	0.17	2.71	2.49	0.12	0.35	(0.23)
Dec-92	87.6	0.9	N/A	N/A	6.77	(0.49)	4.57	4.97	(0.24)	(0.09)	(0.15)
Jun-93	77.1	(10.5)	N/A	N/A	5.96	(0.81)	6.89	7.79	(0.14)	0.10	(0.25)
Dec-93	72.9	(4.1)	N/A	N/A	5.77	(0.19)	2.67	3.01	0.05	0.16	(0.11)
Jun-94	77.0	4.1	N/A	N/A	7.10	1.33	(3.87)	(4.34)	0.10	0.02	0.08
Dec-94	78.3	1.3	N/A	N/A	7.81	0.71	0.99	0.86	0.26	0.10	0.17
Jun-95	64.9	(13.4)	105.5	N/A	6.17	(1.64)	11.44	11.80	(0.11)	0.21	(0.32)
Dec-95	64.9	0.0	92.2	(13.3)	5.71	(0.46)	6.31	6.66	0.21	0.13	0.09
Jun-96	58.2	(6.7)	101.4	9.3	6.91	1.20	(1.21)	(1.88)	0.29	0.18	0.11
Dec-96	56.2	(2.0)	111.0	9.6	6.30	(0.61)	4.90	4.88	0.19	0.15	0.04
Jun-97	54.3	(2.0)	91.1	(19.9)	6.49	0.19	3.09	2.74	0.48	0.19	0.29
Dec-97	67.2	13.0	94.8	3.7	5.81	(0.68)	6.36	6.83	(0.15)	(0.24)	0.09

EXHIBIT 4.16 (Continued)

Semi-annual Period Ending	Lehman Credit Index Treasury OAS (bps)	Change in Lehman Credit Index Treasury OAS (bps)	Treasury Implied Volatility (bps/year)	Change in Treasury Implied Volatility (bps/year)	10 Yr. Constant Maturity Treasury Rate (%)	Change in Constant Maturity Treasury Rate (%)	LBAG Total Return (%)	LBGC Total Return (%)	LBAG Excess Return vs. Treasuries (%)	LBGC Excess Return vs. Treasuries (%)	LBAG Outperformance vs. LBGC (%)
Jun-98	77.1	9.8	81.1	(13.7)	5.50	(0.31)	3.93	4.17	(0.01)	(0.06)	0.05
Dec-98	117.8	40.8	104.8	23.7	4.65	(0.85)	4.58	5.09	(0.76)	(0.66)	(0.10)
Jun-99	111.9	(5.9)	106.3	1.5	5.90	1.25	(1.37)	(2.28)	0.32	0.36	(0.04)
Dec-99	110.8	(1.1)	106.0	(0.2)	6.28	0.38	0.56	0.13	0.49	0.26	0.23
Jun-00	158.8	47.9	103.5	(2.6)	6.10	(0.18)	3.99	4.18	(0.91)	(1.12)	0.21
Dec-00	189.9	31.1	112.1	8.6	5.24	(0.86)	7.35	7.36	(0.31)	(0.44)	0.12
Jun-01	149.2	(40.6)	99.8	(12.2)	5.28	0.04	3.62	3.51	0.88	1.22	(0.34)
Dec-01	164.0	14.8	115.0	15.2	5.09	(0.19)	4.66	4.82	(0.36)	(0.04)	(0.33)
Jun-02	169.7	5.7	110.6	(4.5)	4.93	(0.16)	3.79	3.26	0.23	(0.50)	0.73
Dec-02	168.7	(1.0)	119.3	8.7	4.03	(0.90)	6.23	7.53	0.04	(0.12)	0.16
Jun-03	113.9	(54.9)	109.7	(9.6)	3.33	(0.70)	3.93	5.23	1.20	1.62	(0.41)
Dec-03	88.8	(25.1)	117.1	7.5	4.27	0.94	0.17	(0.53)	0.33	0.70	(0.37)
Jun-04	93.3	4.5	90.7	(26.4)	4.73	0.46	0.15	(0.19)	0.14	0.01	0.13
Dec-04	75.0	(18.2)	91.8	1.1	4.23	(0.50)	4.18	4.39	0.89	0.79	0.10
Jun-05	85.7	10.7	86.4	(5.5)	4.00	(0.23)	2.51	2.75	(0.13)	(0.32)	0.19

EXHIBIT 4.17   Duration-Adjusted Performance of the LBAG Relative to the LBGC versus Changes in Treasury Implied Volatility, June 1995 to June 2005

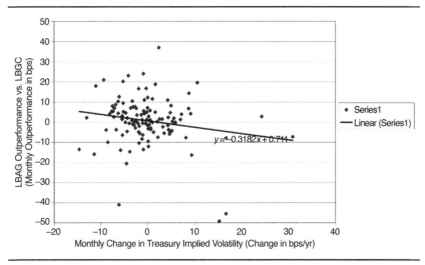

EXHIBIT 4.18   Duration-Adjusted Performance of the LBAG relative to the LBGC versus Changes in Lehman Credit Index OAS, June 1985 to June 2005

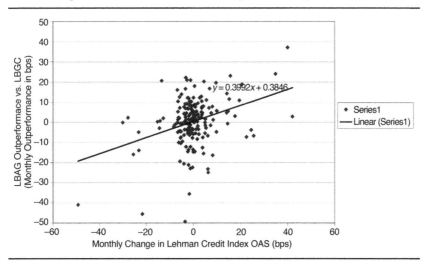

risk characteristics complementary to the liability structure of the assets; and (3) has a relatively neutral market bias associated with it. Unfortunately, no bogey satisfies all of these requirements, and the trade-offs can be costly. It is important to fully understand what the bogey represents to ensure the robustness of the asset allocation decision.

The choices are difficult. Ultimately, correct macroeconomic forecasts will dominate the active/passive choice. Will volatility increase or diminish, and when? Will rates go up or down, and when? What influences volatility? How do interest rates and volatility changes trade off? When does the volatility/interest-rate forecast favor one index over the other? These are the tough questions that you should be asking your active manager or your passive index.

The move to passive management reinforces Say's Law, which holds that supply creates its own demand. Passive investment portfolios have done well in spite of their main investment criterion: buy whatever is produced, independent of price or value considerations. Thus, passive management relies upon the market forces to ensure that assets are appropriately priced.

The LBAG has enjoyed preferential bogey status for more than a decade. The philosophical rationalization for the LBAG bogey is based upon its "market" composition. Essentially, the LBAG is a rule based index predicated upon buying a proportionate share of all investment grade issuance. The greater the amount issued, the greater the ownership, despite the credit quality deterioration associated with greater debt. The composition and duration of the bogey are determined by the issuers—not the investor. This dynamic imposes boundaries on spreads for the various asset classes in the bond universe and imposes a time-varying duration/convexity mismatch for a liability-based investor. If the liability based class of investors were to alter their framework from a "buy what is issued" rule to an asset/liability matching rule, the implications on asset class spreads and yield curve shape could be substantial as longer duration portfolios are created. Relative values of bonds (option adjusted spreads) vary over time and are significantly influenced by their clientele.

Narrow indexes, such as the LBGC, have performed very well at times due to the circumstances—radically lower rates and increased volatility, both of which benefited long duration, call-protected portfolios. During periods of reduced volatility and/or higher rates, the LBAG has performed well. The past is prologue: Today's investment choice will be judged by tomorrow's circumstances.

THE EXLUSION OF TREASURY INFLATION PROTECTED SECURITIES

Treasury Inflation Protected Securities (TIPS) are bonds issued by the U.S. Government. TIPS, where the coupon and principal are indexed to the realized rate of inflation. In 1999, these securities represented 7% of the U.S. Treasury's issuance of debt, and still represent about 7% of the U.S. Treasury's issuance of debt in June 2005. They were originally included in the Lehman Brothers indexes and subsequently excluded. Presumably, this exclusion is due to the difficulty in computing the TIPS' duration. This, however, is not a robust reason. Arguably, the calculation of the duration of mortgage securities is even more uncertain.

A consistent application of the standard that the index contains that which is sold would suggest that TIPS should be included in the indexes. It seems appropriate to include these securities and extraordinary to exclude them. For our purposes, it is important to understand that the addition of these securities to the indexes would alter the investment dynamics. If TIPS were included in the indices, the effect would be to:

1. Increase direct exposure to real interest rates
2. Increase quality
3. Increase call protection
4. Decrease volatility

The inclusion of TIPS, while complicating the dynamics, would be an appropriate and necessary choice given the volume of supply of these securities.

THE IMPORTANCE OF CHANGES IN THE SHAPE OF YIELD CURVE

Change in the shape of the yield curve is another important risk factor. Given that the LBGC, LBAG and portfolio managers' portfolios have varying sensitivities to shifts in various portions of the yield curve, changes in the shape of the yield curve may have a significant impact in relative performance—especially when the shape of the yield curve changes frequently or dramatically. Generally speaking, the cash flows of the LBAG are more heavily weighted in the intermediate portion of the yield curve relative to those of the LBGC. Thus, a steepening yield curve would favor the LBAG, while a flattening yield curve would favor the LBGC; ceteris paribus. Changes in the shape of the yield curve can also affect duration, call and put option values, prepayment behavior, and can have other more subtle effects.

The yield curve effect is not included in this analysis. The difficulty in bond investment analysis is extremely complex when yield curve shape changes are included. These complexities, including the potential correlation between interest rates and volatility are beyond the scope of this chapter. Professional bond portfolio managers must understand these uncertain linkages if they hope to succeed.

INDEX CONSCIOUSNESS

The extraordinary increased volatility of interest rates during the 1970s and 1980s and the reduction in volatility in the 1990s has resulted in considerable volatility in returns. Portfolios with different durations are likely to have substantial deviations in returns when interest rates are volatile. The historical return differences between the LBGC and the Salomon Brothers Long Corporate Index illustrate this point. Many market participants were apparently surprised by the amount of price volatility that their bond portfolios experienced in the 1960s and 1970s. In an effort to control portfolio return variability relative to the "market," some bond managers adopted portfolio constraints wherein their duration risk relative to the market index was bounded. The movement to this new investment strategy helped control variability but reduced the potential gains through the use of expert macroeconomic analysis and interest-rate forecasting. The movement to this policy is an admission of a flawed investment theory, risk aversion, and/or an uncertain conviction in forecasting capability. This chapter has emphasized the importance of the contribution of good interest-rate and volatility forecasts with consistent period-dependent asset selection.

SOME IMPORTANT MISCELLANEOUS COMMENTS ABOUT INDEXES

The first version of this paper appeared in 1986. The author of that paper was perplexed by the peculiar behavior of the plan sponsor community. The well-educated community requires and understands rigorous modern finance statistical methods. A compelling risk/reward statistical argument resulted in the transition from the Long Salomon Bond Index to the LBGC just after interest rates hit a historical high. At the time, the high interest rates caused, oddly enough, the durational difference (risk) of long bonds and 10-year bonds to approach each other. The subsequent transition to the LBAG occurred shortly thereafter, resulting in a further reduction in duration and call protection at a time when interest rates were very high. Subsequently, there was a movement to a "core-plus" concept represented by the *Lehman Universal Index* (LUNV), which coincided with the end of one of the most remarkable decades of growth in U.S. history. A move to the LUNV implied a further reduction in: (1) duration, (2) call protection, and (3) quality.

Exhibits 4.19, 4.20, and 4.21 demonstrate changes in the composition of the LBAG and LBGC over time. We note that these changes were due to a shift in investor demand. The reduced demand for longer duration assets, due to the shift towards lower duration benchmarks, caused the supply of longer duration bonds to fall (as reflected in Exhibit 4.19).

Callable corporate bonds underperformed following the surge of interest rate volatility in the late 1970s and early 1980s. Following the underperformance, the demand for callable corporate bonds fell to such a level that it was more economical for issuers to sell noncallable bonds instead of callable bonds. Exhibit 4.20 shows that the change in the convention regarding the callability of corporate bonds—in the 1970s and early 1980s, corporate bonds were typically callable, while corporate bonds are generally not callable today. The shift from the issuance

EXHIBIT 4.19 Concentration of 10-Year-Plus Maturity Bonds in LBAG and LBGC versus Date

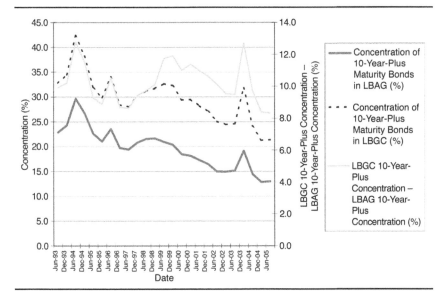

EXHIBIT 4.20 Concentration of Callable Bonds in Lehman Credit Index versus Date

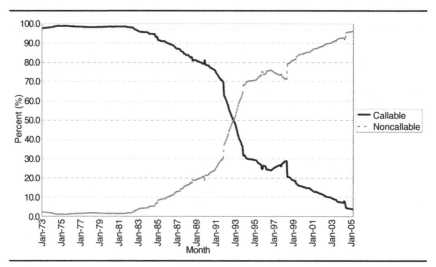

EXHIBIT 4.21 Concentration of Corporate Bonds and MBS in LBAG and LBGC versus Date

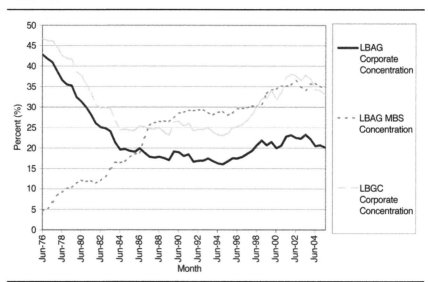

of callable to noncallable bonds reflects the innovations in the fixed income market over time, which allow risks to be bundled together or separated. In the early 1970s, it is likely that corporate bond fixed income managers did not fully value the embedded short call option in callable corporate bonds—and thus it was to the issuers' advantage to sell callable corporate bonds. Given the underperformance of callable corporate bonds in the late 1970s and 1980s, corporate bond fixed income managers became well aware of the drawbacks of callable corporate bonds. Given that corporate bond specialists tend to be more comfortable analyzing credit risk rather than interest rate risk, it is likely that such managers would tend to undervalue corporate bonds with embedded interest rate risk—especially after underperforming following an interest rate volatility bet that went awry. Consequently, the demand for corporate bonds fell to such a level that it was more economic for issuers to sell noncallable bonds instead of callable bonds.

Given the substantial appreciation of U.S. residential real estate, the numerous innovations in the securitization technologies, the continued growth of Fannie Mae and Freddie Mac, and the strengthened requirements for holding whole loans on bank balance sheets, it is no wonder that the mortgage-backed securities market has experienced explosive growth over the last three decades. Exhibit 4.21 shows that the declining concentration of corporate bonds in the LBAG has been offset by an increasing concentration of fixed-rate MBS (recall that the LBGC does not include MBS).

The authors remain skeptical of the "historically blind," but empirically rigorous, approach of the herd. A study of financial history over longer periods of time reveals gradual transitions to greater risk followed by abrupt periods of wealth destruction and risk aversion. This is due to the fact that all agents in the process—especially plan sponsors and investment managers—are judged over relatively short time periods. Thus, decision making will tend to be based upon a short time horizon instead of over the significantly longer life of the plan.

Important macroeconomics and microeconomic phenomena result from the plan sponsors' bogey selection. Exhibit 4.22 summarizes plan sponsors' shifts in bogey selection over time, the resulting microeconomic impact, macroeconomic impact, and the effect on the plans.

The move of the herd from one bogey to another initially results in a shift in the demand curve for a sector, which is soon followed by a shift in the supply curve. The demand curve shift reinforces the asset allocation realignment, as prices of the newly added asset class are bid up. When more and more of the herd enter, assets are bid up ever more; further reinforcing the original statistical analysis and creating a more powerful updated statistical study. Eventually, supply catches up to the

EXHIBIT 4.22 Plan Sponsors' Shifts in Bogey Selection over Time, and Resulting Microeconomic Impact, Macroeconomic Impact, and Effect on the Plans

	Microeconomic	Macroeconomic	Effect on the Plan
1. Salomon Brothers Long Corporate Index → LBGC	Substitution of issuance of intermediate debt in lieu of longer bonds	More risky capital structure	Increases duration gap of assets and liabilities (generally pension plan liabilities have durations of 10+ years)
2. LBGC → LBAG	Financing of mortgage industry from banking industry to longer-term investors. Securitization of asset markets	Cheaper cost of debt to consumers; results in more robust housing industry, consumer demand and household leverage; potential moral hazard risk in loan origination	Increases duration gap of assets and liabilities (generally pension plan liabilities have durations of 10+ years)
3. LBAG → LUNV	Financing of emerging market and high-yield debt market	Reduces cost of debt to highly leveraged producers; encourages more debt and leverage; increases risk of plan assets and reduces value of bond portfolio as deflationary hedge	Increases duration gap of assets and liabilities (generally pension plan liabilities have durations of 10+ years)

fresh demand resulting in a more leveraged economy and a reduced quality of plan assets.

Exhibit 4.23 summarizes the microeconomic impact, macroeconomic impact and the effect on the plans as a result of a potential shift from the LBAG to the Lehman Brothers Long Government Credit Index (LBLGC), assuming no leverage. Note that the LBLGC only includes bonds from the LBGC that have a maturity of 10+ years—consequently, the LBLGC has a much longer duration (11.20 years as of 6/2005) than both the LBGC (5.26 years as of 6/2005) and the LBAG (4.16 years as of 6/2005).

CONCLUSION

The asset allocation decision remains the most important decision for the plan sponsor. Today, there exists a broad menu of bogey choices in the U.S. bond market, each representing a slightly different set of risk characteristics. But there is no "bogey for all seasons." Each bogey performs well in any particular period given a particular set of market circumstances. Ultimately, the plan sponsor's choices are: (1) match duration of assets/liabilities; (2) select a bogey representative of the investable universe; (3) optimize portfolio mix based upon historical risk/return data; or (4) maximize some other objective. The decisions are quite important as 4 trillion dollars of defined benefit pension plan assets are at risk.

EXHIBIT 4.28 Microeconomic Impact, Macroeconomic Impact, and Effect on Plans as a Result of a Potential Shift from the LBAG to the LBLGC (Assuming That Plans Do Not Permit Leverage)

	Microeconomic	Macroeconomic	Effect on the Plan
1. LBAG → LBLGC	Reduced financing of mortgage industry from banking industry to longer-term investors. Decline in securitization of asset markets. Richening of longer dura-tion bonds relative to shorter duration bonds leads to a flattening of the yield curve. Cheapening of the MBS sector leads to an expansion Fannie Mae and Freddie Mac's retained portfolios, and increased implied volatility as Fannie Mae and Freddie Mac attempt to hedge their increased prepayment risk of their larger portfolios.	Higher cost of debt to consumers. Results in weaker housing industry, consumer demand and reduced household leverage.	Decreases duration gap of assets and liabilities (generally pension plan liabilities have durations of 10+ years).

CHAPTER 5

Liability-Based Benchmarks

Lev Dynkin, Ph.D.
Managing Director
Lehman Brothers

Jay Hyman, Ph.D.
Senior Vice President
Lehman Brothers

Bruce D. Phelps, Ph.D., CFA
Senior Vice President
Lehman Brothers

Plan sponsors and investment managers are well acquainted with market-based, fixed income indices (e.g., the Lehman Government/Credit Index). These indices are defined as a set of well-publicized rules that govern which bonds are added and deleted. When a market-based index reflects the risk preferences of the plan sponsor and the investment opportunities facing the investment manager, the index serves as a useful tool for performance evaluation and risk analysis. In other words, the index is a "neutral" benchmark, and the manager is evaluated based on performance versus the index. While the sponsor may impose some additional investment constraints (e.g., credit and issuer concentration and limits on deviations from the index), the sponsor otherwise wants the manager to be unfettered within the confines of the index in the search for added returns.

However, some investment managers must operate in a more constrained environment. A plan's assets may be "dedicated" to satisfying a well-defined liability schedule and assets must be managed to satisfy those liabilities.[1] In these cases, the sponsor specifies, based on risk preferences, the universe of bonds in which the manager may invest and the liability schedule that must be satisfied. Often the investable universe is defined as a market-based index. However, the index usually has a term structure that is very different from the liability schedule (e.g., the liability schedule may have a longer duration than the market index).

The manager now has two goals: produce added returns to help the plan achieve its long-term investment goals and, simultaneously, keep the portfolio's term structure aligned with the liability schedule. How does the sponsor evaluate the manager's performance? If the manager underperforms the market index, was it due to the manager's poor sector and security selection or the manager's correct structuring of the portfolio to satisfy the liability term structure? What is needed is a "neutral" benchmark that reflects both goals of the plan sponsor. The manager's performance can then be properly compared with the return on the "neutral" benchmark.

USEFULNESS OF LIABILITY-BASED BENCHMARKS

A liability-based benchmark is a "neutral" benchmark that gives the sponsor and manager a performance yardstick incorporating both the term structure constraints imposed by the liability schedule and the investment restrictions imposed by the sponsor's risk preferences. Sponsors can be confident that if they hold the positions underlying the liability benchmark, they will meet their liability schedules while satisfying their investment restrictions. This makes the liability benchmark a "neutral" benchmark.

A liability-based benchmark can also retain many of the desirable attributes of a market-based index: Benchmark returns are calculated using market prices, the investment manager can replicate the benchmark, and the benchmark is well defined so that the sponsor and manager can actively monitor and evaluate its risk and performance. Furthermore, if the liability benchmark contains published market-based indices or marketable securities, its performance can be calculated and published by third-party index or market data providers.

---

[1] A dedicated portfolio refers to a portfolio of marketable securities that services a prescribed set of liabilities. There are various ways to construct a dedicated portfolio: cash-matched, immunization, horizon matched, and contingent immunization. For an analysis of these various approaches see Martin L. Leibowitz, "Duration, Immunization and Dedication," in Frank J. Fabozzi (ed.), *Investing: The Collected Works of Martin L. Leibowitz* (Chicago: Probus Publishing, 1992).

Because the liability benchmark reflects the sponsor's liability schedule and investment restrictions, a manager can directly evaluate an investment portfolio against the benchmark. Using standard portfolio analytics, the manager can estimate tracking error, perform scenario analysis, and evaluate individual security swaps. Also, because the liability benchmark is a "neutral" benchmark, its performance can be compared directly with the manager's performance. This greatly facilitates sponsor-manager communication.

TYPES OF LIABILITY-BASED BENCHMARKS

A liability-based benchmark reflects the term structure of the liability schedule and the investment restrictions of the plan sponsor. Two possible ways to construct a liability benchmark are:

1. Use market-based indices that reflect the sponsor's investment restrictions to construct a *composite benchmark* that reflects the liability term structure. For example, if the liability schedule is longer duration than the Lehman Aggregate Index, a composite index of the Credit and Aggregate indices and a custom long Treasury strips index could be created matching the duration of the liability schedule and the sponsor's investment restrictions.[2]

   More complicated composite indices may contain several indices weighted so as to achieve various diversification goals and duration, convexity, and yield targets. Despite matching a targeted duration, however, composite benchmarks may still have cash flow distributions that differ significantly from the liability schedule. Consequently, the composite benchmark and the liability schedule may diverge due to non-parallel shifts in the yield curve. In addition, as the underlying market indices are a set of rules and not a fixed set of bonds, the characteristics of the indices change over time, which may make frequent rebalancing necessary.[3]

   Care must be taken in using composite benchmarks. Suppose the liability schedule is concentrated in the near-term years. The temptation may be to use a short credit index as one of the indices in the com-

---

[2] For more on the construction of liability-based composite benchmarks see Boyce I. Greer, "Market-Oriented Benchmarks for Immunized Portfolios," *Journal of Portfolio Management* (Spring 1992), pp. 26–35.

[3] Rebalancing composite benchmarks, however, is straightforward. *POINT*, the Lehman Brothers portfolio analytics system, can calculate and update the desired index weights automatically to keep duration and sector exposures on target.

posite. However, the short credit index may introduce an unintended bias into the composite benchmark. For example, the industrial sector accounts for 37% of the 0–4 duration bucket of the Credit Index, whereas it accounts for 45.5% in the overall index. Consequently, using the 0–4 duration credit subindex in the composite may inadvertently underweight industrial paper in the composite benchmark.

2. Create a *portfolio benchmark* by selecting bonds from the investable universe such that the portfolio's cash flows closely match the liability schedule and the overall portfolio satisfies the sponsor's investment restrictions.

Because bonds in a portfolio benchmark are selected so that their overall characteristics match the investment restrictions, the risk described above of unintended biases with composite benchmarks is eliminated.

Unlike a composite benchmark that consists of indices and their set of rules, a portfolio benchmark consists of a set of bonds. By design, a portfolio benchmark is explicitly structured to track a given liability schedule over time, reducing the need for rebalancing. However, the relatively few bonds in the portfolio benchmark (compared with the many bonds in the indices underlying a composite benchmark) make the portfolio benchmark susceptible to idiosyncratic risk. Consequently, in sectors in which there is significant event risk (e.g., corporates), great care must be taken to reduce idiosyncratic risk by holding many different issuers.[4]

In this chapter, we present our method for constructing liability-based portfolio benchmarks.

BUILDING A LIABILITY-BASED PORTFOLIO BENCHMARK

The traditional dedication approach is to minimize the cost of a portfolio funding a liability schedule subject to constraints such as requiring that the duration and convexity of the portfolio match those of the liabilities. Other constraints, such as sector weights and a sufficient number of issu-

---

[4] A methodology for constructing replicating credit portfolios that minimizes event risk is explained in Lev Dynkin, Jay Hyman, and Vadim Konstantinovsky, "Sufficient Diversification in Credit Portfolios," *Journal of Portfolio Management* (Fall 2002), pp. 89–114. For example, the Lehman Credit Index can be replicated with a 100-bond portfolio such that it will not underperform the index by more than 35 bps with 95% confidence. The key is to hold most of the 100 issues in the BBB category: using 62 BBB bonds to replicate the BBB-quality sector having a 31% market weight in the Credit Index.

ers in the portfolio, ensure portfolio diversification. Overall, these optimization constraints help keep the portfolio's cash flows "matched" with the liabilities, while also adhering to the sponsor's investment guidelines. This traditional dedication approach is a linear optimization problem, as the objective function and constraints are linear equations.

A different approach is used to construct a liability-based portfolio benchmark. The idea is to construct a portfolio such that its cash flows mimic as closely as possible the cash flows of the liability schedule subject to the portfolio investment constraints. In other words, the objective is to minimize the absolute value of the difference between each liability cash flow and the available cash flow from the portfolio at the time of each liability cash flow.

Since portfolio benchmark cash flows are unlikely to fall on the exact date of the liability cash flows, portfolio cash flows are either reinvested forward or, if permitted, discounted back to a liability cash flow date. Consequently, a portfolio's available cash flow at each liability cash flow date is the amount of portfolio cash that can be delivered to that date. To illustrate, consider a liability cash flow L_t that occurs at time t (Exhibit 5.1). There are several cash flows (assume, for simplicity, that they are zero coupon bonds) available that could possibly meet this liability cash flow. Two of these cash flows (P_1 and P_2) occur before and another one (P_3) occurs after the liability cash flow. However, depending on the assumptions allowed in the portfolio construction process, all three cash flows (if purchased in sufficient quantity) could satisfy the liability cash flow L_t.

Consider cash flow P_1, which occurs before L_t. If the reinvestment rate, r, is assumed to equal zero, then a face amount of cash flow P_1 equal to L_t could be purchased today. When P_1 is received at maturity, it could be held until time t and would be sufficient to satisfy L_t. If the reinvestment rate were greater than zero, then less P_1 would be needed today to satisfy L_t. However, both P_1 and P_2 could each be carried forward to time t to satisfy completely the liability requirement.

EXHIBIT 5.1 Borrowing and Lending to Fund a Liability

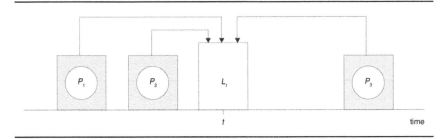

Now consider cash flow P_3 that is received after the liability cash flow requirement. If borrowing is not allowed, then P_3 cannot satisfy L_t. However, if borrowing is permitted, then, at time t, cash could be borrowed against P_3 (at the assumed borrowing rate) in order to satisfy the liability cash flow L_t.

In the more general case, there are many liability cash flows of varying amounts and many feasible bonds, each with its many cash flows comprising periodic coupon payments and return of principal at maturity (Exhibit 5.2). To create a portfolio benchmark, our job is to select a set of bonds whose combined available cash flows at each liability payment date (given the reinvestment and borrowing rate assumptions) will most closely match the liability cash flows. The portfolio benchmark is the solution to this optimization problem.

To set up the optimization problem, the liability schedule is first defined according to the amount of cash flow required at each time period. A feasible set of bonds is then identified as a candidate for the benchmark. For example, if bonds must be rated Aa2 or better, then the feasible set would be constrained to contain bonds rated only Aa2 or better. Then a series of investment restrictions are specified that further constrains bonds selected from the feasible set for the benchmark. For example, the benchmark may be required to have an asset mix of 60% governments and 40% corporates, with no single corporate issuer with more than 2% weight in the benchmark portfolio. Finally, a reinvestment rate (r) is specified (it may be zero), and borrowing is either denied or permitted at a specified rate (b).[5]

EXHIBIT 5.2   More General Case of Borrowing and Lending to Fund a Liability

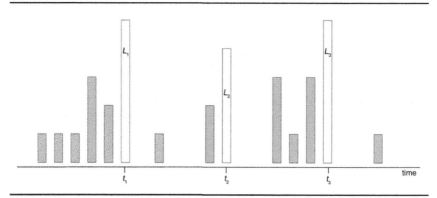

Note: All cash flow boxes should touch the horizontal time axis.

---

[5] To be conservative and insure that all liability payments have sufficient cash, the sponsor could assume that the reinvestment rate equals zero and prohibit borrowing.

The goal of the optimization program is to select bonds for a portfolio benchmark such that the cash flows are as "close as possible" to the liability cash flow. In other words, the program minimizes

$$\sum_{t=1}^{n} \frac{\left| \mathrm{CF}_t(L) - \mathrm{CF}_t(P) \right|}{(1 + \mathrm{IRR})^t}$$

subject to the specified constraints.[6] $\mathrm{CF}_t(L)$ represents the nominal liability cash flow at time t. $\mathrm{CF}_t(P)$ represents the nominal amount of portfolio cash flow that can be made available at time t either from a portfolio cash flow that occurs exactly at time t or earlier cash flows reinvested forward to time t and, if permitted, later cash flows discounted back to time t.

Mechanically, the program works as follows. All available portfolio cash flows that occur before each liability cash flow at time t are reinvested forward to time t at rate r. If borrowing is allowed, then all available portfolio cash flows that occur after time t are discounted back to time t. The program then selects the portfolio of bonds whose cash flows minimize the sum of the absolute values of the cash flow differences across all time periods in which a liability cash flow occurs.

To build intuition for the optimization program, consider the case of two equal liability cash flows, L_1 and L_2. There are two possible bonds, P_1 and P_2. Bond P_1 has one cash flow that occurs before L_1 and whose nominal value equals $(L_1 + L_2)$. Bond P_2 has two equal cash flows with one occurring before L_1 and the other occurring after L_1 but before L_2. Each cash flow's nominal value equals L_1 (and L_2). (Exhibit 5.3 illustrates the cash flows.) Further, assume that the reinvestment rate is zero and that borrowing is not allowed. Finally, the market value of bond P_1 is 95, whereas the market value of bond P_2 equals 100.

Both bonds would fully satisfy the liability schedule. However, bond P_1 would do so at lower cost than bond P_2. Which bond does the optimizer select? The sum of the differences in cash flow between each lia-

---

[6] Essentially, to achieve the closest match, we would like to minimize the "distance" between the portfolio cash flows and those of the liabilities. This could be expressed using the "least-mean-squares" approach, in which we minimize the sum of the squared differences, or by the absolute value approach shown above. Neither of these objective functions is linear. We have chosen to work with the formulation based on absolute values because it can be converted to a linear program. To accomplish this, the problem variables, which represent the cash flow carryovers from one vertex to the next (which can be positive or negative), are each split into two nonnegative variables, one representing a reinvestment and the other a loan. A linear program is used to minimize the weighted sum of all of these variables, using weights that make the problem equivalent to the absolute value minimization shown here.

EXHIBIT 5.3   Portfolio Benchmark Approach Selects Bond P_2 over Bond P_1

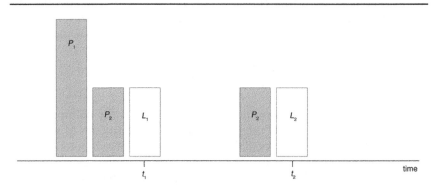

bility cash flow and the available cash flow is less for bond P_2 than for bond P_1. Why is this? Both P_1 and P_2 exactly fund the liability cash flow at t_2, but P_1 must do this by overfunding the liability cash flow at time t_1. In other words, bond P_2 matches the liability schedule more closely than does bond P_1. Consequently, the optimizer will select bond P_2 over bond P_1. This example highlights that the portfolio benchmark approach selects the best matching portfolio, not necessarily the least expensive portfolio, even if it also satisfies the liability schedule.

The term $(1 + IRR)^t$ in the denominator above is an additional discount factor for which IRR is the internal rate of return on the benchmark portfolio. This discount term essentially says that the optimization program cares more about minimizing near-term cash flow mismatches than more distant mismatches.

The solution of this optimization program is a liability-based benchmark portfolio of marketable securities whose cash flows are as close as possible to the liability cash flows. Note that this approach does not minimize the cost of the benchmark portfolio, as is the case for other dedication programs. Here, the goal is to create a portfolio benchmark whose cash flows closely mimic the liability schedule and meet investment constraints: a "neutral" benchmark.

EXAMPLE: CREATING COMPOSITE AND PORTFOLIO BENCHMARKS

Recently, a fund manager working with a plan sponsor, decided to create a benchmark for a fixed liability stream (Exhibit 5.4) with a duration of 12.5. The sponsor's investment restrictions required the benchmark to

EXHIBIT 5.4 Liability Schedule

Year	Amount	Year	Amount
1	$0	17	$7,400,380
2	0	18	6,475,332
3	0	19	6,475,332
4	0	20	5,550,285
5	0	21	5,550,285
6	0	22	4,625,237
7	0	23	4,625,237
8	0	24	3,700,190
9	36,631,879	25	3,700,190
10	24,236,243	26	2,775,142
11	20,351,044	27	2,775,142
12	15,355,787	28	1,850,095
13	15,355,787	29	1,850,095
14	8,325,427	30	925,047
15	8,325,427	31	925,047
16	7,400,380		

EXHIBIT 5.5 Composite Benchmark Weights

Index	Weight (%)
Long Corporate (A3 and higher)	40
CMBS	10
Long Government	23.1
Treasury Strip (18 years +)	26.9

have an asset mix of 50% government, 40% corporate, and 10% CMBS. The minimum credit quality allowed was A3.

To create a *composite benchmark*, at least three different subindices are needed, one for each asset class. A fourth subindex is needed in order for the composite index to match the duration target of 12.5. A long corporate index containing only quality A3 and higher is 40% of the composite benchmark, the CMBS index is 10%, and the remaining 50% is split between the Long Government Index and a custom Treasury strips index containing strips of 18 years and longer. The weights of these two government indices, 23.1% and 26.9%, are such that they add up to 50% and produce an overall composite benchmark duration of 12.5. The weights are presented in Exhibit 5.5.

Exhibit 5.6 compares the cash flows of the composite benchmark with those of the liability schedule. Note that while the duration of the composite benchmark matches that of the liability schedule, there are considerable mismatches in the timing of cash flows. It is likely that cash flows could be more closely matched if additional subindices, appropriately weighted, were added to the composite benchmark.

To create a *portfolio benchmark,* a set of about 1,000 bonds was chosen as the feasible set from which the optimizer can select bonds for the portfolio. Only bullet corporate and agency bonds were considered (so the cash flows would not fluctuate with interest rates) and only strips represented the Treasury sector. The bulk of the feasible set is corporate bonds, with good representation in all corporate sectors. This is desirable, as the portfolio benchmark must contain many corporate names for appropriate diversification.

The optimization problem was set up with constraints that reflect the investment restrictions: an asset mix of 50% government, 40% corporate, and 10% CMBS and a minimum credit quality of A3 for all issues. In addition, the 40% of the portfolio in corporates was further constrained to have the same proportional industry and quality breakdown as the Credit Index. No credit sector and no issuer was allowed to make up more than 22% and 1%, respectively, of the overall bench-

EXHIBIT 5.6   Cash Flow Comparison: Composite Benchmark versus Liability Schedule

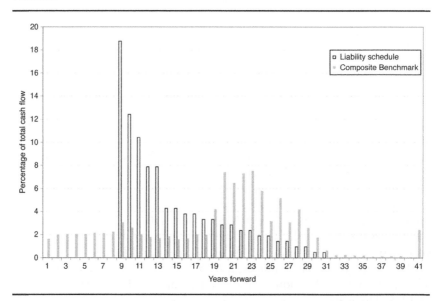

mark. (If desired, separate diversification constraints can be imposed by sector or by quality, to reflect varying levels of protection from event risk.) As a result, the resulting portfolio benchmark consisted of approximately 100 securities.

Exhibit 5.7 compares the cash flows of the portfolio benchmark with those of the liability schedule. Overall, the portfolio benchmark cash flows closely match the liability cash flows. Note, however, that the first liability cash flow (year 9) is mostly pre-funded by the portfolio. This is to be expected, given the investment constraints, as 40% of the portfolio must be invested in corporates that predominantly pay a coupon. Consequently, the portfolio benchmark receives coupon payments in the first eight years that must be reinvested to meet the first liability cash flow in year 9.

Because the portfolio benchmark reflects the liability structure and the investment constraints, the sponsor and investment manager can use the portfolio benchmark as a "neutral" benchmark: The manager can construct a portfolio using the benchmark as his or her bogey, and the sponsor can appropriately evaluate the manager's performance relative to the benchmark. The manager can also use the portfolio benchmark to identify the sources of risk in the investment portfolio relative to the benchmark and, therefore, relative to the liability structure. This is accomplished using the Lehman Brothers Global Risk Model, which will identify

EXHIBIT 5.7   Cash Flow Comparison: Portfolio Benchmark versus Liability Schedule

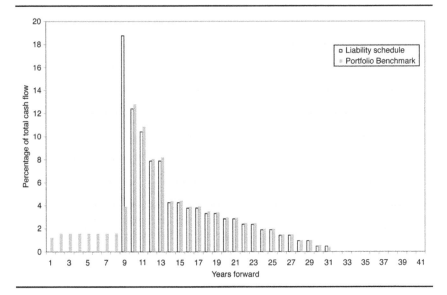

sources of risk (i.e., tracking error) and suggest trades from a manager-selected list of bonds in order to reduce both systematic and security-specific risk. The risk model will also suggest trades to move the portfolio toward matching the portfolio benchmark in yield curve, sector, and quality exposures. In general, if the manager wishes to deviate from the "neutral" benchmark, the risk model can estimate the potential tracking error.

CONCLUSION

A liability-based benchmark retains many of the desirable attributes of a market-based index while simultaneously more closely matching the sponsor's liability term structure. A liability benchmark is a "neutral" benchmark, allowing the sponsor to evaluate appropriately the manager's performance and allowing the manager actively to monitor investment risk and opportunities. Two types of liability benchmarks are composite benchmarks (using market-based indices) and portfolio benchmarks (using a fixed portfolio of bonds). Portfolio benchmarks have two advantages: less frequent rebalancing and reduced risk of introducing unintended biases into the benchmark. Care must be taken, however, to minimize idiosyncratic risk in a portfolio benchmark by holding many different issuer names in the portfolio.

In this chapter we deal with fixed, not inflation-linked, liabilities. However, the methodology we present could be adapted to build an inflation-protected liability benchmark in either of two very different ways. The first possibility would require no changes to the methodology described here, except that the universe of securities from which the benchmark is constructed would contain only inflation-linked bonds. The main drawback of this approach is the relatively limited selection of bonds available in this category, which will both hamper our ability to match arbitrary cash flow streams and restrict benchmark diversification. Another limitation of this approach is that it only addresses inflation that is linked to a CPI-type inflation index, not to a wage inflation index which is sometimes used to adjust future nominal liabilities. A second approach would be to match the liability cash flow stream using a benchmark composed of nominal bonds, as described in this chapter. An overlay portfolio of inflation swaps (either CPI or wage index linked) could then be used to swap the cash flows of this bond portfolio for an inflation-linked cash flow stream. The main limitation of this approach is the heavy reliance on inflation swaps, which is an emerging market and may raise questions of liquidity and price transparency, and may not be allowed in many portfolios.

Whether liabilities are fixed or inflation-linked, plan sponsors and managers are adopting the portfolio benchmark approach to liability benchmark construction and are utilizing fixed income, quantitative portfolio management tools to implement this strategy.

CHAPTER 6

Risk Budgeting for Fixed Income Portfolios

Frederick E. Dopfel, Ph.D.
Managing Director
Client Advisory Group
Barclays Global Investors

Institutional investors often experience difficulties implementing their asset allocation plans for fixed income portfolios. Disappointing performance may result from unknown and unmeasured exposures, inefficient allocation to managers, and the absence of a risk control methodology. In short, investors lack a scientific way of risk budgeting for portfolios of fixed income managers.

Because risk budgeting is critical, one must begin with an understanding of the risk exposures contributed by each fixed income manager. One of the keys is to understand the normal portfolios, or "styles," of the managers to separate active systematic exposures from active residual exposures. Some active exposures reflect persistent biases, but other exposures reflect tactical bets on credit spreads and durations, or assumptions about the ability of active managers to produce pure alpha. By understanding the sources of active exposures, investors can improve their projection of each manager's impact within the larger portfolio and, thereby, improve the allocation of the risk budget.

Fixed income managers should be viewed like securities in a mean-variance framework. With this perspective, the question of how to structure portfolios of managers is an optimization problem that can be solved when one has an understanding of the managers' risk exposures, correlations and projected alphas. Optimal manager portfolios minimize uncompensated risks and yield the lowest risk for a given expected alpha. This chapter provides tools and examples for an investor to optimize the structure of a portfolio of fixed income managers. With this approach, a strategy can be implemented to control risk while adding value to the investor's overall portfolio.

First, benchmarks are discussed and active risk is defined in the context of the benchmark. Next, the sources of risk exposures are explored and the concept of the normal portfolio, or style analysis, is applied to identify, measure and separate a manager's active exposures. Finally, optimal risk budgeting is illustrated with a case study that demonstrates how to blend managers with diverse styles, control risk, and structure an optimal portfolio of fixed income managers.

BENCHMARKS AND RISK

Understanding fixed income benchmarks is critical to risk budgeting because portfolio risk, and overall performance, is defined *relative to the benchmark*. Portfolio active return is defined as:

$$
\begin{array}{r}
\text{Total return of fixed income portfolio} \\
\underline{- \;\text{Total return of fixed income benchmark}} \\
= \;\text{Active return}
\end{array} \qquad (6.1)
$$

Active return is measured by the portfolio's return in excess of the benchmark return. The average active return that is uncorrelated with benchmark component returns is often called *alpha*. Active risk is measured by the volatility (standard deviation) of the active returns and is often called *tracking error.*

The benchmark for fixed income assets follows directly from the strategic asset allocation policy that describes the allocation across asset classes. Implicit in this allocation is a clear definition of a benchmark for each asset class including fixed income. In the United States, institutional investors typically allocate 30% to 40% of total assets to fixed income investments, often benchmarked to the Lehman Brothers Aggregate Bond Index. A customized benchmark may be defined to have different weightings of sectors of the Lehman Aggregate or to include other bond index components including high yield, non-U.S. bonds (developed and emerging) and Treasury Inflation Protection Securities (TIPS). In other countries, fixed income benchmarks may include a blend of regional and global indexes that combine credit and government securities.

The investor may also set a target interest rate duration for the fixed income portfolio that could be different from the natural duration of the benchmark. Matching the duration of the liabilities is intended to lower net surplus risk. This decision is in the realm of strategic asset allocation policy rather than risk budgeting. Derivative instruments can be used to extend duration, enabling the investor to separate the duration-matching objective from the risk-budgeting decision.

The fixed income portion of asset allocation policy is implemented by hiring a mix of active and passive (index) fixed income managers. The risk-budgeting issue can be entirely circumvented by investing solely in an index fund or a combination of index funds that represent the investor's benchmark. Instead, most institutional investors attempt to outperform their benchmark with actively managed fixed income portfolios. The result is that investors are accepting active risk exposures from individual managers and the portfolio at large.

We consider an example of the distribution of active returns for an individual manager and for a portfolio of managers. Panel A of Exhibit 6.1 shows the histogram of monthly active returns for an individual fixed income manager with a core mandate over a 10-year period. This manager has a slight positive average alpha over the period; but there is a wide distribution with 56% of the monthly returns showing positive alpha and 44% showing negative alpha. The distribution is shaped like a normal distribution with a mean that is slightly positive and a standard deviation of 0.20% monthly (0.71% annually) that reflects the active risk, or tracking error, of the manager. The next step for the investor is to consider hiring additional managers with a goal of reducing risk by diversification of exposures.

Panel B of Exhibit 6.1 shows the histogram of monthly active returns for an equal-weighted portfolio of four managers with similar average risk over the same 10-year period. Again, the mean of the distribution is slightly positive, and here the active risk of 0.17% monthly (0.58% annually) has been only slightly reduced through diversification. Ideally, tracking error of a portfolio of four managers should be one-half that of just one manager. But in this example, the average correlation between managers is 30%, which severely limits the potential benefits of naïve diversification. Because of the correlation between managers, there is a decreasing marginal impact as successive managers are added. A pair-wise correlation of 30% to 35% between active returns of managers, as in this example, is fairly typical of a random sample of managers. Exhibit 6.2 demonstrates the loss in efficiency from naïve diversification if the managers are so correlated compared with no correlation.[1] Even with many managers, the active risk is reduced by no more than one-third of the average risk per manager.

This point is the key problem in active risk budgeting—how to allocate assets to managers to control risk and obtain the most favorable distribution of active returns. To obtain the full benefits of diversification, it is important to first understand the sources of active risk and causes of correlation, the topic of the next section.

EXHIBIT 6.1 Comparison of Returns for an Individual Manager versus a Portfolio of Managers
Panel A: Monthy Active Returns of an Individual Manager

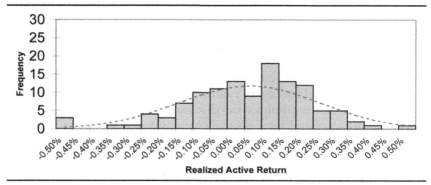

Panel B: Monthly Active Return of Portfolio of Four Managers

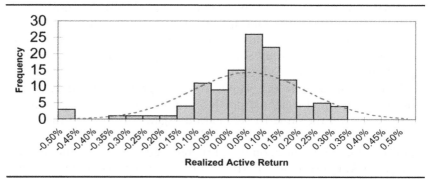

Source: eVestment Alliance and Barclays Global Investors.

---

[1] Assume an equal-weighted portfolio of n managers where each manager has active risk σ and each has active exposure that is correlated ρ (pair-wise) to every other manager; the active risk of the portfolio is $\sigma_p = \sigma\sqrt{1/n + \rho(1 - 1/n)}$. If the managers are uncorrelated, then risk declines to zero as the number of managers gets large: $\sigma_p = \sigma/\sqrt{n} \to 0$. However, even with a large number of managers, if they are correlated, there is lower bound on active risk: $\sigma_p \to \sigma\sqrt{\rho}$.

EXHIBIT 6.2   Impact of Manager Correlation on Portfolio Risk

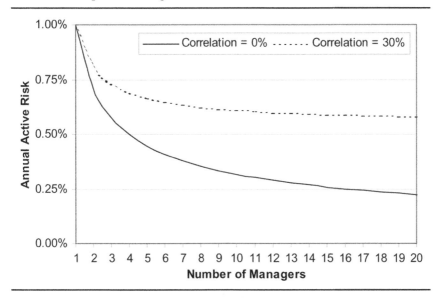

EXHIBIT 6.3   Sources of Fixed Income Active Exposures

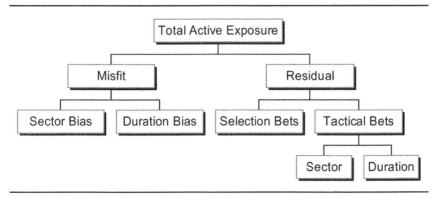

SOURCES OF RISK

Active risk results from *misfit* and *residual* exposures. The structure of fixed income active exposures, both at the manager level and the investor level, are categorized in Exhibit 6.3.

Misfit, also referred to as *style bias*, is the *persistent* difference between the sector and duration exposures of a portfolio compared with the exposures of the investor's fixed income benchmark. Active fixed income managers often have average exposures that are different from the benchmark of the investor but also different from the manager's own *stated* benchmark. The source of misfit may be a bias in exposure to sectors or a bias to shorter or longer duration. Style bias may be an explicit decision by the manager to focus its investment efforts in some preferred domain, or it may be an incidental result of its investment process to generate alpha. Whether intentional or not, the presence of bias in the portfolio, if uncorrected, produces systematic exposures that impact the investor's asset allocation policy. Bias is *not* skill-based and does *not* provide value-added to investor utility.

Hiring managers with similar style biases is the major cause of correlation between managers' active returns, diluting the benefits of diversification. In practice, sector biases reflected in the normal portfolio are a material component of active risk at the manager level and the investor level. For example, it is common practice for core managers to take a sustained overweight in credit and underweight in government sectors. Within the credit overweight there may be an additional bias toward higher quality or lower quality. In addition, some managers hold sectors that are not represented by the benchmark, such as foreign debt or high-yield debt, adding to misfit. This is typical and has even come to be expected of core plus managers. Sector biases reflected in the normal portfolio also affect the average duration of the portfolio because the various sectors have different durations that also change over time. This dynamic is especially felt for the MBS/securitized sector that comprises approximately 40% of the Lehman Aggregate and whose duration is highly sensitive to rate levels and refinancing activity, but sustained duration biases typically consume a small portion of the fixed income manager's active risk budget.

Exposures that are *not* persistent but instead vary relative to average exposures are not a style bias but instead are defined as residual exposures. Unlike style bias, residual exposures are skill-based active exposures and have the *potential* to add value to investor utility. But any non-zero expected alpha is conditional on the investor's belief in the ability of skillful managers.

Residual exposures may be further broken down into *selection bets* and *tactical bets*. Selection bets reflect exposures from individual security selection, and are commonly made in credit risk selection and mortgage selection. In practice, selection bets consume a significant part of a typical fixed income manager's active risk budget while the relative weight of residual tactical bets varies a great deal from manager to manager. Tactical bets are distinguished from other residual exposures as they reflect market-timing activity on forecasted sector spreads and yield curve changes. These exposures are distinguished from persistent sector and duration biases because they are timed and more frequently changed.

The overall impact of residual risk or misfit risk individually on total active risk is always somewhat less than the sum of residual risk or misfit risk on a stand-alone basis because risks—as we define them—are not additive. Measured by standard deviation, risk adds in the squares as follows:

$$\text{Active risk}^2 = \text{Misfit risk}^2 + \text{Residual risk}^2 \qquad (6.2)$$

To understand how managers can be blended to obtain the full benefits of diversification, the active return distributions of any manager (or portfolio) should be decomposed into misfit risk and residual risk. But separating active risk into its components requires an understanding of each manager's normal portfolio. The procedure for determining normal portfolios is the topic of the next section.

NORMAL PORTFOLIOS AND STYLE ANALYSIS

The concept of the normal portfolio may be applied at the manager level or at the overall portfolio level. In either case, it refers to longer-term "average" positions taken with regard to market risk factors. For example, the portfolio may show persistent over- or underweight to credit with respect to the benchmark, or the portfolio may show persistent shorter or longer duration relative to the benchmark duration. In essence, the normal portfolio represents the style of the portfolio, or its "home position" or "natural benchmark." It helps to clarify what the investor may expect absent of skill, and it determines the benchmark for measurement of skill-based performance.

Estimating the normal portfolio is often referred to as style analysis. By measuring a manager's current and historic average exposures, an investor seeks insight on the manager's forward-looking exposures to sector and duration risk. Estimation of the normal portfolio can be informed by an analysis of actual holdings. But in many cases, the holdings data needed are not detailed enough or are incomplete. It is often more convenient—and in some cases more accurate—to use *returns-based style analysis* to determine historical fixed income style.[2] Returns-based style analysis compares actual manager returns with market factor returns to determine a manager's *effective* style. Since its introduction, this robust technique has been popular

---

[2] For the original development, see William F. Sharpe, "Asset Allocation: Management Style and Performance Measurement," *Journal of Portfolio Management* (Winter 1992), pp. 7–19. For later adaptations for the fixed income asset class, see Frederick E. Dopfel, "Fixed-Income Style Analysis and Optimal Manager Structure," *Journal of Fixed Income* (September 2004), pp. 32–43.

with consultants and investors for understanding equity exposures in terms of value versus growth and large-cap versus small-cap market factors. However, it has not been applied as broadly to fixed income as to equity managers. Style analysis can be used to help define managers' exposures relative to the investor's benchmark and facilitate a better understanding of forward-looking exposures of portfolios of managers.

Style analysis applies a regression-like process to a manager's historical returns compared with several market-related style factors. The technique determines the average historic portfolio weights for various style buckets. For fixed income, the appropriate market factors are macrosector and duration factors, as shown in Exhibit 6.4. These factors cover the three macrosectors of the Lehman Aggregate—government, investment-grade credit, and MBS/securitized—plus high yield. In addition, the government sector is broken down into three maturity buckets that may further explain duration exposures that are not sufficiently explained by sectors. This set of style factors is just one of a large set of possibilities. This approach is very suitable for most cases that involve core and core plus managers combined with high-yield managers. In practice, the style factors utilized will depend on the characteristics of the managers considered, the managers' normal portfolios, and the investor's benchmark.

Exhibit 6.5 shows the normal portfolio (or style) of a manager benchmarked to the Lehman Aggregate and the apparent misfit based

EXHIBIT 6.4 Style Factors for Fixed Income Managers

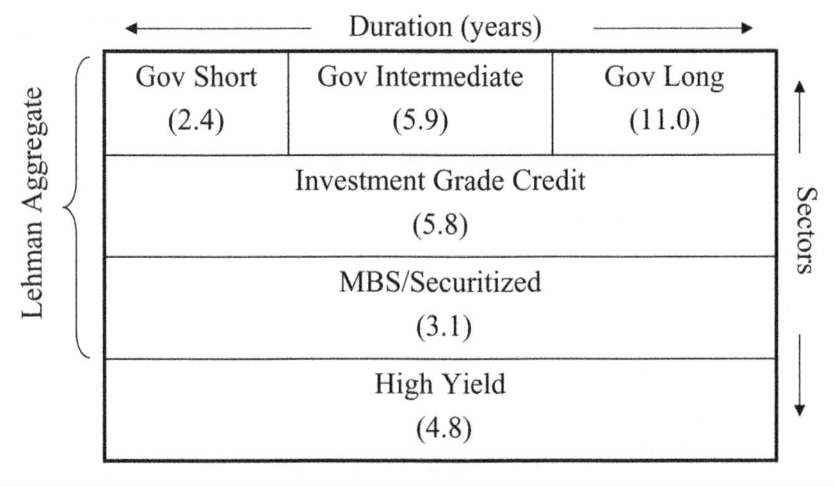
Duration (years)
Gov Short (2.4)
Gov Intermediate (5.9)
Gov Long (11.0)
Investment Grade Credit (5.8)
MBS/Securitized (3.1)
High Yield (4.8)
Lehman Aggregate
Sectors

* Estimated duration as of 12/31/2004.

Source: Barclays Global Investors and LehmanLive.com.

EXHIBIT 6.5 Example Style Analysis of a Core Manager

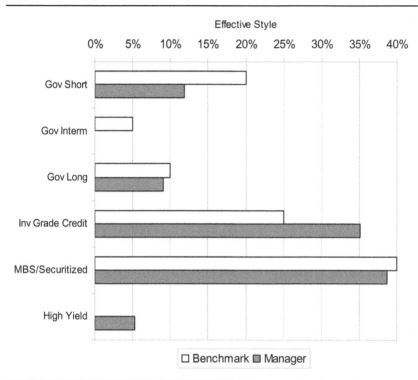

Source: Barclays Global Investors.

on examining active returns over a 36-month period. This manager, the same core manager depicted in Exhibit 6.1, shows a 10% overweight to credit and a 14% underweight to government. There is also an apparent exposure of 5% to high yield even though the manager's investment objective does not include high-yield securities. One explanation is that there is a tilt toward lower-quality securities within the credit portfolio that is picked up by the analysis as a high-yield credit spread. Further, there appears to be a "barbelling" of the term structure within the government sector (i.e., holdings within this sector convey the shape of a barbell). By looking at the relative weighting of longer maturity versus shorter maturity components of the Lehman Aggregate—as well as measuring the impact of sector biases on duration—one can observe a slightly higher duration bias of approximately 0.2 years. These style factors explain 99% of the variance in the manager's *total* returns and explain 72% of the variance in the manager's *active* returns.

The manager is a medium-low active risk manager with overall annual active risk of 0.90% over the 36-month period. This is slightly higher than the 0.71% tracking error that was observed over the 10-year period noted above. The style analysis enables the total active risk to be decomposed into the risk associated with style bias (misfit) and the residual risk as in equation (6.2). In this example, the misfit risk is 0.77%, and the residual risk is 0.48%. We can verify that $(0.48)^2 + (0.77)^2 = (0.90)^2$. The manager has a very material misfit that consumes about half of its total risk budget on unrewarded misfit risk. Further, this could convey misfit to the overall plan unless there are managers with opposite biases to bring the portfolio back to benchmark.

At first blush, it would seem optimal to always balance holdings in order to protect the integrity of the investor's intended asset allocation policy benchmark—eliminate misfit and reduce misfit risk to zero. But it is difficult to find managers with complementary styles such that when aggregated they exactly match the investor's overall benchmark. In fact, it may be optimal (within the set of alternatives available to the investor) to have some amount of misfit if the expected alpha generated by managers contributing to misfit is enough to compensate for a slight amount of misfit risk. This situation is common for institutional portfolios, and even optimal portfolios often maintain a moderate amount of misfit risk.

Defining the normal portfolio and risk components of individual managers are important steps for understanding each manager's potential contribution to overall portfolio risk. But the goal of risk budgeting is to determine the best blend of managers to reduce unrewarded risk and maximize expected alpha at any risk budget. The proposed methodology to achieve this goal and a case study illustrating this methodology are described in the next section.

OPTIMAL RISK BUDGETING

Risk budgeting, or building an ideal portfolio of managers, is an optimization problem.[3] The objective is the maximization of expected alpha for a given level of expected risk. Equivalently, the objective may be restated

---

[3] For the general foundations of active management, see Richard C. Grinold and Ronald N. Kahn, *Active Portfolio Management*, 2nd ed. (New York: McGraw-Hill, 2000). For the development of manager structure optimization, see Barton M. Waring, Duane Whitney, John Pirone, and Charles Castille, "Optimizing Manager Structure and Budgeting Manager Risk," *Journal of Portfolio Management* (Spring 2000), pp. 90–104. For application of these approaches to the fixed income asset class, see Dopfel, "Fixed-Income Style Analysis and Optimal Manager Structure."

as the minimization of expected active risk (tracking error) for a given level of expected alpha. The decision variables are the percentage holdings allocations, or risk budget allocations, to the various candidate managers. The mathematics of this problem is very similar to the strategic asset allocation problem and the solution is similarly a set of optimal portfolios at various risk levels. A case study will be used to illustrate the principles of optimal risk budgeting. The hypothetical investor has a portfolio of five managers—an index manager, two core managers, one core plus manager and a mortgage specialist. Further, the investor has a Lehman Aggregate benchmark.

Assumptions for the Case Study

Establishing meaningful forward-looking assumptions about managers is essential for successful risk budgeting. First we must have a thorough understanding of each manager's projected normal portfolio. The stated benchmark of the managers (except for the specialist) is the Lehman Aggregate, though the normal portfolios of these managers may differ. As noted previously, analysis of the manager's historical exposures, revealed by style analysis, is a good start in understanding the manager's normal portfolio; however, these are just historical estimates and it is important to have a sufficient dialogue with the manager to understand expected forward-looking style exposures.

Exhibit 6.6 shows the list of managers and manager style assumptions for our case example using the style analysis framework shown in Exhibit 6.4. Manager A is an index fund, and its normal portfolio is the Lehman Aggregate benchmark. Manager B is a risk-controlled core manager whose normal portfolio has a 5% overweight to investment-grade credit and MBS/securitized sectors. Manager C is a core manager similar in style to the example manager presented in panel A of Exhibit

EXHIBIT 6.6   Manager Style Assumptions

Manager	Type	Gov. Short	Gov. Interm	Gov. Long	Inv. Grade Credit	MBS/ Securitized	High Yield
A	Lehman Index	20%	5%	10%	25%	40%	0%
B	Core Risk Controlled	15%	0%	10%	30%	45%	0%
C	Core	5%	0%	15%	35%	40%	5%
D	Specialist	0%	0%	0%	0%	100%	0%
E	Core Plus	0%	0%	20%	25%	45%	10%

6.1 and Exhibit 6.5. The manager's normal portfolio has a barbell maturity structure in the government sector, a 10% credit overweight, plus exposure to the high-yield sector. Manager D is a specialist in mortgages and has a pure exposure to the MBS/Securitized sector, and Manager E is described as core plus. The core plus manager has mortgage and high-yield overweights, and has exposures to longer maturities in the government sector.

Exhibit 6.7 shows the assumptions for current holdings of the managers, the expected alphas, expected active risks, and expected information ratios. A byproduct of the manager style analysis is an examination of a manager's residual exposures. The standard deviation of the residuals is usually a good estimate for the expected forward-looking residual risk. The exhibit includes the residual risk and misfit risk components of total active risk consistent with the normal portfolio assumptions of Exhibit 6.6. As expected, the misfit risks of the core, core plus and specialist managers are material components of total active risks for each manager. Instead, the misfit of the risk-controlled core manager does not add materially to its total active risk. After style correction, the residual active returns of all the managers are assumed to be uncorrelated. In practice, this assumption should be tested because it is not uncommon to find some correlations between managers. The residual correlations may be caused by commonality in the active management processes of the managers or by the presence of common systematic biases of the managers that is not captured by a simple style analysis framework.

The average of the residuals is *not* a good estimate of expected alpha. Forecasting expected alpha is a challenging process, and the temptation to use historical alphas must be avoided. Instead, the investor must carefully estimate forward-looking alpha based on an under-

EXHIBIT 6.7   Manager Alpha and Active Risk Assumptions

Manager	Type	Current Holdings	Expected Alpha	Misfit Risk	Residual Risk	Total Active Risk	Expected Information Ratio
A	Lehman Index	25%	0.00%	0.00%	0.00%	0.00%	—
B	Core Risk Controlled	0%	0.40%	0.22%	0.60%	0.64%	0.63
C	Core	25%	0.45%	0.81%	1.00%	1.29%	0.35
D	Specialist	25%	0.50%	1.30%	1.20%	1.77%	0.28
E	Core Plus	25%	0.65%	1.18%	2.00%	2.32%	0.28
	Total	100%	0.40%	0.39%	0.63%	0.75%	0.53

standing of the bets a manager is taking and the degree of above-average skill applied to each. Exhibit 6.7 includes estimates of expected alpha for each manager. While the higher risk managers are portrayed as having higher expected alpha, this is not necessarily the case. Higher risk is rewarded by higher expected returns for systematic exposures but *not* for active exposures. Further, any alpha estimate must be reality-tested against norms that one associates with superior performance. One check is to compute the expected information ratio for each manager, defined as the expected alpha divided by the active risk. A manager with upper-decile skill may correspond to an information ratio of 1.0, but simply average skill has an expected information ratio of zero. Exhibit 6.7 also shows the calculated expected performance of the portfolio for current holdings equally weighted to the index, core, core plus and specialist managers. The overall active risk budget is 0.75%, and (based on the expected alphas of the managers) the overall expected alpha is 0.40%.

Optimal Allocations for the Case Study

The important question for optimal risk budgeting is whether the investor may prefer an allocation to managers that is different from current holdings. At a minimum, the allocations to managers ought to be *mean-variance efficient*, as usually described by an efficient frontier. Exhibit 6.8 presents the *active efficient frontier* in alpha space based on the case

EXHIBIT 6.8   Active Efficient Frontier

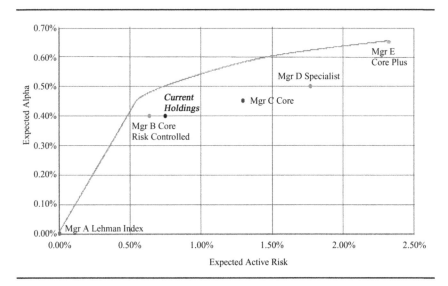

study's assumptions about managers. (Alpha space measures expected alpha and expected total active risk.) Each manager is plotted in the exhibit as well as the portfolio of current holdings. The current holdings portfolio is apparently inefficient because it falls below the active efficient frontier. At the current active risk budget of 0.75%, the active efficient frontier indicates it is possible to increase expected alpha from 0.40% to 0.50% without adding active risk.

Exhibit 6.9 shows the optimal allocation to managers for various risk budgets. At the same risk budget, the optimal allocations to managers change to include larger allocations to the risk-controlled core manager and to the specialist manager, smaller allocations to the core and core plus managers, and no allocation to the index manager. This allocation provides the highest possible expected alpha at the current risk budget. These changes in manager allocations can be rationalized by observing that the risk-controlled core manager can provide a higher expected information ratio—or a higher expected alpha per unit of active risk—than the other core manager. Also, the specialist manager, while having the same expected information ratio of the core plus manager, has lower active risk. This demonstrates an important principle for risk budgeting: The desired allocations for a best active portfolio are directly related to expected information ratio and inversely related to expected risk.

Exhibit 6.9 shows other optimal allocations that are the basis for the active efficient frontier of the case study. First, it is possible to have *no* active risk by allocating the entire portfolio to the index manager. This point is represented at the origin of the active efficient frontier—

EXHIBIT 6.9 Optimal Manager Allocations Depending on Risk Budget

Manager/Type	Current Holdings	Optimal Allocations			
A Lehman Index	25%	100%	54%	8%	0%	0%
B Core Risk Controlled	0%	0%	28%	55%	29%	6%
C Core	25%	0%	8%	16%	19%	20%
D Specialist	25%	0%	7%	15%	29%	38%
E Core Plus	25%	0%	3%	6%	23%	36%
Active Risk Budget	0.75%	0.00%	0.25%	0.50%	0.75%	1.00%
Misfit Risk	0.40%	0.00%	0.13%	0.26%	0.40%	0.49%
Residual Risk	0.64%	0.00%	0.21%	0.42%	0.63%	0.87%
Expected Alpha	0.40%	0.00%	0.20%	0.40%	0.50%	0.57%
Information Ratio	0.53	—	0.80	0.80	0.67	0.57

expected alpha of 0% and active risk of 0%. Moving to a very low risk budget of 0.25% active risk, the expected alpha is 0.20%. At this risk level, the allocation to the index manager is reduced by almost half, the risk-controlled core manager is allocated 28%, with the higher risk core, core plus and specialist managers comprising only 18% of the total allocation. The degree of misfit is slight, with misfit risk of 0.13% adding only 0.04% to total active risk for this portfolio. At the other extreme, an active risk budget of 1.00%, the largest allocations go to the higher risk managers. While the higher risk managers have higher expected alphas, they are less efficient than the two core managers as measured by incremental return per unit of risk. The resulting portfolio has an expected information ratio of 0.57, less efficient than the portfolios at lower risk budgets, shown to have an expected information ratio of 0.80. A contributing factor to the inefficiency of the higher risk portfolio is the misfit risk of 0.49% that adds 0.13% to total active risk and reflects unrewarded systematic biases.

At a 0.50% active risk budget, the index allocation is only 8% while 55% of the portfolio is allocated to the risk-controlled core manager. It is interesting to note that, at this risk budget, it is possible to attain the same expected alpha of 0.40% as with current holdings but at lower risk. Furthermore, any of the efficient portfolios with risk budgets of 0.50% to 0.75% (inclusive) dominate the portfolio of current holdings because they provide an equal or higher expected alpha *and* an equal or lower active risk. In practice, the investor faced with this opportunity set is advised to select among these efficient portfolios instead of the inefficient current holdings. Making this change is contingent on the investor's full confidence in his assumptions for expected alpha. The process of reviewing assumptions and then checking the sensibility of the analysis is a worthwhile exercise to ensure that the assumptions are realistic and that the investor's holdings are self-consistent.

Active versus Passive Management

There has been a long debate on the question of the ideal active versus passive allocation. The preceding analysis of optimal risk budgets definitively answers the question under the assumptions of the case study. The portfolio with the highest expected *information ratio* (IR) of 0.80, the high IR portfolio, corresponds to a risk budget of 0.54%. The high IR portfolio is also the lowest risk portfolio on the efficient frontier that is all active, with no allocation to the index manager. Below that risk level, the mean-variance efficient portfolios are all a combination of the index manager and the high IR portfolio. For those portfolios, the expected information ratio is constant at 0.80 in that lower range of risk levels. Above that risk level, the portfolios are entirely active (with no passive index allocation) and show a diminishing expected information ratio at higher risk levels.

The optimal mix of active and passive investment depends on both the risk budget and on the investor's forecast of the performance of the active managers. If the active risk budget was higher than the norm, then active management would be favored to an even greater extent, and the reverse is true for lower risk budgets. If the assumptions about the expected alphas of the managers are high, then an optimal portfolio is more likely to favor active management, and this can be calculated repeating the same techniques used in the case study. Conversely, if expected alphas are low, then passive management is favored; clearly, if there is no positive expected alpha, then there should be no active management in an optimal portfolio. Stated differently, any portfolio that is other than 100% passive is implicitly assuming that managers have skill in generating a positive expected alpha.

Setting the Risk Budget

The active-passive decision and the overall optimal holdings decision have been shown to be heavily dependent on the established risk budget for the fixed income portfolio. So the question here is how much risk is appropriate? The typical range for active risk of institutional portfolios of fixed income managers is roughly 0.40% to 1.00%. The higher end of the range is typical of portfolios incorporating a high-yield component and the lower end of the range is typical of portfolios composed primarily of core and index managers. Modern portfolio theory does not prescribe what level of active risk an investor should bear even in the presence of skill, only that the decisions on investment allocation ought to be mean-variance efficient. But there are a few considerations that may help address this issue.

One consideration is fees. For example, consider an investor taking only 0.40% active risk with its portfolio of active managers and producing an expected information ratio of 0.5 before fees. If fees are 0.30%, then the net effect of active management is calculated $0.5 \times 0.40\%$ − $0.30\% = -0.10\%$. At this low risk level and expected information ratio, the net-of-fees expected alpha is *negative*! Clearly, we need either a higher information ratio or lower fees or both. After all, what we are really seeking is not just expected alpha but *expected alpha net of fees and costs*.

It is helpful to note that much active risk is taken in other asset classes and that it adds up across all asset classes; that is, at the total portfolio level. Representative values for medium-sized institutional investors are 1.5% tracking error for domestic equities and 2.0% tracking error for international equities portfolios, but often much less than

1.0% tracking error for the fixed income portfolio. At the margin, the allocation to fixed income active risk typically adds less than 0.1% to active risk at the overall plan level. Investors could clearly add more active risk *if* they were confident they had identified profitable opportunities to do so. At the margin, more active management should occur wherever the expected information ratio is the highest.

It is possible that investors are not taking enough active risk in their fixed income portfolios. How should the investor go about spending active risk while seeking higher alpha? Some investors are addressing this issue by reducing the index allocation and replacing it with risk-controlled core managers. Risk-controlled managers usually do not deviate from benchmark style, and—assuming skill—can add expected alpha efficiently (without misfit risk). Another opportunity is portable alpha strategies.

Portable Alpha

The concept of *portable alpha* involves taking nonsystematic returns (alpha) from a source outside an asset class and by *bondization*, fitting the return stream properly into the asset class. For example, suppose an investor has determined that some selected hedge fund, market neutral and long-short strategies have the potential to generate high expected information ratios in the presence of skill. Further, suppose these strategies are designed to have a cash benchmark. It is possible, with derivatives, to change the effective systematic exposure of these investments from cash to the investor's fixed income benchmark or a near equivalent. In this instance, the investor can be described as considering the use of portable alpha strategies in the fixed income portfolio. These strategies, in the presence of skill, show great promise compared with traditional active strategies because of the beneficial impact of relieving the long-only constraint.[4] With proper planning, these strategies can be blended with existing portfolios to improve overall portfolio performance.

SUMMARY

This chapter began with an explanation of the challenges that face investors who wish to control risk in a portfolio of fixed income managers. Fixed income managers frequently share common exposures that are dif-

---

[4] For a discussion of the impact of the long-only constraint and other constraints on portfolio efficiency, see Roger Clarke, Harindra de Silva, and Steven Thorley, "Portfolio Constraints and the Fundamental Law of Active Management," *Financial Analysts Journal* (September/October 2002), pp. 48–66.

ferent than stated benchmarks and, as a result, cause higher correlations between managers' returns and unanticipated risks in the portfolio. The unanticipated risks reduce the efficiency of naive diversification and require improved approaches for risk budgeting.

To reap the full benefit of diversification, it is necessary to understand the sources of active exposures associated with managers' normal portfolios and with their residuals. These insights help in developing meaningful forward-looking inputs to better estimate expected alpha and expected risk at the fixed income portfolio level.

Optimal risk budgeting identifies mean-variance efficient portfolios of fixed income managers, providing the highest expected alpha for a given active risk budget. The managers that are most desirable in the solution are those who can provide the highest possible expected information ratios after adjustment for style biases. Managers of all types—index, core, core plus, high yield, specialist and others—can be considered and blended into an optimal portfolio.

This chapter has shown how portfolios of fixed income managers can be built on a more scientific basis. The process starts by understanding the exposures managers are taking with style analysis and follows with the disciplined process of generating meaningful forward-looking assumptions. Finally, risk budgeting for fixed income portfolios can be solved as an optimization problem that generates mean-variance efficient portfolios and determines optimal holdings at the desired risk budget.

PART

Three

Fixed Income Modeling

CHAPTER 7

Understanding the
Building Blocks for OAS Models

Philip O. Obazee*
Vice President
Delaware Investments

Investors and analysts continue to wrestle with the differences in *option-adjusted spread* (OAS) values for securities that they see from competing dealers and vendors. Portfolio managers continue to pose fundamental questions about OAS with which we all struggle in the financial industry. Some of the frequently asked questions are:

▦ How can we interpret the difference in dealers' OAS values for a specific security?
▦ What is responsible for the differences?
▦ Is there really a correct OAS value for a given security?

In this chapter, we examine some of the questions about OAS analysis, particularly the basic building block issues about OAS implementation. Because some of these issues determine "good or bad" OAS results, we believe there is a need to discuss them. To get at these fundamental issues, we hope to avoid sounding pedantic by relegating most of the notations and expressions to footnotes.

Clearly, it could be argued that portfolio managers do not need to understand the OAS engine to use it but that they need to know how to

---

* This chapter was written while Philip Obazee was vice president, Quantitative Research, First Union Securities, Inc.

131

apply it in relative value decisions. This argument would be correct if there were market standards for representing and generating interest rates and prepayments. In the absence of a market standard, investors need to be familiar with the economic intuitions and basic assumptions made by the underlying models. More important, investors need to understand what works for their situation and possibly identify those situations in which one model incorrectly values a bond. Exhibit 7.1 shows a sample of OAS analysis for passthrough securities. Although passthroughs are commoditized securities, the variance in OAS results is still wide. This variance is attributable to differences in the implementation of the respective OAS models.

Unlike other market measures, for example, the yield to maturity and the weighted average life of a bond, which have market standards for calculating their values, OAS calculations suffer from the lack of a standard and a black-box mentality. The lack of a standard stems from the required inputs in the form of interest rate and prepayment models that go into an OAS calculation. Although there are many different interest rate models available, there is little agreement on which one to use. Moreover, there is no agreement on how to model prepayments. The black-box mentality comes from the fact that heavy mathematical machinery and computational algorithms are involved in the development and implementation of an OAS model. This machinery is often so cryptic that only a few initiated members of the intellectual tribe can decipher it. In addition, dealers invest large sums in the development of their term structures and prepayment models and, consequently, they are reluctant to share it.

EXHIBIT 7.1   Selected Sample of OAS Analysis Results[a]

Security Name	FUSI OAS	Major Vendor Espiel OAS	Major Street Firm OAS
FNCL600	122	118	119
FNCL650	115	113	113
FNCL700	113	117	112
GN600	106	114	100
GN650	101	111	101
GN700	100	116	103
FNCI600	95	98	103
FNCI650	94	99	103
FNCI700	92	101	103

[a] As of July 12, 2000, close.
Source: First Union Securities, Inc. (FUSI).

In this chapter, we review some of the proposed term structures and prepayments. Many of the term structure models describe "what is" and only suggest that the models could be used. Which model to use perhaps depends on the problem at hand and the resources available. In this chapter, we review some of the popular term structure models and provide some general suggestions on which ones should *not* be used.

Investors in *asset-backed securities* (ABS) and *mortgage-backed securities* (MBS) hold long positions in noncallable bonds and short positions in *call* (prepayment) options. The noncallable bond is a bundle of zero-coupon bonds (e.g., Treasury strips), and the call option gives the borrower the right to prepay the mortgage at any time prior to the maturity of the loan. In this framework, the value of MBS is the difference between the value of the noncallable bond and the value of the call (prepayment) option. Suppose a theoretical model is developed to value the components of ABS/MBS. The model would value the noncallable component, which we loosely label the *zero-volatility component*, and the *call option component*. If interest rate and prepayment risks are well accounted for, and if those are the only risks for which investors demand compensation, one would expect the theoretical value of the bond to be equal to its market value. If these values are not equal, then market participants demand compensation for the unmodeled risks. One of these unmodeled risks is the forecast error associated with the prepayments. By this, we mean the actual prepayment may be faster or slower than projected by the model. Other unmodeled risks are attributable to the structure and liquidity of the bond. In this case, OAS is the market price for the unmodeled risks.

To many market participants, however, OAS indicates whether a bond is mispriced. All else being equal, given that interest rate and prepayment risks have been accounted for, one would expect the theoretical price of a bond to be equal to its market price. If these two values are not equal, a profitable opportunity may exist in a given security or a sector. Moreover, OAS is viewed as a tool that helps identify which securities are cheap or rich when the securities are relatively priced.

The zero-volatility component of ABS/MBS valuation is attributable to the pure interest rate risk of a known cash flow—a noncallable bond. The forward interest rate is the main value driver of a noncallable bond. Indeed, the value driver of a noncallable bond is the sum of the rolling yield and the value of the convexity. The rolling yield is the return earned if the yield curve and the expected volatility are unchanged. Convexity refers to the curvature of the price-yield curve. A noncallable bond exhibits varying degrees of positive convexity. Positive convexity means a bond's price rises more for a given yield decline than it falls for the same yield. By unbundling the noncallable bond components in ABS/MBS to their zero-coupon bond components, the rolling yield becomes dominant. This is what is meant by zero-volatility component—that is, the component of the yield spread that is attributable to no change in the expected volatility.

The call option component in ABS/MBS valuation consists of intrinsic and time values. To the extent the option embedded in ABS/MBS is the delayed American exercise style—in other words, the option is not exercised immediately but becomes exercisable any time afterward—the time value component dominates. Thus, in valuing ABS/MBS, the time value of the option associated with the prepayment volatility needs to be evaluated. To evaluate this option, OAS analysis uses an option-based technique to evaluate ABS/MBS prices under different interest rate scenarios. OAS is the spread differential between the zero-volatility and option value components of MBS. These values are expressed as spreads measured in basis points. Exhibit 7.2 shows the FNMA ("Fannie Mae") 30-year current-coupon OAS over a 3-year period.

The option component is the premium paid (earned) from going long (shorting) a prepayment option embedded in the bond. The bondholders are short the option, and they earn the premium in the form of an enhanced coupon. Mortgage holders are long the prepayment option, and they pay the premium in spread above the comparable Treasury. The option component is the cost associated with the variability in cash flow that results from prepayments over time.

The two main inputs into the determination of an OAS of a bond are as follows:

■ Generate the cash flow as a function of the principal (scheduled and unscheduled) and coupon payments
■ Generate interest rate paths under an assumed term structure model

EXHIBIT 7.2 FNMA 30-Year Current-Coupon OAS

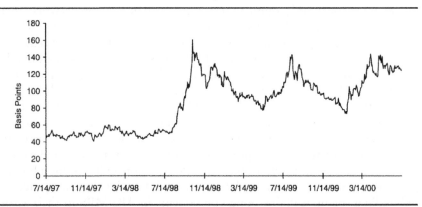

Source: First Union Securities, Inc.

At each cash flow date, a spot rate determines the discount factor for each cash flow. The present value of the cash flow is equal to the sum of the product of the cash flow and the discount factors.[1] When dealing with a case in which uncertainty about future prospects is important, the cash flow and the spot rate need to be specified to account for the uncertainty. The cash flow and spot rate become a function of time and the state of the economy. The time consideration is that a dollar received now is worth more than one received tomorrow. The state of the economy consideration accounts for the fact that a dollar received in a good economy may be perceived as worth less than a dollar earned in a bad economy. For OAS analysis, the cash flow is run through different economic environments represented by interest rates and prepayment scenarios. The spot rate, which is used to discount the cash flow, is run through time steps and interest rate scenarios. The spot rate represents the instantaneous rate of risk-free return at any time, so that $1 invested now will have grown by a later time to $1 multiplied by a continuously compounded rollover rate during the time period.[2] Arbitrage pricing theory stipulates the price one should pay now to receive $1 at later time is the expected discount of the payoff.[3] So by appealing to the arbitrage pricing theory, we are prompted to introduce an integral representation for the value equation; in other words, the arbitrage pricing theory allows us to use the value additivity principle across all interest rate scenarios.

---

[1] In the world of certainty, the present value is

$$PV = \sum_{i=1}^{n} \frac{cf_i}{(1+r_i)^i}$$

where, r_i is the spot rate applicable to cash flow cf_i. In terms of forward rates, the equation becomes

$$PV = \sum_{i=1}^{n} \frac{cf_i}{(1+f_1)(1+f_2)...(1+f_n)}$$

where f_i is the forward rate applicable to cash flow cf_i.

[2]
$$\$1\left[\exp\left(\int_t^T r(u)du\right)\right]$$

[3] $p(t, T) = E\left[\exp\left(-\int_t^T r(u)du\right)\bigg| F_t\right]$

Note that the expectation is taken under some risk-adjusted probability measure. See footnote 12 for more details.

IS IT EQUILIBRIUM OR AN ARBITRAGE MODEL?

Market participants are guided in their investment decision making by received economic philosophy or intuition. Investors, in general, look at value from either an absolute or relative value basis. Absolute value basis proceeds from the economic notion that the market clears at an exogenously determined price that equates supply-and-demand forces. Absolute valuation models are usually supported by general or partial equilibrium arguments. In implementing market measure models that depend on equilibrium analysis, the role of an investor's preference for risky prospects is directly introduced. The formidable task encountered with respect to preference modeling and the related aggregation problem has rendered these types of models useless for most practical considerations. One main exception is the present value rule that explicitly assumes investors have a time preference for today's dollar. Where the present value function is a monotonically decreasing function of time, today's dollar is worth more than a dollar earned tomorrow. Earlier term structure models were supported by equilibrium arguments, for example, the Cox, Ingersoll, and Ross (CIR) model.[4] In particular, CIR provides an equilibrium foundation for a class of yield curves by specifying the endowments and preferences of traders, which, through the clearing of competitive markets, generates the proposed term structure model.

Relative valuation models rely on arbitrage and dominance principles and characterize asset prices in terms of other asset prices. A well-known example of this class is the Black-Scholes[5] and Merton[6] option-pricing model. Modern term-structure models, for example, Hull and White,[7] Black-Derman-Toy (BDT),[8] and Heath, Jarrow, and Morton (HJM),[9] are based on arbitrage arguments. Although relative valuation models based on arbitrage principles do not directly make assumptions

[4] J. Cox, J. Ingersoll, and S. Ross, "A Theory of the Term Structure of Interest Rates," *Econometrica* 53 (1985), pp. 385–408.
[5] F. Black and M. Scholes, "The Pricing of Options and Corporate Liabilities," *Journal of Political Economy* 81 (1973), pp. 637–654.
[6] R. Merton, "The Theory of Rational Option Pricing," *Bell Journal of Economics and Management Science* 4 (1974), pp. 141–183.
[7] J. Hull and A. White, "Pricing Interest Rate Derivatives Securities," *Review of Financial Studies* 3 (1990), pp. 573–592.
[8] F. Black, E. Derman, and W. Toy, "A One Factor Model of Interest Rates and Its Application to Treasury Bond Options," *Financial Analysts Journal* 46 (1990), pp. 33–39.
[9] D. Heath, R. Jarrow, and A. Morton, "Bond Pricing and the Term Structure of Interest Rates: A New Methodology for Contingent Claims Valuation," *Econometrica* 60 (1992), pp. 77–105.

about investors' preferences, there remains a vestige of the continuity of preference, for example, the notion that investors prefer more wealth to less. Thus, whereas modelers are quick in attributing "arbitrage-freeness" to their models, assuming there are no arbitrage opportunities implies a continuity of preference that can be supported in equilibrium. So, if there are no arbitrage opportunities, the model is in equilibrium for some specification of endowments and preferences. The upshot is that the distinction between equilibrium models and arbitrage models is a stylized fetish among analysts to demarcate models that explicitly specify endowment and preference sets (equilibrium) and those models that are outwardly silent about the preference set (arbitrage). Moreover, analysts usually distinguish equilibrium models as those that use today's term structure as an output and no-arbitrage models as those that use today's term structure as an input.

Arbitrage opportunity exists in a market model if there is a strategy that guarantees a positive payoff in some state of the world with no possibility of negative payoff and no initial net investment. The presence of arbitrage opportunity is inconsistent with economic equilibrium populated by market participants that have increasing and continuous preferences. Moreover, the presence of arbitrage opportunity is inconsistent with the existence of an optimal portfolio strategy for market participants with nonsatiated preferences (prefer more to less) because there would be no limit to the scale at which they want to hold an arbitrage position. The economic hypothesis that maintains two perfect substitutes (two bonds with the same credit quality and structural characteristics issued by the same firm) must trade at the same price is an implication of no arbitrage. This idea is commonly referred to as the *law of one price*. Technically speaking, the fundamental theorem of asset pricing is a collection of canonical equivalent statements that implies the absence of arbitrage in a market model. The theorem provides for weak equivalence between the absence of arbitrage, the existence of a linear pricing rule, and the existence of optimal demand from some market participants who prefer more to less. The direct consequence of these canonical statements is the pricing rule: the existence of a positive linear pricing rule, the existence of positive risk-neutral probabilities, and associated riskless rate or the existence of a positive state price density.

In essence, the pricing rule representation provides a way of correctly valuing a security when the arbitrage opportunity is eliminated. A fair price for a security is the arbitrage-free price. The arbitrage-free price is used as a benchmark in relative value analysis to the extent that it is compared with the price observed in actual trading. A significant difference between the observed and arbitrage-free values may indicate the following profit opportunities:

- If the arbitrage price is above the observed price, all else being equal, the security is *cheap* and a *long position* may be called for.
- If the arbitrage price is below the observed price, all else being equal, the security is *rich* and a *short position* may be called for.

In practice, the basic steps in determining the arbitrage-free value of the security are as follows:

- Specify a model for the evolution of the underlying security price.
- Obtain a risk-neutral probability.
- Calculate the expected value at expiration using the risk-neutral probability.
- Discount this expectation using the risk-free rates.

In studying the solution to the security valuation problem in the arbitrage pricing framework, analysts usually use one of the following:

- *Partial differential equation* (PDE) framework
- *Equivalent martingale measure* framework

The PDE framework is a direct approach and involves constructing a risk-free portfolio, then deriving a PDE implied by the lack of arbitrage opportunity. The PDE is solved analytically or evaluated numerically.[10]

Although there are few analytical solutions for pricing PDEs, most of them are evaluated using numerical methods such as lattice, finite difference, and Monte Carlo. The equivalent martingale measure framework uses the notion of arbitrage to determine a probability measure under which security prices are martingales once discounted. The new

---

[10] For example, the PDE for a zero-coupon bond price is

$$\frac{\partial p}{\partial t} + \frac{1}{2}\sigma^2\frac{\partial^2 p}{\partial r^2} + (\mu - \lambda\sigma)\frac{\partial p}{\partial r} - rp = 0$$

where

p = zero-coupon price
r = instantaneous risk-free rate
μ = the drift rate
σ = volatility
λ = market price of risk

To solve the zero-coupon price PDE, we must state the final and boundary conditions. The final condition that corresponds to payoff at maturity is $p(r, T) = k$.

probability measure is used to calculate the expected value of the security at expiration and discounting with the risk-free rate.

WHICH IS THE RIGHT MODEL OF THE INTEREST RATE PROCESS?

The bare essential of the bond market is a collection of zero-coupon bonds for each date, for example, now, that mature later. A zero-coupon bond with a given maturity date is a contract that guarantees the investor $1 to be paid at maturity. The price of a zero-coupon bond at time t with a maturity date of T is denoted by $P(t, T)$. In general, analysts make the following simplifying assumptions about the bond market:

- There exists a frictionless and competitive market for a zero-coupon bond for every maturity date. By a *frictionless market*, we mean there is no transaction cost in buying and selling securities and there is no restriction on trades such as a short sale.
- For every fixed date, the price of a zero-coupon bond, $\{P(t, T); 0 \leq t \leq T\}$, is a stochastic process with $P(t, t) = 1$ for all t. By *stochastic process*, we mean the price of a zero-coupon bond moves in an unpredictable fashion from the date it was bought until it matures. The present value of a zero-coupon bond when it was bought is known for certain and it is normalized to equal one.
- For every fixed date, the price for a zero-coupon bond is continuous in that at every trading date the market is well bid for the zero-coupon bond.

In addition to zero-coupon bonds, the bond market has a money market (bank account) initialized with a unit of money.[11] The bank account serves as an accumulator factor for rolling over the bond.

A term-structure model establishes a mathematical relationship that determines the price of a zero-coupon bond, $\{P(t, T); 0 \leq t \leq T\}$, for all dates t between the time the bond is bought (time 0) and when it matures (time T). Alternatively, the term structure shows the relationship between the yield to maturity and the time to maturity of the bond. To compute the value of a security dependent on the term structure, one needs to specify the dynamic of the interest rate process and apply an

---

[11] The bank account is denoted by

$$B(t) = \exp\left[\int_0^t r(u)\,du\right]$$

and $B(0) = 1$.

arbitrage restriction. A term-structure model satisfies the arbitrage restriction if there is no opportunity to invest risk-free and be guaranteed a positive return.[12]

To specify the dynamic of the interest rate process, analysts have always considered a dynamic that is mathematically tractable and anchored in sound economic reasoning. The basic tenet is that the dynamic of interest rates is governed by time and the uncertain state of the world. Modeling time and uncertainty are the hallmarks of modern financial theory. The uncertainty problem has been modeled with the aid of the probabilistic theory of the stochastic process. The stochastic process models the occurrence of random phenomena; in other words, the process is used to describe unpredictable movements. The stochastic process is a collection of random variables that take values in the state space. The basic elements distinguishing a stochastic process are state space[13] and index parameter,[14] and the dependent relationship among the random variables (e.g., X_t).[15] The Poisson process and Brownian motion are two fundamental examples of continuous time stochastic processes. Exhibits 7.3 and 7.4 show the schematics of the Poisson process and Brownian motion.

In everyday financial market experiences, one may observe, at a given instant, three possible states of the world: Prices may go up a tick, decrease a tick, or do not change. The ordinary market condition characterizes most trading days; however, security prices may from time to time

---

[12] Technically, the term-structure model is said to be arbitrage-free if and only if there is a probability measure Q on Ω ($Q \sim P$) with the same null:

$$Z(t, T) = \frac{P(t, T)}{B(t)}, 0 \leq t \leq T$$

set as P, such that for each t, the process is a martingale under Q.

[13] State space is the space in which the possible values of X_t lie. Let S be the state space. If $S = (0, 1, 2...)$, the process is called the discrete state process. If $S = \Re(-\infty, \infty)$ that is the real line, and the process is called the real-valued stochastic process. If S is Euclidean d-space, then the process is called the d-dimensional process.

[14] Index parameter: If $T = (0, 1...)$, then X_t is called the *discrete-time stochastic process*. If $T = \Re_+[0, \infty)$, then X_t is called a *continuous-time stochastic process*.

[15] Formally, a stochastic process is a family of random variables $X = \{x_t; t \in T\}$, where T is an ordered subset of the positive real line $\Re_+$. A stochastic process X with a time set $[0, T]$ can be viewed as a mapping from $\Omega \times [0, T]$ to $\Re$ with $x(\omega, t)$ denoting the value of the process at time t and state ω. For each $\omega \in \Omega$, $\{x(\omega, t); t \in [0,T]\}$ is a sample path of X sometimes denoted as $x(\omega, \bullet)$. A stochastic process $X = \{x_t; t \in [0, T]\}$ is said to be adapted to filtration F if x_t is measurable with respect to F_t for all $t \in [0, T]$. The adaptedness of a process is an informational constraint: The value of the process at any time t cannot depend on the information yet to be revealed strictly after t.

EXHIBIT 7.3   Poisson Process

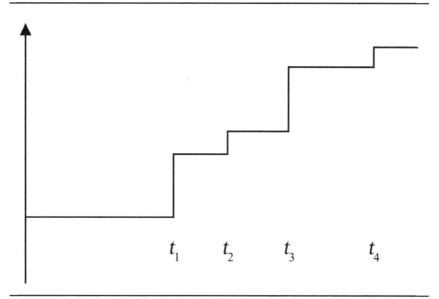

t_1 t_2 t_3 t_4

Source: First Union Securities, Inc.

EXHIBIT 7.4   Brownian Motion Path

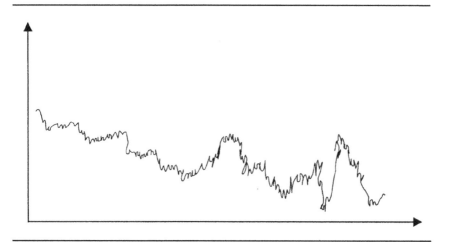

Source: First Union Securities, Inc.

exhibit extreme behavior. In financial modeling, there is the need to distinguish between rare and normal events. Rare events usually bring about discontinuity in prices. The Poisson process is used to model jumps caused by rare events and is a discontinuous process. Brownian motion is used to model ordinary market events for which extremes occur only infrequently according to the probabilities in the tail areas of normal distribution.[16]

Brownian motion is a continuous martingale. Martingale theory describes the trend of an observed time series. A stochastic process behaves like a martingale if its trajectories display no discernible trends.

- A stochastic process that, on average, increases is called a *submartingale*.
- A stochastic process that, on average, declines is called a *supermartingale*.

Suppose one has an interest in generating a forecast of a process (e.g., R_t – interest rate) by expressing the forecast based on what has been observed about R based on the information available (e.g., F_t) at time t.[17] This type of forecast, which is based on conditioning on information observed up to a time, has a role in financial modeling. This role is encapsulated in a martingale property.[18] A martingale is a process, the expectation for which future values conditional on current information are equal to the value of the process at present. A martingale embodies the notion of a fair gamble: The expected gain from participating in a

---

[16] A process X is said to have an independent increment if the random variables $x(t_1) - x(t_0), x(t_2) - x(t_1) \ldots$ and $x(t_n) - x(t_{n-1})$ are independent for any $n \geq 1$ and $0 \leq t_0 < t_1 < \ldots < t_n \leq T$. A process X is said to have a stationary independent increment if, moreover, the distribution of $x(t) - x(s)$ depends only on $t - s$. We write $z \sim N(\mu, \sigma^2)$ to mean the random variable z has normal distribution with mean μ and variance σ^2. A standard Brownian motion W is a process having continuous sample paths, stationary independent increments and $W(t) \sim N(\mu, t)$ (under probability measure P). Note that if X is a continuous process with stationary and independent increments, then X is a Brownian motion. A strong Markov property is a memoryless property of a Brownian motion. Given X as a Markov process, the past and future are statistically independent when the present is known.

[17] We write:

$$E_t[R_t] = E[R_T|F_t], \quad t < T$$

[18] More concretely, given a probability space, a process $\{R_t\ t \in (0, \infty)\}$ is a martingale with respect to information sets F_t, if for all $t > 0$,

1. R_t is known, given F_t, that is, R_t is F_t adapted;
2. Unconditional forecast is finite; $E|R_t| < \infty$; and
3. If

$$E_t[R_t] = R_T, \quad \forall t < T$$

with a probability of 1. The best forecast of unobserved future value is the last observation on R_t.

family of fair gambles is always zero and, thus, the accumulated wealth does not change in expectation over time. Note the actual price of a zero-coupon bond does not move like a martingale. Asset prices move more like submartingales or supermartingales. The usefulness of martingales in financial modeling stems from the fact one can find a probability measure that is absolutely continuous with objective probability such that bond prices discounted by a risk-free rate become martingales. The probability measures that convert discounted asset prices into martingales are called equivalent martingale measures. The basic idea is that, in the absence of an arbitrage opportunity, one can find a synthetic probability measure Q absolutely continuous with respect to the original measure P so that all properly discounted asset prices behave as martingales. A fundamental theorem that allows one to transform R_t into a martingale by switching the probability measure from P to Q is called the *Girsanov Theorem*.

The powerful assertion of the Girsanov Theorem provides the ammunition for solving a stochastic differential equation driven by Brownian motion in the following sense: By changing the underlying probability measure, the process that was driving the Brownian motion becomes, under the equivalent measure, the solution to the differential equation. In financial modeling, the analog to this technical result says that in a risk-neutral economy assets should earn a risk-free rate. In particular, in the option valuation, assuming the existence of a risk-neutral probability measure allows one to dispense with the drift term, which makes the diffusion term (volatility) the dominant value driver.

To model the dynamic of interest rates, it is generally assumed the change in rates over instantaneous time is the sum of the drift and diffusion terms (see Exhibit 7.5).[19] The drift term could be seen as the average movement of the process over the next instants of time, and the diffusion is the amplitude (width) of the movement. If the first two moments are sufficient to describe the distribution of the asset return, the drift term accounts for the mean rate of return and the diffusion accounts for the standard deviation (volatility). Empirical evidence has suggested that interest rates tend to move back to some long-term average, a phenomenon

---

[19] In particular, assume

$$dX(t) = \alpha(t, X(t))dt + \beta(t, X(t))dW(t)$$

for which the solution $X(t)$ is the factor. Depending on the application, one can have n-factors, in which case we let X be an n-dimensional process and W an n-dimensional Brownian motion. Assume the stochastic differential equation for $X(t)$ describes the interest process $r(t)$, (i.e., $r(t)$ is a function of $X(t)$). A one-factor model of interest rate is

$$dr(t) = \alpha(t)dt + \beta(t)dW(t)$$

EXHIBIT 7.5 Drift and Diffusion

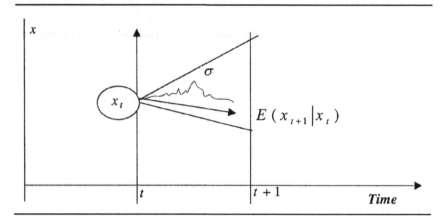

Source: First Union Securities, Inc.

known as mean reverting that corresponds to the Ornstein-Ulhenbeck process (see Exhibit 7.6).[20] When rates are high, mean reversion tends to cause interest rates to have a negative drift; when rates are low, mean reversion tends to cause interest rates to have a positive drift.

The highlights of the preceding discussion are as follows:

- The modeler begins by decomposing bonds to their bare essentials, which are zero-coupon bonds.
- To model a bond market that consists of zero-coupon bonds, the modeler makes some simplifying assumptions about the structure of the market and the price behaviors.
- A term structure model establishes a mathematical relationship that determines the price of a zero-coupon bond and, to compute the value of a security dependent on the term structure, the modeler needs to specify the dynamic of the interest rate process and apply arbitrage restriction.
- The stochastic process is used to describe the time and uncertainty components of the price of zero-coupon bonds.
- There are two basic types of stochastic processes used in financial modeling: The Poisson process is used to model jumps caused by rare events, and Brownian motion is used to model ordinary market events for which extremes occur only infrequently.

---

[20] This process is represented as

$$dr = a(b - r)dt + \sigma r^\beta dW$$

where, a and b are called the *reversion speed* and *level*, respectively.

EXHIBIT 7.6   Process with Mean Reversion (Ornstein-Uhlenbeck Process)

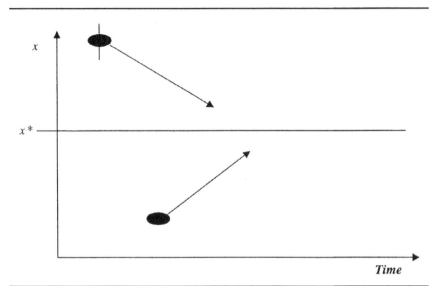

Source: First Union Securities, Inc.

▪ We assume the market for zero-coupon bonds is well bid; that is, the zero-coupon price is continuous. Brownian motion is the suitable stochastic process to describe the evolution of interest rates over time. In particular, Brownian motion is a continuous martingale. Martingale theory describes the trend of the observed time series.

▪ Once we specify the evolution of interest rate movements, we need an arbitrage pricing theory that tells us the price one should pay now to receive $1 later is an expected discounted payoff. The issue to be resolved is, What are the correct expected discount factors to use? The discount must be determined by the market and based on risk-adjusted probabilities. In particular, when all bonds are properly risk-adjusted, they should earn risk-free rates; if not, arbitrage opportunity exists to earn riskless profit.

▪ The risk-adjusted probability consistent with the no-arbitrage condition is the equivalent martingale measure; it is the probability measure that converts the discounted bond price to a martingale (fair price). The elegance of the martingale theory is the "roughs and tumbles" one finds in the world of partial differentiation are to some extent avoided and the integral representation it allows fits nicely with Monte Carlo simulations.

Several term structure models have been proposed with subtle differences. However, the basic differences amount to how the dynamic of the interest rate is specified, the number of factors that generate the rate process, and whether the model is closed by equilibrium or arbitrage arguments. Some of the most popular term-structure models can be summarized in Exhibit 7.7.

EXHIBIT 7.7   Summary of Popular Term-Structure Models

Hull and White (1990)/Extended Vasicek (1977)

Assumptions
- Evolution of interest rates is driven by the short rate (one factor).
- Short rates are normally distributed.
- Instantaneous standard deviation of the short rate is constant.
- Short rates are mean reverting with a constant reversion rate.

Model
- Extended Vasicek model.
- The two volatility parameters are a and θ.
- a determines the relative volatilities of long and short rates, and the high value of a causes short-term rate movement to dampen such that long-term volatility is reduced.
- θ determines the overall volatility.
- The short-rate dynamic is
  $$dr = [\theta(t) - ar] + \sigma dW$$

Issues
- Computational advantages (speed and convergence).
- Analytical solution exists for pricing some European-style derivatives.
- Normally distributed interest rates imply a finite probability of rates becoming zero or negative.

Ho and Lee (HL, 1986)

Assumptions
- Evolution of interest rates is driven by the short rate (one factor).
- Short rates are normally distributed.
- Instantaneous standard deviation of the short rate is constant.
- Short rates are not mean reverting.

Model
- The short-rate process is assumed to be an arithmetic process.
- In continuous time, the short-rate dynamic of HL is
  $$dr = \theta(t) + \sigma dW$$
- $\theta(t)$ makes the model consistent with the initial term structure, and it can be seen approximately as the slope of the forward curve.

EXHIBIT 7.7   (Continued)

Issues
- Computational advantages (speed and convergence).
- Closed-form solution exists for pricing European-style derivatives.
- Nonexistence of a mean-reverting parameter on the model simplifies the calibration of the model-to-market data.
- Normally distributed interest rates imply a finite probability of rates becoming zero or negative.
- Nonexistence of mean reversion in the model implies all interest rates have the same constant rate, which is different from market observations (the short rate is more volatile than the long rate).

Cox, Ingersoll, and Ross (CIR, 1985)

Assumptions
- Evolution of interest rates is driven by the short rate (one factor).
- Short rates are normally distributed.
- Instantaneous standard deviation of the short rate is constant times the square root of the interest rate.
- Short rates are mean reverting with a constant reversion rate.

Model
- The short-rate process is assumed to be a square root process.
- In continuous time, the short-rate dynamic of CIR is

    $dr = a[\theta - r] + \sigma r^{1/2} dW$

Issues
- Eliminating the possibility of negative interest rates.
- Analytical solution is difficult to implement, if you find one.
- Popular among academics because of its general equilibrium overtone.

Black-Derman-Toy (BDT, 1990)

Assumptions
- Evolution of interest rates is driven by the short rate (one factor).
- Short rates are log normally distributed, and short rates cannot become negative.
- Instantaneous standard deviation of the logarithmic short rate is constant.
- The reversion rate is a function of the short-rate volatility.

Model
- In continuous time, the short-rate dynamic of BDT is

    $d\mathrm{Log}(r) = [\theta(t) + (\sigma'(t)/\sigma(t))\mathrm{Log}(r)]dt + \sigma(t)dW$

    where $\sigma'(t)/\sigma(t)$ is the reversion rate that is a function of the short-rate volatility, $\sigma'(t)$ and its derivative with respect to time, $\sigma'(t)$.

Issues
- Eliminating the possibility of negative interest rates.
- No closed-form solution.

EXHIBIT 7.7   (Continued)

Black and Karasinski (BK, 1991)

Assumptions
- Separates the reversion rate and volatility in BDT.
- Provides a procedure for implementing the model using a binomial lattice with time steps of varying lengths.

Model
- In continuous time, the short-rate dynamic of BK is
  $$d\text{Log}(r) = [\theta(t) + a(t)\text{Log}(r)]dt + \sigma(t)dW$$

Issues
- Whether mean reversion and volatility parameter should be functions of time; by making them a function of time, the volatility can be fitted at time zero correctly, however, the volatility structure in the future may be dramatically different from today.

Heath, Jarrow, and Morton (HJM, 1992)

Assumptions
- Evolution of interest rates is driven by the forward rates (one factor or multifactor).
- Involves specifying the volatilities of all forward rates at all times.
- Non-Markovian.
- Expected drift of forward rate in risk-neutral world is calculated from its volatilities.

Model
- The HJM model characterizes the fundamental stochastic process for the evolution of forward rates across time. The model takes as a given the initial forward rate curve and imposes a fairly general stochastic structure on it. By using the equivalent martingale technique, the model shows the condition that the evolution of forward rates must satisfy to be arbitrage-free. The basic condition is the existence of a unique equivalent martingale measure under which the prices of all bonds, risk-adjusted in terms of money market account, are martingales. HJM describes the evolution of forward curves as follows:

  $$df(t, T) = \mu(t, T, \omega)dt + \sum_{i=1}^{n} \sigma_i(t, T, \omega)dW_i(t)$$

  or,

  $$f(t, T) = f(0, T) + \int_0^t \mu(v, T, \omega)dv + \int_0^t \sum_{i=1}^{n} \sigma_i(v, T, \omega)dW_i(v)$$

EXHIBIT 7.7   (Continued)

---

where $\mu(t, T, \omega)$ is the random drift term of the forward rate curve, $\sigma(t, T, \omega)$ is the stochastic volatility function of the forward rate curve and the initial forward rate curve $f(0, t)$ is taken as a given. Taking the spot rate at time t to be the instantaneous forward rate at time t, that is

$$r(t) \equiv \lim_{T \to t} f(t, T)$$

we can write

$$r(t) = f(0, t) + \int_0^t \mu(v, t, \omega) dv + \int_0^t \sum_{i=1}^n \sigma_i(v, t, \omega) dW_i(v)$$

Notice the spot rate equation is similar to the forward-rate process with explicit differences in time and maturity arguments.

Issues
- Difficult to implement.
- Instantaneous forward rate is not a market observable.
- Useful in valuing path-dependent securities such as mortgages.

Which of these models to use in OAS analysis depends on the available resources. Where resource availability is not an issue, we favor models that account for the path-dependent nature of mortgage cash flows. Good rules-of-thumb in deciding which model to use are as follows:

- *Flexibility:* How flexible is the model?
- *Simplicity:* Is the model easy to understand?
- *Specification:* Is the specification of the interest rate process reasonable?
- *Realism:* How real is the model?
- *Good fit:* How well does the result fit the market data?
- *Internal consistency rule:* A necessary condition for the existence of market equilibrium is the absence of arbitrage, and the external consistency rule requires models to be calibrated to market data.

First Union Securities, Inc.'s (FUSI) proprietary interest rate model is based on the HJM framework.

TERM STRUCTURE MODELS: WHICH IS THE RIGHT APPROACH FOR OAS?

Numerical schemes are constructive or algorithmic methods for obtaining practical solutions to mathematical problems. They provide methods for effectively finding practical solutions to asset pricing PDEs.

The first issue in a numerical approach is discretization. The main objective for discretizing a problem is to reduce it from continuous parameters formulation to an equivalent discrete parameterization in a way that makes it amenable to practical solution. In financial valuation, one generally speaks of a continuous-time process in an attempt to find an analytical solution to a problem; however, nearly all the practical solutions are garnered by discretizing space and time. Discretization involves finding numerical approximatizations to the solution at some given points rather than on a continuous domain.

Numerical approximation may involve the use of a pattern, lattice, network, or mesh of discrete points in place of the (continuous) whole domain, so that only approximate solutions are obtained for the domain in the isolated points, and other values such as integrals and derivatives can be obtained from the discrete solution by the means of interpolation and extrapolation.

With the discretization of the continuous domain come the issues of adequacy, accuracy, convergence, and stability. Perhaps how these issues are faithfully addressed in the implementation of OAS models speaks directly to the type of results achieved. Although these numerical techniques—lattice methods, finite difference methods, and Monte Carlo methods—have been used to solve asset pricing PDEs, the lattice and Monte Carlo methods are more in vogue in OAS implementations.

Lattice Method

The most popular numerical scheme used by financial modelers is the lattice (or tree) method. A lattice is a nonempty collection of vertices and edges that represent some prescribed mathematical structures or properties. The node (vertex) of the lattice carries particular information about the evolution of a process that generates the lattice up to that point. An edge connects the vertices of a lattice. A lattice is initialized at its root, and the root is the primal node that records the beginning history of the process.

The lattice model works in a discrete framework and calculates expected values on a discrete space of paths. A node in a given path of a nonrecombining lattice distinguishes not only the value of the underlying claim there but also the history of the path up to the node. A bushy tree represents every path in the state space and can numerically value path-dependent claims. A node in a given path of a bushy tree distinguishes not only the value of the underlying claim there but also the history of the path to the node. There is a great cost in constructing a bushy tree model. For example, modeling a 10-year Treasury rate in a binary bushy tree with each time period equal to one coupon payment would require a tree with 2^{20} (1,048,576) paths. Exhibit 7.8 shows a schematic of a bushy tree.

EXHIBIT 7.8   Bushy or Nonrecombining Tree

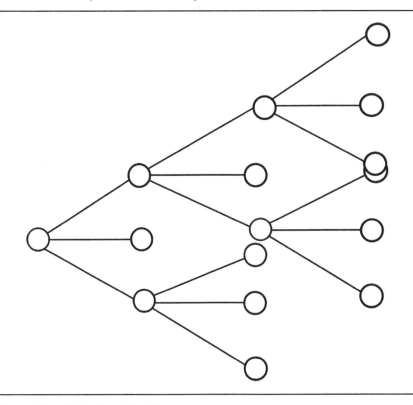

Source: First Union Securities, Inc.

In a lattice construction, it is usually assumed the time to maturity of the security, T, can be divided into discrete (finite and equal) time-steps M, $\Delta t = T/M$. The price of the underlying security is assumed to have a finite number of "jumps" (or up-and-down movements) N between the time-steps Δt. In a recombining lattice, the price or yield of the underlying security is assumed to be affected by N and not the sequences of the jumps. For computational ease, N is usually set to be two or three; the case where $N = 2$ is called *binomial lattice* (or tree), and $N = 3$ is the *trinomial lattice*. Exhibits 7.9 and 7.10 show the binomial and trinomial lattices, respectively, for the price of a zero-coupon bond.

Monte Carlo Method

The Monte Carlo method is a numerical scheme for solving mathematical models that involve random sampling. This scheme has been used to solve

EXHIBIT 7.9   Binomial Lattice for the Price of a Zero-Coupon Bond

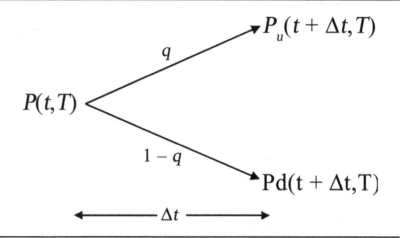

Source: First Union Securities, Inc.

EXHIBIT 7.10   Trinomial Lattice for the Price of a Zero-Coupon Bond

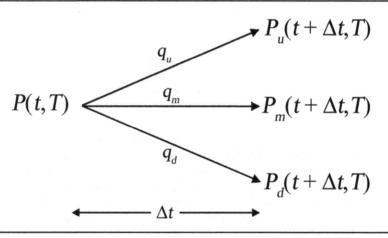

Source: First Union Securities, Inc.

problems that are either deterministic or probabilistic in nature. In the most common application, the Monte Carlo method uses random or pseudo-random numbers to simulate random variables. Although the Monte Carlo method provides flexibilities in dealing with a probabilistic problem, it is not precise especially when one desires the highest level of accuracy at a reasonable cost and time.

Aside from this drawback, the Monte Carlo method has been shown to offer the following advantages:

- It is useful in dealing with multidimensional problems and boundary value problems with complicated boundaries.
- Problems with random coefficients, random boundary values, and stochastic parameters can be solved.
- Solving problems with discontinuous boundary functions, nonsmooth boundaries, and complicated right-hand sides of equations can be achieved.

The application of the Monte Carlo method in computational finance is predicated on the integral representation of security prices. The approach taken consists of the following:

- Simulating in a manner consistent with a risk-neutral probability (equivalent martingale) measure the sample path of the underlying state variables.
- Evaluating the discounted payoff of the security on each sample path.
- Taking the expected value of the discounted payoff over the entire sample paths.

The Monte Carlo method computes a multidimensional integral— the expected value of discounted cash flows over the space of sample paths. For example, let $f(x)$ be an integral function over d-dimensional unit hypercube, then a simple (or crude) estimate of the integral is equal to the average value of the function f over n points selected at random (more appropriately, pseudorandom) from the unit hypercube. By the law of large numbers,[21] the Monte Carlo estimate converges to the value as n tends to infinity. Moreover, we know from the central limit theorem that the standard error of estimate tends toward zero as $1/(\sqrt{n})$. To improve on the computational efficiency of the crude Monte Carlo method, there are several variance-reduction techniques available. These techniques are discussed in the appendix to this chapter. Exhibit 7.11 shows a crude Monte Carlo simulation of the short-rate process.

---

[21] *Strong Law of Large Numbers.* Let $X = X_1, X_2 \ldots$ be an independent identically distributed random variable with $E(X^2) < \infty$ then the mean of the sequence up to the nth term, though itself a random variable, tends as n get larger and larger, to the expectation of X with probability 1. That is,

$$P\left(\lim_{n \to \infty}\left(\frac{1}{n}\sum_{i=1}^{n} X_i\right) = E(X)\right) = 1$$

EXHIBIT 7.11   A Hypothetical Crude Monte Carlo Simulation of the
Short-Rate Process

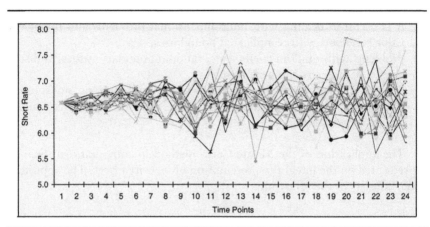

Source: First Union Securities, Inc.

IS THERE A RIGHT WAY TO MODEL PREPAYMENTS?

Because cash flows are one of the most important inputs in determining
the value of a security, there has to be a model for cash flow. The cash
flow model consists of a model for distributing the coupon and scheduled principal payments to the bondholders, as contained in the deal
prospectus, and a prepayment model that projects unscheduled principal payments. The basic types of prepayment models are as follows:

- *Rational prepayment models.* These models apply an option-theoretic
  approach and link prepayment and valuation in a single unified framework.
- *Econometric prepayment models.* This class of models is based on
  econometric and statistical analysis.
- *Reduced-form prepayment models.* This type of model uses past
  prepayment rates and other endogenous variables to explain current
  prepayment. It fits the observed prepayment data unrestricted by
  theoretical consideration.

The reduced-form prepayment model is the most widely used approach
among dealers and prepayment vendors because of its flexibility and
unrestricted calibration techniques. The basic determinants of the voluntary and involuntary components of total prepayments are collateral

and market factors. Collateral factors are the origination date, *weighted average coupon* (WAC) and weighted average maturity, and the market-related factors are benchmark rates and spreads. A simple generalized version of such a model defines total prepayment (voluntary and involuntary) as follows:

$$TP_{CPR} = \text{Turnover} + \text{Rate-Refi} + \text{Curing} + \text{Default}$$

This expression is not necessarily a linear function and could get complicated quickly. It is usually easier to identify a set of model parameters and fit its relationship to observed historical prepayment data. For example, in FUSI proprietary model for a particular category of collateral is defined by specifying the values of numerous parameters that control the projected effects of various contributions to total prepayments. The control parameters that we identify:

- *Seasoning period.* The number of months over which base voluntary prepayments (housing turnover, cash-out refinancing and credit upgrades but not rate refinancing or defaults) are assumed to increase to long-term levels.
- *Housing turnover.* Turnover is the long-term rate at which borrowers in a pool prepay their mortgages because they sell their homes.
- *Default.* Default is expressed as a percentage of the PSA Standard Default Assumption (SDA) or a loss curve.
- *Credit curing.* This is the long-term rate at which borrowers prepay their mortgages because improved credit and/or increased home prices enable them to get better rates and/or larger loans. As the pool burns out, the rate of curing declines.
- *Maximum rate-related conditional prepayment rate (CPR).* This occurs when rates fall below the saturation point for rate-related financing.
- *Maximum rate-related CPR for burnout.* The CPR is lower for a pool that has experienced no prior rate-related refinancing. The lower the ratio, the faster the pool burns out.
- *Refinancing threshold.* This is the amount by which the current market loan rate must fall below the collateral WAC to trigger rate-related financing.
- *Curing threshold.* This is the amount by which the current market loan rate must increase above the collateral WAC to eliminate curing-related financing.
- *Yield-curve sensitivity.* This sensitivity is the maximum yield-curve correction of rate-related CPR that occurs when the yield-curve slope rises above/falls below the historical average.

▦ *Half-life burnout.* This is the time frame in years that a collateral pool must be fully refinancable to reduce interest rate sensitivity 50% of the way from maximum rate-related CPR to maximum rate-related CPR for burnout.

To calibrate these parameters, we developed a database of mortgage loan groups. The collateral groups backing each deal are assigned a prepayment model based on the percentile ranking of their initial credit spread. We define this spread as the collateral WAC minus the Treasury yield at the time of origination. The rationale for our approach is that borrowers who pay a higher credit spread tend to be less creditworthy. Moreover, these borrowers tend to have more opportunities to lower their rate by curing their credit problem, but they are less able to refinance in response to declining rates. Exhibit 7.12 details the specific parameter values assigned to each FUSI prepayment model. Exhibit 7.13 shows the aggregate historical CPR versus FUSI's model projection for EQCC Home Equity Loan Trust.

CONCLUSION

In this chapter, we examined some of the foundational issues that explain: (1) why there is a difference in dealers' OAS values for a specific bond; (2) what may be responsible for the differences; and (3) why one OAS value may be more correct than another. As a general guideline, we urge portfolio managers to get familiar with the economic intuitions and basic assumptions made by the models. We believe the reasonableness of the OAS values produced by different models should be considered. Moreover, because prepayment options are not traded in the market, calibrating OAS values using the prices of these options is not possible. With respect to the basic building block issues, the key points that we made in this report are as follows:

▦ Interest rate models, which are closed by precluding arbitrage opportunities, are more tractable and realistic.
▦ Interest rate models that account for the path-dependent natures of ABS and MBS cash flows are more robust.
▦ With the path-dependent natures of ABS and MBS cash flows come the difficulties of implementation, in particular, the speed of calculation; the toss-up here is between the lattice and Monte Carlo schemes. There is a tendency for market participants to believe that because we are talking about interest rate scenarios, the ideal candidate for the

EXHIBIT 7.12 Agency, Whole, and Home Equity Loan Collateral Parameters

Agency and Whole Loan Collateral

Name	FN30yr	FN15yr	FN7yr	FN5yr	GN30yr	GN15yr	JUMBO	JUMBO15	JUMBO7	ALTER	ALTER15	ALTER7	ARM_AGY	ARM_JUMBO	ARM_ALTER
Seas. Prd.	24	22	20	15	26	22	22	20	18	16	15	14	20	16	14
Turnover CPR	6.5%	7.5%	7.0%	9.0%	6.5%	7.0%	5.5%	5.5%	7.0%	5.5%	6.0%	7.0%	9.0%	8.0%	8.0%
%SDA	0%	0%	0%	0%	0%	0%	75%	75%	75%	125%	125%	125%	0%	75%	125%
Max. Curing CPR	2.5%	2.0%	6.0%	6.5%	2.0%	3.5%	2.0%	2.5%	7.0%	14.0%	15.0%	15.0%	2.5%	8.0%	16.0%
Curing CPR (BO)	2.5%	2.0%	2.0%	3.0%	2.0%	1.0%	2.0%	2.5%	2.0%	6.0%	7.0%	8.0%	1.0%	3.0%	8.0%
Max. Refi. CPR	52.0%	50.0%	53.0%	45.0%	50.0%	48.0%	62.0%	55.0%	60.0%	50.0%	35.0%	35.0%	35.0%	40.0%	30.0%
Max. Refi. CPR (BO)	14.0%	11.0%	20.0%	15.0%	12.0%	8.0%	14.0%	12.0%	20.0%	10.0%	10.0%	12.0%	8.0%	8.0%	8.0%
Refi. Threshold	0.50%	0.70%	0.50%	0.75%	0.60%	1.00%	0.20%	0.25%	0.50%	0.10%	0.75%	0.75%	1.00%	0.50%	1.00%
Curing Threshold	2.50%	2.50%	2.50%	2.50%	2.50%	2.50%	2.50%	2.00%	1.50%	1.50%	1.50%	1.50%	1.50%	1.50%	2.00%
Yield Curve CPR	10.0%	15.0%	0.0%	-5.0%	10.0%	8.0%	15.0%	20.0%	0.0%	8.0%	10.0%	0.0%	-35.0%	-35.0%	-30.0%
Half-Life (BO)	1.25	1.00	1.00	1.00	1.25	1.00	1.25	1.00	1.00	1.00	1.00	1.00	1.00	1.00	1.00
Ref. Category	AGY	AGY	AGY	AGY	AGY	AGY	A+	A+	A+	A-	A-	A-	AGY	A+	A-

Home Equity Loan Collateral

Name	FIX_LO	FIX_MID	FIX_HI	ARM_LO	ARM_MID	ARM_HI	LTV 125	Home Impr.	CRA	Vendee	FIX_RASC	ARM_HELOC	FIX_MANHS	FIX_HI	ARM_MANHS
Seas. Prd.	14	15	16	12	13	14	26	14	30	20	14	10	26	18	12
Turnover CPR	5.0%	4.0%	3.0%	8.0%	6.0%	5.0%	6.0%	4.0%	3.5%	4.0%	4.0%	3.0%	4.0%	4.0%	5.0%
%SDA	325.00%	750.00%	1,200.00%	500.00%	1,000.00%	1,500.00%	1,000.00%	750.00%	150.00%	400.00%	325.00%	1,350.00%	600.00%	900.00%	900.00%
Max. Curing CPR	20.0%	26.0%	24.0%	28.0%	38.0%	45.0%	14.0%	18.0%	1.0%	2.0%	24.0%	38.0%	6.5%	8.5%	8.0%
Curing CPR (BO)	12.0%	14.0%	16.0%	10.0%	12.0%	14.0%	14.0%	10.0%	1.0%	1.0%	12.0%	20.0%	5.0%	6.0%	4.0%
Max. Refi. CPR	14.0%	10.0%	8.0%	18.0%	12.0%	8.0%	20.0%	15.0%	20.0%	24.0%	24.0%	2.0%	5.0%	3.0%	3.0%
Max. Refi. CPR (BO)	10.0%	6.0%	4.0%	8.0%	5.0%	4.0%	16.0%	8.0%	10.0%	8.0%	10.0%	1.0%	2.0%	1.0%	1.0%
Refi. Threshold	0.75%	1.00%	1.50%	0.75%	1.00%	1.00%	1.50%	1.38%	0.50%	1.50%	0.75%	2.00%	1.00%	1.00%	0.75%
Curing Threshold	2.50%	3.25%	3.75%	2.50%	2.75%	3.50%	3.50%	2.50%	1.00%	1.00%	1.50%	3.75%	2.00%	2.00%	2.00%
Yield Curve CPR	4.0%	3.0%	2.0%	-20.0%	-10.0%	-5.0%	1.0%	3.0%	5.0%	5.0%	8.0%	-1.0%	1.0%	1.0%	-2.0%
Half-Life (BO)	1.00	1.00	1.20	0.90	0.90	0.90	3.00	2.00	1.00	1.00	1.40	1.00	0.80	0.80	0.80
Ref. Category	LO	MID	HI	LO	MID	HI	HI	HI	A+	LO	LO	HI	MID	HI	HI

Note: BO: burnout; CPR: constant prepayment rate; Refi: refinancing; SDA: standard default assumption; Seas Prd: seasoning period.
Source: First Union Securities, Inc.

EXHIBIT 7.13   Aggregrate Historical CPR versus FUSI Model for
EQCC Home Equity Loan Trust

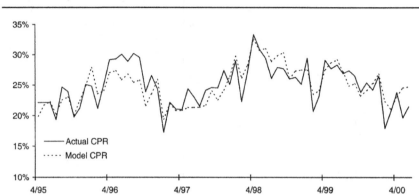

Source: First Union Securities, Inc. (FUSI).

job would be Monte Carlo techniques, but this should not necessarily
be the case. Although lattice implementation could do a good job, the
success of this scheme depends highly on ad hoc techniques that have
not been time-tested. Hence, whereas the OAS implementation
scheme is at the crux of what distinguishes good or bad results, the
preferred scheme is an open question that critically depends on available resources.

- We favor reduced-form prepayment models because of their flexibility
and unrestricted calibration techniques. In particular, a model that
explicitly identifies its control parameters and is amenable to the per-
turbation of these parameters is more robust and transparent.

As a final thought, we rehash two of the questions we asked at the
beginning of this chapter. How do we interpret the differences in dealers' OAS value for a specific security? On this question, we paraphrase
John Maynard Keynes who said that when news in the market is interpreted differently by market participants, then we have a viable market.
In our case, we believe decisions by dealers, vendors, and portfolio managers to choose one interest rate and prepayment model over others and
the different approaches they take in implementing these models largely
account for the wide variance in OAS results, which precipitates a hunt-
for-value mentality that augurs well for the market. Moreover, to com-
plicate the issue, the lack of a market for tradable prepayment options
makes calibrating the resulting OAS values dicey at best. On the question of whether there is a correct OAS value for a given security, we say

it is a state of nirvana that we would all treasure. However, we believe examining the change in OAS value over time, the sensitivity of OAS parameters, and their implications to relative value analysis are some of the important indicators of the reasonableness of OAS value.

APPENDIX: VARIANCE-REDUCTION TECHNIQUES

Antithetic Variates

The most widely used variance-reduction technique in financial modeling is the antithetic variates. Suppose f has a standard normal distribution, then by symmetrical property of normal distribution so does $-\phi$. Antithetic variates involve taking the same set of random numbers but changing their sign, that is, replacing ϕ by $-\phi$ and simulating the rate paths using ϕ and $-\phi$. The antithetic variates technique increases efficiency in pricing options that depend monotonically on inputs (e.g., average options).

Control Variates

Loosely speaking, the principle behind the control variates technique is "use what you know." The idea is to replace the evaluation of unknown expectations with the evaluation of the difference between the unknown quantity and another expectation whose value is known. Suppose there is a known analytical solution to value a security that is similar to the one we want to simulate. Let the values estimated by Monte Carlo simulation be ξ_1' and ξ_2', respectively. If the accurate value of the known security is ξ_2, then an improved estimate for the value of the simulated security is $\xi_1' - \xi_2' + \xi_2$. The notion here is that the error in ξ_1' will be the same as error in ξ_2', and the latter is known.

Moment Matching

Let X_i, $i = 1, 2,..., n$, be independent standard normals used in a simulation. The sample moment of n Xs will not exactly match those of the standard normal. The idea of moment matching is to transform the Xs to match a finite moment of the underlying population. One drawback of moment matching is that a confidence interval is not easy to obtain.

Stratified and Latin Hypercube Sampling

Stratified sampling seeks to make the inputs to simulation more regular than random inputs. It forces certain empirical probabilities to match theoretical probabilities. The idea is, suppose we want to generate 250 normal random variates as inputs to a simulation. The empirical distribution of an independent sample $X_1, X_2, ..., X_{250}$ will look roughly like the normal density. The tails of the distribution—often the most important part—are underrepresented. Stratified sampling can be used to force exactly one observation to lie between the $(i-1)$th and the ith percentile, $j = 1, 2, ..., 250$, thus producing a better match to normal distribution.

$X_1, X_2, ..., X_{250}$ are highly dependent, thus complicating the estimation of standard error. Latin hypercube sampling is a way of randomly sampling n points of a stratified sample while preserving some of the regularity property of stratification.

Importance Sampling

The key observation that an expectation under one probability measure can be expressed as an expectation under another by appealing to the Radon Nikodym theorem is the foundation for this method. In a Monte Carlo simulation, the change of measure is used to try to obtain a more efficient estimator.

Conditional Monte Carlo

A direct consequence of Jensen inequality for condition expectation says that for any random variables X and Y, $\text{Var}[E(X|Y) \leq \text{Var}[X]]$. In replacing an estimator with its conditional expectation, we reduce variance essentially because we are doing a part of the integration analytically and leaving less for Monte Carlo simulation.

Low-Discrepancy Sequences

These sequences use preselected deterministic points for simulation. Discrepancy measures the extent to which the points are evenly dispersed throughout a region: The more evenly dispersed the points are, the lower the discrepancy. Low-discrepancy sequences are sometimes called quasi-random even though they are not random.

CHAPTER 8

Fixed Income Risk Modeling

Ludovic Breger, Ph.D.
Vice-President
Fixed Income Research
MSCI Barra

Oren Cheyette, Ph.D.
Executive Director
Fixed Income Research
MSCI Barra

Most asset owners have traditionally viewed fixed income securities as a relatively safe asset class—a haven from volatility in equity and other markets. While it is certainly true that government bonds are generally a low-risk asset class for domestic investors in developed markets, long-term government bonds can be every bit as risky as a diversified equity portfolio. More generally, many fixed income securities, such as mortgage backed securities (MBSs), collateralized debt obligations (CDOs), or high-yield bonds can be relatively risky investments.

Driven by a variety of pressures, including requirements from asset owners and regulators, there is a continuing demand in the financial community for improved tools for quantitative risk forecasting of fixed income portfolios. Risk analysis is the art and science of forecasting portfolio return variability. It involves several components. One is the choice of the risk measure. Typical in the asset management community is use of the width of the expected return distribution, commonly the standard deviation. An alternative, widely used in the banking world, is a loss value measure such as value-at-risk (VaR), but this is less relevant for asset managers who are more concerned with return measures and performance relative to a benchmark.[1]

A second component is the method of forecasting a portfolio return distribution. Standard approaches include using the historical return distribution for portfolio assets to estimate their future return distribution and using a factor model to characterize asset returns, together with a model for predicting future factor return distributions. Although sometimes used in the equity world (though it suffers when attempting to scale to large portfolios), the first approach is not useful in the fixed income world—because there are very obvious market factors affecting all assets, because of the very large number of individual securities (in the millions), and because of the finite lives and time dependent characteristics of the assets.

This chapter will focus on fixed income risk modeling using factor models to forecast portfolio return standard deviation. Conceptually, this is a relatively straightforward problem, although as with many other aspects of life in the bond world, practical implementations are full of challenges. Our focus is primarily on forecasting at the intermediate horizon of one month. However, most if not all of the ideas presented here are applicable both at longer and shorter horizons. Forecasting at daily or even intraday horizons presents significant challenges with respect to problems such as timing and synchronization, and is beyond the scope of this article.

The chapter is organized as follows. The first section describes in details a general framework for analyzing the risk of portfolios of fixed income securities. In the following sections, we discuss each risk component individually, and then present a method to aggregate components and create a global risk model. The last section shows the risk of several typical standard benchmarks.

MODELING FRAMEWORK

Understanding and forecasting risk accurately consists in identifying the factors that drive the price of securities in the marketplace and adequately capturing these factors in a model. We observe historical asset returns, and our challenge is to explain them in terms of a minimal set of explanatory market factors, whose return distribution (along with

---

[1] VaR has also come in for significant criticism on grounds of, among other things, failure to have good additive properties, and failure to measure the magnitude of expected loss above the VaR threshold. See Philippe Artzner, Freddy Delbaen, Jean-Marc Eber, and David Heath, "Coherent Measures of Risk," *Mathematical Finance* 9, no. 3 (1999), pp. 203–228.

that of the residual asset returns) then serves as the basis for asset or portfolio risk forecasts.

The task of return attribution is to identify a set of common factors, whose changes f_i^t "explain" the excess returns (returns over the risk-free rate) r_k^t of the assets we are concerned with. In general, there is considerable arbitrariness in the identification of the factors, but some choices are more natural or straightforward than others. Return attribution then amounts to solving by regression the relationship

$$r_k^t = X_k^t \cdot f^t + \varepsilon_k^t \tag{8.1}$$

This equation states that the excess return to asset k over a period starting at time t is equal to the dot product of the common factor returns f_i^t with the asset's exposure to each, X_k^t, plus a residual asset-specific return ε_k^t. Note that the common factor returns f_i^t do not depend on the asset. Given the assets' exposures (which may be time dependent), we can solve by regression for the f_i^t to minimize the size of the unexplained residuals ε_k^t.

Many of the factors driving bond returns can be understood by examining the basic valuation formulas or algorithms. The simplest arbitrage free model of security valuation, applicable to default-free bonds with fixed cashflows serves as a useful starting point for understanding more detailed models. The bond value is the sum of cashflows present values with discount rates given by the term structure of interest rates:

$$P = \sum_{i=1}^{N} CF_i e^{-r_i t_i} \tag{8.2}$$

The present value P of a bond is the sum of cash flows CF_i at times t_i discounted by the interest rates r_i.

For a fixed coupon Treasury bond, the cash flows are the coupon, and the interest rates are the prevailing risk-free rates. The valuation formula becomes more complex as soon as we leave the realm of plain vanilla government securities. In the general case, the cash flows are not known in advance and may be state or even history dependent, and the discount factors include a spread and must be computed pathwise. The spread is a shorthand means to capture the excess return required by investors to compensate for various risks, most importantly default and liquidity.

In general, for risk modeling purposes, we can take the valuation model as a black box with various inputs, such as the term structure, spread, volatility forecast and prepayment model, and derive risk forecasts without further reference to the model details. (Of course, this is predicated on someone having built a good valuation black box that can be relied on to take all the necessary inputs and provide an accurate present value output.) The inputs for equation (8.2) and more complicated valuation models are useful for identifying the sources of market risk. One immediately sees from equation (8.2), for example, that a government bond is exposed to risk factors defined by changes in interest rates at different maturities. We discuss the various sources of risk in more detail in the next sections.

A detailed understanding of correlations between asset returns is also required to accurately estimate the risk of a portfolio. Estimating correlations directly is in practice impossible as unknowns severely out-number observations even in relatively small portfolios. Fortunately, the factor attribution of equation (8.1), allows us to model the asset return correlations in terms of a relatively small number of factor covariances.

Because, by construction, factor and specific returns are uncorrelated, and because specific returns are also uncorrelated with each other (leaving aside the correlation of bonds from a common issuer):

$$\sigma^2 = {}^T h \cdot \Sigma \cdot h \tag{8.3}$$

with

$$\Sigma = {}^T X \cdot \Phi \cdot X + \Delta \tag{8.4}$$

where

h = the vector of portfolio holdings
Σ = the covariance matrix of asset returns
Φ = the covariance matrix of factor returns
Δ = the diagonal matrix of specific variances

Equation (8.4) yields active risk forecasts when h is a vector of active holdings—that is, when the portfolio weights are relative to those of a benchmark.

The data that can go into computing factor returns, of course, depend on what the factors are. It may include bond and index level data as well as currency exchange rates. Given a set of factor return series, we seek a forecast of the factor covariance matrix. The simplest approach is to use the sample covariance matrix of the full return history. If the underlying return-generating process is fixed—that is, time independent—this is an optimal estimator. In practice, however, this condition is unlikely to be met: external circumstances change, markets change, and it seems reasonable to expect the dynamics of the term structure to vary in time. Forecasts based on equal weighting of historical data gradually become less and less sensitive to the arrival of new information. Although the forecasts are extremely stable (which can be an attractive feature), the price of this stability is that the forecasts become nonresponsive to changes in the dynamics.

A simple method for addressing this variation is to weight recent returns more heavily than older ones in the analysis, with weight proportional to an exponential of the age of the data. The weight of returns from time t in the past relative to the most recent returns is $e^{-t/\tau}$, where τ is the time scale.[2] The optimal time constant τ can be obtained empirically using, for instance, a maximum-likelihood estimator. However, particularly volatile series may benefit from a different treatment (see the Currency Returns section).

This is our multi-factor framework for forecasting risk. Note that factors are descriptive and not explanatory. In other words, they permit one to forecast risk without necessarily being identified with the underlying economic forces that drive interest rates or bond spreads.

We now proceed with an identification of the factors and the calculation of their returns.

INTEREST RATE RISK

Interest rate or term-structure risk arises from movements in the reference, or "benchmark" interest rate curve. If we exclude currency risk, it is the dominant source of risk, at least for most investment-grade bonds. Building a term structure risk model entails first choosing the benchmark curve. Domestic government bond yields are the choice in most markets, but there are important exceptions that can lead to some complications.

The Eurozone presents a particularly complex picture. On the one hand, the LIBOR/swap curve has emerged as the preferred benchmark for corporate debt due to the absence of a natural government yield curve and the development of a liquid swap market. On the other hand, domestic government debt continues to trade relative to its local government benchmark, and although yields have converged, some differences clearly remain that invite choosing a different government benchmark curve in each legacy market. Overall, the benchmark curve is debt-type and country dependent.

---

[2] The half-life is then $\sigma \ln 2$.

In some smaller markets, the absence of a liquid market for government debt makes the LIBOR/Swap curve the only available benchmark. In a few extreme cases such as in markets affected by extremely high inflation, there is little reliable interest rate data and the best we can do is come up with some reasonable short interest rate.

As long as common factors accurately describe (1) interest rate risk and (2) risk with respect to the benchmark, risk forecasts are in fact not benchmark dependent. Yet, selecting a suboptimal benchmark may limit our ability to correctly identify and hedge a critical factor. For instance, even in markets where securities are quoted off the swap curve, changes in government yields are the dominant underlying source of risk. This is not as clear when interest rate risk is expressed with respect to the swap curve. One approach is to use the government term structure as local benchmark whenever possible and include a swap "intermediate" factor that can be added to the government-based interest rate factors to allow interest rate to be expressed with respect with the swap curve. This swap factor will be described in more details in the next section. In markets where the benchmark is already the LIBOR/Swap curve, there is obviously no need for a swap factor.

Within a given market, as defined by the currency, it may not be appropriate to value all bonds in relation to a single benchmark. This is the case for U.S. municipal bonds, which, thanks to their tax-exempt status, trade at prices affected by various tax rates as well as by the issuer's creditworthiness. It is also the case for *inflation protected bonds* (IPBs), which offer investors a "real" inflation-adjusted yield. Such securities are weakly correlated with other assets classes and require IPB-specific, real yield risk factors.

What should the interest rate factors be? Key rate factors, which are rate changes at standard maturities—such as, 1, 3, and 6 months and 1, 2, 3, 5, 7, 10, and 30 years—seems a natural and somewhat appealing choice. However, because changes in rates for different maturities are highly correlated, using so many factors is unnecessary. Correlations of interest rate changes approach one for nearby maturities and are positive between all maturities in all markets we have studied. This is a consequence of there being a dominant, approximately maturity independent factor driving the changes in the key rates. Using principal component analysis (that is, extracting the eigenvectors of the covariance matrix of the spot rate changes $\Delta s(t, T_i)$), we find that this leading principal component together with the next two account for about 98% of the key rate covariance matrix (the exact fraction depending on the market). That is, reconstructing the key rate covariance matrix from just these three factors leaves an average fractional error in the matrix elements of around 2%. Based on their shapes, shown in Exhibit 8.1 for the U.S. government bond

EXHIBIT 8.1   U.S. Dollar Interest Rate Risk Factor Shapes

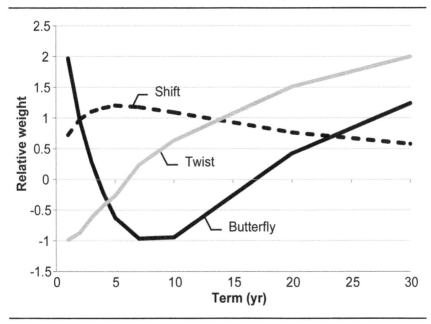

yield curve, the three principal components are referred to as "shift," "twist," and "butterfly" (STB). In this case, equation (8.1) takes the form

$$r_k^t = - \sum_{i \in S, T, B} D_k^i \cdot r_{STB, i}^t + \varepsilon_k^t \qquad (8.5)$$

where are the S, T, and B "durations" of bond k, while $r_{STB, i}^t$ are the S, T, and B factor returns.

Typical shift, twist, and butterfly volatilities are shown in Exhibit 8.2. Shift-like changes are the dominant source of risk in all cases with annualized volatilities ranging from roughly 40 to over 400 bps/yr. Aside from differences of scale, the character of term structure risk is relatively homogeneous across most major markets. A rule of thumb is that twist volatilities are usually about half of shift volatilities, while butterfly volatilities are in turn half of the twist volatilities. Not surprisingly, the largest volatilities are observed for emerging markets such as China, and IPB real yield curves are less volatile than their nominal government counterparts.

The interest rate risk of any given bond depends first on the bond's exposures to the factors and, to a much lesser degree, on correlations

EXHIBIT 8.2   Interest Rate Factor Volatilities on December 31, 2004

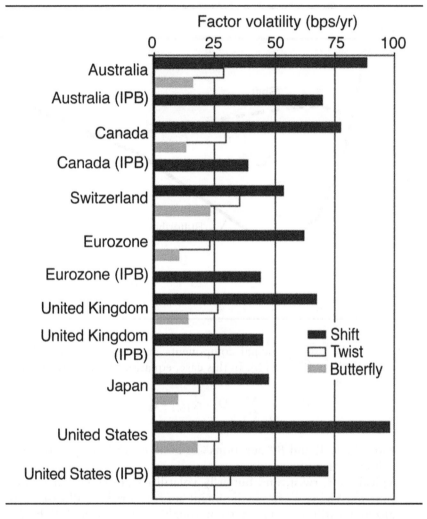

between factors.[3] Exhibit 8.3 gives examples of risk decompositions for three sovereign bonds. The annualized risk of a straight bond issued by the U.S. Treasury varies from about 1% to over 10%, depending on its duration. Korean domestic government bonds have comparable risk characteristics.

---

[3] This is because principal components are, by construction, only weakly correlated. (They are not uncorrelated because we estimate their returns by regression on bond returns rather than from the key rate returns.)

EXHIBIT 8.3   Examples of Interest Rate Risk Breakdown on December 31, 2004

	Exposure			Risk (bps/yr)			
	Shift	Twist	Butterfly	Shift	Twist	Butterfly	Total
U.S. Treasury 5.25% 11/15/2028	9.9	18.7	2.4	967	503	42	1,091
U.S. Treasury 1.625% 02/28/2006	1.0	–0.8	1.8	98	22	32	105
Korean Republic 4.75% 09/17/2013	6.7	2.9	1.6	575	124	25	589

SPREAD RISK—THE CONVENTIONAL APPROACH

International bond portfolios were not long ago still mostly composed of government bonds. The recent explosion of the global corporate credit market now provides asset managers with new opportunities for higher returns and diversification. Unlike government debt, however, corporate debt is exposed to credit and liquidity risk, which are manifest as changes in valuation relative to the benchmark yield curve. For modeling purposes, such changes can again be decomposed into a systematic component that describes, for instance, a market-wide jump in the spread of A-rated utility debt and can be captured by common spread factors, and a bond-specific component. This section discusses model market-wide spread risk, while the next section will address specific spread risk and default risk.

Data considerations are crucial in choosing factors. We can virtually always construct term structure risk factors, whereas spread factors are more data-dependent. In other words, the choice of factors will be limited in markets with little corporate debt. Spread factors should increase the investor's insight and be easy to interpret. Meaningful factors will, in practice, be somewhat connected to the portfolio assets and construction process and allow a detailed analysis of market risk without threatening parsimony.

Swap Spread Factors

In markets with a government bond benchmark yield curve, the spread of LIBOR and swap rates over government rates provides a useful measure of the combination of a liquidity premium on government bonds and the market price of the credit risk on high-grade debt (generally taken as equivalent to a AA-agency rating). In markets with a corporate bond market that is not deep or transparent enough for estimation of a detailed credit risk model, we can use this LIBOR/swap spread as a proxy factor for modeling risk of high-grade bonds relative to the government curve. Given the high correlation of credit spreads of high-grade issuers, this single-factor model is a reasonable approximation. We can also account for the greater risk of lower-quality issuers by using the ratio of bond spread to LIBOR/swap spread as a measure of exposure to the swap risk factor. Linear dependence turns out to overestimate the spread risk of lower-quality bonds, but a sublinear power law generally does a fair job across the markets, where we do have more detailed corporate bond data for comparison.

Swap spread volatilities for several currencies are shown in Exhibit 8.4, with values that vary from about 15 bps/yr to 40 bps/yr. Also showed are the resulting spread risks in the euro and sterling markets for several rating categories. We see in the next paragraphs that the swap model predicts reasonably accurately both the absolute magnitude of the spread risk in each market and their relative values.

In many emerging markets, the swap curve is the benchmark and we cannot build a swap spread factor. We need a reasonable alternative basis for a simple spread risk model.

The answer is yes. One natural approach would be to replace the swap spread by an average credit spread derived from a representative set of domestic corporate bonds. In practice, liquidity issues make with this apparently simple scheme hard to implement. There are often a very limited number of outstanding corporate bonds available in each market. Because many of them are infrequently traded, a model builder is not in a position to obtain accurate prices in these illiquid markets.

An alternative approach is to construct the factor from a universe of arguably more liquid external debt. Consider for instance Asian emerging markets; there are at least two indices that track the performance of Asian U.S. dollar-denominated debt with respect to the U.S. sovereign benchmark: HSBC's Asian U.S. Dollar Bond Index (ADBI) and JP Morgan's Asian Composite Index (JACI). Although these indexes track external debt whereas we are interested in domestic debt, some simple considerations suggest that they may still be useful for the purpose of deriving an average measure of domestic spread risk.

Spreads between corporate and benchmark yields compensate investors for credit risk, liquidity, and, in some cases disparate tax treatments. In practice, emerging market spreads are mostly determined by credit risk considerations. Creditworthiness is attached to the issuer and is to a large extent independent of the market on which a bond is issued. As a result, differential credit spreads between two issuers are also market-independent and we can write for instance:

$$s_{\text{Yuan, CM}} - s_{\text{Yuan, Gov}} \approx s_{\text{US\$, CM}} - s_{\text{US\$, Gov}} \qquad (8.6)$$

EXHIBIT 8.4   Examples Annualized Swap Spread Volatilities

Examples of Annualized Swap Spread Volatilities on December 31, 2004

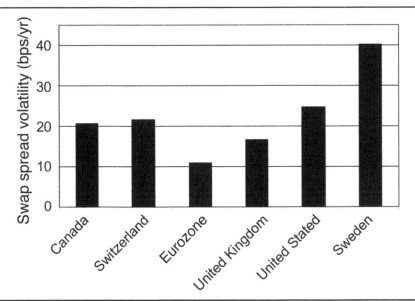

Comparison Between Typical Euro and Sterling Spread Volatilities Computed Using the Swap Factor for Different Rating Categories

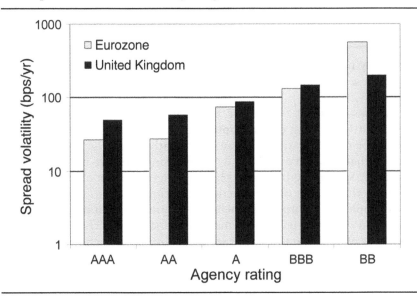

where $s_{\text{Yuan, CM}}$ (respectively $s_{\text{Yuan, Gov}}$) is the spread of a bond issued by China Mobile (respectively the Chinese government) on the Chinese domestic market, and $s_{\text{US\$, CM}}$ (respectively $s_{\text{US\$, Gov}}$) is the spread of a U.S. dollar-denominated bond issued by China Mobile (respectively the Chinese government).

Although not all issuers are simultaneously active on both the euro-dollar market and their domestic market, we can extend equation 8.2 to all issuers with comparable characteristics so that

$$\bar{s}_{\text{Yuan, Corp}} - \bar{s}_{\text{Yuan, Gov}} \approx \bar{s}_{\text{US\$, Corp}} - \bar{s}_{\text{US\$, Gov}} \qquad (8.7)$$

where $\bar{s}_{\text{Yuan, Corp}}$ (respectively $\bar{s}_{\text{Yuan, Gov}}$) is the average spread of investment grade corporate bonds (respectively Chinese government) bonds on the Chinese domestic market $\bar{s}_{\text{US\$, Corp}}$ (respectively $\bar{s}_{\text{US\$, Gov}}$) is the average spread of U.S. dollar-denominated bonds issued by Chinese investment grade companies (respectively the Chinese government).

$\bar{s}_{\text{US\$, Gov}}$ is typically reported in an index such as JACI or ADBI. A quasi-sovereign spread can be used when the sovereign spread is not available. It is also possible to derive $\bar{s}_{\text{US\$, Corp}}$ from one or more sub-components of the same indices. In other words, we can construct a proxy for the local credit spread factor using an global emerging market credit index and, as described earlier, scale it to account for varying credit qualities.

DETAILED CREDIT SPREAD FACTORS

Accurately modeling spread risk in major markets such as the U.S. dollar or Japanese yen market requires detailed currency-dependent, "credit blocks."

Various considerations drive the choice of spread factors. Factors built on little data can end up capturing a large amount of idiosyncratic risk and be representative of a few issuers rather than the market. A corollary is that it is often wiser to avoid building separate factors for thin industries. Spread factors should be meaningful for the investor, and be related to the process of constructing a portfolio.

A simple and natural approach is to capture fluctuations in the average spread of bonds with the same sector and rating. There is unfortunately not enough data to construct sector-by-rating factors for all low-grade ratings and the simplest alternative is then to construct rating-based factors. A typical sector and rating breakdown for the euro and U.S. dollar markets is given in Exhibit 8. 5.

EXHIBIT 8.5 Sector and Rating Breakdown in the Euro and U.S. Dollar Spread
Risk Models
A nondomestic sovereign bond is exposed to the factor corresponding to its sector
and rating. Due to the limited number of high-yield bonds outstanding, some noninvestment grade factors are only broken down by ratings.

Euro		U.S. Dollar	
Sectors	Ratings	Sectors	Ratings
		Domestic agency	
Agency	AAA		
Financial	AA	Energy	AAA
Foreign sovereign	A	Financial	AA
Energy	BBB	Foreign agency and local	A
Industrial		Industrial	BBB
Pfandbrief		Foreign sovereign, Supranational	BB
Supranational		Telecom	B
Telecom		Transportation	
Utility		Utility	
	BB		
	B		CCC
	CCC		

Note that using market-adjusted ratings as opposed to conventional
agency ratings can increase the explanatory power of sector-by-rating
spread factors. The idea is to adjust the rating of bonds with a spread
that is too different from the average spread observed within their rating category. For instance, a AA-rated, euro-denominated bond with a
spread equal to 200 bps would be reclassified as having an implied BBB
rating.[4] Credit spreads are computed with respect to the local swap
curve to accommodate for the swap spread factor.

Arbitrage considerations indicate that the spread risk of issues from
the same obligor should be independent of the market. Why then do we
need different credit factors for the different markets? After all, a model
with only one set would be more parsimonious. Empirical evidence simply shows that spread risk is indeed currency dependent.[5]

Volatilities for selected factors are displayed in Exhibit 8.6. Spread
risk in the euro and U.S. markets is on average quite different, particu-

---

[4] For further details on this point, see Ludovic Breger, Lisa Goldberg, and Oren
Cheyette, "Market Implied Ratings," *Risk* (July 2003), pp. S21–S22.

EXHIBIT 8.6   Euro and U.S. Dollar Spread Factor Volatilities as of December 31, 2004

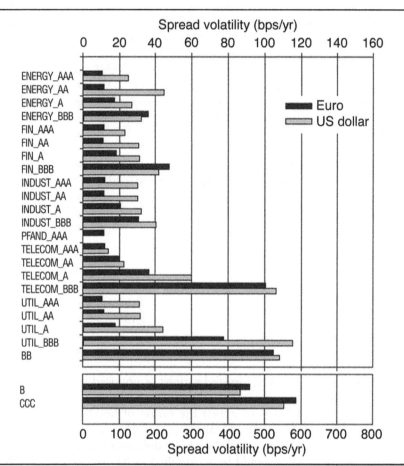

larly for high-grade securities. Looking now in more details, sterling factors tend to be more volatile than euro factors for AAA, AA and A ratings, and less volatile for lower ratings. This is a trend already seen in that confirms that the swap factor would be a simpler but meaningful alternative. Significant differences exist for individual factors that illustrate the need for currency-dependent factors (see for instance the Telecom A and BBB factors). Also note how the high volatilities of the

[5] For further discussion of this issue, see Alec Kercheval, Lisa Goldberg, and Ludovic Breger, "Modeling Credit Risk: Currency Dependence in Global Credit Markets," *Journal of Portfolio Management* (Winter 2003), pp. 90–100.

Energy, Utility and especially Telecom factors reflect the recent turmoil in these industries.

Each corporate bond is only exposed to one of these factors, with an exposure equal to the spread duration. For a fixed rate bond, this will generally be numerically close to the shift factor exposure. Empirically, the spread risk of almost all AAA-, A-, and A-rated bonds will be less than their interest rate risk, and it is only for BBB-rated bonds and in some very specific market sectors such as Energy and Telecoms that spread risk becomes comparable to or exceeds interest rate risk. Spread risk is the dominant source of systematic risk for high-yield instruments.

Emerging Markets Spread Factors

Emerging debt can be issued either in the local currency (i.e., Croatia issuing in kuna) or in any other external currencies (i.e., Mexico issuing in euros, sterlings, or U.S. dollars). These two types of debt do not carry the same risk,[6] and need to be modeled independently. "Internal" risk was discussed in the interest rate and swap-spread risk sections. We will now address external risk.

A rather natural approach is to expose emerging market bonds to a spread factor. The sovereign spread factor turns out to be a poor candidate as the risk of emerging market debt strongly depends on the country of issue. Exhibit 8.7 shows average Argentinean monthly spread changes from June 30, 1999 to June 30, 2002 for U.S. dollar-denominated debt. The collapse of the peso, the illiquidity of the financial system and other economic fallout are all reflected in Argentinean spreads. Chilean spreads remained virtually unaffected despite a strong economic link between the two countries. As a result, any accurate model needs at least one factor per country of issue.

The amount of data available for building emerging market spread factors is unfortunately rather limited. First, there are often at best only a few bonds issued by sovereign issuers in emerging markets. The second problem is that these are mostly U.S. dollar-denominated. Even when some bonds denominated in, say, euro are available, there is generally little returns history. In some cases, a risk model will even be asked to forecast the risk of obligors that just started issuing in a specific currency. Because the risk of an emerging market bond is directly related to the creditworthiness of the sovereign issuer, which is independent of the currency of denomination, we can actually borrow from the history of U.S. dollar-denominated emerging

---

[6] External debt is more risky than internal debt. In principle, a national government can raise taxes or print money to service its internal debt. A shortage of external currency can be more of a problem. This is reflected in the agency credit ratings for emerging market issuers.

EXHIBIT 8.7   Examples of Spread Returns for Two Emerging Markets

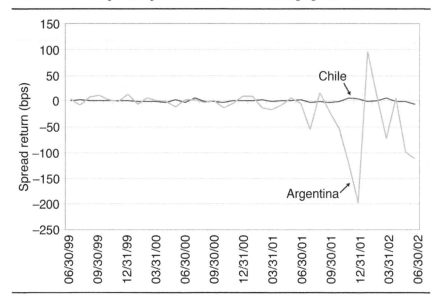

market returns to forecast spread volatilities in any major currencies. Spread return data can be obtained from an index such as JP Morgan Emerging Markets Bond Index Global (EMBIG).

Strictly speaking, these factors are applicable only to sovereign and sovereign agency issuers, based on the inclusion criteria for, say, EMBIG if we happen to use this particular index to estimate emerging markets spread factors. However, most obligors domiciled in these markets carry a risk at least as great as the corresponding sovereign issuer, so that it is reasonable to map the higher-grade corporate issuers to the same factor.

Emerging market spread volatilities are showed in Exhibit 8.8. The spread risk of Latin American and African obligors tend to be above average, Argentina leading the list with spread risk comparable to a B- to CCC-rated corporate. The risk of Asian issuers is on the other hand below average and of the same magnitude as interest rate risk. We clearly observe a rich spectrum of risk characteristics that confirms the need to build a separate factor for each market.

EMPIRICAL CREDIT RISK

The foregoing discussion has focused largely on securities with relatively low credit risk: so-called investment-grade bonds. Their returns

EXHIBIT 8.8   Emerging Market Spread Volatilities as of December 31, 2004

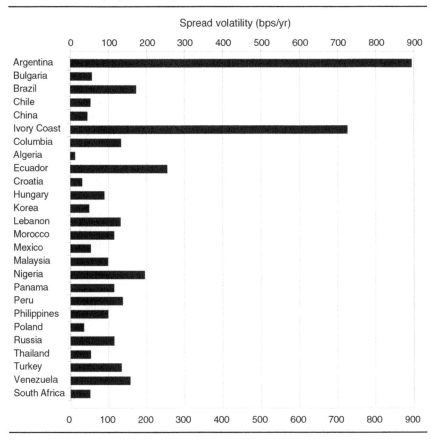

are explained by changes in the term structure and comparatively small spread changes—indeed, above and below investment-grade bonds are empirically distinguished by the fact that interest rate risk is the largest source of risk for the former, while credit risk often becomes the largest source for the latter.

The basis for the risk models discussed earlier is, effectively, the attribution of bond excess return to interest rates and common spreads as

$$r_B^t = r_{GOV}^t + (-D_S)\Delta s_B^t + \varepsilon_B^t \qquad (8.8)$$

This equation explains a bond's return in terms of the return to an equivalent (in the sense of interest rate exposures) government bond, r_{GOV}, a market spread factor return Δs_B, with exposure $-D_S$ (the negative of the spread duration), and a residual ε_B^t. This model does quite well at explaining returns of high quality bonds, with cross-sectional R^2 as high as 80% (meaning that 20% or less of the cross-sectional variance of bond returns is unexplained). But as we move down the credit quality spectrum, the performance of this return model decreases steadily. By the time we get to the low quality end of the high yield universe, the fraction of overall bond return variance explained by equation drops below 20%. In other words, as a group, the returns of CCC-rated bonds are substantially explained neither by interest rate movements nor by sector and rating-based spread changes. Exhibit 8.9 shows this systematic decline in model explanatory power (data points labeled "Equation 8.8").

High-yield bond returns are not, as this might seem to imply, mostly issue specific. They are, however, mostly *issuer* specific. Not surprisingly, returns of bonds of lower credit quality are strongly linked to returns on the issuer's equity. This is certainly what we expect based on quantitative models of capital structure dating back to Merton,[7] where equity is viewed as a call option on the firm's assets with a strike price equal to the firm's liabilities, and a bond is a combination of riskless debt and a short put option on the firm's assets. The Merton model,

EXHIBIT 8.9   Fraction of Bond Return Variance Explained by Equations (8.8), (8.9), and (8.10) Grouped by Whole Credit Rating (Average of S&P and Moody's) for U.S. Dollar Bonds, 1996 to 2003

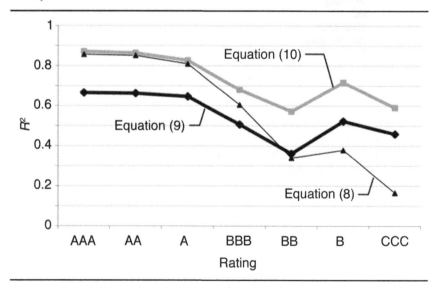

[7] Robert C. Merton, "On the Pricing of Corporate Debt: The Risk Structure of Interest Rates," *Journal of Finance* (May 1974), pp. 449–470.

based on a highly simplified firm capital structure, makes specific predictions for the relation between bond return, interest rate changes, and equity return. The model is too simplified for general application, but it is qualitatively correct: as creditworthiness decreases (default risk increases), a firm's bonds' returns become more correlated with its equity returns, and less correlated with returns of default-free bonds.

We can use the market's assessment of bond credit quality, as measured by its spread over the benchmark, as the input to an empirical model of return linkage. We replace equation (8.8) by an alternative relationship linking the return of a corporate bond to the benchmark return and to the issuer's equity:

$$r_B^t = \beta_{IR} r_{GOV}^t + \beta_E r_E^t + \varepsilon_B^t \qquad (8.9)$$

where r_E^t is the equity return, and β_{IR} and β_E are exposures. Note that the residual ε_B^t will not have the same value when estimating equation (8.9) as in the context of equation (8.8). Comparing the two equations, there are two key differences: (1) the bond's exposure to the benchmark return r_{GOV} is now *scaled* by the exposure β_{IR}, which we expect to be close to one for high quality bonds, and to decrease with decreasing credit quality and (2) the common-factor spread return, which is not issuer-specific, has been replaced by exposure to the issuer's equity return, β_E.

Equation (8.8) serves as the basis for estimating the common factor spread changes Δs_B^t —that is, they are not exogenously specified. By contrast, the explanatory returns in equation (8.9), r_{GOV}^t and r_E^t are both exogenous to the model—that is, they are determined independently of the bond returns r_B^t. Equation (8.8) serves as the basis for estimating the exposures β_{IR} and β_E. The market perception of an issuer's credit quality can be gauged by observing the spreads on the issuer's bonds, so we expect to find that β_{IR} and β_E depend on that spread. A detailed study[8] reveals that β_{IR} is only a function of the bond spread and not of the other bond or equity attributes (as far as we have been able to determine). β_E depends also on the bond duration (higher for longer duration, not surprisingly), and we have preliminary, unpublished evidence of dependence on firm capitalization and the market liquidity of the firm's equity.

For risk prediction purposes, we build a heuristic model of β_E. A simplified version of this model is shown graphically in Exhibit 8.10. As the curve labeled "Equation (8.9)" in Exhibit 8.9 indicates, this model performs significantly better for low quality debt than does equation (8.8). This is not the case for high-grade bonds for which endogenously

---

[8] Oren Cheyette and Tim Tomaich, "Empirical Credit Risk," 2003, Barra Working Paper, http://papers.ssrn.com/sol3/papers.cfm?abstract_id=415080.

EXHIBIT 8.10   Spread Dependence of β_{IR} and β_E for U.S., U.K., and Euro Domestic Corporate Issues, 1996 to 2003

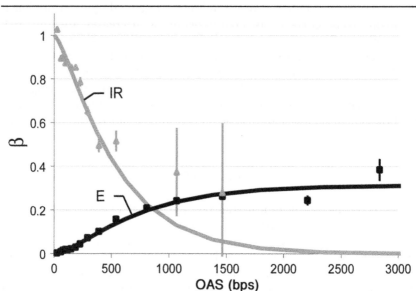

Note: Data points are based on OLS regression on data binned by spread (OAS). Error bars are based on bootstrap analysis. Curves are nonlinear least squares fits of heuristic functional forms to the aggregate data.

determined market spreads evidently provide significant explanatory power. We can gain the benefits of both models by fitting market spread changes to the residuals of equation (8.9). The return attribution equation becomes

$$r_B^t = \beta_{IR} r_{GOV}^t + \beta_E r_E^t + (-D_S)\Delta s_B^t + \eta_B^t \qquad (8.10)$$

where η_B^t is the remaining residual return. The resulting model has R^2's as shown in the upper curve of Exhibit 8.9, performing similarly to the "rates + spreads" model for high-grade credits, and outperforming both models for weaker credits.

For risk forecasting purposes, we replace the interest rate exposures of our original model, such as the shift, twist and butterfly exposures of equation (8.10), with exposures scaled by the factor β_{IR}, bond by bond, and add equity market exposures, scaled by the factor β_E. For example, a Ford Motor bond with a duration of five years and a spread of 180 bps over the government curve, has an estimated β_{IR} of 0.81 and a β_E of

0.036. So the bond's interest rate exposures are reduced from their "naive" values by approximately 19% and it has a small but nonzero exposure to Ford equity. As shown in Panel A of Exhibit 8.11, the empirical credit risk model implies relatively small changes in risk exposures for investment grade portfolios, but a significant decrease in interest rate exposure, and nontrivial equity market exposure for high-yield portfolios (Exhibit 8.11, Panel B). Although the equity market exposure is represented in these figures simply as exposure to a single market factor (equivalent to standard equity β), in practice we drill down to the multiple factor exposures of the equity risk model implied by the exposures to individual firms.

IMPLIED PREPAYMENT RISK

Some markets, in particular the United States, Denmark, and Japan, have securitized mortgages (MBS) that are largely free of credit risk. As with other fixed income securities, interest rate movements affect MBS values through changing discount factors. In addition, because of the borrowers' prepayment options in the underlying loans, MBS have characteristics similar to those of callable bonds. Unlike callable bonds, however, for which the issuers' refinancing strategies are assumed to be close to optimal, mortgage borrowers may be slow to refinance when it would be financially favorable and to prepay (possibly for noneconomic reasons) when it is financially unfavorable. For valuation, this behavior is generally modeled through a prepayment model, giving the projected paydown rate on an MBS as a function of the security's characteristics and the current and past economic state. The need for a prepayment model introduces a new source of potential market risk for MBS investors, attributable to model misspecification, changing expectations, or changing market price of risk for exposure to prepayment uncertainty independent of interest rate risk.

One method for accounting for the valuation impact of prepayment risk and uncertainty is through the use of an implied prepayment model,[9] which uses observed market valuations to infer the market price of prepayment risk or, equivalently, to adjust modeled prepayment rates according to market expectations. The calibration is designed to equalize OASs within a universe of MBS's chosen to broadly sample the range of prepayment exposures.

---

[9] Oren Cheyette, "Implied Prepayments," *Journal of Portfolio Management*, Fall 1996, pp. 107–115.

EXHIBIT 8.11   Empirical Duration Adjustment and Equity Market Exposure

Panel A: Adjusted Portfolio Duration and Equity Market for the Corporate Component of the Investment-Grade Lehman Aggregate U.S. Bond Index in March 2003 and June 2004

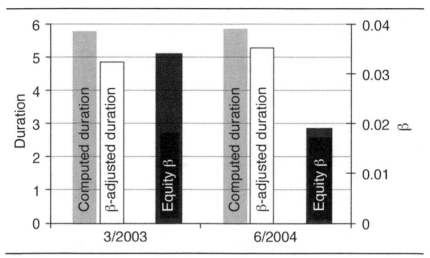

Note: The effect of bond market spread tightening is visible in the substantial decrease in equity exposure over the 15-month interval between the comparison dates.

Panel B: Adjusted Portfolio Duration and Equity Market for the Corporate Component of the Merrill Lynch High Yield Master Index in March 2003 and June 2004

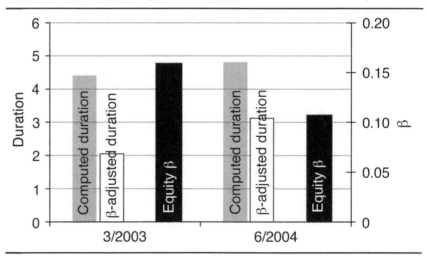

Note: The empirical credit risk model has a much more dramatic effect on the factor exposures for this portfolio than for the investment grade Lehman portfolio.

The actual implementation of an implied prepayment model in the context of a multifactor risk model simply consists in adding one or more factors to capture changes in market prepayment expectations or (equivalently, for pricing) the market price of prepayment risk. In the simplest case we add just one factor for each major program type. The returns to this factor are obtained as follows. First, we obtain OAS returns for an expanded universe of MBS within the same program, including *to-be-announced issues* (TBAs) and more seasoned generics. Then, by regression, we obtain returns for a spread factor and a prepayment factor. Exposures to the spread factor are spread durations. Exposures to the prepayment factor are determined by shocking the overall speed of the prepayment model and observing percentage sensitivity of the valuation model. The sign convention is such that premiums generally have positive prepayment exposure, and discounts negative. Typical prepayment exposures range from −0.01 to 0.06. For example, if an MBS with prepayment exposure of 0.05 were revalued subject to a 10% increase in prepayment speeds, its price would drop by about half a percent (0.05 times 0.1). Prepayment factor volatilities are usually on the order of one, yielding a prepayment risk that can be as large as 6% for highly exposed securities. (To date, we have implemented this model only for the US market.)

The addition of refinancing factors results in a distinct improvement in the explanatory power of the factor model. For example, from 1996 through 2003, a model that includes a prepayment factor captures on average 18% more of the variance of the monthly returns of conventional 30-year issues than a spread-only model,[10] In some months with small spread returns, the prepayment factor by itself accounts for 50% or more of the observed returns variation.

IMPLIED VOLATILITY RISK

The value of instruments with no embedded options is only a function of the current term structure. In contrast, the uncertain character of future interest rates has a significant impact on the analysis of instruments with optionality, for example callable bonds, mortgage passthroughs, or explicit options like caps and swaptions. Such instruments are exposed to the market's varying expectation of the volatility of the term structure, or equivalently, to variations in the market price of risk for interest rate volatility. The basic idea underlying a simple implied volatility risk

---

[10] As measured by the R^2 (coefficient of determination) of the models for a common universe of mortgages.

model is to calibrate a stochastic interest rate model to match observed market prices of interest rate options. The variation over time of the calibration constants then gives rise to implied risk factors.

Consider for instance a *Mean-Reverting Gaussian* (MRG) model, also called the Hull-White model,[11] which assumes that the increment to the short rate dr is a normal random variable with reversion to a long-term mean. In this model, there is a closed form for the price of European swaptions, and given a term structure, we can adjust the model parameters to fit the market prices of swaptions that have a LIBOR at various tenors and expiries. Now fully specified, the MRG model determines the volatility of all forward rates, spot rates, and yields.

Exposure of a security to the implied volatility factor is then determined by numerical differentiation, analogously to duration. In MSCI Barra's model implementation, the factor is the logarithm of the 10-year yield, which has the advantage of capturing volatility of the portion of the term structure relevant for most optionable bonds and MBSs. If we denote the factor by V, the exposure of a security is then the percentage change in price per unit increase of V, that is, per percentage change in 10-year volatility. In practice, one computes this derivative as follows:

$$D_{IV} = \frac{1}{P}\frac{\partial P}{\partial V} = \frac{1}{P}\frac{\partial P}{\partial \sigma}\left(\frac{\partial V}{\partial \sigma}\right)^{-1} \tag{8.11}$$

where P is the security price and σ is the volatility of the short rate.

For MBSs and callable bonds, this exposure is typically negative, because they contain embedded short option positions. Increased volatility (positive factor return) increases the value of the implicit short call position, resulting in a negative asset return. For these securities, exposures generally range between 0 and –0.06. In the major markets, the volatility of V is usually on the order 0.2 yr^{-1}, yielding an implied volatility risk that can reach 1% for bond with at-the-money embedded options.

SPECIFIC RISK

Specific return is residual return not explained by common factors. For securities without significant default risk, this is generally viewed as some form of asset-level basis risk. For bonds, such as, domestic govern-

[11] See for instance Oren Cheyette, "Interest Rate Models," Chapter 1 in Frank J. Fabozzi (ed.), *Interest Rate, Term Structure, and Valuation Modeling* (Hoboken, NJ: John Wiley & Sons, 2002).

ment bonds, this can be straightforwardly forecasted from the standard deviations of the residuals. (More careful modeling would account for liquidity effects such as those affecting benchmark bonds.)

Bonds bearing significant default risk have a firm-specific contribution to their risk. The size of this risk can be forecast reasonably straightforwardly with a reduced form model based on credit migration probabilities. Historical credit migration rates are reported by the major rating agencies, and can be used to estimate future probabilities. Given these probabilities, the specific return variance of the bonds from an issuer can be written as

$$\sigma_{spec}^2 = \sum_j p_{i \to j} [D(s_j - s_i) - r_m]^2 + p_{i \to d}(1 - R - r_m)^2 \qquad (8.12)$$

where

$p_{i \to j}$	=	the one-period probability of transitioning from rating i to j
$p_{i \to d}$	=	the one-period default probability
D	=	the bond's spread duration
s_i	=	the average spread level observed amongst bonds with rating i
R	=	the recovery as a fraction of market value (for which we use a standard 50% estimate)

$$r_m = \left[\sum_j p_{i \to j} D(s_i - s_j) \right] + p_{i \to j}(1 - R)$$

is the mean expected return.

The main premise of this model is that the variance of issuer-specific bond returns arises from credit events. Empirically, credit events of sufficient magnitude to cause one or two whole-step rating changes make the largest contribution to the variance. Note that we are not concerned in this formula with the lag between credit events and agency rating changes. We care only about the average rate of such events, and as long as agency ratings eventually reflect credit quality changes, the reported transition probabilities give good estimates for the rate of these events.

Outside of the U.S. market, there is neither sufficient breadth of credit quality nor sufficient history to reliably estimate the small probabilities of large credit events. However, the main rating firms combine non-U.S. and U.S. data to give global credit migration rates based on historical experience. We use these reported global estimates of $p_{i \to j}$ and $p_{i \to d}$ as the basis for the credit-specific risk model.

The model also requires average spread levels observed within each rating category. Because these levels are market-dependent, so are the credit event risk forecasts. A consequence is that this approach can only be implemented in highly liquid markets, where there are enough corporate to robustly estimate average spread levels—in practice, markets for which we can construct sector-by-rating credit factors.

Given the transition probabilities and spread levels for the different rating classes, the model estimates the distribution of issuer-specific bond returns in a linear approximation from the spread differences and the bond duration. The return variance is then computed from the discrete distribution.

In markets where there is not enough data to construct this detailed model—for example, because there are not enough corporate bonds with reported prices across the full range of ratings—the simplest solution is a linear model of residual spread volatility, increasing as a function of spread level:

$$\sigma_{\text{spec}} = (a + b \cdot s)D \qquad (8.13)$$

where s is the bond's spread and D is the bond's duration. The two constants a and b are fitted in each market using observed residual returns.

CURRENCY RISK

Unhedged currency risk is a potentially large source of risk for global investors. In addition to being a large source of return volatility, currency risk can be highly variable in time. We therefore need a model capable of quickly adjusting to new risk regimes and responsive to new data. Various forms of General Auto-Regressive Conditional Heteroskedastic (GARCH) models have been used to this effect. Such models express current return volatility as a function of previous returns and forecasts. For instance, the GARCH(1,1) model takes the form:

$$\sigma_t^2 = \omega^2 + \beta(\sigma_{t-1}^2 - \omega^2) + \gamma(r_{t-1}^2 - \omega^2) \qquad (8.14)$$

where

σ_t^2 = conditional variance forecast at time t
ω^2 = unconditional variance forecast
β = persistence
γ = sensitivity
r_{t-1} = observed return from $t-1$ to t

The constants β and γ are required to be nonnegative, and in order to avoid runaway behavior, the condition $\beta + \gamma \leq 1$ also must hold. The larger the sensitivity γ, the more responsive the model is to a new large return. Conversely, larger values of the persistence β imply more weight given to a longer history.

Using daily exchange rates insures the convergence of GARCH parameters and minimizes the noise in forecasts based on a short history. To get a monthly risk forecast $\sigma_{t,n}$ from the one-day forecast of equation (8.14), we use the scaling formula, which follows from iteration of equation (8.14):

$$\sigma_{t,n}^2 = n\omega^2 + \frac{1-(\beta+\gamma)^n}{1-(\beta+\gamma)}(\sigma_t^2 + \omega^2) \tag{8.15}$$

where n is the number of business days in a month, typically 20 or 21.

Exhibit 8.12 shows U.S. dollar versus euro returns from 1994 to 2000. Note how volatility forecasts (gray lines) quickly adjust to periods of small or large returns. The overall currency risk is large compared to interest rate risk. From the perspective of a U.S. investor, a German gov-

EXHIBIT 8.12   U.S. Dollar Against Euro Currency Returns and Volatility

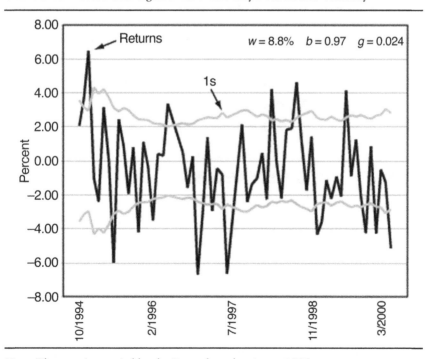

Note: The euro is proxied by the Deutschmark prior to 1999.

ernment bond with a 5-year duration has annualized interest rate risk of about 350 bps and currency risk of about 800 bps. The volatilities of several other currencies from a U.S. dollar perspective are plotted in Exhibit 8.13, and typically range from roughly 6.5% to 10% per year.

GLOBAL MODEL INTEGRATION

Common factors, returns, exposures, and a specific risk model: everything is there except for one last critical ingredient: the covariance matrix. Building a sensible covariance matrix for more than a few factors is a complicated task that involves solving several problems.

Coping with Incomplete Return Series

Factor return series also often have different lengths, with some series starting earlier than others. Return series can also have gaps. A consequence is that the matrix whose elements are given by the standard pairwise formula for the covariance of two series will not, in general, be positive semidefinite, and is, therefore, not a covariance matrix. A standard estimation technique in this situation is the EM algorithm.[12] The

EXHIBIT 8.13   Examples of Foreign Exchange Volatilities on December 31, 2004

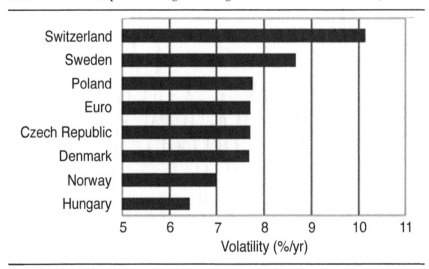

___

[12] Details on the algorithm can be found in. A.P. Dempster, N.M. Laird, and D.B. Rubin, "Maximum Likelihood from Incomplete Data Using the EM Algorithm," *Journal of the Royal Statistical Society* (Series B, Volume 39, 1977), pp. 1–38.

product of this algorithm is a maximum likelihood estimator for the covariance matrix of the observed incomplete data.

Global Integration

Barra's latest global fixed income model includes nearly 500 factors, yielding over 120,000 covariances. (This does not include the covariances of fixed income factors with equity factors, which are relevant for modeling high-yield bonds as described earlier.) In many cases, the factor returns series include no more than 30 to 40 periods. With such a small sample size compared to the number of factors, we have a severely underdetermined problem and are virtually assured that the covariance forecasts will show a large degree of spurious linear dependence among the factors. One consequence is that it becomes possible to create portfolios with artificially low risk forecasts (for example, by use of an optimizer). The structure of these portfolios would be peculiar—e.g., they might be overweight Japanese banks, apparently hedged by an underweight in euro industrial and telecom.

Reducing the number of factors would compromise the accuracy of our risk analysis at the local level. However, we have seen for instance that the higher grade developed credit markets are largely independent so that we do not need all cross-currency covariances to describe the coupling between these two markets. Using our knowledge of the market in a more systematic fashion could go a long way in reducing the spurious correlations amongst factors.

The structured approach presented in Stefek et al. is one solution to this problem.[13] In this method, factor returns are decomposed into a global component and a purely local component, exactly as we already decomposed asset returns into systematic and nonsystematic returns. For instance, in the U.S. dollar market we can write

$$f_{USD} = X_{f_{USD}} \cdot g_{USD} + \varepsilon_{f_{USD}} \qquad (8.16)$$

where

f_{USD} = the vector of factor returns for the U.S. market
g_{USD} = the vector of global factor returns for the U.S. market
X_{USD} = the exposure matrix of the U.S. local factors to the U.S. global factors
ε_{USD} = the vector of residual factor returns not explained by global factors or purely local returns.

---

[13] Stefek et al., "The Barra Integrated Model," Barra Research Insight, 2002.

Equation (8.16) can be easily extended to all the original factors in the model. Because purely local returns are now by construction uncorrelated across markets and also uncorrelated with global returns, the covariance matrix can then be written as

$$F = XG^T X + \Lambda \qquad (8.17)$$

where

G = the covariance matrix of global factors
X = the exposure matrix of the local factor to the global factors
Λ = the covariance matrix of local factors

The choice of global factors is based on econometric considerations. For instance, there is a strong link between interest rates across currencies, especially for the major markets. Given that interest rate risk is a critical component of fixed income risk, we want to insure that correlations between interest rate factors in different market are modeled as accurately as possible. This can be achieved by making the shifts, twists, and butterflies, and implied volatility factors global. We also found that to a large degree, credit factors behave independently of factors in other markets. As a result, we know that we gain very little by choosing more than a few global credit factors in each developed market. However, the link between major credit markets appears to become stronger as credit quality decreases. In choosing global factors, we also want enough granularity to capture such nuances. One possible approach is to create two global average investment-grade spread factors as well as an average high-yield spread factor in markets where there is a reasonably developed speculative debt.

Global factors could typically include:

- The shift, twist, and butterfly and implied volatility factors.
- The swap spread factors
- AAA/AA and A/BBB average high-grade credit spread factors in the Eurozone, United States, United Kingdom, Japan, Canada, and Switzerland
- Average high-yield credit spread factors in the Eurozone, United States, United Kingdom, and Japan
- An average emerging market spread

Unfortunately, we cannot stop there and use equation (8.17). The benefit of using global factors is that they help compute cross-market terms and constitute the skeleton of the matrix. The drawback is a loss of resolution at the local level. A solution to this problem is to replace local blocks by a local covariance matrix computed using the EM algorithm and the full set of original local factors, or "scale" local covariance blocks.[14]

At this point, we have a method for building a model that reconciles two conflicting goals, that is, provide a wide coverage of markets and securities while permitting an accurate and insightful analysis, particularly at the local level.

THE MODEL IN ACTION

The risk characteristics of several typical indices are presented in Exhibit 8.14. We find again that currency risk dominates by far local risk. U.S. investors holding an unhedged portfolio of yen-denominated bonds incur a currency risk that is about four times larger that the interest rate risk. For investment-grade portfolios, interest rate risk represents most of the local risk. It is only for high-yield and emerging market portfolios that spread risk contributes a significant portion of local risk. In fact, for an index such as JP Morgan EMBIG, spread is about the same as interest rate risk. Local risk is the smallest in the yen market and the largest in the U.S. dollar market owing to the relatively large U.S. interest rate factor volatilities (see Exhibit 8.2).

For diversified portfolios in which bonds with embedded options (including mortgages) represent only a small fraction of the total value, there is very little volatility and prepayment risk. However, such risks can become more significant in portfolios of mortgages and can even exceed spread risk, as in the U.S. mortgage index as shown in the exhibit.

SUMMARY

Although the models and methodologies that we have described in this chapter are for the most part relatively standard, two are more recent additions to the realm of risk management. The first is the inclusion of equity exposure in the modeling of fixed income risk. The second is a structural method to aggregate single-market models into a global risk model.

Adequately measuring risk requires sophisticated methods and considerable care. A good risk model should, at a minimum, provide a broad coverage without sacrificing accuracy, retain details but remain parsimonious and be responsive to market changes. The sources of risk are many, and their respective importance depends on the asset. Certainly, there is no shortage of challenges.

---

[14] Stefek *et al.*, "The Barra Integrated Model."

EXHIBIT 8.14 Annualized Risk for Different Indices on December 31, 2004

Portfolio	Total Risk	Interest Rate Risk	Spread Risk	Currency Risk	Other Risk
Merrill Lynch U.S. Domestic Master	4.23%	4.40%	0.61%	N/A	Prepayment 0.0023% Volatility 0.0024%
Merrill Lynch U.S. MBS	3.62%	3.49%	1.16%	N/A	Prepayment 0.32% Volatility 0.48%
Merrill Lynch EMU Broad Market Index	9.93%	3.25%	0.22%	8.50%	
NIKKO BPI	10.50%	2.55%	0.20%	10.36%	
JP Morgan EMBIG	8.34%	6.66%	5.64%	N/A	

Note: The authors thank Avaneesh Krishnamoorthy for assistance with the risk computation.

CHAPTER 9

Multifactor Risk Models and Their Applications*

Lev Dynkin, Ph.D.
Managing Director
Lehman Brothers

Jay Hyman, Ph.D.
Senior Vice President
Lehman Brothers

The classical definition of investment risk is uncertainty of returns, measured by their volatility. Investments with greater risk are expected to earn greater returns than less risky alternatives. Asset allocation models help investors choose the asset mix with the highest expected return given their risk constraints (for example, avoid a loss of more than 2% per year in a given portfolio).

Once investors have selected a desired asset mix, they often enlist specialized asset managers to implement their investment goals. The performance of the portfolio is usually compared with a benchmark that reflects the investor's asset selection decision. From the perspective of most asset managers, risk is defined by performance relative to the benchmark rather than by absolute return. In this sense, the least-risky

* Wei Wu coauthored the original version of the paper from which this chapter is derived. The authors would like to thank Jack Malvey for his substantial contribution to this paper and Ravi Mattu, George Williams, Ivan Gruhl, Amitabh Arora, Vadim Konstantinovsky, Peter Lindner, and Jonathan Carmel for their valuable comments.

195

investment portfolio is one that replicates the benchmark. Any portfolio deviation from the benchmark entails some risk. For example, to the manager of a bond fund benchmarked against the High Yield Index, investing 100% in U.S. Treasuries would involve a much greater long-term risk than investing 100% in high-yield corporate bonds. In other words, benchmark risk belongs to the plan sponsor, while the asset manager bears the risk of deviating from the benchmark.

In this chapter we discuss a risk model developed at Lehman Brothers that focuses on portfolio risk relative to a benchmark.[1] The risk model is designed for use by fixed income portfolio managers benchmarked against broad market indices.

QUANTIFYING RISK

Given our premise that the least-risky portfolio is the one that exactly replicates the benchmark, we proceed to compare the composition of a fixed income portfolio to that of its benchmark. Are they similar in exposures to changes in the term structure of interest rates, in allocations to different asset classes within the benchmark, and in allocations to different quality ratings? Such portfolio versus benchmark comparisons form the foundation for modern fixed income portfolio management. Techniques such as "stratified sampling" or "cell-matching" have been used to construct portfolios that are similar to their benchmarks in many components (i.e., duration, quality, etc.). However, these techniques can not answer quantitative questions concerning portfolio risk. How much risk is there? Is portfolio A more or less risky than portfolio B? Will a given transaction increase or decrease risk? To best decrease risk relative to the benchmark, should the focus be on better aligning term-structure exposures or sector allocations? How do we weigh these different types of risk against each other? What actions can be taken to mitigate the overall risk exposure? Any quantitative model of risk must account for the magnitude of a particular event as well as its likelihood. When multiple risks are modeled simultaneously, the issue of correlation also must be addressed.

The risk model we present in this article provides quantitative answers to such questions. This multifactor model compares portfolio and benchmark exposures along all dimensions of risk, such as yield curve movement, changes in sector spreads, and changes in implied vol-

---

[1] Since the time of the preparation of this chapter, the Lehman Brothers risk model has been significantly updated, following the general approach outlined in this chapter.

atility. Exposures to each *risk factor* are calculated on a bond-by-bond basis and aggregated to obtain the exposures of the portfolio and the benchmark.

Tracking error, which quantifies the risk of performance difference (projected standard deviation of the return difference) between the portfolio and the benchmark, is projected based on the differences in risk factor exposures. This calculation of overall risk incorporates historical information about the volatility of each risk factor and the correlations among them. The volatilities and correlations of all the risk factors are stored in a covariance matrix, which is calibrated based on monthly returns of individual bonds in the Lehman Brothers Aggregate Index dating back to 1987. The model is updated monthly with historical information. The choice of risk factors has been reviewed periodically since the model's introduction in 1990. The model covers U.S. dollar-denominated securities in most Lehman Brothers domestic fixed rate bond indices (Aggregate, High Yield, Eurobond). The effect of nonindex securities on portfolio risk is measured by mapping onto index risk categories. The net effect of all risk factors is known as *systematic risk*.

The model is based on historical returns of individual securities and its risk projections are a function of portfolio and benchmark positions in individual securities. Instead of deriving risk factor realizations from changes in market averages (such as a Treasury curve spline, sector spread changes, etc.) the model derives them from historical returns of securities in Lehman Indices. While this approach is much more data and labor intensive, it allows us to quantify residual return volatility of each security after all systematic risk factors have been applied. As a result, we can measure nonsystematic risk of a portfolio relative to the benchmark based on differences in their diversification. This form of risk, also known as concentration risk or security-specific risk, is the result of a portfolio's exposure to individual bonds or issuers. Nonsystematic risk can represent a significant portion of the overall risk, particularly for portfolios containing relatively few securities, even for assets without any credit risk.

PORTFOLIO MANAGEMENT WITH THE RISK MODEL

Passive portfolio managers, or "indexers," seek to replicate the returns of a broad market index. They can use the risk model to help keep the portfolio closely aligned with the index along all risk dimensions. Active portfolio managers attempt to outperform the benchmark by positioning the portfolio to capitalize on market views. They can use the risk model to quantify the risk entailed in a particular portfolio position relative to the market. This information is often incorporated into the performance review process, where returns achieved by a particular strategy are weighed against the risk taken. Enhanced indexers express views against the index, but limit the amount of risk assumed. They can use the model to keep risk within acceptable limits and to highlight unanticipated market exposures that might arise as the portfolio and index change over time. These management styles can be associated with approximate ranges of tracking errors. Passive managers typically seek tracking errors of 5 to 25 basis points per year. Tracking errors for enhanced indexers range from 25 to 75 basis points, and those of active managers are even higher.

WHY A MULTIFACTOR MODEL?

With the abundance of data available in today's marketplace, an asset manager might be tempted to build a risk model directly from the historical return characteristics of individual securities. The standard deviation of a security's return in the upcoming period can be projected to match its past volatility; the correlation between any two securities can be determined from their historical performance. Despite the simplicity of this scheme, the multifactor approach has several important advantages. First of all, the number of risk factors in the model is much smaller than the number of securities in a typical investment universe. This greatly reduces the matrix operations needed to calculate portfolio risk. This increases the speed of computation (which is becoming less important with gains in processing power) and, more importantly, improves the numerical stability of the calculations. A large covariance matrix of individual security volatilities and correlations is likely to cause numerical instability. This is especially true in the fixed income world, where returns of many securities are very highly correlated. Risk factors may also exhibit moderately high correlations with each other, but much less so than for individual securities.[2]

A more fundamental problem with relying on individual security data is that not all securities can be modeled adequately in this way. For illiquid securities, pricing histories are either unavailable or unreliable; for new securities, histories do not exist. For still other securities, there may be plenty of reliable historical data, but changes in security characteristics make this data irrelevant to future results. For instance, a ratings upgrade of an issuer would make future returns less volatile than those

---

[2] Some practitioners insist on a set of risk factors that are uncorrelated to each other. We have found it more useful to select risk factors that are intuitively clear to investors, even at the expense of allowing positive correlations among the factors.

of the past. A change in interest rates can significantly alter the effective duration of a callable bond. As any bond ages, its duration shortens, making its price less sensitive to interest rates. A multifactor model estimates the risk from owning a particular bond based not on the historical performance of that bond, but on historical returns of all bonds with characteristics similar to those currently pertaining to the bond.

In this chapter, we present the risk model by way of example. In each of the following sections, a numerical example of the model's application motivates the discussion of a particular feature.

THE RISK REPORT

For illustration, we apply the risk model to a sample portfolio of 57 bonds benchmarked against the Lehman Brothers Aggregate Index. The model produces two important outputs: a tracking error summary report and a set of risk sensitivities reports that compare the portfolio composition to that of the benchmark. These various comparative reports form the basis of our risk analysis, by identifying structural differences between the two. Of themselves, however, they fail to quantify the risk due to these mismatches. The model's anchor is, therefore, the tracking error report, which quantifies the risks associated with each cross-sectional comparison. Taken together, the various reports produced by the model provide a complete understanding of the risk of this portfolio versus its benchmark.

From the overall statistical summary shown in Exhibit 9.1, it can be seen that the portfolio has a significant term-structure exposure, as its duration (4.82) is longer than that of the benchmark (4.29). In addition, the portfolio is overexposed to corporate bonds and under exposed to Treasuries. We see this explicitly later in the sector report; it is reflected in the statistics in Exhibit 9.1 by a higher average yield and coupon. The overall annualized tracking error, shown at the bottom of the statistics report, is 52 bps. Tracking error is defined as one standard deviation of the difference between the portfolio and benchmark annualized returns. In simple terms, this means that with a probability of about 68%, the portfolio return over the next year will be within ±52 bps of the benchmark return.[3]

---

[3] This interpretation requires several simplifying assumptions. The 68% confidence interval assumes that returns are normally distributed, which may not be the case. Second, this presentation ignores differences in the expected returns of portfolio and benchmark (due, for example, to a higher portfolio yield). Strictly speaking, the confidence interval should be drawn around the expected outperformance.

EXHIBIT 9.1   Top-Level Statistics Comparison
Sample Portfolio versus Aggregate Index, September 30, 1998

	Portfolio	Benchmark
Number of Issues	57	6,932
Average Maturity/Average Life (years)	9.57	8.47
Internal Rate of Return (%)	5.76	5.54
Average Yield to Maturity (%)	5.59	5.46
Average Yield to Worst (%)	5.53	5.37
Average Option-Adjusted Convexity	0.04	−0.22
Average OAS to Maturity (bps)	74	61
Average OAS to Worst (bps)	74	61
Portfolio Mod. Adjusted Duration	4.82	4.29
Portfolio Average Price	108.45	107.70
Portfolio Average Coupon (%)	7.33	6.98
Risk Characteristics		
Estimated Total Tracking Error (bps/year)	52	
Portfolio Beta	1.05	

Sources of Systematic Tracking Error

What are the main sources of this tracking error? The model identifies
market forces influencing all securities in a certain category as *systematic risk factors*. Exhibit 9.2 divides the tracking error into components
corresponding to different categories of risk. Looking down the first column, we see that the largest sources of systematic tracking error
between this portfolio and its benchmark are the differences in sensitivity to term structure movements (36.3 bps) and to changes in credit
spreads by sector (32 bps) and quality (14.7 bps). The components of
systematic tracking error correspond directly to the groups of risk factors. A detailed report of the differences in portfolio and benchmark
exposures (sensitivities) to the relevant set of risk factors illustrates the
origin of each component of systematic risk.

Sensitivities to risk factors are called *factor loadings*. They are
expressed in units that depend on the definition of each particular risk
factor. For example, for risk factors representing volatility of corporate
spreads, factor loadings are given by spread durations; for risk factors
measuring volatility of prepayment speed (in units of PSA), factor loadings are given by "PSA Duration." The factor loadings of a portfolio or
an index are calculated as a market-value weighted average over all con-

stituent securities. Differences between portfolio and benchmark factor loadings form a vector of *active portfolio exposures*. A quick comparison of the magnitudes of the different components of tracking error highlights the most significant mismatches.

EXHIBIT 9.2   Tracking Error Breakdown for Sample Portfolio
Sample Portfolio versus Aggregate Index, September 30, 1998

	Tracking Error (bps/Year)		
	Isolated	Cumulative	Change in Cumulative[a]
Tracking Error Term Structure	36.3	36.3	36.3
Nonterm Structure	39.5		
Tracking Error Sector	32.0	38.3	2.0
Tracking Error Quality	14.7	44.1	5.8
Tracking Error Optionality	1.6	44.0	−0.1
Tracking Error Coupon	3.2	45.5	1.5
Tracking Error MBS Sector	4.9	43.8	−1.7
Tracking Error MBS Volatility	7.2	44.5	0.7
Tracking Error MBS Prepayment	2.5	45.0	0.4
Total Systematic Tracking Error			45.0
Nonsystematic Tracking Error			
Issuer specific	25.9		
Issue specific	26.4		
Total	26.1		
Total Tracking Error			52

	Systematic	Nonsystematic	Total
Benchmark Return Standard Deviation	417	4	417
Portfolio Return Standard Deviation	440	27	440

[a] Isolated Tracking Error is the projected deviation between the portfolio and benchmark return due to a single category of systematic risk. Cumulative Tracking Error shows the combined effect of all risk categories from the first one in the table to the current one.

EXHIBIT 9.3   Term Structure Report
Sample Portfolio versus Aggregate Index, September 30, 1998

	Cash Flows		
Year	Portfolio	Benchmark	Difference
0.00	1.45%	1.85%	−0.40%
0.25	3.89	4.25	−0.36
0.50	4.69	4.25	0.45
0.75	4.34	3.76	0.58
1.00	8.90	7.37	1.53
1.50	7.47	10.29	−2.82
2.00	10.43	8.09	2.34
2.50	8.63	6.42	2.20
3.00	4.28	5.50	−1.23
3.50	3.90	4.81	−0.92
4.00	6.74	7.19	−0.46
5.00	6.13	6.96	−0.83
6.00	3.63	4.67	−1.04
7.00	5.77	7.84	−2.07
10.00	7.16	7.37	−0.21
15.00	4.63	3.88	0.75
20.00	3.52	3.04	0.48
25.00	3.18	1.73	1.45
30.00	1.22	0.68	0.54
40.00	0.08	0.07	0.01

Because the largest component of tracking error is due to term structure, let us examine the term structure risk in our example. Risk factors associated with term structure movements are represented by the fixed set of points on the theoretical Treasury spot curve shown in Exhibit 9.3. Each of these risk factors exhibits a certain historical return volatility. The extent to which the portfolio and the benchmark returns are affected by this volatility is measured by factor loadings (exposures). These exposures are computed as percentages of the total present value of the portfolio and benchmark cash flows allocated to each point on the curve. The risk of the portfolio performing differently from the benchmark due to term structure movements is due to the differences in the portfolio and benchmark exposures to these risk factors and to their volatilities and correlations. Exhibit 9.3 compares the term structure exposures of the portfolio and benchmark for our example. The Difference column shows the portfolio to be overweighted in the 2-year section of the curve, underweighted in the 3- to 10-year range, and overweighted at the long end. This makes the portfolio longer than the benchmark and more barbelled.

The tracking error is calculated from this vector of differences between portfolio and benchmark exposures. However, mismatches at different points are not treated equally. Exposures to factors with higher volatilities have a larger effect on tracking error. In this example, the risk exposure with the largest contribution to tracking error is the overweight of 1.45% to the 25-year point on the curve. While other vertices have larger mismatches (e.g., –2.07% at 7 years), their overall effect on risk is not as strong because the longer duration of a 25-year zero causes it to have a higher return volatility. It should also be noted that the risk caused by overweighting one segment of the yield curve can sometimes be offset by underweighting another. Exhibit 9.3 shows the portfolio to be underexposed to the 1.50-year point on the yield curve by –2.82% and overexposed to the 2.00-year point on the curve by +2.34%. Those are largely offsetting positions in terms of risk because these two adjacent points on the curve are highly correlated and almost always move together. To eliminate completely the tracking error due to term structure, differences in exposures to each term structure risk factor need to be reduced to zero. To lower term structure risk, it is most important to focus first on reducing exposures at the long end of the curve, particularly those that are not offset by opposing positions in nearby points.

The tracking error due to sector exposures is explained by the detailed sector report shown in Exhibit 9.4. This report shows the sector allocations of the portfolio and the benchmark in two ways. In addition to reporting the percentage of market value allocated to each sector, it shows the contribution of each sector to the overall spread duration.[4] These contributions are computed as the product of the percentage allocations to a sector and the market-weighted average spread duration of the holdings in that sector. Contributions to spread duration (factor loadings) measure the sensitivity of return to systematic changes in particular sector spreads (risk factors) and are a better measure of risk than simple market allocations. The rightmost column in this report, the difference between portfolio and benchmark contributions to spread duration in each sector, is the exposure vector that is used to

---

[4] Just as traditional duration can be defined as the sensitivity of bond price to a change in yield, spread duration is defined as the sensitivity of bond price to a change in spread. While this distinction is largely academic for bullet bonds, it can be significant for other securities, such as bonds with embedded options and floating-rate securities. The sensitivity to spread change is the correct measure of sector risk.

EXHIBIT 9.4 Detailed Sector Report
Sample Portfolio versus Aggregate Index, September 30, 1998

Detailed Sector	Portfolio			Benchmark			Difference	
	% of Portf.	Adj. Dur.	Contrib. to Adj. Dur.	% of Portf.	Adj. Dur.	Contrib. to Adj. Dur.	% of Portf.	Contrib. to Adj. Dur.
Treasury								
Coupon	27.09	5.37	1.45	39.82	5.58	2.22	−12.73	−0.77
Strip	0.00	0.00	0.00	0.00	0.00	0.00	0.00	0.00
Agencies								
FNMA	4.13	3.40	0.14	3.56	3.44	0.12	0.57	0.02
FHLB	0.00	0.00	0.00	1.21	2.32	0.03	−1.21	−0.03
FHLMC	0.00	0.00	0.00	0.91	3.24	0.03	−0.91	−0.03
REFCORP	3.51	11.22	0.39	0.83	12.18	0.10	2.68	0.29
Other Agencies	0.00	0.00	0.00	1.31	5.58	0.07	−1.31	−0.07
Financial Institutions								
Banking	1.91	5.31	0.10	2.02	5.55	0.11	−0.11	−0.01
Brokerage	1.35	3.52	0.05	0.81	4.14	0.03	0.53	0.01
Financial Cos.	1.88	2.92	0.06	2.11	3.78	0.08	−0.23	−0.02
Insurance	0.00	0.00	0.00	0.52	7.47	0.04	−0.52	−0.04
Other	0.00	0.00	0.00	0.28	5.76	0.02	−0.28	−0.02
Industrials								
Basic	0.63	6.68	0.04	0.89	6.39	0.06	−0.26	−0.01
Capital Goods	4.43	5.35	0.24	1.16	6.94	0.08	3.26	0.16
Consumer Cycl.	2.01	8.37	0.17	2.28	7.10	0.16	−0.27	0.01
Consum. Non-cycl.	8.88	12.54	1.11	1.66	6.84	0.11	7.22	1.00
Energy	1.50	6.82	0.10	0.69	6.89	0.05	0.81	0.05
Technology	1.55	1.58	0.02	0.42	7.39	0.03	1.13	−0.01
Transportation	0.71	12.22	0.09	0.57	7.41	0.04	0.14	0.04
Utilities								
Electric	0.47	3.36	0.02	1.39	5.02	0.07	−0.93	−0.05
Telephone	9.18	2.08	0.19	1.54	6.58	0.10	7.64	0.09
Natural Gas	0.80	5.53	0.04	0.49	6.50	0.03	0.31	0.01
Water	0.00	0.00	0.00	0.00	0.00	0.00	0.00	0.00
Yankee								
Canadians	1.45	7.87	0.11	1.06	6.67	0.07	0.38	0.04
Corporates	0.49	3.34	0.02	1.79	6.06	0.11	−1.30	−0.09
Supranational	1.00	6.76	0.07	0.38	6.33	0.02	0.62	0.04
Sovereigns	0.00	0.00	0.00	0.66	5.95	0.04	−0.66	−0.04
Hypothetical	0.00	0.00	0.00	0.00	0.00	0.00	0.00	0.00
Cash	0.00	0.00	0.00	0.00	0.00	0.00	0.00	0.00

EXHIBIT 9.4   (Continued)

Detailed Sector	Portfolio % of Portf.	Portfolio Adj. Dur.	Portfolio Contrib. to Adj. Dur.	Benchmark % of Portf.	Benchmark Adj. Dur.	Benchmark Contrib. to Adj. Dur.	Difference % of Portf.	Difference Contrib. to Adj. Dur.
Mortgage								
Conventnl. 30 yr.	12.96	1.52	0.20	16.60	1.42	0.24	−3.64	−0.04
GNMA 30 yr.	7.53	1.23	0.09	7.70	1.12	0.09	−0.16	0.01
MBS 15 yr.	3.52	1.95	0.07	5.59	1.63	0.09	−2.06	−0.02
Balloons	3.03	1.69	0.05	0.78	1.02	0.01	2.25	0.04
OTM	0.00	0.00	0.00	0.00	0.00	0.00	0.00	0.00
European & International								
Eurobonds	0.00	0.00	0.00	0.00	0.00	0.00	0.00	0.00
International	0.00	0.00	0.00	0.00	0.00	0.00	0.00	0.00
Asset Backed	0.00	0.00	0.00	0.96	3.14	0.03	−0.96	−0.03
CMO	0.00	0.00	0.00	0.00	0.00	0.00	0.00	0.00
Other	0.00	0.00	0.00	0.00	0.00	0.00	0.00	0.00
Totals	100.00		4.82	100.00		4.29	0.00	0.54

compute tracking error due to sector. A quick look down this column shows that the largest exposures in our example are an underweight of 0.77 years to Treasuries and an overweight of 1.00 years to consumer noncyclicals in the industrial sector. (The fine-grained breakdown of the corporate market into industry groups corresponds to the second tier of the Lehman Brothers hierarchical industry classification scheme.) Note that the units of risk factors and factor loadings for sector risk differ from those used to model the term structure risk.

The analysis of credit quality risk shown in Exhibit 9.5 follows the same approach. Portfolio and benchmark allocations to different credit rating levels are compared in terms of contributions to spread duration. Once again we see the effect of the overweighting of corporates: There is an overweight of 0.80 years to single As and an underweight of −0.57 years in AAAs (U.S. government debt). The risk represented by tracking error due to quality corresponds to a systematic widening or tightening of spreads for a particular credit rating, uniformly across all industry groups.

As we saw in Exhibit 9.2, the largest sources of systematic risk in our sample portfolio are term structure, sector, and quality. We have therefore directed our attention first to the reports that address these risk components; we will return to them later. Next we examine the reports explaining optionality risk and mortgage risk, even though these risks do not contribute significantly to the risk of this particular portfolio.

Exhibit 9.6 shows the optionality report. Several different measures are used to analyze portfolio and benchmark exposures to changes in

EXHIBIT 9.5 Quality Report
Sample Portfolio versus Aggregate Index, September 30, 1998

	Portfolio			Benchmark			Difference	
Quality	% of Portf.	Adj. Dur.	Cntrb. to Adj. Dur.	% of Portf.	Adj. Dur.	Cntrb. to Adj. Dur.	% of Portf.	Cntrb. to Adj. Dur.
Aaa+	34.72	5.72	1.99	47.32	5.41	2.56	−12.60	−0.57
MBS	27.04	1.51	0.41	30.67	1.37	0.42	−3.62	−0.01
Aaa	1.00	6.76	0.07	2.33	4.84	0.11	−1.33	−0.05
Aa	5.54	5.67	0.31	4.19	5.32	0.22	1.35	0.09
A	17.82	7.65	1.36	9.09	6.23	0.57	8.73	0.80
Baa	13.89	4.92	0.68	6.42	6.28	0.40	7.47	0.28
Ba	0.00	0.00	0.00	0.00	0.00	0.00	0.00	0.00
B	0.00	0.00	0.00	0.00	0.00	0.00	0.00	0.00
Caa	0.00	0.00	0.00	0.00	0.00	0.00	0.00	0.00
Ca or lower	0.00	0.00	0.00	0.00	0.00	0.00	0.00	0.00
NR	0.00	0.00	0.00	0.00	0.00	0.00	0.00	0.00
Totals	100.00		4.82	100.00		4.29	0.00	0.54

the value of embedded options. For callable and putable bonds, the difference between a bond's static duration[5] and its option-adjusted duration, known as *reduction due to call*, gives one measure of the effect of optionality on pricing. This reduction is positive for bonds trading to maturity and negative for bonds trading to a call. These two categories of bonds are represented by separate risk factors. The exposures of the portfolio and benchmark to this reduction, divided into option categories, constitute one set of factor loadings due to optionality. The model also looks at option delta and gamma, the first and second derivatives of option price with respect to security price.

The risks particular to mortgage-backed securities consist of spread risk, prepayment risk, and convexity risk. The underpinnings for MBS sector-spread risk, like those for corporate sectors, are found in the detailed sector report shown in Exhibit 9.4. Mortgage-backed securities are divided into four broad sectors based on a combination of originating agency and product: conventional 30-year; GNMA 30-year; all 15-year; and all balloons. The contributions of these four sectors to the

[5] *Static duration* refers to the traditional duration of the bond assuming a fixed set of cash flows. Depending on how the bond is trading, these will be the bond's natural cash flows either to maturity or to the most likely option redemption date.

EXHIBIT 9.6 Optionality Report: Sample Portfolio versus Aggregate Index, September 30, 1998

Optionality	% of Portfolio	Duration	Contrib. to Duration	Adjusted Duration	Contrib. to Adj. Dur.	Reduction Due to Call
Portfolio						
Bullet	63.95	5.76	3.68	5.76	3.68	0.00
Callable Traded to Maturity	4.74	10.96	0.52	10.96	0.52	0.00
Callable Traded to Call	4.26	8.43	0.36	4.97	0.21	0.15
Putable Traded to Maturity	0.00	0.00	0.00	0.00	0.00	0.00
Putable Traded to Put	0.00	0.00	0.00	0.00	0.00	0.00
MBS	27.04	3.28	0.89	1.51	0.41	0.48
ABS	0.00	0.00	0.00	0.00	0.00	0.00
CMO	0.00	0.00	0.00	0.00	0.00	0.00
Others	0.00	0.00	0.00	0.00	0.00	0.00
Totals	100.00		5.45		4.82	0.63
Benchmark						
Bullet	57.53	5.70	3.28	5.70	3.28	0.00
Callable Traded to Maturity	2.66	9.06	0.24	8.50	0.23	0.01
Callable Traded to Call	7.06	6.93	0.49	3.56	0.25	0.24
Putable Traded to Maturity	0.35	11.27	0.04	9.64	0.03	0.01
Putable Traded to Put	0.78	11.59	0.09	5.77	0.04	0.05
MBS	30.67	3.25	1.00	1.37	0.42	0.58
ABS	0.96	3.14	0.03	3.14	0.03	0.00
CMO	0.00	0.00	0.00	0.00	0.00	0.00
Others	0.00	0.00	0.00	0.00	0.00	0.00
Totals	100.00		5.17		4.29	0.88

EXHIBIT 9.6 (Continued)

Option Delta Analysis

Option Delta	Portfolio			Benchmark			Difference	
	% of Portf.	Delta	Cntrb. to Delta	% of Portf.	Delta	Cntrb. to Delta	% of Portf.	Cntrb. to Delta
Bullet	63.95	0.000	0.000	57.53	0.000	0.000	6.43	0.000
Callable Traded to Matur.	4.74	0.000	0.000	2.66	0.057	0.002	2.08	-0.002
Callable Traded to Call	4.26	0.474	0.020	7.06	0.584	0.041	-2.80	-0.021
Putable Traded to Matur.	0.00	0.000	0.000	0.35	0.129	0.001	-0.35	-0.001
Putable Traded to Put	0.00	0.000	0.000	0.78	0.507	0.004	-0.78	-0.004
Totals	72.96		0.020	68.38		0.047	4.58	-0.027

Option Gamma Analysis

Option Gamma	Portfolio			Benchmark			Difference	
	% of Portf.	Delta	Cntrb. to Delta	% of Portf.	Delta	Cntrb. to Delta	% of Portf.	Cntrb. to Delta
Bullet	63.95	0.0000	0.0000	57.53	0.0000	0.0000	6.43	0.0000
Callable Traded to Matur.	4.74	0.0000	0.0000	2.66	0.0024	0.0001	2.08	-0.0001
Callable Traded to Call	4.26	0.0059	0.0002	7.06	0.0125	0.0009	-2.80	-0.0006
Putable Traded to Matur.	0.00	0.0000	0.0000	0.35	-0.0029	-0.0000	-0.35	0.0000
Putable Traded to Put	0.00	0.0000	0.0000	0.78	-0.0008	-0.0000	-0.78	0.0000
Totals	72.96		0.0002	68.38		0.0009	4.58	-0.0007

portfolio and benchmark spread durations form the factor loadings for mortgage sector risk. Exposures to prepayments are shown in Exhibit 9.7. This group of risk factors corresponds to systematic changes in prepayment speeds by sector. Thus, the factor loadings represent the sensitivities of mortgage prices to changes in prepayment speeds (PSA durations). Premium mortgages show negative prepayment sensitivities (i.e., prices decrease with increasing prepayment speed), while those of discount mortgages will be positive. To curtail the exposure to sudden changes in prepayment rates, the portfolio should match the benchmark contributions to prepayment sensitivity in each mortgage sector. The third mortgage-specific component of tracking error is due to MBS volatility. Convexity is used as a measure of volatility sensitivity because volatility shocks will have the strongest impact on prices of those mortgages whose prepayment options are at the money (current coupons). These securities tend to have the most negative convexity. Exhibit 9.8 shows the comparison of portfolio and benchmark contributions to convexity in each mortgage sector, which forms the basis for this component of tracking error.

Sources of Nonsystematic Tracking Error

In addition to the various sources of systematic risk, Exhibit 9.2 indicates that the sample portfolio has 26 bp of nonsystematic tracking error or special risk. This risk stems from portfolio concentrations in individual securities or issuers. The portfolio report in Exhibit 9.9 helps elucidate this risk. The rightmost column of the exhibit shows the percentage of the portfolio's market value invested in each security. As the portfolio is relatively small, each bond makes up a noticeable fraction. In particular, there are two extremely large positions in corporate bonds, issued by GTE Corp. and Coca-Cola. With $50 million a piece, each of these two bonds represents more than 8% of the portfolio. A negative credit event associated with either of these firms (i.e., a downgrade) would cause large losses in the portfolio, while hardly affecting the highly diversified benchmark. The Aggregate Index consisted of almost 7,000 securities as of September 30, 1998, so that the largest U.S. Treasury issue accounts for less than 1%, and most corporate issues contribute less than 0.01% of the index market value. Thus, any large position in a corporate issue represents a material difference between portfolio and benchmark exposures that must be considered in a full treatment of risk.

    The magnitude of the return variance that the risk model associates with a mismatch in allocations to a particular issue is proportional to the square of the allocation difference and to the residual return variance estimated for the issue. This calculation is shown in schematic

EXHIBIT 9.7   MBS Prepayment Sensitivity Report
Sample Portfolio versus Aggregate Index, September 30, 1998

MBS Sector	Portfolio % of Portfolio	Portfolio PSA Sens.	Portfolio Cntrb. to PSA Sens.	Benchmark % of Portfolio	Benchmark PSA Sens.	Benchmark Cntrb. to PSA Sens.	Difference % of Portfolio	Difference Cntrb. to PSA Sens.
Coupon < 6.0%								
Conventional	0.00	0.00	0.00	0.00	1.28	0.00	0.00	0.00
GNMA 30 yr.	0.00	0.00	0.00	0.00	1.03	0.00	0.00	0.00
15-year MBS	0.00	0.00	0.00	0.14	0.01	0.00	−0.14	0.00
Balloon	0.00	0.00	0.00	0.05	−0.08	0.00	−0.05	0.00
6.0% ≤ Coupon < 7.0%								
Conventional	2.90	−1.14	−0.03	5.37	−1.05	−0.06	−2.48	0.02
GNMA 30 yr.	0.76	−1.19	−0.01	1.30	−1.11	−0.01	−0.53	0.01
15-year MBS	3.52	−0.86	−0.03	3.26	−0.88	−0.03	0.26	0.00
Balloon	3.03	−0.54	−0.02	0.48	−0.73	0.00	2.55	−0.01
7.0% ≤ Coupon < 8.0%								
Conventional	4.93	−2.10	−0.10	8.32	−2.79	−0.23	−3.39	0.13
GNMA 30 yr.	4.66	−3.20	−0.15	3.90	−2.82	−0.11	0.76	−0.04
15-year MBS	0.00	0.00	0.00	1.83	−1.92	−0.04	−1.83	0.04
Balloon	0.00	0.00	0.00	0.25	−1.98	−0.01	−0.25	0.01
8.0% ≤ Coupon < 9.0%								
Conventional	5.14	−3.91	−0.20	2.26	−4.27	−0.10	2.87	−0.10
GNMA 30 yr.	0.00	0.00	0.00	1.71	−4.71	−0.08	−1.71	0.08
15-year MBS	0.00	0.00	0.00	0.31	−2.16	−0.01	−0.31	0.01
Balloon	0.00	0.00	0.00	0.00	−2.38	0.00	0.00	0.00
9.0% ≤ Coupon < 10.0%								
Conventional	0.00	0.00	0.00	0.54	−6.64	−0.04	−0.54	0.04
GNMA 30 yr.	2.11	−7.24	−0.15	0.62	−6.05	−0.04	1.49	−0.12
15-year MBS	0.00	0.00	0.00	0.04	−1.61	0.00	−0.04	0.00
Balloon	0.00	0.00	0.00	0.00	0.00	0.00	0.00	0.00
Coupon ≥ 10.0%								
Conventional	0.00	0.00	0.00	0.10	−8.14	−0.01	−0.10	0.01
GNMA 30 yr.	0.00	0.00	0.00	0.17	−7.49	−0.01	−0.17	0.01
15-year MBS	0.00	0.00	0.00	0.00	0.00	0.00	0.00	0.00
Balloon	0.00	0.00	0.00	0.00	0.00	0.00	0.00	0.00
Subtotals								
Conventional	12.96		−0.34	16.6		−0.43	−3.64	0.09
GNMA 30 yr.	7.53		−0.31	7.70		−0.26	−0.16	−0.06
15-year MBS	3.52		−0.03	5.59		−0.07	−2.06	0.04
Balloon	3.03		−0.02	0.78		−0.01	2.25	−0.01
Totals	27.04		−0.70	30.67		−0.76	−3.62	0.07

EXHIBIT 9.8   MBS Convexity Analysis
Sample Portfolio versus Aggregate Index, September 30, 1998

MBS Sector	% of Portfolio	Con-vexity	Cntrb. to Convexity	% of Portfolio	Con-vexity	Cntrb. to Convexity	% of Portfolio	Cntrb. to Convexity
	Portfolio			Benchmark			Difference	
Coupon < 6.0%								
Conventional	0.00	0.00	0.00	0.00	−0.56	0.00	0.00	0.00
GNMA 30 yr.	0.00	0.00	0.00	0.00	−0.85	0.00	0.00	0.00
15-year MBS	0.00	0.00	0.00	0.14	−0.88	0.00	−0.14	0.00
Balloon	0.00	0.00	0.00	0.05	−0.48	0.00	−0.05	0.00
6.0% ≤ Coupon < 7.0%								
Conventional	2.90	−3.52	−0.10	5.37	−3.19	−0.17	−2.48	0.07
GNMA 30 yr.	0.76	−3.65	−0.03	1.30	−3.13	−0.04	−0.53	0.01
15-year MBS	3.52	−1.78	−0.06	3.26	−2.06	−0.07	0.26	0.00
Balloon	3.03	−1.50	−0.05	0.48	−1.11	−0.01	2.55	−0.04
7.0% ≤ Coupon < 8.0%								
Conventional	4.93	−3.39	−0.17	8.32	−2.60	−0.22	−3.39	0.05
GNMA 30 yr.	4.66	−2.40	−0.11	3.90	−2.88	−0.11	0.76	0.00
15-year MBS	0.00	0.00	0.00	1.83	−1.56	−0.03	−1.83	0.03
Balloon	0.00	0.00	0.00	0.25	−0.97	0.00	−0.25	0.00
8.0% ≤ Coupon < 9.0%								
Conventional	5.14	−1.27	−0.07	2.26	−1.01	−0.02	2.87	−0.04
GNMA 30 yr.	0.00	0.00	0.00	1.71	−0.56	−0.01	−1.71	0.01
15-year MBS	0.00	0.00	0.00	0.31	−0.93	0.00	−0.31	0.00
Balloon	0.00	0.00	0.00	0.00	−0.96	0.00	0.00	0.00
9.0% ≤ Coupon < 10.0%								
Conventional	0.00	0.00	0.00	0.54	−0.80	0.00	−0.54	0.00
GNMA 30 yr.	2.11	−0.34	−0.01	0.62	−0.36	0.00	1.49	−0.01
15-year MBS	0.00	0.00	0.00	0.04	−0.52	0.00	−0.04	0.00
Balloon	0.00	0.00	0.00	0.00	0.00	0.00	0.00	0.00
Coupon ≥ 10.0%								
Conventional	0.00	0.00	0.00	0.10	−0.61	0.00	−0.10	0.00
GNMA 30 yr.	0.00	0.00	0.00	0.17	−0.21	0.00	−0.17	0.00
15-year MBS	0.00	0.00	0.00	0.00	0.00	0.00	0.00	0.00
Balloon	0.00	0.00	0.00	0.00	0.00	0.00	0.00	0.00
Subtotals								
Conventional	12.96		−0.33	16.6		−0.42	−3.64	0.08
GNMA 30 yr.	7.53		−0.15	7.70		−0.16	−0.16	0.02
15-year MBS	3.52		−0.06	5.59		−0.10	−2.06	0.04
Balloon	3.03		−0.05	0.78		−0.01	2.25	−0.04
Totals	27.04		−0.59	30.67		−0.69	−3.62	0.10

EXHIBIT 9.9 Portfolio Report: Composition of Sample Portfolio, September 30, 1998

#	CUSIP	Issuer Name	Coup.	Maturity	Moody	S&P	Sect.	Dur. W	Dur. A	Par Val.	%
1	057224AF	Baker Hughes	8.000	05/15/04	A2	A	IND	4.47	4.47	5,000	0.87
2	097023AL	Boeing Co.	6.350	06/15/03	Aa3	AA	IND	3.98	3.98	10,000	1.58
3	191219AY	Coca-Cola Enterprises Inc.	6.950	11/15/26	A3	A+	IND	12.37	12.37	50,000	8.06
4	532457AP	Eli Lilly Co.	6.770	01/01/36	Aa3	AA	IND	14.18	14.18	5,000	0.83
5	293561BS	Enron Corp.	6.625	11/15/05	Baa2	BBB+	UTL	5.53	5.53	5,000	0.80
6	31359MDN	Federal Natl. Mtg. Assn.	5.625	03/15/01	Aaa+	AAA+	USA	2.27	2.27	10,000	1.53
7	31359CAT	Federal Natl. Mtg. Assn.-g	7.400	07/01/04	Aaa+	AAA+	USA	4.66	4.66	8,000	1.37
8	FGG06096	FHLM Gold 7-Years Balloon	6.000	04/01/26	Aaa+	AAA+	FHg	2.55	1.69	20,000	3.03
9	FGD06494	FHLM Gold Guar. Single Fam.	6.500	08/01/08	Aaa+	AAA+	FHd	3.13	1.95	23,000	3.52
10	FGB07098	FHLM Gold Guar. Single Fam.	7.000	01/01/28	Aaa+	AAA+	FHb	3.68	1.33	32,000	4.93
11	FGB06498	FHLM Gold Guar. Single Fam.	6.500	02/01/28	Aaa+	AAA+	FHb	5.00	2.83	19,000	2.90
12	319279BP	First Bank System	6.875	09/15/07	A2	A−	FIN	6.73	6.73	4,000	0.65
13	339012AB	Fleet Mortgage Group	6.500	09/15/99	A2	A+	FIN	0.92	0.92	4,000	0.60
14	FNA08092	FNMA Conventional Long T.	8.000	05/01/21	Aaa+	AAA+	FNa	2.56	0.96	33,000	5.14
15	31364FSK	FNMA MTN	6.420	02/12/08	Aaa+	AAA+	USA	2.16	3.40	8,000	1.23
16	345397GS	Ford Motor Credit	7.500	01/15/03	A1	A	FIN	3.62	3.62	4,000	0.65
17	347471AR	Fort James Corp.	6.875	09/15/07	Baa2	BBB−	IND	6.68	6.68	4,000	0.63
18	GNA09490	GNMA I Single Family	9.500	10/01/19	Aaa+	AAA+	GNa	2.69	1.60	13,000	2.11
19	GNA07493	GNMA I Single Family	7.500	07/01/22	Aaa+	AAA+	GNa	3.13	0.75	30,000	4.66
20	GNA06498	GNMA I Single Family	6.500	02/01/28	Aaa+	AAA+	GNa	5.34	3.14	5,000	0.76
21	362320AQ	GTE Corp.	9.375	12/01/00	Baa1	A	TEL	1.91	1.91	50,000	8.32

EXHIBIT 9.9 (Continued)

#	CUSIP	Issuer Name	Coup.	Maturity	Moody	S&P	Sect.	Dur. W	Dur. A	Par Val.	%
22	458182CB	Int.-American Dev. Bank-G	6.375	10/22/07	Aaa	AAA	SUP	6.76	6.76	6,000	1.00
23	459200AK	Intl. Business Machines	6.375	06/15/00	A1	A+	IND	1.58	1.58	10,000	1.55
24	524909AS	Lehman Brothers Inc.	7.125	07/15/02	Baa1	A	FIN	3.20	3.20	4,000	0.59
25	539830AA	Lockheed Martin	6.550	05/15/99	A3	BBB+	IND	0.59	0.59	10,000	1.53
26	563469CZ	Manitoba Prov. Canada	8.875	09/15/21	A1	AA-	CAN	11.34	11.34	4,000	0.79
27	58013MDE	McDonalds Corp.	5.950	01/15/08	Aa2	AA	IND	7.05	7.05	4,000	0.63
28	590188HZ	Merrill Lynch & Co.-Glo.	6.000	02/12/03	Aa3	AA-	FIN	3.77	3.77	5,000	0.76
29	638585BE	Nationsbank Corp.	5.750	03/15/01	Aa2	A+	FIN	2.26	2.26	3,000	0.45
30	650094BM	New York Telephone	9.375	07/15/31	A2	A+	TEL	2.43	3.66	5,000	0.86
31	654106AA	Nike Inc.	6.375	12/01/03	A1	A+	IND	4.30	4.30	3,000	0.48
32	655844AJ	Norfolk Southern Corp.	7.800	05/15/27	Baa1	BBB+	IND	12.22	12.22	4,000	0.71
33	669383CN	Norwest Financial Inc.	6.125	08/01/03	Aa3	AA-	FIN	4.12	4.12	4,000	0.62
34	683234HG	Ont. Prov. Canada-Global	7.375	01/27/03	Aa3	AA-	CAN	3.67	3.67	4,000	0.65
35	744567DN	Pub. Svc. Electric + Gas	6.125	08/01/02	A3	A-	ELU	3.36	3.36	3,000	0.47
36	755111AF	Raytheon Co.	7.200	08/15/27	Baa1	BBB	IND	12.61	12.61	8,000	1.31
37	761157AA	Resolution Funding Corp.	8.125	10/15/19	Aaa+	AAA+	USA	11.22	11.22	17,000	3.51
38	88731EAF	Time Warner Ent.	8.375	03/15/23	Baa2	BBB-	IND	11.45	11.45	5,000	0.90
39	904000AA	Ultramar Diamond Sham.	7.200	10/15/17	Baa2	BBB	IND	10.06	10.06	4,000	0.63

EXHIBIT 9.9 (Continued)

#	CUSIP	Issuer Name	Coup.	Maturity	Moody	S&P	Sect.	Dur. W	Dur. A	Par Val.	%
40	912810DB	U.S. Treasury Bonds	10.375	11/15/12	Aaa+	AAA+	UST	6.30	6.38	10,000	2.17
41	912810DS	U.S. Treasury Bonds	10.625	08/15/15	Aaa+	AAA+	UST	9.68	9.68	14,000	3.43
42	912810EQ	U.S. Treasury Bonds	6.250	08/15/23	Aaa+	AAA+	UST	13.26	13.26	30,000	5.14
43	912827XE	U.S. Treasury Bonds	8.875	02/15/99	Aaa+	AAA+	UST	0.37	0.37	9,000	1.38
44	912827F9	U.S. Treasury Bonds	6.375	07/15/99	Aaa+	AAA+	UST	0.76	0.76	4,000	0.61
45	912827R4	U.S. Treasury Bonds	7.125	09/30/99	Aaa+	AAA+	UST	0.96	0.96	17,000	2.59
46	912827Z9	U.S. Treasury Bonds	5.875	11/15/99	Aaa+	AAA+	UST	1.06	1.06	17,000	2.62
47	912827T4	U.S. Treasury Bonds	6.875	03/31/00	Aaa+	AAA+	UST	1.42	1.42	8,000	1.23
48	9128273D	U.S. Treasury Bonds	6.000	08/15/00	Aaa+	AAA+	UST	1.75	1.75	11,000	1.70
49	912827A8	U.S. Treasury Bonds	8.000	05/15/01	Aaa+	AAA+	UST	2.31	2.31	9,000	1.50
50	912827D2	U.S. Treasury Bonds	7.500	11/15/01	Aaa+	AAA+	UST	2.72	2.72	10,000	1.67
51	9128272P	U.S. Treasury Bonds	6.625	03/31/02	Aaa+	AAA+	UST	3.12	3.12	6,000	0.96
52	9128273G	U.S. Treasury Bonds	6.250	08/31/02	Aaa+	AAA+	UST	3.45	3.45	10,000	1.60
53	912827L8	U.S. Treasury Bonds	5.750	08/15/03	Aaa+	AAA+	UST	4.22	4.22	1,000	0.16
54	912827T8	U.S. Treasury Bonds	6.500	05/15/05	Aaa+	AAA+	UST	5.33	5.33	1,000	0.17
55	9128273E	U.S. Treasury Bonds	6.125	08/15/07	Aaa+	AAA+	UST	6.90	6.90	1,000	0.17
56	949740BZ	Wells Fargo + Co.	6.875	04/01/06	A2	A−	FIN	5.89	5.89	5,000	0.80
57	961214AD	WestPac Banking Corp.	7.875	10/15/02	A1	A+	FOC	3.34	3.34	3,000	0.49

form in Exhibit 9.10 and illustrated numerically for our sample portfolio in Exhibit 9.11. With the return variance based on the square of the market weight, it is dominated by the largest positions in the portfolio. The set of bonds shown includes those with the greatest allocations in the portfolio and in the benchmark. The large position in the Coca-Cola bond contributes 21 bps of the total nonsystematic risk of 26 bps. This is due to the 8.05% overweighting of this bond relative to its position in the index and the 77 bps monthly volatility of nonsystematic return that the model has estimated for this bond. (This estimate is based on bond characteristics such as sector, quality, duration, age, and amount outstanding.) The contribution to the annualized tracking error is then given by

$$\sqrt{12 \times (0.0805 \times 77)^2} = 21$$

While the overweighting to GTE is larger in terms of percentage of market value, the estimated risk is lower due to the much smaller nonsystematic return volatility (37 bps). This is mainly because the GTE issue has a much shorter maturity (12/2000) than the Coca-Cola issue (11/

EXHIBIT 9.10   Calculation of Variance Due to Special Risk (Issue-Specific Model)[a]

	Portfolio Weights	Benchmark Weights	Contribution to Issue-Specific Risk
Issue 1	w_{P_1}	w_{B_1}	$(w_{P_1} - w_{B_1})^2 \sigma_{\varepsilon_1}^2$
Issue 2	w_{P_2}	w_{B_2}	$(w_{P_2} - w_{B_2})^2 \sigma_{\varepsilon_2}^2$
. . .			
Issue $N-1$	$w_{P_{N-1}}$	$w_{B_{N-1}}$	$(w_{P_{N-1}} - w_{B_{N-1}})^2 \sigma_{\varepsilon_{N-1}}^2$
Issue N	w_{P_N}	w_{B_N}	$(w_{P_N} - w_{B_N})^2 \sigma_{\varepsilon_N}^2$
Total Issue-Specific Risk			$\sum_{i=1}^{N} (w_{P_i} - w_{B_i})^2 \sigma_{\varepsilon_i}^2$

[a] w_{P_i} and w_{B_i} are weights of security i in the portfolio and in the benchmark as a percentage of total market value. $\sigma_{\varepsilon_i}^2$ is the variance of residual returns for security i. It is obtained from historical volatility of security-specific residual returns unexplained by the combination of all systematic risk factors.

EXHIBIT 9.11 Illustration of the Calculation of Nonsystematic Tracking Error

CUSIP	Issuer	Coupon	Maturity	Spec. Risk Vol. (bps/Mo.)	% of Portf.	% of Benchmark	Diff.	Contrib. Tracking Error (bps/Mo.)
097023AL	Boeing Co.	6.350	06/15/03	44	1.58	0.01	1.58	2
19219AY	Coca-Cola Enterprises Inc.	6.950	11/15/26	77	8.06	0.01	8.05	21
362320AQ	GTE Corp.	9.375	12/01/00	37	8.32	0.01	8.31	11
532457AP	Eli Lilly Co.	6.770	01/01/36	78	0.83	0.01	0.82	2
563469CZ	Manitoba Prov. Canada	8.875	09/15/21	73	0.79	0.01	0.79	2
655844AJ	Norfolk Southern Corp.	7.800	05/15/27	84	0.71	0.02	0.70	2
755111AF	Raytheon Co.	7.200	08/15/27	85	1.31	0.01	1.30	4
761157AA	Resolution Funding Corp.	8.125	10/15/19	19	3.51	0.12	3.39	2
8731EAF	Time Warner Ent.	8.375	03/15/23	80	0.90	0.02	0.88	2
912810DS	U.S. Treasury Bonds	10.625	08/15/15	17	3.43	0.18	3.25	2
912810EC	U.S. Treasury Bonds	8.875	02/15/19	18	0.00	0.49	−0.49	0
912810ED	U.S. Treasury Bonds	8.125	08/15/19	18	0.00	0.47	−0.47	0
912810EG	U.S. Treasury Bonds	8.750	08/15/20	18	0.00	0.54	−0.54	0
912810EL	U.S. Treasury Bonds	8.000	11/15/21	17	0.00	0.81	−0.81	0
912810EQ	U.S. Treasury Bonds	6.250	08/15/23	19	5.14	0.46	4.68	3
912810FB	U.S. Treasury Bonds	6.125	11/15/27	20	0.00	0.44	−0.44	0
FGB07097	FHLM Gold Guar. Single Fam. 30 yr	7.000	04/01/27	16	0.00	0.56	−0.56	0
FGB07098	FHLM Gold Guar. Single Fam. 30 yr	7.000	01/01/28	15	4.93	0.46	4.47	2
FNA06498	FNMA Conventional Long T. 30 yr	6.500	03/01/28	15	0.00	1.16	−1.16	1
FNA07093	FNMA Conventional Long T. 30 yr	7.000	07/01/22	16	0.00	0.65	−0.65	0
FNA07097	FNMA Conventional Long T. 30 yr	7.000	05/01/27	16	0.00	0.69	−0.69	0
FNA08092	FNMA Conventional Long T. 30 yr	8.000	05/01/21	17	5.14	0.24	4.90	3
GNA07493	GNMA I Single Fam. 30 yr	7.500	07/01/22	16	4.66	0.30	4.36	2

2026). For bonds of similar maturities, the model tends to assign higher special risk volatilities to lower-rated issues. Thus, mismatches in low-quality bonds with long duration will be the biggest contributors to non-systematic tracking error. We assume independence of the risk from individual bonds, so the overall nonsystematic risk is computed as the sum of the contributions to variance from each security. Note that mismatches also arise due to bonds that are underweighted in the portfolio. Most bonds in the index do not appear in the portfolio, and each missing bond contributes to tracking error. However, the percentage of the index each bond represents is usually very small. Besides, their contributions to return variance are squared in the calculation of tracking error. Thus, the impact of bonds not included in the portfolio is usually insignificant. The largest contribution to tracking error stemming from an underweighting to a security is due to the 1998 issuance of FNMA 30-year 6.5% passthroughs, which represents 1.16% of the benchmark. Even this relatively large mismatch contributes only a scant 1 bp to tracking error.

This nonsystematic risk calculation is carried out twice, using two different methods. In the issuer-specific calculation, the holdings of the portfolio and benchmark are not compared on a bond-by-bond basis, as in Exhibits 9.10 and 9.11, but are first aggregated into concentrations in individual issuers. This calculation is based on the assumption that spreads of bonds of the same issuer tend to move together. Therefore, matching the benchmark issuer allocations is sufficient. In the issue-specific calculation, each bond is considered an independent source of risk. This model recognizes that large exposures to a single bond can incur more risk than a portfolio of all of an issuer's debt. In addition to credit events that affect an issuer as a whole, individual issues can be subject to various technical effects. For most portfolios, these two calculations produce very similar results. In certain circumstances, however, there can be significant differences. For instance, some large issuers use an index of all their outstanding debt as an internal performance benchmark. In the case of a single-issuer portfolio and benchmark, the issue-specific risk calculation will provide a much better measure of nonsystematic risk. The reported nonsystematic tracking error of 26.1 bps for this portfolio, which contributes to the total tracking error, is the average of the results from the issuer-specific and issue-specific calculations.

Combining Components of Tracking Error

Given the origins of each component of tracking error shown in Exhibit 9.2, we can address the question of how these components combine to form the overall tracking error. Of the 52 bps of overall tracking error (TE), 45 bps correspond to systematic TE and 26 bps to nonsystematic

TE. The net result of these two sources of tracking error does not equal their sum. Rather, the squares of these two numbers (which represent variances) sum to the variance of the result. Next we take its square root to obtain the overall TE ($[45.0^2 + 26.1^2]^{0.5} = 52.0$). This illustrates the risk-reducing benefits of diversification from combining independent (zero correlation) sources of risk.

When components of risk are not assumed to be independent, correlations must be considered. At the top of Exhibit 9.2, we see that the systematic risk is composed of 36.3 bp of term structure risk and 39.5 bp from all other forms of systematic risk combined (nonterm structure risk). If these two were independent, they would combine to a systematic tracking error of 53.6 bps ($[36.3^2 + 39.5^2]^{0.5} = 53.6$). The combined systematic tracking error of only 45 bps reflects negative correlations among certain risk factors in the two groups.

The tracking error breakdown report in Exhibit 9.2 shows the subcomponents of tracking error due to sector, quality, and so forth. These subcomponents are calculated in two different ways. In the first column, we estimate the isolated tracking error due to the effect of each group of related risk factors considered alone. The tracking error due to term structure, for example, reflects only the portfolio/benchmark mismatches in exposures along the yield curve, as well as the volatilities of each of these risk factors and the correlations among them.

Similarly, the tracking error due to sector reflects only the mismatches in sector exposures, the volatilities of these risk factors, and the correlations among them. However, the correlations between the risk factors due to term structure and those due to sector do not participate in either of these calculations. Exhibit 9.12 depicts an idealized covariance matrix containing just three groups of risk factors relating to the yield curve (Y), sector spreads (S), and quality spreads (Q). Panel A in Exhibit 9.12 illustrates how the covariance matrix is used to calculate the subcomponents of tracking error in the isolated mode. The three shaded blocks represent the parts of the matrix that pertain to: movements of the various points along the yield curve and the correlations among them ($Y \times Y$); movements of sector spreads and the correlations among them ($S \times S$); and movements of quality spreads and the correlations among them ($Q \times Q$). The unshaded portions of the matrix, which deal with the correlations among different sets of risk factors, do not contribute to any of the partial tracking errors.

The next two columns of Exhibit 9.2 represent a different way of subdividing tracking error. The middle column shows the *cumulative tracking error*, which incrementally introduces one group of risk factors at a time to the tracking error calculation. In the first row, we find 36.3 bps of tracking error due to term structure. In the second, we see that if

EXHIBIT 9.12   Illustration of "Isolated" and "Cumulative" Calculations of Tracking Error Subcomponents[a]

Panel A. Isolated Calculation of Tracking Error Components

$Y \times Y$	$Y \times S$	$Y \times Q$
$S \times Y$	$S \times S$	$S \times Q$
$Q \times Y$	$Q \times S$	$Q \times Q$

Panel B. Cumulative Calculation of Tracking Error Components

$Y \times Y$	$Y \times S$	$Y \times Q$
$S \times Y$	$S \times S$	$S \times Q$
$Q \times Y$	$Q \times S$	$Q \times Q$

[a] Y is for yield curve risk factors; S is for sector-spread risk factors; Q is for credit quality spread risk factors.

term structure and sector risk are considered together, while all other risks are ignored, the tracking error increases to 38.3 bps. The rightmost column shows that the resulting "change in tracking error" due to the incremental inclusion of sector risk is 2.0 bps. As additional groups of risk factors are included, the calculation converges toward the total systematic tracking error, which is obtained with the use of the entire matrix. Panel B in Exhibit 9.12 illustrates the rectangular section of the covariance matrix that is used at each stage of the calculation. The incremental tracking error due to sector reflects not only the effect of the $S \times S$ box in the diagram, but the $S \times Y$ and $Y \times S$ cross terms as well. That is, the partial tracking error due to sector takes into account the correlations between sector risk and yield curve risk. It answers the question, "Given the exposure to yield curve risk, how much more risk is introduced by the exposure to sector risk?"

The incremental approach is intuitively pleasing because the partial tracking errors (the "Change in Tracking Error" column of Exhibit 9.2) add up to the total systematic tracking error. Of course, the order in which the various partial tracking errors are considered will affect the magnitude of the corresponding terms. Also, note that some of the partial tracking errors computed in this way are negative. This reflects negative correlations among certain groups of risk factors. For example, in Exhibit 9.2, the incremental risk due to the MBS sector is –1.7 bps.

The two methods used to subdivide tracking error into different components are complementary and serve different purposes. The isolated calculation is ideal for comparing the magnitudes of different types of risk to highlight the most significant exposures. The cumulative approach produces a set of tracking error subcomponents that sum to the total systematic tracking error and reflect the effect of correlations among different groups of risk factors. The major drawback of the cumulative approach is that results are highly dependent on the order in which they are computed. The order currently used by the model was selected based on the significance of each type of risk; it may not be optimal for every portfolio/benchmark combination.

Other Risk Model Outputs

The model's analysis of portfolio and benchmark risk is not limited to the calculation of tracking error. The model also calculates the absolute return volatilities (sigmas) of portfolio and benchmark. *Portfolio sigma* is calculated in the same fashion as tracking error, but is based on the factor loadings (sensitivities to market factors) of the portfolio, rather than on the differences from the benchmark. Sigma represents the volatility of portfolio returns, just as tracking error represents the volatility of the return difference between portfolio and benchmark. Also like tracking error, sigma consists of systematic and nonsystematic components, and the volatility of the benchmark return is calculated in the same way. Both portfolio and benchmark sigmas appear at the bottom of the tracking error report (Exhibit 9.2). Note that the tracking error of 52 bps (the annualized volatility of return difference) is greater than the difference between the return volatilities (sigmas) of the portfolio and the benchmark (440 bps – 417 bps = 23 bps). It is easy to see why this should be so. Assume a benchmark of Treasury bonds, whose entire risk is due to term structure. A portfolio of short-term, high-yield corporate bonds could be constructed such that the overall return volatility would match that of the Treasury benchmark. The magnitude of the credit risk in this portfolio might match the magnitude of the term structure risk in the benchmark, but the two would certainly not cancel each other out. The tracking error in this case might be larger than the sigma of either the portfolio or the benchmark.

In our example, the portfolio sigma is greater than that of the benchmark. Thus, we can say that the portfolio is "more risky" than the benchmark—its longer duration makes it more susceptible to a rise in interest rates. What if the portfolio was shorter than the benchmark and had a lower sigma? In this sense, we could consider the portfolio to be less risky. However, tracking error could be just as big given its capture of the risk of a yield curve rally in which the portfolio would lag. To reduce the risk of underperformance (tracking error), it is necessary to match the risk exposures of portfolio and benchmark. Thus, the reduction of tracking error will typically result in bringing portfolio sigma nearer to that of the benchmark; but sigma can be changed in many ways that will not necessarily improve the tracking error.

It is interesting to compare the nonsystematic components of portfolio and benchmark risk. The first thing to notice is that, when viewed in the context of the overall return volatility, the effect of nonsystematic risk is negligible. To the precision shown, for both the portfolio and benchmark, the overall sigma is equal to its systematic part. The portfolio-level risk due to individual credit events is very small when compared to the total volatility of returns, which includes the entire exposure to all systematic risks, notably yield changes. The portfolio also has significantly more nonsystematic risk (27 bps) than does the benchmark (4 bps), because the latter is much more diversified. In fact, because the benchmark exposures to any individual issuer are so close to zero, the nonsystematic tracking error (26 bps) is almost the same as the nonsystematic part of portfolio sigma. Notice that the nonsystematic risk can form a significant component of the tracking error (26.1 bps out of a total of 52 bps) even as it is a negligible part of the absolute return volatility.

Another quantity calculated by the model is beta, which measures the risk of the portfolio relative to that of the benchmark. The beta for our sample portfolio is 1.05, as shown at the bottom of Exhibit 9.1. This means that the portfolio is more risky (volatile) than the benchmark. For every 100 bps of benchmark return (positive or negative), we would expect to see 105 bps for the portfolio. It is common to compare the beta produced by the risk model with the ratio of portfolio and benchmark durations. In this case, the duration ratio is 4.82/4.29 = 1.12, which is somewhat larger than the risk model beta. This is because the duration-based approach considers only term-structure risk (and only parallel shift risk at that), while the risk model includes the combined effects of all relevant forms of risk, along with the correlations among them.

RISK MODEL APPLICATIONS

In this section we explore several applications of the model to portfolio management.

Quantifying Risk Associated with a View

The risk model is primarily a diagnostic tool. Whatever position a portfolio manager has taken relative to the benchmark, the risk model will quantify how much risk has been assumed. This helps measure the risk of the exposures taken to express a market view. It also points out the potential unintended risks in the portfolio.

Many firms use risk-adjusted measures to evaluate portfolio performance. A high return achieved by a series of successful but risky market plays may not please a conservative pension plan sponsor. A more modest return, achieved while maintaining much lower risk versus the benchmark, might be seen as a healthier approach over the long term. This point of view can be reflected either by adjusting performance by the amount of risk taken or by specifying in advance the acceptable level of risk for the portfolio. In any case, the portfolio manager should be cognizant of the risk inherent in a particular market view and weigh it against the anticipated gain. The increasing popularity of risk-adjusted performance evaluation is evident in the frequent use of the concept of an *information ratio*—portfolio outperformance of the benchmark per unit of standard deviation of observed outperformance. Plan sponsors often diversify among asset managers with different styles, looking for some of them to take more risk and for others to stay conservative, but always looking for high information ratios.

Risk Budgeting

To limit the amount of risk that may be taken by its portfolio managers, a plan sponsor can prescribe a maximum allowable tracking error. In the past, an asset management mandate might have put explicit constraints on deviation from the benchmark duration, differences in sector allocations, concentration in a given issuer, and total percentage invested outside the benchmark. Currently, we observe a tendency to constrain the overall risk versus the benchmark and leave the choice of the form of risk to the portfolio manager based on current risk premia offered by the market. By expressing various types of risk in the same units of tracking error, the model makes it possible to introduce the concept of opportunistic risk budget allocation. To constrain specific types of risk, limits can be applied to the different components of tracking error produced by the model. As described above, the overall tracking error represents the best way to quantify the net effect of multiple dimensions of risk in a single number.

With the model-specific nature of tracking error, there may be situations where the formal limits to be placed on the portfolio manager must be expressed in more objective terms. Constraints commonly found in investment policies include limits on the deviation between the portfolio and the benchmark, both in terms of Treasury duration and in spread duration contributions from various fixed income asset classes. Because term structure risk tends to be best understood, many organizations have firm limits only for the amount of duration deviation allowed. For example, a portfolio manager may be limited to ±1 around benchmark duration. How can this limit be applied to risks along a different dimension?

The risk model can help establish relationships among risks of different types by comparing their tracking errors. Exhibit 9.13 shows the tracking errors achieved by several different blends of Treasury and spread product indices relative to the Treasury Index. A pure Treasury composite (Strategy 1) with duration one year longer than the benchmark has a tracking error of 85 bps per year. Strategies 2 and 3 are created by combining the investment-grade Corporate Index with both intermediate and long Treasury Indices to achieve desired exposures to spread duration while remaining neutral to the benchmark in Treasury duration. Similar strategies are engaged to generate desired exposures to spread duration in the MBS and high-yield markets. As can be seen in Exhibit 9.13, an increase in pure Treasury duration by 1 (Strategy 1) is equivalent to an extension in corporate spread duration by 2.5, or an extension in high-yield spread duration by about 0.75. Our results with MBS spreads show that an MBS spread duration of 1 causes a tracking error of 58 bps, while a duration of 1.5 gives a tracking error of 87 bps. A simple linear interpolation would suggest that a tracking error of 85 bps (the magnitude of the risk of an extension of duration by 1) thus corresponds to an extension in MBS spread duration of approximately 1.47.

Of course, these are idealized examples in which spread exposure to one type of product is changed while holding Treasury duration constant. A real portfolio is likely to take risks in all dimensions simultaneously. To calculate the tracking error, the risk model considers the correlations among the different risk factors. As long as two risks along different dimensions are not perfectly correlated, the net risk is less than the sum of the two risks. For example, we have established that a corporate spread duration of 2.5 produces roughly the same risk as a Treasury duration of 1, each causing a tracking error of about 85 bps. For a portfolio able to take both types of risk, an investor might allocate half of the risk budget to each, setting limits on Treasury duration of 0.5 and on corporate spread duration of 1.25. This should keep the risk within the desired range of tracking error. As shown in Exhibit 9.13, this combination of risks produces a tracking error of only 51 bps. This method of allocating risk under a total risk budget (in terms of equivalent duration mismatches) can provide investors with a method of controlling risk that is easier to implement and more conservative than a direct limit on tracking error. This macroview of risk facilitates the capablity to set separate but uniformly expressed limits on portfolio managers responsible for different kinds of portfolio exposures.

EXHIBIT 9.13 "Risk Budget": An Example Using Components of Treasury and Spread Indices Relative to a Treasury Benchmark

Index	Treasury	Intermediate Treasury	Long Treasury	Corporate	MBS	High Yield
Duration	5.48	3.05	10.74	5.99	3.04	4.68
Spread Duration	0.00	0.00	0.00	6.04	3.46	4.58

Strategy No.	Risk Strategy	Tsy. Dur. Diff.	Spread Dur. Diff.	% Interm. Treasury	% Long Treasury	% Sprd. Sector	Tracking Error versus Tsy. Index (bps/yr.)
	Treasury Index			68.40	31.60	0.00	0
1	Treasury Duration	1.0	0.00	55.40	44.60	0.00	85
2	Corp. Spread Duration	0.0	1.00	58.17	25.27	16.56	34
3		0.0	2.50	42.83	15.78	41.39	85
4	Treas. Dur. & Corp. Sprd. Dur.	0.5	1.25	49.12	30.19	20.70	51
5	MBS Spread Duration	0.0	1.00	39.46	31.64	28.90	58
6		0.0	1.47	25.99	31.65	42.36	85
7		0.0	1.50	24.99	31.66	43.35	87
8	High-Yield Spread Duration	0.0	0.75	55.50	28.13	16.38	84
9		0.0	1.00	51.19	26.97	21.83	119

EXHIBIT 9.14   A Simple Diversification Trade:
Cut the Size of the Largest Position in Half

Issuer	Coupon	Maturity	Par Value ($000s)	MV ($000s)	Sector	Quality	Dur Adj.
Sell: Coca-Cola Enterprises Inc.	6.95	11/15/2026	25000	27053	IND	A3	12.37
Buy: Anheuser-Busch Co., Inc.	6.75	12/15/2027	25000	26941	IND	A1	12.86

Projecting the Effect of Proposed Transactions on Tracking Error

Proposed trades are often analyzed in the context of a 1-for-1 (substitution) swap. Selling a security and using the proceeds to buy another may earn a few additional basis points of yield. The risk model allows analysis of such a trade in the context of the portfolio and its benchmark. By comparing the current portfolio versus benchmark risk and the pro forma risk after the proposed trade, an asset manager can evaluate how well the trade fits the portfolio. Our portfolio analytics platform offers an interactive mode to allow portfolio modifications and immediately see the effect on tracking error.

For example, having noticed that our sample portfolio has an extremely large position in the Coca-Cola issue, we might decide to cut the size of this position in half. To avoid making any significant changes to the systematic risk profile of the portfolio, we might look for a bond with similar maturity, credit rating, and sector. Exhibit 9.14 shows an example of such a swap. Half the position in the Coca-Cola 30-year bond is replaced by a 30-year issue from Anheuser-Busch, another single-A rated issuer in the beverage sector. As shown later, this transaction reduces nonsystematic tracking error from 26 bps to 22 bps. While we have unwittingly produced a 1 bp increase in the systematic risk (the durations of the two bonds were not identical), the overall effect was a decrease in tracking error from 52 bps to 51 bps.

Optimization

For many portfolio managers, the risk model acts not only as a measurement tool but plays a major role in the portfolio construction process. The model has a unique optimization feature that guides investors to transactions that reduce portfolio risk. The types of questions it addresses are: What single transaction can reduce the risk of the portfolio relative to the benchmark the most? How could the tracking error be reduced with minimum turnover? The portfolio manager is given an opportunity to intervene at each step in the optimization process and select transactions that lead to the desired changes in the risk profile of the portfolio and are practical at the same time.

As in any portfolio optimization procedure, the first step is to choose the set of assets that may be purchased. The composition of this investable universe, or bond swap pool, is critical. This universe should be large enough to provide flexibility in matching all benchmark risk exposures, yet it should contain only securities that are acceptable candidates for purchase. This universe may be created by querying a bond database (selecting, for instance, all corporate bonds with more than $500 million outstanding that were issued in the last three years) or by providing a list of securities available for purchase.

Once the investable universe has been selected, the optimizer begins an iterative process (known as *gradient descent*), searching for 1-for-1 bond swap transactions that will achieve the investor's objective. In the simplest case, the objective is to minimize the tracking error. The bonds in the swap pool are ranked in terms of reduction in tracking error per unit of each bond purchased. The system indicates which bond, if purchased, will lead to the steepest decline in tracking error, but leaves the ultimate choice of the security to the investor. Once a bond has been selected for purchase, the optimizer offers a list of possible market-value-neutral swaps of this security against various issues in the portfolio (with the optimal transaction size for each pair of bonds), sorted in order of possible reduction in tracking error. Investors are free to adjust the model's recommendations, either selecting different bonds to sell or adjusting (e.g., rounding off) recommended trade amounts.

Exhibit 9.15 shows how this optimization process is used to minimize the tracking error of the sample portfolio. A close look at the sequence of trades suggested by the optimizer reveals that several types of risk are reduced simultaneously. In the first trade, the majority of the large position in the Coca-Cola 30-year bond is swapped for a 3-year Treasury. This trade simultaneously changes systematic exposures to term structure, sector, and quality; it also cuts one of the largest issuer exposures, reducing nonsystematic risk. This one trade brings the overall tracking error down from 52 bps to 29 bps. As risk declines and the portfolio risk profile approaches the benchmark, there is less room for such drastic improvements. Transaction sizes become smaller, and the improvement in tracking error with each trade slows. The second and third transactions continue to adjust the sector and quality exposures and fine-tune the risk exposures along the curve. The fourth transaction addresses the other large corporate exposure, cutting the position in GTE by two-thirds. The first five trades reduce the tracking error to 16 bps, creating an essentially passive portfolio.

EXHIBIT 9.15 Sequence of Transactions Selected by Optimizer Showing
Progressively Smaller Tracking Error, $000s
Initial Tracking Error: 52.0 bps

Transaction # 1		
Sold:	31,000 of Coca-Cola Enterprises	6.950 2026/11/15
Bought:	30,000 of U.S. Treasury Notes	8.000 2001/05/15
Cash Left Over:	−17.10	
New Tracking Error:	29.4 bps	
Cost of this Transaction:	152.500	
Cumulative Cost:	152.500	

Transaction # 2		
Sold:	10,000 of Lockheed Martin	6.550 1999/05/15
Bought:	9,000 of U.S. Treasury Notes	6.125 2007/08/15
Cash Left Over:	132.84	
New Tracking Error:	25.5 bps	
Cost of this Transaction:	47.500	
Cumulative Cost:	200.000	

Transaction # 3		
Sold:	4,000 of Norfolk Southern Corp.	7.800 2027/05/15
Bought:	3,000 of U.S. Treasury Bonds	10.625 2015/08/15
Cash Left Over:	−8.12	
New Tracking Error:	23.1 bps	
Cost of this Transaction:	17.500	
Cumulative Cost:	217.500	

Transaction # 4		
Sold:	33,000 of GTE Corp.	9.375 2000/12/01
Bought:	34,000 of U.S. Treasury Notes	6.625 2002/03/31
Cash Left Over:	412.18	
New Tracking Error:	19.8 bps	
Cost of this Transaction:	167.500	
Cumulative Cost:	385.000	

Transaction # 5		
Sold:	7,000 of Coca-cola Enterprises	6.950 2026/11/15
Bought:	8,000 of U.S. Treasury Notes	6.000 2000/08/15
Cash Left Over:	−304.17	
New Tracking Error:	16.4 bps	
Cost of this Transaction:	37.500	
Cumulative Cost:	422.500	

An analysis of the tracking error for this passive portfolio is shown in Exhibit 9.16. The systematic tracking error has been reduced to just 10 bps and the nonsystematic risk to 13 bps. Once systematic risk drops below nonsystematic risk, the latter becomes the limiting factor. In turn, further tracking error reduction by just a few transactions becomes much less likely. When there are exceptionally large positions, like the two mentioned in the above example, nonsystematic risk can be reduced quickly. Upon completion of such risk reduction transactions, further reduction of tracking error requires a major diversification effort. The critical factor that determines nonsystematic risk is the percentage of the portfolio in any single issue. On average, a portfolio of 50 bonds has 2% allocated to each position. To reduce this average allocation to 1%, the number of bonds would need to be doubled.

EXHIBIT 9.16   Tracking Error Summary
Passive Portfolio versus Aggregate Index, September 30, 1998

	Tracking Error (bps/year)		
	Isolated	Cumulative	Change
Tracking Error Term Structure	7.0	7.0	7.0
Nonterm Structure	9.6		
Tracking Error Sector	7.4	10.5	3.5
Tracking Error Quality	2.1	11.2	0.7
Tracking Error Optionality	1.6	11.5	0.3
Tracking Error Coupon	2.0	12.3	0.8
Tracking Error MBS Sector	4.9	10.2	−2.1
Tracking Error MBS Volatility	7.2	11.1	0.9
Tracking Error MBS Prepayment	2.5	10.3	−0.8
Total Systematic Tracking Error		10.3	
Nonsystematic Tracking Error			
Issuer specific	12.4		
Issue specific	3.0		
Total	12.7		
Total Tracking Error Return		16	

	Systematic	Nonsystematic	Total
Benchmark Sigma	417	4	417
Portfolio Sigma	413	13	413

The risk exposures of the resulting passive portfolio match the benchmark much better than the initial portfolio. Exhibit 9.17 details the term structure risk of the passive portfolio. Compared with Exhibit 9.3, the overweight at the long end is reduced significantly. The overweight at the 25-year vertex has gone down from 1.45% to 0.64%, and (perhaps more importantly) it is now offset partially by underweights at the adjacent 20- and 30-year vertices. Exhibit 9.18 presents the sector risk report for the passive portfolio. The underweight to Treasuries (in contribution to duration) has been reduced from −0.77% to −0.29% relative to the initial portfolio (Exhibit 9.4), and the largest corporate overweight, to consumer noncyclicals, has come down from +1.00% to +0.24%.

Minimization of tracking error, illustrated above, is the most basic application of the optimizer. This is ideal for passive investors who want their portfolios to track the benchmark as closely as possible. This method also aids investors who hope to outperform the benchmark mainly on the

EXHIBIT 9.17   Term Structure Risk Report for Passive Portfolio, September 30, 1998

Year	Cash Flows		
	Portfolio	Benchmark	Difference
0.00	1.33%	1.85%	−0.52%
0.25	3.75	4.25	−0.50
0.50	4.05	4.25	−0.19
0.75	3.50	3.76	−0.27
1.00	8.96	7.37	1.59
1.50	7.75	10.29	−2.54
2.00	8.30	8.09	0.21
2.50	10.30	6.42	3.87
3.00	5.32	5.50	−0.19
3.50	8.24	4.81	3.43
4.00	6.56	7.19	−0.63
5.00	5.91	6.96	−1.05
6.00	3.42	4.67	−1.24
7.00	5.75	7.84	−2.10
10.00	6.99	7.37	−0.38
15.00	4.00	3.88	0.12
20.00	2.98	3.04	−0.05
25.00	2.37	1.73	0.64
30.00	0.47	0.68	−0.21
40.00	0.08	0.07	0.01

EXHIBIT 9.18 Sector Risk Report for Passive Portfolio, September 30, 1998

Detailed Sector	Portfolio % of Portfolio	Portfolio Adj. Dur.	Portfolio Contrib. to Adj. Dur.	Benchmark % of Portfolio	Benchmark Adj. Dur.	Benchmark Contrib. to Adj. Dur.	Difference % of Portfolio	Difference Contrib. to Adj. Dur.
Treasury								
Coupon	40.98	4.72	1.94	39.82	5.58	2.22	1.16	−0.29
Strip	0.00	0.00	0.00	0.00	0.00	0.00	0.00	0.00
Agencies								
FNMA	4.12	3.40	0.14	3.56	3.44	0.12	0.56	0.02
FHLB	0.00	0.00	0.00	1.21	2.32	0.03	−1.21	−0.03
FHLMC	0.00	0.00	0.00	0.91	3.24	0.03	−0.91	−0.03
REFCORP	3.50	11.22	0.39	0.83	12.18	0.10	2.68	0.29
Other Agencies	0.00	0.00	0.00	1.31	5.58	0.07	−1.31	−0.07
Financial Institutions								
Banking	1.91	5.31	0.10	2.02	5.55	0.11	−0.11	−0.01
Brokerage	1.35	3.52	0.05	0.81	4.14	0.03	0.53	0.01
Financial Cos.	1.88	2.92	0.05	2.11	3.78	0.08	−0.23	−0.02
Insurance	0.00	0.00	0.00	0.52	7.47	0.04	−0.52	−0.04
Other	0.00	0.00	0.00	0.28	5.76	0.02	−0.28	−0.02
Industrials								
Basic	0.63	6.68	0.04	0.89	6.39	0.06	−0.26	−0.01
Capital Goods	2.89	7.88	0.23	1.16	6.94	0.08	1.73	0.15
Consumer Cycl.	2.01	8.37	0.17	2.28	7.10	0.16	−0.27	0.01
Consum. Non-cycl.	2.76	12.91	0.36	1.66	6.84	0.11	1.10	0.24
Energy	1.50	6.82	0.10	0.69	6.89	0.05	0.81	0.05
Technology	1.55	1.58	0.02	0.42	7.39	0.03	1.13	−0.01
Transportation	0.00	0.00	0.00	0.57	7.41	0.04	−0.57	−0.04
Utilities								
Electric	0.47	3.36	0.02	1.39	5.02	0.07	−0.93	−0.05
Telephone	3.69	2.32	0.09	1.54	6.58	0.10	2.15	−0.02
Natural Gas	0.80	5.53	0.04	0.49	6.50	0.03	0.31	0.01
Water	0.00	0.00	0.00	0.00	0.00	0.00	0.00	0.00
Yankee								
Canadians	1.45	7.87	0.11	1.06	6.67	0.07	0.38	0.04
Corporates	0.49	3.34	0.02	1.79	6.06	0.11	−1.30	−0.09
Supranational	1.00	6.76	0.07	0.38	6.33	0.02	0.62	0.04
Sovereigns	0.00	0.00	0.00	0.66	5.95	0.04	−0.66	−0.04
Hypothetical	0.00	0.00	0.00	0.00	0.00	0.00	0.00	0.00
Cash	0.00	0.00	0.00	0.00	0.00	0.00	0.00	0.00
Mortgage								
Conventional 30 yr.	12.96	1.52	0.20	16.60	1.42	0.24	−3.64	−0.04
GNMA 30 yr.	7.53	1.23	0.09	7.70	1.12	0.09	−0.17	0.01
MBS 15 yr.	3.52	1.95	0.07	5.59	1.63	0.09	−2.07	−0.02
Balloons	3.02	1.69	0.05	0.78	1.02	0.01	2.24	0.04
OTM	0.00	0.00	0.00	0.00	0.00	0.00	0.00	0.00
European & International								
Eurobonds	0.00	0.00	0.00	0.00	0.00	0.00	0.00	0.00
International	0.00	0.00	0.00	0.00	0.00	0.00	0.00	0.00
Asset Backed	0.00	0.00	0.00	0.96	3.14	0.03	−0.96	−0.03
CMO	0.00	0.00	0.00	0.00	0.00	0.00	0.00	0.00
Other	0.00	0.00	0.00	0.00	0.00	0.00	0.00	0.00
Totals	100.00		4.35	100.00		4.29	0.00	0.00

basis of security selection, without expressing views on sector or yield curve. Given a carefully selected universe of securities from a set of favored issuers, the optimizer can help build security picks into a portfolio with no significant systematic exposures relative to the benchmark.

For more active portfolios, the objective is no longer minimization of tracking error. When minimizing tracking error, the optimizer tries to reduce the largest differences between the portfolio and benchmark. But what if the portfolio is meant to be long duration or overweighted in a particular sector to express a market view? These views certainly should not be "optimized" away. However, unintended exposures need to be minimized, while keeping the intentional ones.

For instance, assume in the original sample portfolio that the sector exposure is intentional but the portfolio should be neutral to the benchmark for all other sources of risk, especially term structure. The risk model allows the investor to keep exposures to one or more sets of risk factors (in this case, sector) and optimize to reduce the components of tracking error due to all other risk factors. This is equivalent to reducing all components of tracking error but the ones to be preserved. The model introduces a significant penalty for changing the risk profile of the portfolio in the risk categories designated for preservation.

Exhibit 9.19 shows the transactions suggested by the optimizer in this case.[6] At first glance, the logic behind the selection of the proposed transactions is not as clear as before. We see a sequence of fairly small transactions, mostly trading up in coupon. Although this is one way to change the term structure exposure of a portfolio, it is usually not the most obvious or effective method. The reason for this lies in the very limited choices we offered the optimizer for this illustration. As in the example of tracking error minimization, the investable universe was limited to securities already in the portfolio. That is, only rebalancing trades were permitted. Because the most needed cash flows are at vertices where the portfolio has no maturing securities, the only way to increase those flows is through higher coupon payments. In a more realistic optimization exercise, we would include a wider range of maturity dates (and possibly a set of zero-coupon securities as well) in the investable universe to give the optimizer more flexibility in adjusting portfolio cash flows. Despite these self-imposed limitations, the optimizer succeeds in bringing down the term structure risk while leaving the sector risk almost unchanged. Exhibit 9.20 shows the tracking error break-

---

[6] Tracking error does not decrease with each transaction. This is possible because the optimizer does not minimize the tracking error itself in this case, but rather a function that includes the tracking error due to all factors but sector, as well as a penalty term for changing sector exposures.

EXHIBIT 9.19   Sequence of Transactions Selected by Optimizer,
Keeping Exposures to Sector, $000s
Initial Tracking Error: 52.0 bp

Transaction # 1		
Sold:	2,000 of Coca-Cola Enterprises	6.950 2026/11/15
Bought:	2,000 of Norfolk Southern Corp.	7.800 2027/05/15
Cash Left Over:	−235.19	
New Tracking Error:	52.1 bps	
Cost of this Transaction:	10.000	
Cumulative Cost:	10.000	

Transaction # 2		
Sold:	2,000 of Coca-Cola Enterprises	6.950 2026/11/15
Bought:	2,000 of New York Telephone	9.375 2031/07/15
Cash Left Over:	−389.36	
New Tracking Error:	50.1 bps	
Cost of this Transaction:	10.000	
Cumulative Cost:	20.000	

Transaction # 3		
Sold:	10,000 of U.S. Treasury Bonds	6.250 2023/08/15
Bought:	10,000 of New York Telephone	9.375 2031/07/15
Cash Left Over:	−468.14	
New Tracking Error:	47.4 bps	
Cost of this Transaction:	50.000	
Cumulative Cost:	70.000	

Transaction # 4		
Sold:	2,000 of Coca-Cola Enterprises	6.950 2026/11/15
Bought:	2,000 of FHLM Gold Guar. Single Fam.	7.000 2028/01/01
Cash Left Over:	−373.47	
New Tracking Error:	46.0 bps	
Cost of this Transaction:	10.000	
Cumulative Cost:	80.000	

Transaction # 5		
Sold:	6,000 of U.S. Treasury Bonds	6.250 2023/08/15
Bought:	6,000 of GNMA I Single Fam.	7.500 2022/07/01
Cash Left Over:	272.43	
New Tracking Error:	47.2 bps	
Cost of this Transaction:	30.000	
Cumulative Cost:	110.000	

EXHIBIT 9.19   (Continued)

Transaction # 6		
Sold:	1,000 of Norfolk Southern Corp.	7.800 2027/05/15
Bought:	1,000 of U.S. Treasury Notes	6.125 2007/08/15
Cash Left Over:	343.44	
New Tracking Error:	46.4 bps	
Cost of this Transaction:	5.000	
Cumulative Cost:	115.000	
Transaction # 7		
Sold:	2,000 of Norfolk Southern Corp.	7.800 2027/05/15
Bought:	2,000 of Anheuser-Busch Co., Inc.	6.750 2027/12/15
Cash Left Over:	587.60	
New Tracking Error:	45.7 bps	
Cost of this Transaction:	10.000	
Cumulative Cost:	125.000	

EXHIBIT 9.20   Summary of Tracking Error Breakdown for Sample Portfolios

Tracking Error Due to:	Original Portfolio	Swapped Coca-Cola	Passive	Keep Sector Exposures
Term Structure	36	37	7	12
Sector	32	32	7	30
Systematic Risk	45	46	10	39
Nonsystematic Risk	26	22	13	24
Total	52	51	16	46

down for the resulting portfolio. The term structure risk has been reduced from 36 bps to 12 bps, while the sector risk remains almost unchanged at 30 bps.

Proxy Portfolios

How many securities does it take to replicate the Lehman Corporate Index (containing about 4,500 bonds) to within 25 bps/year? How close could a portfolio of $50 million invested in 10 MBS securities get to the MBS index return? How many high-yield securities does a portfolio need to hold to get sufficient diversification relative to the High-Yield Index? How could one define "sufficient diversification" quantitatively? Investors asking any of these questions are looking for "index proxies"—portfolios with a small number of securities that nevertheless closely match their target indices.

Proxies are used for two distinct purposes: passive investment and index analysis. Both passive portfolio managers and active managers with no particular view on the market at a given time might be interested in insights from index proxies. These proxy portfolios represent a practical method of matching index returns while containing transaction costs. In addition, the large number of securities in an index can pose difficulties in the application of computationally intensive quantitative techniques. A portfolio can be analyzed against an index proxy of a few securities using methods that would be impractical to apply to an index of several thousand securities. As long as the proxy matches the index along relevant risk dimensions, this approach can speed up many forms of analysis with only a small sacrifice in accuracy.

There are several approaches to the creation of index proxies. Quantitative techniques include stratified sampling or cell-matching, tracking error minimization, and matching index scenario results. (With limitations, replication of index returns can also be achieved using securities outside of indices, such as Treasury futures contracts.[7] An alternative way of getting index returns is entering into an index swap or buying an appropriately structured note.) Regardless of the means used to build a proxy portfolio, the risk model can measure how well the proxy is likely to track the index.

In a simple cell-matching technique, a benchmark is profiled on an arbitrary grid that reflects the risk dimensions along which a portfolio manager's allocation decisions are made. The index contribution to each cell is then matched by one or more representative liquid securities. Duration (and convexity) of each cell within the benchmark can be targeted when purchasing securities to fill the cell. We have used this technique to produce proxy portfolios of 20 to 25 MBS passthroughs to track the Lehman Brothers MBS Index. These portfolios have tracked the index of about 600 MBS generics to within 3 bps per month.[8]

To create or fine-tune a proxy portfolio using the risk model, we can start by selecting a seed portfolio and an investable universe. The tracking error minimization process described above then recommends a sequence of transactions. As more bonds are added to the portfolio, risk decreases. The level of tracking achieved by a proxy portfolio depends on the number of bonds included. Panel A in Exhibit 9.21 shows the annualized tracking errors achieved using this procedure, as a function of the number of bonds, in a proxy for the Lehman Brothers Corporate Bond Index. At first, adding more securities to the portfolio reduces tracking error rap-

---

[7] *Replicating Index Returns with Treasury Futures*, Lehman Brothers, November 1997.
[8] *Replicating the MBS Index Risk and Return Characteristics Using Proxy Portfolios*, Lehman Brothers, March 1997.

idly. But as the number of bonds grows, the improvement levels off. The breakdown between systematic and nonsystematic risk explains this phenomenon. As securities are added to the portfolio, systematic risk is reduced rapidly. Once the corporate portfolio is sufficiently diverse to match index exposures to all industries and credit qualities, nonsystematic risk dominates, and the rate of tracking error reduction decreases.

Panel B in Exhibit 9.21 illustrates the same process applied to the Lehman Brothers High-Yield Index. A similar pattern is observed:

EXHIBIT 9.21   Corporate Proxy—Tracking Error as a Function of Number of Bonds (Effect of Diversification)
Panel A. Proxy for Corporate Bond Index

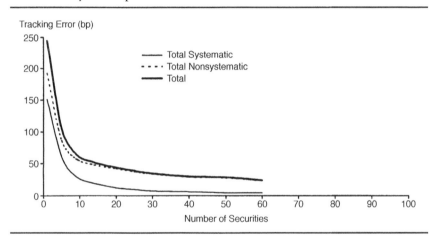

Panel B. Proxy for High-Yield Index

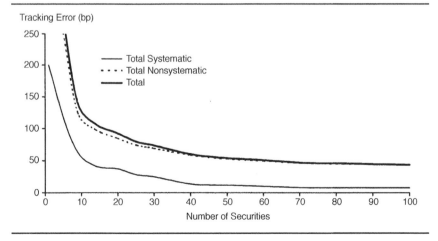

Tracking error declines steeply at first as securities are added; tracking error reduction falls with later portfolio additions. The overall risk of the high-yield proxy remains above the investment-grade proxy. This reflects the effect of quality on our estimate of nonsystematic risk. Similar exposures to lower-rated securities carry more risk. As a result, a proxy of about 30 investment-grade corporates tracks the Corporate Index within about 50 bp/year. Achieving the same tracking error for the High-Yield Index requires a proxy of 50 high-yield bonds.

To demonstrate that proxy portfolios track their underlying indices, we analyze the performance of three proxies over time. The described methodology was used to create a corporate proxy portfolio of about 30 securities from a universe of liquid corporate bonds (minimum $350 million outstanding). Exhibit 9.22 shows the tracking errors projected at the start of each month from January 1997 through September 1998, together with the performance achieved by portfolio and benchmark. The return difference is sometimes larger than the tracking error. (Note that the monthly return difference must be compared to the monthly tracking error, which is obtained by scaling down the annualized tracking error by $\sqrt{12}$.) This is to be expected. Tracking error does not constitute an upper bound of return difference, but rather one standard deviation. If the return difference is normally distributed with the standard deviation given by the tracking error, then the return difference should be expected to be within ±1 tracking error about 68% of the time, and within ±2 tracking errors about 95% of the time. For the corporate proxy shown here, the standard deviation of the return difference over the observed time period is 13 bps, almost identical to the projected monthly tracking error. Furthermore, the result is within ±1 tracking error in 17 months out of 24, or about 71% of the time.

Exhibit 9.23 summarizes the performance of our Treasury, corporate, and mortgage index proxies. The MBS Index was tracked with a proxy portfolio of 20 to 25 generics. The Treasury index was matched using a simple cell-matching scheme. The index was divided into three maturity cells, and two highly liquid bonds were selected from each cell to match the index duration. For each of the three proxy portfolios, the observed standard deviation of return difference is less than the tracking error. The corporate portfolio tracks as predicted by the risk model, while the Treasury and mortgage proxies track better than predicted. The corporate index proxy was generated by minimizing the tracking error relative to the Corporate Index using 50 to 60 securities. Being much less diversified than the index of about 4,700 securities, the corporate proxy is most exposed to nonsystematic risk. In the difficult month of September 1998, when liquidity in the credit markets was severely stemmed, this resulted in a realized return difference three times the projected tracking error.

EXHIBIT 9.22 Corporate Proxy Portfolio: Comparison of Achieved Results with Projected Tracking Errors

Date	Annual Tracking Error (bps)	Monthly Tracking Error (bps)	Return (%/mo.) Proxy	Return (%/mo.) Index	Return Difference (bps/Mo.)	Ret. Diff./ Monthly Tracking Error
Jan-97	48	14	0.15	0.14	0	0.03
Feb-97	48	14	0.37	0.42	−5	−0.34
Mar-97	48	14	−1.60	−1.56	−4	−0.30
Apr-97	47	14	1.60	1.52	8	0.60
May-97	48	14	1.14	1.13	1	0.04
Jun-97	48	14	1.42	1.42	0	0.03
Jul-97	47	14	3.62	3.66	−4	−0.27
Aug-97	48	14	−1.48	−1.48	0	−0.01
Sep-97	47	14	1.65	1.75	−10	−0.72
Oct-97	48	14	1.43	1.27	16	1.13
Nov-97	49	14	0.60	0.57	4	0.25
Dec-97	49	14	1.33	1.06	27	1.88
Jan-98	49	14	1.36	1.19	17	1.19
Feb-98	46	13	0.05	−0.03	8	0.59
Mar-98	46	13	0.39	0.37	2	0.16
Apr-98	45	13	0.75	0.63	12	0.93
May-98	44	13	1.22	1.19	3	0.24
Jun-98	45	13	0.79	0.74	6	0.42
Jul-98	45	13	−0.18	−0.10	−8	−0.63
Aug-98	44	13	0.76	0.47	29	2.26
Sep-98	44	13	3.62	3.24	38	2.99
Oct-98	46	13	−1.40	−1.54	15	1.11
Nov-98	45	13	2.04	1.88	16	1.20
Dec-98	47	14	0.17	0.29	−12	−0.87
Std. Dev.:					13	

	Number	Percentage
Observations within +/− 1 × tracking error	17	71%
Observations within +/− 2 × tracking error	22	92%
Total number of observations	24	

EXHIBIT 9.23 Summary of Historical Results of
Proxy Portfolios for Treasury, Corporate, and MBS Indices, in bps per Month

	Treasury		Corporate		MBS	
	Tracking Error	Return Difference	Tracking Error	Return Difference	Tracking Error	Return Difference
Jan-97	5.5	−1.7	13.9	0.4	4.3	0.8
Feb-97	5.2	−0.6	13.9	−4.7	4.3	−0.3
Mar-97	5.5	−1.8	13.9	−4.2	4.0	2.9
Apr-97	5.5	1.7	13.6	8.2	4.3	−3.3
May-97	5.8	−0.3	13.9	0.6	4.0	1.6
Jun-97	6.6	3.5	13.9	0.4	4.0	−0.5
Jul-97	6.6	3.8	13.6	−3.7	4.0	−2.5
Aug-97	6.9	−3.8	13.9	−0.1	4.3	1.5
Sep-97	6.4	1.5	13.6	−9.8	4.3	−1.2
Oct-97	6.4	3.2	13.9	15.7	4.0	−0.6
Nov-97	6.1	−2.3	14.1	3.5	4.0	0.8
Dec-97	6.6	6.0	14.1	26.6	4.0	−2.4
Jan-98	6.6	1.0	14.1	16.9	4.3	1.8
Feb-98	6.6	−1.8	13.3	7.8	4.9	2.2
Mar-98	6.6	1.8	13.3	2.1	4.0	−1.9
Apr-98	6.6	−1.8	13.0	12.1	4.6	−0.9
May-98	6.6	3.8	12.7	3.1	4.6	−0.3
Jun-98	7.8	−1.4	13.0	5.5	4.9	0.4
Jul-98	7.5	−1.7	13.0	−8.2	4.3	−1.3
Aug-98	7.5	−0.6	12.7	28.7	4.3	−3.4
Sep-98	8.1	−6.1	12.7	38.0	4.0	−1.7
Oct-98	7.8	5.4	13.3	14.7	4.0	3.4
Nov-98	7.8	−4.9	13.0	15.6	4.6	−1.8
Dec-98	6.1	−2.7	13.6	−11.8	4.3	−1.6
Mean	6.6	0.0	13.5	6.6	4.3	−0.3
Std. Dev.		3.2		12.5		1.9
Min		−6.1		−11.8		−3.4
Max		6.0		38.0		3.4

A proxy portfolio for the Lehman Brothers Aggregate Index can be constructed by building proxies to track each of its major components and combining them with the proper weightings. This exercise clearly illustrates the benefits of diversification. The aggregate proxy in Exhibit 9.24 is obtained by combining the government, corporate, and mort-

EXHIBIT 9.24   Effect of Diversification—Tracking Error versus Treasury, Corporate, MBS, and Aggregate

Index	No. of Bonds in Proxy	No. of Bonds in Index	Tracking Error (bps/Year)
Treasury	6	165	13
Government	39	1,843	11
Corporate	51	4,380	26
Mortgage	19	606	15
Aggregate	109	6,928	10

gage proxies shown in the same exhibit. The tracking error achieved by the combination is smaller than that of any of its constituents. This is because the risks of the proxy portfolios are largely independent.

When using tracking error minimization to design proxy portfolios, the choice of the "seed" portfolio and the investable universe should be considered carefully. The seed portfolio is the initial portfolio presented to the optimizer. Due to the nature of the gradient search procedure, the path followed by the optimizer depends on the initial portfolio. The seed portfolio produces the best results when it is closest in nature to the benchmark. At the very least, asset managers should choose a seed portfolio with duration near that of the benchmark. The investable universe, or bond swap pool, should be wide enough to offer the optimizer the freedom to match all risk factors. But if the intention is to actually purchase the proxy, the investable universe should be limited to liquid securities.

These methods for building proxy portfolios are not mutually exclusive, but can be used in conjunction with each other. A portfolio manager who seeks to build an investment portfolio that is largely passive to the index can use a combination of security picking, cell matching, and tracking-error minimization. By dividing the market into cells and choosing one or more preferred securities in each cell, the manager can create an investable universe of candidate bonds in which all sectors and credit qualities are represented. The tracking error minimization procedure can then match index exposures to all risk factors while choosing only securities that the manager would like to purchase.

Benchmark Selection: Broad versus Narrow Indices

Lehman Brothers' development has been guided by the principle that benchmarks should be broad-based, market-weighted averages. This leads to indices that give a stable, objective, and comprehensive representation of the selected market. On occasion, some investors have expressed a preference for indices composed of fewer securities. Among the rationales, transparency of pricing associated with smaller indices and a presumption that smaller indices are easier to replicate have been most commonly cited.

We have shown that it is possible to construct proxy portfolios with small numbers of securities that adequately track broad-based benchmarks. Furthermore, broad benchmarks offer more opportunities for outperformance by low-risk security selection strategies.[9] When a benchmark is too narrow, each security represents a significant percentage, and a risk-conscious manager might be forced to own nearly every issue in the benchmark. Ideally, a benchmark should be diverse enough to reduce its nonsystematic risk close to zero. As seen in Exhibit 9.2, the nonsystematic part of sigma for the aggregate index is only 4 bps.

Defining Spread and Curve Scenarios Consistent with History

The tracking error produced by the risk model is an average expected performance deviation due to possible changes in all risk factors. In addition to this method of measuring risk, many investors perform "stress tests" on their portfolios. Here scenario analysis is used to project performance under various market conditions. The scenarios considered typically include a standard set of movements in the yield curve (parallel shift, steepening, and flattening) and possibly more specific scenarios based on market views. Often, though, practitioners neglect to consider spread changes, possibly due to the difficulties in generating reasonable scenarios of this type. (Is it realistic to assume that industrial spreads will tighten by 10 bps while utilities remain unchanged?) One way to generate spread scenarios consistent with the historical experience of spreads in the marketplace is to utilize the statistical information contained within the risk model.

For each sector/quality cell of the corporate bond market shown in Exhibit 9.25, we create a corporate subindex confined to a particular cell and use it as a portfolio. We then create a hypothetical Treasury bond for each security in this subindex. Other than being labeled as belonging to the Treasury sector and having Aaa quality, these hypothetical bonds are identical to their corresponding real corporate bonds. We run a risk model comparison between the portfolio of corporate bonds versus their hypothetical Treasury counterparts as the benchmark. This artificially forces the portfolio and benchmark sensitivity to term structure, optionality, and any other risks to be neutralized, leaving only sector and quality risk. Exhibit 9.25 shows the tracking error components due to sector and quality, as well as their combined effect. Dividing these tracking errors (standard deviations of return differences) by the average dura-

---

[9] *Value of Security Selection versus Asset Allocation in Credit Markets: A "Perfect Foresight" Study*, Lehman Brothers, March 1999.

EXHIBIT 9.25 Using the Risk Model to Define Spread Scenarios Consistent with History

		Dur.	Annual Tracking Error (%)			Spread Volatility (bps)			
		(Years)	Sector	Quality	Both	Sector	Quality	Both	Monthly
U.S. Agencies	Aaa	4.54	0.26	0.00	0.26	6	0	6	2
Industrials	Aaa	8.42	2.36	0.00	2.36	28	0	28	8
	Aa	6.37	1.72	0.57	2.03	27	9	32	9
	A	6.97	1.89	0.82	2.43	27	12	35	10
	Baa	6.80	1.87	1.36	2.96	27	20	43	13
Utilities	Aaa	7.34	1.62	0.13	1.65	22	2	22	6
	Aa	5.67	1.21	0.45	1.39	21	8	25	7
	A	6.03	1.33	0.63	1.67	22	10	28	8
	Baa	5.68	1.36	1.01	2.07	24	18	36	11
Financials	Aaa	4.89	1.41	0.00	1.41	29	0	29	8
	Aa	4.29	1.31	0.34	1.50	30	8	35	10
	A	4.49	1.31	0.49	1.65	29	11	37	11
	Baa	4.86	1.58	0.86	2.14	32	18	44	13
Banking	Aa	4.87	1.23	0.44	1.40	25	9	29	8
	A	5.68	1.43	0.62	1.72	25	11	30	9
	Baa	5.06	1.27	1.13	2.11	25	22	42	12
Yankees	Aaa	6.16	1.23	0.06	1.26	20	1	20	6
	Aa	5.45	1.05	0.49	1.27	19	9	23	7
	A	7.03	1.62	0.89	2.17	23	13	31	9
	Baa	6.17	1.51	1.36	2.60	24	22	42	12

tions of the cells produces approximations for the standard deviation of spread changes. The standard deviation of the overall spread change, converted to a monthly number, can form the basis for a set of spread change scenarios. For instance, a scenario of "spreads widen by one standard deviation" would imply a widening of 6 bps for Aaa utilities, and 13 bps for Baa financials. This is a more realistic scenario than an across-the-board parallel shift, such as "corporates widen by 10 bps."

Hedging

Because the covariance matrix used by the risk model is based on monthly observations of security returns, the model cannot compute daily hedges. However, it can help create long-term positions that over time perform better than a naïve hedge. This point is illustrated by a historical simulation of a simple barbell versus bullet strategy in Exhibit 9.26, in which a combination of the 2- and 10-year on-the-run Treasuries is used to hedge the on-the-run 5-year. We compare two methods of calculating the relative weights of the two bonds in the hedge. In the first method, the hedge is rebalanced at the start of each month to match the duration of the 5-year Treasury. In the second, the model is engaged on a monthly basis to minimize the tracking error between the portfolio of 2- and 10-year securities and the 5-year benchmark. As shown in Exhibit 9.26, the risk model hedge tracks the performance of the 5-year bullet more closely than the duration hedge, with an observed tracking error of 19 bps/month compared with 20 bps/month for the duration hedge.

The duration of the 2- and 10-year portfolio built with the minimal tracking error hedging technique is consistently longer than that of the 5-year. Over the study period (1/1994–2/1999), the duration difference averaged 0.1 years. This duration extension proved very stable (standard deviation of 0.02) and is rooted in the shape of the historically most likely movement of the yield curve. It can be shown that the shape of the first principal component of yield curve movements is not quite a parallel shift.[10] Rather, the 2-year will typically experience less yield change then the 5- or 10-year. To the extent that the 5- and 10-year securities experience historically similar yield changes, a barbell hedge could benefit from an underweighting of the 2-year and an overweighting of the 10-year security. Over the 62 months analyzed in this study, the risk-based hedge performed closer to the 5-year than the duration-based hedge 59% of the time.

EXHIBIT 9.26 Historical Performance of a Two-Security Barbell versus the 5-Year On-the-Run Treasury Bullet; Duration-Based Hedge versus a Tracking Error-Based Hedge, January 1994 to February 1999

| | | Duration Hedge | | Tracking Error Hedge | | % of Months Tracking Improved |
		Return	Duration	Return	Duration	
2–10 vs. 5	Mean	0.03	0.00	0.03	0.10	59%
	Std. Dev.	0.20	0.00	0.19	0.02	
2–30 vs. 5	Mean	0.04	0.00	0.04	0.36	62%
	Std. Dev.	0.36	0.00	0.33	0.03	

[10] *Managing the Yield Curve with Principal Component Analysis*, Lehman Brothers, November 1998.

A similar study conducted using a 2- and 30-year barbell versus a 5-year bullet over the same study period (1/1994–2/1999) produced slightly more convincing evidence. Here, the risk-based hedge tracked better than the duration hedge by about 3 bps/month (33 bps/month tracking error versus 36 bps/month) and improved upon the duration hedge in 60% of the months studied. Interestingly, the duration extension in the hedge was even more pronounced in this case, with the risk-based hedge longer than the 5-year by an average of 0.36 years.

Estimating the Probability of Portfolio Underperformance

What is the probability that a portfolio will underperform the benchmark by 25 bps or more over the coming year? To answer such questions, we need to make some assumptions about the distribution of the performance difference. We assume this difference to be distributed normally, with the standard deviation given by the tracking error calculated by the risk model. However, the risk model does not provide an estimate of the mean outperformance. Such an estimate may be obtained by a horizon total return analysis under an expected scenario (e.g., yield curve and spreads unchanged), or by simply using the yield differential as a rough guide. In the example of Exhibit 9.1, the portfolio yield exceeds that of the benchmark by 16 bps, and the tracking error is calculated as 52 bps. Exhibit 9.27 depicts the normal distribution with a

EXHIBIT 9.27   Projected Distribution of Total Return Difference (in bps/year) between Portfolio and Benchmark, Based on Yield Advantage of 16 bps and Tracking Error of 52 bps, Assuming Normal Distribution

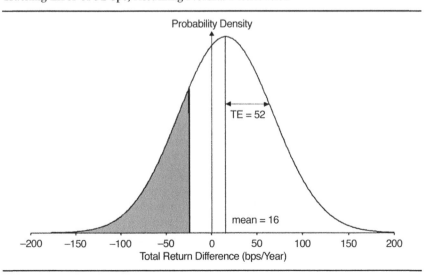

mean of 16 bps and a standard deviation of 52 bps. The area of the shaded region, which represents the probability of underperforming by 25 bps or more, may be calculated as

$$N[(-25) - 16)/52] = 0.215 = 21.5\%$$

where $N(x)$ is the standard normal cumulative distribution function. As the true distribution of the return difference may not be normal, this approach must be used with care. It may not be accurate in estimating the probability of rare events such as the "great spread sector crash" in August 1998. For example, this calculation would assign a probability of only 0.0033 or 0.33% to an underperformance of −125 bps or worse. Admittedly, if the tails of the true distribution are slightly different than normal, the true probability could be much higher.

Measuring Sources of Market Risk

As illustrated in Exhibit 9.2, the risk model reports the projected standard deviation of the absolute returns (sigma) of the portfolio and the benchmark as well as that of the return difference (tracking error). However, the detailed breakdown of risk due to different groups of risk factors is reported only for the tracking error. To obtain such a breakdown of the absolute risk (sigma) of a given portfolio or index, we can measure the risk of our portfolio against a riskless asset, such as a cash security. In this case, the relative risk is equal to the absolute risk of the portfolio, and the tracking error breakdown report can be interpreted as a breakdown of market sigma.

Exhibit 9.28 illustrates the use of this technique to analyze the sources of market risk in four Lehman Brothers indices: Treasury, (investment grade) Corporate, High-Yield Corporate, and MBS. The results provide a clear picture of the role played by the different sources of risk in each of these markets. In the Treasury Index, term structure risk represents the only significant form of risk. In the Corporate Index, sector and quality risk add to term structure risk, but the effect of a negative correlation between spread risk and term structure risk is clearly visible. The overall risk of the Corporate Index (5.47%) is less than the term structure component alone (5.81%). This reflects the fact that when Treasury interest rates undergo large shocks, corporate yields often lag, moving more slowly in the same direction. The High-Yield Index shows a marked increase in quality risk and in nonsystematic risk relative to the Corporate Index. But, the negative correlation between term-structure risk and quality risk is large as well, and the overall risk (4.76%) is less than the term structure risk (4.98%) by even more than it is for corpo-

EXHIBIT 9.28 Risk Model Breakdown of Market Risk (Sigma) to Different Categories of Risk Factors (Isolated Mode) for Four Lehman Brothers Indices, as of September 30, 1998, in Percent per Year

Index:	Treasury	Corporate	High Yield	MBS
Duration (years)	5.58	6.08	4.74	1.37
Convexity	0.69	0.68	0.20	−2.19
Term Structure Risk	5.25	5.81	4.98	3.25
Nonterm Structure Risk	0.17	2.14	5.20	2.28
Risk Due to:				
Corp. Sector	0.00	1.50	1.21	0.00
Quality	0.00	0.84	4.67	0.00
Optionality	0.01	0.08	0.15	0.00
Coupon	0.17	0.01	0.19	0.00
MBS Sector	0.00	0.00	0.00	1.15
MBS Volatility	0.00	0.00	0.00	1.27
MBS Prepayment	0.00	0.00	0.00	0.73
Total Systematic Risk	5.26	5.47	4.75	2.69
Nonsystematic Risk	0.04	0.08	0.17	0.09
Total Risk (std. dev. of annual return)	5.26	5.47	4.76	2.69

rates. The effect of negative correlations among risk factors is also very strong in the MBS Index, where the MBS-specific risk factors bring the term structure risk of 3.25% down to an overall risk of 2.69%.

SUMMARY

In this chapter, we described a risk model for dollar-denominated government, corporate, and mortgage-backed securities. The model quantifies expected deviation in performance ("tracking error") between a portfolio of fixed income securities and an index representing the market, such as the Lehman Brothers Aggregate, Corporate, or High-Yield Index.

The forecast of the return deviation is based on specific mismatches between the sensitivities of the portfolio and the benchmark to major market forces ("risk factors") that drive security returns. The model uses historical variances and correlations of the risk factors to translate the structural differences of the portfolio and the index into an expected tracking error. The model quantifies not only this systematic market risk, but security-specific (nonsystematic) risk as well.

Using an illustrative portfolio, we demonstrated the implementation of the model. We showed how each component of tracking error can be traced back to the corresponding difference between the portfolio and benchmark risk exposures. We described the methodology for the minimization of tracking error and discussed a variety of portfolio management applications.

Interest Rate
Risk Management

Measuring Plausibility of Hypothetical Interest Rate Shocks

Bennett W. Golub, Ph.D.
Managing Director
Risk Management and Analytics Group
BlackRock Financial Management, Inc.

Leo M. Tilman
Chief Institutional Strategist and Senior Managing Director
Bear Stearns

Many areas of modern portfolio and risk management are based on how portfolio managers see the U.S. yield curve evolving in the future. These predictions are often formulated as hypothetical *shocks* to the spot curve that portfolio managers expect to occur over the specified *horizon*. Via key rate durations as defined by Thomas Ho[1] or as implied by principal component durations,[2] these shocks can be used to assess the impact of implicit duration and yield curve bets on a portfolio's

---

[1] Thomas S. Y. Ho, "Key Rate Durations: Measures of Interest Rate Risks," *Journal of Fixed Income* (September 1992), pp. 29–44
[2] Bennett W. Golub and Leo M. Tilman, "Measuring Yield Curve Risk Using Principal Component Analysis, Value-at-Risk, and Key Rate Durations," *Journal of Portfolio Management* (Summer 1997), pp. 72–84.

The authors would like to thank Yury Geyman, Lawrence Polhman, Ehud Ronn, Michael Salm, Irwin Sheer, Pavan Wadhwa, and Adam Wizon for their helpful comments and feedback.

return. Other common uses of hypothetical interest rate shocks include various what-if analyses and stress tests, numerous duration measures of a portfolio's sensitivity to the slope of the yield curve, and so on.

The human mind can imagine all sorts of unusual interest rate shocks, and considerable time and resources may be spent on investigating the sensitivity of portfolios to these interest rate shocks without questioning their *historical plausibility*. Our goal in this chapter is to define what historical plausibility is and how to measure it quantitatively. In order to achieve that, we employ the approaches suggested by principal component analysis. We introduce the framework that derives statistical distributions and measures historical plausibility of hypothetical interest rate shocks thus providing historical validity to the corresponding yield curve bets.

We start with a brief overview of the principal component analysis and then utilize its methods to directly compute the probabilistic distribution of hypothetical interest rate shocks. The same section also introduces the notions of *magnitude plausibility* and *explanatory power* of interest rate shocks. Then we take the analysis one step further and introduce the notion of *shape plausibility*. We conclude by establishing a relationship between the shape of the first principal component and the term structure of volatility and verify the obtained results on the historical steepeners and flatteners of U.S. Treasury spot and on-the-run curves.

PROBABILISTIC DISTRIBUTION OF HYPOTHETICAL INTEREST RATE SHOCKS

The U.S. Treasury spot curve is continuous. This fact complicates the analysis and prediction of spot curve movements, especially using statistical methods. Therefore, practitioners usually *discretize* the spot curve, presenting its movements as changes of key rates—selected points on the spot curve.[3] Changes in spot key rates are assumed to be random variables which follow a multivariate normal distribution with zero mean and the covariance matrix computed from the historical data. There exist different ways to estimate the parameters of the distribution of key rates: equally weighted, exponentially weighted, fractional exponentially weighted, and the like. Although extensive research is being conducted on the connection between the appropriate estimation procedures and different styles of money management, this issue is

---

[3] See Ho, "Key Rate Durations: Measures of Interest Rate Risks."

beyond the scope of this chapter. Ideas presented below are invariant over the methodology used to create the covariance matrix ($\mathfrak{I}$) of key rate changes. We assume that the covariance matrix $\mathfrak{I}$ is given.

Principal component analysis is a statistical procedure which significantly simplifies the analysis of the covariance structure of complex systems such as interest rate movements. Instead of key rates, it creates a new set of random variables called principal components. The latter are the special linear combinations of key rates designed to explain the variability of the system as parsimoniously as possible. The output of the principal component analysis of the RiskMetrics™ monthly dataset is presented in Exhibit 10.1.

The data in Exhibit 10.1 can be interpreted as follows: Over 92% of the historical interest rate shocks are "explained" by the first principal component, over 97% by the first two, and over 98% by the first three. Also note that the "humped" shape of the first principal component is similar to that of the term structure of volatility of changes in spot rates. Later in this chapter we will demonstrate that this is a direct implication of the high correlation between U.S. spot key rates.[4]

Because key rates and principal components are random variables, any hypothetical (and, to that matter, historical) interest rate shock is a particular realization of these variables. We will use the subscripts KR and PC to indicate whether we are referring to a key rate or principal component representation of interest rate shocks. For instance,

$$\vec{X} = (x_1, ..., x_n)^T_{KR}$$

is an interest rate shock formulated in terms of changes in key rates. As mentioned earlier, our goal in this chapter is to analyze the shape and magnitude plausibility of hypothetical interest rate shocks and derive statistical distribution of interest rate shocks of a *given shape.* We start with the following definition.

Let

$$\vec{X} = (x_1, ..., x_n)^T_{KR}$$

---

[4] For a detailed discussion of principal components and their use in portfolio and risk management see Golub and Tilman, "Measuring Yield Curve Risk Using Principal Component Analysis, Value-at-Risk, and Key Rate Durations."

EXHIBIT 10.1 Principal Components Implied by JP Morgan RiskMetrics™ Monthly Dataset, September 30, 1996

	3 Mo	1 Yr	2 Yr	3 Yr	5 Yr	7 Yr	10 Yr	15 Yr	20 Yr	30 Yr
Annualized ZCB Yield Vol (%)	9.63	16.55	18.33	17.82	17.30	16.62	15.27	14.25	13.26	12.09
One Std Dev of ZCB Yields (bps)	52	96	113	112	113	11	104	101	97	83
Correlation Matrix										
3 mo	1.00	0.80	0.72	0.68	0.65	0.61	0.58	0.54	0.51	0.46
1 yr	0.80	1.00	0.91	0.91	0.89	0.87	0.85	0.81	0.78	0.76
2 yr	0.72	0.91	1.00	0.99	0.97	0.95	0.93	0.89	0.85	0.84
3 yr	0.68	0.91	0.99	1.00	0.99	0.97	0.96	0.92	0.90	0.88
5 yr	0.65	0.89	0.97	0.99	1.00	0.99	0.98	0.96	0.93	0.92
7 yr	0.61	0.87	0.95	0.97	0.99	1.00	0.99	0.98	0.96	0.95
10 yr	0.58	0.85	0.93	0.96	0.98	0.99	1.00	0.99	0.98	0.97
15 yr	0.54	0.81	0.89	0.92	0.96	0.98	0.99	1.00	0.99	0.98
20 yr	0.51	0.78	0.85	0.90	0.93	0.96	0.98	0.99	1.00	0.99
30 yr	0.46	0.76	0.84	0.88	0.92	0.95	0.97	0.98	0.99	1.00

EXHIBIT 10.1 (Continued)

PC No	Eig Val	Vol PC	Var Expl	CVar Expl	Principal Components									
					3 Mo	1 Yr	2 Yr	3 Yr	5 Yr	7 Yr	10 Yr	15 Yr	20 Yr	30 Yr
1	9.24	3.04	92.80	92.80	11.09	28.46	35.69	36.37	36.94	36.30	34.02	32.40	30.33	25.71
2	0.48	0.69	4.80	97.60	43.93	48.66	34.19	20.37	5.23	-9.32	-18.63	-30.09	-37.24	-36.94
3	0.13	0.36	1.27	98.87	42.43	54.93	-44.61	-35.28	-21.02	-8.43	0.31	19.59	27.12	17.76
4	0.06	0.25	0.62	99.49	76.77	-61.47	9.21	-0.18	-0.01	-2.08	-0.65	10.46	11.30	-0.31
5	0.02	0.14	0.20	99.69	12.33	-4.93	-55.03	-3.84	38.06	47.35	33.64	-21.36	-35.74	-14.98
6	0.01	0.10	0.11	99.79	8.94	0.33	18.59	-11.83	-15.02	-2.14	19.64	-44.15	-30.58	77.03
7	0.01	0.09	0.09	99.88	3.02	-0.79	-38.42	49.35	45.01	-48.00	-28.08	-10.93	7.76	27.93
8	0.00	0.07	0.06	99.94	3.26	-1.14	-24.96	66.51	-66.82	17.27	13.02	-0.70	-2.46	-1.38
9	0.00	0.06	0.03	99.97	0.76	-0.46	-1.46	-0.97	0.21	60.38	-72.73	-20.12	19.52	16.59
10	0.00	0.05	0.03	100.00	0.54	0.00	-2.53	1.32	-0.42	5.15	-27.03	67.98	-64.58	21.03

ZCB = Zero-coupon bond
Eig Val = Eigenvalues (i.e., principal component variances) × 10,000
Vol PC = Volatility of principal components × 100
Var Expl = Percentage of variance explained
CVar Expl = Cumulative percentage of variance explained

and

$$\vec{Y} = (y_1, ..., y_n)_{KR}^T$$

be spot curve shocks represented as vectors of key rate changes. We will say that

$$\vec{X} \text{ and } \vec{Y}$$

have the *same shape* if they differ only by a factor, that is,

$$(y_1, ..., y_n)^T = (c \times x_1, ..., c \times x_n)^T$$

where c is a real number. (See Exhibit 10.2.)

As this section will show, it turns out that all interest rate shocks of a given *shape* correspond to the realizations of an underlying standard normal random variable. Once we know that, we can talk about the probability associated with a given shock (i.e., given realization). For instance, if a given interest rate shock corresponds to a three standard deviation realiza-

EXHIBIT 10.2   Interest Rate Shocks of the Same Shape

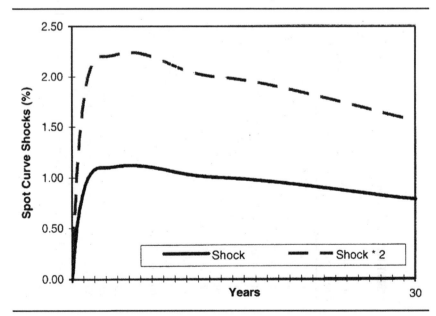

tion of this underlying standard normal random variable, we conclude that it is improbable. While deriving the probabilistic distribution of hypothetical interest rate shocks, we utilize approaches used while constructing principal components. Namely, we start with the discussion of how to compute *one standard deviation principal component shocks* used in a variety of instances including principal component durations. Relationships discussed below apply to random variables and their realizations alike.

Let

$$\vec{X} = (x_1, ..., x_n)_{KR}^T$$

be a spot curve shock formulated in terms of changes in key rates. Let

$$\vec{X} = (p_1, ..., p_n)_{PC}^T$$

be a representation of the *same* interest rate shock $\vec{X}$ corresponding to the coordinate system of principal components (x_i and p_i are the particular realizations of key rates and principal components respectively). Then the relationship between the two representations of the same vector $\vec{X}$ is given by

$$\begin{bmatrix} p_1 \\ ... \\ p_n \end{bmatrix} = \begin{bmatrix} pc_{1,1} & \cdots & pc_{1,n} \\ ... & ... & ... \\ pc_{n,1} & \cdots & pc_{n,n} \end{bmatrix} \times \begin{bmatrix} x_1 \\ ... \\ x_n \end{bmatrix} \tag{10.1}$$

where $\Omega = \{pc_{i,j}\}$ is a matrix whose rows are principal component coefficients. They are the unit vectors of the form

$$\begin{bmatrix} pc_{i,1} & \cdots & pc_{i,n} \end{bmatrix}$$

If K_i are [random] changes in key rates, then the principal components are defined as the following linear combinations

$$pc_{i,1} \times K_1 + ... + pc_{i,n} \times K_n$$

of key rate changes. From the linear algebra viewpoint, the matrix Ω allows us to translate the representation of an interest rate shock in one coordinate system (key rates) into another (principal components). The matrix Ω is orthogonal by construction, i.e., $\Omega^{-1} = \Omega^T$. Therefore, we can rewrite equation (10.1) as follows:

$$
\begin{bmatrix} x_1 \\ \dots \\ x_n \end{bmatrix} = \begin{bmatrix} pc_{1,1} & \dots & pc_{n,1} \\ \dots & \dots & \dots \\ pc_{1,n} & \dots & pc_{n,n} \end{bmatrix} \times \begin{bmatrix} p_1 \\ \dots \\ p_n \end{bmatrix} \tag{10.2}
$$

or simply

$$
\begin{bmatrix} x_1 \\ \dots \\ x_n \end{bmatrix} = \sum_{i=1}^{n} \begin{bmatrix} pc_{i,1} \\ \dots \\ pc_{i,n} \end{bmatrix} \times p_i \tag{10.3}
$$

Equation (10.3) allows us to interpret an arbitrary interest rate shock $\vec{X}$ as a *sum of principal component coefficients that are multiplied by a realization of the appropriate principal component.*

For example, consider a one standard deviation shock corresponding to the first principal component (PC_1). The realization of such event in terms of principal components is given by

$$
(\sqrt{\lambda_1}, 0, \dots, 0)_{PC}^{T}
$$

where $\sqrt{\lambda_1}$ is the one standard deviation of PC_1. In terms of key rate changes, however, via equation (10.3) this shock has the following familiar representation

$$
(\sqrt{\lambda_1} \times pc_{1,1}, \dots, \sqrt{\lambda_1} \times pc_{1,n})_{KR}
$$

The splined shapes of the first three principal components are presented in Exhibit 10.3.

Principal components constitute an orthogonal basis PC in the space of spot curve movements. By definition, the i-th principal components is obtained from the covariance matrix $\mathcal{S}$ of key rate changes via the following optimization problem:

- Compute the remaining variability in the system not explained by the first $i - 1$ principal components.
- Find a linear combination of key rates that explains as much of the remaining variability as possible.
- The i-th principal component should be orthogonal to all the previously selected $i - 1$ principal components.

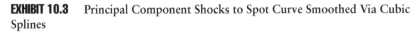

EXHIBIT 10.3 Principal Component Shocks to Spot Curve Smoothed Via Cubic Splines

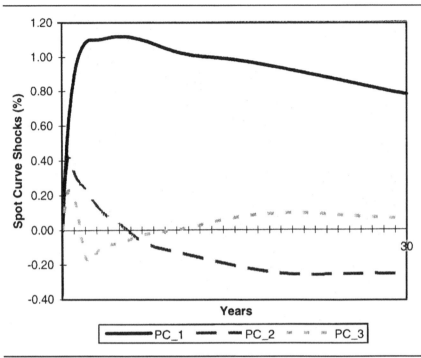

Clearly, in an n-dimensional linear space of spot curve movements, there exist orthogonal *bases other than the one consisting of principal components*. Surprisingly, this fact will help us derive the distribution of interest rate shocks of a given shape.

Suppose

$$\vec{Y} = (y_1, \ldots, y_n)_{KR}$$

is a hypothetical interest rate shock defined in terms of key rate changes. We claim that

$$\vec{Y}$$

corresponds to a particular realization of some standard normal random variable y. In other words, all interest rate shocks of a given shape are in one-to-one correspondence with the set of realizations of y.

Therefore, we can speak about the probability of $\vec{Y}$ occurring. We will now construct y and establish its relationship with $\vec{Y}$.

Let

$$\vec{y} = (\hat{y}_1, \ldots, \hat{y}_n)_{KR}$$

be a unit vector whose shape is the same as that of $\vec{Y}$, that is,

$$\hat{y}_i = y_i / \sqrt{\sum_{i=1}^{n} y_i^2}$$

Similarly to the way we define principal components, define a new random variable Y to be the linear combination

$$Y = \sum_{i=1}^{n} \hat{y}_i \times K_i$$

where $\hat{y}_i$ are real numbers and K_i are changes in key rates (random variables). Then the variance of Y is given by

$$\sigma^2(Y) = (\hat{y}_1, \ldots, \hat{y}_n) \times \Im \times (\hat{y}_1, \ldots, \hat{y}_n)^T \qquad (10.4)$$

We will now construct a new coordinate system in the space of spot curve changes. It will correspond to the new orthogonal basis B (different from principal components) such that Y is the first element in B. We modify the principal component optimization problem as follows:

- On the first step, instead of selecting a linear combination of changes in key rates that explains the maximum amount of variance, select Y.
- On each following step, find a linear combination of key rates that explains the maximum of the remaining variability in the system
- Every newly selected element of the basis B should be orthogonal to all previously selected elements of B.

As a result, we have selected a set of n orthogonal variables that explain the total historical variability of interest rate movements. Moreover, Y is the first element in this basis. Define $y = Y/\sigma(Y)$, then y is a standard normal variable. The analog of equation (10.3) in this new coordinate system is given by

$$
\begin{bmatrix} x_1 \\ \dots \\ x_n \end{bmatrix} = \begin{bmatrix} \hat{y}_1 \\ \dots \\ \hat{y}_n \end{bmatrix} \times Y + \dots \tag{10.5}
$$

or simply

$$
\begin{bmatrix} x_1 \\ \dots \\ x_n \end{bmatrix} = \begin{bmatrix} \sigma(Y) \times \hat{y}_1 \\ \dots \\ \sigma(Y) \times \hat{y}_n \end{bmatrix} \times y + \dots \tag{10.6}
$$

where

$$
(\sigma(Y) \times \hat{y}_1, \dots, \sigma(Y) \times \hat{y}_n)_{KR}^T
$$

is the one standard deviation shock corresponding to Y. Therefore, due to orthogonality, *every interest rate shock whose shape is the same as that of*

$$
\vec{Y} \ (\text{and} \ \vec{y})
$$

corresponds to a particular realization of the standard normal variable y.
For example, consider 10 key rates ($n = 10$) and suppose $\vec{Y}$ is a 200 bps parallel spot curve shock:

$$
\vec{Y} = (200, \dots, 200)_{KR}
$$

Then

$$
\vec{y} = (1/\sqrt{10}, \dots, 1/\sqrt{10})_{KR}
$$

is the corresponding unit vector which has the same shape as $\vec{Y}$. Using the RiskMetrics^{TM} dataset, we can compute the standard deviation of the corresponding random variable Y. It can be shown that the "one standard deviation parallel shock" on September 30, 1996 was 92 bps. Therefore, since we started with a parallel 200 bps spot curve shock, it implies a 200/92 = 2.17 standard deviation realization in the underlying standard normal variable. Then the probability of an annualized parallel shock over 200 bps is 0.015.

The magnitude of a one standard deviation parallel shock varies with the total variability in the market. Thus, on February 4, 1997 the one standard deviation parallel shock was 73 bps and the probability of a parallel shock being over 200 bps was 0.003.

Ability to derive the distribution of interest rate shocks of a given shape leads us to the following important concepts.

Parallel First Principal Component

Many practitioners believe that it is convenient and intuitive to force the first principal component duration to equal effective duration.[5] To achieve this, we need to assume that the first principal component is a parallel spot curve shock. However, unlike the first principal component, a parallel spot curve shock is correlated with steepness and curvature (second and third principal components, respectively). Therefore, immunization and simulation techniques involving principal components become more complicated. Via the method introduced above, we can create a new coordinate system which has a parallel shock as the first basis vector. In this case, since we need to maintain orthogonality in the new coordinate system, the shapes of steepness and curvature will change. Nevertheless, the first three factors still explain a vast majority of the total variability in the system. We believe, however, that the humped shape of the first principal component should not be ignored. As discussed below, it is meaningful and can be used as a tool while placing yield curve bets.

Explanatory Power of a Given Curve Shock

Among all interest rate shocks, the first principal component has the maximum explanatory power by construction. For instance, Exhibit 10.1 indicates that the first principal component "explains" 92% of the recent historical spot curve movements. The number 92% is the ratio of the variance of the first principal component to the total variance in the system (sum of all principal components' variances). We now know how to compute a "one standard deviation shock" of a given shape as well as its variance via equation (10.4). The ratio of the variance of the parallel shock to the total variance in the system in the above example is 87%. This means that on September 30, 1996 a parallel spot curve shock "explained" 87% of the historical spot curve movements. We call the ratio of the percentage of total variability explained by a given shock to the percentage of total variability explained by the first principal component the *explanatory power* of the given shock. The explanatory

---

[5] Ram Wilner, "A New Tool for Portfolio Managers: Level, Slope, and Curvature Durations," *Journal of Fixed Income* (June 1996), pp. 48–59.

power of the first principal component is 1; that of a parallel spot shock in the given example is 95%.

Magnitude Plausibility of a Given Curve Shock

Once we know how many standard deviations k of the underlying standard normal variable a given interest rate shock Y implies, we can talk about the historical magnitude plausibility $mpl(Y)$ of this shock. Let Ψ denote the event "we guessed the direction of change in rates." We define the magnitude plausibility of a given interest rate shock $\vec{Y}$ as

$$mpl(\vec{Y}) = Prob(y > |k| \mid \Psi) \tag{10.7}$$

We can simplify equation (10.7) as follows:

$$mpl(\vec{Y}) = 2 \times Prob(y > |k|) \tag{10.8}$$

For example, the magnitude plausibility of a 200 bps spot curve shock is 3% whereas the magnitude plausibility of a 25 bps parallel spot curve shock is 78%.

The interest rate shock used by Klaffky, Ma, and Nozari to compute what they call short-end duration (SEDUR) is defined as a 50-basis-point steepener at the short end.[6] (See Exhibit 10.4.) It can be shown that the explanatory power of SEDUR is 38% and the magnitude plausibility is 54%.

SHAPE PLAUSIBILITY

The previous section deals with the quantitative measurement of the *magnitude plausibility* of a given spot curve shock. Thus we start with an interest rate shock of a *given shape* and then derive its distribution, which is used to determine if the magnitude of the given shock is reasonable given the recent covariance of interest rates. However, the issue of whether the shape of the shock is plausible from the historical perspective is never considered. This section deals with an independent assessment of the *shape plausibility* of interest rate shocks.

---

[6] Thomas E. Klaffky, Y. Y. Ma, and Ardavan Nozari, "Managing Yield Curve Exposure: Introducing Reshaping Durations," *Journal of Fixed Income* (December 1992), pp. 5–15. Note that SEDUR shock is applied to the on-the-run curve. To perform principal component decomposition, we first need to analytically transform it into a shock to the spot curve.

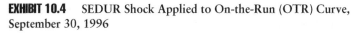

EXHIBIT 10.4   SEDUR Shock Applied to On-the-Run (OTR) Curve,
September 30, 1996

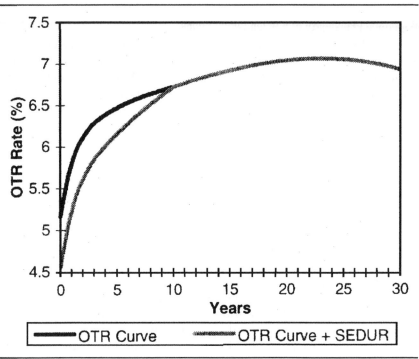

Principal components are the latent factors that depict the historical dynamics of interest rates. Therefore, we have a specific notion of plausibility at hand. The "most plausible" or "ideal" shock is the one whose "decomposition" into principal components is exactly that of the system (Exhibit 10.1):

$$\lambda = \{92.80, 4.80, 1.27, \dots 0.03\}$$

In other words, the first principal component should "contribute" 92.8% to the "ideal" shock, the second should contribute 4.8%, the third 1.3%, and so on. The measure of plausibility should be defined in a way that the plausibility of an "ideal" shock is 1. On the other hand, it is natural to consider "the least plausible" shock to be the last principal component which has the least explanatory power and therefore is the least probable one. Clearly, the decomposition of the least plausible shock into principal components is $\gamma = \{0, \dots 0, 100\}$. Thus, the measure of plausibility should be defined in a way that the plausibility of the least plausible shock is 0. Any other shock $\vec{X}$ will be somewhere in between the "ideal" and "the least plausible" shocks, and will have plausibility $spl(\vec{X})$ between 0 and 1. Below we present one such measure of plausibility.[7]

Write a hypothetical interest rate shock $\vec{X}$ in terms of principal components:

$$\vec{X} = (p_1, ..., p_n)_{PC}$$

Since $\vec{X}$ is a vector, it is reasonable to define the "contribution" of the i-th principal component in $\vec{X}$ based on the percentage of the squared length of $\vec{X}$ due to p_i, i.e.,

$$\hat{p}_i = p_i^2 / \sum_{i=1}^{n} p_i^2$$

Hence, to measure the shape plausibility of $\vec{X}$ is equivalent to measuring *how different the vector $\hat{p} = \{\hat{p}_i\}$ is from the "ideal" shock*. Let $D(\hat{p}, \hat{\lambda})$ be the "distance" between $\vec{X}$ and the ideal shock. Since the maximum distance between any two vectors is the distance $D(\hat{\lambda}, \hat{\gamma})$ between an "ideal" and "the least plausible" shocks, there is a way to normalize the measure of plausibility and present it as a number between 0 and 1.

We define the shape plausibility of $\vec{X}$ as

$$spl(\vec{X}) = 1 - \frac{D(\hat{p}, \hat{\lambda})}{D(\hat{\gamma}, \hat{\lambda})} \tag{10.9}$$

where

$$D(\hat{a}, \hat{\lambda}) = D(\{\hat{a}_i\}, \{\hat{\lambda}_i\}) = \sum |\hat{a}_i - \hat{\lambda}_i| \tag{10.10}$$

The functional form of the "distance" measure in equation (10.10) is not unique. We have experimented with several other functional repre-

---

[7] For alternative approaches, see "measures of consistency" introduced by P. M. Brusilovsky and L. M. Tilman ("Incorporating Expert Judgement into Multivariate Polynomial Modeling," *Decision Support Systems* (October 1996), pp. 199–214). One may also think of the explanatory power of a shock as an alternative measure of shape plausibility.

sentations only to discover that they fail to effectively differentiate between shapes of interest rate shocks, thus making the mapping spl: $\vec{X} \rightarrow [0, 1]$ almost a step function.

For example, to measure the shape plausibility of SEDUR, write its decomposition into principal components along with that of the "ideal" and "least plausible" shocks (Exhibit 10.5). It can be shown via equations (10.9) and (10.10) that $spl(SEDUR) = 0.41$. This means that from the historical perspective, the shape of SEDUR shock is not very plausible. Therefore, one may question the meaningfulness of the corresponding duration.

It remains to note that all characteristics of a given interest rate shock, such as "explanatory power," "magnitude plausibility," and "shape plausibility" depend on historical data and may vary dramatically over time.

FIRST PRINCIPAL COMPONENT AND THE TERM STRUCTURE OF VOLATILITY

Changes in U.S. Treasury spot rates are generally highly correlated. This fact has significant implications in interpreting the shape of the first principal component. This section deals with this issue. We claim that when spot rates are highly correlated, the shape of the first principal component resembles the shape of the term structure of volatility (TSOV) of changes in spot rates. The above statement provides the intuition behind the reason why, according to Ehud Ronn, "large-move days reflect more of a level [first principal component] shift in interest rates."[8] It also enables us to conclude that on days when the market moves substantially (e.g., more than two standard deviations) the relative changes in spot rates are almost solely a function of their historical volatilities. We now provide the informal proof of the above claim.

Let r_i and r_j be spot rates of maturities i and j respectively. Let σ_i and σ_j be the volatilities of *changes* of r_i and r_j respectively, while $pc_{1,i}$ and $pc_{1,j}$ be the coefficients of the first principal component corresponding to r_i and r_j. The statement *"the shape of the first principal component resembles that of TSOV of spot rate changes"* is equivalent to the following identity:

$$\frac{\sigma_i}{\sigma_j} \approx \frac{pc_{1,i}}{pc_{1,j}} \tag{10.11}$$

[8] E. I. Ronn, "The Impact of Large Changes in Asset Prices on Intra-Market Correlations in the Stock and Bond Markets," Working Paper, University of Texas in Austin, 1996.

EXHIBIT 10.5   Shape Plausibility and Principal Component Decomposition

Shock	Spl (.)	\multicolumn{10}{c}{Principal Component Decomposition (%)}
		1	2	3	4	5	6	7	8	9	10
Ideal	1.00	92.80	4.80	1.27	0.62	0.20	0.11	0.09	0.06	0.03	0.03
Least Plausible	0.00	0.00	0.00	0.00	0.00	0.00	0.00	0.00	0.00	0.00	100.00
SEDUR	0.41	34.67	59.58	0.67	1.87	0.17	0.30	1.08	0.02	1.62	0.02

Our argument is based on the following representation of the principal component coefficients:[9]

$$pc_{1,i} = \frac{\rho_{1,i} \times \sigma_i}{\sqrt{\lambda_1}}; \quad pc_{1,j} = \frac{\rho_{1,j} \times \sigma_j}{\sqrt{\lambda_1}} \tag{10.12}$$

where $\rho_{1,i}$ and $\rho_{1,j}$ are the correlations between the first principal component and the rates r_i and r_j respectively. Note that because all spot key rates are highly correlated, they are also highly correlated with the principal components, that is, $\rho_{1,i} \approx \rho_{1,j}$, and then equation (10.11) yields

$$\frac{pc_{1,i}}{pc_{1,j}} = \frac{\rho_{1,i} \times \sigma_i}{\sqrt{\lambda_1}} \Big/ \frac{\rho_{1,j} \times \sigma_j}{\sqrt{\lambda_1}} = \frac{\rho_{1,i}}{\rho_{1,j}} \times \frac{\sigma_i}{\sigma_j} \approx \frac{\sigma_i}{\sigma_j} \tag{10.13}$$

There are a number of interesting implications of the above result. For instance, *when the market rallies, the long end of the spot curve steepens, and when the market sells off, the long end of the spot curve flattens.* To see that just notice that since the historical volatility of the 10-year rate is higher than the historical volatility of the 30-year rate, therefore, the changes in the former are generally larger than those in the latter. Therefore when the market rallies, according to the shape of the first principal component, the 10-year rate should decrease more than the 30-year rate; hence the spot curve should steepen.

U.S. Treasury bond market data seems to support this result:[10] Over the 4-year period November 1992 to November 1996, the ratio of bull steepenings to bull flattenings of the spot curve was 2.5:1, and the ratio of bear flattenings to bear steepenings was 2.75:1. If we study the steepeners/flatteners of the on-the-run Treasury curve instead, we notice that

---

[9] See R. A. Johnson and D. W. Wichern, *Applied Multivariate Statistical Analysis* (Englewood Cliffs, NJ: Prentice-Hall, 1982).

while bull steepening and bear flattening patterns dominate, the proportions are different: over the same time period, the ratio of bull steepenings to bull flattenings of the OTR Treasury curve was 1.6:1, and the ratio of bear flattenings to bear steepenings was 6.5:1.

CONCLUSION

One of the advantages of key rate durations is the ability to estimate the instantaneous return on a portfolio given a hypothetical curve shift. The latter does not require us to do any additional simulations. Until now, sensitivity analysis was never concerned with the issue of whether the utilized hypothetical shocks were plausible from a historical perspective. The measures of plausibility of interest rate shocks introduced in this chapter constrain interest rate shocks used in sensitivity analysis and portfolio optimization. They provide discipline to the scenario analysis by excluding historically implausible interest rate shocks from the consideration. The framework which allows us to compute the distribution of interest rate shocks of a given shape is important by itself. As we explain elsewhere,[11] we utilize the knowledge about these distributions to simulate interest rate shocks and make conscious trade-offs between the value surface and the yield curve dynamics while computing value-at-risk.

---

[10] Monthly changes in the level and steepness of the U.S. spot and OTR curves were considered. We define the market as "bull" if the 10-year spot (OTR) key rate fell more that 5 bps, "bear" if it rose more that 5 bps, and "neutral" in other instances. Likewise, a change in the slope of the spot (OTR) curve is defined as a "steepening" if the spread between the 2-year and 30-year increased by more than 5 bps, "flattening" if it decreased by more than 5 bps, and "neutral" otherwise.

[11] See Chapter 5 in Bennett W. Golub and Leo M. Tilman, *Risk Management: Approaches for Fixed Income Markets* (New York: John Wiley & Sons, 2000).

CHAPTER 11

Hedging Interest Rate Risk with Term Structure Factor Models

Lionel Martellini, Ph.D.
Professor of Finance, EDHEC Graduate School of Business
Scientific Director of EDHEC Risk and Asset Management Research Center

Philippe Priaulet, Ph.D.
Fixed Income Strategist, HSBC
Associate Professor, Mathematics Department, University of Evry Val d'Essonne

Frank J. Fabozzi, Ph.D., CFA
Frederick Frank Adjunct Professor of Finance
School of Management
Yale University

Michael Luo, CFA
Executive Director/Global Investor Group
Morgan Stanley

Portfolio managers seek to control or hedge the change in the value of a bond position or a bond portfolio to changes in risk factors. The relevant risk factors can be classified into two types: *term structure risk factors* and *nonterm structure risk factors*. The former risks include parallel and nonparallel shifts in the term structure. Nonterm structure risk includes sector risk, quality risk, and optionality risk. Multifactor risk models that focus only on hedging exposure to interest rate risks are referred to as *term structure factor model*.

Exposure to changes in interest rates is most often measured in terms of a bond or portfolio's *duration*. This is a one-dimensional measure of the bond's sensitivity to interest rate movements. There is one complication, however: The value of a bond, or a bond portfolio, is affected by changes in interest rates of all possible maturities (i.e., changes in the term structure of interest rates). In other words, there is more than one risk factor that affects bond returns, and simple methods based upon a one-dimensional measure of risk such as duration will not allow portfolio managers to properly manage interest rate risks.[1] Hence the need for term structure factor models.

In this chapter, we show how term structure factor models can be used in interest rate risk management. These models have been designed to better account for the complex nature of interest rate risk. Because it is never easy to hedge the risk associated with too many sources of interest rate uncertainty, it is always desirable to try and reduce the number of term structure risk factors, and identify a limited number of common factors. There are several ways in which this can be done and it is important to know the exact assumptions one has to make in the process, and try to evaluate the robustness of these assumptions with respect to the specific scenario a portfolio manager has in mind.

We first briefly review the traditional duration hedging method, which is still heavily used in practice and has been illustrated in several chapters in this book. The approach is based on a series of very restrictive and simplistic assumptions, including the assumptions of a small and parallel shift in the yield curve. We then show how to relax these assumptions and implement hedging strategies that are robust with respect to a wider set of possible yield curve changes. We conclude by analyzing the performance of various hedging techniques in a realistic situation, and we show that satisfying hedging results can be achieved by using a three-factor model for the yield curve dynamics.

DEFINING INTEREST RATE RISK(S)

The first fundamental fact about interest rate risk management can be summarized by the following statement: bond prices move inversely to market yields.[2] More generally, we define as interest rate risk the poten-

---

[1] This complication is not specific to the fixed income environment. In the world of equity investment, it has actually long been recognized that there may be more than one rewarded risk factors that affect stock returns. A variety of more general multifactor models, economically justified either by equilibrium or arbitrage arguments, have been applied for risk management and portfolio performance evaluation.

[2] There are some derivative mortgage products that do not possess this property.

tial impact on a bond portfolio value of any given change in the location and shape of the yield curve.

To further illustrate the notion of interest rate risk, we consider a simple experiment. A portfolio manager wishes to hedge the value of a bond portfolio that delivers deterministic cash flows in the future, typically cash flows from fixed-coupon Treasury securities. Even if these cash flows are known in advance, bond prices change in time, which leaves an investor exposed to a potentially significant capital loss.

To fix the notation, we consider at date t a bond (or a bond portfolio) that delivers m certain cash flows CF_i at future dates t_i for $i = 1, ...,$ m. The price V of the bond (expressed as a percentage of the face value) can be written as the sum of the future cash flows discounted with the appropriate zero-coupon rate with maturity corresponding to the maturity of the cash flows:

$$V_t = \sum_{i=1}^{m} \frac{CF_i}{[1 + R(t, t_i - t)]^{t_i - t}} \tag{11.1}$$

where $R(t, t_i - t)$ is the associated zero-coupon rate, starting at date t for a remaining maturity of $t_i - t$ years.

We see in equation (11.1) that the price V_t is a function of m interest rate variables $R(t, t_i - t)$. This suggests that the value of the bond is subject to a potentially large number m of risk factors. For example, the price of a bond with annual cash flows up to a 10-year maturity is affected by potential changes in 10 zero-coupon rates (i.e., the term structure of interest rates). To hedge a position in this bond, we need to be hedged against a change of all of these 10 risk factors.

In practice, it is not easy to perform risk management in the presence of many risk factors. In principle, one must design a *global portfolio* in such a way that the portfolio is insensitive to all sources of risk (the m interest rate variables and the time variable t).[3] A global portfolio is one that contains the original portfolio plus any hedging instruments used to control the original portfolio's interest rate risk. One suitable way to simplify the problem is to reduce the number of risk factors. Everything we cover in this chapter can be seen as a variation on the theme of reducing the dimensionality of the interest rate risk management problem.

---

[3] In this chapter, we do not consider the change of value due to time because it is a deterministic term. We only consider changes in value due to interest rate variations. For details about the time value of a bond, see Don M. Chance and James V. Jordan, "Duration, Convexity, and Time as Components of Bond Returns," *Journal of Fixed Income* (September 1996), pp. 88–96.

We first consider the simplest model for interest rate risk management, also known as *duration hedging*, which is based on a single risk variable, the yield to maturity of this portfolio.

HEDGING WITH DURATION

The intuition behind duration hedging is to bypass the complexity of a multidimensional interest rate risk by identifying a single risk factor that will serve as a "proxy" for the whole term structure. The proxy measure used is the yield of a bond. In the case of a bond portfolio, it is the average portfolio yield.

First Approximation: Using a One-Order Taylor Expansion

The first step consists in writing the price of the portfolio V_t (in percent of the face value) as a function of a single source of interest rate risk, its yield to maturity y_t, as shown:

$$V_t = V(y_t) = \sum_{i=1}^{m} \frac{CF_i}{[1+y_t]^t} \qquad (11.2)$$

In this case, we can see clearly that the interest rate risk is (imperfectly) summarized by changes of the yield to maturity y_t. Of course, this can only be achieved by losing much generality and imposing important, rather arbitrary and simplifying assumptions. The yield to maturity is a complex average of the entire term structure, and it can only be assimilated to the term structure if the term structure happens to be flat (i.e., the yield to maturity is the same for each maturity).

A second step involves the derivation of a *Taylor expansion* of the value of the portfolio V as an attempt to quantify the magnitude of value changes that are triggered by small changes y in yield. Before showing how this is done, let us briefly review what a Taylor expansion is. A Taylor expansion is a tool used in calculus to approximate the change in the value of a mathematical function due to a change in a variable. The change can be approximated by a series of "orders," with each order related to the mathematical derivative of the function. When one refers to approximating a mathematical function by a first derivative, this means using a Taylor expansion with only the first order. Adding to the approximation from the second order to the approximation from the first order improves the approximation.

Let us return now to approximating the change in value of a bond when interest rates change. The mathematical function is equation (11.2), the value of a bond portfolio. The function depends on the yield. We denote dV as the change in the value of the portfolio triggered by small changes in yield denoted by dy. The approximate *absolute* change in the value of the portfolio triggered by small changes in yield is using a Taylor expansion is

$$dV(y) = V(y+dy) - V(y) = V'(y)dy + o(y) \approx \$Dur(V(y))dy \quad (11.3)$$

where

$$V'(y) = -\sum_{i=1}^{m} \frac{(t_i - t)F_i}{(1 + y_t)^{t_i - t + 1}}$$

which is the derivative of the bond value function with respect to the yield to maturity, This value is known as the *dollar duration of the portfolio V*, denoted by $duration, and $o(y)$ a negligible term.

Dividing equation (11.3) by $V(y)$ we obtain an approximation of the *relative* change in value of the portfolio as

$$\frac{dV(y)}{V(y)} = \frac{V'(y)}{V(y)}dy + o_1(y) \cup MD(V(y))dy \quad (11.4)$$

where

$$MD(V(y)) = -\frac{V'(y)}{V(y)}$$

is known as the modified duration of portfolio V.

The $duration and the modified duration enable us to compute the absolute profit and loss for the portfolio (absolute P&L) and relative P&L of portfolio V for a small change Δy of the yield to maturity. That is,

$$\textit{Absolute } P \,\&\, L \approx N_V \times \$Dur \times \Delta y$$

$$\textit{Relative } P \,\&\, L \approx -MD \times \Delta y$$

where N_V is the face value of the portfolio.

Performing Duration Hedging

We attempt to hedge a bond portfolio with face value N_V, yield to maturity y and price denoted by $V(y)$. The idea is to consider one hedging instrument with face value N_H, yield to maturity y_1 (*a priori* different from y) whose price is denoted by $H(y_1)$ and build a global portfolio with value V^* invested in the initial portfolio and some quantity ϕ of the hedging instrument.

$$V^* = N_V V(y) + \phi N_H H(y_1)$$

The goal is to make the global portfolio insensitive to small interest rate variations. Using equation (11.3) and assuming that the yield to maturity curve is only affected by parallel shifts so that $dy = dy_1$, we obtain

$$dV^* \approx [N_V V'(y) + \phi N_H H'(y_1)]dy = 0$$

which translates into

$$\phi N_H \$Dur(H(y_1)) = -N_V \$Dur(V(y))$$

$$\phi N_H H(y_1)MD(H(y_1)) = -N_V V(y)MD(V(y))$$

so that we finally get

$$\phi = -\frac{N_V \$Dur(V(y))}{N_H \$Dur(H(y_1))} = -\frac{N_V V(y)MD(V(y))}{N_H H(y_1)MD(H(y_1))} \tag{11.5}$$

The optimal amount invested in the hedging instrument is simply equal to the opposite of the ratio of the $duration of the bond portfolio to hedge by the $duration of the hedging instrument, when they have the same face value.

When the yield curve is flat, which means $y = y_1$, equation (11.5) simplifies to

$$\phi = -\frac{N_V V(y)D(V(y))}{N_H H(y)D(H(y))}$$

where the Macaulay duration $D(V(y))$ is defined as

$$D(V(y)) = -(1+y)MD(V(y)) = \frac{\sum_{i=1}^{m} \frac{(t_i - t)F_i}{(1+y)^{t_i - t}}}{V(y)}$$

In practice, it is preferable to use futures contracts or swaps instead of bonds to hedge a bond portfolio because of significantly lower costs and higher liquidity. For example, using futures as hedging instruments, the hedge ratio ϕ_f is equal to

$$\phi_f = -\frac{N_V \$Dur_V}{N_F \$Dur_{\text{CTD}}} \times cf \tag{11.6}$$

where N_F is the size of the futures contract. $\$Dur_{\text{CTD}}$ is the $duration of the cheapest to deliver as cf is the conversion factor.

Using standard swaps, the hedge ratio ϕ_s is

$$\phi_s = -\frac{N_V \$Dur_V}{N_F \$Dur_S} \tag{11.7}$$

where N_S is the nominal amount of the swap and $\$Dur_S$ is the $duration of the fixed coupon bond forming the fixed leg of the swap contract.[4]

Duration hedging is very simple. However, one should be aware that the method is based upon the following, very restrictive, assumptions:

- It is explicitly assumed that the value of the portfolio could be approximated by its first order Taylor expansion. This assumption is all the more disputable that changes of the interest rates are larger. In other words, the method relies upon the assumption of small yield to maturity changes. This is why the hedging portfolio should be re-adjusted reasonably often.
- It is also assumed that the yield curve is only affected by parallel shifts. In other words, interest rate risk is simply considered as a risk on the general level of interest rates.

In what follows, we attempt to relax both assumptions to account for more realistic changes in the term structure of interest rates.

---

[4] For examples of hedging with futures, see Chapter 57. Examples of hedging portfolios constructed with futures contracts and swaps, see Lionel Martellini, Philippe Priaulet, and Stéphane Priaulet, *Fixed-Income Securities: Valuation, Risk Management and Portfolio Strategies* (Chichester: John Wiley and Sons, 2003).

RELAXING THE ASSUMPTION OF A SMALL SHIFT

We have argued that $duration provides a convenient way to estimate the impact of a *small* change dy in yield on the value of a bond or a portfolio.

Using a Second-Order Taylor Expansion

Duration hedging only works effectively for small yield changes, because the price of a bond as a function of yield is nonlinear. In other words, the $duration of a bond changes as the yield changes. When a portfolio manager expects a potentially large shift in the term structure, a convexity term should be introduced and the price change approximation can be improved if one can account for such nonlinearity by explicitly introducing the convexity term.

Let us take the following example to illustrate this point. We consider a 10-year maturity and 6% annual coupon bond trading at par. Its modified duration and convexity are equal to 7.36 and 57.95, respectively.[5] We assume that the yield to maturity goes suddenly from 6% to 8% and we re-price the bond after this large change. The new price of the bond, obtained by discounting its future cash flows, is now equal to $86.58, and the exact change of value amounts to –$13.42 (= $86.58 – $100). Using a first-order Taylor expansion, the change in value is approximated by –$14.72 (= –$100 × 7.36 × 0.02), which overestimates the decrease in price by $1.30. We conclude that a first-order Taylor expansion does not provide us with a good approximation of the bond price change when the variation of its yield to maturity is large.

If a portfolio manager is concerned about the impact of a larger move dy on a bond portfolio value, one needs to use (at least) a second-order version of the Taylor expansion as given below.

$$dV(y) = V'(y)dy + \frac{1}{2}V''(y)(dy)^2 + o((dy)^2)$$
$$\approx \$Dur(V(y))dy + \frac{1}{2}\$Conv(V(y))(dy)^2$$
(11.8)

where the quantity V'' also denoted $\$Conv(V(y))$ is known as the $convexity of the bond V.

Dividing equation (11,8) by $V(y)$, we obtain an approximation of the relative change in value of the portfolio as

$$\frac{dV(y)}{V(y)} \approx -MD(V(y))dy + \frac{1}{2}RC(V(y))(dy)^2$$

---

[5] Note that convexity can be scaled in various ways.

where $RC(V(y))$ is called the (relative) convexity of portfolio V.

We now reconsider the previous example and approximate the bond price change by using equation (11.8). The bond price change is now approximated by $-\$13.56$ ($= -14.72 + (100 \times 57.95 \times 0.02^2/2)$). We conclude that the second-order approximation is better suited for larger interest rate deviations.

Performing Duration-Convexity Hedging

Hedging by taking into consideration first and second orders is called *duration-convexity hedging*. To perform a duration-convexity hedge, a portfolio manager needs to introduce two hedging instruments. We denote the with value of the two hedging instructions by H_1 and H_2. The goal is to obtain a portfolio that is both \$duration neutral and \$convexity neutral. The optimal quantity (ϕ_1, ϕ_2) of these two hedging instruments to hold is then given by the solution to a system of equations, at each date, assuming that $dy = dy_1 = dy_2$. The system of equations consists of two equations and two unknowns and can easily be solved algebraically.

More formally, the system of equations is

$$\begin{cases} \phi_1 N_{H_1} H'_1(y_1) + \phi_2 N_{H_2} H'_2(y_2) = -N_V V'(y) \\ \phi_1 N_{H_1} H''_1(y_1) + \phi_2 N_{H_2} H''_2(y_2) = -N_V V''(y) \end{cases}$$

which can be rewritten as

$$\begin{cases} \phi_1 N_{H_1} \$Dur(H_1(y_1)) + \phi_2 N_{H_2} \$Dur(H_2(y_2)) \\ \quad = -N_V \$Dur(V(y)) \\ \phi_1 N_{H_1} \$Conv(H_1(y_1)) + \phi_2 N_{H_2} \$Conv(H_2(y_2)) \\ \quad = -N_V \$Conv(V(y)) \end{cases} \tag{11.9}$$

or

$$\begin{cases} \phi_1 N_{H_1} H_1(y_1) MD(H_1(y_1)) + \phi_2 N_{H_2} H_2(y_2) MD(H_2(y_2)) \\ \quad = -N_V V(y) MD(V(y)) \\ \phi_1 N_{H_1} H_1(y_1) RC(H_1(y_1)) + \phi_2 N_{H_2} H_2(y_2) RC(H_2(y_2)) \\ \quad = -N_V V(y) RC(V(y)) \end{cases}$$

RELAXING THE ASSUMPTION OF A PARALLEL SHIFT

Duration and duration-convexity hedging are based on single-factor models because only one interest rate is being considered. In this section, we look at how we can go beyond a single-factor model to a term structure factor model.

Accounting for the Presence of Multiple-Risk Factors

A major shortcoming of single-factor models is that they imply that all possible zero-coupon rates are perfectly correlated, making bonds redundant assets. We know, however, that rates with different maturities do not always change in the same way. In particular, long-term rates tend to be less volatile than short-term rates. An empirical analysis of the dynamics of the interest rate term structure suggests that two or three factors account for most of the yield curve changes. They can be interpreted, respectively, as a level, slope, and curvature factors (see below). This strongly suggests that a term structure factor model should be used for pricing and hedging fixed income securities.

There are different ways to generalize duration hedging to account for nonparallel deformations of the term structure. The common principle behind all techniques is the following. Going back to equation (11.1), let us express the value of the portfolio using the entire curve of zero-coupon rates, where we now make explicit the time-dependency of the variables. Hence, we consider V_t to be a function of the zero-coupon rates $R(t, t_i - t)$, which will be denoted by R_t^i in this section for simplicity of exposition. The risk factor is the yield curve as a whole, *a priori* represented by m components, as opposed to a single variable, the yield to maturity y.

The main challenge is then to narrow down this number of factors in the least arbitrary way. The good news is that one can show that a limited number (two or three) of suitably designed risk factors can account for a large fraction of the information in the whole term yield curve dynamics. There are two ways to accomplish that. The first is to use a functional form term structure model. The other method is to use statistical analysis using a technique called principal component analysis (PCA) to identify the typical yield curve movement factors. We are going to explain both methodologies in detail in the following sections.

Hedging Using a Three-Factor Term Structure Model of the Yield Curve

The idea here consists of using a model for the zero-coupon rate function. We detail below the Nelson and Siegel model,[6] as well as the

---

[6] Charles R. Nelson and Andrew F. Siegel, "Parsimonious Modeling of Yield Curves," *Journal of Business* (October 1987), pp. 473–489.

Svensson model (or extended Nelson and Siegel) model.[7] One may alternatively use the Vasicek model,[8] the extended Vasicek model, or the Cox-Ingersoll-Ross (CIR) (1985) model,[9] among many others.[10]

Nelson-Siegel and Svensson Models

Nelson and Siegel suggested modeling the continuously compounded zero-coupon rates $R^C(0, \theta)$ as

$$R^C(0,\theta) = \beta_0 + \beta_1 \left[\frac{1 - \exp(-\theta/\tau_1)}{\theta/\tau_1} \right] + \beta_2 \left[\frac{1 - \exp(-\theta/\tau_1)}{\theta/\tau_1} - \exp(-\theta/\tau_1) \right]$$

a functional form that was later extended by Svensson as

$$R^C(0,\theta) = \beta_0 + \beta_1 \left[\frac{1 - \exp(-\theta/\tau_1)}{\theta/\tau_1} \right] + \beta_2 \left[\frac{1 - \exp(-\theta/\tau_1)}{\theta/\tau_1} - \exp(-\theta/\tau_1) \right]$$
$$+ \beta_3 \left[\frac{1 - \exp(-\theta/\tau_2)}{\theta/\tau_2} - \exp(-\theta/\tau_2) \right]$$

where

$R^C(0, \theta)$ = the continuously compounded zero-coupon rate at time zero with maturity θ

β_0 = the limit of $R^C(0, \theta)$ as θ goes to infinity (in practice, β_0 should be regarded as a long-term interest rate)

β_1 = the limit of $R^C(0, \theta) - \beta_0$ as θ goes to 0 (in practice, β_1 should be regarded as the short- to long-term spread)

β_2 and β_3 are curvature parameters. τ_1 and τ_2 are scale parameters that measure the rate at which the short-term and medium-term components decay to zero.

---

[7] Lars Svensson, "Estimating and Interpreting Forward Interest Rates: Sweden 1992–94," *CEPR discussion paper 1051* (October 1994).

[8] Oldrich A. Vasicek, "An Equilibrium Characterisation of the Term Structure," *Journal of Financial Economics* (November 1977), pp. 177–188.

[9] John C. Cox, Jonathan E. Ingersoll, and Stephen A. Ross, "A Theory of the Term Structure of Interest Rates," *Econometrica* (March 1985), pp. 385–407.

[10] For details about these models, see Lionel Martellini and Philippe Priaulet, *Fixed-Income Securities: Dynamic Methods for Interest Rate Risk Pricing and Hedging* (Chichester: John Wiley & Sons, 2000).

As shown by Svensson, the extended form is a more flexible model for yield curve estimation, in particular in the short-term end of the curve, because it allows for more complex shapes such as U-shaped and hump-shaped curves. The parameters β_0, β_1, β_2, and β_3 are typically estimated on a daily basis by using an *ordinary least squares* (OLS) optimization program, which consists, for a basket of bonds, in minimizing the sum of the squared spread between the market price and the theoretical price of the bond as obtained with the model.[11] On June 9, 2005, the continuously compounded zero-coupon yield curve can be described by the following set of parameters of the Svensson model: $\beta_0 = 5.17\%$, $\beta_1 = -1.16\%$, $\beta_2 = -0.006\%$, $\beta_3 = -1.73\%$, and $\tau = 5.43$, as shown in Exhibit 11.1.

We can see that the evolution of the zero-coupon rate $R^C(0, \theta)$ is entirely driven by the evolution of the beta parameters, the scale parameters being fixed.

In an attempt to hedge a bond, for example, one should design a global portfolio with the bond and hedging instrument, so that the portfolio achieves a neutral sensitivity to each of the beta parameters. Before

EXHIBIT 11.1   Observed Continuously Compounded Zero-Coupon Yield Curve and Model Yield Curve Using the Svensson Model: June 9, 2005

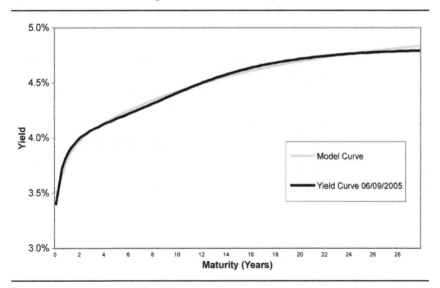

Note: Parameters for Svensson Model: $\beta_0 = 5.17\%$, $\beta_1 = -1.16\%$, $\beta_2 = -0.006\%$, $\beta_3 = -1.73\%$, $\tau = 5.43$

---

[11] For more details, see Martellini, Priaulet, and Priaulet, *Fixed-Income Securities: Valuation, Risk Management and Portfolio Strategies.*

the method can be implemented, one needs to compute the sensitivities of any arbitrary portfolio of bonds to each of the beta parameters.

Consider a bond which delivers principal or coupon and principal payments denoted by F_i at dates θ_i, for $i = 1, \ldots, m$. Its price P_0 at date $t = 0$ is given by the following formula

$$P_0 = \sum_{i=1}^{m} F_i e^{-\theta_i R^C(0, \theta_i)}$$

In the Nelson and Siegel and Svensson models, we can calculate at date $t = 0$ the \$durations $D_i = \partial P_0 / \partial \beta_i$ for $i = 0, 1, 2, 3$ of the bond P to the parameters β_0, β_1, β_2, and β_3. They are given by the following formulas[12,13]

$$
\begin{cases}
D_0 = -\sum_i \theta_i F_i e^{-\theta_i R^C(0, \theta_i)} \\[2ex]
D_1 = -\sum_i \theta_i \left[\dfrac{1 - \exp(-\theta_i / \tau_1)}{\theta_i / \tau_1} \right] F_i e^{-\theta_i R^C(0, \theta_i)} \\[2ex]
D_2 = -\sum_i \theta_i \left[\dfrac{1 - \exp(-\theta_i / \tau_1)}{\theta_i / \tau_1} - \exp(-\theta_i / \tau_1) \right] F_i e^{-\theta_i R^C(0, \theta_i)} \\[2ex]
D_3 = -\sum_i \theta_i \left[\dfrac{1 - \exp(-\theta_i / \tau_2)}{\theta_i / \tau_2} - \exp(-\theta_i / \tau_2) \right] F_i e^{-\theta_i R^C(0, \theta_i)}
\end{cases}
\tag{11.10}
$$

Hedging Method

The next step consists of creating a global portfolio that would be unaffected by (small) changes of parameters β_0, β_1, β_2, and β_3. This portfolio will be made of:

---

[12] Of course, \$duration is only obtained in the Svensson model.

[13] An example of calculation of the level, slope and curvature \$durations is given in Martellini, Priaulet, and Priaulet, *Fixed-Income Securities: Valuation, Risk Management and Portfolio Strategies*. See also Andrea J. Heuson, Thomas F. Gosnell Jr., and W. Brian Barrett, "Yield Curve Shifts and the Selection of Immunization Strategies," *Journal of Fixed Income* (September 1995), pp. 53–64, and Ram Willner, "A New Tool for Portfolio Managers: Level, Slope and Curvature Durations," *Journal of Fixed Income* (June 1996), pp. 48–59.

■ The bond portfolio to be hedged whose price and face value are denoted by P and N_P

■ Four hedging instruments whose prices and face values are denoted by G_i and N_{G_i} for $i = 1, 2, 3,$ and 4

Therefore, we look for the quantities q_0, q_1, q_2, and q_3 to invest, respectively, in the four hedging instruments G_0, G_1, G_2, and G_3 so as to satisfy the following linear system:

$$\begin{cases} q_1 N_{G_1}\dfrac{\partial G_1}{\partial B_0} + q_2 N_{G_2}\dfrac{\partial G_2}{\partial B_0} + q_3 N_{G_3}\dfrac{\partial G_3}{\partial B_0} + q_4 N_{G_4}\dfrac{\partial G_4}{\partial B_0} = -N_P D_0 \\[2mm] q_1 N_{G_1}\dfrac{\partial G_1}{\partial B_1} + q_2 N_{G_2}\dfrac{\partial G_2}{\partial B_1} + q_3 N_{G_3}\dfrac{\partial G_3}{\partial B_1} + q_4 N_{G_4}\dfrac{\partial G_4}{\partial B_1} = -N_P D_1 \\[2mm] q_1 N_{G_1}\dfrac{\partial G_1}{\partial B_2} + q_2 N_{G_2}\dfrac{\partial G_2}{\partial B_2} + q_3 N_{G_3}\dfrac{\partial G_3}{\partial B_2} + q_4 N_{G_4}\dfrac{\partial G_4}{\partial B_2} = -N_P D_2 \\[2mm] q_1 N_{G_1}\dfrac{\partial G_1}{\partial B_3} + q_2 N_{G_2}\dfrac{\partial G_2}{\partial B_3} + q_3 N_{G_3}\dfrac{\partial G_3}{\partial B_3} + q_4 N_{G_4}\dfrac{\partial G_4}{\partial B_3} = -N_P D_3 \end{cases} \quad (11.11)$$

In the Nelson and Siegel model, we only have three hedging instruments because there are only three parameters.

From equation (11.10), we can see that the hedging method has a potential problem as how to hedge the bond with uncertain cash flow. For example, the largest sector in U.S. debt market is the mortgage-backed securities (MBS) market. More specifically, it is the market for residential MBS. The cash flow is very much dependent on the interest rate level and interest rate paths. It will be difficult to calculate the D_0, D_1, D_2, and D_3 for these bonds from any closed-form functions. Potentially, we could find the corresponding yield curve shift for the parameter β_i and can then shock the yield curve with corresponding curve shift to calculate the price sensitivities using advanced analytical system such as Yield Book®. When we employ this approach to calculate \$durations D_i, the methodology becomes very similar to the hedging method we are going to discuss in the next section.

Regrouping Risk Factors Through a Principal Component Analysis

The purpose of PCA is to explain the behavior of observed variables using a smaller set of unobserved implied variables. From a mathematical standpoint, it consists of transforming a set of m-correlated variables into a reduced set of orthogonal variables that reproduce the original information present in the correlation structure. This tool can yield interesting results, especially for the pricing and risk management of correlated positions. Using PCA with historical zero-coupon rate curves (both from the Treasury and Interbank markets), it has been observed that the first three principal components of spot curve changes, which can be interpreted as level, slope, and curvature factors, explain the main part of the returns variations on fixed income securities over time.[14]

Using a PCA of the yield curve, we may now express the change $dR(t, \theta_k) = R(t + 1, \theta_k) - R(t, \theta_k)$ of zero-coupon rate $R(t, \theta_k)$ with maturity θ_k at date t as a function of changes in the principal components (unobserved implicit factors):

$$dR(t, \theta_k) = \sum_{l=1}^{m} c_{lk} C_t^l + \varepsilon_{tk}$$

where c_{lk} is the sensitivity of the kth variable to the lth factor defined as

$$\frac{\Delta(dR(t, \theta_k))}{\Delta(C_t^l)} = c_{lk}$$

which amounts to individually applying a, say, 1% variation to each factor, and computing the absolute sensitivity of each zero-coupon yield curve with respect to that unit variation.

---

[14] Studies of the U.S. market include Robert Litterman and Jose Scheinkman, "Common Factors Affecting Bond Returns," *Journal of Fixed Income* (September 1991), pp. 54–61; Joel R. Barber and Mark L. Copper, "Immunization Using Principal Component Analysis," *Journal of Portfolio Management* (Fall 1996), pp. 99–105, and; Bennett W. Golub and Leo M. Tilman, "Measuring Yield Curve Risk Using Principal Components Analysis, Value at Risk, and Key Rate Durations," *Journal of Portfolio Management* (Summer 1997), pp. 72–84. For France, see Martellini and Priaulet, *Fixed-Income Securities: Dynamic Methods for Interest Rate Risk Pricing and Hedging*. For Italy, see Rita L. D'Ecclesia and Stavros Zenios, "Risk Factor Analysis and Portfolio Immunization in the Italian Bond Market," *Journal of Fixed Income* (September 1994), pp. 51–58. For Germany and Switzerland, see Alfred Bühler and Heinz Zimmermann, "A Statistical Analysis of the Term Structure of Interest Rates in Switzerland and Germany," *Journal of Fixed Income* (December 1996), pp. 55–67. For Belgium, France, Germany, Italy, and the United Kingdom, see Sandrine Lardic, Philippe Priaulet, and Stephane Priaulet, "PCA of Yield Curve Dynamics: Questions of Methodologies," *Journal of Bond Trading and Management* (April 2003), pp. 327–349.

These sensitivities are commonly called the *principal component $durations*. C_t^l is the value of the *l*th factor at date *t*, and ε_{tk} is the residual part of $dR(t, \theta_k)$ that is not explained by the factor model.

One can easily see why this method has become popular. Its main achievement is that it allows for the reduction of the number of risk factors with an optimally small loss of information. At Morgan Stanley, for example, PC analysis on the monthly yield curve data going back 15 years is used. The three principal components shown in Exhibit 11.2 are identified that are consistent with those of other studies for the United States and other countries: level, twist, and curvature. Since these three factors, regarded as risk factors, explain 97% of the variance in interest rate changes, there is no need to use more than three hedging instruments. The changes of value of a fixed income portfolio can then be expressed as

$$dV_t^* \approx \sum_{k=1}^{m} \left(\frac{\partial V_t}{\partial R(t, \theta_k)} + \sum_{j=1}^{3} \phi_t^j \frac{\partial H_t^j}{\partial R(t, \theta_k)} \right) dR(t, \theta_k)$$

We then use

$$dR(t, \theta_k) \approx \sum_{l=1}^{3} c_{lk} C_t^l$$

EXHIBIT 11.2   Three Principal Components Identified

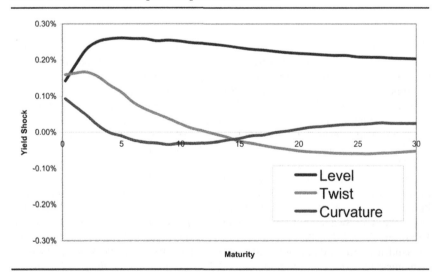

to obtain

$$dV_t^* \approx \sum_{k=1}^{m} \left(\frac{\partial V_t}{\partial R(t, \theta_k)} + \sum_{j=1}^{3} \phi_t^j \frac{\partial H_t^j}{\partial R(t, \theta_k)} \right) \sum_{l=1}^{3} c_{kl} C_t^l$$

or

$$dV_t^* \approx \sum_{k=1}^{m} \left(c_{1k} \frac{\partial V_t}{\partial R(t, \theta_k)} + \sum_{j=1}^{3} \phi_t^j c_{1k} \frac{\partial H_t^j}{\partial R(t, \theta_k)} \right) C_t^1$$

$$+ \sum_{k=1}^{m} \left(c_{2k} \frac{\partial V_t}{\partial R(t, \theta_k)} + \sum_{j=1}^{3} \phi_t^j c_{2k} \frac{\partial H_t^j}{\partial R(t, \theta_k)} \right) C_t^2$$

$$+ \sum_{k=1}^{m} \left(c_{3k} \frac{\partial V_t}{\partial R(t, \theta_k)} + \sum_{j=1}^{3} \phi_t^j c_{3k} \frac{\partial H_t^j}{\partial R(t, \theta_k)} \right) C_t^3$$

The first term in the above expression commonly called the *principal component $duration* of portfolio V^* with respect to factor 1.

If we want to set the (first order) variations of the hedged portfolio V_t^* to zero for any possible change in interest rates $dR(t, \theta_k)$, or equivalently for any possible evolution of the C_t^l terms, we may take as a sufficient condition, for $l = 1, 2, 3$

$$\sum_{k=1}^{m} \left(c_{lk} \frac{\partial V_t}{\partial R(t, \theta_k)} + \sum_{j=1}^{3} \phi_t^j c_{lk} \frac{\partial H_t^j}{\partial R(t, \theta_k)} \right) = 0$$

This is a neutral principal component $durations objective.

Finally, on each possible date, we are left with three unknowns ϕ_t^j and three linear equations. Let us introduce the following matrix notation

$$H_t' = \begin{bmatrix} \sum_{k=1}^{m} c_{1k} \frac{\partial H_t^1}{\partial R(t, \theta_k)} & \sum_{k=1}^{m} c_{1k} \frac{\partial H_t^2}{\partial R(t, \theta_k)} & \sum_{k=1}^{m} c_{1k} \frac{\partial H_t^3}{\partial R(t, \theta_k)} \\ \sum_{k=1}^{m} c_{2k} \frac{\partial H_t^1}{\partial R(t, \theta_k)} & \sum_{k=1}^{m} c_{2k} \frac{\partial H_t^2}{\partial R(t, \theta_k)} & \sum_{k=1}^{m} c_{2k} \frac{\partial H_t^3}{\partial R(t, \theta_k)} \\ \sum_{k=1}^{m} c_{3k} \frac{\partial H_t^1}{\partial R(t, \theta_k)} & \sum_{k=1}^{m} c_{3k} \frac{\partial H_t^2}{\partial R(t, \theta_k)} & \sum_{k=1}^{m} c_{3k} \frac{\partial H_t^3}{\partial R(t, \theta_k)} \end{bmatrix}$$

and

$$\Phi_t = \begin{bmatrix} \phi_t^1 \\ \phi_t^2 \\ \phi_t^3 \end{bmatrix} ; \ V_t' = \begin{bmatrix} -\displaystyle\sum_{k=1}^{m} c_{1k}\dfrac{\partial V_t}{\partial R(t,\theta_k)} \\ -\displaystyle\sum_{k=1}^{m} c_{2k}\dfrac{\partial V_t}{\partial R(t,\theta_k)} \\ -\displaystyle\sum_{k=1}^{m} c_{3k}\dfrac{\partial V_t}{\partial R(t,\theta_k)} \end{bmatrix}$$

We then have the system

$$H_t'\Phi_t = V_t'$$

The solution is given by

$$\Phi_t = (H_t')^{-1}V_t' \tag{11.12}$$

COMPARATIVE ANALYSIS OF VARIOUS HEDGING TECHNIQUES

We now analyze the hedging performance of three methods in the context of a specific bond portfolio. The methods we consider in this horse race are the duration hedge, the duration/convexity hedge, and Morgan Stanley PCA hedge.

We consider a bond portfolio whose features are summarized in Exhibit 11.3. The price is expressed in percentage of the face value, which is equal to $100 million. This is a 5% coupon mortgage-backed security on June 9, 2005. We compute the *yield to maturity* (YTM), the $duration, the $convexity, and the level, slope and curvature $durations of the bond portfolio using Yield Book® (Citigroup).

To hedge the bond portfolio, we use three plain vanilla swaps whose features summarized in Exhibit 11.4. $duration, $convexity, level, slope and curvature $durations are those of the fixed coupon bond contained in the swap estimated using the PCA model. The principal amount of the swaps is $1 million. They all have an initial price of zero.

To measure the performance of the three hedging methods, we assume 10 different possible changes in the yield curve. On June 9, 2005, the continuously compounded zero-coupon yield curve can be

EXHIBIT 11.3 Characteristics of the Bond Portfolio to Be Hedged

				Level	Slope	Curvature
Price	YTM	$Duration	$Convexity	D_0	D_1	D_2
998.13	5.017%	–3,334.5	–247,930	–832	–239.5	8.0

EXHIBIT 11.4 Characteristics of the Swap Instruments

				Level	Slope	Curvature
Maturity	Swap Rate	$Duration	$Convexity	D_0	D_1	D_2
2 years	3.972%	–190.6	456	–44.2	–32.3	–9.2
10 years	4.365%	–808.6	7,615	–210.4	–25.9	22.3
30 years	4.684%	–1,620.4	37,171	–345.8	60.3	–19.4

described by the following set of parameters of the Nelson and Siegel model: $\beta_0 = 5.07\%$, $\beta_1 = -1.39\%$, $\beta_2 = -3.82\%$, and $\tau = 5.43$. These 10 scenarios are obtained by assuming the following changes of the beta parameters in the Nelson and Siegel model:

▨ Small parallel shifts with $\beta_0 = +0.1\%$ and $\beta_0 = -0.1\%$
▨ Large parallel shifts with $\beta_0 = +1\%$ and $\beta_0 = -1\%$
▨ Decrease and increase of the spread short to long-term spread with $\beta_1 = +1\%$ and $\beta_1 = -1\%$
▨ Curvature moves with $\beta_2 = +0.6\%$ and $\beta_2 = -0.6\%$
▨ Flattening and steepening moves of the yield curve with ($\beta_0 = -0.4\%$, $\beta_1 = +1.2\%$) and ($\beta_0 = +0.4\%$, $\beta_1 = -1.2\%$)

The six last scenarios, which represent nonparallel shifts, are displayed in Exhibits 11.5, 11.6, and 11.7.

Duration hedging is performed with the 10-year maturity swap using equation (11.7), leading us to enter into 41.2 payer swaps. Duration/convexity hedging is performed with the 2-year and 10-year maturity swaps using equation (11.9), leading us to enter into 2,086 2-year maturity receiver swaps and 450 10-year maturity payer swaps. The PCA hedge is performed with the three swaps using equation (11.12), leading us to enter into 54.3 2-year maturity payer swaps, 26.7 10-year maturity payer swaps, and 0.85 30-year maturity payer swaps. Results are given in Exhibit 11.8, where we display the change in value of the global portfolio (which aggregates the change in value on the bond portfolio and the hedging instruments) assuming that the yield curve scenario occurs

EXHIBIT 11.5 New Yield Curve after an Increase (β_1 = +1%) and a Decrease (β_1 = –1%) of the Slope Factor

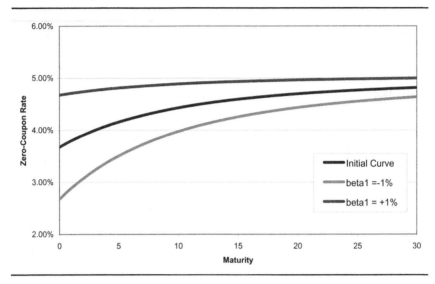

EXHIBIT 11.6 New Yield Curve after an Increase and a Decrease of the Curvature Factor (β_2 = +0.6%) and (β_2 = –0.6%)

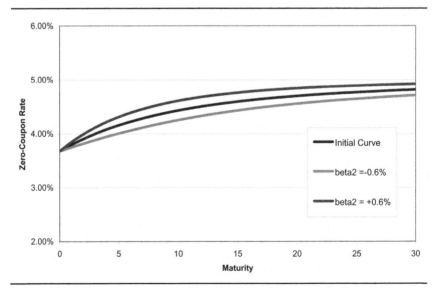

EXHIBIT 11.7   New Yield Curve after a Flattening Movement ($\beta_0 = -0.4\%$, $\beta_1 = +1.2\%$) and a Steepening Movement ($\beta_0 = +0.4\%$, $\beta_1 = -1.2\%$)

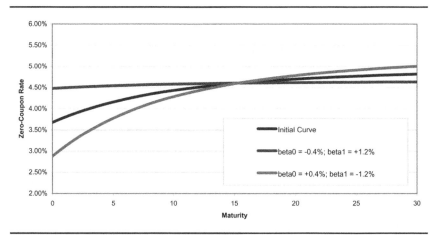

EXHIBIT 11.8   Hedging Errors in $ of the Three Different Methods, Duration, Duration/Convexity and PCA $Durations

Yield Curve Scenario	No Hedge	Duration	Duration/ Convexity	PCA $Durations
$\beta_0 = +0.1\%$	−349,053	−17,231	−1,589	−16,908
$\beta_0 = -0.1\%$	324,201	−10,833	2,096	−10,604
$\beta_0 = +1\%$	−4,220,793	−1,041,694	340,962	−1,014,059
$\beta_0 = -1\%$	1,915,014	−1,585,511	−107,538	−1,558,049
$\beta_1 = +1\%$	−2,142,260	−580,316	−13,729,309	−236,490
$\beta_1 = -1\%$	1,597,426	−35,078	−14,183,446	−373,634
$\beta_2 = +0.6\%$	448,033	−137,739	3,402,569	−39,596
$\beta_2 = -0.6\%$	−518,543	57,142	−3,370,193	−38,150
$\beta_0 = +0.4\%$, $\beta_1 = -1.2\%$	3,090,905	930,839	−30,444,748	177,515
$\beta_0 = -0.4\%$, $\beta_1 = +1.2\%$	−2,671,371	−450,240	30,523,703	291,193

instantaneously. This change of value can be regarded as the hedging error for the strategy. It would be exactly zero for a perfect hedge.

The value of the bond portfolio is equal to \$99,813,500.[15] With no hedge, we clearly see that the loss in portfolio value can be significant in all adverse scenarios.

As expected, duration hedging appears to be effective only for small parallel shifts of the yield curve. The hedging error is negative for large parallel shifts because of the negative convexity of the portfolio. For nonparallel shifts, the loss incurred by the global portfolio can be very significant. For example, the portfolio value increases by \$930,839 in the scenario when $\beta_0 = -0.4\%$ and $\beta_1 = +1.2\%$ and drops by \$450,240 in the $\beta_0 = +0.4\%$ and $\beta_1 = -1.2\%$ scenario. As also expected, duration/ convexity hedging is better than duration hedging when large parallel shifts occur. On the other hand, it appears to be ineffective for all other scenarios, even if the hedging errors are still better (smaller) than those obtained with duration hedging. Finally, we see that the PCA hedging scheme is a relative reliable method for all kinds of yield curve scenario. The nonparallel shift scenarios were generated using Nelson-Siegel method. Had we generated the yield curve shocks using the principal components, the hedging error will be minimal since the hedge ratios are constructed by those yield curve shocks.

SUMMARY

A decline (rise) in interest rates will cause a rise (decline) in bond prices, with the most volatility in bond prices occurring in longer maturity bonds and bonds with low coupons. As a stock risk is usually proxied by its beta, which is a measure of the stock sensitivity to market movements, bond price risk is most often measured in terms of the bond interest-rate sensitivity, or duration. This is a convenient one-dimensional measure of the bond's sensitivity to interest-rate movements.

Duration provides a portfolio manager with a convenient hedging strategy: to offset the risks related to a small change in the level of the yield curve, one should optimally invest in a hedging asset a proportion equal to the opposite of the ratio of the (dollar) duration of the bond portfolio to be hedged by the (dollar) duration of the hedging instrument.

---

[15] Opposite results in terms of hedging errors would be obtained if the investor was short the bond portfolio.

Duration hedging is convenient because it is very simple. On the other hand, it is based upon the following, very restrictive, assumptions: (1) It is explicitly assumed that changes in the yield curve will be small; and (2) it is also assumed that the yield curve is only affected by parallel shifts. An empirical analysis of bond markets suggests, however, that large variations can affect the yield-to-maturity curve and that three main factors (level, slope and curvature) have been found to drive the dynamics of the yield curve. This strongly suggests that duration hedging is inefficient in many circumstances.

In this chapter, we go "beyond duration" by relaxing the two aforementioned assumptions. Relaxing the assumption of a small change in the yield curve can be performed though the introduction of a convexity adjustment in the hedging procedure. Convexity is a measure of the sensitivity of $duration with respect to yield changes. Accounting for general, nonparallel deformations of the term structure is not easy because it increases the dimensionality of the problem. Because it is never easy to hedge the risk associated with too many sources of uncertainty, it is always desirable to try and reduce the number of risk factors and identify a limited number of common factors. This can be done in a systematic way by using an appropriate statistical analysis of the yield-curve dynamics. Alternatively, one may choose to use a model for the discount rate function.

Finally, we analyzed the performance of the various hedging techniques in a realistic situation, and we show that satisfying hedging results can be achieved by using a principal component hedging method.

CHAPTER 12

Scenario Simulation Model for Fixed Income Portfolio Risk Management

Farshid Jamshidian, Ph.D.
Coordinator of Quantitative Research
NIB Capital Bank
and
Professor of Applied Mathematics
FELAB, University of Twente

Yu Zhu, Ph.D.
Professor of Finance
China Europe International Business School
and
Senior Consultant
Fore Research & Management, LP

The risk of a fixed income portfolio is often measured by one or two risk parameters, such as duration or convexity. These are important portfolio sensitivities, but more and more portfolio managers start to look at more comprehensive risk measurements, such as *Value-at-Risk* (VaR). In recent years, VaR has been considered as one of the most significant market risk measures by banks and other financial institutions. It is defined as the expected loss from an adverse market movement with a specified probability over a period of time. Similar concepts such as credit-VaR can be applied to measure a portfolio's credit risk. The Bank for International Settlement (BIS) and other regulators have allowed banks to use their internal model to measure the market risk exposure, expressed in terms of VaR. In the new capital adequacy framework endorsed by Group of Ten recently (Basel II), banks will be allowed to use "internal ratings-based" ("IRB") approaches to credit risk.

There are several commonly applied methods to calculate VaR. One simplest method is "delta approximation." It uses variance-covariance matrix of market variables and the portfolio's sensitivities with each of the market variables (delta) to approximate the potential loss of the portfolio value. This method critically depends on two dubious assumptions: the normality assumption of portfolio value, and the linearity assumption of the relationship between transactions' prices and market variables.

In general, however, most fixed income securities and interest rate derivatives have nonlinear price characteristics. Thus, Monte Carlo simulation is a more appropriate method to estimate their market exposures. A common implementation is based on the joint lognormality assumption of market variables to generate a large number of market scenarios using their historical variance-covariance matrix. Then, transaction values for each scenario are calculated and aggregated. From the obtained distribution of the portfolio value, VaR can be easily estimated. The difficulty with the Monte Carlo approach is its computational burden. In order to obtain a reliable estimation, the sample size has to be large. In the case of large multicurrency portfolios, the required huge sample size often makes the approach impractical. Choosing a smaller sample size would result in a distorted distribution, defeating the purpose of adopting the Monte Carlo approach.

The scenario simulation model described in this article is an alternative approach to estimate VaR.[1] The model approximates a multidimensional lognormal distribution of interest rates and exchange rates by a multinomial distribution of key factors. While it allows very large samples, the number of portfolio evaluations is limited. As a result, a great computational efficiency has been obtained in comparison with conventional Monte Carlo methods.

A portfolio's VaR is only a point estimate of its risk-return profile. The market turmoil in the fall of 1998 taught us that we should not rely

---

[1] The authors have developed the scenario simulation model to meet the challenge of accurately and efficiently evaluating both the market exposure and credit exposure of a fixed income derivative portfolio. While at Sakura Global Capital (SGC), the authors applied it to estimate SGC's value at risk, credit reserve, and credit exposures. It was also applied to SGC's triple-A derivative vehicle, Sakura Prime.

on a single number to manage a portfolio's risk. We should look at the whole return distribution in addition to VaR. The scenario simulation model provides the entire distribution of future portfolio returns. From this, not only VaR, but standard deviation and other measures of risk, such as "coherent measures of risk," can be computed.[2] The importance of stress testing should never be overlooked. In this regard, we believe that the Scenario Simulation model fits the needs of risk management better than conventional Monte Carlo method.

The concept of VaR is not restricted to the market risk. For the risk management of a fixed income portfolio, it is important to examine not only the market risk of the portfolio, but also its overall risk exposures. The scenario simulation model can be applied in estimating a portfolio's overall risk profile of joint market risk, credit risk, and country risk events.

In this chapter, we describe the model in two stages: single currency scenario simulation and multicurrency scenario simulation, and then discuss its applications in risk management. Some of the model's mathematical assumptions are listed in the chapter's appendix.[3]

SINGLE-CURRENCY SCENARIO SIMULATION

The traditional method to evaluate a derivative portfolio's risk exposure is to use Monte Carlo simulation. Given the current yield curve and the covariance matrix of the risk factors that drive the yield curve evolution process, we can use Monte Carlo technique to generate a large number of possible yield curves for a horizon date. All these simulated yield curves represent the assumed distribution of yield curves. For example, suppose a USD yield curve can be described by the following 11 "key rates": 6-month, 1-, 2-, 3-, 4-, 5-, 7-, 10-, 15-, 20-, and 30-year zero coupon rates. From historical data, we can estimate the volatilities and correlation matrix of these key rates. We can generate 10,000 yield curves, each with equal probability, to simulate this 11-factor model. All transactions are then valued along each path and aggregated, and the portfolio's market risk exposure can be estimated by the obtained portfolio value sample distribution.

Though the above Monte Carlo method is robust, the computational burden it imposes is rather heavy. For a portfolio of 100 transactions, 1 million transaction valuations would be required in a simulation with

---

[2] P. Artzner, F. Delbaen, J.-M. Eber, and D. Heath, "Thinking Coherently," *Risk* (November 1997), pp. 68–71.
[3] F. Jamshidian and Y. Zhu, "Scenario Simulation: Theory and Methodology," *Finance and Stochastics* 1 (1997), pp. 43–67.

10,000 paths, in addition to curve generation, transaction value aggregation, and other computations. Moreover, unless the sample size is very large, there are possibilities that the Monte Carlo sample may not cover adequately the tails of the distribution, which are of significance in evaluating a portfolio's risk exposure.

The scenario simulation model takes a different approach. Unlike the traditional Monte Carlo simulation, which uses a large number of yield curves, each with the same probability, we generate say, a set of 105 yield curves with different assigned probabilities. Each of the curves is called a "scenario." It has been numerically demonstrated that this set of scenario curves gives a description of yield curve distribution as good as or better than the Monte Carlo method with a moderate sample size.

Exhibit 12.1 illustrates the methodology of the single currency scenario simulation model. First, a principal component analysis is performed on the historical covariance (correlation) matrix. Empirical evidence has shown that the first three principal components can often explain 90%–95% of the variations, hence three factors should be sufficient for most risk management applications.[4]

As an example, using RiskMetrics data as of 4/7/1999, we obtain the first three principal components for the correlation matrices of euro yield curve movements:

0.476	0.465	0.874	0.915	0.965	0.946	0.949	0.918	0.893
−0.863	−0.869	0.038	0.125	0.089	0.083	0.118	0.206	0.225
0.065	0.047	−0.470	−0.314	−0.107	−0.139	0.230	0.304	0.367

EXHIBIT 12.1 Diagram of Single Currency Scenario Simulation Model

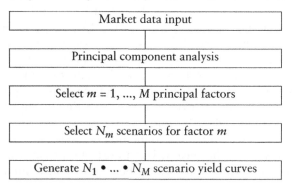

Market data input

Principal component analysis

Select $m = 1, ..., M$ principal factors

Select N_m scenarios for factor m

Generate $N_1 \bullet ... \bullet N_M$ scenario yield curves

---

[4] A working group of BIS studied various methodologies of measuring aggregate market risk, including scenario generating using principal component analysis. See M. Loretan, "Generating Market Risk Scenarios Using Principal Components Analysis: Methodological and Practical Considerations," Federal Reserve Board (March 1997).

The columns corresponding to zero coupon rates with maturities of 6 month, 1, 2, 3, 4, 5, 7, 9 and 10 years, respectively. The numbers in the first row are all of the same sign, and, except for the short end, the magnitude of those numbers are close to each other. Therefore, the first principal factor is often explained as a "parallel shift" factor. Similarly, the second factor can be called a "twist" factor and the third factor a "butterfly" factor.

By examining the principal components for yield curve movements in other currencies, these three factors can also be identified. The following are the first three principal components for JPY and USD yield curves from the same RiskMetrics data set. For this example, we selected 12 key rates for JPY. There are three more columns in JPY which represent one month and three month rates in the front and 20-year zero-coupon rate in the last column. In USD, we added 30-year zero-coupon rate as an additional key rate. Comparing with the euro curve, JPY has larger twist and butterfly factors. One may also notice that for the time period that the data set was generated, the USD curve movements were mainly in parallel in the maturity range longer than one year.

JPY Principal Components

0.340	0.440	0.407	0.423	0.892	0.945	0.962	0.965	0.938	0.913	0.883	0.731
−0.750	−0.810	−0.716	−0.819	−0.141	−0.043	0.019	0.141	0.297	0.343	0.376	0.461
−0.419	0.014	0.420	0.298	−0.170	−0.166	−0.176	−0.094	−0.008	0.039	0.127	0.365

USD Principal Components

−0.073	−0.120	−0.062	0.123	−0.962	−0.980	−0.982	−0.983	−0.994	−0.990	−0.987	−0.975	−0.890
0.691	0.852	0.888	0.766	−0.009	−0.006	−0.002	−0.037	−0.018	−0.001	0.007	−0.011	−0.042
−0.656	−0.397	0.392	0.582	−0.003	0.008	0.017	−0.002	0.007	0.015	0.022	0.036	0.051

In the scenario simulation model, each selected factor is discretized by a binomial distribution. Since the first principal factor is most important, seven scenarios ($N_1 = 7$) are selected; for the second principal factor five scenarios ($N_2 = 5$) are selected; and three scenarios are selected for the third factor ($N_3 = 3$).[5] Altogether, there are ($n_1 = 0,...,6$; $n_2 = 0,...,4$; $n_3 = 0,...,2$) possible scenarios, and the total number of scenarios is $7 \times 5 \times 3 = 105$. Because all principal factors are independent of each other, the probability of yield curve scenario can be calculated easily. As an example, the probability of scenario ($n_1 = 4$, $n_2 = 2$, $n_3 = 1$) is equal to

---

[5] The actual number of factors and the number of scenarios for each factor should be determined empirically.

$$^{15}\!/_{64} \times {}^{3}\!/_{8} \times {}^{1}\!/_{2} = {}^{45}\!/_{1024} \approx 4.395\%$$

Exhibits 12.2 through 12.4 show the Japanese yen scenario yield curves over a 1-year horizon.[6] All curves are implied zero coupon swap curves, and in each exhibit the middle curve is the current yield curve one year forward. The seven curves in Exhibit 12.2 are generated using only the first principal factor. It shows that the changes in the yield levels resemble parallel shifts. Exhibits 12.3 and 12.4 demonstrate that the second factor and the third factor reflect the twist and the "butterfly" movements of yield curve, respectively. Each curve in Exhibits 12.2 to 12.4 is associated with a probability of the corresponding scenario. For example, the third curve from the top in Exhibit 12.2 represents scenario (4,2,1) whose probability is 4.395%.

As a consequence of smaller number of scenario yield curves, the required number of transaction valuations is much smaller. For a 100-transaction portfolio, the required number of transaction valuations becomes 10,500, about 1% of the traditional Monte Carlo requirement with 10,000 paths. This is a very significant saving in computation time. We have tested the model extensively by estimating the market risk exposures of swaps, caps and floors, swaptions and other derivatives in

EXHIBIT 12.2 JPY Yield Curve Scenarios
Factor 1 Only

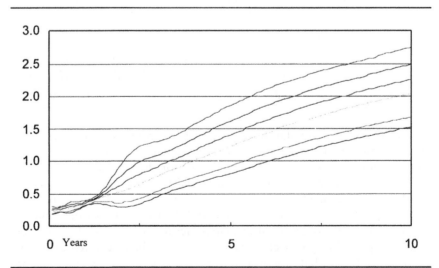

---

[6] The scenario curves are based on Japanese yen swap yield curve as of 5/3/1999.

EXHIBIT 12.3   JPY Yield Curve Scenarios
Factor 2 Only

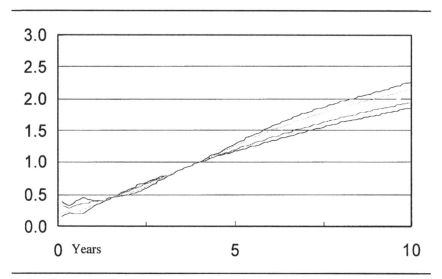

EXHIBIT 12.4   JPY Yield Curve Scenarios
Factor 3 Only

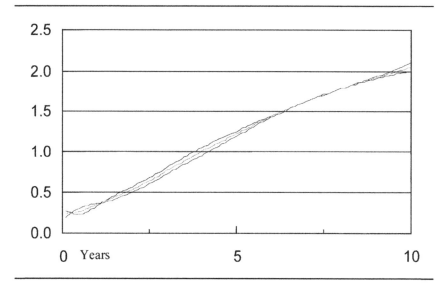

various currencies using both traditional Monte Carlo method and the scenario simulation model. The simulated portfolio exposure distributions from the two methods are strikingly similar: There are no significant differences in their estimated means, standard deviation, and various percentiles.

MULTICURRENCY SCENARIO SIMULATION

The advantage of the scenario simulation model becomes more evident when the portfolio consists of fixed income securities and derivatives in multiple currencies. Suppose there are six currencies in the portfolio, and each currency yield curve can be described by 10 key rates. The total number of factors is therefore 65, including the five exchange rates. If we select three principal factors for each currency curve, the total number of factors can be reduced to 23. Obviously to generate a good representation of a 65-factor (or even a 23-factor) joint distribution utilizing a traditional Monte Carlo method, the sample size has to be very large. As in the single currency case, for such a large sample size, generating curves and valuing transaction along each path would require extremely lengthy computations.

The scenario simulation model employs a different method in dealing with multicurrency portfolios. The method is computationally very efficient while generating excellent representation of the risk exposure distribution. Exhibit 12.5 illustrates the model methodology. First, scenario simulations of each currency portfolio are performed. If three factors and a total of 105 scenarios for each currency curve are used, and seven scenarios for each exchange rate are selected, each currency port-

EXHIBIT 12.5   Diagram of Multicurrency Scenario Simulation

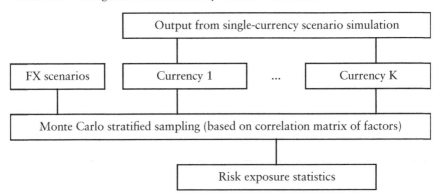

folio will have an output with $105 \times 7 = 735$ joint interest rate and exchange rate scenarios, except for the base currency portfolio which has 105 scenarios. Then, to obtain the risk exposure of the whole portfolio, joint market scenarios based on the correlation matrix of principal factors and exchange rates are generated. A method, which we call *stratified sampling*, is applied to generate the distribution. It is a Monte Carlo method, but the discretization feature of single-currency simulation is preserved. For a given joint multicurrency market scenario, the portfolio value $V(s)$ is simply

$$V(s) = \sum_{k=1}^{K} X_k(s) \times V_k(s)$$

where X_k is the exchange rate and V_k is the portfolio value of currency k. Using this method, even though the Monte Carlo has multimillion paths, only 105 yield curves need to be generated for each currency and 105 values calculated for each transaction.

In summary, the scenario simulation model makes the simulation computationally practical to apply to a very large multicurrency portfolio with fixed income securities and derivatives.

VALUE-AT-RISK ESTIMATION AND STRESS TESTING

There are many different ways to calculate VaR, but the most popular method is the delta approximation method. The method assumes that portfolio returns are normally distributed and linearly related to market variables. Therefore, the calculation of VaR only requires the variance-covariance matrix of market variables and the portfolio's sensitivities to these market variables (delta). The method is easy to understand and the computation is very efficient. Unfortunately, both assumptions are, practically speaking, incorrect: portfolio returns often deviate from normal distribution, and not only delta, but also gamma (second order derivative of portfolio value to market variables) and, to lesser extent, other higher moments contribute to portfolio returns. To obtain more accurate VaR, a Monte Carlo simulation can be employed. However, as discussed above, the computation efficiency becomes a serious concern.

The scenario simulation model provides an effective alternative to the delta approximation method and the traditional Monte Carlo method. We can directly apply the model by valuing each transaction say, 105 times, and obtain the portfolio's profit and loss distribution, and with it, the portfolio risk exposure statistics. The portfolio's VaR is simply one of the portfolio risk statistics:

$$VaR = \max\{v: \text{Probability}[\Delta V(s) \le v] \le 1 - \alpha\}$$

where α is the confidence level and $\Delta V(s)$ is the change in portfolio value at scenario (s). This is much more efficient than the traditional Monte Carlo method, but for calculating VaR, the calculation can be further simplified by taking advantage of portfolio's delta and gamma. Usually, these risk parameters are readily available to risk managers. Suppose that δ and γ are the delta and gamma of the k-th currency portfolio. Delta is a vector whose i-th component is defined as the first order derivative of the market value V_k with respect to y_i, the i-th bucket forward rate. Gamma in general is a matrix of the second order derivatives of V_k with respect to y. At a given yield curve scenario s, its portfolio value change can be approximated by

$$\Delta V_k(s) \approx \delta \times \Delta y(s) + \frac{1}{2}\Delta y(s)^T \times \gamma \times \Delta y(s)$$

where $\Delta y(s)$ represents the vector of forward rates changes from the current yield curve to the given scenario curve. In contrast to the full simulation method, which requires each transaction be valued in all scenarios, with this method, the delta and gamma of each transaction are calculated only once, using the current yield curves. Once calculated, the delta and gamma are applied in the above approximation formula for each scenario. Thus, it greatly simplifies the single currency scenario simulation. After the completion of these calculations for each currency, the portfolio's profit and loss distribution and VaRs at various confidence levels can be obtained by the stratified sampling.

Exhibit 12.6 shows VaR calculation results using the scenario simulation model for three simple derivative transactions, all denominated in USD and with $100 million notional. The first transaction is a 5-year market rate swap (Party A receives fixed rate and pays six month LIBOR); the second transaction Party A sells a 5-year 6% cap, and the third is a 1-year payer swaption into 5-year swap with fixed rate at 7%. One day, 14-day and 28-day VaRs are calculated using 99% confidence level. For one day VaR, all three methods give similar results. In all cases, the method using both delta and gamma gives a closer approximation to the full simulation results than the delta only method. As expected, the gamma's contribution becomes significant when the horizon goes beyond one day. For example, for the long swaption position,

EXHIBIT 12.6   VaR Using Scenario Simulation Model
$100 million swap (receiving fixed)

Method	One day	14 days	28 days
Full simulation	$707,225	$2,722,285	$3,918,261
Delta only	716,559	2,825,615	4,115,313
Delta and gamma	713,272	2,774,731	4,007,411

$100 million cap (short position)

Method	One day	14 days	28 days
Full simulation	$507,230	$2,045,630	$3,019,888
Delta only	500,220	1,960,242	2,848,081
Delta and gamma	511,402	2,121,828	3,181,208

$100 million 1-year payer swaption (long position)

Method	One day	14 days	28 days
Full simulation	$382,031	$1,226,831	$1,580,740
Delta only	392,103	1,407,511	1,944,209
Delta and gamma	378,259	1,205,577	1,554,154

Three-transaction portfolio

Method	One day	14 days	28 days
Full simulation	$792,650	$2,975,627	$4,206,118
Delta only	808,052	3,188,506	4,645,768
Delta and gamma	796,169	3,007,058	4,278,876

because the gamma is significantly positive, the delta only approximation overestimates 14-day and 28-day VaR by 15% and 23%, respectively. By incorporating gamma, the difference between the full
simulation and the approximation is less than 2%. The last panel of
Exhibit 12.6 shows VaRs of the portfolio with these three transactions.

    The scenario simulation model can also be applied to perform stress
testing. One of the lessons people learned from the market crisis in the
fall of 1998 is that Value-at-Risk analysis has to be supplemented by
stress testing. Many risk managers use the data from extraordinary historical market events such as 1987 market crash to stress testing their

portfolios. It is also important to stress test the assumptions of VaR models such as volatilities and correlations. Because of its computational efficiency, the scenario simulation model is particularly suitable for such testing. Furthermore, the scenario simulation model allows risk managers to examine portfolio's risk exposures within the tail of a given distribution. Unlike other methods, the discretization of the scenario simulation model makes it possible to identify specific stress scenarios under which the portfolio may become vulnerable.

Portfolio's Credit Risk Exposure

The importance of credit risk management of a fixed income portfolio can never be overemphasized. Traditional credit analyses, credit ranking or rating, and other fundamental analyses are essential. More and more portfolio managers are going beyond the traditional credit risk measures and starting to quantify a portfolio's potential credit exposures under normal as well as stressed situations.

There are three basis ingredients to estimate a portfolio's potential credit risk:

1. Market value profile for bonds and transactions for each issuer/counterparty
2. The default probability distribution of issuers and/or counterparties
3. Recovery-rate distribution

A portfolio will suffer a credit loss if an issuer or a counterparty defaults, the market value of the portfolio with respect to the issuer or the counterparty is positive, and the recovery rate is less than 100%. We have the following basic credit risk model:

Credit loss = Max (0, Mark-to-market value) × (1 − Recovery rate) × d

where d equals 1 if the counterparty defaults, and 0 otherwise. Clearly estimating credit risk is related to market risk estimation, but it is more complicated. In fact, all the above three ingredients are random, and they are usually correlated with each other. The focus of market risk management is usually on the portfolio's potential losses over a short horizon such as one day or a few days. To have a good understanding of credit risk, however, we need to look at a longer horizon, even the entire life of the transaction. There are significant differences in hedging these two risk types. The recent development of credit derivatives market creates possibilities for portfolio managers to hedge credit exposure, but it is still far more difficult than to hedge portfolio's market risk.

The scenario simulation model can be applied to estimate a portfolio's credit risk exposure as well as its joint market and credit risk exposure. For a given market scenario (s), we define the credit risk exposure with respect to an issuer or a counterparty at time t as

$$V_t^+(s) = \max\{V_t(s),0\}$$

Using the scenario simulation model, $V_t^+(s)$ for all scenarios selected and for various horizons t are readily available, and credit risk parameters such as maximum credit exposure with a given confidence level can be calculated. Given default probability distribution for the counterparty, the required credit reserve amount, defined as the discounted expected default loss with respect to the counterparty, can be computed. In addition, the correlation of defaults among different issuers and/or counterparties can be incorporated into the scenario simulation model. For example, in the Gaussian copula approach, the joint default distribution $(d_1, d_2, ..., d_n)$ can be mapped into a Gaussian distribution $\varphi(x_1, x_2, ..., x_n; \Sigma)$, where Σ is the correlation matrix.[7] The default scenarios can then be generated to compute the potential credit losses under various market scenarios.

Exhibits 12.7 through 12.9 illustrate the simulation results for a multi-currency swap portfolio. The portfolio contains more than 300 interest rate and currency swaps in five different currencies. Exhibit 12.7 shows the portfolio's market exposure over a 1-month period. Not surprisingly, the simulated distribution looks quite symmetric. In fact, it is not too different from a normal distribution. When default risk is taken into account, the joint market and credit exposure (Exhibit 12.8) is no longer symmetric. Exhibit 12.9 illustrates the portfolio's potential loss distribution due to default.

More often than not, when estimating credit risk, people make more simplified assumptions. One typical assumption is parallel shifts of interest rates. We use the following example to illustrate the importance of yield curve modeling. It should be noted ignoring yield curve twists and butterfly may cause significant errors in credit risk estimation.

Suppose a JPY swap portfolio has two swaps:

1. 5-year swap with 2 billion yen notional paying fixed at 1.6% and receiving LIBOR
2. 10-year swap with 1 billion yen notional receiving 2.5% and paying LIBOR

---

[7] See D. Li, "On Default Correlation: A Copula Approach," *Journal of Fixed Income* 9 (March 2000), pp. 43–54.

EXHIBIT 12.7   Market-Exposure Distribution
Sample Portfolio of Swaps

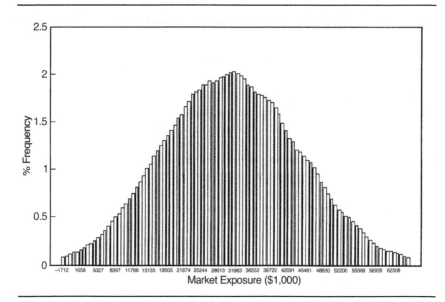

EXHIBIT 12.8   Joint-Exposure Distribution
Sample Portfolio of Swaps

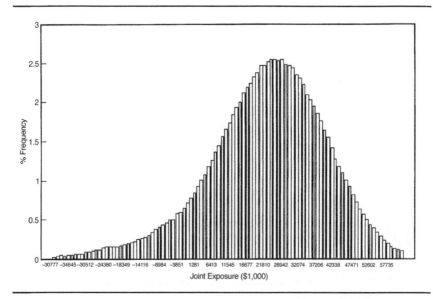

EXHIBIT 12.9   Default-Loss Distribution
Sample Portfolio of Swaps

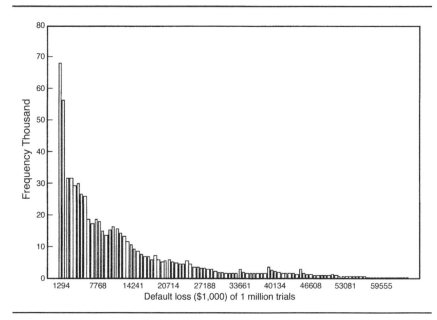

Exhibit 12.10 shows the expected credit exposure of the portfolio. Within the scenario simulation framework, we use two methods: One applies 1-factor yield curve model, which is similar to the assumption of parallel shift; and the other method employs 3-factor model. The difference is quite significant, especially in 1 to 2 years. Exhibit 12.11 makes a similar comparison for the maximum credit exposure with 95% confidence level. Here the large difference occurs in the time period of 2 to 3 years.

CONCLUSION

The scenario simulation model described in this chapter is an innovative alternative to the traditional risk management methods such as the Monte Carlo or the delta approximation methods. The computational efficiency comes from selecting principal factors at single-currency level, and stratified sampling at multicurrency stage. Because of the efficiency, the model can afford a large sample size in order to obtain a very satisfactory representation of return distribution for multicurrency fixed income portfolios.

EXHIBIT 12.10 Credit Mean Profile
JPY Swaps

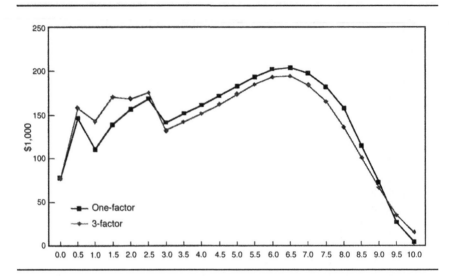

EXHIBIT 12.11 Maximum Credit Exposure

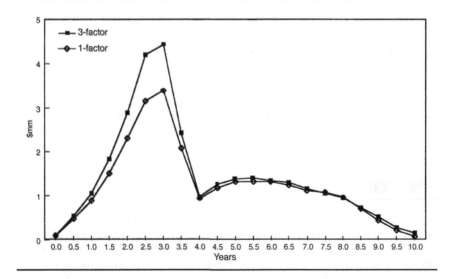

APPENDIX: SCENARIO SIMULATION MODEL

1. *Single-Currency Yield Curve Modeling*
We use a vector of key zero coupon rates to describe a yield curve.

$$\{r_1, ..., r_i, ..., r_n\}$$

We assume that these rates are correlated with a correlation matrix R, and the stochastic process of each key rate is described by the following equation:

$$\frac{dr_i}{r_i} = \mu_i(t)dt + \sigma_i dz_i$$

When yield curve scenarios are simulated over long time horizons such as in the case of estimating credit exposures, we incorporate mean reversions into the processes. In the scenario simulation model, we assume that

$$dz_i = -kz_i(t)dt + dB_i$$

where $z_i(t)$ are Orestein-Uhlenbeck processes with distribution of

$$N\left(0, \sqrt{\frac{1 - e^{-2kt}}{2k}}\right)$$

2. *Reduction of Dimensionality by Principal Component Analysis*
We can find eigenvectors of the correlation matrix R by solving the following equations:

$$R\beta_j = \lambda_j\beta_j \qquad j = 1,...,n$$

Define the principal factor dw_j by

$$dw_j = \frac{1}{\lambda_j}\sum_{k=1}^{n} \beta_{kj}dz_k \qquad j = 1,...,n$$

Then, we have

$$dz_i = \sum_{j=1}^{n} \beta_{ij} dw_j \qquad i = 1,\ldots,n$$

Note that principal factors are orthogonal to each other. As we discussed above, in general, the first three principal factors are able to capture most of the variations of the yield curve movements; therefore, we can approximate dz_i by

$$dz_i \approx \beta_{i1} dw_1 + \beta_{i2} dw_2 + \beta_{i3} dw_3$$

The residuals are usually quite small. It is straightforward to derive an approximation model for the yield curve movements:

$$\frac{dr_i(t)}{r_i(t)} = \mu_i(t)dt + \delta_{i1} dw_1 + \delta_{i2} dw_2 + \delta_{i3} dw_3$$

where

$$\delta_{ij} = \sigma_i \beta_{ij}$$

3. *Discretization of Principal Factors*
The approximation yield curve model reduces the dimension from n-factor model to a 3-factor model. A Monte Carlo simulation model can be directly built on the approximation model. However, in order to enhance the computational efficiency, we discretize the principal factors according to a binomial distribution. The probability distribution of a binomial variable is as follows

$$\text{Probability}(i) = 2^{-m} \frac{m!}{i!(m-i)!} \qquad i = 0,\ldots,m$$

For example, for seven binomial states ($m = 6$), the corresponding probabilities for state $i = 0, 1, \ldots, 6$ are

$$\tfrac{1}{64}, \tfrac{6}{64}, \tfrac{15}{64}, \tfrac{20}{64}, \tfrac{15}{64}, \tfrac{6}{64}, \tfrac{1}{64}$$

Roughly speaking, seven scenarios are almost as good as 64 Monte Carlo states, and we do not need to generate random numbers. In scenario simulation, we apply a binomial approximation for each principal factor. For example, we may select 7, 5, and 3 scenarios for the first, second, and third factor, respectively. In this case, the total number of yield curves generated is equal to $7 \times 5 \times 3 = 105$ scenarios. The probability of each yield curve scenario can be calculated by directly multiplying the probabilities of corresponding states of the binomial distributions.

4. Joint-Probability Distribution in Multicurrency Scenario Simulation
The multicurrency scenario simulation model addresses the problem of creating correlated yield curve scenarios in multiple currencies. The model discretizes joint distribution of yield curves of all currencies in such a way that the marginal distribution of each currency is discretized binomial, as described in the previous section. Let

$$a_{i+1} = \Psi^{-1}(F(i)) \quad i = 0,...,m; \quad (a_0 = -\infty, a_{m+1} = +\infty)$$

where Ψ represent cumulative distribution functions of the normal distributions, and F represent cumulative distribution functions of the binomial distributions. Thus, a_i $(i =0,..., m+1)$ are the points on the real line such that the area under the normal curve on the segment $[a_i, a_{i+1}]$ equals the binomial probability of state i. For example, if $m = 6$, we have

$$a_1 = -2.15387, a_2 = -1.22986, a_3 = -0.40225, a_4 = 0.40225, a_5 = 1.22986,$$
$$a_6 = 2.15387$$

The area under the normal curve on $[a_0, a_1]$ is equal to $1/64$, the probability of the first state in this seven states binomial distribution.

Define function $B^{(m)}$ on the real line with values in the set $\{0,...,m\}$:

$$B^{(m)}(Z) = i \quad \text{if } a_i \leq z < a_{i+1}$$

If Z is a normally distributed with mean zero and variance one, then $B^{(m)}(Z)$ is binomially distributed with $m + 1$ states.

Now we expand the above discussion into the multidimensional case. If X is a k-dimensional normal variate with correlation matrix Q,

$$X = (X_1,...,X_k) \sim N(0,Q)$$

each X_i having mean zero and variance one, define its discretization:

$$B^{(m)} = (B^{(m)}(X_1), ..., B^{(m)}(X_k))$$

Each coordinate of $B^{(m)}$ is binomially distributed and equals the discretization of the corresponding component of X. In this sense this discretization preserves the stratification.

To generate correlated multicurrency yield curve scenarios requires random samples of $B^{(m)}$. First, we generate a multivariate $N(0,Q)$ normal deviate $x = (x_1, ..., x_k)$, then simply find between which a_i and a_{i+1} each x_j lies, and thus form $(B^{(m)}(x_1), ..., B^{(m)}(x_k))$. Recall each $B^{(m)}(x_i)$ represents a currency yield curve scenario. The above procedure thus generates one set of yield curve scenarios for all currencies.

The joint probability density of $B^{(m)}$ can be written as

$$\mathrm{prob}(B^{(m)} = i_1, ..., i_k) = \int_{a_{i_1}}^{a_{i_1+1}} ... \int_{a_{i_k}}^{a_{i_k+1}} p(x_1, ..., x_k) dx_1 ... dx_k$$

where $p(x) = p(x_1, ..., x_k)$ is the multivariate normal density function of X with correlation matrix Q.

5. *Distribution of a Multicurrency Portfolio*
To calculate the risk exposure of a multicurrency fixed income portfolio, the exchange rates have to be incorporated into the model. In the scenario simulation model, the exchange rate scenarios are generated in a way similar to the yield curve scenarios. For example, we may assume that each exchange rate $X = X(t)$ is lognormally distributed as

$$X(t) = f(t)e^{\sigma_x w_x(t)}$$

where $f(t)$ is the forward exchange rate for the horizon t. Binomial discretization can be applied to generate exchange rate scenarios at the horizon t. Assume there are a total of k currencies, including the home currency (say, USD). If V_i is the i-th currency portfolio value, and X_i is the exchange rate of the i-th currency. Then total value of portfolio is simply

$$V = X_1 V_1 + X_2 V_2 + ... + X_k V_k$$

Once the scenarios are generated, portfolio value can be calculated directly. The distribution of the portfolio value can be generated by a large sample of interest rate and exchange rate scenarios.

Credit Analysis and Credit Risk Management

Valuing Corporate Credit: Quantitative Approaches versus Fundamental Analysis

Sivan Mahadevan
Executive Director
Morgan Stanley

Young-Sup Lee
Vice President
Morgan Stanley

Viktor Hjort
Vice President
Morgan Stanley

David Schwartz*

Stephen Dulake*

In this chapter, we compare fundamental approaches to valuing corporate credit with quantitative approaches, commenting on their relative merits and predictive powers. On the quantitative front, we first review structural models, such as KMV and CreditGrades™, which use information from the equity markets and corporate balance sheets to deter-

---

* David Schwartz and Stephen Dulake were employed at Morgan Stanley when this chapter was written.

mine default probabilities or fair market spreads. Second, we describe reduced form models, which use information from the fixed income markets to directly model default probabilities. Third, we review simple statistical techniques such as factor models, which aid in determining relative value. With respect to fundamental approaches, we examine rating agency and credit analyst methodologies in detail.

QUANTITATIVE APPROACHES TO VALUING CORPORATE CREDIT

Quantitative approaches for analyzing credit have existed for decades but have surged in popularity over the last few years. This is due in large part to several trends in the credit markets:

- As credit spreads have widened and default rates have increased, investors have looked to increase their arsenal of tools for analyzing corporate bonds. Quantitative models can be used to provide warning signals or to determine whether the spread on a corporate bond adequately compensates the investor for the risk.
- The number of investors interested in credit products has grown worldwide. In part, this can be attributed to declining yields on competing investments and the expansion of the European corporate bond market following the introduction of the euro. Commercially available credit models have been developed to meet the growing investor demand.
- The rapidly expanding credit derivatives market, which includes credit default swaps and collateralized debt obligations, has spurred a new generation of quantitative models. For derivative products, quantitative techniques are critical for valuation and hedging.
- Risk management has become increasingly important for financial institutions. The need to compute Value-at-Risk and determine appropriate regulatory capital reserves has led to the development of sophisticated quantitative credit models.

In this section, we introduce some popular quantitative techniques for analyzing individual credits. (We discuss quantitative methods for portfolio products later in this chapter.) The goal of these methods is to estimate default probabilities or fair market spreads. Although many different quantitative techniques are practiced in the market, we focus on two different approaches for modeling default: structural models and reduced form models.

Structural models use information from the equity market and corporate balance sheets to model a corporation's assets and liabilities.

Default occurs when the value of the corporation's assets falls below its liabilities. Structural models are used to infer default probabilities and fair market spreads. KMV and CreditGrades are two commercial examples of this approach.

Unlike structural models, *reduced form models* rely on information from the fixed income market, such as asset swap spreads or default swap spreads. In these models default probabilities are modeled directly, similar to the way interest rates are modeled for the purpose of pricing fixed income derivatives. These models are particularly useful for pricing credit derivatives and basket products.

For comparison to default-based models, we briefly present a simple *factor model* of corporate spreads. It focuses on the *relative* pricing of credit, using linear regression to determine which bonds are rich or cheap. The factors used in the model include credit rating, leverage (total debt/EBITDA), duration, and recent equity volatility.

Structural Models

In the structural approach, we model the assets and liabilities of a corporation, focusing on the economic events that trigger default. Default occurs when the value of the firm's assets falls below its liabilities. The inputs to the model are the firm's liabilities, as projected from its balance sheet, as well as equity value and equity volatility. An option pricing model is used to infer the value and volatility of the firm's assets.

To see why an option pricing model is at the heart of the structural approach, consider a simple firm that has issued a single one-year zero-coupon bond with a face value of $100 million. A stylized balance sheet for this firm is shown in Exhibit 13.1.

The key insight comes from examining the values of the equity and debt in one year, when the debt matures. If in one year the value of assets is $140 million, then the $100 million due to bondholders will be paid, leaving the value of equity at $40 million. On the other hand, if in one year the value of assets is $60 million, equity holders can "walk

EXHIBIT 13.1   Stylized Balance Sheet

Assets	Claims on Assets
Assets of the firm	*Liabilities (Debt)*
	1-year zero-coupon bond with face value of $100 million
	Equity
	Common shares

Source: Morgan Stanley.

away," turning over the $60 million in assets to the bondholders. Because equity holders have limited liability, the value of equity is $0. The payoff diagram for equity and debt holders in one year as a function of assets is shown in Exhibit 13.2.

From the hockey-stick shape of the payoff diagram for equity holders, it is clear that equity can be thought of as a call option on the assets of the firm. In this example, the strike is the face value of the debt, $100 million. Similarly, the zero-coupon corporate bond is equivalent to being long a risk-free zero-coupon bond and short a put option on the assets of the firm.

With the key insight that equity can be considered a call option on the assets of the firm, the rest of the structural approach falls into place. Exhibit 13.3 shows the steps involved in implementing a structural model. Equity value and volatility, along with information on the firm's liabilities, are fed into an option pricing model in order to compute the implied value and volatility of the firm's assets. Having computed the value and volatility of the firm's assets, we can determine how close the firm is to default. This "distance to default" can be translated into a probability of default, or it can be used to determine the fair spread on a corporate bond.

EXHIBIT 13.2   Value of Equity and Debt in One Year

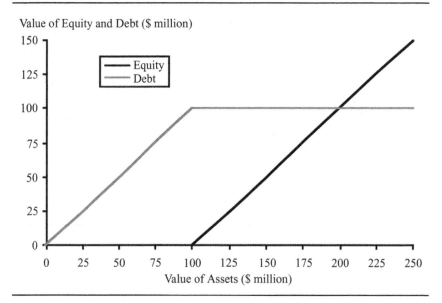

Source: Morgan Stanley.

EXHIBIT 13.3   Implementation of a Structural Model

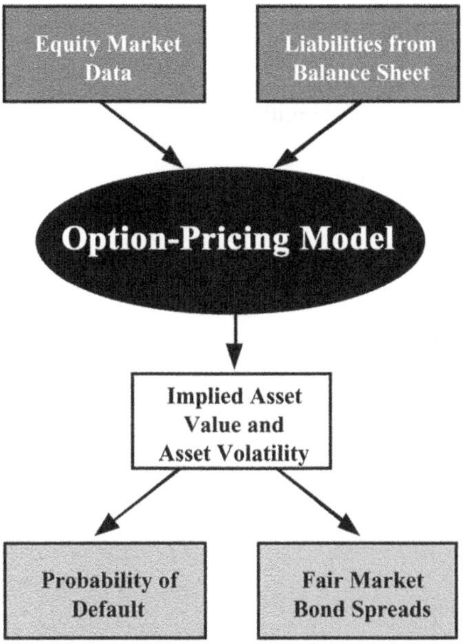

Source: Morgan Stanley.

Example: Merton's Original Model

To illustrate the calculations behind structural models, we consider the original structural model described by Robert Merton.[1] We revisit our simple firm, which has a single 1-year zero-coupon bond outstanding with a face value of $100 million. Furthermore, assume that the equity is valued at $30 million and has a volatility of 60%, and that the risk-free interest rate is 4%. These parameters are summarized in Exhibit 13.4.

Step 1: Computing Asset Value and Volatility
In Merton's original approach, equity is valued as a call option on the firm's assets using the Black-Scholes option pricing formula (N refers to the cumulative normal distribution function):

$$E = AN(d_1) - Fe^{-rT}N(d_2)$$

---

[1] Robert C. Merton, "On the Pricing of Corporate Debt: The Risk Structure of Interest Rates," *Journal of Finance* 29 (1974), pp. 449–470.

EXHIBIT 13.4   Parameters for Structural Model Example

Inputs

Value of Equity	$E = \$30$ million
Volatility of Equity	$\sigma_E = 60\%$
Face Value of Debt	$F = \$100$ million
Maturity of Debt	$T = 1$ year
Risk-free Interest Rate	$r = 4\%$

Outputs

Value of Assets	$A = ?$
Volatility of Assets	$\sigma_A = ?$

Source: Morgan Stanley.

where

$$d_1 = \frac{\log(A/F) + (r + \sigma_A^2/2)T}{\sigma_A \sqrt{T}}$$

and

$$d_2 = d_1 - \sigma_A \sqrt{T}$$

In the Black-Scholes framework, there is also a relationship between the volatility of equity and the volatility of assets:[2]

$$\sigma_E = \sigma_A N(d_1)\frac{A}{E}$$

The Black-Scholes formula and the relationship between equity volatility and asset volatility provide two equations, which we must solve for the two unknown quantities: the value of assets (A) and the volatility of assets (σ_A). Solving the equations yields $A = \$125.9$ million and $\sigma_A = 14.7\%$.[3]

Step 2a: Computing Fair Market Spreads
Having computed the implied asset value and volatility, we can now determine the implied spread on the zero-coupon bond over the risk-

---

[2] This equation is derived from Ito's lemma. For details, see John C. Hull, *Options Futures and Other Derivatives*, 3rd ed. (Upper Saddle River, NJ: Prentice Hall, 1997).

[3] These two equations can be solved simultaneously in a spreadsheet by an iterative procedure (e.g., Goal Seek or Solver in Excel).

free rate. To do this, we note that the value of the debt is equal to the value of the assets minus the value of the equity. That is, the value of the debt equals $125.9 million – $30 million = $95.9 million. Since the face value of the debt is $100 million, we can easily determine that the yield on the zero-coupon bond is 4.22%, which corresponds to a spread of 22 basis points over the risk-free rate.

At this point, it is worth noting that it is difficult to get "reasonable" short-term spreads from Merton's original model. In part, the reason for this is that the asset value is assumed to follow a continuous lognormal process, and the probability of being significantly below a static default threshold after only a short amount of time is low. In this example, the spread of 22 basis points probably underestimates what would be the observed spread in the market. In practice, adjustments are made to Merton's basic structural model in order to produce more realistic spreads.

Step 2b: Computing Distance to Default and Probability of Default One popular metric in the structural approach is the "distance to default." Shown graphically in Exhibit 13.5, the distance to default is the difference between a firm's asset value and its liabilities, measured in units of the standard deviation of the asset value. In short, it is the number of standard deviations that a firm is from default. In the Black-

EXHIBIT 13.5   Distance to Default

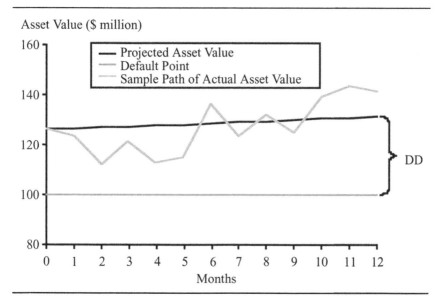

Source: Morgan Stanley.

Scholes-Merton framework, the distance to default is equal to d_2, from above. Using the values of A and σ_A computed earlier, we calculate the distance to default to be 1.76. In other words, the projected asset value is 1.76 standard deviations above the default threshold.

The distance to default, d_2, is important because it is used to compute the probability of default. In the Black-Scholes-Merton framework, the risk-neutral probability of default is $N(-d_2)$. In our example, the risk-neutral probability of default is $N(-1.76)$, which equals 3.1%.

Recovery Rates   In Merton's model, recovery rates are determined implicitly. In this example, if the value of assets in one year is $80 million, then the corporation defaults, and bondholders recover $80 million. We can also compute the expected recovery rate (under the risk-neutral measure). Conditional on the default of the company, the expected value of assets to be recovered by debtholders is given by $AN(-d_1)/N(-d_2)$. In this example, expected recovery value is $90.7 million. This is higher than we would likely observe, for the same reason that the model underestimates short-term spreads.

Extending Merton's Original Model

The original Merton model outlined above features a firm with a single zero-coupon bond and a single class of equity. Models used in practice are more elaborate, incorporating short-term and long-term liabilities, convertible debt, preferred equity, and common equity. In addition, models used in practice are more sophisticated in order to produce more realistic spreads, default probabilities, and recovery rates. The following list of modeling choices is representative of some of the more popular extensions to Merton's original model:

- The default threshold need not be a constant level. It can be projected to increase or decrease over time.
- Default can occur at maturity, on coupon dates or continuously. Exhibit 13.6 shows three possible paths for a firm's asset value over the next year. In Merton's original model, where default can only occur at maturity, the firm defaults only in asset value path C, where the recovery rate is 80%. If the default barrier is continuous, the firm defaults in asset value paths B and C, as soon as the asset value hits the default barrier. The recovery rate would be determined separately.
- The default threshold can have a random component, reflecting imperfect information about current and future liabilities. Indeed, current liabilities may not be observable with sufficient accuracy, for example, because the balance sheet is out of date. Similarly, it is not easy to pre-

EXHIBIT 13.6   Sample Asset Value Paths

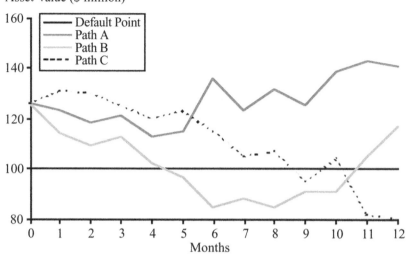

Source: Morgan Stanley.

dict how management will refinance debt or adjust debt levels in the future in response to changing economic conditions.

■ Asset value need not follow a lognormal distribution. For example, it can have jumps, reflecting unanticipated surprises that cause asset value to decrease sharply. The option-pricing model can be different from the Black-Scholes model, and equity can be modeled as a perpetual option. In addition, asset value and volatility can be inferred from the equity markets in a more robust way, using an iterative procedure that incorporates time series information.

■ Firm behavior can be incorporated into a structural model. One example is a "target leverage" model, in which the initial capital structure decision can be altered. The level of debt changes over time in response to changes in the firm's value, so that the Debt/Assets ratio is meanreverting. In this model, the firm tends to issue more debt as asset values rise.[4]

■ In a "strategic debt service" model, there is an additional focus on the incentives that lead to voluntary default and the bargaining game that occurs between debt and equity holders in the event of distress. These

---

[4] Pierre Collin-Dufresne and Robert Goldstein, "Do Credit Spreads Reflect Stationary Leverage Ratios?" *Journal of Finance* 56 (2001), pp. 1928–1957.

models acknowledge the costs associated with financial distress and the possibility of renegotiation before liquidation.[5]

Commercial Implementations of the Structural Approach

Commercial implementations, such as KMV and CreditGrades, have refined the basic Merton model in different ways. Each strives to produce realistic output that can be used by market participants to evaluate potential investments.

KMV has extended the basic structural model according to the Vasicek-Kealhofer (VK) model. The primary goal of the model is to compute real-world probabilities of default, which are referred to as *Expected Default Frequencies*, or EDF™s. The model assumes that the firm's equity is a perpetual option, and default occurs when the default barrier is crossed for the first time. A critical feature of KMV's implementation is the sophisticated mapping between the distance to default and the probability of default (EDF). The mapping is based on an extensive proprietary database of empirical default and bankruptcy evidence. As such, the model produces real-world, not risk-neutral, probabilities.[6]

CreditGrades, a more recent product, is an extension of Merton's model that is primarily focused on computing indicative credit spreads. In the CreditGrades implementation, the default barrier has a random component, which is a significant driver of short-term spreads. Default occurs whenever the default threshold is crossed for the first time. Parameters for the model have been estimated in order to achieve consistency with historical default swap spreads.[7]

Advantages of Structural Models

There are seven advantages of structural models:

- Equity markets are generally more liquid and transparent than corporate bond markets, and some argue that they provide more reliable information. Using equity market information allows fixed income instruments to be priced independently, without requiring credit spread information from related fixed income instruments.
- Structural models attempt to explain default from an economic perspective. They are oriented toward the fundamentals of the company, focusing on its balance sheet and asset value.

---

[5] For a simple example, see Suresh Sundaresan, *Fixed Income Markets and Their Derivatives*, 2nd ed. (Cincinnati, OH: South-Western, 1997).

[6] *Modeling Default Risk*, KMV LLC, January 2002.

[7] *CreditGrades Technical Document*, RiskMetrics Group, Inc., May 2002.

- Credit analysts' forecasts can be incorporated into the model to enhance the quality of its output. For example, balance sheet projections can be used to create a more realistic default threshold. The model can also be run under different scenarios for future liabilities.
- Structural models are well-suited for handling different securities of the same issuer, including bonds of various seniorities and convertible bonds.
- A variety of structural models are commercially available. They can be used as a screening tool for large portfolios, especially when credit analyst resources are limited.
- Structural models can be enhanced, for example, to incorporate firm behavior. Examples include target leverage models and strategic debt service models.
- Default correlation can be modeled quite naturally in the structural framework. In a portfolio context, correlation in asset values drives default correlation.

Disadvantages of Structural Models

The disadvantages of structural models are as follows:

- If equity prices become irrationally inflated, they may be poor indicators of actual asset value. The Internet and telecom bubbles of the past few years are perhaps the most striking examples. Generally, users of structural models must believe that they can reasonably imply asset values from equity market information. This can become a significant issue when current earnings are low or negative and equity valuations are high.
- Bond prices and credit default swap spreads, which arguably contain valuable information about the probability of default, are outputs of the model, not inputs.
- In Merton's structural model, implied credit spreads on short-term debt and very high quality debt are very low when compared to empirical data. Refinements to the model have alleviated this problem, at the expense of simplicity.
- The determination of a unique arbitrage-free option price implicitly assumes that the value of the whole firm is tradable and available as a hedge instrument, which is a questionable assumption. In addition, it may not be clear how to best model a firm's asset value.
- Structural models can be difficult to calibrate. In practice, asset values and volatilities are best calibrated using time-series information. Assumptions for equity volatility can have a significant impact on the model.

▓ Structural models can be complex, depending on the capital structure of the issuer and the level of detail captured by the model. An issuer may have multiple classes of short-term and long-term debt, convertible bonds, preferred shares, and common equity.

▓ It can be difficult to get reliable, current data on a firm's liabilities. Issues regarding transparency and accounting treatment are, of course, not unique to structural models. In addition, once adequate information on the liabilities is obtained, the information must be consolidated to project a default barrier.

▓ Notwithstanding innovations such as target leverage models and strategic debt service models, it is difficult to model future corporate behavior.

▓ It can be difficult to model a firm that is close to its default threshold, since firms will often adjust their liabilities as they near default. Firms will vary in terms of their ability to adjust their leverage as they begin to encounter difficulties. (For this reason, KMV reports a maximum EDF of 20%.)

▓ Financial institutions should be modeled with caution, since it can be harder to assess their assets and liabilities. In addition, since financial institutions are highly regulated, default may not be the point where the value of assets falls below the firm's liabilities.

▓ Structural models are generally inappropriate for sovereign issuers.

Reduced Form Models

In the reduced form approach, default is modeled as a surprise event. Rather than modeling the value of a firm's assets, here we directly model the probability of default. This approach is similar to the way interest rates are modeled for the purpose of pricing fixed income derivatives. Unlike the structural models described above, the inputs for reduced form models come from the fixed income markets in the form of default swap spreads or asset swap spreads.

The quantity we are actually modeling in the reduced form approach is called the *hazard rate*, which we denote by $h(t)$. The hazard rate is a *forward* probability of default, similar to a forward interest rate. The hazard rate has the following interpretation: Given that a firm survives until time t, $h(t)\Delta t$ is the probability of default over the next small interval of time Δt.

For example, assume that the hazard rate is constant, with $h = 3\%$. Conditional on a firm surviving until a given date in the future, its probability of default over the subsequent one day (0.0027 years) is approximately $h\Delta t = 3\% \times 0.0027 = 0.008\%$.

Letting τ represent the time to default, the hazard rate is defined mathematically as follows:

$$h(t) = \frac{\text{Prob}(\tau \leq t + \Delta t \,|\, \tau > t)}{\Delta t}$$

Three features of hazard rates make them particularly useful for modeling default.

Even though the hazard rate is an instantaneous forward probability of default, it tells us the probability of default over any time horizon. For example, assume a constant hazard rate. The probability of a bond defaulting in the next t years is $1 - e^{-ht}$. If $h = 3\%$, the probability of the firm defaulting in the next two years is $1 - e^{-0.03(2)} = 5.82\%$. A graph of the cumulative default probability when $h = 3\%$ is shown in Exhibit 13.7.

Hazard rates can be inferred from the fixed income markets, in the form of default swap spreads or asset swap spreads. For example, assuming a constant hazard rate, the default swap premium is approximately equal to $h \times (1 - Expected\ Recovery\ Rate)$. If the default swap premium is 180 basis points and the expected recovery rate is 40%, we can set $h = 1.80\%/(1 - 0.40) = 3\%$.

Hazard rates are convenient for running simulations to value derivative and credit portfolio products. In a portfolio context, a simulation

EXHIBIT 13.7   Cumulative Probability of Default—3% Hazard Rate

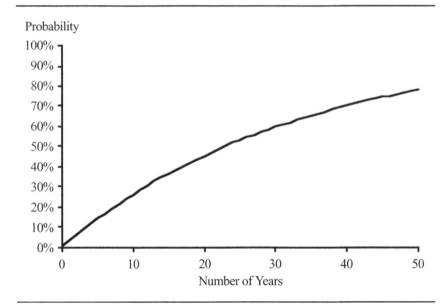

Source: Morgan Stanley.

would allow for defaults to be correlated. Assuming a constant hazard rate, we can simulate the time to default as follows: We can repeatedly generate values between 0 and 1 for the uniform random variable U and use the relation $\tau = -\log(U)/h$ for the time to default. For example, with $h = 3\%$, if in the first path of a simulation $U = 0.757$, the corresponding time until default is $-\log(0.757)/0.03 = 9.28$ years.

In the examples above, we have assumed that hazard rates are constant. The real exercise, however, is to *model* the hazard rates. Like interest rates, hazard rates are assumed to have a term structure, and they are assumed to evolve randomly over time. Models for interest rates, such as a lognormal model or the Cox-Ingersoll-Ross model, can be used to model hazard rates. In addition, it is not uncommon for models of hazard rates to incorporate jumps that occur at random times. Hazard rate models are typically calibrated to a term structure of default swap spreads or asset swap spreads.

Advantages of Reduced Form Models
The advantages of reduced form models are as follows:

- Reduced form models are calibrated to the fixed income markets in the form of default swap spreads or asset swap spreads. It is natural to expect that bond markets and credit default swap markets contain valuable information regarding the probability of default.
- Reduced form models are extremely tractable and well-suited for pricing derivatives and portfolio products. The models are calibrated to correctly price the instruments that a trader will use to hedge.
- In a portfolio context, it is easy to generate correlated hazard rates, which lead to correlated defaults.
- Hazard rates models are closely related to interest rate models, which have been widely researched and implemented.
- Reduced form models can incorporate credit rating migration. However, for pricing purposes, a risk-neutral ratings transition matrix must be generated.
- Reduced form models can be used in the absence of balance sheet information (e.g., for sovereign issuers).

Disadvantages of Reduced Form Models
The disadvantages of reduced form models are as follows:

- Reduced form models reveal limited information about the fixed income securities that are used in their calibration.

▪ Reduced form models can be sensitive to assumptions, such as the volatility of the hazard rate and correlations between hazard rates.
▪ Even if hazard rates are highly correlated, the occurrences of default may not be highly correlated. For this reason, practitioners pay careful attention to which particular process hazard rates are assumed to follow. Models with jumps have been used to ameliorate this problem.
▪ Whereas there is a large history on interest rate movements that can be used as a basis for choosing an interest rate model, hazard rates are not directly observable. (Only the events of default are observable.) Thus, it may be difficult to choose between competing hazard rate models.

Factor Models

For comparison to the default-based pricing models described above, we include a brief discussion of a simple factor model of investment grade corporate spreads.[8] Unlike the structural and reduced form models, the factor model does not attempt to model default in order to gain insight into fair market prices. Rather, it is a simple statistical approach to the *relative* pricing of credit and used to determine which bonds are rich or cheap.

This factor model uses linear regression to attribute spreads to various characteristics of the bonds being analyzed. The idea is to quantify the importance of various drivers of corporate bond spreads. The residual from the regression is used to indicate rich and cheap securities. Some potential factors for investment grade credit are shown in Exhibit 13.8. Later in this chapter, in the section on Historical Analysis of Quantitative and Fundamental Approaches, we review the performance of this factor model, along with other quantitative and fundamental approaches.

FUNDAMENTAL APPROACHES TO VALUING CORPORATE CREDIT

Fundamental approaches for analyzing credit have been practiced for decades, most often by buy- and sell-side credit analysts and rating agency analysts. To give readers a sense of how credit analysts analyze the creditworthiness of companies, we summarize and generalize the credit analyst approach based on Morgan Stanley experiences. We also describe the process rating agencies go through to arrive at credit ratings (based on their own published research). Our conclusions are as follows:

---

[8] For details, see "A Model of Credit Spreads," *Morgan Stanley Fixed Income Research*, November 1999.

EXHIBIT 13.8 Sample Factor Model Inputs

Factor	Type	Description
Total Debt/EBITDA	Numeric	Measure of leverage
Rating	Numeric	Scaled to a numeric value
Watchlist	{-2,-1,0,1,2}	On watchlist, negative or positive
Duration	Numeric	Modified duration
Stock Returns	Numeric	1-year total return
Stock Volatility	Numeric	Price volatility over last 90 days
Quintile of Debt Outstanding	{1,2,3,4,5}	E.g., top 20% = 5th quintile
10- to 15-year Maturity	Numeric	Years to maturity >10 but <15
Gaming	{0,1}	E.g., casinos
Cyclical	{0,1}	E.g., retail, autos
Finance	{0,1}	E.g., banks, finance, brokerage
Technology	{0,1}	E.g., software, hardware
Global	{0,1}	Global bond
AAA/AA	{0,1}	Rated Aaa/AA or Aa/AA or split
Yankee	{0,1}	Yankee bond

Source: Morgan Stanley.

- In some cases, there may be no substitute for the credit expert who can formulate subjective views on business, financial, and strategic risks associated with a company or industry.
- Special considerations such as pension liabilities and off-balance-sheet items, which have been a focus in the market recently, can be easily incorporated by credit analysts.
- The motivation for changing the capital structure of a company, and the likelihood of such a change occurring, can drive the valuation of corporate credit in a significant manner. Credit analysts can have important subjective views on capital structure changes.
- Rating agency approaches focus on determining probability of default and loss severity by evaluating the financial state of a company, with future scenarios weighted in a probabilistic framework. The agencies aim to establish stable credit ratings.
- In general, fundamental approaches do not directly lead to market prices. Valuations are usually made in a relative value context.

Credit Analysis Principles: Disaggregating Credit Risk

At the company level, the objective is to use information from the financial statement to assess the firm's capacity and willingness to service a given level of debt. There is specific emphasis on the predictability and variability of corporate cash flows.

Credit risk can be decomposed into a number of constituents, each of which must be considered (see Exhibit 13.9). Specifically, a basic assessment of credit risk at the company level should involve a consideration of three sorts of risk:

- *Business risk*. Described as the quality and stability of operations over the business cycle, which implies judgment as to the predictability of corporate cash flows.
- *Financial risk*. Whether or not current cash flow generation and profitability are sufficient to support debt levels, ratings levels, and, therefore, credit quality levels.
- *Strategy risk*. Considering potential event risk, for example, what's the probability of a change in company strategy by management? What are the probability and credit quality implications of executing a certain acquisition? External risks, such as asbestos- or tobacco-related litigation or the advent of 3G technology, would also be considered here.

Clearly, business, financial, and strategy risks are not mutually exclusive, but rather interdependent. There is no unique way of weighting or combining these factors. It is at the discretion of the analyst and will vary on a company-to-company basis. The task is to determine what the market thinks about each of these risks and in what combination. Only then can one make some judgment as to relative richness or cheapness.

EXHIBIT 13.9   Industrial Credit Research

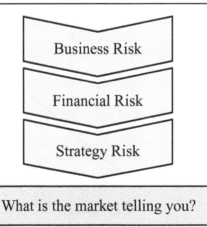

Source: Morgan Stanley.

Capital Structure Changes and the Equity Option

There is one aspect of strategic risk that links together the quantitative structural approach and the fundamental approach. In the Merton framework, the face value of outstanding debt is the strike price of the call option equityholders have on the company's assets. The strike price changes when the capital structure of a company changes, which is very much a part of the strategic risk a credit analyst has to measure.

Consider again our original example of a corporation which has a single zero-coupon bond outstanding with a face value of $100 million that will mature in one year. If the total value of the firm's assets is $100 million or less in one year's time, the value of the firm's equity is zero and stockholders simply "walk away," leaving bondholders to recover what value they can from the firm's assets. Now, if the starting position of the corporation were $120 million in debt, as opposed to $100 million, the strike price of the option which bondholders implicitly write to stockholders is raised by $20 million (the increase in the face value of the amount of debt outstanding). Exhibit 13.10 shows the original and new payoff structures associated with this change in the firm's capital structure.

In the quantitative section, we discussed how extensions to the classic Merton framework address a changing strike price (e.g., modeling the default barrier as a random process). However, analysts can also have a view or assign a probability to the magnitude and timing of a

EXHIBIT 13.10   The Value of Equity in One Year

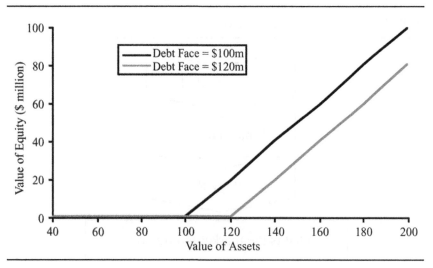

Source: Morgan Stanley.

capital structure change. If the magnitude and likelihood of this change is high, then it will dominate any valuation of a credit, whether fundamental or quantitative, so it should be factored in correctly.

Developing a Framework for Thinking About "The Management Option"

What motivates a firm's management to exercise this sort of capital structure option? More important from a creditor perspective, can we develop a conceptual framework that gives us some insight as to when a firm's management might be inclined to effect a change in the capital structure? At this point, at the expense of stating the obvious, it is worth highlighting that changes in a firm's capital structure do not always put bondholders at a disadvantage relative to shareholders.

The Weighted Average Cost of Capital

In thinking about the opportunities available to a firm's management, we have found it increasingly useful to think within a *weighted average cost of capital* (WACC) framework. By way of definition:

$$\text{WACC} = Q_d \cdot C_d + Q_e \cdot C_e$$

Q_d and Q_e represent the amount of debt and equity, respectively, as percentage of total enterprise value, and C_d and C_e represent their respective costs. These are in turn defined as

$$C_d = (r + \text{BS}) \times (1 - \tau)$$

$$C_e = r + (\beta \times \text{ERP})$$

Here r is the risk-free rate (or benchmark government bond yield), BS is the borrowing spread on top of the risk-free rate, τ is the corporate tax rate, β is a measure of the volatility of the company's stock vis-à-vis the broader equity market, and ERP is the market-wide equity risk premium.

Mapping the WACC to credit ratings, one would typically expect to observe the "hockey stick" profile shown in Exhibit 13.11. Remember, interest is tax deductible and dividends are only distributed after taxes, although this tax treatment may change in the future. This is why, as more debt is added to the balance sheet and the firm migrates down the ratings spectrum, we initially observe a negatively sloped WACC curve. Beyond a certain point, however, the incremental tax benefit associated with adding more debt to the balance sheet is more than offset by a combination of a higher borrowing spread and a rising β. Thus, when

EXHIBIT 13.11   A Stylized Version of the Weighted Average Cost of Capital

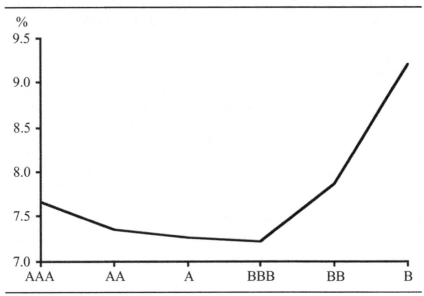

Source: Morgan Stanley.

we map the WACC to leverage and credit ratings, we observe an eventual shift from a negatively sloped to a positively sloped curve.

The WACC is a theoretical concept, but it provides an extremely useful framework for thinking about the circumstances in which management might change the firm's capital structure. A WACC framework helps us put bounds on the risk-reward structure associated with the "management option." Specifically, we believe that it is at the tails of the leverage distribution, where the risk–reward mismatch associated with a change in the capital structure is greatest, and therefore the incentive to change the capital structure is arguably the greatest. For example, at the high end of the ratings spectrum, there is a strong incentive for a company to increase leverage and lower its cost of capital. Similarly, the incentive to pursue a strategy of balance sheet reparation is much stronger at the opposite end of the leverage distribution.

The Operating Environment: Industry Analysis

Any fundamental assessment of corporate credit risk for a given company must necessarily extend beyond the latest set of financials and consider the "macro" operating environment including issues related to industry structure and evolution, the regulatory environment and barriers to entry. (See Exhibit 13.12.)

EXHIBIT 13.12   Forces Shaping the Operating Environment

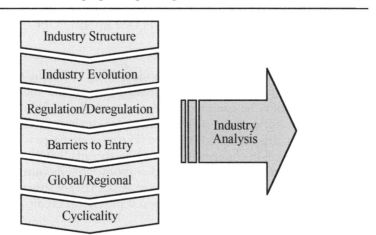

Source: Morgan Stanley.

To illustrate the questions that one typically asks, it is important to consider whether, for example, we are dealing with a monopoly or a highly competitive business from an industry structure perspective. Barriers to entry have clear implications for pricing and earnings power. Is the business global or regional? For example, in the case of autos, what is the viability of a regional car maker in a global business?

On the regulatory front, deregulation has been a clear driver of capital structure and credit quality trends in the utility sector. Again, what is important from a credit risk perspective are the *ex ante* and *ex post* implications of any regulatory change on pricing power and the ability for a company to generate cash flow and support a given level of debt and credit quality.

Regarding industry evolution, a classic case in point is the telecommunications business and the advent of 3G technology. As has been the case with deregulation in the utility sector, 3G has been the principal driver of the telecom credit quality rollercoaster in 2000 and 2001.

The Output from Credit Analysts: Determining Relative Value and Spreads

At this point, a natural question to ask is how credit analysts translate their company-specific analyses into a spread? In our experience, we find that credit analysts formulate appropriate valuation levels through a relative value framework based on comparability. Such a framework takes the current market level for spreads as given and suggests valuations through a peer group of comparable credits. Statements such as "company X should trade 20 basis points behind company Y" are common, however subjective they may appear. We explore the importance of ratings versus sectors in determining these peer groups in the next section.

Comparability: Sectors versus Ratings

Given the focus by credit analysts on identifying and utilizing an appropriate peer group for determining spreads, how should such a group of comparable credits be constructed? As an example, in Exhibit 13.13 we present intersector correlation coefficients for single-A rated segments of MSCI's Euro Corporate Credit Index. The average pairwise correlation coefficient of weekly changes in asset swap spreads is 0.28, quite low in our opinion. Similarly, for BBB-rated corporate bonds (not shown), the average pairwise correlation coefficient is 0.24. From this analysis we can conclude that peer groupings, based purely on credit ratings, may not be appropriate.

What is the degree of correlation within a given sector between different credits with different ratings? We have focused our example on two of the more liquid sectors in the European credit markets: autos and telecommunications. Exhibit 13.15 presents the results of this exercise for the auto sector. We have selected five credits rated mid-A to mid-BBB with relatively liquid bonds of similar maturities outstanding. The lowest pairwise correlation in the auto sector, at 0.31 between Ford and Renault, is higher than the average observed for either single As or triple Bs (see Exhibit 13.15). The average pairwise correlation for the auto sector is 0.62, which would suggest that sector groupings are more important than ratings groups, at least when considering the auto sector.

The results for the telecom sector are shown in Exhibit 13.14. Again, we have selected a group of credits that cover a reasonable spectrum of European credits. The average pairwise correlation for the telecom sector is 0.40, which is again higher than that observed between different sectors within a given rating class.

Rating Agency Approaches

No institution wields as much influence on how the market perceives the credit quality of an individual borrower as the credit rating agencies. The agencies themselves see their role as being the providers of truly independent credit opinions, and as such, helping to overcome the information asymmetry between borrowers and lenders. With such monumental influence on pricing decisions, rating agencies, unsurprisingly, regularly receive criticism for not achieving all of their aims. Market participants have traditionally criticized the agencies for being too slow to react to new information. Lately the criticism has tended to be that agencies are

EXHIBIT 13.13 Single As—Sector Correlation Coefficients Based on Weekly Asset Swap Spread Changes End-1999 to Present

	Banks	Nonbank Fins	Con Disc	Con Staples	Energy	Industrials	Technology	Telecoms	Utilities
Banks	1								
Nonbank Fins	0.55	1							
Con Disc	0.41	0.59	1						
Con Staples	0.23	0.24	0.33	1					
Energy	0.30	0.32	0.33	0.23	1				
Industrials	0.26	0.30	0.44	0.21	0.33	1			
Technology	0.10	0.01	0.11	0.13	0.16	-0.04	1		
Telecoms	0.17	0.11	0.40	0.22	0.12	0.22	0.37	1	
Utilities	0.44	0.45	0.37	0.41	0.31	0.36	0.11	0.31	1

Source: Morgan Stanley.

EXHIBIT 13.14 Telecoms—Cross-Credit Correlation Coefficients

	VOD	TELECO	OTE	BRITEL	FRTEL	DT	TIIM	OLIVET	KPN
VOD	1								
TELECO	0.29	1							
OTE	0.21	0.31	1						
BRITEL	0.54	0.04	0.37	1					
FRTEL	0.47	0.13	0.48	0.68	1				
DT	0.41	−0.17	0.39	0.66	0.83	1			
TIIM	0.60	0.39	0.35	0.61	0.60	0.44	1		
OLIVET	0.53	0.49	0.20	0.33	0.25	0.06	0.77	1	
KPN	0.33	0.23	0.39	0.36	0.58	0.39	0.53	0.38	1

Source: Morgan Stanley.

EXHIBIT 13.15 Autos—Cross-Credit Correlation Coefficients

	GM	DCX	FIAT	RENAUL	F
GM	1				
DCX	0.84	1			
FIAT	0.80	0.67	1		
RENAUL	0.34	0.42	0.50	1	
F	0.82	0.77	0.73	0.31	1

Source: Morgan Stanley.

too quick to change opinions. Nevertheless, given the crucial role the agencies play in the capital markets, it is important to understand the rating process and the factors that influence the agencies' decisions.[9]

Reducing Information Asymmetry

Corporate borrowers have access to more detailed information on their businesses and credit profiles than do lenders. This is particularly true for capital market lenders. For commercial banks, which work closely with their clients, lending decisions are based on a detailed understanding of the borrowers. The process of lending is characterized by constant monitoring of credit quality and actively using covenants to restrict potentially credit-detrimental activities of borrowers. Ultimately, banks can agree to restructure loans as a final attempt to recover funds before allowing default.

The capital markets, on the other hand, are anonymous to the borrowers in the sense that borrowers will never know nor control who ultimately lent them the money. Precisely because of this distance between borrowers and lenders, bond investors rely on credit analysts to bridge the information asymmetry.

Arriving at a Rating

Credit-rating agencies try to assess the probability of default and loss severity. The product of the two yields the expected loss. Based on this, a rating is produced. The rating is expected, over time, to map to a subsequent expected loss, based on historical experience. The process involves three main steps:

- *Evaluating the financial status.* Observing hard facts associated with the financial state of a particular company.
- *Evaluating management.* Subjectively evaluating the ability and interest in maintaining a particular credit profile.
- *Conducting scenario analysis.* Making assumptions about the probability of various scenarios that may impact the future credit profile.

Finally, arriving at a particular rating requires anchoring the two components, default probability and loss severity, to the historical experience. In estimating the default probability, rating agencies target relative risk over time. In estimating loss severity, analysts evaluate security and seniority, as well as sector differences. In addition, recovery rates may differ over time and across jurisdictions.

---

[9] For a more comprehensive survey, see Euro Credit Basis Report: "What's Going on at the Rating Agencies?" *Morgan Stanley Fixed Income Research*, May 31, 2002.

Creditworthiness Is a Stable Concept

Underlying this process lies a crucial assumption: Creditworthiness is a stable concept. Fundamentally, creditworthiness changes only gradually over time or at least is only confirmed over time. In theory, this ought to make multinotch rating changes unlikely, and the rating agencies therefore use tools such as outlooks and watch lists to flag changes. Even these, however, tend to have a built-in lag. Moody's, for instance, has an 18-month horizon for its outlooks and 90 days for its Watch List, whereas S&P targets 90 days for its CreditWatch listings, with a longer but unspecified time-horizon for Outlooks. This gradual approach gives credit ratings a serially correlated pattern. This is also what creates the impression that ratings activity lags the market so significantly.

Have the Agencies Changed Their Approach?

The rating agencies have been criticized for the market-lagging approach and serially correlated ratings pattern. The main criticism is that the approach causes ratings to lag their information content, and therefore lose their value as investor protection. In the case of Enron, for example, senior bonds and loans were already trading below 20 cents to the dollar when the company was downgraded to noninvestment grade, which was less than a week before the company filed for Chapter 11 bankruptcy protection.

In response to this criticism, Moody's put its ratings process under review early in 2002. Moody's asked investors whether they wanted ratings decisions to be quicker and more severe. The use of so-called market-based tools for evaluating credit was also suggested. The answer to the consultation was overwhelmingly "no." Investors showed little interest for a quicker ratings process, nor did they show any interest in the use of market-based tools to enhance the process. What there was a need for, according to the published feedback, was transparency.[10]

Standard & Poor's, has not (publicly) put its process up for review, but has increasingly focused on issues that will enhance and complement the information content of the ratings. In particular, S&P has (1) begun surveying its corporate issuers for information on *ratings contingent commitments*, such as ratings triggers; (2) indicated that it will start rating the transparency, disclosure, and corporate governance practices of the companies in the S&P 500; (3) introduced Core Earnings, a concept reflecting the agency's belief of how fundamental earnings performance *should* be reflected; and (4) introduced liquidity reports on individual companies.[11]

---

[10] *Understanding Moody's Corporate Bond Ratings and Ratings Process*, Moody's, May 2002.

[11] *Enhancing Financial Transparency: The View from Standard & Poor's*, S&P, July 2002.

HISTORICAL ANALYSIS OF QUANTITATIVE AND FUNDAMENTAL APPROACHES

While we have focused our efforts so far on describing quantitative and fundamental approaches to valuing corporate credit, we have yet to comment on their predictive powers. In this section we compare historical performance studies of our factor model, KMV EDFs, a quantifiable measure of the fundamental approach based on free cash flow changes, and rating agency approaches. Our conclusions are as follows:

▨ Our simple statistical factor model was a good predictor of *relative* spread movements over short time periods.
▨ KMV EDFs were good predictors of default and performed consistently over different categories of risk over one-year time horizons.
▨ Market-implied default probabilities (i.e., using spread as a predictor) overestimated default in most cases, given risk premiums inherent in market spreads. However, they were inconsistent predictors of default at different risk levels over one-year time horizons.
▨ Changes in free cash flow generation relative to debt (a fundamental measure of credit quality improvement) were a good predictor of *relative* spread movements over one-year time periods.
▨ Over long periods of time for the market at large, actual ratings migration and default behavior have been consistent with ratings expectations, based on Moody's and S&P data.
▨ While not always easily observable, market participants should understand the time period for which an indicator is useful. Equity and bond market valuations could be short- or long-term, as can analyst views. We have included our findings in the above points.

While our studies were performed on samples of different sizes based on the availability of reliable data, we believe the data sets are comparable and do not contain any systematic biases.

Statistical Factor Model Historical Study

We conducted a 16-month historical study (March 2001 through June 2002) of our factor model results (described in the Quantitative Approaches section) to test the predictive power of such a model. The factors used in the model are listed in Exhibit 13.16.

The study included a universe of 2,000 investment grade corporate bonds. A linear regression was conducted each month where we calculated a residual (i.e., actual spread minus the model's predicted spread) for each bond in the universe. A positive residual value indicates cheapness of the credit, while a negative value suggests richness. Rich-cheap residuals are

EXHIBIT 13.16   Factors Used in the Model

Factor	Type	Description
Total Debt/EBITDA	Numeric	Measure of leverage
Rating	Numeric	Scaled to a numeric value
Watchlist	{–2,–1,0,1,2}	On watchlist, negative or positive
Duration	Numeric	Modified duration
Stock Returns	Numeric	1-year total return
Stock Volatility	Numeric	Price volatility over last 90 days
Quintile of Debt Outstanding	{1,2,3,4,5}	E.g., top 20% = 5th quintile
10- to 15-Year Maturity	Numeric	Years to maturity >10 but < 15
Gaming	{0,1}	E.g., casinos
Cyclical	{0,1}	E.g., retail, autos
Finance	{0,1}	E.g., banks, finance, brokerage
Technology	{0,1}	E.g., software, hardware
Global	{0,1}	Global bond
AAA/AA	{0,1}	Rated Aaa/AA or Aa/AA or split
Yankee	{0,1}	Yankee bond

Source: Morgan Stanley.

not statistically significant unless their magnitudes are at least twice the standard error of the regression (standard deviation of all the residuals), which, in our experience, can be over 30 bps in a given month.

The results of our study show that the factor model is quite successful at determining relative value among bonds. The factor model's cheapest decile tightened significantly more than other bonds in nine of 16 months. Similarly, its richest decile significantly widened in nine of the 16 months. In Exhibit 13.17 we show the cumulative spread changes for richest and cheapest deciles (which are recomputed every month) and for the entire universe. The cheapest decile tightened an average of 160 bps versus the entire universe, while the richest decile widened 70 bps over that same period.

KMV EDFs Are Not as Useful for Relative Value

Since many market participants are attempting to use KMV EDF data to predict relative spread changes, we studied how well this worked. It is important to note, however, that KMV is meant to be a predictor of default, not spreads.

In studying how well KMV predicted spread changes, we determined richness and cheapness by comparing KMV EDFs to market-implied probabilities of default. These implied default probabilities are derived from the market spread and an assumed recovery rate.

EXHIBIT 13.17   Factor Model Performance

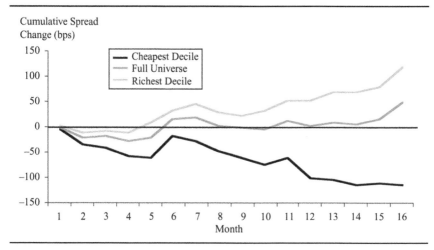

Source: Morgan Stanley.

EXHIBIT 13.18   KMV Spread Model Performance

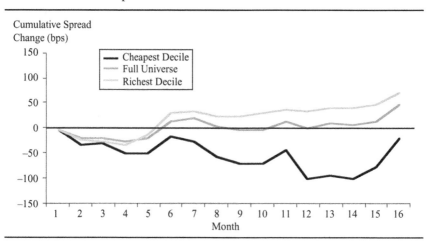

Source: Morgan Stanley, KMV.

Similarly to our factor model study, we observed the ensuing month's spread change for the cheapest and richest deciles of this EDF-based relative value measure. The results for the EDF signals, shown in Exhibit 13.18, are not as compelling as the factor model. In the EDF study, the cheapest bonds rallied by 68 bps, while the richest widened by only 24 bps.

The fact that KMV EDFs are poorer predictors of relative spread movements than our factor model does not surprise us. EDFs are designed to be predictors of default probability, not spread movement. To test this hypothesis, we conducted a default probability study using over 800 investment-grade and high-yield issuers covered by KMV for the years 2000 and 2001. We ranked all companies by their prior year-end EDFs, divided the universe into deciles based on absolute EDFs, and calculated the average EDF for each decile. If EDFs are a good predictor of the actual probability of default, companies in each decile should default over the next year by roughly that same average EDF. Exhibit 13.19 shows the results for our study for years 2000 and 2001. Our conclusions are as follows:

■ KMV default predictions were within 0% to 3% of actual default experience within each decile.
■ During 2001, a more active year for corporate defaults than 2000, KMV default predictions were remarkably close to actual default experience, particularly in the highest deciles (those with the highest default probabilities).

We believe these results are robust, demonstrating that KMV EDFs are good predictors of default, at least over this period. Furthermore, our study did not show that KMV EDFs raised too many false negatives (high EDFs that were disproportionate to default experience), a common market criticism. Default experience was consistent with default probability.

Spreads Were Less Reliable Predictors of Default
For comparison, we investigated whether the market itself was a good predictor of default. If this were true, then tools such as KMV might not be as useful, since the information would be already priced into the market.

To answer this question, we conducted a study comparing 1-year market-implied default rates with actual default experience, where market-implied rates are derived from market spreads and a recovery rate assumption. Our study included over 1,200 issuers over the 2000 and 2001 periods. As in the KMV study, we ranked each year's starting implied default probabilities and divided the population into deciles. We compared each average to the actual default rate experienced over the following year. Exhibit 13.20 shows the results of our study. Our conclusions are as follows. First, market-implied default rates overestimated default for most of the high-risk deciles by 5% to 8% and by 1% to 3% for the low-risk deciles. The overestimation is understandable, given that the market has priced in an additional risk premium and liquidity premium However, during 2001, market-implied default rates for the highest risk decile actually underestimated default despite the risk premium.

EXHIBIT 13.19   EDF as Predictor of Default Year 2000 and 2001
Panel A. Year 2000

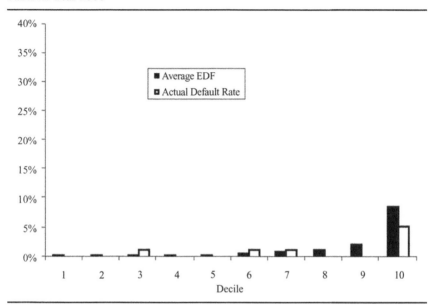

Panel B. Year 2001

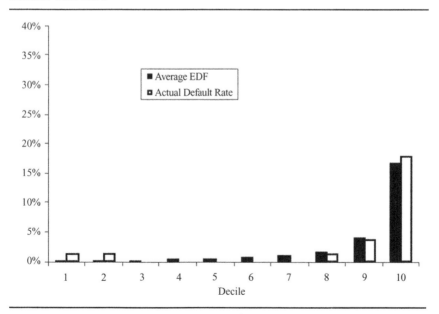

Source: Morgan Stanley, KMV.

EXHIBIT 13.20 Spread-Implied Default Probability as Predictor of Default Year 2000 and 2001

Panel A. Year 2000

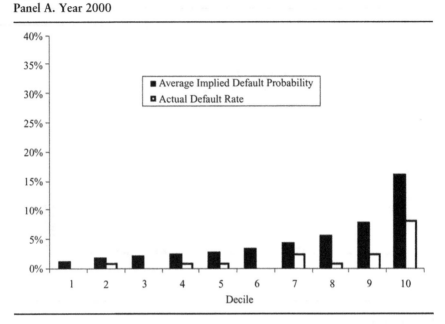

Panel B. Year 2001

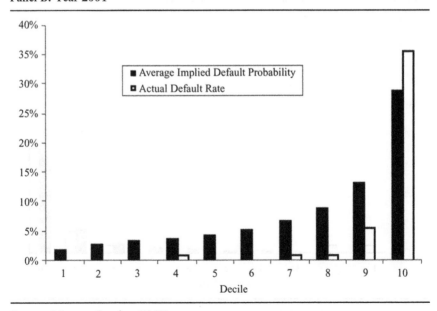

Source: Morgan Stanley, KMV.

Free Cash Flow Good at Relative Value

Empirically testing the fundamental approach to credit analysis is not a straightforward task given the subjective nature of the output. Instead, we focus our empirical testing on a simple metric that captures some of what analysts attempt to understand: free cash flow generation.

We first tested the hypothesis that free cash flow generation is a good predictor of relative spread in 2001.[12] Results from that study are presented in Exhibits 13.21 and 13.22, based on a universe of approximately 200 nonfinancial U.S. corporate issuers. The study was backward looking in the sense that the universe was sorted into quintiles based on spread performance during calendar year 2000 (see Exhibit 13.21), and then free cash flow dynamics were observed for these quintiles from 1998 through 1999 (see Exhibit 13.22). We observed that companies within the poorest performing quintile experienced lower levels of free cash flow generation in 1999 relative to 1998. The best performers through 2000, on the other hand, generated more cash in 1999 relative to 1998.

Exhibit 13.23 shows median spread performance versus free cash flow trends for the major sectors. Again, prior free cash flow trends are reasonably descriptive of subsequent performance.

EXHIBIT 13.21 Calendar 2000 Median Spread Performance: Spread Widening versus Treasuries

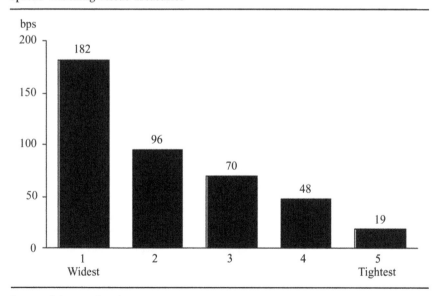

Source: Morgan Stanley.

---

[12] See "The Bottom Line," *Morgan Stanley Fixed Income Research*, February 27, 2001.

EXHIBIT 13.22   Median Free Cash Flow/Debt Changes: 1998 versus 1999

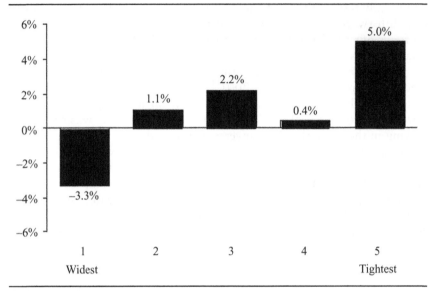

Source: Morgan Stanley.

EXHIBIT 13.23   Sector 1998–1999 Free Cash Flow and 2000 Spread Performance

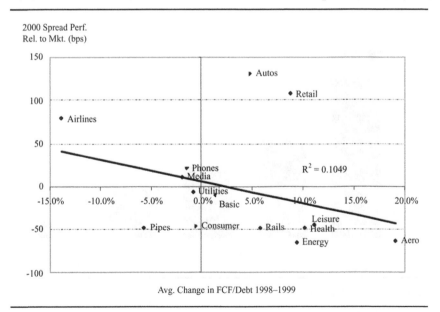

Source: Morgan Stanley.

EXHIBIT 13.24   Sector 1999–2000 Free Cash Flow Changes versus 2001 Spread Performance

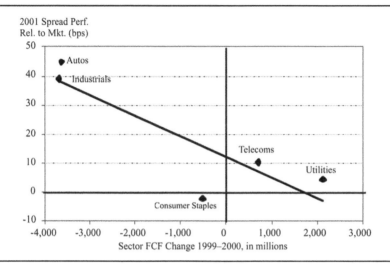

Source: Morgan Stanley.

We conducted a similar study for European issuers more recently (spread changes in 2001 based on free cash flow dynamics from 1999 to 2000). In Exhibit 13.24 we show the free cash flow sector relationships based on a universe of the top 50 nonfinancial European corporate bond issuers, which account for about 70% to 80% of all European corporate debt outstanding. Again, we believe that free cash flow generation was a good predictor of spread change.

Ratings Are Consistent with Historical Experience

Ratings agencies have been criticized for being both too slow and too quick in their ratings decisions. The agencies, for their part, consider it their job to produce ratings that, over time, match a default rate (expected loss), which in turn is based on historical experience. Hence, when judging the performance of the agencies, one needs to focus on the historical relationship between ratings and default rates.

Exhibit 13.26 shows average cumulative default rates by rating using Moody's historical data from 1970–2001. The data show a strong correlation between ratings and default rates. Over a 5-year horizon, for instance, the cumulative default rate of Baa-rated companies is almost 14 times that of Aaa-rated companies. Similarly, the cumulative default rate of speculative grade companies is almost 23 times that of investment-grade companies.

EXHIBIT 13.25   S&P Average Cumulative Default Rates (1987–2000)

Outlook	Rating	Year 1 (%)	Year 2 (%)	Year 3 (%)
Stable	AAA	0.00	0.00	0.00
Negative	AAA	0.00	0.00	0.00
Positive	AA	0.00	0.00	0.00
Stable	AA	0.00	0.03	0.07
Negative	AA	0.10	0.22	0.35
Positive	A	0.00	0.00	0.00
Stable	A	0.03	0.05	0.07
Negative	A	0.07	0.21	0.29
Positive	BBB	0.10	0.33	0.33
Stable	BBB	0.15	0.20	0.39
Negative	BBB	0.19	0.52	1.04
Positive	BB	0.12	1.30	2.35
Stable	BB	0.34	1.72	3.59
Negative	BB	2.64	6.86	10.44
Positive	B	2.42	7.55	12.63
Stable	B	2.76	8.45	12.80
Negative	B	9.65	18.05	23.72
Positive	CCC	2.08	2.08	6.25
Stable	CCC	7.84	15.16	20.42
Negative	CCC	29.18	37.95	44.53

Source: S&P.

Exhibit 13.25 illustrates the relationship between ratings outlooks and subsequent defaults. Speculative-grade issuers with negative outlooks are, on average, nearly five times more likely to default than those with positive outlooks. The multiple is highest for the 1-year default rate, in which companies with negative outlooks are over nine times more likely to default.

QUANTITATIVE APPROACHES TO VALUING CREDIT PORTFOLIO PRODUCTS

While we have focused our efforts on understanding how to value corporate credit in a single-name context, the portfolio perspective is important as well. At one level, a portfolio can simply be thought of as an aggregation of individual investments. In this respect, nearly every investor in the credit markets is managing a credit portfolio, some relative to a benchmark (which is also an aggregation of single names), others to a set of liabilities or investment guidelines.

EXHIBIT 13.26 Moody's Average Cumulative Default Rates by Letter Rating, 1970–2001

	1	2	3	4	5	6	7	8	9	10	11	12	13	14	15	16	17	18	19	20
Aaa	—	—	—	0.04	0.14	0.25	0.37	0.49	0.64	0.79	0.96	1.15	1.36	1.48	1.60	1.74	1.88	2.03	2.03	2.03
Aa	0.02	0.04	0.08	0.20	0.31	0.44	0.56	0.69	0.79	0.89	1.01	1.18	1.37	1.64	1.76	1.90	2.13	2.31	2.62	2.87
A	0.02	0.07	0.21	0.35	0.51	0.68	0.87	1.07	1.32	1.57	1.84	2.09	2.38	2.62	2.97	3.35	3.78	4.30	4.88	5.44
Baa	0.15	0.46	0.97	1.44	1.95	2.54	3.16	3.75	4.40	5.09	5.85	6.64	7.42	8.23	9.10	9.94	10.76	11.48	12.05	12.47
Ba	1.27	3.57	6.20	8.83	11.42	13.75	15.63	17.58	19.46	21.27	23.23	25.36	27.38	29.14	30.75	32.62	34.24	35.68	36.88	37.97
B	6.66	13.99	20.51	26.01	31.00	35.15	39.11	42.14	44.80	47.60	49.65	51.23	52.91	54.70	55.95	56.73	57.20	57.20	57.20	57.20
Caa-C	21.99	34.69	44.43	51.85	56.82	62.07	66.61	71.18	74.64	77.31	80.55	80.55	80.55	80.55	80.55	80.55	80.55	80.55	80.55	80.55
Investment Grade	0.06	0.19	0.38	0.65	0.90	1.19	1.50	1.81	2.15	2.15	2.51	2.89	3.30	3.72	4.15	4.60	5.08	5.58	6.55	6.96
Speculative Grade	4.73	9.55	13.88	17.62	20.98	23.84	26.25	28.42	30.40	32.31	34.19	36.05	37.83	39.44	40.84	42.37	43.67	44.78	45.71	46.58
AllCorps	1.54	3.08	4.46	5.65	6.67	7.57	8.34	9.04	9.71	10.37	11.03	11.70	12.36	12.98	13.58	14.22	14.84	15.42	15.96	16.43

In the total return world, investors are focused on relative portfolio return with respect to their bogeys, and their exposures to individual credits and credit sectors are generally calculated in this relative framework. Given the relatively large size of investment portfolios, the weights of issuers and sectors tend to be proportional to the market. Asset-liability managers focus efforts on forecasting liabilities and finding the portfolios that most efficiently match these liabilities given investment guidelines. Their choices of individual credits and sectors can also be thought of in a relative framework with respect to their guidelines and tolerances for risk.

Absolute return portfolio products, such as synthetic baskets and CDOs, require a somewhat different thought process. First, price volatility at the single-name level is not as important as the projected default behavior of the portfolio. Second, the portfolios themselves are generally small enough that issuer and sector weights do not have to be proportional to the market. Structurers and managers have much more freedom in constructing these portfolio products. Third, for tranched portfolio products, such as CDOs, valuation is not as simple as adding up the values of the individual credits. For these products, default correlation directly affects the value of a given tranche.

The Importance of Default Correlation

The single-name models of default presented earlier in this chapter provide a starting point for understanding the default distribution of a portfolio. However, the models need to be extended to account for the expected interrelationship between these credits over the term of the portfolio product. Default correlation is the glue that defines these interrelationships.

Why is default correlation so important? Default correlation does not affect the expected number of defaults in a portfolio, but it greatly affects the probability of experiencing any given number of defaults. For example, if default correlation is high, the probability of extreme events (very few defaults or many defaults) will increase, even if the expected number of defaults does not change.

The effect of positive default correlations can be quite significant. In Exhibits 13.27 through 13.29, we show the default distribution given by our model for a portfolio of 100 assets, assuming that each has a 10% probability of default and that all pairs of assets have either a 1%, 4%, or 8% default correlation. The greater the positive default correlation, the greater the "fat tail" that the distribution will have. At high correlation levels, the default distribution stands in sharp contrast to the binomial distribution, which features a more symmetric, bell-shaped curve.

EXHIBIT 13.27   Number of Defaults: Default Correlation = 1%

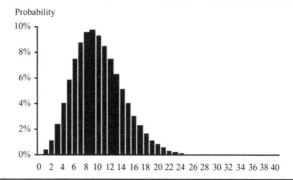

Source: Morgan Stanley.

EXHIBIT 13.28   Number of Defaults: Default Correlation = 4%

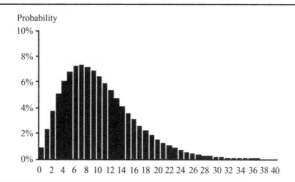

Source: Morgan Stanley.

EXHIBIT 13.29   Number of Defaults: Default Correlation = 8%

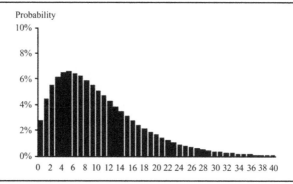

Source: Morgan Stanley.

The traditional measure of default correlation is a correlation between binary (0 or 1) random variables. Specifically, for an issuer X, we define the random variable d_X as follows:

$$d_X = \left\{ \begin{array}{l} 1, \text{ if issuer X defaults over a given horizon} \\ 0, \text{ otherwise} \end{array} \right\}$$

The default correlation between two issuers A and B over a given time horizon is the correlation between d_A and d_B. The formula is given by

$$\rho(d_A, d_B) = \frac{p_{A \text{ and } B} - p_A p_B}{\sqrt{p_A(1 - p_A)p_B(1 - p_B)}}$$

Here, p_A is the probability that A defaults, p_B is the probability that B defaults, and $p_{A \text{ and } B}$ is the joint probability that both A and B default over the horizon being considered.

Default probabilities and default correlations are the key ingredients for determining the distribution of the number of defaults. However, it is important to note that knowing default probabilities and correlations does not quite give us everything we need to construct a default distribution. For example, even if we knew the default probabilities for corporations A, B, and C, as well as all default correlations, we still would not know the probability that all three issuers default over the given time horizon.[13]

Inferring Default Correlation

Default correlation cannot be easily observed from history. Historical data on defaults for various sectors is relatively scarce. Moreover, the historical data might not be easily applicable to the two unique companies being considered, or it may not give a satisfactory forward-looking estimate of default correlation. For these reasons, we examine the practice of inferring default correlation from observable market data.

We assume that we have already computed the individual probabilities of default for issuers A and B, perhaps by the structural approach or the reduced form approach, both of which were outlined earlier in this chapter. In order to calculate default correlation using the formula given above, we need to compute $p_{A \text{ and } B}$, the joint probability that A and B both default over the time horizon.

---

[13] For this reason, "copula functions" are often used in modeling defaults. A copula function generates a complete distribution given a set of individual probabilities and a set of correlations. There are a variety of copula functions that have been used in practice.

One simple approach to computing the joint probability of default is based on the structural model. However, rather than focusing on asset values and asset volatilities, we can exploit the fact that we already know the individual default probabilities for A and B and use standardized normal random variables to simplify the calculations.

First, we compute the implied default threshold for each asset, that is, the default barriers that match the default probabilities. These barriers are given by $z_A = N^{-1}(p_A)$ and $z_B = N^{-1}(p_B)$, respectively, where N^{-1} represents the inverse normal cumulative distribution function. For example, if $p_A = 5\%$, the implied default threshold would be $N^{-1}(0.05) = -1.645$. In other words, a standard normal random variable has a 5% chance of being below -1.645.

Second, we use the correlation between asset values in order to compute the joint probability that both A and B default. This probability is given by the bivariate normal distribution function, M:

$$p_{A \text{ and } B} = M(z_A, z_B; \text{Asset Correlation}_{A, B})$$

For example, if $p_A = 5\%$, $p_B = 10\%$, and the asset correlation is 30%, then $p_{A \text{ and } B} = 1.22\%$. The default correlation is given by

$$\rho(d_A, d_B) = \frac{p_{A \text{ and } B} - p_A p_B}{\sqrt{p_A(1 - p_A)p_B(1 - p_B)}}$$

Using this formula, we compute that the default correlation equals 11.1%. As in this example, default correlations will typically be substantially lower than asset correlations.

It is important to note that asset correlation, like asset value, may be a difficult parameter to observe, so equity correlation is often used as a proxy. This approximation often works well. However, equity correlations may be markedly different from asset correlations for firms with asset values near their default points, or for highly leveraged firms that are very sensitive to interest rates, such as financials and utilities.

Using Default Correlation

Default correlation has two key applications for absolute return portfolio products. First, default correlation is critical for the valuation of tranched portfolio products such as CDOs. For example, the reduced form models presented earlier in this chapter can be easily extended to account for default correlation, and a simulation could be run to determine the value of a given tranche. Second, default correlation can be used to construct a portfolio. For example, a default correlation matrix would be a key input to a portfolio optimization process, where the objective is to minimize the variance of the fraction of the portfolio that defaults, subject to various constraints. For absolute return products, the use of these quantitative techniques is becoming increasingly widespread.

CONCLUSION

Clearly the topics we have discussed in this chapter are individually worthy of much more in-depth research. Our purpose in juxtaposing them in this chapter is to help investors gain insight into valuing corporate credit and select the most appropriate approach, or combinations of approaches, for a given situation. These approaches each have their benefits and drawbacks, and we recommend that investors think about a given company along the three dimensions noted earlier to help decide which approach is best:

- Distance to default
- Leverage, or the ability to service debt from operations
- The management option to change the capital structure

Another issue which can dictate the usefulness of the various approaches is investor profile. In particular, it is important to distinguish those investors who are sensitive to mark-to-market fluctuations from those who are focused on absolute return to maturity. The latter may find the long-term signals provided by credit analysts, rating agencies, and quantitative models to be more important than the near-term risks priced into the market. Furthermore, as we highlighted in our section on credit portfolios, an investor's benchmark is also an important consideration, as those portfolios that are not forced to be anchored to the market can apply methods to find value relative to the market.

Finally, it is important to understand that credit investors, traders, and analysts do not have to select a single approach to value corporate credit as combinations of approaches may prove to be particularly insightful. For example, credit analysts could find structural models very useful in measuring the sensitivity of company valuations to changes in balance sheet items and cash flow projections. Similarly, investors and traders may combine analysts' projections for a company with structural models to understand the potential impact corporate actions could have on valuation. In conclusion, rather than idealistically selecting a single approach, we encourage market participants to understand all approaches and select the best method or combinations of methods for a given investment situation.

CHAPTER 14

An Introduction to Credit Risk Models

Donald R. van Deventer, Ph.D.
Chairman and Chief Executive Officer
Kamakura Corporation

One of the most interesting and complex aspects of credit risk modeling is the web of commercial links between participants in the credit markets. Investment bankers who structure collateralized debt obligations want only semitransparency in credit risk modeling. Models have to be good enough to convince investors to buy collateralized debt obligations but not so good that investors realize they are being sold a package of securities at a price of 103 that actually has a mark to market value of 98. Commercial vendors of default probabilities and risk management software have rarely made public disclosure of the credit models they sell commercially, although this is changing as a result of the Basel II Capital Accords of the Basel Committee on Banking Supervision. Some of these vendors are owned in part by the investment banks who structure CDOs, whose vested interest is clear. Other vendors are owned by rating agencies, whose conflict of interest is subtle but massive enough to be a major focus of the U.S. Congress. U.S. Representative Michael G. Oxley (R-Ohio), Chairman of the House Financial Services Committee, said the following in his opening statement in April 2003 hearings on rating agencies:

> The similarities between the potential conflicts of interest presented in this area (rating agencies) and those that were addressed in the area of accounting firms in Sarbanes-Oxley are impossible to ignore.

355

   The conflicts that Representative Oxley addressed in this statement refer to obvious conflict between the provision of risk management services to clients by the rating agencies who then in turn opine on the risk of the same company. There is another conflict of interest, however, that is potentially more serious. Rating agencies make more money when more securities are rated. For corporate bonds, where 20 to 25 years of ratings accuracy statistics are published annually by the rating agencies, the pressure for accurate credit ratings helps keep the temptation to rate companies as less risky than they are (so more debt will be issued and more ratings fees paid) under control. In the collateralized debt obligation market, ratings histories and performance studies are rare and the temptations to "overrate" tranches are great. The key tests for credit model accuracy are essential both as a matter of corporate governance and as a check for a bias that might be financially useful to the vendor.

   This chapter introduces the topic of credit risk modeling by first summarizing the key objectives of credit risk modeling.[1] We then discuss ratings and credit scores, contrasting them with modern default probability technology. Next, we discuss why valuation, pricing and hedging of credit risky instruments are even more important than knowing the default probability of the issuer of the security. We review some empirical data on the consistency of movements between common stock prices and credit spreads with some surprising results. This background is very useful for our discussion of structural models of risky debt and more modern reduced form models of risky debt. We conclude with a summary of recent empirical results on model performance and the key conclusions of this overview.

KEY OBJECTIVES IN CREDIT RISK MODELING

In short, the objectives of the credit risk modeling process are to provide an investor with practical tools to "buy low/sell high."[2] Robert Merton, in

---

[1] The reader needs to be extremely conscious of the economic interests of the providers of credit risk information and software services. As a first step in that awareness, the author is a shareholder in Kamakura Corporation, a provider of default probabilities, default correlations, and enterprise risk management solutions, including credit risk. Much of what follows stems from that company's efforts to bring transparency to a market where most of the market participants have some of the conflicts of interest listed above.

[2] For a detailed discussion of the objectives of the credit risk modeling process, see Donald R. van Deventer and Kenji Imai, *Credit Risk Models and the Basel Accords* (Hoboken, NJ: John Wiley & Sons, 2003).

a 2002 story retold by van Deventer, Imai, and Mesler,[3] explained how Wall Street has worked for years to get investors to focus on expected returns, ignoring risk, in order to get investors to move into higher risk investments. In a similar vein, investment banks have tried to get potential investors in collateralized debt obligations (CDOs) to focus on "expected loss" instead of market value and the volatility of that market value on a CDO.

This means that we need more than a default probability. The default probability provides some help in the initial yes/no decision on a new transaction, but it is not enough information to make a well informed yes/ no, buy/sell decision as we discuss below. Once the transaction is done, we have a number of very critical objectives from the credit risk modeling process. We need to know the value of the portfolio, the risk of the portfolio (as measured most importantly by the random variation in its value) and the proper hedge of the risk if we deem the risk to be beyond our risk appetite. Indeed, the best single sentence test of a credit model is "What is the hedge?" If one cannot answer this question, the credit modeling effort falls far short of normal risk management standards. It is inconceivable that an interest rate risk manager could not answer this question. Why should we expect any less from a credit risk manager, who probably has more risk in his area of responsibility than almost any one else?

RATINGS AND "CREDIT SCORES" VERSUS DEFAULT PROBABILITIES

Despite Representative Oxley's comments above and our concerns about conflict of interest, the rating agencies have played a major role in fixed income markets around the world for decades. Even "rating agencies" of consumer debt, the credit bureaus, play prominently in the banking markets of most industrialized countries. Why do financial institutions use ratings and credit scores instead of default probabilities?

As a former banker myself, I confess that the embarrassing answer is "There is no good reason" to use a rating or a credit score as long as the default probability modeling effort is a sophisticated one and the inputs to that model are complete.

Ratings have a lot in common with interest accrual based on 360 days in a year. Both ratings and this interest accrual convention date from an era that predates calculators and modern default probability

---

[3] Donald R. van Deventer, Kenji Imai, and Mark Mesler, *Advanced Financial Risk Management: Tools and Techniques for Integrated Credit Risk and Interest Rate Risk Management* (Hoboken, NJ: John Wiley & Sons, 2004).

technology. Why use a debt rating updated every 1 to 2 years when one can literally have the full term structure of default probabilities on every public company updated daily or in real time? In the past, there were good reasons for the reliance on ratings:

- Default probability formulas were not disclosed, so proper corporate governance would not allow reliance on those default probabilities.
- Default probability model accuracy was either not disclosed or disclosed in such a way that weak performance was disguised by selecting small sectors of the covered universe for testing.
- Default probability models relied on old technology, like the Merton model of risky debt and its variants, that has long been recognized as out of date.
- Default probability models implausibly relied on a single input (the unobservable value of company assets), ignoring other obvious determinants of credit risk like cash flow coverage, the charge card balance of the CEO of a small business, or the number of days past due on a retail credit.

With modern credit technology, none of these reasons are currently valid because there is a rich, modern credit technology available with full disclosure and an unconstrained ability to take useful explanatory variables. In this vein, ratings suffer from a number of comparisons to modern credit models:

- Ratings are discrete with a limited number of grades. Default probabilities are continuous and run (or should run) from 0 to 100%.
- Ratings are updated very infrequently and there are obvious barriers that provoke even later than usual response from the rating agencies, like the 2004 downgrade from AAA to AA– for Merck, a full three weeks after the withdrawal of its major drug Vioxx crushed the company's stock price. Default probabilities can adjust in real time if done right.
- Ratings have an ambiguous maturity, which we discuss in the next section. The full term structure of default probabilities is available and the obvious impact of the business cycle is observable: The full default probability term structure rises and falls through the business cycle, with short-term default probabilities rising and falling more dramatically than long-term default probabilities. Exhibit 14.1 illustrates this cyclical rise and fall for the last 15 years for Bank of America Corporation and Wachovia, two of the largest U.S. bank holding companies, using the reduced form model default probabilities discussed below and provided by Kamakura Corporation.

EXHIBIT 14.1   Five-Year Default Probabilities for Bank of America and Wachovia: 1990–2005

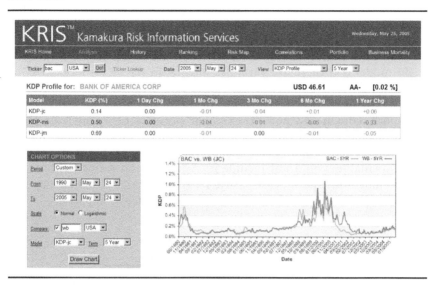

The cyclical rise and fall of default probabilities for both banks are very clear and show the impact of the business cycle in 1990–1991, a mini recession in 1994–1995, and the most recent recession. By way of contrast, Standard & Poor's only changed its ratings on Bank of America twice in the 1995–2005 period.

What about consumer and small business "credit scores"? Like ratings and the interest accrual method mentioned above, these date from an era were there was limited understanding of credit risk in the financial community. Vendors of credit scores had two objectives in marketing a credit risk product: to make it simple enough for any banker to understand and to avoid angering consumers who may later learn how they are ranked under the credit measure. The latter concern is still, ironically, the best reason for the use of credit scores instead of default probabilities today on the retail side. From a banker's perspective, though, the score hides information that is known to the credit score vendor. The credit scoring vendor is actually using the statistical techniques we describe below to derive a default probability for the consumer. They then hide it, by scaling the default probability to run from some arbitrary range like 600 to 1,000 with 1,000 being best. One scaling that does this, for example is the formula:

Credit score = 1,000 − 4 (Consumer 1-year default probability)

This scaling formula hides the default probability that Basel II requires and modern bankers are forced to "undo" by analyzing the mapping of credit scores to defaults. This just wastes everyone's time for no good reason other than the desire to avoid angering retail borrowers with a cold-hearted default probability assessment.

The only time a rating or credit score can outperform a modern credit model is if there are variables missing in the credit model. As of this writing, for example, the SK Group in Korea still had a convicted felon as the head of a business unit over the objections of many investors, both Korean and non-Korean. The presence of a convicted felon on the management team is an obvious negative from a credit quality point of view, but it is an event that happens so rarely that even the best model available would not include it. A judgmental rating in this case would embed this special case easily. This, however, is a rare case and in general a first class modeling effort will be consistently superior.

WHAT DOES "THROUGH THE CYCLE" REALLY MEAN?

Financial market participants often comment that default probabilities span a specific period of time (30 days, 1 year, 5 years) while ratings are "through the cycle" ratings. What does "through the cycle" really mean?

Exhibit 14.2 provides the answer. It shows the term structure of default probabilities for General Motors on May 24, 2005 and November 28, 1997. The November 1997 term structure was quite low because business conditions at the time were excellent. Looking at the right hand side of the curve, we can see that both default probability curves are converging and, if the graph is continued to a long enough maturity, will both hit about 50 basis points for a very long-term default probability.

This is consistent with the "long-run" default experience for both GM's old Standard and Poor's rating of BBB– (43 basis points average, 1-year loss experience over 22 years) and its recently assigned BB+ rating (52 basis points, 1 year average loss experience over the same period). "Through the cycle" has a very simple meaning—it is a very long-term default probability that is totally consistent with the term structure of default probabilities of a well-specified model. What is the term? The major rating agencies are currently reporting 20 to 25 years of historical experience, so the answer is 20 to 25 years.

EXHIBIT 14.2   Term Structure of Default Probabilities for General Motors on May 24, 2005 and November 28, 1997

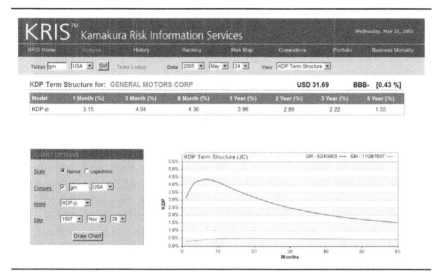

VALUATION, PRICING, AND HEDGING

Earlier in this chapter, we said the best one sentence test of a credit model is "what is the hedge?" That statement is no exaggeration because, in order to be able to specify the hedge, we need to value the risky credit (or portfolio of risky credits). If we can value the credits, we can price them as well. If we can value them, we can stress test that valuation as macroeconomic factors driving default probabilities shift. The pervasive impact of macroeconomic factors on default probabilities Exhibit 14.1 shows for Bank of America and Wachovia make obvious is documented by van Deventer and Imai.[4] With this valuation capability, we can meet one of the key objectives specified in this chapter: We know the true value of everything we own and everything Wall Street wants us to buy or sell. We can see that the CDO tranche offered at 103 is in reality only worth 98 in the example we noted earlier. This capability is essential to meet modern risk management standards. Just as important, it is critical insurance against becoming yet another victim of Wall Street.

---

[4] Van Deventer and Imai, *Credit Risk Models and the Basel Accords.*

EMPIRICAL DATA ON CREDIT SPREADS AND
COMMON STOCK PRICES

Before exploring the nature and performance of modern credit models, it is useful to look at the relationship between stock prices and credit spreads. Van Deventer and Imai print in its entirety a useful data series of new issue credit spreads compiled over a 9-year period beginning in the mid-1980s by First Interstate Bancorp.[5] First Interstate at the time was the seventh largest bank holding company, one of the largest debt issuers in the United States, and a company whose rating ranged from AA to BBB during the course of the data series. The credit spreads were the average credit spread quoted for a new issue of noncall debt of $100 million by six investment banking firms, with the high and low quotations throw out. Data were collected weekly for 427 weeks. No yield curve smoothing or secondary market bond prices were necessary to get the spreads, as the spreads themselves were the pricing quotation.

Jarrow and van Deventer first used this data to test the implications of credit models.[6] They reported the following findings on the relationship between credit spreads and equity prices:

- Stock prices and credit spreads moved in opposite directions during the week 172 to 184 times (depending on the maturity of the credit spread) of the 427 observations.
- Stock prices and credit spreads were both unchanged only 1 to 3 observations.
- In total, only 40.7% to 43.6% of the observations were consistent with the Merton model (and literally any of its single factor variants) of risky debt.

This means that multiple variables are impacting credit spreads and stock prices, not the single variable (the value of company assets) that is the explanatory variable in any of the commercially available implementations of default probabilities that are Merton related. We address this issue in detail in our discussion of the Merton model and its variants in

---

[5] Van Deventer and Imai, *Credit Risk Models and the Basel Accords*.
[6] Robert A. Jarrow and Donald R. van Deventer, "Integrating Interest Rate Risk and Credit Risk in Asset and Liability Management," in *Asset and Liability Management: The Synthesis of New Methodologies* (London: Risk Publications, 1998) and Robert A. Jarrow and Donald R. van Deventer, "Practical Usage of Credit Risk Models in Loan Portfolio and Counterparty Exposure Management: An Update," Chapter 19 in David Shimko (ed.), *Credit Risk Models and Management* (London: Risk Publications, 1999).

the following section. The summary data on the First Interstate stock price and credit spreads is reproduced in Exhibit 14.3.

STRUCTURAL MODELS OF RISKY DEBT

Modern derivatives technology was the first place analysts turned in the mid-1970s as they sought to augment Altman's early work on corporate default prediction with an analytical model of default.[7] The original work in this regard was done by Black and Scholes[8] and Merton.[9] This early work and almost all of the more recent extensions of it share a common framework:

■ The assets of the firm are perfectly liquid and are traded in efficient markets with no transactions costs.
■ The amount of debt is set at time zero and does not vary.
■ The value of the assets of the firm equals the sum of the equity value and the sum of the debt value, the original Modigliani and Miller assumptions.

All of the analysts using this framework conclude that the equity of the firm is some kind of option on the assets of the firm. An immediate implication of this is that one variable (except in the cases of random interest rates assumed below), the random value of company assets, completely determines stock prices, debt prices, and credit spreads. Except for the random interest rate versions of the model, this means that when the value of company assets rises, then stock prices should rise and credit spreads should fall. Exhibit 14.3 rejects the hypothesis that this result is true by 23.5% to 24.9% standard deviations using the First Interstate data described earlier. In fact, as the First Interstate data show, relative movements of stock prices and credit spreads move in the direction implied by various versions of the Merton model only 40.7% to 43.6% of the time. Van Deventer and Imai report on a similar analysis for a large number of companies with more than 20,000 observations and find similar results.[10]

---

[7] Edward I. Altman, "Financial Bankruptcies, Discriminant Analysis and the Prediction of Corporate Bankruptcy," *Journal of Finance* (September 1968), pp. 589–609.
[8] Fischer Black and Myron Scholes, "The Pricing of Options and Corporate Liabilities," *Journal of Political Economy* (May–June 1973), pp. 637–654.
[9] Robert C. Merton, "On the Pricing of Corporate Debt: The Risk Structure of Interest Rates," *Journal of Finance* 29 (1974), pp. 449–470.
[10] Van Deventer and Imai, *Credit Risk Models and the Basel Accords*.

EXHIBIT 14.3 Analysis of Changes in First Interstate Bancorp Credit Spreads and Stock Prices

	SPREAD					
	2 Years	3 Years	5 Years	7 Years	10 Years	Total
Total Number of Data Points	427	427	427	427	427	2,135
Data Points Consistent with Merton						
Opposite Move in Stock Price and Spreads	179	178	183	172	184	896
Stock Price and Credit Spreads Unchanged	3	3	1	2	2	11
Total Consistent	182	181	184	174	186	907
Percent Consistent With Merton Model	42.6%	42.4%	43.1%	40.7%	43.6%	42.5%
Standard Deviation	2.4%	2.4%	2.4%	2.4%	2.4%	1.1%
Standard Deviations from 100% Consistency	−23.9	−24.1	−23.7	−24.9	−23.5	−53.8
Standard Deviations from 50% Consistency	−3.1	−3.2	−2.9	−3.9	−2.7	−7.0

Source: Donald R. van Deventer and Kenji Imai, *Credit Risk Models and the Basel Accords* (Hoboken, NJ: John Wiley & Sons, 2003).

Given this inconsistency of actual market movements with the strongly restrictive assumption that only one variable drives debt and equity prices, why did analysts choose the structural models of risky debt in the first place? Originally, the models were implemented on the hope (and sometimes belief) that performance must be good. Later, once the performance of the model was found to be poor, this knowledge was known only to very large financial institutions that had an extensive credit model testing regime. One very large institution, for example, told the author in 2003 that it had known for years that the most popular commercial implementation of the Merton model of risky debt was less accurate than the market leverage ratio in the ordinal ranking of companies by riskiness. The firm was actively using this knowledge to arbitrage market participants who believed, but had not confirmed, that the Merton model of risky debt was accurate. We report on the large body of test results that began to enter the public domain in 1998 in a later section.

As analysts began to realize there were problems with the structural models of risky debt, active attempts were made to improve the model. Here is a brief listing of the types of assumptions that can be used in the structural models of risky debt.[11]

Pure Black-Scholes/Merton Approach

The original Merton model assumes interest rates are constant and that equity is a European option on the assets of the firm. This means that bankruptcy can occur only at the maturity date of the single debt instrument issued by the firm. Lando notes a very important liability of the basic Merton model as the maturity of debt gets progressively shorter: ". . . when the value of assets is larger than the face value of debt, the yield spreads go to zero as time to maturity goes to 0 in the Merton model."[12] This is a critical handicap in trying to use this one-period model as a complete valuation framework. If credit spreads are unrealistic, we cannot achieve accuracy in our one sentence credit model test: What's the hedge?

Note here that allowing for various classes of debt is a very modest extension of the model. Allowing for subordinated debt does not change the probability of default. The implicit loss given default will simply be higher for the subordinated debt issue than it will for the senior debt issue.

---

[11] For a summary of the extensions of the model, see Chapter 2 in David Lando, *Credit Risk Modeling* (Princeton, NJ: Princeton University Press, 2004).

[12] Lando, *Credit Risk Modeling*, p. 14.

Merton Model with Stochastic Interest Rates

The Merton model with stochastic interest rates was published by Shimko, Tejima and van Deventer in 1993.[13] This modest extension of the original Merton framework simply combined Merton's own model for options when interest rates are random with the structural credit risk framework. The model has the virtue of allowing two random factors (the risk-free, short-term rate of interest and the value of company assets, which can have any arbitrary degree of correlation). It provides at least a partial explanation of the First Interstate results discussed above, but it shares most of the other liabilities of the basic Merton approach.

The Merton Model with Jumps in Asset Values

One of the most straightforward ways in which to make credit spreads more realistic is to assume that there are random jumps in the random value of company assets, overlaid on top of the basic Merton assumption of geometric Brownian motion (i.e., normally distributed asset returns and lognormally distributed asset values). This model produces more realistic credit spread values but Lando concludes, ". . . while the jump-diffusion model is excellent for illustration and simulating the effects of jumps, the problems in estimating the model make it less attractive in practical risk management."[14]

Introducing Early Default in the Merton Structural Approach

In 1976, Black and Cox allowed default to occur prior to the maturity of debt if the value of company assets hits a deterministic barrier that can be a function of time. The value of equity is the equivalent of a "down and out" call option. When there are dividend payments, modeling gets much more complicated. Lando summarizes key attributes of this modeling assumption: "While the existence of a default barrier increases the probability of default in a Black-Cox setting compared with that in a Merton setting, note that the bond holders actually take over the remaining assets when the boundary is hit and this in fact leads to higher bond prices and lower spreads."[15]

Other Variations on the Merton Model

Other extensions of the model summarized by Lando include:

---

[13] David C. Shimko, Naohiko Tejima, and Donald R. van Deventer, "The Pricing of Risky Debt when Interest Rates are Stochastic," *Journal of Fixed Income* (September 1993), pp. 58–66.
[14] Lando, *Credit Risk Modeling*, p. 27.
[15] Lando, *Credit Risk Modeling*, p. 33.

- A Merton model with continuous coupons and perpetual debt
- Stochastic interest rates and jumps with barriers in the Merton model
- Models of capital structure with stationary leverage ratios

Ironically, all current commercial implementations of the Merton model for default probability estimation are minor variations on the original Merton model or extremely modest extensions of Black and Cox.[16] In short, at best 29-year old technology is being used. Moreover, all current commercial implementations assume interest rates are constant, making failure of the "What's the hedge test" a certainty for fixed income portfolio managers, the primary users of default technology. All of the problems raised in the previous section on the First Interstate dataset remain for all current commercial implementations. That has much to do with the empirical results summarized below.

REDUCED FORM MODELS OF RISKY DEBT

The many problems with the major variations on the Merton approach led Jarrow and Turnbull[17] to elaborate on a reduced form model originally introduced by Merton. In his options model for companies where the stock price is lognormally distributed, Merton allowed for a constant instantaneous default intensity. If the default event occurred, the stock price was assumed to go to zero. Merton derived the value of options on a defaultable common stock in a constant interest rates framework. Van Deventer shows how to use this Merton "reduced form" model to imply default probabilities from observable put and call options.[18]

Jarrow and Turnbull adopted this default intensity approach as an alternative to the Merton structural approach. They did so under the increasingly popular belief that companies' choices of capital structure vary dynamically with the credit quality of the firm, and that the assets they hold are often highly illiquid, contrary to the assumptions in the structural approach. Duffie and Singleton,[19] Jarrow,[20] and many others

---

[16] Fischer Black and John C. Cox, "Valuing Corporate Securities: Some Effects of Bond Indenture Provisions," *Journal of Finance* 31 (1976), pp. 351–367.

[17] Robert A. Jarrow and Stuart Turnbull, "Pricing Derivatives on Financial Securities Subject to Credit Risk," *Journal of Finance* 50 (1995), pp. 53–85.

[18] Donald R. Van Deventer, "Asset and Liability Management in Enterprise Wide Risk Management Perspective," Forthcoming in Michael Ong (ed.), *Risk Management: A Modern Perspective* (London, UK: Risk Publications, 2005).

[19] Darrell Duffie, and Kenneth Singleton, "Modeling Term Structures of Defaultable Bonds," *Review of Financial Studies*, 12 (1999), pp. 197–226.

[20] Robert A. Jarrow, "Technical Guide: Default Probabilities Implicit in Debt and Equity Prices," *Kamakura Corporation Technical Guide*, 1999, revised 2001.

have dramatically increased the richness of the original Jarrow-Turnbull model to include the following features:

■ Interest rates are random.
■ An instantaneous default intensity is also random and driven by interest rates and one or more random macroeconomic factors.
■ Bonds are traded in a less liquid market and credit spreads have a "liquidity premium" above and beyond the loss component of the credit spread.
■ Loss given default can be random and driven by macroeconomic factors as well.

Default intensities and the full term structure of default probabilities can be derived in two ways:

■ By implicit estimation, from observable bond prices, credit default swap prices, or options prices or any combination of them
■ By explicit estimation, using a historical default database

Formally, the former method produces "risk-neutral" default probabilities and the latter method produces "empirical" or actual default probabilities. An increasing amount of research suggests that these two sets of default probabilities are the same (because of diversification of portfolios in the face of macro factors driving correlated default) or so close in magnitude that the differences are not statistically significant. This is particularly likely when one allows for a "liquidity premium" in excess of the loss component of credit spreads or credit default swap quotes.[21]

The first commercial implementation on a sustained basis of the latter approach was the 2002 launch of the Kamakura Risk Information Services multiple models default probability service, which includes both Merton and reduced form models benchmarked in historical default data bases.

In deriving default probabilities from historical data, financial economists have converged on a hazard rate modeling estimation procedure using logistic regression, where estimated default probabilities $P[t]$ are fitted to a historical database with both defaulting and non-defaulting observations and a list of explanatory variables X_i. Logistic regression produces the best fitting coefficients using a maximum likelihood approach:

---

[21] This is described in Chapter 18 of Van Deventer, Imai, and Mesler, *Advanced Financial Risk Management: Tools and Techniques for Integrated Credit Risk and Interest Rate Risk Management.*

$$P[t] = 1/[1 + \exp(-\alpha - \Sigma_{i = 1, n}\beta_i X_i)]$$

This simple equation makes obvious the most important virtue of the reduced form approach. The reduced form approach can employ any variable, without restriction, that improves the quality of default prediction, because any variable can contribute in the equation above including Merton default probabilities if they have explanatory power. This means that the reduced form approach can never be worse than the Merton model because the Merton model can always be an input. The reverse in not true—the charge card balance of the chief executive officer is a well known predictor of small business default, but the Merton default formulas do not have the flexibility to use this insight.

In short, reduced form models can be the result of unconstrained variable selection among the full set of variables that add true economic explanatory power to default prediction. The Merton model, in any variation, is a constrained approach to default estimation because the mathematical formula for the model does not allow many potential explanatory variables to be used.

Most importantly, the logistic regression approach provides a solid opportunity to test whether in fact the Merton model does have the problems one would predict from the First Interstate data discussed above. We turn to that task now.

EMPIRICAL EVIDENCE ON MODEL PERFORMANCE

Shumway and Bharath conduct an extensive test of the Merton approach.[22] They test two hypotheses. Hypothesis 1 is that the Merton model is a "sufficient statistic" for the probability of default, that is, a variable so powerful that in a logistic regression like the formula in the previous section no other explanatory variables add explanatory power. Hypothesis 2 is the hypothesis that the Merton model adds explanatory power even if common reduced form model explanatory variables are present. They specifically test modifications of the Merton structure disclosed by Moody's/KMV and their clients in numerous publications, although full disclosure has never been made. The Shumway and Bharath conclusions, based on all publicly traded firms in the United States (except financial firms) using quarterly data from 1980 to 2003 are as follows:

---

[22] Tyler Shumway and Sreedhar T. Bharath, "Forecasting Default with the KMV-Merton Model," University of Michigan and Stanford University Graduate School of Business, December 2004.

- "We conclude that the KMV-Merton model does not produce a sufficient statistic for the probability of default[.]" [23]
- "Models 6 and 7 include a number of other covariates: the firm's returns over the past year, the log of the firm's debt, the inverse of the firm's equity volatility, and the firm's ratio of net income to total assets. Each of these predictors is statistically significant, making our rejection of hypothesis one quite robust. Interestingly, with all of these predictors included in the hazard model, the KMV-Merton probability is no longer statistically significant, implying that we can reject hypothesis two[.]"[24]
- "Looking at CDS implied default probability regressions and bond yield spread regressions, the KMV-Merton probability does not appear to be a significant predictor of either quantity when our naïve probability, agency ratings and other explanatory variables are accounted for."[25]

These conclusions have been confirmed by Kamakura Corporation in four studies done annually in each year beginning in 2004. The current Kamakura default data base includes more than 1.4 million monthly observations on all public companies in North America from 1990 to October 2004, including 1,746 defaulting observations. Both hypothesis 1 and 2 were tested in the context of a "hybrid" model which adds the Kamakura Merton implementation as an additional explanatory variable alongside the Kamakura reduced form model inputs. In every case, we agree with Shumway and Bharath that hypothesis 1 can be strongly rejected. Kamakura has found 44 other variables that are statistically significant predictors of default even when Merton default probabilities are added as an explanatory variable.

Somewhat different from Shumway and Bharath, we find that the Merton default probability has weak statistical significance when added as an explanatory variable to these other 44 variables, but the coefficient on the Merton default probability has the wrong sign: When Merton default probabilities rise, the predicted hybrid default probabilities fall. This is because Merton default probabilities are highly correlated with other variables like the market leverage ratio (which was mentioned above as out predicting the KMV Merton implementation) and the ratio of total liabilities to total assets. It is an interesting economet-

---

[23] From the abstract of Shumway and Bharath, "Forecasting Default with the KMV-Merton Model."

[24] Shumway and Bharath, "Forecasting Default with the KMV-Merton Model," p. 16.

[25] Shumway and Bharath, "Forecasting Default with the KMV-Merton Model," p. 23.

ric question whether the Merton input variable should be retained in such an event. Moody's/KMV has indirectly confirmed these findings in Bohn, Arora, and Korablev,[26] in which the firm for the first time releases quantitative test results on their Merton implementation. In that paper, the authors report on relative accuracy of their proprietary Merton implementation relative to the more standard Merton implementation; they state that on a relatively easy data set (1996–2004 with small firms and financial institutions excluded) the proprietary Merton implementation has a *receiver operating characteristics* (ROC) accuracy ratio 7.5% higher than the standard Merton implementation.[27] This puts the accuracy of the KMV model more than 5% below that reported on a harder data set (all public firms of all sizes, including banks, 1990 to 2004) in the Kamakura Risk Information Services Technical Guide, Version 4.0.[28] The accuracy is also well below reduced form model accuracy published in van Deventer and Imai[29] and van Deventer, Imai, and Mesler.[30] The standard Merton accuracy ratio reported by Bohn, Arora, and Korablev is identical to that reported by Kamakura on a harder data set. It is not surprising that there were no comparisons to reduced form models using logistic regression in Bohn, Arora, and Korablev.

Key Conclusions on Credit Risk Modeling

From the outset, a careful examination of the age of Merton technology leaves one with the concern that the Merton approach is just, well, old. Indeed, Bohn, Arora and Korablev confirm that their commercial implementation is a minor variation on the Black-Cox model from 1976. The First Interstate data first analyzed by Jarrow and van Deventer (1998) leads one to worry that a model that attempts to explain both stock price movements and bond price movements with only one random variable (the value of company assets) is a model that is a poor approx-

---

[26] Jeffrey Bohn, Navneer Arora, and Irina Korablev, "Power and Level Validation of the EDF[tm] Credit Measure in North America," Moody's KMV memorandum, March 18, 2005.

[27] Bohn, Arora, and Korablev, "Power and Level Validation of the EDF[tm] Credit Measure in North America," p.16. The difference is 15% on the equivalent cumulative accuracy profile basis, which is scaled from 0 to 100, compared to a 50–100 scale for the ROC accuracy ratio.

[28] *Kamakura Risk Information Services, Technical Guide, Version 4.0*, February 2005, monograph, Kamakura Corporation.

[29] Van Deventer and Imai, *Credit Risk Models and the Basel Accords*.

[30] Van Deventer, Imai, and Mesler, *Advanced Financial Risk Management: Tools and Techniques for Integrated Credit Risk and Interest Rate Risk Management*.

imation to what are clearly securities affected by multiple variables. As Kamakura reported, more than 44 variables have been identified as default predictors even when the Merton model is present as an explanatory variable. Shumway and Bharath provide confirmation that the Merton approach is not necessary as an input in a properly specified reduced form model.

In addition to much higher accuracy that comes from the reduced form approach is a complete valuation, pricing and hedging framework. That allows us to answer the key one sentence credit model test "What's the hedge?" in a concrete way. We turn to that task in the next chapter.

CHAPTER 15

Credit Derivatives and Hedging Credit Risk

Donald R. van Deventer, Ph.D.
Chairman and Chief Executive Officer
Kamakura Corporation

In Chapter 14, a wide range of potential models for measuring and managing credit risk were discussed. As explained in that chapter, the best single sentence credit model test was the question "What's the hedge?" With that comment in mind, we examine now practical tools for hedging credit risk at both the transaction level and the portfolio level. Our major focus will be the interaction between the credit modeling technologies and traded instruments that would allow one to mitigate credit risk. We start with a discussion linking credit modeling and credit portfolio management in a practical way. We then turn to the much discussed credit default swap market as a potential hedging tool, followed by an examination of collateralized debt obligations (CDOs) in the same manner. Finally, state-of-the art is discussed: hedging transaction level and portfolio credit risk using hedges that involve macroeconomic factors that are traded in the marketplace. The final section summarizes the conclusions.

CREDIT PORTFOLIO MODELING: WHAT'S THE HEDGE?

One of the reasons that the popular Value-at-Risk (VaR) concept has been regarded as an incomplete risk management tool is that it provides little or no guidance on how to hedge if the VaR indicator of risk levels is regarded as too high. In a more subtle way, the same criticisms apply to many of the key modeling technologies discussed in the previous chapter. In this chapter we summarize the virtues and the vices from a hedging perspective of both various credit modeling techniques and credit derivative instruments traded in the marketplace. One of the key issues that requires a lot of attention in credit portfolio modeling is the impact of the business cycle on default probabilities. Default probabilities rise and fall when the economy weakens and strengthens. This is both obvious and so subtle that almost all commercially available modeling technologies ignore it. It is easy to talk about it and hard to do.

Exhibit 15.1 shows the cyclical rise and fall in 5-year reduced form default probabilities for Citigroup and Ford Motor Company for 1990 to 2005.[1] The exhibit shows the obvious correlation in default probabilities for both companies as they rise or fall in the 1990–1991 recession and in the recession spanning 1999 to 2003, depending on the sector.

With this common knowledge as background, we begin with the hedging implications of the Merton model at the individual transaction and portfolio level.[2]

EXHIBIT 15.1   Cyclical Rise and Fall in 5-Year Reduced Form Default Probabilities: Citigroup and Ford Motor Company, 1990–2005

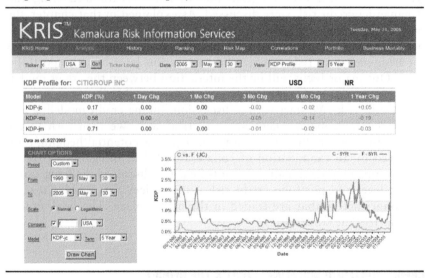

[1] Default probabilities presented in this chapter are supplied by Kamakura Corporation.
[2] Robert C. Merton, "On the Pricing of Corporate Debt: The Risk Structure of Interest Rates," *Journal of Finance* 29 (1974), pp. 449–470.

The Merton Model and Its Variants: Transaction Level Hedging

As of this writing, every publicized commercial implementation of the Merton model or its variants have one principal assumption in common: The only random factor in the model is the "value of company assets." Regardless of the variety of Merton model used, all models of this type have the following attributes in common when the value of company assets rises:

- Stock prices rise
- Debt prices rise
- Credit spread falls

From a theoretical point of view, there are three obvious ways to think about hedging in the Merton context:

- Hedge a long position in the debt of the firm with a short position in the assets of the company.
- Hedge a long position in the debt of the firm with a short position in the common stock of the company.
- Hedge a long position in the debt of the firm with a short position in another debt instrument of the company.

The first hedging strategy is consistent with the assumptions of the Merton model and all of its commercial variants, because assets of the firm are assumed to be traded in perfectly liquid efficient markets with no transactions costs. Unfortunately, for most industrial companies, this is a very unrealistic assumption. Investors in General Motors cannot go long or short auto plants in any proportion. The third hedging strategy is also not a strategy that one can use in practice, although the credit derivative instruments we discuss in the next section provide a variation on this theme.

From a practical point of view, shorting the common stock is the most direct hedging route and the one that combines a practical hedge and one consistent with the theory model. Unfortunately, however, even this hedging strategy has severe constraints that restrict its practical use. Specifically, even if the Merton model or its variant are true, mathematically, the first derivative of the common stock price with respect to the value of company assets approaches zero as the company becomes more and more distressed. When the value of company assets is well below the amount of debt due, the common stock will be trading just barely above zero. One would have to short more and more equity to offset further falls in debt prices, and at some point a hedging strategy that shorts even 100% of the company's equity becomes too small to fully offset the risk still embedded in debt prices. In short, even if the Merton model is literally true, the model fails the hedging test ("What's the hedge?") for deeply distressed situations.

What about companies that are not yet severely distressed? The First Interstate data described in the previous chapter show that for one-week time horizons, the First Interstate stock price and credit spreads moved in the direction predicted by the Merton model and all of its commercial variants less than half the time. As explained by Jarrow and van Deventer,[3] it was this fact that made Merton hedging of a long position in First Interstate debt (1) almost always less effective than a reduced form model hedge and (2) often worse than no hedge at all. Over the sample period used by Jarrow and van Deventer, First Interstate's debt ratings varied from AA to BBB. They analyzed the debt and equity hedge ratios produced by the Merton model (and its variants) and tested for biases that would reduce hedging errors. The results of that analysis showed that a common stock hedge in the *opposite direction* of that indicated by the Merton model (and its variants) would have improved results. That is, one should have gone long the equity even if one is long the debt, not short the equity. Jarrow and van Deventer are careful to point out that this strategy is certainly not recommended. They make the point that the Merton model is clearly missing key variables that would allow credit spreads and equity prices to move in either the same direction or the opposite direction as these input variables change. None of the Merton models in commercial use have this flexibility and, therefore, any hedge ratios they imply are quite suspect.

What about companies that are not investment grade but do not yet fall in the "severely distressed" category? It is in this sector that individual transaction hedging using Merton-type intuition is potentially the most useful. Most of the research that has been done in this regard has been done on a proprietary basis on Wall Street. Even if the Merton model hedging is useful for companies in the BB- and B-rating grade, how effective can it be in protecting the owner of a bond once rated AA when it sinks to a distressed CCC? Whether or not hedging errors in the AA to BBB and CCC ratings ranges more than offset hedging benefits in the BB and B range is an important question. Modern corporate gover-

---

[3] Robert A. Jarrow and Donald R. van Deventer, "Integrating Interest Rate Risk and Credit Risk in Asset and Liability Management," in *Asset and Liability Management: The Synthesis of New Methodologies* (London: Risk Publications, 1998) and Robert A. Jarrow and Donald R. van Deventer, "Practical Usage of Credit Risk Models in Loan Portfolio and Counterparty Exposure Management: An Update," Chapter 19 in David Shimko (ed.), *Credit Risk Models and Management* (London: Risk Publications, 1999).

nance requires that users of the Merton model have evidence that it works in this situation, rather than relying on a belief that it works.

There are a few more points that one needs to make about the Merton model and all of its commercial variants when it comes to transaction level hedging:

- The Merton model default probability is *not an input* in this calculation for the same reason that the return on the common stock is not an input in the Black-Scholes options model. The Merton model and all of its commercial variants incorporate all possible probabilities of default that stem from every possible variation in the value of company assets.
- Loss given default is also *not an input* in this calculation because all possible loss given defaults (one for each possible ending level of company asset value) are analyzed by the model.

Given the value of company assets, we should know the hedge ratio. If instead we are given the Merton (or its variants) default probability, we do not know the hedge ratio without full disclosure of how the default probability was derived. Any failure to make this disclosure is a probable violation of the new Basel capital accords from the Basel Committee on Banking Supervision.

The Merton Model and Its Variants: Portfolio Level Hedging

One of the attractive things about the Merton model, in spite of the limitations mentioned above, is its simple intuition. We know that the basic businesses of Ford and General Motors are highly correlated, so it is a small logical step to think about how the assets of the two companies must be closely correlated. As we discussed in the previous chapter, one has to make a very substantial set of additional assumptions if one wants to link the macroeconomic factors that drive correlated defaults to the value of company assets in the Merton framework or any of its one-factor commercial variants. Let us assume away those complexities and assume that we know the returns on the assets of Ford have a 0.25 correlation with the returns on the assets of General Motors. Note that the 0.25 correlation *does not* refer to the following:

- The correlation in the default probabilities themselves.
- The correlation in the events of default, defined as the vector of 0s and 1s at each time step where 0 denotes no default and 1 denotes default.

These are different and mathematically distinct definitions of correlation. Jarrow and van Deventer show some of the mathematical links between these different definitions of correlation.[4]

Once we have the correlation in the returns on the value of company assets, we can simulate correlated default as follows:

- We generate N random paths for the values of company assets of GM and Ford that show the assumed degree of correlation.
- We next calculate default probability that would prevail, given that level of company assets, at that point in time in the given scenario.
- We then simulate default/no default.

For any commercial variant of the Merton model, an increase in this "asset correlation" results in a greater degree of bunching of defaults from a time perspective. This approach is a common first step for analysts evaluating first-to-default swaps and CDOs because they can be done in common spreadsheet software packages with a minimum of difficulty.

There are some common pitfalls to beware of in using this kind of analysis that are directly related to the issues raised about the Merton framework and its commercial variants in the previous chapter:

- If one is using the original Merton model of risky debt, default can happen at only one point in time: the maturity date of the debt. This assumption has to be relaxed to allow more realistic modeling.
- If one is using the "down and out option" variation of the Merton model, which dates from 1976, one has to specify the level of the barrier that triggers default at each point in time during the modeling period.

Unless one specifically links the value of company assets to macroeconomic factors, the portfolio simulation has the same limitations from a hedging point of view as a single transaction. As explained earlier, the hedge using a short position in the common stock would not work for deeply troubled companies from a theoretical point of view and it does not work for higher rated credits (BBB and above) from an empirical point of view.

If one does link the value of company assets to macroeconomic factors, there is still another critical and difficult task one has to undertake to answer the key question: "What's the hedge?" One needs to convert the single period, constant interest rates Merton model or Merton vari-

---

[4] Robert A. Jarrow and Donald R. van Deventer, "Estimating Default Correlations using a Reduced Form Model," *Risk* (January 2005), pp. 83–88.

ant to a full valuation framework for multiperiod fixed income instruments, many of which contain a multitude of embedded options (like a callable bond or a line of credit). As Lando discusses, this is not a trivial set of issues to deal with.[5] Most importantly, moving to a multiperiod framework with random interest rates leads one immediately to the reduced form model approach, where it is much easier for the default probability models to be completely consistent within the valuation framework. We turn to that task now.

Reduced Form Models: Transaction Level Hedging

One of the many virtues of the reduced form modeling approach is that it explicitly links factors driving default probabilities, like interest rates and other macroeconomic factors, to the default probabilities themselves. Just as important, the reduced form framework is a multiperiod no arbitrage valuation framework in a random interest rate context. Once we know the default probabilities and the factors driving them, credit spreads follow immediately as does valuation. Valuation, even when there are embedded options, often comes in the form of analytical closed-form solutions. More complex options require numerical methods that are commonly used on Wall Street.

Suffice to say that for any simulated value of the risk factors driving default, there are two valuations that can be produced in the reduced form framework. The first valuation is the value of the security in the event that the issuer has not defaulted. This value can be stress tested with respect to the risk factors driving default to get hedge ratios with respect to the nondiversifiable risk factors. The second value that is produced is the value of the security given that default has occurred. In the reduced form framework of Duffie and Singleton[6] and Jarrow,[7] this loss given default can be random and is expressed as a fraction of the defaultable instrument one instant prior to default.

These default-related jumps in value have two components. The first part is the systematic (if any) dependence of the loss given default or recovery rate on macroeconomic factors. The second part is the issuer-specific default event, because (conditional on the current values of the

---

[5] David Lando, *Credit Risk Modeling* (Princeton, NJ: Princeton University Press, 2004).

[6] Darrell Duffie and Kenneth Singleton, "Modeling Term Structures of Defaultable Bonds," *Review of Financial Studies*, 12 (1999), pp. 197–226.

[7] Robert A. Jarrow, "Technical Guide: Default Probabilities Implicit in Debt and Equity Prices," *Kamakura Corporation Technical Guide*, 1999, revised 2001; and "Default Parameter Estimation Using Market Prices," *Financial Analysts Journal* 57 (September–October 2001), pp. 75–92.

risk factors driving default for all companies) the events of default are independent. At the individual transaction level, this idiosyncratic company-specific component can only be hedged by shorting a defaultable instrument of the same issuer or a credit default swap of that issuer.

At the portfolio level, this is not necessary. We explain why next.

Reduced Form Models: Portfolio Level Hedging

One of the key conclusions of a properly specified reduced form model is that the default probabilities of each of N companies at a given point in time are independent, conditional on the values of the macroeconomic factors driving correlated defaults. That is, as long as none of the factors causing correlated default have been left out of the model, then by definition given the value of these factors default is independent.

This powerful result means that individual corporate credit risk can be diversified away, leaving only the systematic risk driven by the identified macroeconomic variables. This means that we can hedge the portfolio with respect to changes in these macroeconomic variables like we do in every hedging exercise: We mark to market the portfolio on a credit-adjusted basis and then stress test with respect to one macroeconomic risk factor. We calculate the change in value that results from the macroeconomic risk factor shift and this gives us the "delta." We then can calculate the equivalent hedging position to offset this risk.

This exercise needs to be done for a wide range of potential risk factor shifts, recognizing that some of the macroeconomic risk factors are in fact correlated themselves. Van Deventer, Imai, and Mesler outline procedures for doing this in great detail.[8]

We turn now to commonly used credit-related derivative instruments and discuss what role they can play in a hedging program.

CREDIT DEFAULT SWAPS AND HEDGING

Credit default swaps in their purest form provide specific credit protection on a single issuer. They are particularly attractive when the small size of a portfolio (in terms of issuer names) or extreme concentrations in a portfolio rule out diversification as a vehicle for controlling the idiosyncratic risk associated with one portfolio name.

---

[8] Donald R. van Deventer, Kenji Imai, and Mark Mesler, *Advanced Financial Risk Management: Tools and Techniques for Integrated Credit Risk and Interest Rate Risk Management* (Hoboken, NJ: John Wiley & Sons, 2004).

Generally speaking, credit default swaps should only be used when diversification does not work. As we discuss in a later section, dealing directly in the macroeconomic factors that are driving correlated default is much more efficient both in terms of execution costs and in terms of minimizing counterparty credit risk. Although the odds of a major investment bank acting as counterparty on the trade defaulting at the same time the reference name on the credit default swap defaults is low, it is a concern that should not be ignored. An event that causes a large number of corporate defaults over a short time period would also obviously increase the default risk of the financial institutions that both lend to them and act as intermediaries in the credit default swap market.

Many researchers have begun to find that credit spreads and credit default swap quotations are consistently higher than actual credit loses would lead one to expect.[9] How can such a "liquidity premium" persist in an efficient market? From the perspective of the insurance provider on the credit default swap, in the words of one market participant, "Why would we even think about providing credit insurance unless the return on that insurance was a lot greater than the average losses we expect to come about?" That preference is simple enough to understand, but why doesn't the buyer of the credit insurance refuse to buy insurance that is "overpriced"?

One potential explanation is related to the lack of diversification that individual market participants face even if their employers are fully diversified. An individual fund manager may have only 10 to 20 fixed income exposures and a bonus pool that strictly depends on his ability to outperform a specific benchmark index over a specific period of time. One default may devastate the bonus, even if the fund manager in 1 billion repeated trials may in fact outperform the benchmark. The individual has more reason to buy single-name credit insurance than the employer does because (1) his work-related portfolio is much less diversified than the entire portfolio of the employer; (2) the potential loss of his bonus makes him much more risk averse than the employer; and (3) the employer is much less likely to be aware that the credit insurance is (on average) overpriced than the individual market participant. It remains to be seen whether subsequent research is as consistent with this speculation as the initial research suggests.

We now turn to the collateralized debt obligation market and first to default swaps.

---

[9] See Chapter 18 in van Deventer, Imai, and Mesler, *Advanced Financial Risk Management: Tools and Techniques for Integrated Credit Risk and Interest Rate Risk Management*, for a summary of the research in this area.

COLLATERALIZED DEBT OBLIGATIONS AND HEDGING

In the previous chapter, we consistently stressed that market participants need to be able to determine whether the CDO tranche offered at 103 is in fact worth 98. We know from simple economics that structurers would not be creating CDOs, with all of the expensive documentation and trustee fees, unless they can buy the reference collateral, pay these structuring expenses, and still have plenty of money left over after it is all done. Given this reality, what role do CDOs play in credit risk management?

CDOs are of greatest potential interest to institutions that are very undiversified in corporate fixed income instruments. An example might be a new hedge fund focused on fixed income instruments, a regional bank doing mainly retail business, or a bank in South Africa eager to increase its relative exposure to North American names. Why would such an institution not deal directly in corporate bonds or credit default swaps in order to get this diversification? Better yet, why would the institution not use the approach described in the next section to increase its diversification or decrease its diversification?

These two questions are critical questions for any potential purchaser of CDOs to answer before they make the first trade. One reason may be that the institution is too small to get efficient execution in the bond market or credit default swap market. A devil's advocate might note that if they are too small to get efficient execution in the bond market, they are certainly too small to get efficient execution in the CDO market.

There is another reason why many have attempted diversification via the CDO market in spite of their small size as an institution, high transactions costs, or the fact that the structurer clearly is always taking value out of the structuring process. Sad to say, many have made analytical errors in deciding whether a CDO tranche was "rich or cheap." As noted in the previous chapter, many of the vendors of the default probabilities and risk analysis commonly used by fixed income market participants are directly or indirectly owned by rating agencies or CDO structurers who benefit financially from an increase in CDO issuance. Many of these institutions have actively promoted "expected loss" as the key criterion for deciding whether to buy or sell when in fact it is irrelevant—the real question, which includes analysis of expected loss as part of a complete deal analysis, is whether the CDO tranche offered at 103 is worth 104 or 102. Having answered that question, there is a secondary question that one only deals with if the answer to the first question is higher than 103—should our institution be buying this instrument even if it is attractively priced?

The next section shows that there are many other ways to change the level of diversification in a portfolio even if one's institution is very small without participating in the CDO market. Van Deventer, Imai, and Mesler outline the procedures for a complete analysis of CDOs in great detail.[10] When discussing CDO analysis and rich/cheap analysis with a Wall Street salesman, here are key items to be aware of:

- *Expected loss.* As in the Robert Merton story described in the introduction to the previous chapter, it is common for market participants to get a potential buyer to focus on expected loss rather than whether the fair value is higher or lower than the offered price of 103
- *Correlation in default.* Another common technique to make an offered CDO tranche look better than it in fact is relates to correlation—by systematically understating the correlation in defaults among reference names, the potential buyer will overstate the value of the CDO tranche and perhaps buy when they should not.
- *Pair-wise correlation.* Finally, another tool popular on Wall Street is analysis which assumes that all pairs of reference names have the same pair-wise correlation, regardless of whether the correlation is (1) the correlation in the value of company assets; (2) the correlation in the default probabilities themselves; or (3) the correlation in the events of default. In a five-name, first-to-default basket credit default swap, for example, it is easy to come up with examples of where the change in one pair's pair-wise correlation from the assumed common value can change valuation of the first-to-default swap by 100%. Wall Street encourages use of one correlation value for all pairs, but a correct analysis uses different pair-wise correlations for each pair.

We now turn to portfolio level hedging using traded macroeconomic indices.

PORTFOLIO AND TRANSACTION-LEVEL HEDGING USING TRADED MACROECONOMIC INDICES

In the previous chapter, we explained how the instantaneous probability of default can be specified as a linear function of one or more macroeconomic factors. An example is the case where the default intensity is a

---

[10] Van Deventer, Imai, and Mesler, *Advanced Financial Risk Management: Tools and Techniques for Integrated Credit Risk and Interest Rate Risk Management.*

linear function of the random short term rate of interest r and a macro economic factor with normally distributed return Z:

$$\lambda(t) = \lambda_0 + \lambda_1 r(t) + \lambda_2 Z(t)$$

The constant term in this expression is an idiosyncratic term that is unique to the company. Random movements in the short rate r and the macroeconomic factor Z will cause correlated movements in the default intensities for all companies whose risk is driven by common factors. The default intensity has a term structure like the term structure of interest rates and this entire term structure moves up and down with the business cycle as captured by the macroeconomic factors. The parameters of this reduced from model can be derived by observable histories of bond prices of each counterparty or from observable histories of credit derivatives prices using enterprise wide risk management software.

Alternatively, a historical default database can be used to parameterize the term structure of default probabilities. The most common approach uses logistic regression as described in the previous chapter. For each company, monthly observations are denoted 0 if the company is not bankrupt in the following month and 1 if the company does go bankrupt in the next month. Explanatory variables X_i are selected and the parameters α and β are derived which produce the best fitting predictions of the default probability using the following logistic regression formula:

$$P[t] = \frac{1}{1 + e^{-\alpha - \sum_{i=1}^{n} B_i X_i}}$$

By fitting this logistic regression for each maturity on the default probability term structure, one can build the entire cumulative and annualized default probability term structures for a large universe of corporations. Exhibit 15.2 shows the cumulative term structure of default probabilities for Enron in November 2001, a few days before its default in December 2001.[11]

Alternatively, one can annualize the entire term structure of default probabilities for easy comparison with credit spreads and credit default swap quotations. The resulting curve is downward sloping for high risk credits like Enron (see Exhibit 15.3).

---

[11] Kamakura Risk Information Services, Version 3.0, provided by Kamakura Corporation (www.kamakuraco.com).

EXHIBIT 15.2   Cumulative Term Structure of Default Probabilities for Enron:
November 2001, A Few Days Before December 2001 Default

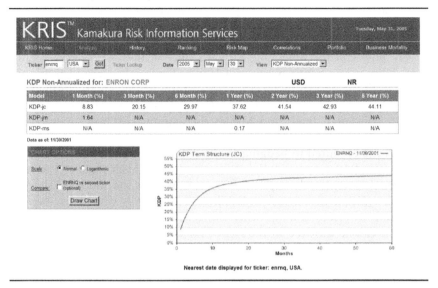

EXHIBIT 15.3   Annualized Term Structure of Default Probabilities for Enron:
November 2001, A Few Days Before December 2001 Default

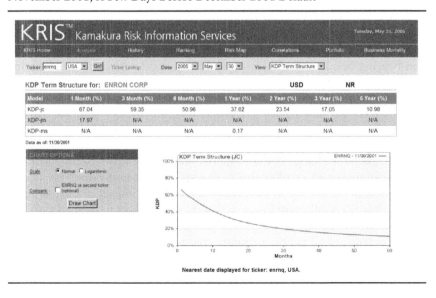

The key advantage of the reduced form approach is that critical macro-economic factors can be linked explicitly to default probabilities as explanatory variables. The result is a specific mathematical link like the linear function of the pure Jarrow reduced form model or the logistic regression formula used for historical database fitting. The logistic regression formula is very powerful for simulating forward since it always produces default probability values between zero and 100%. These values can then be converted to the linear Jarrow form for closed-form mark-to-market values for every transaction in a portfolio, in a CDO or in a first-to-default swap.

Van Deventer, Imai, and Mesler then summarize how to calculate the macroeconomic risk factor exposure as follows.[12] The Jarrow model is much better suited to hedging credit risk on a portfolio level than the Merton model because the link between the (N) macrofactor(s) M and the default intensity is explicitly incorporated in the model. Take the example of Exxon, whose probability of default is driven by interest rates and oil prices, among other things. If $M(t)$ is the macrofactor oil prices, it can be shown that the size of the hedge that needs to be bought or sold to hedge one dollar of risky debt zero-coupon debt with market value v under the Jarrow model is given by

$$\partial v_I(t, T :i)/\partial M(t)$$
$$= -[\partial\gamma_i(t, T)/\partial M(t) + \lambda_2(1 - \delta_i)(T - t)/\sigma_m M(t)]v_I(t, T :i)$$

The variable v is the value of risky zero-coupon debt and γ is the liquidity discount function representing the illiquidities often observed in the debt market. There are similar formulas in the Jarrow model for hedging coupon-bearing bonds, defaultable caps, floors, credit derivatives, and so on.

Van Deventer and Imai[13] show that the steps in hedging the macro-factor risk for any portfolio are identical to the steps that a trader of options has been taking for 30 years (hedging his net position with a long or short position in the common stock underlying the options):

- Calculate the change in the value (including the impact of interest rates on default) of all retail credits with respect to interest rates.
- Calculate the change in the value (including the impact of interest rates on default) of all small business credits with respect to interest rates.
- Calculate the change in the value (including the impact of interest rates on default) of all major corporate credits with respect to interest rates.

[12] Van Deventer, Imai, and Mesler, *Advanced Financial Risk Management: Tools and Techniques for Integrated Credit Risk and Interest Rate Risk Management*.
[13] Donald van Deventer and Kenji Imai, *Credit Risk Models and the Basel Accords* (Hoboken, NJ: John Wiley & Sons, 2003).

■ Calculate the change in the value (including the impact of interest rates on default) of all bonds, derivatives, and other instruments.

■ Add these delta amounts together.

■ The result is the global portfolio delta, on a default adjusted basis, of interest rates for the entire portfolio.

■ Choose the position in interest rate derivatives with the opposite delta.

■ This eliminates interest rate risk from the portfolio on a default adjusted basis.

We can replicate this process for any macroeconomic factor that impacts default, such as exchange rates, stock price indices, oil prices, the value of class A office buildings in the central business district of key cities, and so on.

Most importantly:

■ We can measure the default-adjusted transaction level and portfolio risk exposure with respect to each macroeconomic factor.

■ We can set exposure limits on the default adjusted transaction level and portfolio risk exposure with respect to each macroeconomic factor.

■ We know how much of a hedge would eliminate some or all of this risk.

The reason this analysis is so critical to success in credit risk portfolio management is the all-pervasiveness of correlated risk. Take the Japan scenario. At the end of December 1989, the Nikkei stock price index had reached almost 39,000. Over the course of the next 14 years, it traded as low as 7,000. Commercial real estate prices fell by more than 50%. Single-family home prices fell in many regions for more than 10 consecutive years. More than 135,000 small businesses failed. Six of the 21 largest banks in Japan were nationalized. How would this approach have worked in Japan?

First of all, fitting a logistic regression for small businesses in Japan over this period shows that the properly specified inputs for the Nikkei and the yen/ U.S. dollar exchange rates have t-score equivalents of more than 45 standard deviations from zero in a logistic regression. By stress testing a small business loan portfolio with this knowledge, we would have known how many put options on the Nikkei and put options on the yen were necessary to fully or partially offset credit-adjusted mark to market loan losses, just like the Federal Deposit Insurance Corporation announced it was doing in its 2003 Loss Distribution Model.[14]

This same approach works with:

---

[14] See press release dated December 10, 2003 on www.fdic.gov.

- Retail loan portfolios
- Small business loan portfolios
- Large corporate loan, bond, derivative and other portfolios
- Sovereign and other government exposures

If common factors are found to drive each class of loans, then we have enterprise wide correlations in defaults.

The key to success in this analysis is a risk management software package that can handle it.[15] What is also important in doing the modeling is to recognize that macroeconomic factors which are exchange traded (such as the S&P 500) are much preferred to similar indicators that are not traded (such as the Conference Board index of leading indicators or the unemployment rate).

If one takes this approach, total balance sheet credit hedging is very practical:

- Without using credit derivatives
- Without using first-to-default swaps
- Without using Wall Street as a counterparty from a credit risk point of view

All of these benefits are critical to answer the key question we posed in the previous chapter: "What's the hedge?" We now know how to get the answer.

SUMMARY AND CONCLUSIONS

For too many years, it has been in Wall Street's interest for securities purchasers not to know how to value a first-to-default swap, a loan portfolio or a CDO tranche. As we have shown in this chapter, the tools to do this on a daily basis on the full balance sheet of large financial institution or any subset of it are now available. With these tools at one's disposal, management has much greater control of the risk and returns delivered to investors. We now know how to answer the question "what's the hedge" and how to use the answer to that question to deliver more value-added to investors.

---

[15] See, for example, the Kamakura Risk Manager risk management software system.

CHAPTER 16

Implications of Merton Models
for Corporate Bond Investors

Wesley Phoa
Vice President, Quantitative Research
Capital Strategy Research
The Capital Group Companies

In the 2000–2002 period, and to a lesser extent in 2003, participants in U.S. capital markets observed a strong link between equity markets and corporate bond spreads:

- When stock prices fall, bond spreads tend to widen.
- However, the relationship seems nonlinear: It appears strongest when stock prices are low.

A typical example is shown in Exhibit 16.1, which plots the relationship between the daily stock price of Nextel and the daily spread on its cash pay bonds. When the stock price was over $20, the relationship appeared weak or absent; but when the stock price fluctuated below that level, there was a very strong link.

Have equity and bond markets always behaved like this, or is the recent period anomalous? Exhibit 16.2 plots generic spreads on single-A and single-B rated corporates against the (log of the) U.S. equity index level, using data from the past 10 years. In the period since 1998, there is a strong relationship; but in the 1992–1998 period the relationship seems weaker, if it exists at all. To repeat the question: is the period since 1998 unusual?

The author thanks Eknath Belbase and Ellen Carr for their useful comments.

EXHIBIT 16.1   Nextel: Bond Spread versus Stock Price

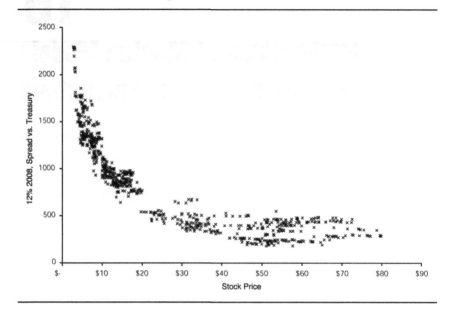

EXHIBIT 16.2   U.S. Equity Market and Corporate Bond Spreads, 1992 to 2002

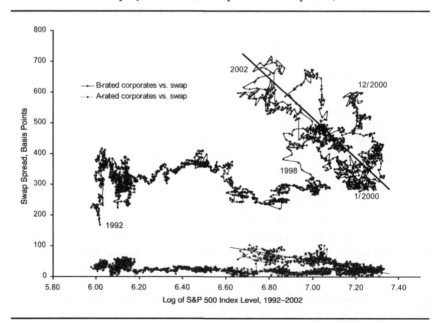

EXHIBIT 16.3   U.S. Equity Market and Corporate Bond Spreads, 1919 to 1943

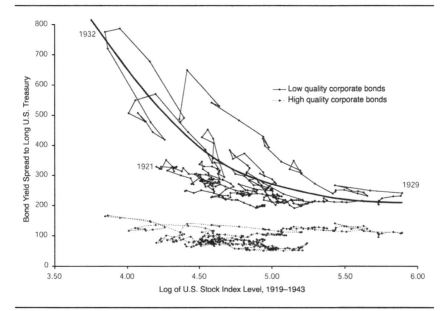

Exhibit 16.3 plots U.S. corporate bond spreads against the U.S. equity index level during the 1919–1943 period. The resemblance to Exhibit 16.1 is striking—there is a clear relationship, which was stronger when equity prices were lower. (Note that spreads on low quality bonds were tighter in 1921 than they were when the equity index revisited comparable levels after the Crash, presumably because firms accumulated more debt in the intervening period.)

Exhibit 16.4 plots spreads on U.S. railroad bonds against the U.S. railroad stock index during the 1857–1929 period. (U.K. gilts are used as a risk-free yield benchmark, consistent with market practice during that period; note that there is no currency component to the spread, because both countries were on the gold standard for almost the whole period.) Exactly the same relationship appears in this graph. Furthermore, deviations from this relationship mostly have reasonable explanations; for example, spreads were unusually wide in the late 1860s/early 1870s, but this was a period when railroads' capital structures were being dishonestly manipulated on a massive scale.

It therefore seems that this link between the equity market and the corporate bond market has always existed. But it was only in the 1970s that a theoretical framework was developed, within which formal models of the relationship could be constructed.

EXHIBIT 16.4   U.S. Railroad Stocks and Railroad Bond Spreads, 1857 to 1929

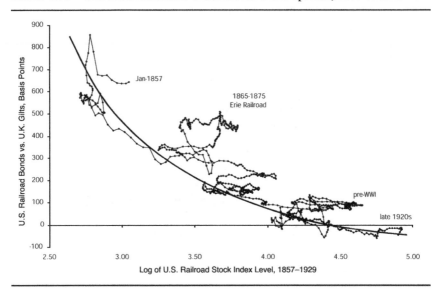

This framework has been the subject of intense academic research, and has been widely adopted by commercial banks as a method for forecasting default rates and pricing loans. Interest from total return investors has been more recent. This article describes the role that equity-based credit risk models have begun to play in the mark-to-market world of a typical corporate bond investor.

MODEL OVERVIEW, USES, AND CAVEATS

Robert Merton proposed in 1974 that the capital structure of a firm can be analyzed using contingent claims theory: Debtholders can be regarded as having sold a put option on the market value of the firm; and equityholders' claim on the firm's value, net of its debt obligations, resembles a call option.[1] In this framework, the meaning of default is that the value of the firm falls to a sufficiently low level that "the put option is exercised" by liquidating the firm or restructuring its debt.

This idea led to the so-called "structural models" of credit risk, which assume that (1) default occurs when the market value of the firm falls below a clearly defined threshold, determined by the size of the

---

[1] Robert C. Merton, "On the Pricing of Corporate Debt: The Risk Structure of Interest Rates," *Journal of Finance* 29 (May 1974), pp. 449–470.

firm's debt obligations; and (2) the market value of the firm can be modeled as a random process in a mathematically precise sense. Taken together, these assumptions make it possible to calculate an estimated default probability for the firm. The precise estimate will depend on the assumed default threshold, the nature and parameters of the random process used to model the firm's value, and possibly other technical details. Different choices lead to different models.[2]

However, all the different structural models have a strong family resemblance. First, they have similar inputs; the key inputs tend to be:

1. The capital structure of the firm.
2. The market value of the firm, usually derived from its stock price.
3. The volatility of the firm's market value, usually derived from stock price volatility.

Second, they make qualitatively similar predictions. In particular, they all imply that:

■ The credit risk of a firm rises as its stock price falls.
■ However, this relationship is nonlinear, and is most apparent when the stock price is fairly low.

This is precisely the pattern observed in Exhibits 16.1 through 16.4.

Since the late 1990s there has been a dramatic rise in the popularity of structural models. KMV Corporation pioneered the approach and built a formidable global client base among commercial banks, but other models have recently gained substantial followings among other capital market participants; these include CSFB's CUSP Model, Risk-Metrics' CreditGrades, Barra's BarraCredit model, and Bank of America's COAS. The Capital Group has developed a proprietary model along similar lines.

This article discusses whether structural models should be of interest to corporate bond investors. It assumes some general familiarity with the theoretical details.

In gauging the reliability and usefulness of structural models of credit risk, it is important to understand that they can be used in a number of different ways. For example,

---

[2] For an overview of structural credit risk models, as well as the alternative "reduced-form" approach commonly used to price credit derivatives, see Kay Giesecke, *Credit Risk Modeling and Valuation: An Introduction*, Humboldt-Universität zu Berlin, August 19, 2002. For a survey of empirical results, see Young Ho Eom, Jean Helwege, and Jingzhi Huang, *Structural Models of Corporate Bond Pricing: An Empirical Analysis*, EFA 2002 Berlin, February 8, 2002.

1. To estimate default risk.
2. To predict rating transitions (especially downgrades).
3. To identify relative value opportunities within a specific firm's capital structure.
4. To predict changes in corporate bond spreads.
5. To identify relative value opportunities within the corporate bond market.
6. To assess the sensitivity of corporate bond spreads to equity prices.

It may turn out that a model performs well in some of these applications, but is useless for others. And it is important to understand that in each case, the key premises differ. Every proposed application of a model assumes that:

1. The assumptions underlying the model are reasonably accurate.

However, all applications except the first, make further strong assumptions about the way in which different market participants process new information relevant to credit risk. Remembering that the key input to these models is the stock price, the corresponding assumptions are:

2. Rating agencies sometimes lag equity markets.
3. Equity and bond markets sometimes process information in inconsistent ways.
4. Bond markets sometimes lag equity markets.
5. Bond markets sometimes process information less efficiently than equity markets.
6. Equity and bond markets eventually process information in consistent ways.

Assumptions 1 and 6, and perhaps 2, are quite plausible; assumptions 3, 4, and 5 are more questionable. Research within the Capital Group has been mainly concerned with the last application: assessing the sensitivity of corporate bond spreads to equity prices. It is, therefore, assumptions 1 and 6 that play the most important role.

To see why assessing equity sensitivity is important, it is helpful to adopt the perspective of asset allocation. One reason to own bonds is that they provide diversification versus equity returns: Bond investments should hold up well in periods where equities have poor returns. For that reason, it is not rational to invest an excessive amount in corporate bonds, which have a high correlation with equities. However, structural models imply, and experience shows, that this correlation varies with equity prices. Therefore, a prudent approach to corporate bond investment in a portfolio context should take equity prices into account. This is the place where structural models can play a crucial role in credit risk management.

A final important use for structural models is the estimation of default correlations (or joint default probabilities), which are crucial in applications such as portfolio credit risk aggregation and CDO modeling. Default correlations are hard to measure, particularly for the investment grade universe. For example, default data is far too sparse; both default and rating transition are hard to use directly because of timing problems; and the use of bond spread data tends to understate correlations. In principle, default correlations can be inferred from the pricing of tranched credit products, but in practice this exercise is highly model-dependent and tends not to lead to consistent estimates.

The Merton approach suggests that default correlations may be inferred from directly observable equity market data. Note that default correlations need not be equal to equity (or firm value) correlations. Nor can one estimate the default correlation just by measuring the correlation of changes in the estimated default probability. However, the calculations do turn out to be computationally tractable.[3]

SOME EMPIRICAL RESULTS

Because the technical details of structural models are covered elsewhere, it seems more helpful to organize the discussion around some empirical illustrations. To begin with, Exhibits 16.5 to 16.9 indicate how the model works, using the example of Nextel Communications.

Exhibit 16.5 shows the historical stock price and "distance to default." The latter is derived from Nextel's enterprise value (determined by its stock price) and the amount of debt in its capital structure; a distinction is made between long- and short-term debt. Note that Nextel's leverage increased during this period, so the fact that the stock price was the same on two different dates does not imply that the distance to default was the same.

Exhibit 16.6 shows the estimated historical volatility of Nextel's enterprise value; this estimate fluctuated between 35% and 60%, as equity volatility varied, so it would clearly not be valid to use a constant volatility input. Note that this volatility is not directly observable, and different models estimate it in different ways. Most models derive it from equity volatility. For example, KMV uses historical equity volatili-

---

[3] For a closed-form formula, see Chunsheng Zhou, *Default Correlation: An Analytical Result*, Finance and Economics Discussion Series 1997–27, Board of Governors of the Federal Reserve System, May 1, 1997.

EXHIBIT 16.5   Nextel: Stock Price and Distance to Default

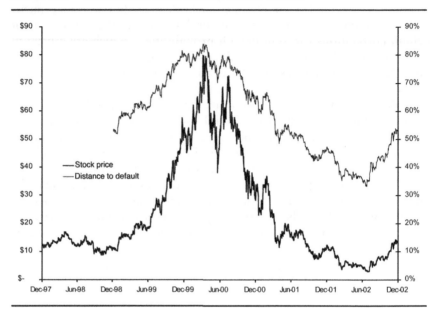

EXHIBIT 16.6   Nextel: Volatility of Enterprise Value

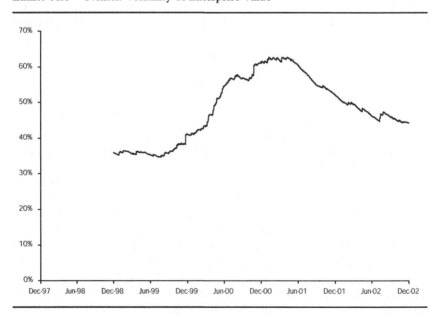

ties computed using a fixed window; the Capital Group's model uses historical volatilities computed using a simple exponentially weighted scheme; and CUSP uses option implied volatilities if they are available, and a GARCH estimate if they are not. There are a few models (such as COAS) that do not look at equity volatility, but use the volatility implied by the market price of debt instead; this is an interesting alternative, though it is impracticable if the bonds are illiquid and/or there is a substantial amount of bank debt in the capital structure.

Exhibit 16.7 shows the historical daily stock price and credit risk measure, labeled "bond risk" on the graph. This is the probability that Nextel's enterprise value will cross the default threshold within the next 12 months; however, since default need not be an automatic event, this risk measure should be interpreted as a "probability of distress," or the probability of a severe financial crisis, rather than a literal default probability.

Exhibit 16.8 shows the historical daily credit risk measure (probability of distress) and the historical daily spread on a specific Nextel cash pay bond. As expected, the bonds tend to widen when the probability of distress rises, and vice versa. Though it does seem that in 2000–2001 the bond market was somewhat slow to respond to an increase in risk.

Exhibit 16.9 is a scatter plot of the bond spread against the probability of distress.In theory, this should be an upward sloping line or

EXHIBIT 16.7   Nextel: Stock Price and Credit Risk Measure

curve, and the observations do show this pattern. That is, the model "works." However, there are two other interesting phenomena:

1. The curve slopes upward more sharply at high levels of risk. This is observed for many high-yield issuers, and may reflect declining recovery value assumptions.
2. In the more recent period, the curve as a whole shifted upward. This is not a widespread phenomenon, and may reflect an increased level of investor risk aversion towards the high yield wireless sector in 2002, independent of current equity prices.

Some additional findings emerge when looking at further examples, this time drawn from the investment-grade universe.

Exhibit 16.10 shows, for Ford, the historical probability of distress and the historical bond spread; as before, the bonds tend to widen when the probability of distress rises, and vice versa. Rating actions are also marked on the graph: The larger white circles indicate Moody downgrades and the smaller circles mark dates when Ford was put on negative watch; gray circles mark more recent rating actions by S&P. In some cases the bonds seemed to widen in response, but in some cases the bonds had clearly widened in anticipation, and often the perfor-

EXHIBIT 16.10 Ford: Credit Risk Measure, Bond Spread, and Rating Actions

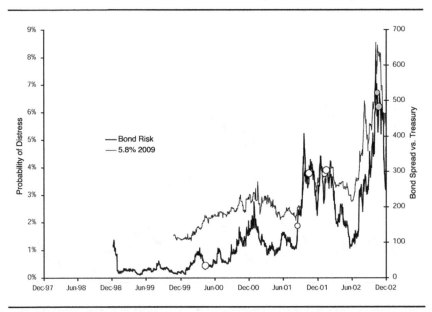

EXHIBIT 16.8   Nextel: Credit Risk Measure and Bond Spread

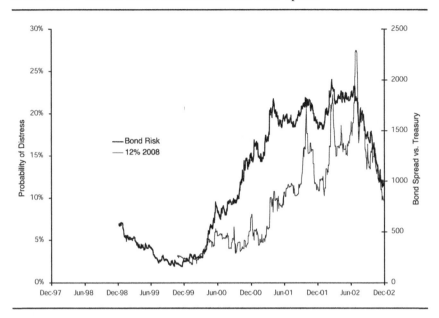

EXHIBIT 16.9   Nextel: Bond Spread versus Credit Risk Measure

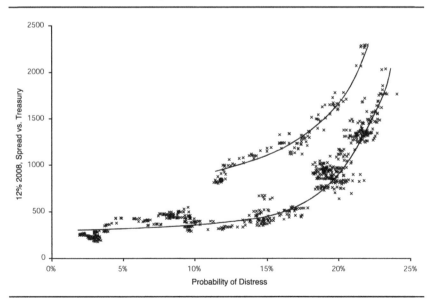

mance of the bonds was not related at all to a rating action. This example shows that for bond investors, predicting rating transitions is not the most important application.

Exhibit 16.11 is a scatter plot of the bond spread against the probability of distress. In this case the observations cluster nicely around an upward sloping straight line. There is an excellent relationship between the actual spread on the bonds and the model's estimate of credit risk. Thus, the model provides a good way to estimate the equity sensitivity of Ford bonds.

Exhibit 16.12 shows a different way of visualizing how this sensitivity has changed over time. The thick solid line shows Ford's historical stock price. The thin dotted line marks the "critical range" where the equity sensitivity of the bonds rises significantly, while the thin solid line marks the point of maximum sensitivity. (Note that if both the capital structure and volatility were constant over time, these lines would be horizontal.)

Exhibit 16.13 shows, for Sprint, a scatter plot of the bond spread against the probability of distress. Again, the observations cluster nicely around an upward sloping straight line, indicating that the model is very consistent with the market behavior of the debt; note that there is more scatter at higher levels of risk. Does scatter represent trading opportunities?

Exhibit 16.14 shows the daily probability of distress, the daily bond spread, and the daily credit default swap spread (CDS) (plus the 5-year

EXHIBIT 16.11   Ford: Bond Spread versus Credit Risk Measure

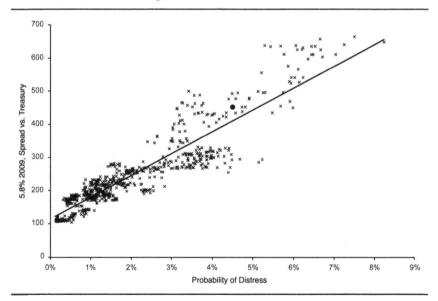

EXHIBIT 16.12 Ford: Stock Price and Critical Range

EXHIBIT 16.13 Sprint: Bond Spread versus Credit Risk Measure

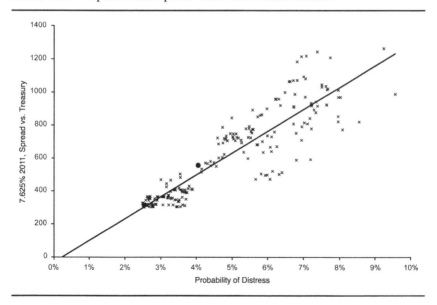

EXHIBIT 16.14 Sprint: Credit Risk Measure, Bond Spread, and Credit Default Swap Spread

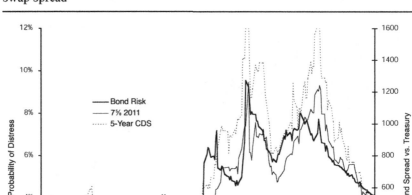

swap spread). An analysis of this data indicates that none of these three markets consistently leads the other two. The bond spread and CDS spread are tightly linked. One market occasionally lags the other, but only by a day. The probability of distress (which reflects the equity market) is much less tightly coupled. It sometimes leads the bond and CDS markets by a week or more—and is for that reason a trading signal—but it also sometimes lags.[4]

Structural models only give useful trading signals to a bond investor when bond markets are less efficient than equity markets (perhaps due

---

[4] Note that if there are cash instruments trading at a significant discount to par, both an implied default probability and an implied recovery rate (for bonds) can be computed from the observed credit default swap basis. Furthermore, a structural model can be used to estimate an "expected recovery rate" based on the conditional mean exceedance (i.e., the mathematical expectation of the firm value conditional on its dropping below the default threshold). A would-be arbitrageur might attempt to profit from discrepancies between the default probabilities and recovery rates implied by the equity and CDS markets. Unfortunately, neither estimate of the recovery rate is very robust. A further problem is that priority of claims is often violated in the event of default and restructuring, which complicates the analysis of specific debt securities.

to the constraints affecting bond investors, and/or their bounded rationality). An example might be when a credit event affects an industry as a whole, causing bond investors to rapidly reduce their industry allocation by selling across the board. This may trigger a uniform widening in bonds across different issuers, even though the actual rise in credit risk may vary from firm to firm.

Finally, the above analysis assumes a constant capital structure going forward. Investors with longer term forecasting horizons might find it useful to extend the model by incorporating discretionary capital structure choices triggered by exogenous factors, such as macroeconomic conditions.[5]

FEEDBACK LOOPS AND CAPITAL STRUCTURE DYNAMICS

As the popularity of structural credit risk models has grown—and particularly since Moody's acquired KMV—some market participants have suggested that the widespread use of these models creates excess volatility in debt markets and even leads to liquidity crises. The underlying complaint is that models that refer to stock prices are in some sense circular.

This concern is most commonly expressed at the level of the individual firm. The use of the KMV model by commercial banks (or hedge funds, who have more recently been competing with banks in certain areas of corporate lending) can lead to an unfortunate feedback loop affecting highly levered companies. When the stock price falls, the model says that the credit risk of the company has risen. This causes banks to restrict access to credit, and also raises financing costs by pushing up bond spreads. This in turn puts financial pressure on the company, leading to a further decline in the stock price. Of course, this can only occur if the firm has an insufficiently liquid balance sheet. During 2002, several high profile firms in the telecommunications and energy sectors are said to have been affected.

It is hard to model this effect at the firm level, but stylized numerical simulations at the industry level provide some interesting results. Consider the following ideal industry model:

▓ The industry begins with a fixed allocation of debt and equity.
▓ Banks provide all the debt, and in doing so maintain fixed capital ratios.

---

[5] See, for example, Robert Korajczyk, and Amnon Levy, "Capital Structure Choice: Macroeconomic Conditions and Financial Constraints," *Journal of Financial Economics* 68 (April 2003), pp. 75–109.

- Banks fund themselves at a constant rate (e.g., a fixed spread over a risk-free rate).
- The industry receives a growing revenue stream which is used to service debt.
- Revenues in excess of debt service increase the industry's equity base.
- Individual issuer defaults occur at a rate predicted by a structural credit risk model.
- The stream of debt service payments causes bank capital to rise.
- Individual issuer defaults trigger loan losses, causing bank capital to fall.
- A fixed percentage of any increase in bank capital is allocated back to the industry.

Exhibits 16.15 and 16.16 compare the impact of two different loan pricing policies, static and risk based. More precisely, the two policies are:

1. New loans priced at the same rate as the original debt.
2. New loans continually repriced with reference to the structural credit risk model.

Risk-based pricing is assumed to use a spread based on the model's estimated default probability times a fixed expected loss rate. This is

EXHIBIT 16.15   Comparative Equity Return Dynamics: Static Loan Pricing

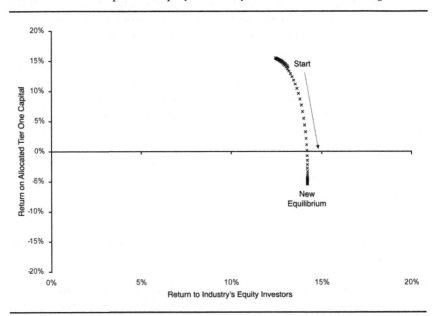

EXHIBIT 16.16   Comparative Equity Return Dynamics: Risk-Based Loan Pricing

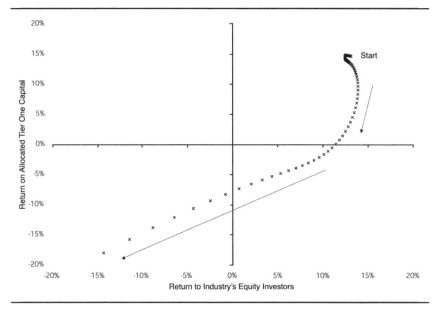

broadly consistent with the policy implied by the forthcoming Basel II regime. It is also assumed that the model is reliable, i.e., the actual default rate is equal to the model's estimated default probability.

In each case the scatter plot compares the returns to industry equity investors and the return on that portion of bank tier-one capital allocated to the industry. The series of points shows how these returns evolve over time (the arrows indicate the direction of time). The model parameters are calibrated so that initial returns to both industry equity investors and bank tier-one capital are quite attractive.

Exhibit 16.15 assumes static loan pricing. In this simulation, returns to both industry equity investors and bank tier-one capital remain high for a while. Then, as leverage rises, there is an increase in the industry default rate. Return on bank capital falls sharply because of credit losses. However, as banks continue to extend loans at the same interest rate, equity returns for industry investors remain high. The benefit of leverage for equity holders offsets the damage done by defaults. Finally an equilibrium is reached in which firms are more highly levered than initially, industry equity returns are higher, but banks suffer constant negative returns on tier-one capital due to the higher equilibrium rate of defaults. (Note that negative returns on lending may be sustainable for some time if they are offset by relationship-based fee income.)

Exhibit 16.16 assumes risk based loan pricing. In this simulation, returns to both industry equity investors and bank tier one capital again remain high for a while. Then, as before, as leverage rises, there is an increase in the industry default rate. Banks adjust loan pricing, but return on bank capital still falls because there is always an existing stock of debt whose interest rate is too low. Meanwhile, return on industry equity capital falls since debt service eats up a higher and higher proportion of revenue. This causes leverage to spiral even higher. Eventually debt service exceeds revenue. There is no equilibrium. Instead, returns on both industry equity and bank capital become increasingly negative until both are wiped out.

These findings should not be taken too literally. The premises are not realistic. For example, it is implausible that banks would be willing to absorb credit losses forever, and it is implausible that the industry would never raise new equity in the capital markets (although this may become extremely difficult in periods of distress). So it is not yet possible to make quantitative real world predictions using this approach. The qualitative results remain a nagging worry rather than a concrete forecast.[6]

Structural models of credit risk can be powerful risk management tools, and perhaps even useful trading tools. Although they only became popular rather recently, they do seem to reflect timeless relationships between the corporate bond and equity markets. However, as the KMV model and its competitors exert an increasing influence on banks' credit decisions, investor behavior and possibly even rating agency actions, it is legitimate to ask whether there is a trade-off between capital market efficiency and market stability.

---

[6] It is surprisingly difficult to devise more realistic models of capital structure dynamics. Even sophisticated models have trouble accounting for the mix of debt and equity observed in the real world; for example, see Mathias Dewatripont and Patrick Legros, *Moral Hazard and Capital Structure Dynamics*, CARESS Working Paper 02-07, July 5, 2002.

CHAPTER 17

Capturing the Credit Alpha

David Soronow, CFA
Senior Associate, Credit Products
MSCI Barra

Defaults and large unexpected credit migrations can have a significant impact on the return of a corporate bond portfolio. Headliners such as Enron, Parmalat, and General Motors act as bitter reminders of the importance of credit risk assessment to the bond portfolio management process. The sheer magnitude of losses triggered by these types of debacles often means that a small number of defaults and credit migrations can negate a year's worth of hard-fought positive returns.

Why does default and credit migration have such a dominating effect on the return of a credit portfolio? The phenomenon is partly explained by the asymmetric nature of the return distribution for a bond. A downside loss associated with default is considerably larger than an upside gain associated with credit improvement. Moreover, rapid deterioration in credit quality occurs more frequently than rapid improvement.

If we could identify in advance the firms that are likely to deteriorate, we should be able to enhance the risk-adjusted return of our portfolio. This begs the question: If defaults and credit migrations contribute so disproportionately to the return of a corporate bond portfolio, why are asymmetric measures of risk (such as probability of default) not more widely utilized for bond portfolio optimization? Walk into any portfolio management shop and you find that mean-variance optimization, with its ubiquitous assumption of normally distributed bond returns, still dominates the landscape even though this assumption is clearly at odds with reality.

The asymmetric nature of the return distribution for a credit portfolio suggests that mean-variance optimization is the wrong tool for credit selection. That said, a major roadblock to employing an asymmetric measure is the difficulty in estimating this measure in the first place. Default is such a rare event that one is usually unable to glean meaningful forward-looking information from analyzing historical bond and default data. To overcome this challenge, asset management firms rely on in-house credit analysts to assess issuer creditworthiness through evaluation of company fundamentals.

In this chapter, we take a different, albeit related, track to that of the fundamental analyst. We investigate a model that utilizes a combination of equity market and financial statement information. We then apply this model within the context of credit selection for a bond portfolio.[1] We demonstrate that equity markets provide ample quantitative information regarding the asymmetry of a bond's return distribution. Exhibit 17.1 provides a preview of our results. It depicts the value of $1 invested in an active portfolio constructed using a default probability-based credit selection method, versus $1 invested in a passive index portfolio. As the exhibit suggests, portfolio return is significantly enhanced through use of this equity-implied default probability measure.

EXHIBIT 17.1 Cumulative Portfolio Value

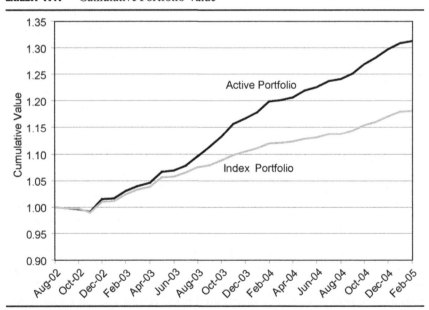

---

[1] This chapter focuses exclusively on the impact of credit selection on portfolio performance. The research studies described herein were constructed so as to isolate returns attributable solely to changes in issuer credit spreads.

DEBT AND EQUITY—THE CAPITAL STRUCTURE LINK

Do equity markets have something valuable to say about bond markets? The answer, of course, is "yes." This should be of no surprise given that both equity and bonds are a reflection of the firm's capital structure. To gain some intuition into why this is so, recall the relation: Assets = Liabilities + Equity. This most fundamental of accounting concepts provide the impetus for using an issuer's equity to evaluate its bonds. As Exhibit 17.2 illustrates, debt and equity securities are intrinsically linked vis-à-vis their claim on the assets of the firm. This relationship is more than just theoretical; capital structure arbitrage hedge funds have been exploiting this relationship for some time.

EXHIBIT 17.2   Firm Assets Decomposition
Default Probability can be derived by modeling the capital structure of a firm.

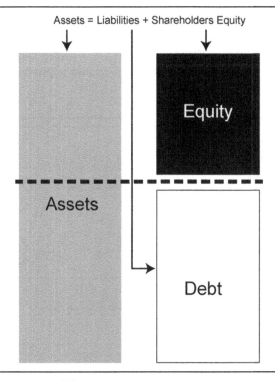

Assets = Liabilities + Shareholders Equity

Equity

Assets

Debt

Note: The reasoning is as follows:
Shareholders have limited liability in that the maximum loss they can experience is the value of their shares (i.e., the stock price can never go below zero). The company will default when equity is worth zero (which is when assets fall below the debt level).

AN EQUITY IMPLIED MEASURE—BARRA DEFAULT
PROBABILITY

In our studies, we use *Barra Default Probability* (BDP) as the equity
implied measure of creditworthiness. The BDP represents the probability that a company will default on its debt obligations over a predefined
period of time. It is computed by explicitly modeling the firm's capital
structure and the evolution of this structure through time. The model
assumes default occurs when the value of the firm's assets crosses a
threshold dictated by the level of the firm's debt obligations. This
assumption stems from the understanding that shareholders have limited liability—they can lose a maximum of their equity stake. As such,
shareholders are forced to default once their equity stake is wiped out.
In the event of default, the shareholders' claim on the assets of the firm
is expunged and debt holders are left with the residual value of the
assets. The inputs to the model include equity market and financial
statement data. Exhibit 17.3 offers a graphical depiction of the model
and its inputs.

The BDP model is similar in flavor to the so-called "structural model"
approach pioneered by Merton[2] in the 1970s and improved upon by many

EXHIBIT 17.3   Barra Default Probabilities

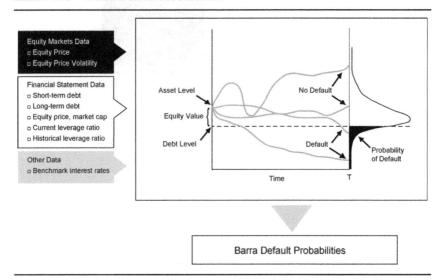

[2] Robert C. Merton, "On the Pricing of Corporate Debt: The Risk Structure of Interest Rates," *Journal of Finance* 29 (1974), pp. 449–470.

researchers in subsequent years.[3] Note that unlike other measures of risk (such as volatility), default probability is an asymmetric measure: BDP measures downside risk specifically. As one would suspect, BDP tends to be highest for highly leveraged firms with high equity volatility.

A natural question to ask is: Why use equity-implied default probability if this same information can be deduced directly from bond spreads? The answer comes down to the observation that bond and equity markets often have differing opinions regarding the creditworthiness of a firm. In essence, there is an advantage to having an additional information source to flag problematic credits. Moreover, equity data tends to be of better quality and higher frequency than data available in bond (or credit default swap) markets.

PREDICTING DEFAULT AND SPREAD JUMPS

A survey of the credit risk literature yields ample material on the performance of various default forecasting models. One of the more popular model tests originates from the field of signal detection theory and is known as *receiver operating characteristic curves* (ROC curves).[4] Exhibit 17.4 presents a sample of the results of our internal ROC studies that assess the power of BDP as a predictor of default and large jumps in the *credit default swap* (CDS) spread. The predictive power of the model is summarized in the ROC accuracy ratio, which is 0.91 for BDP as a predictor of default. For those unfamiliar with ROC curves, we can interpret this number to mean that, on average, only 9% of surviving firms had a BDP above that of the defaulting firms. To put this into perspective, a model with perfect foresight into default has an accuracy ratio of 1, while a model with no predictive power whatsoever has an accuracy ratio of 0.5. The accuracy ratio of 0.91 indicates that BDP does indeed impart valuable information about future defaults.

---

[3] It should be noted that while similar in flavor to a structural model, BDP is actually derived from the Incomplete Information Model (I2)—a hybrid model that has the characteristics of both reduced form and structural models. For a description of hybrid models, see Kay Giesecke and Lisa Goldberg, "The Market Price of Credit Risk," working paper, Cornell University (2003); and Kay Giesecke and Lisa Goldberg, "Forecasting Default in the Face of Uncertainty," *Journal of Derivatives* 12 (2004), pp. 11–25.

[4] Receiver Operating Characteristics curves were first developed during World War II to assess the ability of radar operators in distinguishing legitimate enemy targets from radar signal noise (see J.A. Swets, R.M. Dawes, and J. Monahan, "Better Decisions through Science," *Scientific American* 283, no. 4 (2000), pp. 82–88).

EXHIBIT 17.4   ROC Study Sample

Prediction Study	Sample	Period	Defaults Caught	Nondefaults Caught
Defaults	1,384 U.S. companies	Jan 1998– June 2004	78% of the 89 events	11% of nonevents
Credit Default Swap Spread Jumps[a]	About 500 U.S. companies	July 2002– Feb 2005	71% of 109 events	25% of nonevents

[a] A jump event is defined as credit with an initial 5-year CDS spread of less than 200 bps observed at the beginning of the month, which jumps to a spread of greater than 300 bps during the month.

With our default probability measure in hand, we now investigate credit selection strategies that use this information to our advantage.

PORTFOLIO CONSTRUCTION RULES— A RELATIVE RANKING RULE

In this section we use our BDPs to construct an active bond portfolio and compare our active portfolio to that of a passive index portfolio.

Let us suppose that our portfolio investment mandate dictates the following:

- We are required to be fully invested in credits at all times.
- Our investable universe is defined by the credits represented in a popular index.
- We have full discretion as to which credits to invest in, so long as they are contained in the index.
- We can rebalance our portfolio once per month.
- Our mandate is to outperform the index on a risk-adjusted return basis.

For the purposes of this chapter, a simple selection method is specified:

1. Choose a Benchmark Index.
2. Convert the BDP for each credit into a percentile rank within the names in the index.[5]

---

[5] For example, the highest default probability would be ranked at the 100th percentile.

3. Convert the bond spread for each credit into a percentile rank within the names in the index.
4. At each time step, construct the portfolio based on the following rule: if BDP rank is greater than the bond spread rank in excess of some threshold amount, exclude the issuer from the active portfolio. We refer to this selection rule as the "criterion" and the threshold amount as the "operating point."
5. Distribute the capital evenly across the remaining bonds in the portfolio.
6. Repeat steps one through five at the beginning of each month.

Two important points to note about this method:

1. By converting BDP and bond spreads from an absolute value into a percentile rank, we are normalizing for changes in the general level of spreads and default probabilities. This produces stable results as we move through the economic cycle (i.e., as the market price of risk changes, the volatility of spreads changes, the number of defaults changes, etc.). In contrast, methods that rely solely on the absolute value of default probability tend to produce unstable results.
2. The method relies on BDP ranking relative to bond spread ranking. Our backtests indicate that a criterion based on default probability or bond spread in isolation produces less compelling results for reasons that will be described later in this chapter.

DESCRIPTION OF BACKTESTING FRAMEWORK

Our backtesting framework allows us to evaluate bond returns due to changes in issuer spread and payment of coupons. For simplicity, we assume an equal amount of capital is allocated to each credit in the portfolio. The risk-free rate remains constant during this period in order to negate changes in the portfolio due to changes in benchmark rates. To further isolate the effects of credit selection, we assume each issuer has the same hypothetical 5-year bond that values to par if discounted off the Treasury curve. In addition, CDS spreads are used as a proxy for bond credit spreads.

The rationale for using CDS spread is threefold:

1. CDS isolates for changes in the credit quality of an issuer. In contrast, bond price reflects idiosyncratic features of bond issues (such as embedded options), which may not directly relate to the creditworthiness of an issuer.

2. CDS spread is quoted directly in the market and, therefore, tends to be a closer reflection of actual market credit spreads. In contrast, bond spread must often be inferred by way of an option-adjusted spread model.
3. CDS allows us to negate term-structure inconsistencies across issuers because all CDS spread quotes used in the study are for a 5-year CDS contract.

Note that the method we use is equivalent to constructing a synthetic corporate bond portfolio using positions in CDS, coupled with a position in a 5-year on-the-run U.S. Treasury bond.

While the backtesting results presented in this chapter do not account for transaction costs, our analysis indicates that the return of the active portfolio is reduced by approximately 1% per annum using a transaction cost assumption of 30 basis points per trade.

RESULTS OF BACKTESTING THE CREDIT SELECTION METHOD

We assess the performance of our credit selection method through backtesting. In so doing, we determine what our portfolio return would have been had we followed this strategy over some historical time period. For our backtests, we include approximately 550 U.S. domiciled firms covering the period from August 2002 to February 2005. The total number of firms is taken as our bond index. The portfolio is rebalanced monthly, yielding a data set with roughly 16,300 data points. To put this into perspective, the method evaluates approximately 16,300 individual buy/sell/hold decisions throughout the course of the 30-month period.

Exhibit 17.5 displays the number of firms in the passive index portfolio versus the number of firms in the active portfolio. As the exhibit illustrates, the active portfolio holds approximately half of the firms in the index at any given point in time. This can be "tuned" to any level desired. For example, if the portfolio manager has only a small portion of her portfolio dedicated to credits, she can choose a more selective operating point so that fewer credits are chosen.

Exhibit 17.6 displays the monthly returns of the active portfolio and the index portfolio. Exhibit 17.7 lists the average monthly return and standard deviation of the active portfolio versus the index. We also compute the Information Ratio as a measure of risk-adjusted return.[6]

---

[6] The Information Ratio is the average monthly return divided by the standard deviation of the monthly return.

EXHIBIT 17.5 Number of Credits Held in the Portfolio

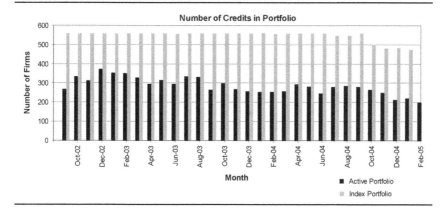

EXHIBIT 17.6 Monthly Portfolio Returns

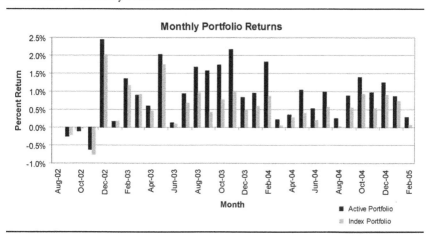

EXHIBIT 17.7 Returns And Standard Deviation of the Portfolios

	Index Portfolio	Active Portfolio	Perfect Foresight
30-month Cumulative Return	18.1%	31.3%	57.7%
30-month Annualized Return	6.9%	11.5%	19.9%
Average Monthly Return	0.55%	0.91%	1.52%
Standard Deviation	0.56%	0.74%	0.68%
Information Ratio	0.998	1.232	2.232

We find that the active portfolio outperforms the index on both an absolute and a risk-adjusted return basis. The annualized return of the active portfolio is 11.5%, versus 6.9% for the index portfolio. From the perspective of risk-adjusted return, the active portfolio earns 1.23% per unit of standard deviation, versus 0.99% for the index portfolio. Thus, the active portfolio's risk-return profile is superior to that of the index portfolio. These results are robust across a large range of operating points and throughout the entire period under consideration.

To ensure the results are not simply a result of chance, we test the same selection method with a signal consisting purely of noise.[7] As expected, we find that the noise-based portfolio is unable to consistently outperform the index across several operating points or on a risk-adjusted return basis. In contrast, the active portfolio outperforms the index across a large range of operating points and on a risk-adjusted return basis.

To gain further insight, we also test the selection method assuming perfect 1-month ahead foresight into credit migrations (see Exhibit 17.6). For example, we would know in advance if a firm is going to migrate from a 5th percentile ranking in the current month, to the 90th percentile ranking in the subsequent month. It turns out that the maximum that could have been earned at this operating point is 19.9% annually.

One may wonder if equity-implied default probability measures are a leading indicator of bond spreads. Our findings suggest that one cannot make any definitive statement as to the ability of an equity-implied model to always lead the bond or credit default swap market. In fact, the two markets tend to operate contemporaneously. However, there are occasions where these two markets offer divergent opinions on the relative creditworthiness of a firm. In these cases, we often find that a greater level of uncertainty exists regarding the state of the company in question. Our results indicate that, on average, the index portfolio was not compensated for bearing the additional risk associated with this uncertainty. Therefore, excluding these credits from the active portfolio yielded superior performance on a risk-adjusted return basis.

CONCLUSION

This chapter demonstrates the use of an equity-implied credit measure within the credit selection process. The results of backtesting demonstrate that it is possible to enhance the risk-adjusted return of a credit

---

[7] Specifically, we create a portfolio by replacing BDP with default probabilities obtained from a random number generator.

portfolio through application of these techniques. Additional empirical work is needed to ascertain the applicability of such methods to other data sets such as European credits, as well as relevant subsets of the data such as investment grade and noninvestment grade groupings.

International
Bond Investing

CHAPTER 18

Global Bond Investing for the 21st Century

Lee R. Thomas, Ph.D
Managing Director
Allianz Global Investors

No single currency dominates global bond markets. Over half the world's bonds are denominated in currencies other than the dollar, and the share of nondollar bonds is growing. In light of this investors can ill afford to neglect the opportunities available in foreign bond markets. Global integration, the end of the Cold War, and the widespread adoption of free markets mean that more and more issuers have access to the world's capital markets. Moreover, the creation of the euro means issuers have a realistic alternative to issuing in dollars. At the same time portfolio managers, encouraged by increasingly cosmopolitan clients offering increasingly liberal investment mandates, are reaching out for superior risk-adjusted return wherever in the world it can be found.

This chapter describes the why and how of investing in global bond markets. The first section surveys the opportunities. After reviewing the size and composition of bond markets around the world, we discuss two ways investors can make the most of them. These two approaches, which we call *tactical* and *strategic*, are complementary. We wrap up the discussion on opportunities in global bond markets by considering whether the many developments that have recently occurred in global bond markets, resulting from the increasing integration of global financial markets and from the creation of the euro, have weakened the arguments for using global bonds. Our conclusion is that the opportunities are changing, not vanishing.

COMPOSITION OF GLOBAL BOND MARKETS

In this section we survey the opportunities available in global bond markets and two complementary approaches to take advantage of these opportunities.

How Large are the Foreign Markets?

What is a "foreign" bond? "Foreign" could refer to the domicile of the issuer, the domicile of the principal buyers, the market in which the bond trades, or the currency in which the bond is denominated. For the purposes of this chapter, foreign bonds refer to issues denominated in a currency different from that ordinarily used by the investor who owns them. A U.S. investor who buys euro-denominated bonds holds "foreign" bonds. So does a German investor who buys U.S. dollar bonds. In light of this definition, exchange rate risk is unique to foreign bonds, and we discuss managing exchange rate risks at some length.

Let us examine the world's major bond markets, by currency of denomination, to show how large the "foreign" bond market is considered from the perspectives of different investors. We start with sovereign bonds, or those issued by governments. As estimated by the investment bank Salomon Smith Barney, at the end of 2004 the sovereign bond markets were dominated by three major currency blocs: the dollar, representing 20% of the total market; the euro, representing 39%; and the yen, representing 30%. Together, all other currencies account for only 11% of the market. When we add nongovernment bonds to the mix the dollar, euro, and yen remain dominant. Accordingly, portfolio managers can think of global bond portfolio allocation largely in terms of these three currency blocs.

In practice many of the smaller bond markets are associated with one of the major blocs, anyway. So, for example, portfolio managers often think of Canadian, Australian, and New Zealand bonds in terms of their yield spreads to the U.S. market, while the United Kingdom, Sweden, and Denmark would be evaluated based on their yield spreads to euro-denominated bonds. This makes the "three-bloc" approach to global bond allocation even more appealing.

The three-bloc approach to global bond markets is new, and it reflects major, recent changes in the structure of the world's bond markets attendant with the creation of the euro in 1999. Understanding these changes will be critical to successfully managing global portfolios.

Once managing global bond portfolios was a top-down game. The major source of return was moving funds from country to country, manipulating a portfolio's interest rate and exchange rate exposures based on a manager's macroeconomic forecast. There were large yield disparities among bonds in different countries, and many countries from which to choose. Each country had its own currency, so there were many exchange rate plays to consider, too.

But the world has changed. First, yield disparities among the major economies have narrowed substantially.[1] As yields converged, the volatility of international yield spreads declined. Second, before January 1, 1999 there were 10 relatively small European markets, rather than one large euro-denominated market. The *European Monetary Union* (EMU) changed that. This change has an obvious implication for the potential for using foreign bond markets for the purpose of diversification. The creation of the euro also reduced the opportunity for an active bond manager to generate excess return, or "alpha," by managing interest rate and currency exposures using top-down macroeconomic analysis. EMU eliminated ten currencies, so that there are far fewer exchange rates to bet on. Again, this means that top-down macroeconomic analysis is becoming less important. Today there are just three major blocs to rotate into and out of, for bonds and currencies. Opportunities to make convergence trades on interest rates—betting that yields everywhere revert towards the global average—are much less plentiful, at least when we consider the developed markets only. One implication of this is that global managers want to range more widely into the bonds of emerging markets. Today the major convergence trading opportunities involve emerging markets, though many emerging markets have become investment grade, eroding the distinction between them and the developed world's bonds.

At the same time, corporate and asset-backed bond markets have started to expand rapidly in Europe and are likely to expand in Asia, too. This increases an active global bond manager's scope to add value using bottom-up, relative value analysis.

So, in addition to sovereign bonds, let us consider "spread product," or nonsovereign bonds, too. When we do we see that the 20% share of the U.S. sovereign market understates the relative importance of the U.S. bond market. The United States has by far the world's largest asset-backed markets (largely mortgages). In the United States, the fixed income market is about 40% government or agency bonds, 40% securitized bonds, and about 20% corporates. In the rest of the world, sovereign debt still dominates (see Exhibit 18.1). When the nonsovereign bond markets are included, the dollar represents about 40% of the global bond markets, about the same share as the euro markets.

---

[1] The exception is yen bonds, which have substantially lower yields than those found elsewhere.

EXHIBIT 18.1   The Composition of Global Bond Markets, March 2005
(Based on the Lehman Global Aggregate Index)

Category	U.S.	Pan-Euro	Asia Pacific	Total
Treasury	10%	23%	17%	50%
Government Related	6	5	2	13
Corporate	7	7	2	16
Securitized	16	5	0	21
Total	39%	40%	21%	100%

EXHIBIT 18.2   Maturity Structure of Global Bonds, March 2005
(Based on the Lehman Global Aggregate Index)

Maturity	Size (MM)	Percentage
1–3	$5,168,090	25.3%
3–5	4,622,182	22.7
5–7	3,101,015	15.2
7-10	4,546,566	22.3
10+	2,954,846	14.5
Total	$20,392,699	100%

The maturity structure of the world's bond markets is shown in Exhibit 18.2, which is based on the Lehman Global Aggregate index, a popular index that includes sovereign and nonsovereign issues. As you can see, about half the world's bonds are 5 years or less in maturity. Only 14% mature in 10 years or more.

A trend in future is likely to be an increase in the share of very long maturity bonds. France recently floated a 50-year issue, for example. This will make it easier to defease the long maturity liabilities associated with ageing populations.

Exhibit 18.3 shows the quality structure of the world's bonds. Most are high quality, with triple-A bonds representing the largest single category, and representing more than half of the total. That is, for most bonds, interest rate and foreign exchange rate risks predominate. Credit risk is comparatively less important. This is changing as more spread product is issued in Europe.

EXHIBIT 18.3   Quality Structure of Global Bonds, March 2005
(Based on the Lehman Global Aggregate Index)

Quality	Size (MM)	Percentage
Aaa	$11,073,460	54.3%
Aa	2,333,046	11.5
A	5,738,461	28.1
Baa	1,247,732	6.1
Total	$20,392,699	100%

USING GLOBAL BONDS

There are two ways to use foreign bonds. The first is tactically, or opportunistically, as a substitute for domestic bonds. Effectively this creates a new market sector which a portfolio manager can use occasionally, to outperform a domestic benchmark. The second approach is to use foreign bonds strategically, as a separate asset class. This typically means constructing a bond portfolio that is benchmarked to one of the major global indices, such as the JP Morgan Government Bond Index, the Salomon World Government Bond Index, or the Lehman Global Aggregate Index, and including it as a permanent part of a client's broad asset allocation. Note that these two approaches can be used in concert.

The Case for Using Foreign Bonds Tactically

Foreign markets expand the tool set a portfolio manager can use to add alpha to outperform a domestic bogey.

Sector rotation is a well known active technique for earning excess return. The active manager shifts funds from sector to sector, based on a forecast of prospective relative performance. Foreign bonds are a sector that can be used sporadically as a substitute for domestic bonds, just as asset-backed securities or corporate bonds are used as tactical substitutes for government bonds by active bond managers. Because economic and interest rate cycles in different countries are often asynchronous, foreign bond markets may occasionally present substantial opportunities compared to an investor's domestic market.

To illustrate the potential excess return foreign bonds can offer, Exhibit 18.4 contrasts the performance of the U.S. bond market, and foreign bonds, in each year from 1999 to 2004.[2] These returns span the range

---

[2] To isolate pure bond market effects, the returns have been hedged into a common currency (U.S. dollars).

of opportunities available to an active country rotation specialist who uses tactical asset allocation to add value, shifting a portfolio between U.S. and foreign bonds each year.

Notice that the difference in return between the U.S. and foreign bond markets in many years has been substantial. Of course, the range of regional returns would be even greater if we factored in exchange rate changes, too. The wide range of outcomes, comparing the best and worst performing market each year, suggests that there is considerable potential to add value by using foreign bonds tactically. In fact, the yearly country bond market performance differences recorded in Exhibit 18.4 are not exceptional. If we look back further, to the inflationary period of the 1970s, the performance differences among national bond market returns were much greater. The difference between the best and worst performing markets averaged about 10% per year during the run-up to EMU.

The differences among bond returns in different countries offer the opportunity for a shrewd active manager to add considerable value to his domestic bogey. Even a small allocation to a foreign bond market—if it is the right market—can add considerable excess return. A manager who can consistently select the world's best foreign markets can handily outperform a domestic benchmark. To demonstrate, Exhibit 18.5 shows how a wealth index would have evolved had an investor with perfect

EXHIBIT 18.4   U.S. and Hedged Foreign Bond Returns, Annual

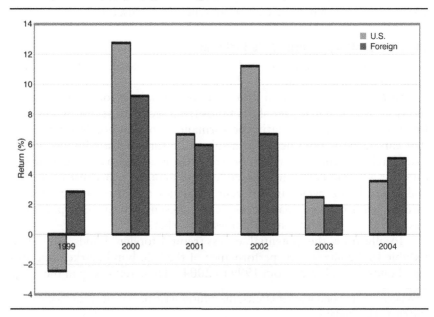

EXHIBIT 18.5　　Growth of $100 with Perfect Foresight

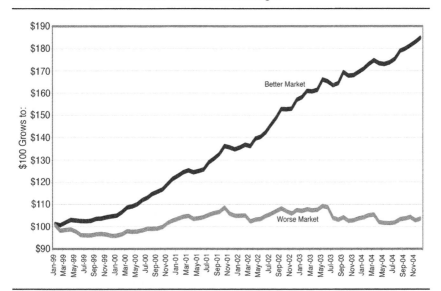

foresight improbably chosen to invest exclusively in the better performing of (1) the U.S. market, and (2) hedged foreign bond markets every
month. It also shows an investor's wealth had the investor been unfortunate enough to have chosen the worse market instead. Choosing the better performing market each year produced an average annual return of
10.3%; choosing the worse performing market produced a return of
only 0.7% per year. Starting with an initial investment of $100, the dif-
ference in terminal wealth (from 1999 to 2004) was $184 compared to
$103.

Clearly, rotation into foreign bond markets can add considerable
value to a domestic bogey, at least in principle. But harvesting this
potential is difficult. First, the manager must choose the right foreign
markets. Then the manager must time the move into foreign bonds
before they outperform domestic bonds, and then rotate back into
domestic bonds when foreign bonds are poised to underperform. Obviously, this requires astute active bond management and a keen sense of
market timing.

It is important to recognize that Exhibit 18.5 shows that foreign
bonds can be a two-edged sword: *Foreign bonds can subtract alpha just
as quickly as they can add it.* More formally, the problem a manager
confronts when using foreign bonds is that they often introduce substantial tracking risk when they are added to a domestic-benchmarked

portfolio. For example, consider the case of a U.S. bond manager who
has been assigned the Lehman Aggregate Bond Index as his bogey.

A 5% excess allocation to mortgages introduces about 8 basis
points of tracking risk.[3] The corresponding figure for overweighting
investment-grade corporate bonds by 5% is approximately 10 basis
points of tracking risk. By comparison, a well diversified, 5% overweight position in foreign bonds adds about 18 basis points of tracking
risk. Notice that this is about twice the risk of an equally overweighted
allocation to mortgages or corporate bonds, even when the foreign
bonds are currency hedged and when the manager rotates into a diversified portfolio of foreign bonds, rather than only choosing one or two
foreign markets. This means that portfolio managers ordinarily commit
only a small portion of their funds to foreign bonds when they are being
evaluated against a domestic benchmark. To encourage a larger foreign
allocation, the manager must be assigned a global benchmark, so that
foreign bonds become a strategic part of his holdings.

The Case for Using Foreign Bonds Strategically

Using foreign bonds tactically depends on effective market timing, so it
only makes sense for active managers. However, both passive and active
managers can use foreign bonds strategically. In other words, the strategic benefits of international bonds do not depend on active management, though active management may enhance them. The distinctive
strategic benefit afforded by foreign bonds is volatility reduction.

Foreign bonds can reduce a portfolio's volatility in two ways. First,
and most obviously, *some foreign bond markets may be less volatile
than a manager's domestic bond market.* If so, they represent good raw
material for creating a lower-risk bond portfolio. To illustrate, Exhibit
18.6 shows volatilities of the U.S. and foreign bond markets calculated
over the 1999 to 2004 period. The foreign returns are shown currency
hedged (into U.S. dollars) in order to eliminate the effects of exchange
rate fluctuations. The more hyperactive bond market (the U.S.) was
more than twice as volatile as hedged foreign markets (WGBI, ex-U.S.).
That means we expect an allocation to foreign bonds to reduce a dollar
bond portfolio's volatility considerably, even ignoring the effects of risk
reduction from diversification, if you currency hedge.

While it may be true that "foreign" markets are individually less risky
than the domestic market for *some* investors—investors domiciled in countries with relatively volatile bond markets (like the United States)—that
obviously cannot be the case for *all* the world's investors. Somebody must

---

[3] Tracking risk is the annualized standard deviation of the difference between the return to the active manager's portfolio, and the return to the bogey.

EXHIBIT 18.6   Bond Market Volatilities, 1999 to 2004

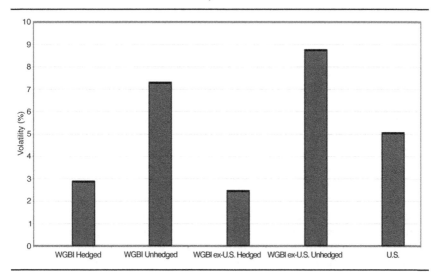

live in the countries that have relatively tranquil markets! Nevertheless, using foreign bonds can, in principle, even benefit investors in countries with relatively low volatility bond markets. Why? The second reason foreign bonds can reduce a portfolio's volatility: *A global index typically has lower risk than the average of its components.* This is because the correlations among bond returns in different countries are not one, so there are diversification benefits to be reaped from holding foreign bonds. For example, during the period 1999 to 2004, the correlation between the Lehman Aggregate index (of U.S. bonds) and the Salomon WGBI ex-U.S.—that is, between U.S. and hedged foreign bonds—was 53%. That means the U.S. bond market statistically "explained" about one-quarter of the variation in foreign bond returns; about three-quarters of foreign bond market volatility was statistically unrelated to what happened in the U.S. markets.[4]

When we think about what drives bond returns, it should not be a surprise that bond markets in different countries are only loosely correlated. Bond yields are primarily driven by three factors: (1) secular economic forces, (2) business cycles, and (3) monetary and fiscal policies. Let us briefly consider these factors.

Structural features of economies, such as different economic factor endowments (labor, capital, and natural resources) and different population demographics, directly influence long-term growth and inflation.

---

[4] That is, the coefficient of determination (R^2) between the U.S. and hedged foreign bond markets was about 0.28%.

They also mean that global shocks have different implications for a country's business cycles. A spike in the price of oil does not affect the Japanese and Norwegian economies in the same way at all. Accordingly, changes in the global economic environment will naturally cause growth and inflation to diverge in different countries.

Economic shocks also elicit different policy responses in different countries. Moreover, policies may differ internationally quite independently of global economic shocks. In short, the fiscal and monetary policies appropriate for one country may not be appropriate or politically feasible in another.

Since structural, political, and cultural differences among countries are not likely to vanish in the early 21st century, it is unlikely that business cycles will become perfectly coordinated, replaced by a single global cycle. In fact, the scope to run independent monetary policies in different countries is one of the most important reasons cited by academic economists for using floating, rather than fixed, exchange rates. Only the adoption of a single global currency would be likely to make yields in different countries' bond markets become perfectly synchronized. That is unlikely in the immediate future.

Because the returns to domestic and foreign bonds have not historically been highly correlated, substantial benefits can, in principle, be realized by combining them in a globally diversified portfolio. To illustrate, we shall now examine the effect of global diversification.

Foreign Bond Diversification: A U.S. Perspective

Exhibit 18.7 shows the effect of global diversification from a U.S. investor's perspective, based on six years of historical data (1999-2004). In Exhibit 18.7 we start in the upper right of the chart with a portfolio consisting of U.S. bonds alone; its historic volatility was about 5%. When we introduce some foreign bonds, to produce a portfolio of 90% U.S. and 10% foreign bonds, we move to the left; the volatility of the resulting portfolio falls to about 4.8%. (Each black diamond represents a 10% reallocation to foreign bonds.) Increasing the international allocation to 30% reduces the volatility still further, to about 4%. In fact, the minimum volatility portfolio historically consisted of 100% foreign bonds and 0% U.S. bonds. The reason the minimum volatility portfolio held no dollar bonds at all was that foreign markets were much more tranquil than the U.S. market. The foreign only portfolio had a volatility of only 2.5%, or about half of the volatility of a U.S.-only bond portfolio.[5] According to

[5] These results use data from 1999 to 2004. The U.S. index is the Lehman Aggregate Index; the foreign index is the Salomon World Government Bond Index (WGBI), ex-U.S.

EXHIBIT 18.7   Diversification into Hedged Foreign Bonds

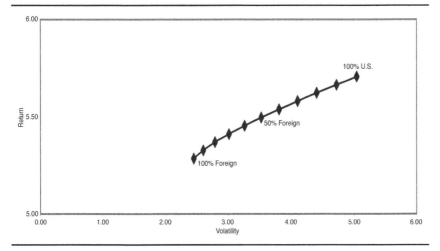

Exhibit 18.7, the effect of a 60% allocation to foreign bonds—about the share in a global index—has been to reduce volatility by one-third or so from a U.S. investor's perspective. But what about return?

As you can see dollar markets were the better performing from 1999 to 2004. (Recall that this period included aggressively loose Federal Reserve monetary policy following the collapse of stock prices and 9/11.) Notice also that the return difference was modest. Does diversification always reduce return? Certainly not. Diversification is the only free lunch in economics; it reduces risk without necessarily reducing expected return.[6]

In the case of foreign bonds there is little reason to expect the reduction in volatility associated with global diversification to be associated with a commensurate reduction in return in the future.[7] Needless to say, a U.S. investor should *not* expect a globally diversified portfolio to earn

---

[6] See André Perold and Evan Schulman, "The Free Lunch in Currency Hedging," *Financial Analysts Journal* (May–June 1988), pp. 45–50; and Lee R. Thomas, "The Performance of Currency Hedged Foreign Bonds," *Financial Analysts Journal* (May–June 1989), pp. 25–31, for a discussion of this "free lunch" argument as applied to global bond diversification.

[7] In principle, we could try to predict the expected return difference between U.S. and foreign bonds using an international *capital asset pricing model* (CAPM). But applying the CAPM requires a number of strong simplifying assumptions that create a highly imprecise forecasts of the future outperformance of foreign bonds. To be conservative an investor should discount both historical data and CAPM-based return projections. Realistically it is not possible to say if foreign bonds or U.S. bonds have higher expected returns in the future.

more than a U.S.-only one in future years. But neither should a U.S. investor expect a globally diversified portfolio to earn significantly less.

Diversification Potential: Foreign Bonds and U.S. Bonds Compared

The preceding section quantified the historic gains from using foreign sovereign bonds to diversify a U.S. Treasury-only bond portfolio. But, are these risk reduction results "good" or "bad"? In other words, how can we calibrate this level of historic risk reduction?

One way a U.S. Treasury-only bond investor can evaluate the diversification benefits provided by foreign bonds is to compare what they have offered historically compared to diversifying into other categories of U.S. bonds, such as mortgage-backed securities or corporate bonds. Exhibit 18.8 shows the returns generated by U.S. Treasury bonds and mortgages, using monthly index data from 1986 to 1999. Exhibits 18.9 and 18.10 show the same data for U.S. Treasury bonds and, respectively, high-yield corporate bonds, and for foreign bonds.

Exhibits 18.8 and 18.9 do not suggest either mortgages or high-yield bonds offered much in the way of diversification potential most of the time. Only in the tails of the distributions—in months when U.S. Treasury bond returns were extreme—do high-yield bonds, and to a lesser extent mortgages, seem to offer modest diversification. Otherwise, the monthly returns are highly correlated. In fact, the correlation between U.S. Treasury returns and mortgage-backed security returns is

EXHIBIT 18.8   U.S. Treasuries and Mortgage Securities, Monthly Returns 1986 to 1999

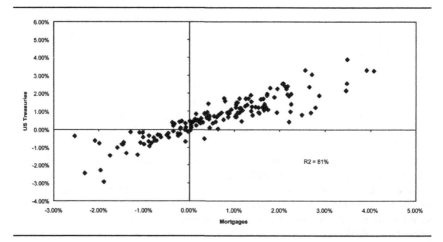

EXHIBIT 18.9   U.S. Treasury and High-Yield Corporate Bonds, Monthly Returns, 1986 to 1999

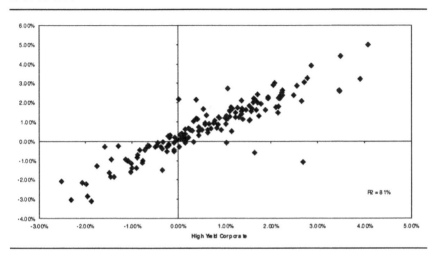

EXHIBIT 18.10   U.S. Treasuries and Hedged Foreign Bonds Monthly Returns, 1986 to 1999

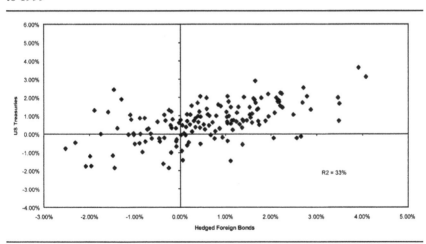

about 0.9. For high-yield bonds, the correlation is also about 0.9. In contrast, Exhibit 18.10 compares U.S. Treasury returns with the returns to foreign bonds, specifically the JP Morgan hedged, non-U.S. bond index. The correlation is only 0.6. (Recall that using Salomon's WGBI, the correlation from 1999 through 2004 was 0.53.)

Diversification Benefits for Non-U.S. Investors

In principle, risk reduction from diversifying should work for bond investors anywhere, not just for U.S. investors. Unfortunately, the U.S. market has been so much more volatile than foreign markets, that there has been little scope for a foreign investor to reduce volatility by diversifying into U.S. bonds.

These historic results, and others, can be summarized as follows: diversification into currency hedged foreign bonds reduces the volatility of a bond portfolio in principle, when compared to investing in a domestic-only portfolio. However, the historic benefits of diversification, and the risk-minimizing weight to allocate to foreign bonds, have varied considerably from country to country. The benefit has been greatest for investors who live in countries with relatively volatile bond markets—the U.S. Historically, during the 1999–2004 period, a U.S. bond investor could have reduced a domestic-only portfolio's volatility by about one-third by allocating 60% of his portfolio to foreign bonds. The corresponding figures for European and Japanese investors were negligible. The U.S. results are consistent with *Modern Portfolio Theory* (MPT): International bond diversification reduces interest rate risk in a bond portfolio. We expect it to continue to do so in the future.

Why Use a Currency Hedged Benchmark?

So far we have looked at diversifying using *currency hedged* foreign bonds. What about using *unhedged* foreign bonds instead?

Unhedged foreign bonds provide risk reduction because their returns are imperfectly correlated with domestic bond returns. That is the good news. Unfortunately, foreign bonds also carry with them exchange rate risk. In an ideal world, that would not matter: exchange rate risks would be self-diversifying. That is, if changes in different exchange rates were uncorrelated, and an investor had enough different countries represented in a bond portfolio, exchange rate risk might diversify itself away. Using the formal language of MPT, we might find that exchange rate risk was unsystematic to a global bond portfolio.

Unfortunately, it is not likely and has not worked that way in practice. Exchange rate changes, observed from the perspective of any single base currency, are correlated. Moreover, the number of countries available to diversify into is relatively small. So foreign exchange rate risk does not just conveniently diversify itself away. Rather, as an investor adds foreign bonds, exchange rate risk accumulates in the portfolio. The result can be catastrophic if an investor's intention is to use foreign bonds to reduce risk.

Consider Exhibit 18.11, which shows global bond diversification from a U.S. investor's perspective *without* currency hedging. Compare it

EXHIBIT 18.11   Diversification with Unhedged Foreign Bonds

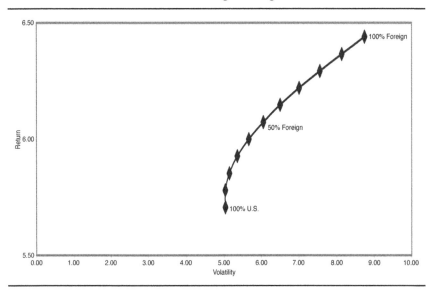

to Exhibit 18.7, which shows diversification from a U.S. investor's perspective *with* currency hedging. They are not at all alike. Foreign bonds
offer no risk reduction. In fact, in Exhibit 18.11, after an investor adds
only about 10% of foreign bonds to the U.S.-only portfolio, its overall
volatility begins to increase.

This results from the exchange rate risk embedded in the foreign
bonds. That is, beyond an allocation of only 10% to foreign bonds, the
disadvantage of increasing foreign exchange rate risk overwhelm the
benefits of falling interest rate risk (the latter resulting from diversification and from the smaller volatility of foreign markets). So the portfolio's total risk begins to increase. Notice that allocating 60% to foreign
markets, to match global market capitalization weighting, produces a
significant increase of volatility.

Exchange rate risk is like toxic waste: it is an unwanted byproduct
of foreign diversification.

Notice in Exhibit 18.11 that continuing to add unhedged foreign
bonds to a U.S. portfolio eventually increases its volatility substantially.
Recall from Exhibit 18.7 that a 60% foreign/40% U.S. portfolio historically had a volatility of 4.5% when the foreign bonds were currency
hedged. The same 60% foreign allocation results in portfolio volatility
of almost 6.5% if an investor does *not* currency hedge. That is, instead
of volatility falling by about a third compared to a U.S.-only bond port-

folio, volatility increases significantly if an investor diversifies instead (using the same allocation) into unhedged foreign bonds.

What about returns? For a U.S. investor, foreign bond returns were higher from 1999 to 2004 when they were unhedged. But in examining historic data, one should be skeptical about projecting differences in hedged and unhedged returns into the future. There is no reason to expect the dollar to fall forever. Sometimes currency hedging increases a foreign bond's return, sometimes it reduces it. Ignoring transactions costs, the expected long-run return from currency hedging is probably about zero. That is, the expected return of hedged and unhedged foreign bonds is about the same.

This is the essence of the "free lunch" argument for hedging. Numerous studies of currency risk premia have found that there is a zero long-run expected return from owning foreign currency. Yet foreign currency holdings clearly have significant volatility, and some of that volatility is transmitted by including foreign bonds in a portfolio if an investor fails to currency hedge. It is incumbent on any portfolio manager to secure the maximum amount of return for each unit of risk he bears. To make an investment with no expected return, but with substantial volatility—like holding a chronic, unmanaged foreign currency exposure in a bond portfolio—would be an investment management cardinal sin. Accordingly, a portfolio manager should think of currency hedging as the base case.

Not currency hedging represents an active strategy that can only be justified if a manager thinks a particular foreign currency will outperform its forward foreign exchange rate. If a manager is doubtful, about a currency's prospects, he or she should currency hedge.

Are the Benefits of Global Diversification Declining?

This chapter is about global bond investing in the markets of the 21st century, not about what an investor could have done in the past. It has become conventional wisdom to observe that global markets are becoming more integrated.[8] As a result, some argue that the benefits of global bond diversification are declining. However, this is not necessarily the

---

[8] For an interesting overview of the evolution of globally integrated markets, see Jeffrey Sachs and Andrew Warner, "Economic Reform and the Process of Global Integration," Brookings Papers on Economic Activity, 1995. They observe that economic and financial integration was probably *greater* at the end of the 19th century than it is today. The degree of integration declined during the interim, but is now rising again. While the future seems to offer more integration, at present most investors in most countries still invest most of their wealth in domestic financial markets. This is formally known as "home country bias."

case in principle. "Integrated" need not mean "highly correlated." Moreover, it does not appear to be the case in practice yet. The risk reduction afforded by foreign bonds depends on the correlation between foreign and domestic bonds: the smaller the better. Critics of global bond diversification are implicitly arguing that closer economic and financial integration across political borders will result in higher bond market correlations. But are domestic and foreign bond market correlations rising through time? Let's examine the evidence during the period of greatest convergence of bond markets, the run-up to EMU.

Exhibits 18.12, 18.13, and 18.14 do not tell a story of generally rising international bond market correlations. They show rolling 3-year correlations of "domestic" and "foreign" bond returns from 1988 to 1999, each from a different national perspective. This was the period of the run-up to EMU, when we might expect to see the greatest increase in bond market integration.

Over this time period there have been periods of increasing correlation and periods of decreasing correlation in various markets, but there are no clear general trends. Japan is the exception, where the domestic market's correlation with foreign bonds has been falling. In fact, upon close examination the most recent data are more consistent with *declining* bond market correlations around the world. Upon reflection, this is not surprising, in light of the markedly asynchronous business cycles in Europe, the United States and Japan from 1995 to 1998. During this period the United States was enjoying a robust expansion, while Europe

EXHIBIT 18.12   Rating 3-Year Correlations: U.S. and Foreign Bonds

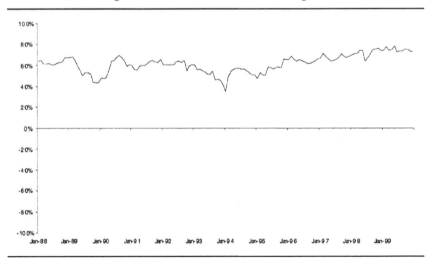

EXHIBIT 18.13   Rolling 3-Year Correlations: German and Foreign Bonds

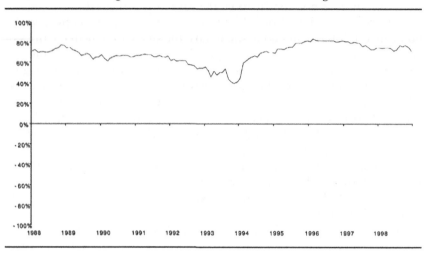

EXHIBIT 18.14   Rolling 3-Year Correlations: Japanese and Foreign Bonds

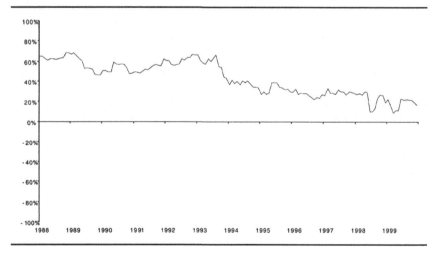

was experiencing a growth recession, and Japan persistently threatened to slip into a depression.

The view that bond correlations are rising around the world may be based on casual observation of the 1994–1995 period. Bond prices fell sharply during 1994, and recovered sharply during 1995, globally. However, inconveniently for the increasing correlation thesis, bond returns substantially diverged again in 1996, when the U.S. market dramatically underperformed the European markets and Japan on a currency-hedged basis. In fact, during 1996 the return spread between the best and worst performing bond markets was unusually large. This is a reminder that a plausible story and casual anecdotes are no substitute for examining the data.

The Effect of EMU

One group of bond markets that certainly has become more correlated is those in Europe. With the advent of EMU on January 1, 1999, 11 government bond markets effectively collapsed into one: a single market for euro-denominated bonds.[9] It is widely anticipated that Sweden, Denmark, and possibly the United Kingdom may join the euro "club" within a decade, raising the total membership to 15 countries. Other countries in Eastern Europe are likely to follow in time.

"Losing" foreign bond markets to EMU obviously reduces the potential efficacy of foreign diversification. One consolation is that the new euro bond market, representing 15 issuing countries, is far more liquid than any of the markets it replaces. Moreover, European spread product opportunities have increased substantially.

In this sense of creating deeper bond markets, the euro already has been a success. One of the reasons for establishing EMU was to create a competitor currency to the U.S. dollar. The economic benefits of this to Europe may be modest, but the political benefits are substantial. Europe wanted to assert that even though it has been in the shadow of the United States since World War II, it is now independent economically and financially. During the first nine months of EMU, 45% of all international bond issuance was denominated in euros, compared to 42% in dollars. Euro bond markets are roughly equal in market capitalization to U.S. bond markets, as of 2005.

The new euro bond market offers more diversity, including opportunities to add value using corporate bonds and asset-backed securities, in addition to its greater liquidity. Most commentators expect the euro market to become more diverse and liquid through time, becoming more like the U.S. bond market.

However, let us ignore all these benefits and ask, how much will the coming of EMU reduce the advantages of global bond diversification? We can only guesstimate the answer to that question, and to do so let's perform the following experiment. Suppose a broad EMU had been

---

[9] Various euro-denominated sovereign bonds trade at yield spreads to each other. These spreads change modestly, but for all practical purposes the Eurozone sovereign bond markets can be considered to be virtually perfectly correlated when constructing global portfolios.

formed in 1986. Specifically, suppose 15 countries' bond markets—Germany, France, Italy, the United Kingdom, the Netherlands, Belgium, Luxembourg, Spain, Portugal, Denmark, Greece, Sweden, Austria, Denmark, and Finland—had been replaced by the German market alone during the 1987 to 1999 period. From a U.S. investor's perspective, how much of the volatility reduction afforded by international diversification would have been sacrificed?

Exhibit 18.15 shows the risk and return combinations that historically accrued to a U.S. investor from 1987-1999 when all 15 European bond markets were available.[10] A U.S. only-portfolio had volatility of 4.5% per year. By placing 70% of the portfolio in the JP Morgan global ex-U.S. index, and 30% in the United States, that volatility could have been reduced to 3%. By way of comparison, Exhibit 18.15 also shows what would have happened if the 15 EMU countries' representation in the JP Morgan index had been replaced by Germany alone. The minimum volatility portfolio would have been marginally less diversified. The volatility of the minimum variance mixed portfolio, 3.4%, still reflects a substantial risk reduction compared to investing in the United States alone. The effect of broad EMU—15 countries, including the

EXHIBIT 18.15   Global Bond Diversification from a U.S. Investor's Perspective (1987–1999): Assumes Broad EMU

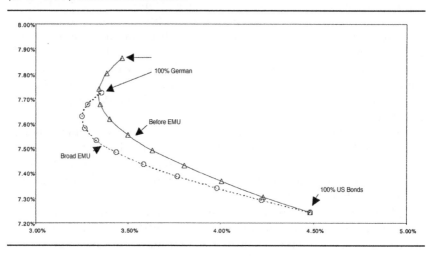

---

[10] The portfolio in Exhibit 18.15 uses the JP Morgan Government Bond Indices and weights. Otherwise, it is like that shown in Exhibit 18.7, which used the Salomon Smith Barney WGBI. Comparison of the two exhibits illustrates that the arguments for global diversification are robust to the way we measure returns

United Kingdom—would have been to increase the volatility of the minimum variance portfolio from 3.3% to 3.4%.

Based on this simulation, the most likely outcome seems to be that EMU will only modestly reduce the diversification benefits of foreign bond markets; it will by no means eliminate them. Moreover, EMU will increase an active manager's opportunity to find attractive "spread product," such as corporate and asset-backed bonds, in Europe—a potentially lucrative compensation for having fewer distinct sovereign bond opportunities within Europe.

A Caveat: Overstating Foreign Bonds' Contribution to Risk Reduction

This chapter looks only at bond portfolios. Few investors own only bonds. Instead, they hold mixed portfolios containing bonds plus, at least, domestic and foreign equities. They may also hold more exotic asset classes, such as real estate, private equity, and commodities (such as gold). If we were to examine foreign bonds' diversification potential when they are held as a part of much broader portfolios of assets, we might find they offer less diversification potential. (In fact, that is exactly what we would find.) So the reader should bear in mind that this chapter deals with foreign bonds *only* when they are held in pure bond portfolios. It is beyond our scope to consider foreign bonds' diversification potential in a broader allocation context.

CONCLUSION

Global bond management is changing rapidly, because it is highly sensitive to two of the most powerful forces influencing the investment management industry today: (1) the increasing sophistication of investing, in terms of the complexity of the instruments used and the analytical power needed to evaluate them and combine them into efficient portfolios; and (2) the globalization of all financial markets. That means that bond portfolio managers have had to acquire new skills, and the future promises no relief from this trend.

Global bond investors must consider all the nuances of domestic bond investing: duration, slope exposure, convexity, and credit issues. In addition they must also understand currencies, sovereign risks, and the differing legal and accounting frameworks that exist in different countries. And they must do all this in an environment that is in a state of flux. Investors should anticipate that the significant changes that occurred in the financial markets during the late years of the 20th century will have a major impact on the philosophy and process of global bond portfolio management during the early years of the 21st century. The most profound changes in the economic and financial landscape have occurred in Europe, but similar changes are occurring in Asia as well.

The first year of EMU was 1999. Yet in that year alone merger and acquisition activity in Europe doubled in value to about $1,200 billion USD. Initially merger activity was largely intranational: Olivetti trying to take over Telecom Italia; Banque National de Paris trying to take over Paribas and Societe Generale. But by the end of 1999, merger and acquisition activity had already spilled across borders—witness the U.K. firm Vodafone's hostile takeover offer for Mannesmann, a German company. That is a trend that is going to accelerate. It will cause new bond issuance, and changing corporate credit risks throughout Europe.

The creation of a single European market, without internal exchange rate risk, means there will be fewer, larger companies. Banks, hobbled by the Basle Capital adequacy regulations and competitive pressures of their own, are lending less. The result is an explosion of corporate bond issuance in Europe.

At the same time, a single European currency and European Central Bank has meant the opportunity to earn an excess return from forecasting interest rates and exchange rates has diminished. Global bond managers really have three currency blocs—dollar, euro, and yen—to choose from, plus emerging markets. The plethora of bond and currency choices that existed before EMU is gone. The implications for bond investors are clear. In the future, global managers will depend far less on top down macroeconomic forecasts, and far more on bottom up relative value analysis (including credit analysis) than they ever have in the past. Global bond investors will, in style anyway, begin more and more to look like U.S. bond investors.

EMU is only one global change that will radically change how global bond portfolios are managed. The late 1960s and 1970s were the era of the Great Inflation, worldwide. The 1980s and 1990s represented the corresponding Great Disinflation. The world now has lower interest rates, and more stable ones. Bond investment strategies that were successful during the inflationary 1970s or the disinflationary 1990s, may no longer work. But new strategies will replace them as the investing environment evolves.

As the world's markets become more integrated in the 21st century—a return to the conditions that prevailed at the beginning of the 20th century—foreign bonds are likely to be seen less as "exotic" instruments and more as part of the investment mainstream. Active managers will use foreign bonds tactically as substitutes for domestic bonds when they manage against a domestic bogey. Or foreign bonds will be used strategically, as a permanent part of an investor's asset allocation, to diversify across the world's three major currencies to secure the benefits of interest rate risk reduction.

To date it has been more common for investors to choose a domestic bond bogey, and permit their active managers to use foreign bonds tactically to add alpha to that bogey. In the future, however, as clients become accustomed to seeing foreign bonds in their portfolios, broader global bogeys are likely to become more common.

In addition to diversification, the main attraction of foreign bonds is that they expand a manager's investment universe. The information ratio achievable by a manager depends on his or her skill, on his or her scope to range over many investment opportunities, and on how correlated the active bets he or she takes are. Most financial markets are mostly efficient most of the time. Inefficiencies—opportunities to add excess return—develop sporadically and unpredictably. The lesson is clear: for a manager to improve his or her information ratio, he or she must search for opportunities anywhere in the world they can be found. Managers must be able to use whatever bond investing style is appropriate for the moment—top-down macroeconomic forecasting, bottom up relative value analysis, sector rotation, credit analysis, and convergence trades, to name just a few. Managers with more tools in their toolbox are likely to outperform a competitor who knows how to use only a few, even if that specialist knows how to use his or her few tools very well. That means neglecting foreign bonds, a whole world of potential opportunities, will almost certainly condemn a manager to the "also ran" category of bond managers in the 21st century.

CHAPTER 19

Managing a Multicurrency Bond Portfolio

Srichander Ramaswamy
Head of Investment Analysis
Bank for International Settlements, Basel, Switzerland

Robert Scott, CFA
Portfolio Manager
Bank for International Settlements, Basel, Switzerland

Investor groups who actively invest in the fixed income market include pension funds, central banks managing foreign exchange reserves, and private individuals seeking regular cash flows. Each of these investor groups may have different risk and return objectives for their investments. These objectives are usually expressed in terms of a benchmark, which then serves as the comparison portfolio to judge the portfolio manager's relative performance. When institutional investors debate the choice of an appropriate benchmark for their fixed income exposure, the relative merits of choosing a single currency versus a multicurrency bond benchmark usually comes up in the debate.

In general, diversifying investments into international bonds in a multicurrency portfolio is an ideal choice for the investor in search of additional sources of risk-reduction and return. Empirical evidence also supports the view that a well-diversified multicurrency bond portfolio generates improved risk-adjusted returns compared to investing only in

The views expressed here are those of the authors and not necessarily the views of the Bank for International Settlements.

the local currency denominated bonds. Based on this evidence, there is a growing trend among institutional investors to invest in a diversified multicurrency bond portfolio. Actively managing this multicurrency portfolio can be an additional source of return, and requires making decisions on interest rate positions for each country, and possibly currency positions, both of which should differ from the sensitivities of the benchmark. A useful approach to position taking is to first determine the macroeconomic forces that drive bond yields, measure market expectations of these variables, and then develop a forecast of these variables.

Managing a multicurrency bond portfolio, however, can be quite challenging due to differing time zones, local market structures, currency management requirements, and the need to monitor monetary policy expectations for different economies. Managing these added complexities requires a well-defined and disciplined investment process that is supported by adequate risk management and portfolio selection tools. In this chapter we address the following issues in the context of managing a multicurrency bond portfolio:

- Benefits of a multicurrency portfolio and the choice of an appropriate benchmark.
- Strategies that can be employed for taking active bets to beat the benchmark returns.
- How to develop models for measuring those active risks.
- Techniques that can be used for portfolio construction and rebalancing.

BENEFITS OF A MULTICURRENCY PORTFOLIO

Between 1995 and 2005, major bond markets have seen significant reductions in short-term interest rates in response (at least in part) to bursting asset bubbles in the United States and Japan. These reductions inevitably have been followed by the search for alternative assets, often called "the search for yield." Instead of increasing duration risk in order to increase returns, many investors have invested in global fixed income securities, which provide scope for introducing currency risk. Exhibit 19.1 shows the increase in international bond holdings of investors in G7 countries between 1997 and 2002.

An important argument that favors introducing international securities into a fixed income portfolio is that this can lead to diversification benefits, and perhaps also provide scope for return enhancement. This is because business cycles across countries are generally not synchronized, and this supports the argument that a well-diversified global portfolio can collect higher risk-adjusted returns than a purely domestic fixed

EXHIBIT 19.1 International Holdings of G7 Government Issued Long-Term Debt Securities in Millions of U.S. Dollars

	1997	2001	2002
Canada	178,077	197,456	212,626
France	105,201	330,614	475,868
Germany	446,277	802,951	1,026,701
Italy	162,562	427,682	583,597
Japan	144,846	168,384	159,613
U.K.	232,448	390,801	435,056
U.S.	885,718	1,663,438	1,885,577

Source: Table 13.2, IMF Coordinated Portfolio Investment Survey, http://www.imf.org/external/np/sta/pi/cpis.htm.

EXHIBIT 19.2 Correlations of Changes in 5-Year Government Benchmark Bond Yields, 1993 to 2004

	Germany	Canada	U.S.	Japan	U.K.	France	Italy
Germany	1.00	0.56	0.67	0.26	0.75	0.92	0.65
Canada		1.00	0.73	0.11	0.59	0.56	0.43
U.S.			1.00	0.13	0.62	0.66	0.47
Japan				1.00	0.10	0.16	0.09
U.K.					1.00	0.76	0.56
France						1.00	0.75
Italy							1.00

Source: Bloomberg, authors' calculations.

income portfolio. Although with the increase of globalization, business cycles in many developed nations have become more synchronized, presumably reducing the main benefit of international diversification, correlations still remain relatively low enough to provide sufficient benefits from diversification. Exhibit 19.2 shows that, although all G7 markets are positively correlated, there is sufficient scope for volatility reduction through the addition of government bonds from other countries.

In order to demonstrate the improved risk-adjusted returns achievable for hedged multicurrency bond portfolio, Exhibit 19.3 shows the total return volatility and risk-adjusted returns for multicurrency portfolios in different base currencies versus investing only in the local currency government bond markets. The figures in Exhibit 19.3 have been computed using market-capitalization-weighted JP Morgan global bond index returns.

EXHIBIT 19.3   Diversification Benefits for Various Base Currencies, 1993 to 2004

Base	Statistic	Global Hedged	Domestic
USD	Return volatility	3.24%	4.73%
	Sharpe ratio	0.94	0.52
JPY	Return volatility	3.17%	4.10%
	Sharpe ratio	0.96	0.91
EUR	Return volatility	3.22%	3.34%
	Sharpe ratio	1.02	0.83

Source: JP Morgan, Bloomberg, authors' calculations.

One can clearly infer from the historical performance reported in Exhibit 19.3 that the hedged multicurrency portfolios perform better on a risk-adjusted basis in all the base currencies investigated here. In general, the lower volatility of total returns of the hedged multicurrency portfolio can lead to lower expected returns for a multicurrency benchmark. However, one could consider introducing some currency risk into the multicurrency fixed income benchmark with the intention of improving the expected returns. In the next section, we describe how an investor can evaluate different alternatives when choosing a multicurrency benchmark for a fixed income portfolio.

Choosing an Appropriate Benchmark

The choice of a benchmark for a multicurrency bond portfolio should reflect the risk preferences of the investor, requiring that the appropriate set of countries, credit class, and maturity be carefully selected. For the sake of simplicity, only selection of sovereign benchmarks is discussed in this section. The decision to invest in corporate and other non-sovereign bonds can be considered separate from the decision to invest in multicurrency international bonds. The number of countries constituent in the benchmark should be numerous, but not to the point of adding unacceptable credit risk. As the number of investment-grade sovereign issuers is limited, the investor must decide on the greatest acceptable amount of credit risk to include in the benchmark.

In constructing the benchmark, the percentage share for each country can be weighted equally, by market capitalization, by *gross domestic product* (GDP) at purchasing power parity or by any other objective criteria. By far the most common method is market capitalization. However, the drawback with this approach is that the most indebted nations make up the largest percentage of the benchmark. For example, as of January 2005, Japan constituted over 29% of the JP Morgan Global Bond Index.

This may represent too much concentration in just one country, which is particularly undesirable if the goal is to increase diversification.

Next, benchmark duration must be considered. The appropriate range will vary according to the investor's risk preference. For central banks, which may have higher liquidity requirements than most investors, duration might be restricted to 2, whereas a pension fund investor might allow duration to lie in the range 5 to 7. One approach for deciding on the duration of the benchmark is to limit the value-at-risk that is acceptable to the investor and choose the duration risk that would give a low probability (perhaps 1%) of losing more than this amount.

The choice of the base currency for the benchmark is usually an easier decision to make. For instance, pension funds and other institutional investors would normally choose the currency of the liabilities that they are trying to immunize. Suppose the pension liabilities are in Swiss francs. Then the base currency of the multicurrency benchmark would also be in Swiss francs, although actual Swiss-franc-denominated securities in the benchmark might be very few. Central banks might choose the base currency as the one in which they hold their foreign exchange reserves, such as U.S. dollar, Japanese yen or euro. There is an increasing trend, however, for central banks to hold a basket of currencies. This may lead to the choice, which is similar for international institutions, of using a basket of currencies such as the *Special Drawing Rights* (SDR) as the base currency. The base currency in the case of an unhedged portfolio (described in more detail below) is just a unit of account for performance and valuation. In the case of a hedged portfolio, all currency positions are hedged with FX swaps, FX forwards, futures, or currency swaps into the base currency.

There are many global fixed income benchmarks available to the investor, many of which include some common subindices (i.e., only 1–3-year maturities, etc.). The investor must weigh the pros and cons of using a readily available benchmark versus a customized benchmark. Country weights in these benchmarks are typically based on the market size of outstanding debt, meaning more indebted countries hold higher weightings in the index, which may not be desirable. The portfolio manager as part of the active process could consider underweighting any country that might be considered too heavily weighted in the benchmark. This type of decision underlines the difficulty of differentiating between benchmark decisions and decisions that are better made by the active portfolio manager. If the investor is making too many exclusions or modifications, particularly if they are thought to be temporary, then these should be reconsidered in favor of allowing the active portfolio manager, who is presumably better able to market time, to make these decisions. Some commonly used global bond indexes include those listed in Exhibit 19.4.

EXHIBIT 19.4   Common Global Benchmarks in USD (Unhedged)

Index	Number of countries	Return 1993–2004	Sharpe Ratio
JP Morgan Global Bond Index	14	7.20%	0.50
Citigroup World Government Bond Index	22	7.28%	0.51
Merrill Lynch Global Sovereign Broad Market Plus Index	31	7.32%	0.52

Source: Bloomberg, authors' calculations.

Hedged versus Unhedged Benchmarks

One can usually distinguish between two general classes of multicurrency benchmarks: hedged and unhedged. In a fully hedged multicurrency benchmark having, say, the euro as the base currency, all non-euro denominated bonds will be fully hedged back into euros. This means that exchange-rate fluctuations do not generally affect the benchmark returns, but relative interest rate movements do. In the unhedged multicurrency benchmark, the foreign currency exposures will not be hedged and, as a result, the benchmark returns will be driven by both the interest rate movements and the exchange rate movements. However, for both types of benchmarks, there will be only one reporting or base reference currency. Multicurrency benchmarks can also have a basket of currencies, such as the SDR, as their reference currency.

While debating the choice between hedged versus unhedged benchmarks, both intuition and empirical evidence would suggest that currency risk cannot be considered as a *systematic* risk for which the investor would normally earn additional expected returns (or risk premia). Intuitively, two investors with different base currencies cannot both invest in the others' currency and both expect positive returns. However, this is not entirely true due to a result known as Siegel's Paradox, which shows that because the reference currency is different, any percentage gain by one currency is not perfectly offset by the same percentage loss in another.[1] Black[2] and Solnik[3] argue that it is this small

---

[1] Siegel's paradox identifies a small difference in expected returns for investors of different base currency even if the expected exchange rate distribution is the same. For example, a euro-based investor and a U.S. dollar based investor both expect the euro to move from 1.30 to 1.40 dollars per euro. For the euro-based investor who buys dollars, this translates to a loss of 7.14% (1/1.4 ÷ 1/1.3 − 1) while for the same currency movement, there is a gain of 7.69% for the dollar based investor who buys euros (1.4/1.3 − 1).

[2] Fischer Black, "Equilibrium Exchange Rate Hedging," *Journal of Finance* 45, no. 3 (July 1990), pp. 899–907.

[3] Bruno Solnik, "Currency Hedging and Siegel's Paradox: On Black's Universal Hedging Rule," *Review of International Economics* 1, no. 2 (June 1993), pp. 180–187.

incongruity that allows the investor to gain a small risk premium from having open currency positions in the portfolio. Despite the argument that suggests investors may collect a small risk premium from holding unhedged currency positions, the empirical evidence strongly favors hedging currency risk. A simple exercise comparing returns for a hedged and unhedged global bond portfolio in Exhibit 19.5 with U.S. dollars as the reference currency shows that the Sharpe ratio for the hedged portfolio is much higher than that of the unhedged portfolio.

These results lend evidence to the theory that currency risk is generally an unrewarded risk. Open currency positions add volatility to the portfolio without adding any appreciable return. However, some research shows that risk premiums can be earned on currency positions when the relative exchange rates are far away from purchasing power parity.[4] These conflicting results suggest that currency risk is something better taken as part of the active portfolio management process as opposed to part of benchmark selection process.

The decision to hedge or not to hedge a multicurrency benchmark is not simply a yes or no decision. In general, one could choose to hedge only a portion of the currency exposure. The percentage of currency exposure that is hedged is often called the *hedge ratio*. A simple exercise of varying the hedge ratio, however, shows that the more hedged the benchmark is, the better is the risk-adjusted returns (see Exhibit 19.6).

The second decision with respect to hedging concerns the type of hedge. Most common hedged multicurrency indices are calculated using monthly forward currency hedges. To replicate this, the investor can simply hedge the spot value of the position with a short-term FX swap or outright forward, where the nominal value of the bond is hedged

EXHIBIT 19.5   Global Government Bond Portfolio Returns Hedged Versus Unhedged, 1993 to 2004

	USD Treasuries	USD Hedged	USD Unhedged
Average Return (1993–2004)	6.44%	7.1%	7.2%
Sharpe ratio	0.50	0.93	0.50
Average Return (1998–2004)	6.33	6.12%	7.46%
Sharpe ratio	0.55	0.85	0.56

Source: JP Morgan and authors' calculations. Average returns are calculated as the average monthly return over the period times 12.

---

[4] See Bernard Dumas, and Bruno Solnik, "The World Price of Foreign Exchange Risk," *Journal of Finance* 50, no. 2 (June 1995), pp. 445–479.

EXHIBIT 19.6   Performance of Global Bond Portfolios in U.S. Dollar with Varying
Hedge Ratios, 1993 to 2004

Hedge Ratio	Return	Sharpe Ratio
100%	7.06%	0.93
75%	7.08%	0.85
50%	7.11%	0.72

Source: JP Morgan, authors' calculations.

against movements in the spot exchange rate. For example, if an investor buys 10 million euro of par value 10-year German bunds, then the investor can hedge it back into U.S. dollars by buying a U.S. dollar FX swap for one-month in maturity.

The choice of the benchmark is without a doubt the most important decision for the investor. Once the range of countries, maturity, credit quality, and hedging method is decided, the investor must decide whether to simply attempt to replicate the returns of the benchmark or to manage actively against the benchmark with the intention of adding value. If the active management route is taken, it is important to remember that most of the returns will still come from the choice of the benchmark, and a much smaller portion of the returns will come from active portfolio management. In the next section, we explore some popular ways of taking active positions against the benchmark in order to generate some excess returns versus the benchmark.

TAKING ACTIVE RISK AGAINST THE BENCHMARK

Actively managing a multicurrency fixed income portfolio entails varying the risk exposures of the portfolio from those of the benchmark. The main element of active risk is market timing, where the portfolio manager varies the risk exposure of the portfolio relative to the benchmark for a period of time in order to benefit from market movements. This can be done by either taking interest rate or currency positions. Security selection can also play an important role in enhancing portfolio returns through the use of relative valuation tools. One area of contention in active management, however, is the assumption of systematic risks that are not contained in the benchmark (e.g., adding corporate bonds to a portfolio with a government bond benchmark). While there are many approaches to making active decisions, the proven drivers of returns to fixed income instruments are mostly macroeconomic variables. Technical and quantitative analysis can often detect short-term anomalies in pricing, but for investment horizons applicable to the average institutional investor, taking active duration, yield curve, and country exposures requires a disciplined investment process supported by macroeconomic forecasts. A brief discussion of market timing, security selection, and benchmark shifting is given below.

Market timing entails varying the systematic risk exposure of the portfolio to take advantage of anticipated market movements. For a fixed income portfolio, the most common way of doing this is by changing the duration, or interest rate sensitivity of the portfolio. For example, suppose a simple benchmark is equally weighted U.S. dollar, euro and yen, all hedged into U.S. dollars. If the portfolio manager believes that yields on the yen-denominated bonds will rise and dollar yields will fall, he or she can increase duration in the U.S. dollar portion and decrease duration in the Japanese yen portion so there is a bullish exposure in the U.S. dollar portion and a bearish exposure in the yen portion. Another example of market timing is the varying of the currency exposure of the portfolio. In the equally weighted portfolio, let us assume that the portfolio manager believes that the yen will appreciate versus the U.S. dollar. Instead of hedging the yen portion of the investments back into U.S. dollars, the portfolio manager could just partially hedge (or abstain from hedging altogether). Because the unit of account in this example is U.S. dollars, if the exchange rate of U.S. dollars per yen rises, the dollar value of the unhedged yen-denominated bonds will rise relative to the benchmark portion of yen-denominated bonds (because the benchmark currency exposures are hedged back into U.S. dollars). By continuously varying the risk exposures over time in anticipation of market movements, the portfolio manager can add value to the returns of the portfolio versus those of the benchmark. This obviously requires that the predictions of movements in interest rates or currencies are more often right than wrong. In the next section we look at some common tools that can be used to improve the chances of correctly anticipating market moves.

Another active management tool available to the portfolio manager is that of *security selection*. By this, is meant the process of distinguishing between two similar securities, searching for the one that will provide slightly better value over the long run. For example, suppose the portfolio manager is selecting Treasury securities for the U.S. dollar portion of a multicurrency portfolio. The portfolio manager currently holds a 4.5% May 2007 bond yielding 3.4%. By selling this bond and buying a similar 3.75% May 2007 bond yielding 3.44%, the portfolio manager may be able to add some value to the portfolio. Since the bonds have different coupons, but the same maturity, it is possible that the extra convexity for the 4.5% bond accounts for the 4 basis point-lower yield, but this is the evaluation that the portfolio manager must make to determine if in fact added value is worth the switch. This process is often called *rich/cheap analysis*.

Active risk is generally not considered as the prolonged addition of systematic risks to the portfolio. Systematic risks, such as duration, credit, prepayment risk, and the like are nondiversifiable risks that provide additional returns over the long run, and are better made as part of the benchmark decision. For example, an active portfolio manager who manages against a 1–3-year government bond benchmark could shift the portfolio to 50% credit (e.g., corporate or agency bonds), which earns a risk premium over the long run due to their higher probability of default. By choosing a benchmark that has 50% exposure to government bonds and 50% exposure to credits, the selector of the benchmark could in theory have also made this "active" decision of not being fully invested in government bonds. Market timing, however, does entail the temporary assumption of more systematic risks when it would be deemed beneficial to do so. Active risk could then be qualified by specifying that on average over a sufficiently long period, the portfolio should have the same risk exposures as the benchmark. For example, over a sufficiently long performance period, say five years, the average duration deviation versus the benchmark would be considered nonactive risk or *benchmark shifting*. This is because the portfolio manager has simply taken more systematic risk on average, which is the goal of the benchmark selection process. The same case can be made for any other type of systematic risk, such as credit and convexity (callable and MBS bonds).

Active portfolio management is generally concerned with market timing and security selection. For the multicurrency portfolio, market timing generally involves taking either interest rate positions or currency positions. They are discussed in more detail in the next section.

Taking Interest Rate Risk

The simplest form of market timing involves varying the portfolio duration relative to the benchmark in order to benefit from anticipated changes in yields. Increasing the interest rate sensitivity can be achieved by selling lower duration bonds and buying higher duration bonds, thus increasing the duration of the portfolio. For a multicurrency portfolio, this is in practice done on a country by country basis. For example, if the yield on yen-denominated bonds is expected to rise, then the duration of the yen bonds, relative to the duration of yen bonds in the benchmark, should be shortened. Therefore, a proper understanding of the drivers of yields for each country in the benchmark is needed. A useful approach to taking positions involves (1) understanding the variables which drive interest rates; (2) estimating the market expectations for these variables; and (3) developing a forecast for these variables. With these three steps accomplished, it is possible to form a view as to the likely direction of interest rates and bond yields for each country in the benchmark and to position the portfolio to best benefit from these anticipated moves. In this section, we look at some practical tools that can be used to accomplish each step.

While there is much debate about the specific factors that actually drive bond yields, the generally accepted categories of variables are consistent with basic macroeconomic theory. The Fisher Hypothesis states that the nominal yield of a bond is the sum of the *expected* real rate of interest and the *expected* rate of inflation over the life of the bond. The current commonly held notion is a slight variation on the *Fisher hypothesis*, arguing that the nominal rate of interest is the sum of the expected real rate plus the expected inflation rate plus a risk premium which varies according to the uncertainty of inflation and real rates. The driver of very short-term nominal interest rates is the central bank which is usually charged with maintaining price stability by raising or lowering the overnight lending rate of interest, effectively increasing or decreasing the real rate of interest, with the eventual goal of moderating price inflation to some desired level.

Fleming and Remolona show that there are at least three categories of economic data that have a measurable impact on bond yields in the United States—labor market variables, aggregate demand variables, and price level variables.[5] The first two categories are commonly associated with influencing the real rate of interest, while the third is associated with the expected inflation component of the Fisher Hypothesis. Within these three categories, surprises in the following statistical data releases were found to have significant effects on U.S. bond yields:

- Consumer Price Index
- Durable Goods Orders
- Housing Starts
- Jobless Rate
- Nonfarm Payrolls
- Producer Price Index
- Leading Economic Indicator
- Retail Sales

---

[5] Michael Fleming and Eli Remolona, "Price Formation and Liquidity in the U.S. Treasury Market: The Response to Public Information," *Journal of Finance* 54, no. 5 (October 1999), pp. 1901–1915.

Some active managers position the portfolio to benefit from announcement effects, or the almost instantaneous yield changes after economic data, especially for data releases such as nonfarm payrolls. Given the high amount of seasonal adjustment,[6] noise, and other transient effects, it may not be a practical approach to base an investment strategy on small deviations in month-to-month data releases. Alternatively, a longer horizon (such as 3- to 6-months) can be used for position taking where no single economic data release dominates returns, but the general evolution of the economy and its implications for real rates and inflation are the real drivers instead.

For each country included in the multicurrency benchmark, the economic variables that are associated with yield moves must be identified. Suppose the portfolio manager identifies five variables for driving U.S. Treasury yields, namely, inflation, GDP growth, monetary policy, labor growth and government debt. The variables that are subsequently identified for driving Japanese or German bond yields may be similar, but have different weights or levels of importance. The challenge for the portfolio manager then is to develop an understanding of the variables that drive bond yields for each country over the horizon that he or she is targeting. If the manager has little expertise in one or several of the countries in the benchmark, a neutral position for that country in the portfolio relative to the benchmark might be the appropriate decision.

Once the driving variables are identified and the relative importance of each is established, the portfolio manager must gather market intelligence indicating what market expectations for these variables are. There are some basic steps the portfolio manager can follow in order to produce a credible estimate of market expectations with which his or her views can be compared. Some tools for measuring the market expectations are discussed in the next section.

Measuring Market Expectations

Measuring market expectations can be rather difficult to do accurately. The most common approach is the survey method, where many market participants and observers are asked their expectation for a key economic variable over some horizon. As these participants respond to the survey, a general consensus emerges before the release of the number. If the data release is as expected, there should be, in theory, only a small

---

[6] Between 1994 and 2004, the average seasonal adjustment to each monthly change in nonfarm payrolls was 715,000 while the average seasonally adjusted change in nonfarm payrolls was 151,000. In other words, the average adjustment was over 4½ times the value of the reported figure, leaving substantial room for noise from the seasonal adjustment process.

market move if any. Often, however, when the data release matches survey numbers, there can still be substantial movements, suggesting that surveys of "experts" may not always capture the market expectation.

Expectations for some variables, however, can be imputed directly from asset prices. The most common variable measured with this approach is monetary policy. In the United States, federal funds futures give an indication of the market expectation for the federal funds rate some months later (reasonable liquidity can be found as far out as six months). For extracting market expectations further out in time, prices of eurodollar futures contracts are often used. The information from these futures contracts can be much more difficult to interpret, however, as they contain a banking deposit credit premium and a term premium (because they are for three month deposits and we are interested in overnight rates). For measuring expectations over a large number of countries, it is quite likely that money market forward rates would need to be used. A quick and simple method for adjusting for the bias in forward rates would be to subtract the average difference between the forward rate (e.g., overnight rate in six months) and the realized spot rate.

While survey methods are commonly used for growth forecasts, there has been a fair amount of research showing that the slope of the yield curve (i.e., the difference in yield between a long maturity and short maturity bond) has good predictive powers for growth several quarters in the future. This relationship, then, can be exploited by using the slope of the yield curve to impute the market expected rate of growth over the next several quarters. For example, an inverted yield curve (where long-term yields are lower than short-term yields) can indicate that the rate of growth might be expected to go negative over the subsequent few quarters.

Market expectations for inflation can be imputed from inflation indexed government bonds. These are available for the United States, United Kingdom, Canada, Japan, France, and several other countries. The difference in yield between a nominal bond and inflation indexed bond of the same maturity can be used as a quick approximation to the average expected rate of inflation over the life of the bond. Most researchers suggest that there is a risk premium incorporated in the nominal bond, and hence, the imputed "expected" inflation may be biased. "Breakeven" inflation is a more common term used, which is simply the average rate of inflation that will ensure the holding period return for both the nominal and inflation indexed bonds to be the same. Even if there is a risk premium in inflation indexed bonds, it is not likely that it varies from day to day. Therefore changes in the breakeven inflation rate are likely to provide good estimates of changes in market expectations of inflation.

After market expectations for the variables that drive yield changes are obtained, the portfolio manager can then develop an independent (and hopefully superior) forecast for these variables.

Developing Forecasts

Once the market estimates of the relevant variables have been established, it is necessary for the portfolio manager to take a view on these estimates. It is the difference in these views that will determine what risk deviations should be taken in the portfolio. The view on future monetary policy is probably the most important decision to take, because market perceptions of future short rates contribute significantly to influencing the entire yield curve. Some tools that can be used to develop a view on monetary policy and support the active portfolio management process are described below.

Developing a "Policy Rule"

Taylor suggested that a useful step in monetary policy transparency was the use of a policy rule.[7] For a central bank such as the U.S. Federal Reserve, which has a two-pillar system targeting price stability and growth, the optimal policy rate *could* be described with a simple rule. Taylor argued that the nominal target rate would equal the sum of some fixed growth rate, say 2%, plus the rate of inflation, plus the average of the inflation gap and the GDP gap. His specification was the following:

$$R_{\text{policy}} = 2\% + \pi_t + \frac{1}{2}(\pi_t - \pi_*) + \frac{1}{2}(\text{GDPgap}_t)$$

where π_t is the current inflation rate at time t, and π_* is the target inflation rate.

Taylor noted that this simple formulation coincidentally described monetary policy from the mid-1980s up until the early 1990s. Unfortunately, policy has deviated from this simple rule many times since the publishing of this paper, but still many market participants use the prescribed rate as an indication of the "neutral" policy rate. For market participants without much expertise in monetary policy, a rough approximation for rates could be established using some type of rule as this. Because the Federal Reserve, however, does not target a particular level of inflation, and it does not explicitly give equal importance to the inflation gap and the GDP gap in its deliberations, it might be possible to improve on the original specification through some simple optimization.

---

[7] John Taylor, "Discretion versus Policy Rules in Practice," *Carnegie–Rochester Conference Series on Public Policy* 39 (1993), pp. 195–214.

Estimating the "target inflation" measure, as well as the fixed growth rate and the weights for the GDP gap and inflation gap might create a potentially better fitting policy rule. The 2% growth rate specified by Taylor might actually be more appropriate at 2.2% (or any other number for that matter). Because many central banks do not target any stated level of inflation, it might be possible that there is some "imputed" target that no one individual is actually aware of. Finally, there is no reason to assume that an equal weighting for the inflation gap and the growth gap is appropriate. It is quite possible that one is more important than the other. One will then have to estimate these unknown variables in the equation given below to better explain short-term interest rates:

$$R_{\text{target}} = \alpha + \pi_t + \beta_1(\pi_t - \beta_2) + (1 - \beta_1)(\text{GDPgap}_t) + \varepsilon_t$$

In the above equation, α is the constant real rate, π_t is the rate of inflation, β_1 is an estimated coefficient for the weight to be placed in the inflation gap, and β_2 is the estimated target inflation rate.

The calculation of the GDP gap in itself can also be difficult. The GDP gap is calculated as the current level of real GDP divided by potential GDP minus one. Potential, however, is a theoretical construct. Two popular solutions usually present themselves to estimate potential GDP. In the United States, for instance, one option is to use a readily usable estimate for potential GDP provided by the Congressional Budget Office. The second option is to estimate it with the use of a filter, such as the Hodrick-Prescott filter.[8] This can prove more fruitful especially when repeating the exercise for several countries.

One has to keep in mind, however, that there is no certainty that this helps "forecast" future policy moves. Nevertheless, a fitted Taylor rule would provide an improved forecast of the future policy moves compared to the original Taylor rule. Although originally intended to describe monetary policy in the United States, the Taylor rule has been found to be a fairly accurate description for monetary policy in Europe as well.[9] Some market participants have begun to look at other drivers of monetary policy to include them in their forecasting rule. These indicators fall under the realm of monetary and financial conditions indices.

---

[8] The *Hodrick-Prescott filter* is a noise filter commonly used for the calculation of potential or trend GDP. The results are comparable to a centred moving average. For more on the topic, see Robert Hodrick and Edward Prescott, "Postwar U.S. Business Cycles: An Empirical Investigation," *Journal of Money, Credit, and Banking* 29, no. 1, (February 1997), pp. 1–16.

[9] See, Stefan Gerlach and Gert Schnabel, "The Taylor Rule and Interest Rates in the EMU Area," Bank for International Settlements Working Papers, No. 73 (August 1999).

Monetary/Financial Conditions and Other Macro Variables

Central banks, particularly those of economies with large external trade balances, often jointly focus on inflation and the exchange rate. In the 1990s for example, the Bank of Canada moved towards tracking what was known as a *Monetary Conditions Index* (MCI), which captured the "interest rate like" properties of currency movements. A 3% rise in the currency for a country with an open economy with a large import/export sector can be likened to a 1% rise in interest rates because both import prices and exports fall, and these together act as a drag on growth. Including some type of MCI into a forecast can improve explanatory power of actual changes in monetary policy.

In the case of Canada, the MCI has been calculated as follows:

$$\Delta \text{MCI} = \frac{1}{4}\Delta \text{CAD} + \frac{3}{4}\Delta 90 \text{ day CP}$$

In this equation, CAD is the Canadian-U.S. dollar exchange rate and 90 day CP is the interest rate on 90-day commercial paper. The Bank of Canada deemed the coefficients of ¼ for the exchange rate and ¾ for the interest rate appropriate, but there is no reason why these cannot be estimated parameters in a Taylor rule type of model.

While it would be naïve to presume that the use of a fitted Taylor rule and the possible inclusion of some type of monetary/financial conditions index will give better than market average predictions for changes in short-term interest rates, it can greatly assist in a forming a consistent approach to forecasting monetary policy particularly across multiple countries.

Forecasts of GDP growth are often done piecemeal, in that each component of growth is dealt with separately using leading data such as surveys of business conditions. In the United States, Japan, and Europe, these advance surveys (such as the IFO in Germany, the Tankan in Japan and ISM in the United States) can help forecast each element of GDP growth. It should be pointed out that these surveys are not of market participants, but of participants in the real economy. Obviously, using the advance data alone will not provide a good forecast for growth that will be much different from market expectations. Nevertheless, it is a starting point for some source data that might be used either in a qualitative assessment, or a quantitative forecasting model.

Developing accurate and reliable forecasts of the variables that drive bond yields is without question the most difficult and most important element in successfully outperforming a benchmark. The need to do this across multiple countries for a multicurrency portfolio greatly complicates the task. Once the portfolio manager is comfortable with both the measure of market expectations, and his or her own forecast for these variables, the next step is to take a position in the portfolio.

Forming a View on Interest Rates

Using some of the tools mentioned above, it is possible to develop a forecast for several of the important economic variables that tend to influence the changes in bond yields. By comparing the forecast values with either the surveyed or otherwise measured market expectations of these variables, it is possible to gauge the likely changes in bond yields should the forecast prove to be correct. The difference between the portfolio manager's forecast and the market expectations will determine the meaning of the forecast with respect to changes in bond yields. This relationship could be implemented in a quantitative manner, where a model is specified for the driver of bond returns for the particular country. This quantitative relationship could take the form where the forecast of the change in the 2-year yield is a function of the following variables:

- Forecast of the monetary policy changes in the next six months
- Forecast of inflation surprises
- Forecast of the GDP gap
- Forecast of the government deficit

If the portfolio manager's forecast for these variables turns out to be correct, he or she might expect to have yields move in the direction and magnitude that the model might suggest. This approach might also be implemented in a more qualitative way. For instance, the portfolio manager might believe that monetary policy will move in line with what the market expects, but that the GDP gap will close faster than is expected by the market. While the monetary policy prediction suggests no action, the GDP forecast implies a rise in real rates, meaning that nominal rates will rise. As a result, the duration for that particular country could be shorter in the portfolio than in the benchmark.

While forecasting interest rate changes presents many challenges in a multicurrency portfolio, modeling changes in *foreign exchange* (FX) rates can be even more challenging. Both in the case of hedged and unhedged multicurrency benchmarks, the decision must be made as to whether or not to take an active currency exposure in the portfolio relative to the benchmark. The next section addresses this decision.

Taking Currency Risk

A typical multicurrency portfolio, whether hedged or unhedged, usually allows for taking FX exposures versus the benchmark. Given the high volatility of many FX pairs, currency positions can add considerable risk to the portfolio, often more than interest rate risk. While discussing the benchmark selection process, we noted that for the most part the FX market is a zero-sum game (except for the gains from Siegel's Paradox). However, this does not rule out the possibility of adding value through market timing of currency positions. There are two typical approaches to forming a view on the currency markets, namely fundamental, which is based on macroeconomic factors, and technical. Much research has shown the significant relationship between currency movement and macroeconomic releases. In addition, technical analysis can potentially add value through filter and momentum trading rules. A dedicated active currency strategy that is independent of the underlying assets, often called a *currency overlay*, has become fairly popular, but is beyond the scope of this chapter.

Macroeconomic Effects

Devising an active strategy for currency position-taking can be done with a similar process to interest rate position-taking. First, the drivers of exchange rates must be determined, then market expectations measured, and finally the difference between the forecast and market expectations will determine the position to be taken. In this section we will briefly discuss some variables that can be used for devising a strategy to take on currency risk. The starting point for any macroeconomic analysis of exchange rates is inevitably the *purchasing power parity* (PPP). This approach is based on the "law of one price," arguing that a basket of goods should cost the same in different countries in terms of a common currency. This means that inflation in one country should be offset by a corresponding decline in the exchange rate.

Empirical evidence is mixed on the predictive power of PPP for exchange rate moves. Clark et al. cite various studies indicating that it can take between three and 12 years for exchange rates to revert to purchasing power parity.[10] By calculating PPP based only on tradable goods allows for some improvement in using PPP for forecasting exchange rates as discussed in Xu.[11] The implication is that inflation differentials are a major factor in driving movements in exchange rates over the long run. Trade balance is also often cited as a driver of FX moves. However, like PPP measures, it cannot be shown to drive FX moves over short- or medium-

---

[10] Peter Clark, Leonardo Bartolini, Tamin Bayoumi, and Steven Symansky, "Exchange Rates and Economic Fundamentals," International Monetary Fund, Occasional Paper 115 (December 1994).

[11] Zhenhui Xu, "Purchasing Power Parity, Price Indices, and Exchange Rate Forecasts," *Journal of International Money and Finance* 22 (February 2003), pp. 105–130.

time periods. Capital market returns can also be regarded as likely drivers of exchange rates. For example, given the high degree of capital mobility, often strong performing equity markets can be highly correlated with FX movements. While there are numerous data releases that have been shown to move FX rates, the general categories are related to either the "law of one price" (i.e., PPP), trade balance, or capital flows.[12]

Technical Trading

Many participants in the FX markets are quick to point out that there seems to be a disproportionately higher number of technical analysts in this field than in other markets. It may come as no surprise then that some researchers have found evidence of excess returns from technical trading models. For instance, Levich and Thomas show that excess returns could be generated by market timing of hedging decisions using technical trading rules.[13] Momentum-based and filter models are common for anticipating exchange rate movements as part of active portfolio management. The weak form market efficiency hypothesis, however, argues that price movements cannot be inferred from past price movements. Despite this evidence, this area is being constantly researched with the intention of finding potential prescriptions for trading rules. Whether one will be found is open to speculation. But one thing that can be said with regards to technical analysis is that a trader who discovers an exploitable pattern in FX data is best served by revealing this information to no one.

MEASURING ACTIVE RISK

In the previous section we described techniques for forming views that would allow the portfolio manager to take active risk versus the benchmark with the intention of generating returns in excess of the benchmark. The active risk that is taken versus the benchmark has to be measured and monitored in order to ensure that the portfolio manager's actions are within the permissible portfolio management guidelines. In this section we develop a risk model to identify the risk exposures and to quantify the relative risk versus the benchmark.

---

[12] For some releases that influence the U.S. dollar/euro exchange rate, see Gabriele Galati and Corinne Ho, "Macroeconomic News and the euro/dollar Exchange Rate," Bank for International Settlement Working Papers, No. 105 (December 2001).

[13] Richard Levich and Lee Thomas, "Internationally Diversified Bond Portfolios: The Merits of Active Currency Risk Management," National Bureau of Economic Research Working Paper 4340 (April 1993).

At a conceptual level, the risk model serves to quantify the relative risk of the portfolio versus a benchmark by identifying a set of risk factors that influence the value of the portfolio and the benchmark. However, for many portfolio managers the risk model also plays an important role in the portfolio construction and rebalancing processes. Furthermore, the risk exposures as measured by the risk model can also serve as a valuable tool for communicating to the client how active risks were taken to add value over the benchmark. To ensure that the risk model can serve all these purposes, it is important that the risk model is kept conceptually simple but yet is able to measure the risks reasonably well. A risk model is deemed to measure risks reasonably well if the estimate of the average ex ante risk measure over a certain time period serves as a good approximation to the ex post risk measure estimated over the same time period. The risk measure that is usually used for making this comparison is the tracking error between the portfolio and the benchmark. Tracking error is defined as the annualized volatility of excess returns between the portfolio and benchmark. The risk model in conjunction with the current risk factor exposures can be used to make a forecast of this excess return volatility, and the forecast of the excess return volatility is referred to as the ex ante tracking error.

Considering that one of the functions of a risk model is to identify the sources of mismatch between the portfolio and the benchmark returns, our first objective will be to select a set of risk factors that can explain changes to the mark to market value of the portfolio. For a multicurrency bond portfolio, an obvious choice for these risk factors would be yield curve shape changes and changes in foreign exchange rate. For modeling yield curve shape changes, it turns out that choosing two or three yield curve risk factors can provide a good trade-off between complexity and accuracy.[14] The risk modeled by the yield curve shape changes and changes to foreign exchange rate is usually referred to as the systematic risk component. In developing the risk model, we will restrict our attention to modeling only the systematic risk component and work with weekly time series data.

Developing a Risk Model

To develop an appropriate risk model for managing a multicurrency bond portfolio, we first have to identify a set of risk factors that model changes

---

[14] For references on multifactor risk models for bond portfolio management see, for example, Lev Dynkin, Jay Hyman, and Wei Wu, "Multi-Factor Risk Models and Their Applications," and Robert C. Kuberek, "Term Structure Factor Models," in Frank J. Fabozzi (ed.), *Professional Perspectives on Fixed Income Portfolio Management*, vol. 2 (Hoboken, NJ: John Wiley & Sons, 2001).

in the mark to market value of the portfolio. We mentioned that yield curve shape changes are important risk factors that influence the portfolio's mark to market value. Given this observation, the question of interest to us is the following: What shape changes need to be taken into account so that a significant part of the valuation changes are explained? To address this question, let us consider an arbitrary shape change to the par yield curve over any one-week time period which is given below:

$$\Delta y_i(t) = y_i(t) - y_i(t-1), \quad i = 1, 2, ..., n \qquad (19.1)$$

In equation (19.1) $\Delta y_i(t)$ denotes the change in par yield over a 1-week period at the ith maturity point of the yield curve. Let us assume that the par yield curve is sampled at the following maturities: 1 year, 2 years, 3 years, 5 years, 7 years, 10 years, 15 years, 20 years, and 30 years. For such a sampling we will have n equal to 9 in equation (19.1). Suppose we wish to model the yield changes at the 9 different maturities using three risk factors. Then the yield changes can be represented in terms of these three risk factors, denoted $F_1(i)$, $F_2(i)$, and $F_3(i)$, as follows:

$$\Delta y_i(t) = a(t)F_1(i) + b(t)F_2(i) + c(t)F_3(i) + e_i(t), \quad i = 1, 2, ..., n \quad (19.2)$$

In equation (19.2) $e_i(t)$ denotes the error term at the ith maturity and $a(t)$, $b(t)$, and $c(t)$ are the coefficients associated with the risk factors at the given time t. If the risk factors are known, the coefficients associated with the risk factors for any given time t can be determined by solving a set of equations that minimize the sum of the squared error terms $e_i(t)$. The solution to this problem formulation can be represented compactly in matrix notation as given below:

$$\vec{x}(t)^T = (F^T F)^{-1} F^T \Delta \vec{y}(t)^T \qquad (19.3)$$

In equation (19.3) the matrix F and vectors $\vec{x}(t)$ and $\Delta \vec{y}(t)$ are given by

$$F = \begin{bmatrix} F_1(i) & F_2(i) & F_3(i) \end{bmatrix}$$

$$\vec{x}(t) = \begin{bmatrix} a(t) & b(t) & c(t) \end{bmatrix}$$

$$\Delta \vec{y}(t) = \begin{bmatrix} \Delta y_1(t) & \Delta y_2(t) & ... & \Delta y_9(t) \end{bmatrix}$$

We have still not indicated how to choose the three risk factors for modeling yield curve changes. One method that can be used is to carry out a principal component decomposition of the yield changes across different maturities over some historical time period, and then to choose the first three principal components as the risk factors. In practice, the chosen risk factors need not be principal components. The advantage of using principal components as the risk factors is that for a given number of risk factors, principal components explain more variance in the data set over the in-sample period than any other set of risk factors. In general, the explanatory power of the principal components will decline out-of-sample. Moreover, principal components change over time and the principal components of yield curves of different countries will have different shapes. As a consequence, principal components sometimes lack an intuitive interpretation of the yield curve shape change they model. To avoid this problem we can consider using a fixed set of risk factors across all yield curves which provide an intuitive interpretation. Exhibit 19.7 shows such a set of risk factors, and Exhibit 19.8 shows the graphical representation of the chosen risk factors.

It is useful to note here that the chosen risk factors have the interpretation of a parallel shift of the yield curve, flattening or steepening of the yield curve, and curvature of the yield curve around the 5-year maturity. But how well do the chosen risk factors model shape changes of different yield curves? To answer this question we can determine the percentage of variance in the original data set which the chosen three risk factors explain. We will describe briefly how this can be done in practice.

Let $\{\Delta\vec{y}(t)\}$ be the vector time series of weekly yield changes for different maturities and the covariance matrix of this vector time series be denoted Σ. For the chosen risk factor matrix F let $\{\vec{e}(t)\}$ denote the vector time series of unexplained yield changes where $\vec{e}(t)$ is given by

EXHIBIT 19.7 Risk Factors Used to Model Yield Curve Changes

Maturity	$F_1(i)$	$F_2(i)$	$F_3(i)$
1 year	−10 bps	4 bps	−1 bps
2 years	−10 bps	3 bps	−0.5 bps
3 years	−10 bps	2 bps	0 bps
5 years	−10 bps	0 bps	1 bps
7 years	−10 bps	−0.4 bps	0.5 bps
10 years	−10 bps	−1 bps	−0.25 bps
15 years	−10 bps	−2 bps	−0.5 bps
20 years	−10 bps	−3 bps	−0.75 bps
30 years	−10 bps	−5 bps	−1.25 bps

EXHIBIT 19.8 Graphical Representation of Risk Factors Used to Model Yield Curve Changes

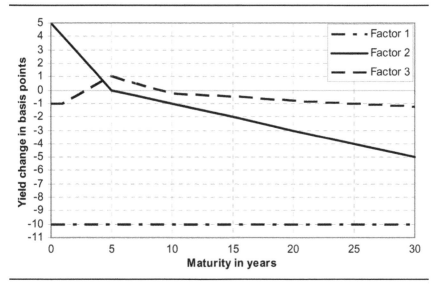

$$\vec{e}(t) = \Delta\vec{y}(t) - \vec{x}(t)F^T$$

Let E denote the covariance matrix of the vector time series $\{\vec{e}(t)\}$. The total variance of the yield changes is given by the sum of the diagonal elements of the covariance matrix Σ, and the unexplained variance as a consequence of using the chosen risk factor is given by the sum of the diagonal elements of the matrix E. Denoting these two variances by $\sigma^2_{\Delta y}$ and σ^2_e, respectively, the percentage variance explained by the chosen risk factors is given by the following equation:

$$\text{Percentage variance explained} = \left(1 - \frac{\sigma^2_e}{\sigma^2_{\Delta y}}\right) \times 100$$

Using constant maturity par yields captured from Reuters data on a weekly frequency for different yield curves over the period October 2000 to October 2004, Exhibit 19.9 shows the percentage of variance explained by the chosen yield curve risk factors across different government bond markets. Also shown in this exhibit is the corresponding variance explained by the first three principal components estimated over the in-sample period.

EXHIBIT 19.9   Variance Explained by Chosen Risk Factors and Principal
Components

Country	Modeled risk factors	Principal components
United States	96.3%	97.7%
Germany	98.1	99.3
Japan	95.5	97.3

We described so far how to choose the yield curve risk factors and
how to estimate the coefficients associated with these risk factors. The
risk factor coefficients have to be recomputed every week assuming that
we use data at weekly frequency for estimating the risk model. Suppose
we have to model 20 yield curves in the multicurrency bond portfolio,
then we need to estimate 60 yield curve risk factor coefficients every
week. Using the time series of these risk factor coefficients we can estimate our risk model if the risks are limited to yield curve exposures.

In a multicurrency portfolio, however, we also have exposures to foreign exchange rates. As a consequence, changes in foreign exchange rates
versus the base currency of the portfolio impacts the mark-to-market
value of the portfolio. In order to model the risk exposure to changes in
foreign exchange rate, let us assume that this risk factor models a 1%
appreciation of the foreign currency against the base currency of the
portfolio. In this case, the coefficient $d(t)$ associated with the chosen risk
factor based on weekly exchange rate data is given by

$$d(t) = 100 \times \frac{X(t) - X(t-1)}{X(t-1)} \tag{19.4}$$

In equation (19.4) $X(t)$ denotes the exchange rate of the foreign currency at time t expressed in units of foreign currency required to buy
one unit of the base currency.

We have now identified all relevant risk factors that can affect the valuation of the portfolio or the benchmark. Constructing the risk model
using this information is quite simple. To see why, we note that a risk
model primarily captures the covariance between the relevant risk factors
so that the comovements between risk factors will be taken into account
when computing the aggregate risk arising from all exposures. In a mathematical sense, the risk model is simply the covariance matrix estimated
using the time series of risk factor coefficients we have estimated. Assuming that we have to take into consideration m yield curves and q exchange
rates, the covariance matrix will have a dimension $(3m + q) \times (3m + q)$.

This covariance matrix, denoted Ω can be estimated using the vector time series of risk factor coefficients given below:

$$\vec{\phi}(t) = [a_1(t), b_1(t), c_1(t), \ldots, a_m(t), b_m(t), c_m(t), d_1(t), \ldots, d_q(t)]$$

Using the risk model, we can compute various portfolio risk measures of interest to us such as ex ante tracking error, beta of the portfolio, or value at risk. This is described in the next section.

Computing Different Risk Measures

In order to compute different risk measures of interest, we first have to compute the risk factor sensitivities for the portfolio and benchmark. Risk factor sensitivity provides a measure of the percentage change in the mark to market value of the portfolio or the benchmark to the predefined risk factors. For instance, if the risk factor sensitivity of the portfolio to a parallel shift of –10 basis points of the U.S. Treasury par yield curve is 25 basis points, then it indicates that the percentage price change of the portfolio to this risk factor is 25 basis points. To compute the risk factor sensitivities for the portfolio, we need to revalue all the securities in the portfolio under the predefined risk factor scenarios.

Suppose we wish to compute the change in market value of a U.S. Treasury bond for a –10 basis points parallel shift of the U.S. Treasury yield curve. Then a fairly good approximation to the price change under the modeled risk factor can be computed using the modified duration D and convexity C of the bond. If Δy denotes the yield change in percentage terms and P_{dirty} the current dirty price for a \$1 par value of the bond, then the price change of the bond due to yield change is given by

$$\Delta P = P_{\text{dirty}} \times \left(-0.01 \times D \times \Delta y + \frac{1}{2} \times 0.0001 \times C \times \Delta y^2 \right)$$

Using this approximation to price change at the bond level, we can compute the price change of the portfolio to the –10 basis points parallel shift of U.S. Treasury yield curve. Specifically, if we are interested in the change in portfolio value to the kth risk factor, then this is given by

$$\Delta M_P^k = \sum_{i=1}^{n} A_i \times \Delta P_i^k \tag{19.5}$$

In equation (19.5) A_i denotes the nominal amount of the ith bond held in the portfolio expressed in the base currency of the portfolio, and

ΔP_i^k is the price change of the ith bond to the kth risk factor. The risk factor sensitivity of the portfolio expressed in basis points to the kth risk factor is given by

$$S_P^k = 10,000 \times \frac{\Delta M_P^k}{M_P}$$

If the risk factor under consideration is the foreign exchange risk, then we need to compute the change in mark to market value of the portfolio for a 1% appreciation of the foreign currency versus the base currency of the portfolio. When computing the mark to market change in portfolio value it is important to also include cash positions held in the portfolio. Extending the approach described here to compute risk factor sensitivities when the portfolio includes derivative instruments such as options, bond futures, and interest rate swaps is fairly straightforward.

Computing the various risk measures given the risk factor sensitivities for the portfolio and benchmark is a simple exercise. Let us denote the vector of risk factor sensitivities for the portfolio and benchmark as $\vec{S}_P$ and $\vec{S}_B$, respectively. Assuming the covariance matrix Ω has been estimated using weekly data, the annualized ex ante tracking error of the portfolio is given by

$$TE = \sqrt{52(\vec{S}_P - \vec{S}_B)^T \Omega(\vec{S}_P - \vec{S}_B)}$$

The scaling factor 52 in the above equation is used to convert the weekly tracking error information computed using the covariance matrix Ω into an annualized one.

The value at risk of the portfolio over a one-week horizon at 95% level of confidence is given by

$$\text{VaR(weekly, 95\%)} = 1.65 \times \sqrt{\vec{S}_P^T \Omega \vec{S}_P}$$

The beta of the portfolio with respect to the benchmark is by definition the covariance between portfolio and benchmark returns divided by the variance of the benchmark returns and is given by

$$\beta = \frac{\vec{S}_P^T \Omega \vec{S}_B}{\vec{S}_B^T \Omega \vec{S}_B}$$

The risk factor sensitivities that we computed for the portfolio and the benchmark can be used to generate a risk attribution report. A risk attribution report provides detailed information on the types of risk exposures taken by the portfolio manager to add value over the benchmark. Such a risk attribution report can be generated by taking the difference between the risk factor sensitivities in basis points between the portfolio and the benchmark, that is,

$$S_P^k - S_B^k$$

and reporting this information for every risk factor modeled. For instance, if the sensitivity to a –10 basis points parallel shift of the U.S. Treasury yield curve is 1 basis point, then it implies that the portfolio will outperform the benchmark by 1 basis point if the specified risk scenario is realised. On the other hand, a –5 basis point sensitivity arising from a foreign currency exposure will have the implication that the portfolio will underperform the benchmark by 5 basis points if the foreign currency appreciates by 1% against the base currency of the portfolio.

Many portfolio managers entrusted with active mandates like to have a measure of the marginal risk contribution of different bets taken against the benchmark. Because risk is usually expressed in terms of tracking error, the marginal tracking error contribution of different risk exposures provides information on risk consumed by those positions. Allocating a certain amount of marginal tracking error to specific risk exposures is becoming popular and is referred to as risk budgeting. In the context of a multicurrency bond portfolio, risk budgets are typically assigned to duration exposures, yield curve exposures, credit exposures, and foreign exchange exposures. Computing the marginal tracking error contribution to such aggregate risk factor exposures is facilitated by computing the marginal tracking error contribution of each risk factor modeled.

The marginal tracking error contribution of the ith risk factor can be regarded as the rate of change of portfolio tracking error with respect to a small percentage change to the risk factor. Using this definition, it can be shown that the marginal tracking error of the ith risk factor (MTE_i) is given by the following relation:

$$\text{MTE}_i = \frac{52 \times (S_P^i - S_B^i) \sum_k \Omega_{ik} \times (S_P^k - S_B^k)}{\text{TE}} \tag{19.6}$$

Because the covariance matrix Ω is computed using weekly data, the scaling factor 52 in equation (19.6) is required to annualize the marginal tracking error. Using equation (19.6) we can compute the marginal tracking error contribution of different aggregate risk factors. For example, to compute the marginal tracking error to parallel shift of all yield curves (duration risk), we need to add up all the marginal tracking error contributions to shift risk factor for every yield curve. Similarly, to compute the marginal tracking error contribution to foreign exchange risk, we need to add up all marginal risk contributions from currency risk. The sum of the marginal tracking error contributions of all risk factors will be equal to the total tracking error of the portfolio.

TOOLS FOR PORTFOLIO CONSTRUCTION AND REBALANCING

We have seen so far in this chapter how to form views that will allow the portfolio manager to take active bets against the benchmark and to quantify the risk exposures arising from such bets using a risk model. In this section we discuss how the portfolio manager's views can be translated into actual trading positions with the help of a portfolio selection tool. Specifically, we discuss how one could formulate an optimization problem that would allow the portfolio manager to rebalance an existing portfolio efficiently. Rebalancing a portfolio efficiently implies that the rebalancing can be done by performing a minimum number of trades. In general, bond futures could be used in a cost effective way to take yield curve exposures assuming that the portfolio has been structured to replicate the benchmark risk characteristics. If such an approach is taken, the portfolio manager would still benefit from an optimization tool that helps in the portfolio construction process for replicating the benchmark risk characteristics. We describe in this section how to formulate such an optimization problem that can be used for either portfolio construction or rebalancing.

Minimizing Transaction Costs

In general, there are several alternative ways in which one can formulate an optimization problem for portfolio selection. Depending on how we formulate the optimization problem, we can get different portfolio compositions that are in some sense optimal in meeting the objectives and constraints of the problem formulation. However, many commonly used problem formulations for selecting an optimal portfolio pay little attention to the transaction costs involved. Ignoring transaction costs can result in the optimal portfolio composition being very expensive to implement, and as a consequence, determining the optimal portfolio composition will turn out to be only a theoretical exercise. In order to ensure that the optimization problem formulated is of practical value, one has to give careful consideration to implementation costs. One way to take into account implementation costs is to minimize the turnover of the portfolio when it is rebalanced to its optimal portfolio composition. In addition to this, if we can reduce the number of actual transactions required to rebalance the portfolio, then the task of rebalancing the portfolio becomes much simpler. Imposing constraints to minimize the number of transactions is usually difficult to enforce in an optimization problem. Certain optimization problem formulations, however, can lead to fewer transactions than others. For example, an optimization problem formulated as a linear programming problem usually gives rise to smaller number of transactions compared to quadratic programming problem formulation. A programming problem is said to be linear if both the objective and constraint functions are linear in the variables we solve for. We will describe later how the portfolio construction or rebalancing problem can be formulated as a linear programming problem that minimizes transaction costs.

To keep the exposition simple, we assume that set of permissible securities that can be bought or sold comprises only bonds. Also for notational simplicity we will assume that only bonds and cash are held in the existing portfolio that has to be rebalanced. Note that the portfolio construction problem can be thought of as rebalancing a portfolio that has only cash holdings, and as such, can be regarded as a special case of a portfolio rebalancing problem.

Suppose the set N_E denotes the set of bonds held in the portfolio before rebalancing, and w_i^E the current weights in the portfolio. Assuming M_p to be the market value of the portfolio that is to be rebalanced, the relative weight of the ith bond held in the portfolio before rebalancing is given by

$$w_i^E = \frac{A_i P_i}{M_p}$$

where A_i is the nominal amount expressed in base currency of portfolio that is invested and P_i is the dirty price for trading one local currency unit of the bond.

To facilitate the formulation of the optimization problem, it is convenient to distinguish between the buy and sell transactions needed to rebalance the portfolio. Let us denote the relative weights of the ith bond bought by w_i^{buy} and the ith bond sold by w_i^{sell}. If bonds cannot be sold short, then we can only sell bonds that are held in the portfolio. The no short sell constraint can be expressed as

$$0 \leq w_i^{\text{sell}} \leq w_i^{E}, \quad i \in \mathbb{N}_E$$

Let the relative weight of the net cash held in the portfolio be denoted w_{cash}. If w_{cash} is positive, we can regard this as cash injection into the portfolio which has to be invested. On the other hand, if w_{cash} is negative, we can regard this as a cash withdrawal from the portfolio that will be financed by selling bonds in the portfolio. Because the buy, sell and cash injection/withdrawal transactions have to balance, we have the following equation:

$$\sum_{i \in \mathbb{N}_P} w_i^{\text{buy}} - \sum_{i \in \mathbb{N}_E} w_i^{\text{sell}} = w_{\text{cash}}$$

Suppose $\mathbb{N}_P$ denotes the set of permissible bonds that can be held in the portfolio and $\mathbb{N}_R$ the set of yield curve risk factors that we have modeled.[15] Then the risk factor sensitivity in basis points of the ith bond that can be bought from the set $\mathbb{N}_P$ to the kth risk factor is by definition given by

$$f_{ik}^{\text{buy}} = 10{,}000 \times \frac{P_i^k - P_i}{P_i} \tag{19.7}$$

In equation (19.7) P_i denotes the current dirty price of the ith bond, and P_i^k the dirty price after a shock to the kth risk factor. Because we wish to distinguish between buy and sell transactions, let f_{ik}^{sell} denote the risk factor sensitivity of the ith bond held in the portfolio to the kth risk factor. The portfolio sensitivity in basis points to various risk factors before rebalancing are given by

$$\sum_{i \in \mathbb{N}_P} w_i^E f_{ik}^{\text{sell}} = S_P^k, \quad k \in \mathbb{N}_R$$

Let us assume that the benchmark sensitivity in basis points to modeled risk factors have also been precomputed, that is, we have computed S_B^k, $k \in \mathbb{N}_R$. The relative risk exposures of the portfolio versus the benchmark in basis points will be the difference between the risk factor sensitivities of the portfolio and the benchmark. This is given by

[15] The desired exposures to foreign exchange risk factors can be gained by doing FX forward contracts and, for that reason do not require being included in the optimization problem formulation.

$$\Psi_k = S_P^k - S_B^k, \quad k \in \mathbb{N}_R \tag{19.8}$$

It is useful to note here that equation (19.8) simply captures the risk attribution report for the portfolio before rebalancing. Some of the risk exposures held may be intentional if the portfolio is being managed actively against the benchmark. Let us assume that the portfolio manager wishes to rebalance the portfolio so that the risk attribution report will have Φ_k as sensitivities to various risk factors. To make this possible the portfolio manager will have to buy and sell bonds or equivalently, rebalance the portfolio. The combined effect of the buy and sell transactions will alter the existing risk factor sensitivities by Δ_k, $k \in \mathbb{N}_R$ which is given by

$$\Delta_k = \Phi_k - \Psi_k, \quad k \in \mathbb{N}_R$$

The changes in the risk factor sensitivities are a consequence of the buy and sells transactions. In this case, the following relationship should be satisfied:

$$\sum_{i \in \mathbb{N}_P} w_i^{\text{buy}} f_{ik}^{\text{buy}} - \sum_{i \in \mathbb{N}_E} w_i^{\text{sell}} f_{ik}^{\text{sell}} = \Delta_k, \quad k \in \mathbb{N}_R$$

We have now defined all the relevant constraints for the optimal portfolio rebalancing problem. Assuming that our objective is to minimize the turnover of the portfolio during the process of rebalancing, the optimization problem to solve is the following:

$$\textit{Minimize:} \quad \sum_{i \in \mathbb{N}_P} w_i^{\text{buy}}$$

Subject to the constraints

$$\sum_{i \in \mathbb{N}_P} w_i^{\text{buy}} f_{ik}^{\text{buy}} - \sum_{i \in \mathbb{N}_E} w_i^{\text{sell}} f_{ik}^{\text{sell}} = \Delta_k, \quad k \in \mathbb{N}_R$$

$$\sum_{i \in \mathbb{N}_P} w_i^{\text{buy}} - \sum_{i \in \mathbb{N}_E} w_i^{\text{sell}} = w_{\text{cash}}$$

$$0 \le w_i^{\text{sell}} \le w_i^E, \quad i \in \mathbb{N}_E$$

$$w_i^{buy} \geq 0, \quad i \in \mathbb{N}_P$$

We note that the objective function and all constraint functions are linear in the variables w_i^{buy} and w_i^{sell}, and hence, the optimization problem formulated is a linear programming problem. Standard software tools can be used to solve this optimization problem. Using w_i^{buy} and w_i^{sell} in conjunction with the market value of the portfolio M_P, the optimal buy and sell transactions to be done can be determined.

Minimizing Tracking Error

The optimal portfolio selection problem we presented in the last section allows for explicit control of the transaction costs by taking this into account in the objective function of the optimization problem. The advantage of such a problem formulation is that we can explicitly specify the desired exposures to different risk factors and, therefore, select portfolios that incorporate specific views of portfolio managers. Many standard portfolio selection software tools available in the market, however, formulate the portfolio selection problem as a quadratic programming problem instead of a linear programming problem. This means that the objective function of the optimization problem is a quadratic function, which is usually the square of the tracking error of the portfolio. Since portfolio turnover is not controlled for explicitly in such a problem formulation, implementing the optimal portfolio composition may involve significant transaction costs.

To illustrate how such an optimization problem can be formulated, let us denote by $\mathbb{N}_P$ the set of permissible bonds that can be included in the portfolio and the benchmark. Clearly, some or many bonds from the permissible set will have zero weights in the portfolio and benchmark. Let us denote the relative weights of the ith bond in the portfolio and benchmark by $w_{P,i}$ and $w_{B,i}$, respectively. Suppose $F = [f_{ik}]$ denotes the risk factor sensitivity matrix and Ω the covariance matrix of the risk factors, then the square of the portfolio tracking error is given by

$$TE^2 = (\vec{w}_P - \vec{w}_B)^T F \Omega F^T (\vec{w}_P - \vec{w}_B)$$

To compute the optimal portfolio weight vector $\vec{w}_p$ that minimizes the square of the portfolio tracking error, we need to solve the following quadratic programming problem:

$$Minimize: (\vec{w}_P - \vec{w}_B)^T F \Omega F^T (\vec{w}_P - \vec{w}_B)$$

Subject to the constraints

$$\sum_{i \in \mathbb{N}_P} w_{P,i} = 1$$

$$w_{P,i} \geq 0, \quad i \in \mathbb{N}_P$$

Note that the quadratic programming problem formulation given above does not take into consideration the existing portfolio weights when the optimal portfolio weights are determined. As a consequence, the rebalancing trades required to implement the optimal portfolio composition can be significant. It is useful to make the observation here that the linear programming problem formulation given earlier can reduce the tracking error of the portfolio to zero by enforcing the following constraints:

$$\vec{w}_P^T F = \vec{w}_B^T F$$

The advantage of such a formulation is that it gives us the additional freedom to minimize transaction costs while forcing the tracking error to be zero. Furthermore, the linear programming problem formulation is computationally more attractive to the quadratic programming problem formulation.

SUMMARY

In this chapter we have discussed the benefits of investing in a multicurrency bond benchmark. Specific benefits that were cited included an improved trade-off between risk and return, and the scope for taking more diversified active bets versus the benchmark to add value. Managing a multicurrency portfolio tends to be more challenging though. This challenge starts with the choice of the benchmark, then the requirement to follow monetary policy developments and exchange rate movements across several economies, and finally the need for proper portfolio selection and risk management tools to aid the portfolio construction process and to manage the active risks taken.

We presented several techniques in this chapter to support the active risk-taking process that included measuring market expectations, developing a modified Taylor rule for forecasting monetary policy changes, and monitoring the monetary/financial conditions indices for certain economies. Although we presented more techniques to support taking interest rate exposures, the techniques for taking currency exposures were more limited. This is because much of the currency risks taken in the context of active portfolio management tend to be driven more by technical trading rules rather than through macroeconomic forecasts.

For the purpose of measuring the active risks, we developed a three-factor yield curve model that is closely related to the technique of principal component decomposition. We also presented how the risk sensitivities to the various risk factors modeled can be computed, and the marginal tracking error contributions to aggregate risk factors can be determined. Subsequently, the formulation of an optimization problem for portfolio selection was presented which minimized the transaction costs during the portfolio implementation process.

CHAPTER 20

A Disciplined Approach to Emerging Markets Debt Investing

Maria Mednikov Loucks, CFA
Managing Director, Emerging Markets Fixed Income
Black River Asset Management

John A. Penicook, Jr., CFA, CPA
Managing Director, Global Head of Fixed Income
UBS Global Asset Management

Uwe Schillhorn, CFA
Executive Director, Head of Emerging Markets Debt
UBS Global Asset Management

Valuation, risk management, and attribution are familiar tools for professional money managers. An *emerging markets debt* (EMD) investor can use these tools to build a disciplined investment framework that captures the unique and constantly evolving nature of the EMD asset class. In this chapter, we outline a complete process for EMD investing, including:

- Benchmark selection

The authors gratefully acknowledge comments and inputs from their colleagues and former colleagues at UBS Global Asset Management—Sandra Bieri, Stefano Cavaglia, Norman Cumming, Christoph Kessler, Yu Chen Lin, Oleg Movchan, Joe Pratt, Günter Schwartz, Parvathy Sree, and Kevin Terhaar.

■ Overall market, country and instrument valuation
■ Portfolio construction and risk management
■ Attribution

The historically high price volatility and low intracountry correlation of EMD creates opportunities for the disciplined investor to outperform his or her benchmark and the peer group. A fundamentally based valuation process provides an anchor to investors when prices fluctuate wildly. Risk management allows the portfolio manager to examine alternative factors that influence a portfolio's return relative to its benchmark. Valuation and risk management come together during portfolio construction so that only well-compensated risks are taken. Finally, attribution provides investors with crucial feedback about the strengths and weaknesses of their investment decisions.

EMERGING MARKETS DEBT INDICES

Although we do not provide a detailed description of emerging market bonds in this chapter, it is worth mentioning several basic characteristics of the asset class before reviewing the selection of an appropriate benchmark.

The EMD universe encompasses both sovereign and corporate issuers; emerging market bonds may be denominated in hard currencies (U.S. dollar, euro, yen) and local currencies. U.S. dollar-denominated, sovereign bonds are the easiest way for investors to gain exposure to EMD because of liquidity and ease of trading. Therefore, this chapter will be written for an investor that gains exposure to EMD mainly through investing in U.S. dollar-denominated sovereign debt. The approach used here can be expanded to include multiple currencies and corporate issuers.

Due to poorly developed domestic capital markets, emerging market issuers must rely on international investors for capital. Although emerging market issuers differ greatly in terms of credit risk, dependence on foreign capital is the most basic common characteristic of the asset class. After the Asian crisis in 1997, investors realized that even investment grade sovereign issuers can run into problems when access to foreign capital is constrained.

The criteria used for issuer inclusion in EMD indices are based either on ratings, similar to other bond indices, or on structural statistics. Non-ratings-based inclusion criteria are favored by investors who believe that emerging market sovereigns share similar risks, particularly the need for foreign capital, regardless of rating.

JP Morgan EMBI Global

The JP Morgan Emerging Markets Bond Index Global (EMBI Global) is currently the most widely used benchmark by EMD investors. The EMBI Global consists of only U.S. dollar-denominated sovereign bonds and does not use ratings as an inclusion criterion for issuers. The EMBI Global contains countries with investment-grade long-term foreign-currency ratings such as China, nonrated issuers such as Nigeria, and defaulted issuers such as Côte d'Ivoire. There are currently 27 issuers in the EMBI Global.[1]

In order for a country to be included in the EMBI Global it must meet either an *income per capita criterion* or a *debt restructuring criterion*. Countries that meet the income per capita criterion are classified in the lower or medium income per capita tier by the World Bank.[2] Countries that meet the debt restructuring criterion have restructured their external or local debt within the last 10 years. Popular emerging markets equity indices also use income per capita to classify countries for inclusion.

Once a country meets the criteria to be included in an EMD index, a particular bond must meet certain liquidity requirements. The liquidity requirements used by EMD indices are stringent in comparison to those used by other bond indices. In order to be included in the EMBI Global, a bond must have at least $500 million face amount outstanding, at least 2.5 years to maturity, verifiable prices, and verifiable cash flows.[3] The liquid nature of the EMBI Global Index facilitates the trading of index swaps and allows investors to quickly implement top down strategy changes.

Issuer Diversification Concerns

Lack of diversification is the greatest complaint voiced by investors regarding the EMD asset class in general and about EMD indices in particular. EMD indices have historically had high exposure to a small number of large individual issuers such as Argentina, Brazil, and Mexico and to the Latin American region overall.

Index providers have responded to investor concerns by switching from ratings-based to GDP/capita-based country inclusion criteria (thus including higher rated sovereigns) and by lowering liquidity requirements. Exhibit 20.1 compares the composition of JP Morgan Emerging Markets Debt indices as of April 1995 and April 2001. Over this period,

---

[1] All EMBI Global statistics are for April 30, 2001, unless stated otherwise.

[2] In 1999, a low or middle per capita income country would have an income per capita less than $9,635.

[3] As of April 30, 2001, the minimum face outstanding for the Lehman Investment Grade Corporate Index and the Merrill Lynch High-Yield Index was $150 million and $100 million, respectively.

EXHIBIT 20.1   Emerging Markets Debt Index Comparison, April 1995 versus April 2001

Date	April 30, 1995	April 30, 2001
Index	JP Morgan EMBI	JP Morgan EMBI Global
Market Capitalization	$59,519 million	$188,022 million
Number of Countries	8	27
Number of Securities	20	130
Percent Latin	88%	65%
Largest Issuer	Brazil (33.4%)	Brazil (19.7%)
Average Quality (Moody's)	Ba3	Ba2/Ba3

the proportion of Latin American issuers in these EMD indices has fallen from 88% to 65%.

There is no argument that EMD indices continue to have extremely poor issuer diversification when compared to U.S. high-yield and U.S. investment-grade credit indices. While most U.S. high-yield and U.S. investment-grade credit indices have hundreds of issuers, the EMBI Global contains only 27 sovereign issuers. Four issuers in the EMBI Global have a market weight in the index that is over 10%: Argentina (19.1%), Brazil (19.7%), Mexico (15.5%), and Russia (10.8%).

The lack of issuer diversification contributes to the large spread volatility of EMD. Between April 1991 and April 2001, the annualized volatility of emerging market spreads was 8.7%, while the annualized volatility of U.S. high-yield spreads was 4.7% over the same time period.[4] The impact of large issuers on spreads is magnified by regional and sometimes global contagion within the asset class.

In order to reduce issuer concentration, some investors have moved towards using EMD indices that are not market-capitalization-weighted. These indices shift a greater weight to countries outside of Latin America and increase the percentage of the index represented by less liquid sovereign issuers. The EMBI Global Constrained, for example, is a non-market-weighted index that limits the face amount of debt that is included in the index from a specific issuer. The EMBI Global Constrained has 53% of its market capitalization in Latin America compared to 65% in the EMBI Global.

---

[4] Monthly EMD spreads from JP Morgan: EMBI (4/1991–2/1996), EMBI+ (3/1996–5/2000), EMBI Global (6/2000–4/2001) adjusted for defaulted issuers; monthly U.S. high yield spreads from Merrill Lynch (option-adjusted spreads used after 12/31/1996).

EXHIBIT 20.2 Comparison of Market-Weighted and Nonmarket-Weighted Indices, April 1994 through April 2001

	EMBI Global[a]	EMBI Global Constrained
Type of Index	Market Weighted	Nonmarket Weighted
Annualized Return	14.25%	14.53%
Standard Deviation[b]	17.28%	16.37%
Sharpe Ratio[c]	0.49	0.53

[a] The EMBI Global Index was introduced by JP Morgan in the summer of 1999. Exhibit 20.2 uses back history that was created by JP Morgan.
[b] Annualized standard deviation measured from monthly returns.
[c] U.S. Eurodeposit rate used as cash in Sharpe ratio formula.

Exhibit 20.2 compares the returns, volatilities, and Sharpe ratios of the EMBI Global Index with those of the EMBI Global Constrained. The exhibit shows that between December 1993 and April 2001, the EMBI Global Constrained had higher annualized returns and lower return standard deviation than the EMBI Global.

An investor should not assume that the higher measured Sharpe ratio of the EMBI Global Constrained is necessarily due to better diversification. Since the EMBI Global Constrained shifts more weight to less liquid and lesser known issuers, a higher return may be necessary to compensate investors for increased risk (similar to the small stock effect in equities). Less liquidity also helps to reduce measured volatility because bonds that trade infrequently appear less volatile even though it is difficult to sell these securities at quoted prices. Managers of funds with regular inflows and outflows may have difficulty managing their exposure relative to an index with high weights in less liquid issuers.

For nonmarket-weighted indices, the increased complexity of the weighting rules make it difficult for managers to predict how market events, such as new issuance, will impact the index. Furthermore, the issuer weighting rules are vulnerable to change by the index provider as the market grows.

When investors decide on the appropriate index to use, they have to weigh the potentially improved diversification offered by a nonmarket-weighted index against the better liquidity and ease of use offered by a market-weighted index. Since an EMD portfolio is usually a small piece of an institutional investor's portfolio, issuer diversification should be less of a concern.

Despite the relatively high volatility of market-weighted EMD indices, their lower correlation with other fixed income markets improves the risk/return characteristics of U.S. bond portfolios. Exhibit 20.3

EXHIBIT 20.3   Yield and Spread Change Correlation Matrix for Various U.S. Fixed Income Sectors, April 1991 through April 2001[a]

	EMD	Treasury/ Agency	Inv Grade Corp	HY Corp
Emerging Markets Debt Spread	1.00			
U.S. Treasury/Agency Yield	(0.01)	1.00		
U.S. Investment Grade Corp Spread	0.33	(0.27)	1.00	
U.S. High Yield Spread	0.34	(0.24)	0.86	1.00

[a] Merrill Lynch monthly data used for Treasury/Agency yields, Investment Grade Corporate spreads and U.S. High Yield spreads (option adjusted spreads used after 12/31/96). EMD monthly spreads from JP Morgan are adjusted for defaulted securities.

shows the correlations between EMD spread changes, U.S. Treasury/agency yield changes, U.S. investment grade corporate spread changes and U.S. high yield spread changes. Yield and spread correlations are measured instead of return correlations to separate the movement of spreads from the movement of Treasuries. Exhibit 20.3 shows that changes in U.S. investment-grade corporate spreads and U.S. high-yield spreads have a high correlation with each other, while changes in EMD spreads have a low correlation with changes in both U.S. investment grade corporate spreads and U.S. high yield spreads. Changes in EMD spreads are uncorrelated with changes in U.S. Treasury/agency yields, while changes in U.S investment grade corporate spreads and U.S. high yield spreads have a negative correlation with changes in U.S. Treasury/agency yields.

For the remainder of this chapter, we will discuss how to manage an EMD portfolio against the EMBI Global. EMBI Global is liquid, transparent and widely used. We think it is an appropriate benchmark for investors that incorporate EMD within a diversified portfolio.

VALUATION OF OVERALL MARKET

This is the first of three sections that describe fundamentally based valuation techniques that can be applied in the management of EMD portfolios. This section will discuss valuation techniques for the overall market; the following sections will discuss valuation techniques for countries and instruments.

From April 1991 to April 2001, EMD has returned 14.02% annually with an annualized volatility of 15.77%.[5] This high volatility was exacerbated by a series of crises beginning with Mexico in 1994.

In 1993, Mexico was rated BB+ by S&P. The increasing importance of NAFTA and the expectation that Mexico would soon be investment grade drove spreads to levels lower than warranted by fundamentals. When Mexico devalued the peso, spreads on Mexican debt widened substantially. This triggered similar spread widening in other emerging market countries, especially in Latin America, because investors feared wide range defaults in the region.

After a successful resolution of Mexico's liquidity crisis, optimism returned to the market. Private capital flows to emerging markets and EMD trading volumes reached unprecedented levels.[6] In 1998, in the aftermath of several Asian devaluations, Russia devalued and defaulted on its domestic debt and part of its external debt. The unwinding of leveraged positions following the Russian default caused an increase in risk aversion leading to a dramatic widening of EMD spreads that was not warranted by fundamentals.

These episodes illustrate that an investor must take into account both the potentially large returns and the considerable risks in the EMD asset class. In evaluating EMD, the following issues should be considered:

- Relationship of EMD spreads to credit quality
- Trends in EMD credit quality
- EMD spreads relative to other asset classes

Relationship between Bond Spreads and Credit Quality

Sovereign credit ratings, provided by the rating agencies, are an assessment of each government's capacity and willingness to repay debt according to its terms.[7] We compare ratings and spreads by assigning a numerical score to the rating of the overall market (calculated by combining historical country ratings according to their market weight).[8] We

---

[5] Emerging debt daily return data from JP Morgan: EMBI (4/1991–2/1996), EMBI+ (3/1996–5/2000), EMBI Global (6/2000–4/2001)

[6] According to the Institute of International Finance, net private capital flows increased from 229 billion USD in 1995 to 330 billion USD in 1996. According to the Emerging Markets Traders Association, trading volume increased from 2.738 trillion USD in 1995 to 5.296 trillion USD in 1996.

[7] David T. Beers and Marie Cavanaugh, "Sovereign Credit Ratings: A Primer," Standard & Poor's Research (December 1998)

[8] We took Moody's sovereign ratings. Our rating score starts with 10 for A3 and then declines one point for each rating. All C-rated sovereigns have a score of 0; non-rated and B3-rated sovereigns have a score of 1. We tried different scaling methods but the essence of the results did not change.

then standardize the two time series (ratings and market spreads) by calculating their z-scores for each month.[9] We inverted the z-score for the spread so that improving credit quality and a declining spread move in the same direction. Exhibit 20.4 plots the standardized rating against the standardized inverted spread of the market to see how closely the spreads move with the credit quality indicated by the rating score.

Spreads had an annualized volatility of 8.7% between April 1991 and April 2001.[10] Since ratings are long term and change infrequently, they do not provide a timely explanation for spread movements. Even the addition of rating outlooks would not greatly increase the movement of rating changes relative to spreads.

The underlying economic fundamentals of a country determine the capacity of a country to pay its debts. A complementary approach to using ratings is to use the macroeconomic fundamentals directly to assess the credit quality of the market. We measure the market-weighted macroeconomic fundamentals of the individual countries and then aggregate them to compute an indicator for the entire market.

The *Market Fundamental Indicator* (MFI) is calculated up from the country level. We use eight macroeconomic variables to calculate a *Country Fundamental Indicator* (CFI) for each country. The variables include short-term serviceability variables such as basic balance, medium-term solvency variables such as debt service ratio, and long-

EXHIBIT 20.4   Emerging Market Debt Spreads (Inverted) versus Market Rating

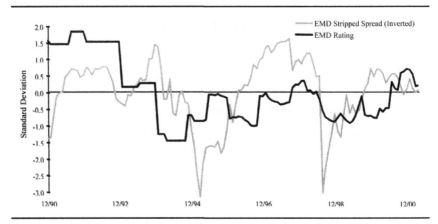

---

[9] The z-score of a value (z) for a variable (v) is calculated as follows: z-score = $(z -$ mean of $v)$/standard deviation of v.

[10] Monthly EMD spreads from JP Morgan adjusted for defaulted issuers from April 1991 to April 2001.

term structural variables such as inflation. Serviceability variables measure short-term debt service and liquidity risks. Solvency variables measure the medium-term financial health of a country. Structural variables are indicators for structural imbalances in the economy that can influence solvency and serviceability in the long run. The definitions of the variables used and an explanation of why these variables are important is provided in a later section describing relative valuations of countries.

To construct a CFI, a country receives a score on each variable for every year.[11] The score is a z-score where the mean and standard deviation are calculated across countries and across time.[12] By calculating the mean and the standard deviation in this fashion, we compare a country's performance both relatively (across country) and historically (across time). A higher CFI signifies better macroeconomic fundamentals. Outliers (such as inflation over 1,000%) distort the mean and standard deviation, so we place limits on variables. Essentially, this method assumes that once a variable reaches a particular threshold, further deterioration has limited negative impact on the economy.

CFIs are combined according to their market weights to calculate the MFI. Political factors are captured in the MFI only in so far as they impact macroeconomic estimates. We can assume that specific political events in the different countries are uncorrelated and neutral for the market as a whole.

Exhibit 20.5 shows the MFI versus the inverted standardized spreads of the market. The historical values for the MFI are calculated from real (ex post) data; the 2001 value is calculated from *Institute of International Finance* (IIF)[13] macroeconomic forecasts.

Three observations can be drawn from Exhibit 20.5:

1. Emerging market spreads (inverted) and macroeconomic fundamentals tend to move in the same direction. Accurate macroeconomic forecasts can therefore serve as useful indicators for the direction of EMD spreads.
2. Spreads are more volatile over short periods than are measurable economic fundamentals. They are influenced by global financial conditions and the relative value of other asset classes. Euphoria and contagion

---

[11] The annual data are updated on a quarterly basis.

[12] The z-score of country A at time t is equal to $(X_{A,t} - \overline{X})/\sigma_X$ where $X_{A,t}$ is the value of variable X in Country A for time t, $\overline{X}$ is the average of variable X across all countries and time periods, and σ_X is the standard deviation of variable X across all countries and time periods. The CFI for country A at time t is the average of the variable z-scores for country A at time t.

[13] The Institute of International Finance, Inc. is a global association of financial institutions created in 1983 in response to the international debt crisis.

EXHIBIT 20.5 Emerging Markets Debt Spreads (Inverted) versus Market Fundamental Indicator

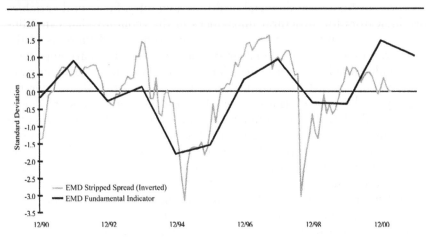

seem to explain at least part of the departure of the spreads from their underlying fundamentals.

3. Economic fundamentals have been on an improving trend since the mid-1990s. The deterioration after the Asian crisis in 1997 and the Russian default in 1998 was much less severe and of shorter duration than the decline of economic fundamentals at the beginning of the 1990s.

Long-Term Credit Trends

We attribute the improvement in economic fundamentals of emerging market countries to structural reforms implemented in the 1990s and to the general acceptance of capitalism and democracy.

Economic crises in emerging markets have often been associated with high fiscal deficits, weak banking systems, or overvalued currencies.[14] Since the mid-1990s, many emerging market countries have improved important parts of their political and economic systems that address these three issues. In addition, many countries have moved away from isolation towards greater integration with the global economy.

---

[14] For an overview of financial crises in Latin America see Sebastian Edwards, *Crisis and Reform in Latin America: From Despair to Hope* (New York: Oxford University Press, 1995).

After initial difficulties, functioning democracies and market economies with low fiscal deficits have been created in most of Eastern Europe. Large parts of the banking systems in many EM countries are now controlled by well capitalized foreign banks. Many large countries in the EMD universe liberalized their exchange rates. Mexico abandoned its pegged exchange rate in 1994; Russia, Turkey, Korea, Thailand, Brazil, and Colombia substituted their managed currency regimes with floating exchange rates between 1997 and 2001.

Trade barriers and ownership restrictions for foreigners have been reduced throughout the emerging world. Most Latin American governments have reduced their stakes in loss-making or inefficiently managed enterprises. According to the Institute of International Finance, net foreign direct investments in emerging markets increased from $81 billion in 1995 to $151 billion in 2000.

Democracy and capitalism are now accepted political and economic models in most emerging market countries. Previously, governments' heavy involvement in the allocation of production factors and the fixing of exchange rates masked the informational value of economic variables and lowered efficiency. Managed exchange rates, fixed domestic interest rates, and bank financing provided no price feedback for policy makers, increasing the risks of periodic crises. Fiscal accounts and financial statements of government-owned enterprises were not transparent and the ruling political class protected itself from being held responsible. Now, market economies give the necessary price feedback to expose bad economic management and the politicians at fault at an early stage. Better functioning democracies and increased political competition have led to the demise of many incompetent and corrupt politicians and have helped market-oriented reformers.

Emerging Markets Debt Relative to Other Asset Classes

In addition to economic fundamentals, investors should consider the attractiveness of other asset classes relative to emerging markets debt. EMD is a small, risky portion of investors' portfolios. Returns in other asset classes can influence the demand for EMD. According to a study by Goldman Sachs,[15] performance of the U.S. stock market and U.S. high-yield spreads are important factors in explaining EMD spreads. In addition to dedicated EMD investors, cross-over investors from other asset classes actively invest in EMD. Because of its similar overall rating, investors view U.S. high yield and EMD as competing asset classes.

---

[15] Alberto Ades, Rumi Masih and Daniel Tenengauzer, "EMD Valuemetrics," Goldman Sachs Emerging Markets Bond Views (October 23, 2000).

Exhibit 20.6 shows that EMD spreads have been higher and more volatile than U.S. high-yield spreads. Market participants have attributed the higher risk premium of EMD relative to U.S. high yield to the following factors:

- EMD historical recovery rates are lower.
- EMD historical volatility is higher.
- EMD is a less diversified asset class.

The first factor (lower historical recovery rates) is based on data that do not reflect the current structure of EMD. The second factor (high volatility adjusted returns) is difficult to assess because of the composition changes and liquidity differences between U.S. high yield and EMD. The third factor (less diversification) is accurate, but it may not be significant to an investor who puts EMD in a diversified portfolio.

The median recovery rate for senior unsecured corporate debt from 1970 to 1998 was 48% according to Moody's survey of defaulted debt. This recovery rate is based on secondary market prices for corporate bonds one month after they default. Recent recovery rates on defaulted corporate debt have been lower than in the past. For EMD sovereign bonds, a recovery rate of only 20% is typically assumed. This is based on secondary market prices for the commercial bank debt restructurings in the 1980s and 1990s. Because EMD sovereigns have moved from

EXHIBIT 20.6   Emerging Markets Debt Spreads versus U.S. High Yield Spreads[a]

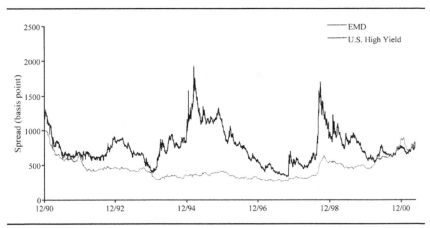

[a] Emerging debt monthly return data from JP Morgan: EMBI (4/1991–2/1996), EMBI+ (3/1996–5/2000), EMBI Global (6/2000–4/2001); U.S. high-yield monthly return data from Merrill Lynch.

bank to bond financing, low historical recovery rates for EMD might not be a good indicator for future recovery rates. According to a study conducted by Deutsche Bank, more recent sovereign defaults suggest that the recovery rates on publicly traded sovereign bonds have been at least as high as those on U.S. corporations.[16]

The restructuring of Russia's defaulted Soviet debt and Ecuador's Brady Bonds in 2000 suggest that EMD recovery rates may be higher than U.S. corporate recovery rates. Before restructuring, Russian and Ecuadorian bonds traded at 33 and 36, respectively. Prior to credit deterioration and subsequent default, these bonds traded around 50. The exact recovery amount for these bonds is difficult to calculate because, being themselves the result of a former debt restructuring, they were not issued at par and traded immediately at deep discounts. But investors that bought these bonds in the secondary market prior to credit deterioration/default realized recovery values even higher than the historical corporate bond recovery rate of 48%.

Exhibit 20.7 shows that historical spread volatility for U.S. high yield has been lower than that of EMD. Because the composition of both markets has changed considerably since the early 1990s, one has to be cautious when using these data to compare the two asset classes.

It is difficult to compare spread volatility in the U.S. high yield market with EMD volatility. In times of high market volatility, U.S. high yield bonds often trade "by appointment" in the secondary market; actual sales often take place two to three points below the quoted bid. EMD has tighter bid-offer spreads and quoted prices are generally executable.

EXHIBIT 20.7 Emerging Markets Debt and U.S. High Yield: Return and Volatility Statistics, April 1991 through April 2001[a]

	Annualized Returns		Sharpe Ratios	
	EMD	USHY	EMD	USHY
3-Year	6.12%	0.98%	0.09	−1.35
5-Year	12.64%	5.60%	0.52	0.39
10-Year	14.02%	9.63%	0.60	2.16

[a] Emerging debt daily return data from JP Morgan: EMBI (4/1991–2/1996), EMBI+ (3/1996–5/2000), EMBI Global (6/2000–4/2001); U.S. high-yield daily return data from Merrill Lynch.

---

[16] Peter Petas and Rashique Rahman, "Emerging Markets versus Corporate Bond Recovery Values," *Deutsche Bank Emerging Markets Weekly* (April 7, 2000), pp. 7–10.

Because EMD consists of a rather small number of different sovereign issuers, as an asset class it is much less diversified than U.S. high yield. The extra risk premium required for this lack of diversification depends on whether EMD is viewed as a standalone asset class or as part of a broader fixed income portfolio. As the previous section on EMD indices shows, compared to U.S. high yield, EMD offers less diversification when combined with U.S. Treasury bonds and more diversification when combined with investment grade U.S. corporate bonds.

RELATIVE VALUATION OF COUNTRIES

Despite the fact that emerging market debt is not a very diversified asset class, the performance of individual bonds often differs significantly. During the year 2000, 10-year bonds in Argentina, Brazil, Colombia, and Mexico returned 4.4%, 13.0%, 1.8%, and 12.7%, respectively. These large performance differences show that even within the same geographical region, country selection can have a substantial impact on portfolio returns.

Relation between Bond Spreads and Credit Quality

Following the approach we used to investigate the price versus value relationship of the overall market, we start by investigating the hypothesis that the movement in country spreads is captured by rating changes. We use Colombia as an example.

On August 11, 1999, Moody's changed Colombia's long-term foreign-currency debt rating from Baa3 to Ba2. As of April 30, 2001, Colombia's Ba2 rating remains unchanged by Moody's. Exhibit 20.8 shows the spread movements of the Colombia Republic 9¾% due 2009 while the Ba2 rating was in place.

The high spread volatility in Exhibit 20.8 cannot be explained by the rating, which remained unchanged during the period. Looking at spread changes for bonds in other countries during a period of unchanged ratings leads to similar conclusions.

Since sovereign bond spreads change significantly without corresponding changes in the underlying country rating, we follow the approach used in the market valuation section and calculate a CFI.[17] Exhibit 20.9 shows spreads versus CFIs for various countries at one point in time. It shows that spreads for countries with similar CFIs vary

---

[17] See market valuation section for a detailed description of how Country Fundamental Indicators (CFI) are calculated.

EXHIBIT 20.8   Spread of Colombia Republic 9¾% due 2009

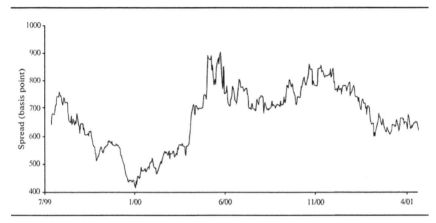

EXHIBIT 20.9   Country Fundamental Indicators versus Country Spreads[a]

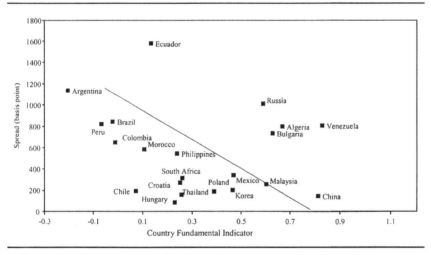

[a] Spreads of 10-year benchmark Eurobonds are used as country spreads. If a country has no Eurobonds, then the country spread is calculated from a liquid Brady substitute.

significantly and that countries with better CFIs don't necessarily have lower spreads. If CFIs explained spreads perfectly, we would see spreads decline with better fundamentals along a line similar to the one drawn on the graph.

Sometimes, discrepancies between CFIs and theoretical spread levels represent opportunities where the market is not properly pricing country risk. Other times, CFIs and theoretical spread levels do not converge because the CFI does not adequately measure a country's credit risk. Potential weaknesses of the CFI include the methodology by which different factors are combined to create the indicator, the lack of a time dimension, and the absence of qualitative variables.

Quantitative and Qualitative Considerations in Assessing Country Risk

A country's bond spreads are related to willingness and capacity to repay its debt. The latter depends directly on the amount of obligations coming due at any point in time and the foreign exchange resources and refinancing opportunities available at that time. CFIs not only contain variables that measure a country's immediate risk (serviceability variables), but they also contain variables that measure the intermediate and long-term risks facing a country (solvency and structural variables). Intermediate and long-term variables, such as the budget deficit and level of inflation, do not directly measure a country's capacity to service the debt in any given period. They do, however, serve as indicators for the quality of economic policy and structural soundness and therefore indirectly determine serviceability by influencing the availability of external financing.

All risk variables (immediate, intermediate, and long-term) have the same weight in the CFI, however their relative importance differs by country. In explaining the spreads and credit worthiness of a country, we look at each variable in the CFI and provide a dynamic analysis of how the different variables might interact. For a given variable, we determine over what time frame it may become important and we analyze how quantitative variables interact (i.e., the transmission mechanisms between variables).

When we valued the overall market, we ignored qualitative variables, such as politics. We assumed that political factors in different countries are independent of each other and that positive developments in some countries would compensate for negative developments in other countries. On an individual country basis, qualitative factors, particularly political factors, become increasingly important, so we include them in our country analysis.

EXHIBIT 20.10   Country Variables along a Timeline

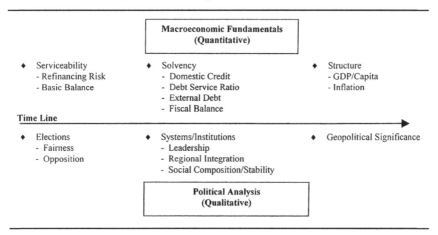

Exhibit 20.10 shows quantitative and qualitative variables that influence credit quality and spreads. The variables are shown along a timeline. Variables on the left side of the exhibit have an immediate impact on credit quality, variables in the middle of the exhibit have a medium-term impact on credit quality, and variables on the right side of the exhibit affect spreads over the long term.

Quantitative Variables

Most emerging market countries depend on continued access to external financial markets to refinance their debt, to stay current on their obligations, to continue to grow, and to reduce their debt ratios. The variables we consider in our analysis measure the external financing needs of a country and the riskiness of a country's financing position. We calculate our quantitative variables from macroeconomic forecasts provided by the IIF.

Serviceability Variables (Immediate Risk)   Serviceability variables measure short-term debt service and liquidity risks. *Refinancing Risk* is an indicator of the size of the debt service that has to be refinanced from external financing sources and is measured as follows:[18]

---

[18] The measure includes only interest payments and debt amortizations for external debt, which is total disbursed debt in foreign currencies owed to nonresidents. Short-term debt has a maturity of one year or less.

Refinancing risk

$$= \left(\begin{array}{c} \text{Short-term} \\ \text{debt stock} \end{array} + \begin{array}{c} \text{Interest} \\ \text{payments} \end{array} + \begin{array}{c} \text{Amortization on medium} \\ \text{and long-term debt} \end{array} \right) / \text{Reserves}$$

A low value indicates less risk.

Different financing sources do not have the same degree of uncertainty. Financing from official sources (multilaterals and bilaterals)[19] does not depend on capital market conditions, but is affected by longer term agreements between the borrower and the creditor. Such flows are not subject to market sentiment. Availability of financing from capital markets is more uncertain. It depends on the ongoing credit assessment of the country by the potential investors and on capital market cycles. A high degree of dependence on financing from capital markets puts a country in a much riskier position than a country that depends on official financing sources.

Basic balance measures the amount of foreign currency (excluding portfolio flows) that enters the country in any given year. A high value indicates less risk.

Basic Balance
= [Current account balance + Foreign direct investment]/[GDP]

In order to pay foreign currency debt service, a country must attract foreign currency inflows through trade (current account) or through capital inflows. Capital flows can be divided between foreign direct investment and portfolio flows. Foreign direct investments are usually based on long-term planning that is less dependent on business cycles and capital market cycles than portfolio investments, while portfolio flows are a riskier source of financing. A negative basic balance would indicate a potential need for riskier sources of financing.

Some countries have exports that are highly dependent on commodity prices. Since commodity prices tend to be much more volatile than prices for other goods and services, the basic balance for these countries is much more volatile.

Solvency Variables (Intermediate Risk)   Strong solvency ratios support a country's access to the external financial market in order to refinance its immediate obligations. The *Domestic Credit Ratio* estimates the ratio of domestic credit to GDP in three years and is computed as follows:

---

[19] This includes financial aid from multilateral institutions such as the International Monetary Fund and the World Bank and bilateral aid and loans from individual countries.

$$\text{Domestic credit ratio} = \frac{\left(1 + \dfrac{\text{Expected 3-year}}{\text{domestic credit growth}}\right) \times \text{Domestic credit}}{\left(1 + \dfrac{\text{Expected 3-year}}{\text{GDP growth}}\right) \times \text{GDP}}$$

A low value indicates less risk.[20]

An efficient allocation of credit to productive investment projects should result in higher GDP growth than credit growth over time. If credit is not allocated efficiently the investment will not produce the desired GDP growth and the domestic credit ratio will increase, indicating overinvestment or credit allocation that is not based on profit maximization.

Inefficient allocation of domestic credit was one of the reasons for the Asian crisis. In 1997 and 1998, South Korea and Malaysia had domestic credit ratios of over 150% and Thailand's domestic credit ratio was above 130%. After having addressed some of the problems in their banking systems, domestic credit ratios in all three countries are declining but remain over 100%, well above the 65% benchmark average.

In countries with low-credit intermediation, credit growth rates can be significantly higher than GDP growth rates over an extended time period without being a sign of inefficient credit allocation. This phenomenon is well captured in the domestic credit ratio because it is a ratio of absolute levels of domestic credit to GDP, projected forward. Only countries with high credit intermediation and inefficient allocation will have a high ratio.

The *External Debt Ratio* and *Debt Service Ratio* are indicators for the size of the debt and debt burden in a given period. The calculation of both ratios follows:[21]

$$\text{External debt ratio} = [\text{External debt}]/[\text{GDP}]$$

$$\text{Debt service ratio} = \frac{(\text{Interest payments} + \text{Amortization on medium and long-term debt})}{(\text{Exports of goods and services} + \text{Income receipts})}$$

---

[20] This is generally the case for emerging market countries but a very low level can also indicate a lack of domestic investment opportunities in the real economy.

[21] The debt service ratio includes only interest payments and debt amortizations for external debt, which is total disbursed debt in foreign currencies owed to nonresidents.

A low value in these variables indicates less risk.

For example, Argentina's debt service ratio exceeds the emerging market country average and has grown from 47% in 1997 to a forecasted 80% in 2001. The debt service ratio is high not only because of Argentina's large interest and amortization payments but also because of Argentina's low exports. Argentina's export to GDP ratio is only 6%. A low export ratio makes it more difficult for Argentina to earn foreign exchange to repay foreign currency denominated debt. In contrast, Chile has a higher debt to GDP ratio but a much lower debt service ratio because of its high level of exports.

Our variables for refinancing risk, debt service ratio, and external debt ratio include corporate and bank obligations because, taken as a whole, corporate and bank debt is a contingent liability for the sovereign. The Republic of Korea provides a recent example of this contingent liability when it assumed a large part of the corporate and bank debt in the 1997 Asian crises.

Primary fiscal balance and interest payments compose the Public Sector Borrowing Requirement, which is measured as follows:[22]

> Public sector borrowing requirement
> = [Primary fiscal balance + Interest payments]/[GDP]

Fiscal deficits add to the refinancing burden because they have to be financed, so a low public sector borrowing requirement indicates less risk.

The composition of the public sector borrowing requirement is important. Primary fiscal deficits are an indicator of current fiscal problems and countries with primary fiscal deficits will have increasing debt service in the future. Large public sector borrowing requirements resulting from high interest payments can be an indicator of past fiscal problems. For example, due to high interest rates on past borrowing, Brazil had a 4.6% public sector borrowing requirement in 2000 despite a significant primary fiscal surplus.

Structural Variables (Long-Term Risk) Structural variables show potential imbalances that could weaken solvency ratios and debt service ability. Structural imbalances, such as low growth or high inflation might not be alarming if they are transitory. The challenge of examining structural variables lies in predicting when the market will focus on them and when they will lead to a deterioration in serviceability and solvency variables and therefore to a rapid increase in bond spreads.

---

[22] Includes central, provincial, and local governments, as well as public sector enterprises.

1. *5-Year Average GDP Per Capita Growth.* Low GDP per capita growth over a sustained period of time make it difficult for a country to reduce poverty, form a stable society and reduce debt ratios. Higher GDP per capita growth rates indicate less risk.

Argentina in 2001 illustrates how sustained structural imbalances can lead to deteriorating debt ratios and make an otherwise manageable refinancing program very hard to achieve. Between 1998 and 2001, Argentina was in a recession with below average GDP per capita growth. Despite a large IMF package that reduced refinancing needs, capital markets closed to Argentina at the beginning of 2001 and Argentine spreads widened dramatically. The market doubted whether the economic and monetary model in Argentina could produce sufficiently high growth to avoid a debt trap in which debt ratios increase past an unsustainable level.

2. *Inflation (Average Change Year-Over-Year).* High inflation numbers, especially when combined with high fiscal deficits, can reflect structural imbalances that require drastic adjustment programs entailing fiscal as well as monetary measures.

In the past, countries have tried to lower inflation by management of the exchange rate. When the government implements a managed exchange rate system, nominal interest rates do not immediately adjust downward, so real interest rates on short term debt instruments (T-bills) become very high. The government creates quasi-arbitrage conditions with no exchange rate risk and high real rates encouraging speculation as investors borrow money at low rates offshore and invest in the domestic T-bill market.

If the government would quickly proceed with the other structural reforms required to put the economy on a sustainable path, interest rates and inflation would decline, the government could free the exchange rate and leveraged positions in the local T-bill market would decline. Unfortunately, an abundance of short-term financing, due to the high real interest rates in T-bills, allows governments to run a fiscal deficit and proceed slowly with structural reforms. High real-interest rates increase the country's debt stock quickly. Eventually, the currency peg breaks (Russia 1998, Turkey 2001) with disastrous results for the local banking system and for investors.

Caveats to Using Publicly Available Statistics

According to IMF methodology, external debt is not only issued in a foreign currency but also in debt held by foreign investors. This distinction is important in countries such as Argentina, where local investors held approximately 60% of foreign currency-denominated debt at the end of 2000. Not including debt held by locals in external debt statistics may understate debt ratios. Statistics regarding the proportion of locally held, foreign currency-denominated bonds vary from country to country.

Publicly available statistics do not take the concessional character of bilateral financing (i.e., financing from one country to another) into account. Bilateral debt service has a political element and may be restructured or rescheduled rather than refinanced. In Ukraine for example, the official data show that external debt service is $8.2 billion in 2001. As a result, the refinancing risk variable for Ukraine is over 800% (versus an average refinancing risk of 176% for all emerging market countries in 2001). Roughly $6.9 billion of Ukraine's obligations is owed to Russia for gas supplies. This debt is political and is likely to be renegotiated rather than paid in cash. Therefore, Ukraine's refinancing risk is effectively lower than it seems from looking at the size of its official debt service.

Domestic debt is excluded from external debt data. Some countries have very large amounts of short-term domestic debt and reliable statistics are often unavailable. It is estimated that Brazil had over $130 billion of short-term domestic debt at the end of 2000 compared to an external debt service of $60.3 billion.

Fiscal accounts in different countries often do not follow the same standard methodology. Differences result from the treatment of provincial balances and balances of government agencies. In Mexico the official deficit in 2000 was 1.1% of GDP versus 4.7% when government agencies and provinces were included.

Qualitative Factors

Anecdotal evidence suggests that certain qualitative variables have in the past often been associated with a change in a country's risk premium. Qualitative factors, even if they are not pressing, need to be constantly monitored because credit events erupt very quickly. By the time an event reaches the headlines of international newspapers, bond spreads have already widened out. Although qualitative weaknesses are often known beforehand, they are not the focus of the market unless they develop into a major problem. Focusing research efforts on pertinent qualitative factors is better than watching events unfold and spreads widen.

Many emerging market countries have defaulted in the past and have gone through periods of sharp economic adjustments and political instability in the last 20 years. Because of the need for many emerging market countries to constantly access international capital markets, the importance of investor confidence in a country's politics and institutions is more important in emerging markets than in developed countries.

Qualitative Factors of Immediate Importance   Issues regarding *fairness of elections* and the political program of *opposition parties* can influence a country's risk premium during the election period. The Peruvian spring 2000 presidential election was colored by allegations that the incumbent president Alberto Fujimori orchestrated election fraud. During the election period, bond spreads in Peru widened out over 200 basis points compared to the JP Morgan EMBI Global. Because of the political pressure resulting from these allegations and the discovery of a widespread corruption scandal within the government, new elections were held in June 2001. One of the main contenders in the new election was ex-president Alan Garcia, who had pushed the country into a debt crisis in 1987 because of his populist politics. Political uncertainty that resulted from the candidacy of Alan Garcia lead to another relative spread widening in Peruvian bonds compared to the EMBI Global of 200 basis points before the elections.

Qualitative Factors of Intermediate and Long-Term Risk   High economic volatility often requires governments in emerging market countries to implement harsh fiscal adjustment programs. *Political leadership* is required to overcome initial resistance of legislators who often respond to particular interest groups instead of following the government's agenda. It is difficult for a government to function effectively when it does not have a majority in congress, when the government coalition is based on a desire for power sharing rather than ideology, or when the President is a weak leader.

Potential *integration* into trading blocks or membership in international organizations that are dominated by industrial countries can be powerful anchors of stability and can greatly accelerate a country's reform process. The European Union, for example, requires prospective new members to pass certain economic and political reforms. Because EU membership is strongly backed by the population of the prospective new member state, there is much less resistance to reforms than in countries that don't have that external anchor. In contrast, Mercosur, the Latin American trading block of Argentina, Brazil, Paraguay, and Uruguay, does not have a strong industrialized country as a member. Although Mercosur led to an improvement in trade among its members, it did not lead to milestone political and economic reforms.

Political crises or violent uprisings occasionally occur in countries that have disenfranchised minority groups. An extreme example is Colombia, where guerilla and paramilitary terrorist activities constantly provide negative headlines and keep risk premiums high. A less dramatic example is the uprising in Chiapas, Mexico in 1994, which contributed to a loss of investor confidence that led to the Mexican crisis in December 1994. Countries that do not have these kinds of social issues, such as Argentina, are likely to avoid this kind of crisis.

The *geopolitical significance* of a country might only become relevant if a country has a major credit crisis. Industrialized countries have in the past, either directly or via multilateral institutions like the IMF, devoted significant resources to prevent economic collapse and political instability in countries if they perceived larger global repercussions. Mexico's common border with the United States and NAFTA membership was a contributing factor in the $48 billion official package for Mexico in 1995. Multilaterals devoted significant financial resources to Russia in 1998 to prevent a devaluation and default; however, the political and economic situation was so chaotic that the problem escalated. Geopolitically less important Ecuador and Ukraine did not enjoy the same kind of support in their latest financial crises; multilaterals actually actively encouraged both countries to default on private creditors.

Valuation Process Example

To make relative value decisions across countries, one must compare the credit quality and pricing of the different countries to each other. The challenge is to have the resources to acquire in depth credit knowledge of every country and to put their credit quality on the same scale, independent from possible biases of individual analysts. A solid starting point is an analysis of the quantitative variables of a country that can be objectively compared to the values of all other countries in the investment universe. This puts countries on a level playing field and focuses research on the relevant variables. As an example for our general valuation process, the following Russia case study starts with a relative valuation of the quantitative variables and then adds qualitative factors to complete the analysis.

Exhibit 20.11 shows a comparison of Russia's quantitative variables in 1995 and 1997 in a radar chart. The serviceability ratios start at the 12 o'clock position of the chart, solvency and structural variables follow clockwise. The mean for each variable is calculated by averaging across countries in the investment universe and is represented by the dotted line in the middle of the graph. The gray line represents Russia's relative position in 1995 and the black line represents its relative position in 1997. Variables are measured in standard deviations from the benchmark average. Variables inside the dotted line are better than average, while variables outside the dotted line are worse than average. The external debt variable for Russia in 1997, for example, was one standard deviation better than the benchmark average. The radar chart

EXHIBIT 20.11 Russian Quantitative Variables in 1995 and 1997 (Radar Chart Comparison)

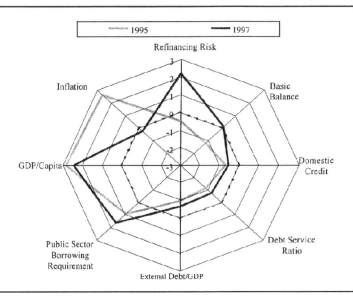

provides a quick overview of the relative weakness and strengths of a country compared to the average country in the benchmark. The radar chart combined with a country's spread relative to the market provides the starting point of our country analysis process.

In 1995, Russia was in the middle of its IMF-led, post-communist macroeconomic stabilization program and was attempting to create a market economy. Inflation was running at over 100%, GDP was declining, and fiscal deficits were high. These weaknesses are clearly shown by the 1995 radar chart. However, external debt write-offs of old Soviet debt left the country with little external debt. Serviceability ratios and solvency ratios (with the exception of public sector borrowing requirement) looked very healthy. To control inflation, Russia's currency was managed in a crawling peg to a basket of Deutschmarks and U.S. dollars. The inflation reduction strategy via a pegging of the exchange rate showed positive results. Inflation declined from 280% in 1992 to 40% in 1996. As described in the section on structural variables, the crawling peg and rapidly declining inflation led to high real-interest rates and a sharp inflow of capital into the local currency-denominated T-bill market. Private and government owned Russian banks provided foreign investors with currency hedges that guaranteed dollar returns far superior to the return on the longer-dated, dollar-denominated Russian Eurobonds.

By 1997, Russia's refinancing position had dramatically worsened and fiscal deficits were still very high. The inflation problem had been reduced but a short-term serviceability problem had been created.

Qualitative variables were worrisome. The country was at war in Chechnya. Red tape, white-collar crime, and corruption were obstacles to foreign investment. Institutions did not work properly, the federal government had little control over the regions, and president Yeltsin had lost his ability to actively lead and govern the country. Exhibit 20.12 shows that Russia's Eurobond spreads, trading only 30 basis points wider than market spreads in the spring 1998, did not reflect the looming quantitative and qualitative risks. Comparing relative spreads with quantitative and qualitative factors in early 1998 supported underweighting Russian bonds in early 1998.

International investors speculated that, because of its geopolitical significance, Russia was "too big to fail" and that the international community would come to rescue if needed. In fact, the IMF approved an $11.2 billion financial support program in July 1998 and immediately disbursed $4.6 billion. A month later, Russia devalued and contemporaneously defaulted on its local currency-denominated T-bills and Soviet era external debt. Russia did not, however, default on its Eurobonds.

Exhibit 20.13 is a radar chart comparing Russian macroeconomic variables in 1997 and 2000. Default on its Soviet-era external debt greatly improved Russia's refinancing picture. Currency depreciation and high oil prices led to an 18% current account surplus and a positive 18.8% basic balance in 2000. Accurate forecasts for Russia's serviceability position in 2000 were available in fall 1999 when Russia's Eurobond spreads were

EXHIBIT 20.12   Spread of Russia Republic 10% due 2007 less Market Spread

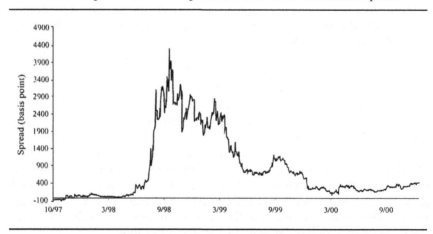

EXHIBIT 20.13 Russian Quantitative Variables in 1997 and 2000 (Radar Chart Comparison)

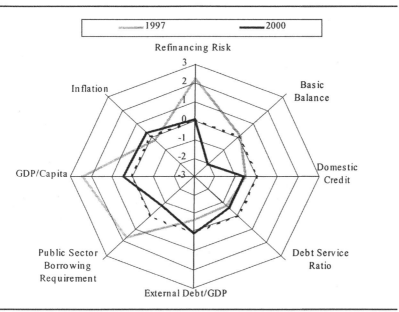

still trading 1,400 basis points above the market as indicated in Exhibit 20.12. Comparing relative spreads with quantitative and qualitative factors in late 1999 supported overweighting Russian bonds.

In spring 2000, the government under President Putin had secured a working coalition in the Duma for the first time since communism and was able to actively approve market friendly and institution building reforms. Although Russia's Eurobond spreads had declined substantially relative to market spreads, improved political conditions supported a continued overweight of Russian bonds in the Spring of 2000.

Overall Market Valuation Implications for Country Selection

Overall market spread expectations should be taken into account in country allocation. EMD country spreads tend to move in the same direction if there are no overriding country issues. When market spreads decline, countries with relatively high spreads (high risk) tend to outperform countries with lower spreads (low risk). If the valuation of the overall market indicates that EMD is undervalued, a portfolio's cash position should be small and the portfolio should have more weight in riskier countries. If the valuation of the overall market indicates that

EMD is overvalued, a portfolio's cash position should be increased and the portfolio should have more weight in defensive, low-risk countries. The risk management and portfolio construction section elaborates further on the relative riskiness of countries.

RELATIVE VALUATION OF INSTRUMENTS

Overall market exposure and country weights are the most important return contributors in emerging markets. Therefore, most research and investor interest is concentrated at the market or country level. However, performance of bonds within the same country can differ substantially and contribute significantly to performance. This section describes features of emerging market bonds that can cause differences in instrument performance and discusses some techniques to value different bonds within the same country.

Analysis of the Eurobond Spread Curve

The purest form of a country's credit risk is represented by internationally issued, bullet-maturity, fixed-coupon Eurobonds; all other instruments usually carry an extra premium to basic Eurobonds. Exhibit 20.14 shows the spreads of Mexican and Argentine dollar-denominated Eurobonds versus their spread duration. Most of the spreads of Eurobonds within the same country can be explained by spread duration, spread convexity, and the implied probability of default.

EXHIBIT 20.14 Eurobond Curves in Mexico and Argentina (4/30/2001)

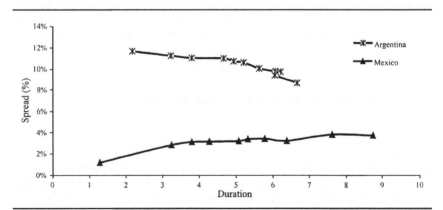

Spread Duration

Spread duration measures the price sensitivity of a bond due to changes in spread (risk premium). The shapes of the two spread curves in Exhibit 20.14 are quite different from each other. Mexico's spreads are much lower and the curve is relatively smooth and upward sloping. Argentina's spreads are much higher, the individual bonds are more scattered, and the curve is inverted.

Mexico's spread curve is a typical upward sloping spread curve. An upward sloping spread curve is consistent with risk aversion if we assume parallel shifts in the spread curve because higher-duration bonds will have greater price volatility than lower-duration bonds.

Spread Convexity

Spread convexity measures the rate of change of duration as spreads change and is used (along with duration) to approximate the change in a bond's price when spreads change.[23] A high convexity adds value to a bond. Due to the long duration and high spread volatility of many sovereign bonds, spread convexity plays a more important role in the management of emerging market bond portfolios than interest rate convexity plays in the management of U.S. corporate bond portfolios. Spread convexity explains the slight downward slope at the very end of the Mexican Eurobond curve because longer maturity bonds have more convexity. The longest instruments on the Mexican Eurobond curve are due in 2016 and 2026. The difference in spread convexity between the Eurobond due in 2026 and the Eurobond due in 2016 is 46.52. If we estimate the potential Mexican Eurobond spread change by their 90-day historic standard deviation (15.5%), then the convexity value of the Eurobond due 2026 is 54 cents ($\frac{1}{2} \times 46.52 \times 0.1552$) higher than that of Eurobond due 2016. A 54-cent convexity value equates to 5 basis points of value in the Eurobond due 2026 relative to the Eurobond due 2016 and may explain why the long end of the Mexican curve is downward sloping.

Implied Probability of Default

Bonds with a very high probability of default trade on a percentage-of-par (i.e., price) basis instead of a spread basis because past debt restructurings have been done on a percentage-of-par basis. In a percentage-of-par restructuring, the potential loss for high-dollar-priced bonds is higher than for low-dollar-priced bonds; this leads to an inverted spread

---

[23] The percentage change in dollar price due to spread movements can be approximated by the following formula: Price change = (Spread duration) × (Spread change) + $\frac{1}{2}$ (Spread convexity) × (Spread change)^2.

curve because shorter bonds typically have higher prices. The precedent of percentage-of-par restructurings is changing. During Ecuador's debt restructuring in the summer of 2000, debt write-offs were calculated on a *net present value* (NPV) basis. If investors expect a NPV-based debt restructuring, an issuer's spread curve should be flat, not inverted.

The inverted spread curve in Argentina in Exhibit 20.14 indicates high default risk and investor expectation of a percentage-of-par debt write-off. Investor expectations regarding the probability of default can be calculated from bond prices. The *implied probability of default* (IPD) is the default probability that sets the expected return on the bond equal to the risk free rate. Therefore, it is also called *risk neutral default probability*. The implied probability of a bond with three years to maturity and annual coupon payments can be calculated by solving the probability tree shown in Exhibit 20.15 for q.

When bonds trade on price and the spread curve is inverted, the IPD of short-duration bonds is higher than the IPD of long-duration bonds. A higher IPD in the short term makes economic sense because high IPD levels are unsustainable for a long period of time (either the country defaults or it overcomes the crisis and default probability starts to decline). Because investors cannot accurately assess a country's default risk in the long run, a country in crisis will have a IPD term structure that is declining for the first few years and then constant after a certain period of time.

EXHIBIT 20.15 Solving for Implied Probability of Default (IPD) using a Probability Tree

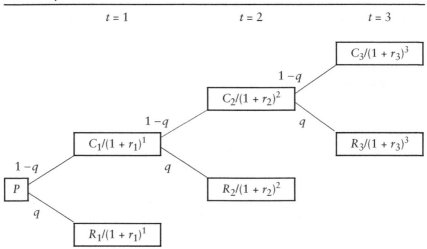

Where P denotes the price of the bond, q is the IPD, C are cash flows (coupons and principal, discounted at the risk free rate, r), and R is the present value of the recovery rate (discounted at the risk-free rate).

Applying the probability tree approach to bonds independent of one another will lead to different IPDs for overlapping cash flows; this is inconsistent. To generate a consistent term structure of default, one can calculate the IPD for short-term bonds and then apply the short-term IPD for the cash flows of longer-term bonds to find the longer term IPD (bootstrapping method). Applying this method to the spread curve in Argentina and assuming that the probability of default remains constant after four years generates the term structure of default probability in Exhibit 20.16.[24]

An investor can use this term structure of default probabilities to calculate consistent prices for long duration bonds. These prices can then be compared to market prices to make relative value decisions.[25]

There are more elaborate ways to calculate IPD such as taking the volatility of a country's credit risk into account. Elaborate methods often suffer from too much complexity and judgmental input. In the end, a model that is able to describe bond price behavior will serve the investor best.

Emerging Market Bonds that Do Not Trade on the Eurobond Spread Curve

So far, we have concentrated our analysis only on Eurobonds. Exhibit 20.17 shows spreads and durations for a variety of U.S. dollar-denomi-

EXHIBIT 20.16 Implied Probability of Default Term Structure in Argentina (4/30/2001)

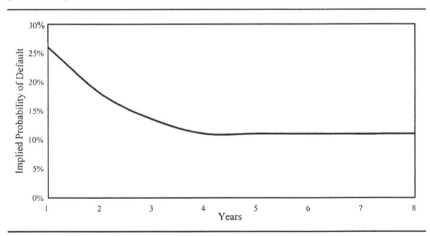

---

[24] Because Argentina does not have a Eurobond with maturity in 2002, we calculated the IPD for the first year from default swap rates.
[25] This approach ignores the influence of different repo rates and differences in default swap rates.

EXHIBIT 20.17   Argentine Instruments: Stripped Spread versus Spread Duration

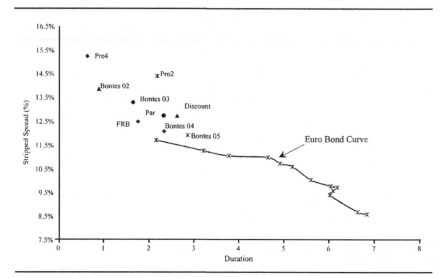

nated bonds in Argentina including Eurobonds, Brady bonds, and domestically issued bonds. Exhibit 20.17 illustrates that Argentine U.S. dollar-denominated bonds can have radically different spreads despite similar durations.

Spread differences between bonds with similar durations can be attributed to differences in credit ranking, collateralization, liquidity and repo rates, and instrument type. Below the characteristics of different EMD instruments relative to basic Eurobonds are outlined.

Credit Ranking

Credit ranking of an emerging market bond depends on the bond's original issuance, the legal status of the bond, payment guarantees, and the identity of the issuer.

Original Issuance   Some bonds are issued as a result of a debt restructuring or forced debt exchange. If a country has insufficient financial resources to service all its debt, it may choose to selectively default on previously restructured debt and continue to service its regularly issued Eurobonds. Eurobonds represent a country's future access to the capital markets, so there is an incentive to service Eurobonds above other types of debt. Sometimes restructured debt has the same legal protection as new Eurobond debt and sometimes it clearly does not; in many cases it is unclear.

Legal recourse for bondholders against sovereigns that selectively default is limited and has only rarely been tested in courts. Brady bonds resulted from a comprehensive sovereign loan restructuring. Because they had been restructured before, Brady bonds were initially rated lower than Eurobonds and traded at significantly higher spreads than Eurobonds. The rating agencies eventually increased the rating of Brady bonds to that of Eurobonds. Many countries have been buying back their Brady bonds or exchanging Brady bonds for Eurobonds. This has led to a reduction in the spread difference between Brady bonds and Eurobonds. Although Brady bonds are legally *pari passu* to sovereign Eurobonds and carry the same rating, in many cases the spread difference between Brady bonds and Eurobonds has not completely gone away.

Russia successfully selectively defaulted on previously restructured *Former Soviet Union* (FSU) bank debt.[26] The FSU bank debt was issued by Vneshekonombank, a fully government-owned export bank in Russia. The market generally viewed the FSU bank debt as obligations of the Russian Republic. When Russia issued its first Eurobond in 1997, it made the Eurobond senior to the FSU debt in order to secure lower funding costs; the prospectus of the new Eurobond did not include cross-default language to the FSU debt.

In 1998, Russia defaulted on its restructured FSU debt, but continued to service its Eurobonds. The subsequent restructuring of the FSU debt resulted in the issuance of more Eurobonds. To make the restructuring acceptable to the holders of the FSU debt, the Russians had to include prospectus language that would prevent the new Eurobonds from being subordinated again to regularly issued Eurobonds. Even so, it is unclear if such language will effectively protect bondholders from a selective default. As of April 2001, Russian Eurobonds that were issued in the FSU debt restructuring still trade at higher spreads than regularly issued Russian Eurobonds.

Due to weak legal protection of sovereign bondholders, the issuer's incentives to selectively default should not be underestimated. History shows that doubts concerning effective subordination leads to a relative spread widening of bonds issued as the result of a debt restructuring, particularly if default risk is high.

Legal Status Usually a sovereign issues domestic currency bonds and notes under domestic law—and foreign currency bonds and notes under New York or United Kingdom law. In some cases, however, sovereigns

---

[26] In contrast, Ecuador unsuccessfully tried to selectively default on part of its Brady bonds in 1999.

issue dollar-denominated instruments under domestic law. The enforcement of claims under domestic law is more difficult because the investor has to go through domestic rather than international courts, so bonds issued under domestic law usually trade at higher spreads than bonds issued under international law.

Exhibit 20.17 illustrates this point by comparing the spreads of the similar duration, dollar-denominated bonds in Argentina. The "Pro2 Bocones" and the "Bonte" due 2004 are domestically issued and the Eurobond due in 2003 is issued under New York law. The spread differential between domestic and internationally issued bonds is directional: It becomes larger when spreads increase and vice versa.

Partial Payment Guarantees Some countries have issued bonds that are partially guaranteed by the World Bank. For example, the cash flows of the Colombia World Bank-backed bond are structured as an annuity payable every six months with the World Bank (rated AAA) guaranteeing the first two consecutive payments. As long as Colombia is current on its interest and amortization payments, the World Bank guarantee will continue to roll forward to the next semiannual payment. If Colombia defaults on its payments to bondholders, the World Bank makes the next payment. This will trigger a default of the Republic of Colombia to the World Bank, which has preferred creditor status. The rating agencies posit that the likelihood of default to the World Bank is much lower than the likelihood of default on regular bonded sovereign debt.[27] Colombian World Bank-backed bonds are rated BBB/Baa1, whereas the Republic of Colombia has a rating of Ba2/BBB.[28]

Partially guaranteed sovereign bonds are relatively new to the market. They are not very well understood and the relative credit quality of guaranteed bonds has not been fully tested. World Bank-backed bonds in Argentina actually widened out relative to the Argentine Eurobonds when Argentina's credit quality deteriorated in the spring of 2000.[29]

---

[27] Standard & Poor's, "How Preferred Creditor Support Enhances Ratings," *Standard & Poor's CreditWeek* (June 1999).

[28] The standard method of comparing spreads of partially guaranteed bonds to spreads of nonguaranteed bonds is to calculate their stripped spreads. The calculation of stripped spreads for collateralized Brady bonds is explained in the section on collateralization. However, applying a similar methodology to partially guaranteed bonds does not take into account the World Bank's preferred creditor status.

[29] Argentine World Bank-backed bonds were issued with an investment-grade rating from S&P. Due to subsequent declines in Argentina's long-term debt rating, the World Bank-backed bonds were downgraded to BB.

Issuer The central government, government agencies, provincial governments, and corporations issue external dollar-denominated bonds. These different issuers within a country have different credit quality. Sovereign bonds issued by the central government generally have lower credit risk than other bonds. There are, however, some cases where corporations have better credit quality than the central government either because of their unique credit features or because they have better access to capital markets. Both Moody's and S&P rate some corporations higher than their sovereign ceiling.

Bonds of government agencies that do not have explicit guarantees from the central government like *Banco Nacional de Desenvolvimento Economico e Social* (BNDES) in Brazil or *Korean Development Bank* (KDB) in Korea usually also have more credit risk and carry an extra spread over sovereign Eurobonds.

The spread difference between riskier bonds and the sovereign Eurobond curve declines when Eurobond spread levels decline and widens when sovereign spreads widens.

Collateralization

The principal payments of some Brady bonds are collateralized by U.S. Treasury zero-coupon bonds. These bonds are effectively a combination of a risk-free Treasury bond and a risky emerging market bond. To compare the risk premium for collateralized bonds to the risk premium of noncollateralized bonds one should calculate spreads after stripping out the collateral. The so-called "stripped spread" is found by discounting the collateral at the appropriate spot interest rate and subtracting this collateral value from the bond's market price. The remainder is the price of the risky sovereign cash flows for which the standard procedure of finding the credit spread can be applied.

Many investors cannot effectively hedge the Treasury component of collateralized Brady bonds and therefore receive a low blended yield, which is a combination of the stripped yield and the yield of U.S. Treasuries. To compensate for the lower blended yield, investors require an extra premium for holding collateralized bonds. Therefore, collateralized bonds trade at higher stripped spreads than noncollateralized bonds.

Liquidity and Repo Market Considerations

Different issuers within a country have different liquidity. Eurobond and Brady bonds issued by the central government can be traded in institutional scale and have better liquidity than other bonds. Liquidity in corporate bonds can be especially poor if the corporation has just one issue outstanding and is not covered by multiple dealers.

In the past, massive short sales of the more liquid bonds have led to very low or even negative repo rates. Investors that hold the shorted bond can generate extra returns in the repo market.

Instrument Type

Not all fixed income instruments are issued as bonds. Some are issued in other legal forms such as trust certificates and loan participations. Because settlement of these alternative issue types is sometimes more complex and some investors cannot invest in these issues for regulatory reasons, these instruments often carry an additional spread over standard bonds.

Country Relative Valuation Implications for Instrument Selection

Country spread expectations should be taken into account during instrument selection. If a country is undervalued and spreads are expected to decline, a portfolio should be overweight long duration bonds if the spread curve is upward sloping; if the spread curve is inverted, a portfolio should be overweight bonds with high implied probability of default (usually shorter duration bonds). Under a declining spread scenario, the following types of bonds would outperform: subordinated bonds, uncollateralized bonds, illiquid bonds, and bonds with a nonstandard structure.

Conversely, if a country is overvalued and spreads are expected to increase, a portfolio should be overweight shorter duration bonds if the spread curve is upward sloping; if the spread curve is inverted, a portfolio should be overweight bonds with a lower dollar price. Under an increasing spread scenario, the following types of bonds would outperform: senior bonds, collateralized bonds, liquid bonds, and bonds with a standard structure. The risk management and portfolio construction section elaborates further on the relative riskiness of countries.

RISK MANAGEMENT AND PORTFOLIO CONSTRUCTION

How does an EMD investor incorporate his views regarding the overall market, relative country attractiveness, and instrument choices into a portfolio? How can an investor incorporate macroeconomic views into an EMD portfolio?

The valuation system described in the previous sections only provides part of the answer to the questions above. A valuation system compares value and price and determines the attractiveness of the overall market and the relative attractiveness of countries and instruments.

A detailed risk management system allows the EMD portfolio manager to incorporate his valuation views in the construction of a portfolio. An active investor establishes country and instrument over/underweights relative to his chosen benchmark. The exposure measurement techniques described in this section are calculated relative to a benchmark unless explicitly stated otherwise. Portfolio exposure can vary from simple percentage over/underweights to elaborate tracking error decomposition. We will discuss the pros and cons of various risk management techniques as they apply to an EMD portfolio.

Basic Exposure Measurement

Percentage market weight is the simplest way to measure risk exposure. It is the exposure of a portfolio to the return of a particular instrument or country. Instrument weights are summed together to calculate the weight for a particular country.

During periods of extreme market distress securities start to trade on a price basis rather than a spread basis.[30] When securities trade on a price basis, percentage exposure correctly measures a portfolio's exposure to a distressed issuer.

In a normal market environment the return of an EMD instrument is influenced by U.S. interest rate risk, instrument spread risk, country spread risk, and overall market spread risk. Percentage market weight does not specifically address these different risks.

An instrument's sensitivity to U.S. interest rate changes and issuer spread changes is measured by an instrument's interest rate duration and spread duration, respectively. Spread duration is higher than interest rate duration for floating rate bonds; interest rate duration is higher than spread duration for collateralized bonds.

U.S. interest rate risk can be measured on an overall portfolio basis by calculating the interest rate duration of the portfolio relative to the benchmark. Investors may choose to hedge U.S. interest rate risk by using U.S. note and bond futures to separate their U.S. interest rate views from their EMD credit views.

While U.S. interest rate exposure is aggregated for the entire portfolio, *contribution to spread duration* (CTD) relative to a benchmark should be shown by country and by instrument so the portfolio manager can determine exactly where credit risk is taken. The calculations for instrument-relative CTD are as follows:

---

[30] When there is a high probability that an issuer will default, securities trade on a price basis rather than a yield or spread basis. This behavior is driven by the market perception that all bonds of a defaulted issuer will be restructured on a percentage-of-par basis as described in the instrument valuation section.

$P(z)$ = weight of instrument z in portfolio
$B(z)$ = weight of instrument z in benchmark
$D(z)$ = spread duration of instrument z

$$\text{Instrument relative CTD} = D(z) \times [P(z) - B(z)]$$

Country-relative CTD is the sum of instrument-relative CTDs for all of the instruments in the country. The spread duration exposure for the overall portfolio is the sum of the CTDs.

Exhibit 20.18 is a risk report for an EMD portfolio relative to the EMBI Global benchmark. U.S. interest rate duration and spread duration are shown for the aggregate portfolio; percentage market weight exposure and relative CTD are broken out by country. Relative U.S. interest rate duration is hedged with U.S. Treasury futures.

The U.S. interest rate duration of the portfolio is similar to that of the benchmark. Despite a cash exposure of 3.4%, the portfolio has more spread duration relative to the benchmark because it has an overweight in higher spread duration instruments.

Country exposures vary depending on the risk measurement methodology used. For example, the portfolio has more percentage market weight exposure in Bulgaria than in Qatar, but Qatar contributes more to the portfolio's spread duration than Bulgaria. These results indicate that the portfolio has more exposure to spread movements in Qatar than in Bulgaria because the portfolio has longer duration Qatar securities. However, the portfolio has more exposure to a massive credit event in Bulgaria than in Qatar because the percentage market weight exposure to Bulgaria is higher.

Beta-Adjusting Spread Durations

Since EMD securities are risky assets, a decrease in investor risk tolerance can lead to an increase in spreads for EMD issuers. However, an increase in spreads for the overall market does not uniformly affect spreads of individual EMD issuers. Spreads of risky credits such as Russia and Brazil tend to increase more during a market selloff than spreads of less risky credits such as Mexico and Poland; risky credits tend to outperform when market spreads decrease. Exhibit 20.19 shows the spread change for the market and for various countries during a market rally and a market sell-off using weekly data.[31] We define a spread decline of 50 or more basis points during a week as a market rally (18 instances) and a spread increase of 50 or more basis points during a week as a market selloff (21 instances).

---

[31] Stripped spread data are from JP Morgan from 12/31/1997 to 4/30/2001. (Data series start at 12/31/1997 because EMBI Global Country Sub-Indices are not available before that date.) EMD market spreads are adjusted for defaulted issuers.

EXHIBIT 20.18   Basic Risk Report, April 30, 2001

	Portfolio	Benchmark	Relative
Cash	3.4%	0.0%	—
Interest Rate Duration	4.92	4.92	1.00
Spread Duration	4.96	4.66	1.06

Country	Percentage Market Weight (%)			Contribution to Spread Duration		
	Portfolio	Benchmark	Difference	Portfolio	Benchmark	Difference
Algeria	—	0.5	(0.5)	—	0.01	(0.01)
Argentina	19.0	19.1	(0.1)	0.65	0.73	(0.08)
Brazil	23.7	19.7	4.0	1.27	0.92	0.35
Bulgaria	5.8	1.9	3.9	0.26	0.08	0.18
Chile	—	0.3	(0.3)	—	0.02	(0.02)
China	—	1.1	(1.1)	—	0.05	(0.05)
Colombia	1.7	1.9	(0.2)	0.08	0.09	(0.01)
Côte d'Ivoire	—	0.1	(0.1)	—	0.00	(0.00)
Croatia	—	0.4	(0.4)	—	0.01	(0.01)
Ecuador	—	1.0	(1.0)	—	0.05	(0.05)
Hungary	—	0.4	(0.4)	—	0.01	(0.01)
Korea	1.7	5.6	(3.9)	0.09	0.21	(0.12)
Lebanon	—	0.3	(0.3)	—	0.00	(0.00)
Malaysia	—	2.5	(2.5)	—	0.13	(0.13)
Mexico	14.3	15.5	(1.2)	0.81	0.83	(0.02)
Morocco	1.1	0.9	0.2	0.03	0.03	0.01
Nigeria	—	1.6	(1.6)	—	0.04	(0.04)
Panama	1.9	2.1	(0.2)	0.15	0.14	0.01
Peru	0.1	1.1	(1.0)	0.01	0.07	(0.06)
Philippines	1.2	2.2	(1.0)	0.09	0.15	(0.06)
Poland	—	1.9	(1.9)	—	0.12	(0.12)
Qatar	3.3	—	3.3	0.31	—	0.31
Russia	19.2	10.8	8.4	1.06	0.56	0.50
South Africa	—	1.0	(1.0)	—	0.06	(0.06)
Thailand	—	0.3	(0.3)	—	0.02	(0.02)
Turkey	—	2.8	(2.8)	—	0.13	(0.13)
Ukraine	0.8	0.4	0.4	0.02	0.01	0.01
Venezuela	2.7	4.8	(2.1)	0.13	0.20	(0.07)
Cash	3.4	—	3.4	—	—	—
Total	100.0	100.0	—	4.96	4.66	0.29

EXHIBIT 20.19   Country Spread Changes During Market Rallies and Sell-Offs, December 1997 through April 2001

| | Average Weekly Spread Δ (bps) | |
Country	Market Rally	Market Selloff
Market	−92	110
Argentina	−75	122
Brazil	−106	123
Bulgaria	−64	81
Colombia	−46	40
Ecuador	−140	158
Korea	−37	29
Mexico	−60	71
Morocco	−58	103
Nigeria	−63	108
Panama	−22	33
Peru	−49	55
Philippines	−41	41
Poland	−17	26
Russia[a]	−310	371
Turkey	−22	44
Venezuela	−132	137

[a] The spread change numbers are very high because the time period examined includes the Russian crisis, which had a significant impact on spreads of other emerging debt countries. To the extent that Russian spread changes influenced market spread changes, the large spread changes in Russia during rallies and sell-offs exaggerate the true market risk in Russia.

Exhibit 20.19 shows that spreads in Brazil, Ecuador, and Russia typically change more than the market spread during rallies and sell-offs, while spreads in Panama, Poland, and Korea change less than the market spread during rallies and sell-offs. Spread changes that are smaller than market spread changes during a rally/sell-off indicate that a country has less market risk but not necessarily less credit risk. For example, Turkey's spreads have increased and decreased dramatically over the time period examined in Exhibit 20.19. However, large spread changes in Turkey have not occurred at the same time as large market spread changes.

Instrument spread sensitivities to country spread movements also vary. The spreads of shorter maturity instruments and instruments with unique structures may increase by more than other bonds within a given country following a negative credit event; similarly, the spreads of these securities decrease by more than other securities following a positive credit event.[32] Exhibit 20.20 compares the spread change for the Brazilian EMBI Global Sub-Index and for various instruments in Brazil during a market rally and a market sell-off using weekly data.[33] We define a spread decline for the Brazilian Sub-Index of 50 or more basis points during a week as a rally (22 instances) and a spread increase of 50 or more basis points during a week as a sell-off (28 instances).

Exhibit 20.20 shows that spreads of collateralized Brady bonds[34] (Pars and Discounts) and short duration Brady bonds (EI) typically change more than the Brazilian Sub-Index spread during rallies and sell-offs, while spreads of Eurobonds and very liquid Bradys (C bond) change less than the Brazilian Sub-Index spread during rallies and sell-offs. The spreads of short duration Brazilian Eurobonds change more relative to other Eurobonds during market rallies and sell-offs.

A portfolio's overall spread duration is an accurate measure of market risk if one assumes that all of the spreads of the countries in the portfolio will increase/decrease by the same amount in response to a negative/positive market credit event. Similarly, a country's contribution to spread duration is an accurate measure of country risk if we assume that the spreads of the instruments within a country will increase/decrease by the same amount in response to a negative/positive country credit event. Exhibits 20.19 and 20.20 indicate that it is not realistic to assume that country and instrument spreads react identically.

Beta-adjusting spread durations can provide portfolio managers with an enhanced tool to measure the sensitivity of their portfolio to changes in overall market spreads and changes in the spreads of a particular country. Each instrument has two betas: a market beta and a country beta. A *market beta* measures an instrument's sensitivity to overall market spread changes; a *country beta* measures a bond's sensitivity to country spread changes. Betas are measured as the coefficient of a regression of the spread change of an instrument against the spread change of the overall market (market beta) or the spread change of a country (country beta). Exhibit 20.21 shows market and country betas for various instruments in Brazil and Panama.[35]

---

[32] For more details, refer to the section on relative valuation of instruments.

[33] Spread data are from JP Morgan from 12/31/1997 to 4/30/2001; EMBI Global Brazil Sub-Index is used for the Brazil country spread.

[34] Spreads for collateralized bonds are shown as stripped spreads (for the calculation of stripped spreads refer to the section on instrument valuation).

[35] Market and country betas are calculated from 18 months of weekly spread data. For instruments with limited history, a substitute instrument with similar characteristics may be used. Post-restructuring data were used for Russia and Ecuador.

EXHIBIT 20.20 Brazilian Instrument Spread Changes During Market Rallies and Sell-Offs, December 1997 through April 2001

Bond	Type	Coupon	Principal	Spread Duration	Average Weekly Spread Δ (bps)	
					Market Rally	Market Sell-Off
Brazil	Index			4.69	−115	118
Republic 11⅝% due 2004ᵃ	Eurobond	Fixed	Bullet	2.44	−120	160
Republic 9⅜% due 2008	Eurobond	Fixed	Bullet	4.81	−92	92
Republic 10⅛% due 2027	Eurobond	Fixed	Bullet	6.65	−81	86
EI	Brady	Floating	Amortizing	2.17	−147	161
FLIRB	Brady	Floating	Amortizing	3.67	−114	120
DCB	Brady	Floating	Amortizing	4.69	−115	116
C	Brady	Step-Up	Amortizing	4.80	−79	92
Par	Brady	Step-Up	Collateralized	2.95	−163	152
Discount	Brady	Floating	Collateralized	3.33	−191	166

ᵃ Due to short data history, the spread changes for the Brazilian Eurobond due 2004 were calculated by taking the ratio of the spread changes for the Eurobond due 2004 and the Eurobond due 2008 (for the period when spread information for the Eurobond due 2004 was available) and multiplying by the spread changes for the Eurobond due 2008 for the entire time period.

EXHIBIT 20.21 Market and Country Betas (Brazil and Panama), April 2001

Bond	Type	Coupon	Principal	Spread Duration	Beta	
					Market	Country
Brazil Republic 9⅜% due 2008	Eurobond	Fixed	Bullet	4.81	0.84	0.77
Brazil Republic 10⅛% due 2027	Eurobond	Fixed	Bullet	6.65	0.94	0.83
Brazil DCB	Brady	Floating	Amortizing	4.69	1.22	1.11
Panama 8¼% due 2008	Eurobond	Fixed	Bullet	5.19	0.50	0.87
Panama 8⅞% due 2027	Eurobond	Fixed	Bullet	9.02	0.53	0.94
Panama PDI	Brady	Floating	Amortizing	7.37	0.55	1.06

In Exhibit 20.21, the market betas for Brazilian instruments are higher than the market betas for Panamanian instruments indicating that Brazilian bonds are more sensitive to EMD spread movements. Within Brazil and Panama, sensitivity to country spread movements varies with Brady bonds having more sensitivity to spread movements than Eurobonds.

Because an instrument's market and country beta measure different sensitivities, the two risks should be shown separately or valuable information is lost. A portfolio's overall spread duration and a country's relative CTD can be adjusted by using market and country betas as follows:

$P(z)$ = weight of instrument z in portfolio
$B(z)$ = weight of instrument z in benchmark
$D(z)$ = spread duration of instrument z
$BC(z)$ = spread beta of instrument z relative to country
$BM(z)$ = spread beta of instrument z relative to overall market

Country beta-adjusted instrument relative CTD = $BC(z) \times D(z) \times [P(z) - B(z)]$

Market beta-adjusted instrument relative CTD = $BM(z) \times D(z) \times [P(z) - B(z)]$

Country beta-adjusted instrument relative CTDs can be combined for all of the instruments within a country to more accurately show a portfolio's sensitivity to changes in spread for the particular country. Country beta-adjusted instrument relative CTDs are only applicable at the country level and should not be summed up to the overall portfolio.

Market beta-adjusted instrument relative CTDs can be combined for all of the instruments within a country to show how a particular country contributes to the overall market risk of the portfolio. Market beta-adjusted instrument relative CTDs can be summed up to measure the market risk of the overall portfolio.

Exhibit 20.22 shows a risk report for an EMD portfolio versus the EMBI Global benchmark. Overall portfolio spread duration is adjusted by the market beta. Country relative CTDs are shown adjusted by market betas and adjusted by country betas.

The risk report in Exhibit 20.22 shows that the relative risk of the portfolio is considerably larger when spread durations are adjusted by a market beta because the portfolio has more exposure to countries that are particularly sensitive to market spread movements. In Exhibit 20.18, the spread duration of the portfolio was 1.06 times the spread duration of the benchmark, while the portfolio's market beta-adjusted spread duration is 1.28 times the benchmark's. Due to the high market sensitivity of Russia, Russia's contribution to the portfolio's risk has increased

EXHIBIT 20.22   Risk Report Containing Beta-Adjustments, April 30, 2001

	Portfolio	Benchmark	Relative
Market Beta-Adjusted Spread Duration	5.90	4.60	1.28

	Market Beta-Adjusted CTD			Country Beta-Adjusted CTD		
	Portfolio	Benchmark	Difference	Portfolio	Benchmark	Difference
Algeria	—	0.00	(0.00)	—	0.01	(0.01)
Argentina	1.14	1.12	0.02	0.75	0.71	0.04
Brazil	1.41	1.05	0.36	1.21	0.89	0.32
Bulgaria	0.24	0.08	0.17	0.25	0.08	0.17
Chile	—	0.00	(0.00)	—	0.02	(0.02)
China	—	0.01	(0.01)	—	0.05	(0.05)
Colombia	0.06	0.06	(0.00)	0.07	0.09	(0.02)
Côte d'Ivoire	—	0.00	(0.00)	—	0.00	(0.00)
Croatia	—	0.01	(0.01)	—	0.01	(0.01)
Ecuador	—	0.06	(0.06)	—	0.05	(0.05)
Hungary	—	0.00	(0.00)	—	0.01	(0.01)
Korea	0.05	0.05	(0.00)	0.22	0.19	0.03
Lebanon	—	0.00	(0.00)	—	0.00	(0.00)
Malaysia	—	0.03	(0.03)	—	0.13	(0.13)
Mexico	0.55	0.53	0.02	0.77	0.75	0.02
Morocco	0.02	0.02	0.00	0.03	0.03	0.01
Nigeria	—	0.03	(0.03)	—	0.04	(0.04)
Panama	0.09	0.08	0.01	0.16	0.14	0.01
Peru	0.00	0.05	(0.05)	0.00	0.07	(0.06)
Philippines	0.09	0.12	(0.03)	0.10	0.16	(0.05)
Poland	—	0.03	(0.03)	—	0.12	(0.12)
Qatar	0.10	—	0.10	0.31	—	0.31
Russia	2.00	0.97	1.04	1.21	0.59	0.62
South Africa	—	0.03	(0.03)	—	0.06	(0.06)
Thailand	—	0.00	(0.00)	—	0.02	(0.02)
Turkey	—	0.07	(0.07)	—	0.13	(0.13)
Ukraine	0.03	0.01	0.01	0.02	0.01	0.01
Venezuela	0.11	0.19	(0.08)	0.11	0.19	(0.07)

from 21% of the portfolio's spread duration to 34% of the portfolio's market beta-adjusted spread duration.[36]

Exhibit 20.18 showed a CTD underweight in Argentina, while Exhibit 20.22 shows a market beta-adjusted CTD overweight in Argentina. The increase in sensitivity to Argentina is due to the portfolio's higher exposure to instruments that are more sensitive to spread movements in Argentina (the portfolio's country beta-adjusted CTD for Argentina is higher than the benchmark's).

Tracking Error Decomposition

Does increasing an overweight to a country with a high market beta necessarily increase the overall risk of a portfolio? Can a risk model capture a portfolio's exposure to an external factor, such as oil prices?

The risk measurement techniques described in the previous sections do not provide a complete picture of a portfolio's risk because they calculate each country's/instrument's risk separately, without taking into account how a particular country's instrument's spread moves relative to other holdings in a portfolio. Increasing an overweight in a country with a large market beta can decrease the overall risk of a portfolio if the particular country has a low correlation with other holdings in a portfolio. Percentage market weights and CTDs (regular and beta-adjusted) do not take into account co-movement between countries, so they cannot tell a portfolio manager what trades will lower the overall risk of an EMD portfolio relative to a benchmark.

Tracking error measurement and decomposition is becoming the industry norm for measuring the risk of a portfolio versus a benchmark. Tracking error decomposition gives EMD managers a more complete picture of how their exposures are contributing to overall portfolio risk. Tracking error measurement incorporates not only the spread volatility of every holding in a portfolio, but also incorporates the correlation between the different countries and instruments within a portfolio and relative to benchmark holdings. Below we describe how a bond risk management system decomposes the tracking error risk of an EMD portfolio.

Tracking error measures (in terms of standard deviations) the risk of a performance difference between a portfolio and its benchmark.[37] To simplify the tracking error discussion, we analyze an EMD portfolio that is hedged against movements in U.S. interest rates and focus on risk from credit spread movements. The tracking error measurement will

---

[36] Exhibit 20.18 shows that Russia's contribution to the portfolio's spread duration is 1.06 (21% of the portfolio's total spread duration of 4.96). Exhibit 20.22 shows that Russia's contribution to the portfolio's market beta-adjusted spread duration is 2.00 (34% of the portfolio's total market beta-adjusted spread duration of 5.90).

take into account the volatilities and correlations of spread changes for all of the countries held in the benchmark and the portfolio. The tracking error measurement will also take into account the specific risk (i.e., the difference in spread change between bonds in the same country).

The matrix formulas used to calculate the tracking error of a portfolio are shown as follows:

$$\text{Tracking error} = (\text{Systematic risk}^2 + \text{Instrument-specific risk}^2)^{\frac{1}{2}}$$

$$
\begin{aligned}
\text{Systematic risk}^2 = \;& (\text{Country-active exposure vector})^T \\
& \times (\text{Country-spread variance/Covariance matrix}) \\
& \times (\text{Country-active exposure vector})
\end{aligned}
$$

$$
\begin{aligned}
\text{Instrument-specific risk}^2 = \;& [(\text{Instrument-active exposure vector})^2]^T \\
& \times [\text{Instrument-residual risk vector}^2]
\end{aligned}
$$

Systematic risks influence all of the bonds within a specific category. In this tracking error model, countries are treated as systematic risks. The systematic risk calculation contains a vector with active exposures across countries and a matrix that contains spread variances and covariances across countries in the portfolio and the benchmark. An active exposure is the difference in risk factor sensitivity between the portfolio and the benchmark. Since the risk in this tracking error model is spread movement, relative CTD is the appropriate risk factor sensitivity. Therefore, the country active exposure vector contains differences in country CTD between the portfolio and the benchmark.

Instrument-specific risk captures performance differences between securities within a specific country. Instrument-relative CTDs are placed in the instrument active exposure matrix. The active exposure vector is multiplied by a vector that contains residual risk information for every instrument in the portfolio and benchmark. Residual risk for a particular instrument measures the standard deviation of the spread difference between the instrument and the corresponding country spread. Factors such as instrument type (Brady, Eurobond, and local issue) and instrument duration influence residual risk.

In calculating overall tracking error, systematic risk and instrument specific risk are assumed to be independent (zero correlation).

---

[37] Assuming a normal distribution and zero value added from the active strategy, a tracking error of 2% for a given period implies that the portfolio will underperform or outperform its benchmark by less than 2% in that period approximately 68% of the time.

Exposure vectors contain relative CTDs for a country or an instrument. Instrument-residual risk vectors are estimated by calculating the historic spread change differences between bonds in the same country. Country spread variance/covariance matrices require more advanced calculations based on historical spread data analysis.

The country-spread variance/covariance matrix is calculated through a process that takes into account the historical correlation of common factors that drive country spreads. For example, the positive correlation between spread movements in Russia and Venezuela is partly due to the fact that both countries are major exporters of energy products (oil and gas). Therefore, oil price is an underlying factor that helps explain the correlation between Russia and Venezuela. This risk model uses the following common factors: regional spread factors (Latin America, Asia, Eastern Europe), quality spread factors (investment grade, noninvestment grade), U.S. equity, oil, U.S. high-yield spreads, and foreign exchange rates (euro/$ and yen/$).

A variance/covariance matrix is calculated for the underlying factors using historical data. Then, analysis is performed to measure the sensitivity of a country's spread movement to the underlying factors. For example, Venezuela is sensitive to Latin American spread movements and oil prices. The underlying factor variance/covariance matrix is combined with the sensitivity analysis to create a country spread variance/covariance matrix that contains all of the countries in the portfolio and in the benchmark.[38]

Exhibit 20.23 shows a risk summary for an EMD portfolio that uses the EMBI Global as its benchmark. The risk summary shows the total tracking error and beta of the portfolio versus its benchmark as well as total volatility for the portfolio and the benchmark. Tracking error, beta, and volatility numbers are further separated into a systematic and an instrument-specific component.

EXHIBIT 20.23 Tracking Error Risk Summary, April 2001

	Risk		
	Total	Systematic	Instrument Specific
Benchmark Volatility	9.3%	9.2%	1.1%
Portfolio Volatility	11.1%	10.9%	1.6%
Expected Tracking Error	2.9%	2.5%	1.4%
Portfolio Beta	1.16	1.15	0.01

---

[38] Using underlying factors to build a variance/covariance matrix facilitates the modeling of countries with limited spread data history and is intuitively more consistent than calculating relationships from historical data.

This exhibit shows that the portfolio is a lot riskier than the benchmark. The expected volatility of the portfolio is 11.1% versus 9.3% for the benchmark and the portfolio has an expected tracking error of 2.9%. The bulk of the risk comes from systematic (i.e., market) rather than instrument-specific risk.

The tracking error model estimates the portfolio beta at 1.16, which is above the relative spread duration of the portfolio measured in Exhibit 20.18 (1.06), but below the relative market beta-adjusted spread duration of the portfolio measured in Exhibit 20.22 (1.28). This makes intuitive sense. The tracking error model and the market beta-adjusted spread duration calculate higher relative risk for the portfolio because they account for both spread duration and the portfolio's overweight in certain high beta countries. The relative risk calculated by the tracking error model is lower than the relative risk of market beta-adjusted spread duration because imperfect correlation between country spread movements decreases the risk of the high-beta portfolio.

Exhibit 20.24 shows a detailed breakout of an EMD portfolio's tracking error across countries. This exhibit shows that the bulk of the portfolio's tracking error risk is explained by overweights in Russia and Brazil, with the overweight in Russia explaining more than half of the portfolio's tracking error. The portfolio's underweight in high volatility Ecuador actually lowers the portfolio's tracking error. Instrument specific risk is important in countries that have a variety of bonds (Bradys's, domestic bonds, etc.) such as Argentina and Brazil. Argentina's contribution to the portfolio's tracking error comes mainly from instrument selection within Argentina.

Exhibit 20.25 provides a summary of the strengths and weaknesses of different portfolio risk management techniques just described.

ATTRIBUTION

A detailed attribution model provides feedback to portfolio managers about the strengths and weaknesses of their decision-making processes. A portfolio manager's valuation process dictates not only an approach to risk management but also the structure of an attribution model. The valuation section described how to evaluate the attractiveness of the market, the relative attractiveness of countries, and the relative attractiveness of instruments within countries. The attribution model provides feedback on each of these decisions.

The return of an emerging market bond can be divided into four components: (1) underlying treasury yield, (2) U.S. yield curve change,

EXHIBIT 20.24   Tracking Error Breakout by Country, April 2001

	Total Contribution	Systematic Contribution	Instrument-Specific Contribution
Total	2.85%	2.47%	1.43%
Algeria	−0.01%	−0.01%	0.00%
Argentina	0.18%	−0.13%	0.60%
Brazil	0.78%	0.69%	0.37%
Bulgaria	0.26%	0.29%	0.01%
Chile	0.03%	0.00%	0.05%
China	0.00%	0.00%	0.00%
Colombia	0.00%	−0.01%	0.01%
Côte d'Ivoire	0.00%	0.00%	0.00%
Croatia	−0.01%	−0.01%	0.00%
Ecuador	−0.08%	−0.10%	0.00%
Hungary	0.00%	0.00%	0.00%
Korea	−0.01%	−0.01%	0.01%
Lebanon	0.00%	0.00%	0.00%
Malaysia	0.00%	0.00%	0.00%
Mexico	0.00%	−0.01%	0.02%
Morocco	0.01%	0.01%	0.00%
Nigeria	−0.01%	−0.01%	0.00%
Panama	0.01%	0.01%	0.00%
Peru	−0.04%	−0.04%	0.00%
Philippines	−0.04%	−0.05%	0.01%
Poland	−0.01%	−0.01%	0.00%
Qatar	0.07%	0.08%	0.01%
Russia	1.72%	1.81%	0.30%
South Africa	0.01%	0.01%	0.00%
Thailand	0.00%	0.00%	0.00%
Turkey	−0.03%	−0.05%	0.02%
Ukraine	0.01%	0.01%	0.00%
Uruguay	0.00%	0.00%	0.00%
Venezuela	0.00%	0.00%	0.01%

EXHIBIT 20.25   Portfolio Risk Management Techniques for EMD Portfolios

Technique	Strengths	Weaknesses
Percentage Weight	- Simple - Useful during periods of distress when securities trade on price	- Does not separate spread risk from U.S. interest rate risk - Volatility and comovement of spreads between countries not evaluated - Cannot calculate overall portfolio risk relative to benchmark
Contribution to Spread Duration (CTD)	- Simple - Captures sensitivity to spread movement - Relative risk for overall portfolio can be calculated	- Not as useful during periods of distress - Volatility and comovement of spreads between countries not evaluated
Beta-Adjusted CTD	- Captures a volatility adjusted sensitivity to spread movement - Relative risk for overall portfolio can be calculated	- Comovement of spreads between countries not evaluated
Tracking Error Decomposition	- Decomposes sensitivity to spread movement adjusted for volatility and comovement of countries - Divides portfolio risk between systematic and security specific risk factors - Allows flexibility to divide portfolio risk along various noncountry dimensions	- Relatively complex. Model is sensitive to assumptions made during construction - Model correlation/volatility assumptions have to be recalibrated if there is a market regime shift

(3) spread yield, and (4) spread change. The U.S. Yield curve change component measures the portion of a bond's return that is explained by movements in the underlying Treasury yield curve. Underlying Treasury yield and spread yield are calculated by dividing up the income and accretion component of a bond's return. The spread change component represents the part of a security's return due to spread tightening/widening. Underlying Treasury yield can be combined with U.S. yield curve change to create a U.S. yield curve factor that represents the total return of the U.S. Treasury instrument equivalent to the EMD instrument. Sim-

ilarly, spread yield and spread change can be combined to create a spread factor.

The components of an emerging market bond's return are then calculated as follows:[39]

$$
\begin{array}{l}
\text{Return of emerging} \\
\text{debt instrument}
\end{array}
=
\begin{array}{l}
\text{Underlying} \\
\text{Treasury yield}
\end{array}
+
\begin{array}{l}
\text{U.S. yield} \\
\text{curve change}
\end{array}
+
\begin{array}{l}
\text{Spread} \\
\text{yield}
\end{array}
+
\begin{array}{l}
\text{Spread} \\
\text{change}
\end{array}
$$

Underlying Treasury yield + Spread yield
= Income and accretion of instrument

U.S. Yield curve factor
= Underlying treasury yield + U.S. yield curve change

Spread factor = Spread yield + Spread change

Return of emerging market debt instrument
= U.S. yield curve factor + Spread factor

The components of an instrument's return are weighted by portfolio and benchmark percentage market weights and differences between the portfolio and benchmark are analyzed within the attribution process. Since U.S. yield curve exposure is measured at the overall portfolio level, it is not necessary to break out the difference between the portfolio's and the benchmark's U.S. yield curve factor by country.

Because valuation and risk management for EMD portfolios is done on the basis of spread movements, an EMD attribution model decomposes the spread factor difference between the portfolio and the benchmark. The spread factor difference between the portfolio and the benchmark is divided into three factors: (1) market effect, (2) country selection, and (3) instrument selection. *Market effect* measures the contribution of the overall portfolio spread duration to the portfolio's relative performance. A portfolio with a spread duration that is greater than the benchmark's will have a positive market effect if the benchmark has a positive spread factor. *Country selection* measures how country relative CTDs contribute to the spread factor difference between the portfolio and the benchmark. Lastly, *instrument selection* measures how instrument relative CTDs contribute to the spread factor difference.[40]

---

[39] The equations show components of the underlying returns, not returns themselves.

[40] For a more detailed discussion on performance attribution for EMD portfolios see Brian Fischer and Fernando Cunha, "Performance Attribution for an Emerging Market External-Debt Portfolio," *JP Morgan Portfolio Strategies* (September 9, 1998).

Exhibit 20.26 shows an attribution report for a single month (April 2001) for an EMD portfolio. The return difference between the portfolio and the benchmark is divided between U.S. yield curve factor and spread factor. Then, spread factor is divided into market effect, country selection, and instrument selection. Country selection and instrument selection are shown by country. Instrument selection contribution can be displayed down to the individual instrument level, but are summarized at the country level in this exhibit.

Exhibit 20.26 shows the portfolio's exposure relative to the benchmark at the beginning of the month both in percentage weight and CTD. Also shown is the spread factor for each country; this is the country's return excluding the effect of U.S. yield curve change and underlying Treasury yield. Turkey, Côte d'Ivoire, and Russia had the largest spread factors, while Peru, Ecuador, and Argentina had the lowest spread factors.

The portfolio in Exhibit 20.26 outperformed the benchmark by 45 basis points. U.S. yield curve and spread factor contributed 7 basis points and 38 basis points, respectively, to the portfolio's relative performance. The portfolio's overall duration overweight is captured by the market effect and explains only 1 basis point of the spread factor. Country selection explains 27 basis points of the spread factor, while instrument selection contributed 10 basis points to the spread factor. Positive contributors to country selection include CTD overweights in Russia and Qatar and CTD underweight in Peru and Argentina. A CTD underweight in Turkey negatively impacted country selection. Issue selection in Korea contributed to performance, while issue selection in Argentina detracted from performance.

CONCLUSION

The volatility of emerging markets debt requires using a fundamental valuation approach as an anchor. The analysis shows that while EMD spreads and macroeconomic fundamentals move in the same direction, spreads are more volatile than fundamentals and EMD fundamentals have been on an improving trend since the mid-1990s.

A distinguishing feature of the EMD asset class is the need of emerging countries to rely on international investors for capital. A systematic framework for evaluating EMD sovereign issuers considers the interaction of quantitative and qualitative factors to determine the probability that a country receives the foreign capital that it needs.

EXHIBIT 20.26 Detailed Attribution by Country, April 30, 2001

Portfolio less Benchmark		Contribution to Spread Factor	
U.S. Yield Curve	0.07%	Market Effect	0.01%
Spread Factor	0.38%	Country Selection	0.27%
Total	0.45%	Instrument Selection	0.10%
		Total	0.38%

Country	Portfolio less Benchmark		Spread Factor	Contrib to Spread Factor	
	Weight	CTD		Country Slct	Instrument Slct
Total	0.00%	0.12	0.69%	0.27%	0.10%
Cash	8.46%	0.00	0.00%	0.00%	0.00%
Algeria	−0.48%	−0.01	1.28%	−0.01%	0.00%
Argentina	−1.01%	−0.10	−2.42%	0.10%	−0.14%
Brazil	1.22%	0.25	−0.23%	−0.04%	0.05%
Bulgaria	3.96%	0.19	−0.48%	−0.03%	0.00%
Chile	−0.27%	−0.02	0.73%	0.00%	0.00%
China	−1.09%	−0.04	0.30%	0.00%	0.00%
Colombia	0.33%	0.01	1.78%	0.00%	0.02%
Côte d'Ivoire	−0.06%	0.00	4.99%	0.00%	0.00%
Croatia	−0.37%	−0.01	0.11%	0.00%	0.00%
Ecuador	−1.04%	−0.05	−5.06%	0.06%	0.00%
Hungary	−0.37%	−0.01	−0.19%	0.00%	0.00%
Korea	−4.52%	−0.15	0.73%	−0.08%	0.10%
Lebanon	−0.28%	−0.01	0.58%	0.00%	0.00%
Malaysia	−2.85%	−0.14	−1.45%	0.05%	0.00%
Mexico	−0.77%	0.01	2.57%	0.00%	0.07%
Morocco	0.19%	0.01	0.70%	0.00%	0.00%
Nigeria	−1.52%	−0.04	4.35%	−0.06%	0.00%
Panama	−0.03%	0.02	3.67%	0.01%	0.00%
Peru	−1.13%	−0.07	−10.60%	0.12%	0.00%
Philippines	−1.01%	−0.06	−0.32%	0.01%	−0.02%
Poland	−2.22%	−0.14	2.13%	−0.04%	0.00%
Qatar	3.23%	0.31	4.14%	0.12%	0.00%
Russia	6.92%	0.43	4.49%	0.35%	0.03%
South Africa	−0.95%	−0.06	1.51%	−0.01%	0.00%
Thailand	−0.34%	−0.02	1.78%	−0.01%	0.00%
Turkey	−2.52%	−0.12	9.34%	−0.23%	0.00%
Ukraine	0.43%	0.01	−0.95%	0.00%	0.00%
Venezuela	−1.91%	−0.06	2.13%	−0.03%	0.00%

Because of the variety of investment alternatives and their widely differing performance characteristics, there are many opportunities for relative value trades across countries and within the same country. High spread volatility and low legal protection make technical, as well as legal, considerations indispensable when evaluating individual bonds.

Due to the high volatility of EMD spreads, a portfolio manager benefits from using a variety of risk management techniques. Adjusting spread duration measurements by a volatility-based beta provides a more complete picture of the portfolio's sensitivity to movements in market spreads. Tracking error decomposition takes into account inter-country correlations and exposures to common risk factors such as oil prices.

All of the stages of a disciplined investment process are connected. After deciding on a benchmark that properly captures the investment universe, the investor considers overall market, country, and instrument valuation when making investment decisions. The different portions of the valuation process are reflected in risk and attribution models in order to assist the investor in portfolio construction and to provide performance feedback on prior decisions.

Index

Wizon, Adam, 249
World Bank, 496, 512
  preferred creditor status, 512
Worldcom, bankruptcy, 8
Worst case return, maximization, 55–56
Wu, Wei, 464

Xu, Zhenhui, 462

Yeltsin, Boris, 504
Yen bonds, exception, 423
Yen-denominated bonds. *See* Unhedged yen-
  denominated bonds
Yield basis, 515
Yield Book, 280
  usage, 284
Yield change, 203
Yield curve, 44
  bets, implicit duration (impact), 249
  butterfly movements, 296
  changes, 466
  dynamics, 268
  exposures, 471
  flatness, 272
  impact, 90
  movements, 242, 308
  parallel shift, 268
  risk factors, 219
  scenarios, defining, 240–241
  segment, 203
  sensitivity, 155
  shape, changes (importance), 89–90
  shock
    explanatory power, 260–261
    magnitude plausibility, 261
  slope, 27

  three-factor term structure model, usage.
    See Hedging
  twist movement, 296
Yield hogs, 29
Yield spread
  management, 10
  volatility, 27–28
Yield-to-maturity, 270
  curve, 289

Zenios, Stavros, 281
Zero-coupon bond
  actual price, movement, 143
  face value, 330
  market, 145
  price, 139
    determination, 144
    equation, 138
Zero-coupon corporate bond, 316
Zero-coupon debt, risk, 386
Zero-coupon price, equation, 138
Zero-coupon rates
  changes, 269, 281
  correlation, 276
  function, 276
Zero-coupon securities, 231
Zero-coupon yield curve, 278
  absolute sensitivity, 281
Zero-sum game, 39
Zero-volatility component, 133. *See also* Asset-
  backed securities; Mortgage-backed secu-
  rities
Zhou, Chunsheng, 395
Zhu, Yu, 21, 293
Zimmermann, Heinz, 281
z-score, 487

Printed and bound by CPI Group (UK) Ltd, Croydon, CR0 4YY

23/04/2025

14660921-0004